PC Repair
Bench Book

PC Repair
Bench Book

Ron Gilster

Wiley Publishing, Inc.

PC Repair Bench Book

Published by
Wiley Publishing, Inc.
10475 Crosspoint Boulevard
Indianapolis, IN 46256
www.wiley.com

Copyright © 2003 by Wiley Publishing, Inc., Indianapolis, Indiana

Published simultaneously in Canada

ISBN: 0-7645-2578-6

Manufactured in the United States of America.

10 9 8 7 6 5 4 3 2 1

1B/RR/QT/QT/IN

For general information on our other products and services or to obtain technical support, please contact our Customer Care Department within the U.S. at (800) 762-2974, outside the U.S. at (317) 572-3993 or fax (317) 572-4002.

Wiley also publishes its books in a variety of electronic formats. Some content that appears in print may not be available in electronic books.

Library of Congress Control Number: 2002114861

WILEY is a trademark of Wiley Publishing, Inc.

Credits

PROJECT EDITOR
Linda Morris

ACQUISITIONS EDITOR
Melody Layne

SR. COPY EDITOR
Teresa Artman

TECHNICAL EDITOR
Dan DiNicolo

EDITORIAL MANAGER
Kevin Kirschner

EDITORIAL ASSISTANT
Amanda Foxworth

VICE PRESIDENT AND EXECUTIVE GROUP PUBLISHER
Richard Swadley

EDITORIAL DIRECTOR
Mary C. Corder

VICE PRESIDENT AND PUBLISHER
Andy Cummings

MEDIA DEVELOPMENT SUPERVISOR
Richard Graves

MEDIA DEVELOPMENT SPECIALIST
Kit Malone

SR. PERMISSIONS EDITOR
Carmen Krikorian

PROJECT COORDINATOR
Bill Ramsey

GRAPHICS AND PRODUCTION SPECIALISTS
David Bartholomew
Jennifer Click
Sean Decker
Heather Pope
Rashell Smith
Jeremey Unger

PROOFREADERS
Laura L. Bowman
John Greenough

INDEXER
Infodex Indexing Services Inc.

About the Author

Ron Gilster has been operating, programming, and repairing computers for more than 30 years, and networking them for more than 13 years. Ron has extensive experience in training, teaching, and consulting in computer-related areas, having spent more than 20 years as a college-level instructor in A+, CCNA, MCSE, MOUS, and computer programming programs. His experience includes mainframes, mini-computers, and virtually every type of personal computer and operating system in use. In addition to a wide range of positions that have included systems programming supervisor, customer service manager, data processing manager, management information systems director, and executive positions in major corporations, Ron has served as a management consultant with both an international accounting firm and his own consulting firm.

He is the author of *A+ Certification For Dummies, Network+ Certification For Dummies, Server+ Certification For Dummies, i-Net+ Certification For Dummies, CCNA For Dummies, Cisco Networking For Dummies, CCDA For Dummies,* and with Curt Simmons, *MCSA All-in-One Desk Reference For Dummies,* plus several books on computer and information literacy and programming.

To my very best fan, friend, and wife — Connie.

Preface

If you've purchased or are considering the purchase of this book, you probably fit into one of the following categories:

◆ You're an experienced PC technician who wants a concise reference on PCs and how to troubleshoot and repair them.

◆ You think that reading this book might be a fun, entertaining way to extend your knowledge of PCs and their components.

◆ You either have or are preparing for A+ certification.

◆ You're a big fan of mine and can hardly wait for my next book.

If you fit into one or more of these descriptions (except the last one, for which I am not qualified in the appropriate medical areas to help you), this is the book for you!

About This Book

If your goal is to discover more about PCs, their components, and how to identify and fix their problems, you're in the right place. In this book, I provide you with some background information on the major component areas of a personal computer and also offer detailed procedures that you can use to resolve many of the common failures and problems that can occur on a user's PC.

I fondly remember the days when I could lift the hood (*bonnet* for my British readers) on my car and not only identify all the parts but also actually repair or replace a broken or malfunctioning component. Sadly, those days are gone, and I must now depend on Mr./Ms. Goodwrench to fix anything under the hood of my car. Luckily, this evolution has not quite transpired on PCs . . . at least not yet. If anything, the components under the hood of the PC have gotten simpler to identify, and problems that occur are getting easier to isolate and resolve.

However, typical users, although growing more and more savvy with software, are reluctant to fix their PCs themselves, preferring to call on Mr./Ms. Gooddriver to fix their PC hardware when something goes wrong. And because not every PC technician can know every problem and the right or best procedure to use when finding and fixing a PC problem, I wrote this book as a guide.

In writing this book, I've made the assumption that you are a PC technician with at least a few months of hands-on experience in the installation, configuration, and repair of PCs as well as a fundamental knowledge of electronics, computers, software, protocols, and troubleshooting procedures. If you're just getting started, though, don't worry that this book makes too many assumptions concerning your knowledge, experience, and abilities. On the contrary, I've tried to present things in such a way that whether you're just getting started or have years of experience, the information, processes, and procedures that I've included are useful.

How to Use This Book

Like with the majority of my other books on PC hardware topics, this book is intended as a reference and troubleshooting guide that you can keep handy on your workbench – hence, the *Bench Book* part of the title. Each major component group is presented first with some general background information to orient you to its operation, compatibilities, and common problems.

This book presents the facts, concepts, processes, and applications that a PC technician needs to know in step-by-step lists, tables, figures, and text without long or (hopefully) boring explanations. The focus is to provide you with information on the how's and why's of PC hardware components and not to impress you with my obviously extensive and impressive knowledge of PCs (nor my modesty, I might add).

Another excellent reference tool that you can use, especially if you're just getting started, is *A+ Certification For Dummies,* 2nd Edition (Wiley Publishing, Inc.). Okay, so this is a shameless plug of another of my books, but it's still a good reference on PCs.

Appendix A includes a list of my favorite PC hardware reference books.

How This Book Is Organized

This book is organized to allow you to find information specific to certain hardware or component groups without the need to wade through stuff you already know. At the beginning of each chapter is a list of topics that you can use as a guide to what's in the chapter.

You'll also find that some topics might be covered in more that one place in the book, with one location providing more information than the other. Some information has a better relationship to certain other areas and is placed into the context of a specific or related issue. Rely on the index of the book to find the specific page where a certain topic, component, or issue is covered. I've also included cross references to other information that you might find useful.

Here are the parts of the book and what they cover.

Part I: The Motherboard and Its Components

This book is organized around the major component areas of a personal computer. Part I begins at the heart of the PC, covering the motherboard, processor, chipset, Basic Input/Output System (BIOS), system resources, memory, and cache memory. Although these components aren't typically the source of a PC problem, it's a good idea that you know and understand their function, fit, and processes in relationship to the other parts of the PC.

Part II: The System Case and Power Supply

The PC's case and power supply are responsible for more PC problems than most people think. I've put them together because they typically come as a combined part and to emphasize their importance to the PC's overall operations.

Part III: Storage Devices

Unfortunately, this part of the book doesn't provide you with a better way to explain to a user the difference between memory and permanent data storage devices; you're still on your own with that. What this part does provide is an in-depth look into the more common data storage devices, such as hard disks, floppy disks, CD-ROMs, and the like. The information included in this part covers the construction, operation, and common issues of data storage devices, which are now an essential part of any PC.

Part IV: Sight and Sound Systems

PCs are designed to provide an interactive processing environment. A user's basic interactive tools are his or her eyes and ears. (Touch, smell, and mental telephony can't be too far off.) The PC's display and sound systems provide the basis for the interaction between the user and the PC. When one of these component groups has a problem, it's typically a BIG problem for the user.

This part of the book deals with the PC's video and display systems and the components of its sound system.

Part V: Printers

If a broken monitor or a quiet sound system causes grief for the user, a broken printer is a major catastrophe. Because of the importance of printers, this part of the book focuses solely on PC printers, their operations, issues, and how to get them back up and running.

Part VI: Keyboards and Pointing Devices

Although speech recognition systems that actually work are on the horizon, the user's main tool for entering data and commands to the PC are still the keyboard and mouse. Because several types of both devices are on the market, when you're presented with a problem in either, you need to know which device type you're working with and what's the best way to fix it.

In addition, this part of the book also looks at other devices used to enter or manipulate data on the PC, such as joysticks, digital tablets, and the like.

Part VII: Communications and Networking

Without including so much information on data communications and network that this book turns into a networking bench book, this part looks at the components and processes used to connect a PC to a local area network (LAN).

Part VIII: Configuring the PC

Most of the configuration tasks on a PC surround the configuration of expansion cards and the ports and connectors through which external peripheral devices are attached to the PC. This part covers the types, compatibilities, installation, and configuration of expansion cards and the PC's external ports and connectors.

Part IX: PC Operating Systems

Have no fear; this part of the book doesn't cover application software or how to create a really nifty document or Web site. What it does cover is the Windows and Linux operating systems and their installation, configuration, and troubleshooting. Installing a new PC often includes either the installation and configuration or the upgrading of an operating system. This part of the book provides information on the more popular Windows operating system versions and a look into the world of Linux.

Part X: Maintaining a PC

The two major parts of PC maintenance are preventive care and optimization, which coincidently are the two chapters in this part. A well-maintained PC has a much better chance for an extended life, and the procedures used to perform an organized and regularly applied preventive maintenance plan are covered. And because you'll occasionally want to try to get just a little better performance out of a PC, here I offer some system optimization techniques. Although it flies in the face of the philosophy that *If it isn't broke, don't fix it,* this might be the part of the book that you refer to the most (or at least you should).

Part XI: Appendix

The appendix gives a complete listing of third-party software and bonus content on the CD-ROM that accompanies this book. Highlights are three bonus appendixes (troubleshooting tips, suggesting software and hardware tools, and a complete glossary), as well as a searchable PDF of the entire text of this book.

Icons Used in This Book

Look to Cross Reference icons to find additional or expanded information on a particular topic.

Note icons provide more information to help you understand a particular point or to make some information more relevant.

Tip icons flag information that can come in extra-handy while working on a PC.

The Caution icon alerts you to some potentially dangerous or treacherous material. Heads up!

Where to Go from Here

Only you know where you need to begin reading this book. If you need more information on motherboards and their components, start with Part I. If you need some advice on working with video or sound on a PC, start with Part IV. There is no right or wrong place to begin working with this book.

Talk to Me

I'd like to hear from you. If any aspect or topic of PC repair isn't covered as well as it should be, or if I've provided more coverage than you think is warranted about a particular topic, please let me know. Or if I've made an error or misstated a fact (it could happen!), I'd appreciate hearing about it. Your feedback is solicited and welcome. You can send e-mail to me at this e-mail address: feedback@rongilster.com.

Acknowledgments

I'd like to acknowledge the contributions of a virtual cast of tens who helped this project along. This includes the very excellent crew from Wiley Publishing, Inc., without whom this book would look like my desktop (not a pretty sight, I might add): Melody Layne, Linda Morris, Teresa Artman, Kim Darosett, and Amanda Foxworth. A special thanks goes to Rashell Smith and David Bartholomew, who did such a wonderful job illustrating this book. I would also like to extend a huge thanks to Dan DiNicolo for challenging me with his absolutely great technical review.

I'd also like to thank the manufacturers, vendors, and suppliers of PC hardware and software that provided photographs and illustrations for the book.

And last, but certainly not least, I'd like to acknowledge the support of my family (Connie, Markus, Jessica, and Carly) and my dear friend and agent (Margot Maley Hutchison), without whom I couldn't have survived this task.

Contents at a Glance

Contents

Part I

The Motherboard and Its Components

Chapter 1

Mastering the Motherboard

IN THIS CHAPTER

The *motherboard*, also known as the system board, main board, or planar board, is a large printed circuit board that includes or provides an interconnect to most of the essential components of the PC:

- Microprocessor (see Chapter 2)

- Expansion bus (see Chapter 2)

- Chipset (see Chapter 3)

- Memory sockets and RAM modules (see Chapter 6)

- Cache memory (see Chapter 7)

- Integrated Drive Electronics (IDE), Enhanced IDE (EIDE), or Small Computer System Interface (SCSI) controllers (see Chapter 11)

- Mouse and keyboard connectors (see Part VI)

- Parallel and serial ports (see Parts V and VI)

AS THIS LIST SHOWS, there is more to working with a motherboard than I can cover in just this one chapter. Motherboards are the glue that binds the PC's components together. I can safely say that virtually every component, internal or peripheral, that's installed on or connected to a PC has some connection (no pun intended!) to the motherboard.

Motherboard manufacturers attempt to differentiate their products and increase their value by integrating a varying combination of devices and controllers into their boards. The upside of including more on the motherboard is a wider compatibility to a wider range of systems and potentially a deeper list of features. The downside is that unless you're very careful when selecting a new motherboard, you might not get the combination or quality of processor or peripheral support that you intended.

Although I assume that you have some background in working with PCs and their components, I want to be sure that you and I are on the same page when it comes to motherboards. In the following sections, I cover what is likely some fundamental material. However, when it comes to motherboards, I'd rather be safe than sorry.

Differentiating Motherboard Designs

If PCs had only a single type and style of motherboards, the task of working with them would be greatly simplified. However, even though most of today's PCs use the ATX (see "Creating the new standard: The ATX" later in this chapter), you can expect to encounter different motherboard form factors on the job. If, after all else has failed, you decide to replace a PC's motherboard, you must match the form factor of the motherboard to the case and its mountings.

Laying out the mainboard

Essentially, the two basic design approaches to PC motherboards are the mainboard (or the true mother-of-all-boards) design and the backplane design.

A *mainboard* design, like the one in Figure 1-1, incorporates the PC's primary system components on a single circuit board. This type of motherboard contains most of the circuitry of a PC and acts as the conduit through which all the PC's operations flow.

On a typical motherboard (see Figure 1-1), you will find the microprocessor, the Basic Input/Output System (BIOS) ROM, the chipset, RAM, expansion cards, perhaps some serial and parallel ports, disk controllers, connectors for the mouse and the keyboard, and possibly a few other components as well.

TIP

Mainboard motherboard designs, although somewhat standard, do vary in the inclusion and placement of system components and interfaces. Before you charge down the road to diagnose, troubleshoot, or replace any motherboard, be very sure that you can at least identify the components indicated in Figure 1-1 on your PC's mainboard.

Connecting to the backplane

There are actually two types of backplane mainboards: passive and active. A *passive backplane mainboard* is only a receiver card with open slots into which a processor card (which contains a central processing unit [CPU] and its support chips) and input/output (I/O) cards that provide bus and device interfaces are plugged. These add-in cards are referred to as *daughterboards*.

The backplane interconnects the system components through a bus structure and provides some basic data buffering services. The backplane design is popular with server-type computers because it can be quickly upgraded or repaired. The backplane design provides the advantage of getting a server back online with only the replacement of a single slotted card, instead of replacing an entire mainboard!

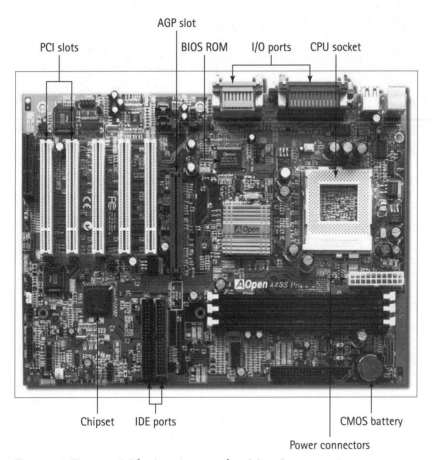

Figure 1-1: The essential (and most common) mainboard components.

Photo courtesy of AOpen, Inc.

An *active backplane* design, also called an *intelligent* backplane, adds some CPU or controller-driven circuitry to the backplane board, which can speed up the processing speed of the system. Even on an active backplane, the CPU is on its own card to provide for easy replacement.

The utility of the backplane design is being challenged by newer motherboards that incorporate the slot-style mountings of Pentium-class processors. The advantage of the active backplane is that the processor can be easily accessed and replaced, but the slot-style motherboards also offer this same advantage.

For purposes of clarity and because they are the most commonly used in PCs, when I refer to a motherboard, I am referring to the mainboard design. When referring to a backplane design, I will specifically say so.

Factoring in the motherboard form

When the original IBM PC was introduced in 1981, it had a simple motherboard designed to hold an 8-bit processor (the Intel 8088), five expansion cards, a keyboard connector, 64–256K RAM (from individual memory chips mounted on the motherboard), a chipset, BIOS ROM, and a cassette tape I/O adapter for permanent storage. The PC was designed to be a desktop computer, and its system case layout dictated the first of what are now called motherboard form factors. Simply, a *form factor* defines a motherboard's size, shape, and how it is mounted to the case. However, form factors have been extended over time to include the system case, the placement and size of the power supply, the power requirements of the system, external connector placements and specifications, and case airflow and cooling guidelines.

Table 1-1 lists the common form factors that have been and are being used in PCs.

TABLE 1-1 MOTHERBOARD FORM FACTORS

Style	Width (inches)	Length (inches)	Design	Case Type
IBM PC	8.5	13	Mainboard	IBM PC
IBM PC XT	8.5	13	Mainboard	IBM PC XT
IBM PC AT	12	11–13	Mainboard	Desktop or tower
Baby AT	8.5	10–13	Mainboard	Desktop or tower
LPX	9	11–13	Backplane	Desktop
Micro-AT	8.5	8.5	Mainboard	Desktop or tower
ATX	12	9.6	Mainboard	Desktop or tower
Mini-ATX	11.2	8.2	Mainboard	Desktop
Mini-LPX	8–9	10–11	Backplane	Desktop
Micro-ATX	9.6	9.6	Mainboard	Desktop
NLX	8–9	10–13.6	Backplane	Desktop
Flex-ATX	9	7.5	Mainboard	Desktop or tower

SETTING THE STANDARD: THE IBM AT

When IBM released its first 16-bit computer, the PC AT, the circuitry added to the motherboard of its predecessor (the PC XT) increased the size of its motherboard and case to 12 inches wide by 13 inches deep. During this time, many clone (non-IBM) manufacturers also began releasing XT-compatible motherboards, which included keyboard connectors, expansion slots, and mounting holes to fit into AT cases. The AT's size, shape, and mounting placements became the first motherboard form factor standard, a standard that has essentially continued through today. Nearly all present-day motherboard form factors are a derivative of the early AT standard.

BRINGING UP THE BABY AT

It wasn't long before clone manufacturers began releasing their own 16-bit PCs and motherboards with higher integration in the supporting chipsets that allowed their motherboard to take a smaller form. This smaller form was called the Baby AT, shown in Figure 1-2, a more compact motherboard that was compatible with AT cases. The Baby AT became very popular because of its size and flexibility and joined the AT motherboard as a de facto standard.

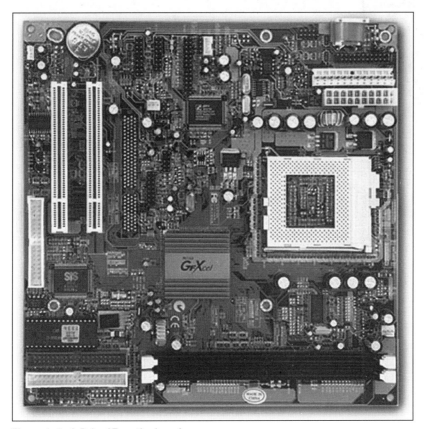

Figure 1-2: A Baby AT motherboard.

TAKING THE STANDARD ONE STEP SMALLER

Most of the PC cases manufactured between 1984 and 1996 were made to house a Baby AT motherboard. However, with still higher integration and further miniaturization of the processor, chipset, and other support components, it became possible to produce an even smaller version of the AT form factor. The Micro-AT motherboard (see Figure 1-3), which is nearly half the size of the Baby AT mainboard, is also compatible with the motherboard mountings in AT and Baby AT cases.

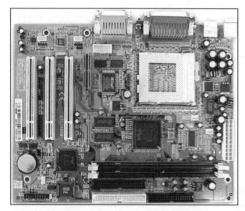

Figure 1-3: A Micro-AT motherboard.

WORKING WITH A LOW PROFILE: LPX AND MINI-LPX

Originally created by Western Digital to provide slimline cases to the consumer market, the LPX and Mini-LPX form factors have produced many variations. Actually, the LPX and Mini-LPX specifications are more of a general motherboard category than a specific form factor with a standard specification, like that of the AT and its derivatives. Manufacturers such as Packard Bell and Compaq used their own proprietary configurations for LPX motherboards in their PCs. Unfortunately, this practice guarantees that their customers cannot typically upgrade their computers without swapping the motherboard.

TIP One quick note on the meaning of form factor names: There aren't any. If the form factor names ever had meanings, they are lost to time.

The LPX style is characterized by a *riser card* that has plugs into a slot in the middle of the motherboard. LPX riser cards typically have two or three expansion slot sockets on them, but the number of sockets available depends on the size of the riser card and whether it has expansion slots on both sides. The motherboard is mounted flat in the LPX case, and the riser card is inserted perpendicularly. This arrangement allows the expansion cards mounted in the riser card to be placed parallel to the motherboard, which allows for a much slimmer case design.

CREATING THE NEW STANDARD: THE ATX

In 1995, Intel released its "next best thing" with the ATX form factor. The ATX is an improvement over preceding form factors because of its published and continuously maintained standard, which guarantees compatibility among all ATX motherboards and cases.

The ATX form factor, shown in Figure 1-4, is based on the Baby AT but is rotated 90 degrees and incorporates unique mounting locations and power supply connections. Unlike many of the previous motherboard form factors, ATX locates its I/O connections so that they're accessible through the back of an ATX case.

The ATX form factor specification incorporates solutions to the performance issues associated with Baby AT and LPX forms. ATX places the CPU and RAM slots out of the way of expansion cards and near the power supply fan, which improves the airflow over the CPU and RAM chips.

Figure 1–4: An ATX motherboard.

Photo courtesy of AOpen, Inc.

Changing the Way the Wind Blows

The original specification for the ATX form pulled air into the system case and inward through the power supply, over the CPU, and out the case vents. The idea was to supposedly eliminate the need for separate CPU fans. The downside was that dust and other airborne particles entered the case and settled inside, which required more preventive maintenance. The lesson learned is that air inflow is less efficient than air outflow; and instead of eliminating fans, many still required additional fans to cool the CPU properly.

More recent ATX versions push the airflow out so that the power supply fan is now venting the case. However, if this still doesn't solve a particular cooling problem, ATX cases typically allow for installing additional case fans. PCs with 3-D video accelerators and other high-heat producing cards or those with multiple hard disk drives might require additional case fans to be installed.

The ATX specification also defines the Mini-ATX sub-specification, which has a board size of 11.2 inches by 8.2 inches. Other sub-specifications of the ATX form factor that you might encounter are the Micro-ATX and the Flex-ATX.

SLIMMING DOWN WITH NLX

NLX is a newer format and standardized low-profile motherboard form factor. It is designed to support a number of current and emerging microprocessor technologies along with many newer developments, including support for Accelerated Graphics Port (AGP) video adapters and tall memory modules (such as dual inline memory modules, or DIMMs). The NLX form provides more flexibility for the system-level design and for easy removal and replacement of the motherboard, allegedly without tools. The NLX motherboard measures about 8 inches by 13.6 inches and uses a plug-in riser board for its expansion bus support. The riser board attaches to the edge of the mainboard, as shown in Figure 1-5.

Three primary influences were behind the development of the NLX standard: processor and system cooling requirements, the number of connectors needed by multimedia hardware, and a further reduction of interior cable clutter. The size and thermal characteristics of newer microprocessors, especially those configured into multiple processor sets, along with the addition of high-performance (and high-heat) graphics adaptors, forced a new look at the airflow in slimline cases. As multimedia systems became more common, the need for more connectors from the motherboard to the outside world also increased. As more internal adapters and controllers were added to the motherboard, the interior of the system case was cluttered with cabling, which impeded repair or upgrade activities.

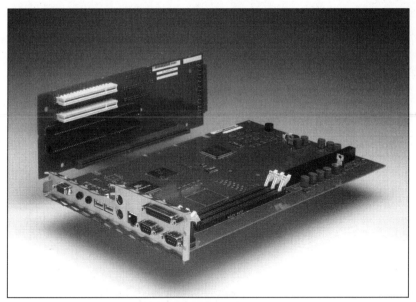

Figure 1-5: The Intel NLX form factor motherboard.

Photo courtesy of Intel Corporation.

Working with the Motherboard

In the vast majority of situations, the problem that you're trying to track down on a PC is not likely to be specifically caused by the motherboard itself. Actually, if the problem is a bad motherboard (not a common event), your only course of action is to replace it. However, sometimes maybe – just maybe – you can check out the motherboard and isolate the problem.

If you do remove an allegedly bad motherboard, you really should test it in a test bed PC before throwing it out. It could actually still be good. And even if a new motherboard fixed its PC's problems, the solution might be more coincidental than anything else.

Using the right tools

The following is a list of the tools that you should have in your toolkit for removing or installing a motherboard:

- ◆ *Dental mirror:* A dental mirror-like tool can be purchased from most tool suppliers, so you don't have to beg your dentist for one. A dental mirror is perfect for seeing around corners in an assembled system, like when you need to see a detail being blocked by a disk drive cage. It can also come in handy when you're trying to attach a connector or a power cord to the back of a PC.

◆ *Digital multimeter:* If the motherboard is running strangely, some of the first places to look are its power connections. A multimeter or a digital voltmeter is a good tool to have for testing the continuity of power cables and the power supply's output.

◆ *Electrostatic discharge (ESD) mat and wrist (or ankle) strap:* If you don't have access to an ESD mat on which you can set any static-sensitive parts that you remove (such as expansion cards or a motherboard), by all means wear an ESD wrist or ankle strap and have plenty of anti-static bags available. Even with an ESD strap in use, never stack unprotected cards or parts on top of one another and always ground yourself to the system case's metal as often as possible.

◆ *Penlight or mini flex-type flashlight:* Having some light to help you see small identifying marks on the motherboard, its chips, and expansion cards can prevent a serious error and save the time removing and reinserting the wrong parts. You might want to consider spare batteries as well.

◆ *Screwdrivers:* Your toolkit should include a collection of screwdrivers that has at least one of each of the following screwdrivers: a standard (slot), a mini-head Phillips (cross-head recess), a standard-size Phillips (magnetic tip optional), and a Torx. Magnetic screwdrivers can be potentially dangerous if used incorrectly, such as gouging the motherboard or blowing an integrated circuit (IC) chip. However, they can come in handy for retrieving a dropped screw or for starting a screw in an inaccessible place.

◆ *Software system testing utilities:* As long as you are able to boot into some operating system, a set of diagnostic utilities (like Norton Utilities) can be among the best tools in your kit. Use these software aids to diagnose a number of suspected motherboard or system performance problems, such as system slow-downs and inexplicable crashes.

◆ *Your eyes, ears, and nose:* Your senses are among your best tools. As corny as that might sound, your senses are probably the tools most often used when you first begin your troubleshooting.

Troubleshooting the motherboard

Before you do anything else, you must remove enough of the case cover so that you can see the CPU and the BIOS ROM. Then get out your penlight and your notebook and pen or pencil. As you move through the next few steps, write down every bit of information that you identify.

1. Identify the processor's class and model.

   What kind of processor is in use? For example, is it an AMD Athlon or an Intel Pentium II or III? What type of mount is in use?

2. Identify the BIOS manufacturer and its revision level.

   Make a note of the Basic Input/Output System (BIOS) in use: for example, a Phoenix BIOS I4HS10 rev 4.05.10. This information can be obtained during the boot sequence (if you're fast!) or from a label on the BIOS ROM chip itself. If the motherboard doesn't have a model number printed on it, motherboard manufacturers commonly have custom BIOS versions for each chipset and motherboard combination, so a motherboard's model number can often be derived from the BIOS serial number and vice versa. Check the BIOS manufacturer's Web site for details. Some sites even offer search tools specifically for this sort of look-up.

3. Identify motherboard manufacturer and model.

   Near an edge of the motherboard, you should find a block of printed information that identifies the manufacturer, the model number, and possibly a revision level. This information is typically silk-screened right on the board.

4. Identify the bus type.

   Which expansion buses are supported on the motherboard, or are any riser boards in use?

Identifying motherboard problems

Three general types of failures are directly related to the motherboard. Failures relating to the motherboard are often disguised as component failures during the boot sequence. (See Chapter 5 for more information on the system boot process.) Motherboard-related failures are typically identified during the Power-On Self-Test (POST) process by a BIOS beep code and any related messages. I've named the three primary boot sequence failure modes: no beep-no boot, beep-no boot, and beep-boot-bam.

   To begin the identification process, power on the PC, listen and look, and then go to the section below that most approximates what you think you heard or saw.

NO BEEP-NO BOOT

The PC's power is on, you can see lights on the front panel, but as near as you can tell, the POST process did not run.

1. Check the main power cord, especially where it connects to the back of the PC, to make sure that it's fully pushed into the connector or receptacle.

   Inspect the power cord for cuts or crimps that might have damaged the inner wires. Inspect the plug head and the female connector of the cord for corrosion or metal damage. Take a look at the connector on the back of the PC to make sure that the prongs aren't bent over and not connecting properly.

2. Check the power source outlet for proper voltage with a multimeter or digital voltage meter (DVM).

   You might find it easier to try plugging the PC into a different outlet (not on the same source). If it works on a different outlet, the problem was the source. If the PC is plugged into a surge suppressing plug strip, the plug strip's varistor could've been blown out by an electrical surge. On those plug strips that have a fuse or circuit breaker, try resetting it.

3. Check the power supply's fan to see whether it's turning.

   If it's not turning, the problem could be in the power supply, and you need to troubleshoot it. See Chapter 9 for information on troubleshooting the power supply.

4. Check the motherboard's power connection.

   If the power supply fan is spinning but nothing else is happening, the power to the motherboard could be faulty. For example, you might have a +12 volts (v) source but no +5v or +3.3v supplies. Possibly the power-good line from the power supply to the motherboard is being set on for some reason. The processes used to diagnose these conditions are covered in Chapter 9.

5. Verify that the power connectors from the power supply are firmly seated and in the correct position.

   Check to make sure that the power connector to the motherboard from the power supply is firmly seated. The type of connector or connectors in use varies with the motherboard's form factor. AT and Baby AT power supplies have two 6-wire connectors that must be connected just so, and an ATX (or any of its derivatives) typically has a single 20-wire connector. See Chapter 9 for more information on the motherboard's power connection.

   The power connectors on an AT or Baby AT motherboard, usually labeled as P8 and P9, attach to the motherboard side-by-side. The trick to making sure that you have them in the right positions is to have all four of the black wires, or ground wires (two on each plug), placed together in the middle. However, be very cautious when connecting the power cable to these connectors; if the orientation of the connectors is wrong, it could damage the motherboard.

   The power connection on ATX or later form factors is keyed with a prong, lip, or finger that prevents it from being connected incorrectly.

6. Confirm that the motherboard's voltage setting jumpers are correctly positioned for the PC's motherboard and CPU combination.

   See the motherboard's documentation for the proper settings of these jumpers.

7. Check for a mismounted or missing processor.

   If the processor has been installed very recently, check how well it's seated in its mounting. Under the heading of *It Could Never Happen:* If the PC is in a public area, such as a laboratory, student lab, library, or another open and unsecured location, there could be a missing processor, memory, or expansion card. Unfortunately, theft is common on PCs to which there is public access.

8. Look for smoke and smell for burnt wire smells.

   A running joke among PC technicians is that the smoke is the magic that makes all electronic and electrical parts work. If the smoke gets out, the PC stops working. Examine the board, chips, and trace pathways for scorch or burn marks or bubbling in the motherboard's substrates that could be associated with excessive heat damage. You might want to use a small magnifying glass to examine the motherboard and its components for heat damage.

9. Reseat expansion cards, memory modules, and, if the PC is older, the ROM BIOS chip.

   You might want to check the mounting of any socket-mounted chips on the motherboard. All chips are subject to *chip creep*, which is the very slight movement of a device out of its socket. Chip creep is the result of thermal shifts caused by powering a PC on (heating it up) and off (cooling it down). If you discover any chips that need to be reseated, you should remove them and check for corrosion on the connector edges – if you find some, use contact cleaner before reinstalling them.

10. Check for electrical shorts.

    Look for anything that could be shorting the motherboard, drives, peripheral cards, or power supply. Screws that fall into the case can lodge under or behind the motherboard or the board retainer tray (if the case has one) and ground the electrical system. In most cases, removing the loose part should solve the problem without any damage to the motherboard or other circuits. If you find a loose screw or the like, or if the motherboard is in contact with the case (where it shouldn't be), don't assume that no damage occurred. Use chipset/memory/CPU test and diagnostic software, such as SiSoft's Sandra, TweakBIOS, or CTCHIPZ, to verify the motherboard's functions.

11. Check the motherboard standoffs.

    If your motherboard is mounted on brass standoffs that hold it off the case tray, verify that paper or plastic washers are inserted between the standoff and the motherboard. If you don't have the little paper or plastic washers, use a small piece of electrical tape over the end of the standoff where it contacts the motherboard. If the standoff is contacting the motherboard directly, it can cause a short in some instances.

12. Disconnect all external connectors — serial, parallel, Universal Serial Bus (USB), keyboard, mouse, and so on — and reboot the system.

    If the system boots, begin a cycle of replacing the connectors one at a time and cold booting the PC each time until the problem reoccurs. If the system fails after a certain device is attached, troubleshoot the connector or the device. See Parts III–VI for information on troubleshooting the connectors and ports for a specific device.

BEEP-NO BOOT

If the PC powers up but the POST process appears to halt after sounding one or more beep, follow this troubleshooting procedure:

1. Make sure that the PC's monitor is on, connected, and operating okay.

    Don't laugh; this head-slapper has stumped more than one experienced tech.

2. Look up the pattern used on the BIOS in your PC.

    Each BIOS manufacturer uses a different and unique pattern of beep tones to signal errors. After you know what you're listening for, attempt to write down the pattern of the beep tones. Remember that tones are short or long with varying-length pauses inserted between beep series. After you are sure of the beep signal pattern (you might need to reboot several times to hear it all), consult your motherboard's documentation or visit the BIOS manufacturer's Web site for the meaning of the beep pattern and a suggested procedure to correct the problem. Understand that every manufacturer has a different meaning for a certain signal pattern, and it can even differ for different revisions of a BIOS from a single manufacturer.

3. Check to make sure that the Complementary Metal-Oxide Semiconductor (CMOS) battery jumper is in the correct position.

    Surprisingly, many new PCs and motherboards are shipped with the CMOS battery jumper in the wrong setting. Check the motherboard's documentation for the correct settings.

4. Inspect the CMOS battery for leaks, corrosion, or burns.

    Depending on the age of the motherboard, the CMOS battery is either a little blue barrel (see Figure 1-6) or something like a big watch battery (a flat silver disk like that shown in Figure 1-7). In either case, it is located on the motherboard near the CMOS chip. You should also check the battery with a multimeter. Maybe it's just time for a new battery. These batteries can go bad and leak chemicals on the motherboard, which can short or melt circuit traces. On that note, look for broken circuit traces on the motherboard or solder blobs accidentally connecting two circuit trace paths.

Figure 1-6: The blue barrel-style CMOS battery.

Figure 1-7: The lithium watch-style CMOS battery.

5. Check the video card by removing and reinstalling it.

   If the beep codes are for something very generic, the problem could be that you just can't see the display. If reinstalling the video card doesn't work, try swapping it out for another video card of the same type, if available.

6. Check for a text message.

   Depending on when the POST detects the error, you might get a text message as a part of the BIOS information. If so, study the information displayed; it can usually provide clues on where the problem is occurring.

If you are familiar with the PC, you should know the sequence of the POST process and what should occur immediately following the last displayed action – the likely point of failure. Otherwise, check with the BIOS or motherboard manufacturer for information on the boot sequence.

7. Remove the RAM chips or modules and try booting with different combinations of memory modules in different slots on the board.

   Memory modules have been known to work great in one (or more) slot(s) but hang the system in another. If the PC includes Level 2 (L2) cache boards, try booting the PC without it.

8. Verify that the RAM chips or modules in use are compatible with the motherboard, chipset, and processor.

   Also be sure that the modules are installed in the proper slot or slots. Some PCs allow single modules, some require module pairs, and still others require four of the same module type to be installed to work. Remember that you can't mix and match memory module types. See Chapter 6 for more information on memory modules.

9. Check the IDE/ATA connection on the motherboard and the boot disk drive.

   You might also want to verify the jumper settings on the disk drives themselves to make sure that the master/slave configuration is properly set.

10. Reseat the expansion cards (see Step 9 in the No Beep-No Boot procedure).

    If the system uses an expansion card IDE controller and you have a spare, replace the installed card with it.

11. Confirm that the motherboard's voltage setting and motherboard speed (multiplier) jumpers are correctly positioned for the PC's motherboard and CPU combination.

    See the motherboard's documentation for the location and proper settings of these jumpers.

12. Verify the system configuration settings in CMOS.

    If you can access the BIOS' set-up program by pressing the access key (usually Delete or a function key), use its reset function to reset the CMOS settings to their default values and reboot. Only do this after you have written down the current settings of the CMOS contents. After resetting the CMOS values, you can begin changing the default settings back to their original values one (or more, but not more than a few related settings) at a time.

13. Remove all the expansion boards, except the video adapter, and reboot.

    If the system reboots, the problem is probably one of the boards or the expansion bus on one of the expansion slots. Begin replacing the boards one at a time, rebooting after each card is installed. If the system fails on a particular card, put it in a different slot and reboot to isolate whether it's the card or the slot that has the problem.

14. Disconnect the system speaker, which could be shorting to the board.

15. Disconnect each of the case-to-motherboard wires, such as the connections to the front panel light-emitting diode (LED) lights and switches.

    Do these one at a time and reboot after removing each one.

16. Check keyboard and mouse connections.

    Verify that they are securely connected to the motherboard.

17. Check whether the keyboard fuse is blown.

    This fuse can blow if a serial mouse is connected to a PS/2 connector through an adapter or if there is an electrical short somewhere in the keyboard. And, if all else has failed, try a different keyboard.

BEEP-BOOT-BAM

In this situation, the PC is powered on, the POST completes and signals an all-clear, but the PC fails at the beginning of the startup sequence or right after the boot completes.

1. Study the BIOS information displayed on the monitor and verify that the boot drive sequence is set correctly.

   If the correct drive is set as the first boot drive, check its power and data connections. If the PC's BIOS supports it, set the boot drive setting to Auto Detect.

2. Check the hard disk drives to ensure that you have only one master disk and one slave disk on each IDE cable.

   If you wish to boot from a hard disk drive (the most common choice), be sure that it is the master disk on the primary IDE channel. See Chapter 10 for more information on IDE disk drives.

3. Check any Small Computer System Interface (SCSI) connections.

   If your primary disk drive is a SCSI drive, be sure that the end device on each chain (internal and external) is terminated. Verify that the SCSI BIOS and the motherboard's BIOS are set to allow a SCSI disk drive to be the boot disk. Verify that the SCSI device ID assigned to the disk drive matches that in the BIOS and also make sure that the SCSI controller is connected to the SCSI drive. Check all SCSI connectors to ensure that they're pushed all the way in.

4. Try a different boot disk drive.

   If the boot still fails, change the boot sequence in the BIOS and attempt to boot off an alternate media (floppy or CD-ROM).

5. Rebuild the master boot record.

   If you can boot with a DOS floppy disk, try using the `FDISK /MBR` command to rebuild the master boot record.

6. Replace the controller card of the boot disk and reboot.

   This, of course, assumes that the boot disk drive is connected to an expansion card controller. If the boot drive is connected to a motherboard (meaning chipset) interface, check the connection. Alternatively, you might want to test the boot drive in another PC.

7. Check the processor fan or heat sink.

   If the disk drives are not the problem, the CPU could be overheating and shutting down. Verify that the processor, processor fan, and heat sink are properly installed. If thermal grease is in use, verify that the fan and/or heat sink are in their proper positions. If thermal grease is not in use, you might want to consider applying it.

8. Check the memory modules as described in Steps 7 and 8 in the "Beep-No Boot" section earlier in the chapter.

9. Confirm that the CPU and chipset are compatible with the operating system.

   You should be able to get this information from either the CPU manufacturer (which might or might not be the chipset manufacturer) or the operating system publisher.

10. Review your motherboard manufacturer's Web site for bulletins of known problems or incompatibilities.

    I had a problem with a VIA chipset motherboard and the AGP video adaptors that I would have never been able to figure out had I not visited the manufacturers' Web sites.

TIP

Find out which chipsets the motherboard manufacturer is using for video, audio, and SCSI, if it is an option. Always go with well-known companies, such as ATI, Creative Labs, and Adaptec, if you have a choice. Generally, information about any known flaws in peripheral controller chipsets is readily available on the Internet or in technical hardware-related magazines. Study up on the components on the motherboard. This will save you from disabling parts of the motherboard in the BIOS or through a jumper or wasting an expansion slot with a redundant replacement card.

Removing a Motherboard

Nothing in a PC has as much potential for disaster as the act of removing or installing its motherboard. However, if you proceed methodically and carefully, you really have nothing to fear and usually much to gain.

Working by the rules

Follow these six general rules when removing a motherboard (or any other component of a PC, for that matter!):

1. **Proceed cautiously.**

   When working on a PC, proceed as if any action you take has the potential to destroy the system – because it can! This is especially true of motherboards.

2. **Write everything down.**

   Even if you've worked on hundreds of PCs and can field strip a PC blindfolded in less than 60 seconds, every PC should be approached as if it is totally unique. Write down every action that you take and make a note of each removed part (and where you store it) so that later when you're trying to reassemble the PC, you can simply reverse your actions and know where you put all the parts.

3. **Draw pictures.**

   Making quick sketches of connector orientations, jumper locations, and the like can be very helpful. Relying on your memory for such things can lead to failed boots, blown components, and fried motherboards.

4. **Label parts.**

   Label each component removed or disconnected from the system in a way that's meaningful to you. You might want to number or letter parts, connectors, and cables and also reference them in your notes – or maybe just label devices by their relationship to other components, such as Drive0, Drive1, and so on.

5. **Protect everything from ESD.**

   And this means you (too)! I don't need to tell you of the dangers of ESD, so this is just a gentle reminder to protect the system and its components whether in or out of the PC.

6. **Use the right tools correctly.**

   Even though you like to use your tweaker for virtually everything, often there is a better and more appropriate tool for any task. Your first task is to protect the motherboard, and using the wrong tool can result in gouged traces, stripped screws, and metallic debris in the system.

Opening the case

The type of system case in use can make removal and installation of a motherboard a snap. On the other hand, a case might be designed for efficient manufacturing but not for ease of repair.

On many newer cases, almost every component is removable — often without the need for the use of many tools beyond a screwdriver. Manufacturers are always looking for ways to reduce the number of hard connectors (such as screws and clips) that hold cases and components together to simplify production and lower costs.

So, under the assumption that opening the case (see the manufacturer's documentation for this activity) is not a big problem, here are some generic guidelines to opening a PC case.

1. Remove all cables from the ports on the back, side, or front of the PC, including the monitor, speakers, and the serial cables, parallel cables, and USB cables of external devices.

   I recommend that you label the cables as to which connector they were attached to *and* create a diagram illustrating the connections and cables.

2. Remove the case cover.

   Every PC case is a little unique, even between models of the same manufacturer. Usually the case is secured with screws around the edge of the rear panel of the PC. However, you'll find new breeds of PCs on which the motherboard, CPU, and memory modules are exposed by simply lifting off the front or side panel, usually without tools. If your PC is one of these, the front or side panel is held in place by spring latches or friction retainers. You might need to slide a locking handle or lift the panel, but typically a strong and steady pull should release the panel. Watch for protruding floppy disk and CD-ROM drives or interior cables that could catch on the panel and be dislodged or damaged in the process. If the panel won't pull off without significant effort or possible damage, stop and look for screws securing it to the chassis.

   Most newer computers have separated the sides of the case to allow only one side to be removed. This exposes the motherboard and its components, which is usually enough for normal maintenance. On others, the entire case slips off the rear of the PC, exposing the motherboard on all sides. Regardless, because complete access is needed to remove the motherboard, remove enough of the case cover to expose both sides of the motherboard, if possible.

3. Remove the retaining screws in the expansion cards.

   Also remove the cables connecting the cards to the computer, such as the drive cables from IDE or SCSI cards and the CD-ROM audio cables on sound cards. Label each cable with a piece of masking tape or with a fine-point marker as to what it is and its orientation. The disk drive data cable should have a red or blue edge to indicate its Pin 1 location. Draw a diagram that shows which expansion card went into which expansion slot. Mark each slot with a number and then label each card with a piece of tape on which you've written the slot number from which it was removed. Include the connecting cables and the device to which each was attached in the diagram.

4. Mark or label the cables that connect directly into the connectors integrated into the motherboard, including the power supply, floppy disk controller, IDE controller, and possibly the sound controller.

   Indicate the device, which is usually printed on the motherboard surface next to each socket, as shown in Figure 1-8. Create a diagram for these cables that indicates the source, destination, orientation, and any special markings on the cable that will be important at reassembly time.

Figure 1–8: The device type is printed on the motherboard for integrated controllers.
Photo courtesy of Intel Corporation.

5. Remove the motherboard's mounting screws.

   Locate the heads of the screws that secure the motherboard to the chassis, and remove the motherboard mounting screws and store them where you can find them later. Be careful not to lose any paper or plastic washers that are on these screws.

6. Lift out the motherboard.

Some PCs have a mounting plate from which the screws must be removed to swing the motherboard out of its mounting. Hold the motherboard by its edges, being careful not to put pressure on or to soil either side of the board. Place the board on an anti-static mat or on an anti-static shipping bag and document any other connectors or mountings that you've not previously noted.

If the motherboard is mounted on brass standoffs that are used to lock the motherboard to the case, remove the screws attaching the board to the brass standoffs and slide it to unlock the standoffs. Lift the board out of the standoff keys and place it on an anti-static surface.

7. To reinstall or replace the motherboard, use your diagrams and notes and reverse the order of operations.

Other considerations

As I describe in this chapter, problems that could be associated with a motherboard are typically problems with one or more of the components mounted on or connected to the motherboard. You'll find the specific information for each of these components in other chapters of this book.

As a general guideline for diagnosing what you think could be motherboard problems, start with the power supply and work through the other components before you begin suspecting the motherboard itself.

Chapter 2

Processors

IN THIS CHAPTER

Unless you're Mr. or Ms. Goodwrench, when you open the hood (*bonnet*, for my British friends) of any new car, what you see might look very technologically impressive, but there isn't much on the engine that you could actually troubleshoot or fix yourself. Not only are special equipment and tools required but a heap of knowledge, training, and experience as well.

Well, the microprocessor (more commonly called the *processor* for short) in a PC is very much like the engine in a new car. After you open the case, you can't do much except admire the technology, engineering, and high-level integration that went into creating that very small package containing more computing power than the mainframes of the '60s and '70s.

For that reason, this chapter is less about troubleshooting a processor and more about

- ◆ Its number systems

- ◆ Logic processing

- ◆ The steps used to install or replace a processor

- ◆ Which processors will fit into which motherboard mountings

IF YOU'RE HOPING to troubleshoot, diagnose, or debug a processor, your advanced degree in electrical engineering will come in very handy. Otherwise, if you're like most folks (including me!), you should just accept some things on faith. However, because nearly everything that goes on inside the PC is controlled one way or another, you should understand some of the characteristics and operational features of a PC processor.

Understanding Processors

PCs are electronic devices, and as such, they internally represent binary numbers with voltage levels. Binary numbers are represented in the PC with only two distinct voltage levels: high and low. In turn, these voltage levels (also called *logic levels*) are used to represent the binary values one and zero. The voltage of a logic level must remain constant so it can be properly registered by the electronic circuitry, which is why microprocessors and their associated support chips require a direct current (DC) power source.

The world of microprocessors is the world of the semiconductor. A *semiconductor* is a material that's not exactly a *conductor* (a material that allows electrical current to pass through it) or an *insulator* (a material that doesn't support the flow of electrical current) that can be made to perform electronically encoded instructions in microscopic-sized environments. Semiconductors are materials that are neither a conductor nor an insulator, such as silicon.

Powering a processor

The amount of power used by a processor is actually very small. In fact, from the 8086 to about halfway through the life cycle of the 486, Intel processors ran on 5 volts (v) of DC. (*nv* DC refers to a certain amount of direct current voltage.) Some 486 processors and most of the Pentiums (and Pentium-class processors) use 3v DC, but some Pentium-class processors use 3.3v DC, 2.5v DC, 2.2v DC, and 1.3v DC. Reducing the voltage of a processor (in addition to speeding up the processing) also reduces the amount of electrical power (important in portables) needed to power the processor and the amount of heat that the processor generates.

Cooling a processor

Prior to the Intel 486, processors were cooled by the case (power supply) fan through *radiant cooling*. Since then, however, processors are cooled with a heat sink, a dedicated processor fan, or both, attached to the surface of the processor packaging. This system was designed to draw the heat up and out of the processor and carry it away on the tines of the heat sink and airflow from the fan.

The Pentium processor was designed to operate at around 185° Fahrenheit (85° Celsius), and the cooling system must keep it at or near this temperature. On the 486, Pentium, and Pentium Pro processors, heat sinks and fans are clipped to the processor or attached with a dielectric gel *(thermal grease)* – or both (see Figure 2-1). Later Pentium models, including the Slot 1 Celeron, the Pentium II, and the Pentium III, use a variation of the Single Edge Contact Cartridge (SECC) packaging, which includes mounting points for fans and heat sinks as part of their design.

Figure 2-1: Microprocessor heat sink and fan.

Photo courtesy of PC Power and Cooling, Inc.

Often the processor is not the only high-heat device inside the computer case. Other high-performance devices, such as accelerated video cards and high-speed hard drives, can cause the inside of a PC's case to heat up. PC case designs must provide enough ventilation to allow cool air to be drawn in and hot air to be expelled. Otherwise the life of the system, including the processor and other heat-sensitive components, will be dramatically shortened.

Packaging the processor

What you see when you look at a microprocessor is actually its packaging. The outer covering of the processor protects its core and serves to both connect and distribute the processor to its mounting socket or slot. Older processor packaging designs were often ceramic, which has excellent heat resistance and heat dissipation properties. However, most of today's processors are now encased in plastic using a type of SECC mounting, which are popular because they're easy to install or remove.

Setting a processor

Pentium-class motherboards typically have one of two types of receptacles into which a processor can be inserted: either a *socket* (a squarish block with pin receptacles and typically a locking arm) or a *slot* (very much like the slots used for expansion cards). The functional differences between a slot and a socket are minimal and are used primarily because of manufacturer (and possibly design) preferences.

Sorting the sockets

Those processor chips that are packaged in the various configurations of the Pin Grid Array (PGA) are mounted on a motherboard using a socket. The two primary socket types used to mount a processor on a motherboard are the Zero Insertion Force (ZIF) and the Low Insertion Force (LIF).

ZIF sockets, which are the most commonly used on today's motherboards, have a lever arm that is used to lock the processor in place. When the ZIF's locking arm is raised, the processor is pushed up out of the mounting's pinholes. When the locking arm is lowered, the pins on the back of the processor are lowered into the mounting holes, provided that you have the processor aligned properly over the holes. The ZIF's arm then is secured under a catch lip to lock the processor in place.

A *LIF socket* has no locking arm, only the pinholes into which the pins on the back of the processor are inserted. To install a processor into a LIF mounting, the processor is placed directly over and aligned with the holes on the mounting. The processor is inserted into the mounting with straight-down and steady, yet gentle, pressure. Take care not to bend the pins by pushing too hard or pushing when the processor is not aligned exactly over the LIP mounting. To remove a processor from a LIF mounting, you should use a chip removal tool (which looks something like a baby crowbar) or a screwdriver, but I don't really recommend it.

Table 2-1 lists the most common socket types, their characteristics, and the processors that each supports.

TABLE 2-1 MICROPROCESSOR SOCKETS

Socket	Pins	Processors Supported	Type
Socket 1	169	AMD 5x86 133 Cyrix 5x86 100–120 Intel 486SX 16–33 Intel 486SX2 50–66 Intel 486SXODP 25–33 Intel 486DX 20–33 Intel 486DX2 50–66 Intel 486DX2ODR 50–66 Intel 486DX2ODPR 50–66 Intel 486DX4 75–120 Intel 486DX4ODR 75–100 Intel 486DX4ODPR 75–100	Low Insertion Force (LIF) or Zero Insertion Force (ZIF)
Socket 2	238	AMD 5x86 133 Cyrix 5x86 100–120 Intel 486SX 25–33 Intel 486SXODP 25–33 Intel 486SX2 50–66 Intel 486SX2ODP 50 Intel 486DX 25–50 Intel 486DXODP 25–33 Intel 486DX2 50–80 Intel 486DX2ODP 50–66 Intel 486DX2ODPR 50–66 Intel 486DX4 75–120 Intel 486DX4ODP 75–100 Intel 486DX4ODPR 75–100 Intel Pentium ODP 63–83	LIF or ZIF
Socket 3	237	AMD 5x86 133 MHz Cyrix 5x86 100–120 MHz Intel 486SX 25–33 MHz Intel 486SXODP 25–33 MHz Intel 486SX2 50–66 MHz Intel 486SX2ODP 50 MHz Intel 486DX 25–50 MHz Intel 486DXODP 25–33 MHz Intel 486DX2 50–80 MHz	LIF or ZIF

Socket	Pins	Processors Supported	Type
		Intel 486DX2ODP 50–66 MHz	
		Intel 486DX2ODPR 50–66 MHz	
		Intel 486DX4 75–120 MHz	
		Intel 486DX4ODP 75–100 MHz	
		Intel 486DX4ODPR 75–100 MHz	
		Intel Pentium ODP 63–83 MHz	
Socket 4	273	Intel Pentium 60–66 MHz	LIF or ZIF
		Intel Pentium Overdrive 120–133 MHz	
Socket 5	296	AMD K5 PR75–PR133 MHz	LIF or ZIF
		Cyrix 6x86L PR120+–PR166+ MHz	
		Intel Pentium 75–133 MHz	
		Intel Pentium ODP 125–166 MHz	
Socket 5	320	AMD K6 166–300 MHz	LIF or ZIF
		AMD K6-2 266–400 MHz	
		Cyrix 6x86MX PR166–PR233 MHz	
		Intel Pentium ODP MMX 125–180 MHz	
		Intel Pentium MMX 166–233 MHz	
Socket 6	235	Intel 486DX4 75–120 MHz	ZIF
Socket 7	296	AMD K5 PR75–PR200 MHz	LIF
		Cyrix 6x86 PR90+–PR200+ MHz	
		Cyrix 6x86L PR120+–PR200+ MHz	
		Intel Pentium 75–200 MHz	
		Intel Pentium ODP 125–166 MHz	
Socket 7	321	AMD K6 166–300 MHz	ZIF
		AMD K6-2 266–550 MHz	
		AMD K6-2+ 450–550 MHz	
		AMD K6-III 400–450 MHz	
		AMD K6-III+ 450–500 MHz	
		Cyrix 6x86MX PR166–PR333 MHz	
		Cyrix M II 233–433 MHz	
		Intel Pentium ODP MMX 125–200 MHz	
		Intel Pentium MMX 166–233 MHz	
Socket 8	387	Intel Pentium Pro 150–200 MHz	LIF or ZIF
		Intel Pentium II Overdrive 300–333 MHz	

Continued

TABLE 2-1 MICROPROCESSOR SOCKETS *(Continued)*

Socket	Pins	Processors Supported	Type
Socket 370	370	Cyrix (VIA) III 533–667 MHz Intel Celeron 300–533 MHz Intel Celeron 500 MHz–1.1 GHz Intel Celeron 1.0 GHz Intel Pentium III 500 MHz–1.13 GHz Intel Pentium III 866 MHz–1.13 GHz Intel Pentium III 1.0–1.33 GHz Intel Pentium IIIS 700 MHz VIA C3 733–800 MHz VIA C3 800–866 MHz VIA C3-T 800–933 MHz VIA C4 1.2–2.0 GHz	ZIF (See Figure 2-2.)
Socket A	462	AMD Athlon 750 MHz–1.4GHz AMD Athlon 4 850 MHz–1.6 GHz AMD Athlon MP 1.0–2.0 GHz AMD Athlon XP 1.5–2.2 GHz AMD Athlon XP Mobile 1.4–1.8 GHz AMD Duron 600–950 MHz AMD Duron 1.0–1.3 GHz	ZIF
Socket 423	423	Intel Celeron 1.7–1.8 GHz Intel Pentium 4 1.3–2.0 GHz Intel Pentium 4 1.6–2.2 GHz	ZIF
Socket 478	478	Intel Celeron 1.7–1.8 GHz Intel Pentium 4 1.4–2.0 GHz Intel Pentium 4 1.6–2.2 GHz Intel Pentium 4 2.0–4.0 GHz	ZIF (See Figure 2-3.)
Socket 603	603	Intel Xeon 1.4–2.0 GHz Intel Xeon 1.8–2.6 GHz Intel Xeon MP 1.4–1.6 GHz	ZIF
PAC 418	418	Intel Itanium 733–800 MHz	Very Light Insertion Force (VLIF)
PAC 611	611	Itanium 2 900 MHz–1.0 GHz	VLIF
Socket 754	754	AMD K8 1.8–2.0 GHz	ZIF (See Figure 2-4.)

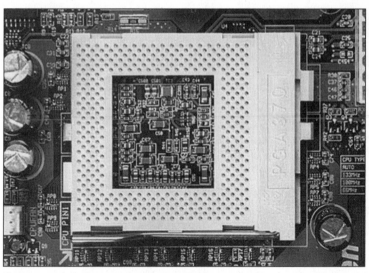

Figure 2-2: A Socket 370 processor mounting.

Figure 2-3: A Socket 478 processor mounting.

Figure 2-4: A Socket 754 processor mounting.

Slot types

Several Pentium-class processors use a slot mounting that is very much like the slots used for expansion cards. Table 2-2 lists the slot types found on many newer motherboards.

TABLE 2-2 MICROPROCESSOR SLOTS

Slot	Pins	Processors Supported	Type
Slot 1 (SC-242)	242	Intel Celeron 266–300 MHz Intel Celeron 300–433 MHz Intel Celeron Pin Grid Array (PGA) 300–533 MHz Intel Celeron 500 MHz–1.1 GHz Intel Pentium Pro 150–200 MHz Intel Pentium II 233–300 MHz Intel Pentium II 266–450 MHz Intel Pentium III 450–600 MHz Intel Pentium III 533 MHz–1.13 GHz	Single Edge Contact Cartridge (SECC: see Figure 2-5); SECC2, Single Edge Processor Package (SEPP)
Slot 2 (SC-330)	330	Intel Pentium II Xeon 400–450 MHz Intel Pentium III Xeon 500–550 MHz Pentium III Xeon 600–1.0 GHz	SECC

Slot	Pins	Processors Supported	Type
Slot A	242	AMD Athlon K7 500–700 MHz AMD Athlon K75 550 MHz–1.0 GHz AMD Athlon 700 MHz–1.0 GHz	
Slot M	418	Intel Itanium	SECC plus PGA

Figure 2-5: Slot 1 connector.

Photo courtesy of AOpen, Inc.

Here is a very good Web site for information on sockets and the processors that fit into them:

`www.pcguide.com/ref/cpu/char/socketSpecifics-c.html`

What's Happening in There? A Quick Look at CPU Operations

A microprocessor is also referred to as a *central processing unit* or *CPU*, which pretty well describes what it does. If you've ever wondered what goes on inside that marvel of modern technology, read on. However, if you've heard it all before, skip this sidebar.

The three types of CPU operations are

◆ Data Transfer

◆ Arithmetic and Logic

◆ Control

Continued

What's Happening in There? A Quick Look at CPU Operations *(Continued)*

Data Transfer Operations

This type of CPU operation consists of instructions that direct the CPU to move data from one location to another. The CPU can move data in a variety of lengths, including bytes, words, *dwords* (32-bit words), or *blocks* (larger groups of bits). The data is moved from *registers* (CPU data holding spaces) inside the processor to memory, from memory to registers, from registers to registers, and from memory to memory. However, in many systems, memory-to-memory commands are executed from direct memory access (DMA) chips to unload this type of action from the CPU. The way that its internal registers are laid out is one of the defining characteristics of an individual CPU line.

Arithmetic and Logic

The brain of a microprocessor is its Arithmetic Logic Unit (ALU). This is where data is used to develop a value or a comparative result. Operands are loaded into specific registers; when an instruction is executed, that places a result in another register, which is often referred to as an *accumulator*. This is one of the most complex portions of the microprocessor. The ALU's *logic gates,* which consist of small networks of transistors, perform all data transformations and combinations requested by an executing instruction. More recent processors include integrated integer and floating-point math co-processors in their ALUs.

Control Unit

If the ALU is the CPU's brain, the Control Unit is its heart. In this portion of the processor, commands, such as tracking program counters, organize return locations for subroutine calls and perform logic jumps. The Control Unit also dynamically maps the virtual memory system to control program segments moving in or out of memory or the hard disk. This part of the CPU is where most of the speed increases are being made through smarter pre-execution and caching of potentially needed instructions. The Control Unit is also where power management functions and processor mode changes are performed.

Differentiating the Microprocessors

Intel is by far the leading manufacturer of the microprocessors used in PCs. Although Intel does have competition from companies like AMD, VIA Cyrix, and a few others, Intel has consistently set the standard by which all processors are measured.

The processors that you're probably most familiar with – most probably the Pentiums – are all Intel processors. Another popular processor manufacturer is

Motorola, which you might have found in an Apple or Macintosh computer or in older computers, such as Altos, Motorola, or Amiga. However, because this book is about PC repair, I am concentrating on the Pentium-class processors. Before you e-mail me with long diatribes about how the Macintosh and Amiga (and the like) are not only PCs but the best PCs, just understand that I omit them only to keep the focus narrow.

To that end, I am also skipping over the early Intel, AMD, and Cyrix (VIA) processors – the 808x, 80286, 80386, the 80486 and their clone equivalents, the AMD 5x86, and the Cyrix 5x86.

Pentium

When it was introduced in 1992, the *Pentium* processor, shown in Figure 2-6, had many new features, including two 8-bit caches (one for data and one for instructions) and a floating-point unit (FPU) that operated as much as five times faster than that of its predecessor, the Intel 80486 (the 486).

Figure 2-6: A Pentium microprocessor.

Photo courtesy of Intel Corporation.

The Pentium used a data bus of 64 bits but kept the 486's 32-bit address bus. It also featured a new superscalar architecture that could execute multiple instructions simultaneously. *Pipelining*, which attempts to sequence the multiple parts of an instruction for faster execution, had been introduced with the 386, but the Pentium took it one step further with dual pipelining. This new technology could execute all of an instruction's parts in a single cycle. Pentium processor speeds ranged from the original Pentium 60 MHz to the Pentium 200 MHz.

A second version of the original Pentium was introduced with MMX (MultiMedia Extensions), shown in Figure 2-7, which had clock speeds ranging from 166 MHz to 233 MHz. The MMX code added an instruction set allowing the FPU to perform the same operation on several pieces of data simultaneously using single instruction multiple data (SIMD). The MMX instructions, which use matrix math (another meaning for MMX), provide added support for compression and decompression algorithms (such as Joint Photographic Experts Group [JPEG], Graphics Interchange Format [GIF], and Motion Picture Experts Group [MPEG]) and 3-D graphics rendering.

Figure 2-7: A Pentium processor with MMX.

Photo courtesy of Intel Corporation.

Cyrix 6x86

Cyrix, now a part of VIA, produced a line of Pentium work-alikes that ranged from its original 6x86-P120 to the 6x86-P200. Because the 6x86-P series had reported heat problems and some alleged incompatibility issues, Cyrix also produced a low-power version called the 6x86L that also operated at a lower temperature. The assumption is that the *L* stood for low temperature, but many contend it stands for *later*.

Cyrix also produced a Socket 7 style processor that required a special motherboard. This processor, the MediaGX, included an onboard sound processor and graphics adaptor. The MediaGX was designed for low-end computers, but its poor graphics quality was largely responsible for its short life.

Other Pentium clones

A few other manufacturers built Pentium-class processors as well. Perhaps the most successful was the K5 line from AMD (Advanced Micro Devices). The 75–166 megahertz (MHz) K5 was AMD's attempt to directly compete with the Pentium, but it suffered from a lack of speed, which was caused by its complexity.

The Integrated Device Technology (IDT) Centaur WinChip C6 (also known as the Evergreen Technologies 200 MxPro) includes MMX extensions, has a large L1 cache, and is less expensive than the Intel 200 MHz Pentium MMX. The WinChip

C6, which was more popular outside the U.S., was available in 180 MHz to 240 MHz versions. Of the MMX clones, the WinChip C6 delivered almost identical performance to the Intel Pentium with MMX.

Pentium Pro

Intel developed the Pentium Pro, shown in Figure 2-8, primarily for use in network servers. It was designed to be used in configurations of one, two, or four processors on specially designed motherboards. The Pentium Pro featured 1 megabit (mb) of advanced Level 2 (L2) cache running at the processor's core clock speed. The 200 MHz Pentium Pro was also designed to support 32-bit operating systems, such as Windows NT and Windows 95.

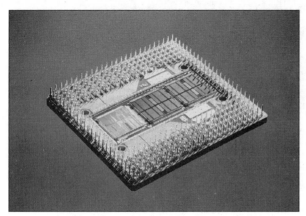

Figure 2-8: The Intel Pentium Pro microprocessor.

Photo courtesy of Intel Corporation.

Pentium II

The Pentium II, shown in Figure 2-9, is really just the Pentium Pro with the MMX instruction set added. When it was released, there was a great to-do over a floating-point math bug in the chip, which Intel promptly fixed. The PII is available in versions with clock speeds of 233 MHz, 266 MHz, and 300 MHz. It is especially well suited for multimedia reproduction that includes full-motion video and 3-D images. Although it has twice the L1 cache of the Pentium Pro at 32KB, its 512KB of L2 cache is only half of that in the Pentium Pro.

Celeron

The Celeron microprocessor (see Figure 2-10) is intended to be a lower-cost alternative of the Pentium II for use in desktop and mobile computers. It uses two mounting styles: the Pentium II's Slot 1 and the Socket 370. The Celeron was originally released with clock speeds ranging from 333 MHz to 500 MHz. The newer Celerons, those with clock speeds of 566 MHz to over 1.0 GHz, are built on the Pentium III core.

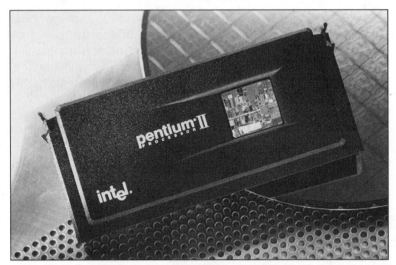

Figure 2-9: The Intel Pentium II microprocessor in the Slot 1 package.

Photo courtesy of Intel Corporation.

Figure 2-10: The Intel Celeron microprocessor showing both the SECC and the Socket 370 configurations.

Photo courtesy of Intel Corporation.

Xeon

The Xeon processor, shown in Figure 2-11, was originally based on the Pentium II and was seen as the successor to the Pentium Pro as a server processor. The Xeon has a range of L2 cache size choices, ranging from 512K, 1MB, and 2MB, which all run at the processor's core clock speed. The Xeon's cache uses Intel's proprietary 512K CSRAM (custom static RAM) chips that can be applied like building blocks to increase the cache size. The Xeon addresses and caches to 64GB of memory by using a 36-bit memory address bus. The Xeon supports four and up to eight CPUs in one server. The Xeon (pronounced *zee*-on) is currently available with speeds up to 2.4 GHz.

Figure 2–11: The Intel Pentium II Xeon processor.

Photo courtesy of Intel Corporation.

AMD K6

The AMD K6, developed to compete with the Pentium MMX, was actually able to out perform it in speed and price. It was available in 166 MHz, 200 MHz, 233 MHz, and 266 MHz versions, as well as a 300 MHz model that used the Super 7 socket style to achieve 100 MHz bus speeds.

Cyrix 6x86MX

Also known as the MII, the Cyrix 6x86MX processor contained virtually the same MMX instruction set as the Pentium MMX. In order to make its processors comparable to Intel's, Cyrix (and later AMD) began using a processor rating (PR) designation for equivalent clock speeds. A PR-166 rating indicated that a processor had the equivalent speeds of 166 MHz. The Cyrix 6x86 processors had PR speeds from PR-166 (on a Socket 7 mounting) to PR-366 (on a Super 7 motherboard).

VIA Cyrix III

The VIA Cyrix III microprocessor, shown in Figure 2-12, runs at clock speeds of 433, 466, 500, and 533 MHz and features some enhanced performance features, such as a 100/133 MHz Front Side Bus and 128K full-speed L1 cache. It also supports both Intel's MMX and AMD's 3DNow, AMD's multimedia extensions.

Figure 2-12: The VIA Cyrix III microprocessor.

Photo courtesy of VIA Technologies, Inc.

AMD K6-2 and K6-III processors

The AMD K6-2 processor has increased an added set of 3-D graphics instructions called 3DNow, which extends the MMX instructions already included in the K6 design. The K6-2 processors are primarily built for the 100 MHz Super 7 socket. K6-2 models are available with clock speeds from 266 MHz to 550 MHz.

A newer model, the K6-2+, has added 128K of L2 cache to the processor and some new power control features.

The K6-III Super 7 processor features 256K of L2 cache and clock speeds from 400 MHz to 600 MHz. A newer model K6-III+ includes 1MB of cache and runs at the same clock speeds as the K6-III.

Intel Pentium III

The Pentium III processor is a network server processor that features speeds that range from 450 MHz to 1 GHz. The Pentium III is packaged in a second-generation single-edge connector package called SECC2, shown in Figure 2-13, which conducts and removes heat better and fits into the Slot 1 bus.

Most Pentium II motherboards can be upgraded for Pentium IIIs with only a flash BIOS (see Chapter 4) upgrade. A newer version of the PIII, which will sport 256K L1 cache and a 133 MHz bus speed, will also be packaged in the less expensive Slot 370-like Flip Chip Pin Grid Assembly (FCPGA).

Figure 2-13: The Pentium III processor in the Slot 1 SECC2 package.

Photo courtesy of Intel Corporation.

AMD Athlon

The new powerhouse on the block is the 1 GHz AMD Athlon, which boasts 22 million transistors, support for Intel's MMX and an enhanced version of AMD's own 3DNow, and improved FPU functions. It can also simultaneously decode more instructions than the Pentium III. Although it plugs into a Slot 1 connector, AMD's Slot A specification is based on the Alpha EV-6 bus, which runs at speeds of 200 MHz to 400 MHz. Other features of the Athlon processor are that it has the first fully pipelined, superscalar FPU for x86 platforms, 256K of L2 cache, and 128K of L1 cache on the chip.

AMD Duron

The AMD Duron processor is a derivative of the AMD Athlon processor. Designed for business and home-user desktop as well as mobile computing, the Duron processor is available at clock speeds ranging from 600 MHz to 1.3 GHz.

Intel Pentium 4

The Intel P4 processor, the latest of the Pentium processors, is available with speeds of 1.6 to 2.8 GHz and is designed for desktop processing.

VIA C3

VIA claims that the C3 processor, shown in Figure 2-14, is the coolest GHz processor available. I'm sure that VIA is proud of it, but *cool* here means that it runs at a lower operating temperature, which saves energy and allows it to run with standard cooling systems and power supplies.

The C3 features a 128KB L1 cache and 64K L2 cache and supports both 3DNow and MMX. The C3 mounts in a Socket 370 mounting.

Figure 2-14: The VIA C3 microprocessor.

Photo courtesy of VIA Technologies, Inc.

Intel Itanium and Itanium 2

The 64-bit Itanium (pronounced eye-*tain*-ee-um) creates a processor architecture specifically designed for use in network servers and high-end workstations. It might not be the fastest (at 833 MHz to 1.0 GHz), but it is very robust and is designed for scalability and high availability, two characteristics very important to networks.

Binary (Logical) Arithmetic Operations

The three main types of CPU binary computation functions are arithmetic, logical, and data shift operations. Each CPU function has a corresponding binary operator: AND, OR, and EXCLUSIVE OR, respectively. These binary operators each require two binary numbers (usually taken from CPU registers), which are combined to derive a third number that is based on the interaction of the original two numbers.

ANDing operations

In an *ANDing* operation, as performing an AND operation is commonly called, the answer can be true (represented by the value 1) only if both of the operands are true.

Binary value 1	1	1	0	0
Binary value 2	1	0	1	0
Result of AND operation	1	0	0	0

The figure here illustrates how this works. First the binary numbers are aligned position-by-position, right to left. Then each pair of bits (one from each number) is combined. Notice how in the leftmost column of the figure that the two ones resulted in a one and that all the other number pairs resulted in a zero. This is because only two trues (ones) will result in a true (one) value. Anything else results in a false (zero) condition.

When AND operations are applied to a bit word, each column is treated as an individual equation, and there is no carry over to adjoining columns. Here is another example:

```
        10010110
AND     11001101

        10000100
```

Only those bit pairs that are both one values (true) result in a one (true). All other combinations of ones and zeroes (including two zeroes) result in a zero (false). The basic logic behind the AND operation is that in order for two bits to result in a true, the first AND the second must both be true.

A common use for the logical AND operator is to mask a binary number. This involves arbitrarily masking out (reducing to 0) a certain portion of the target binary number by applying a second number (the mask) that has zeroes in the positions to be discarded and ones in the positions of the bits to be kept. The AND operator can be used to force zeroes into certain binary positions while leaving the other bits unchanged.

Continued

Binary (Logical) Arithmetic Operations *(Continued)*

The Logical OR

In an OR operation, which also combines two binary number values to achieve a logical result, the result will be true (1) if either of the bits in each column pair is a one (true). See the following figure that illustrates how the logical OR works.

Binary value 1	1	1	0	0
Binary value 2	1	0	1	0
Result of OR operation	1	1	1	0

Notice in the figure that only those columns that have at least one true (1) result in a true. An OR operation is the reverse of the AND operation. The OR function places ones in any non-duplicated positions. Ones can also be forced into specified bit positions without disturbing the surrounding digits. The following is an example of ORing two bytes together:

```
      10010110
OR    11001101

      11011111
```

Any column that has at least one true (1) value results in a true value. Only true values matter; two falses are always false. The logic of the OR function is that any one bit OR the other can be true to result in a true for the pair.

The Exclusive OR operation

An Exclusive OR (XOR) operation requires one, and only one, of the two bit operands to be true exclusive of the other bit's value. So, in the XOR logical operation, if only one bit is true (1), the pair results in a true. If both or neither of the bits is true, the result is false (0). The following figure illustrates this operation of the XOR function.

Binary value 1	1	1	0	0
Binary value 2	1	0	1	0
Result of XOR operation	0	1	1	0

Because the two bits in the leftmost column of the figure are both ones, the XOR operation results in a false. However, in the center two columns, where only one bit is true, the results are both true. Once again, false is false, and only truth matters.

XOR can be used in column style to combine two binary digits to form a third. Here is another example:

```
      10010110
XOR   11001101

      01011011
```

Only the columns where just one of the bits is a one is the result also a one. The logic is that one bit, exclusive of the other bit, can be true to result in a true condition. XOR is often used to find the complement of a bit string. Exclusive ORing any byte with a byte of all ones will produce its complement, as shown in this example:

```
      10010110
XOR   11111111

      01101001
```

Working with Number Systems

The primary storage device inside the computer is the *transistor*, which holds exactly one bit. The transistor stores binary values in the form of electrical voltage levels that are either positive or non-positive. The binary number system matches the capabilities of the transistor perfectly because they both have only two states or values. The computer stores a single binary numeral (either a one or a zero) in a single transistor.

Understanding how 1+1 = 10: The binary system

The binary number system represents values as exponential values of two. Binary is a base two number system like decimal is a base ten number system. Decimal numbers, such as 101, are a combination of various powers of the base ten. The decimal number 101 represents one plus zero tens plus one one-hundred, which is the same as 1 times 10 to the zero power plus 0 times 10 to the first power plus 1 times 10 to the second power:

$$(1 * 10^2) + (0 * 10^1) + (1 * 10^0) = 101$$

Likewise, the number 221 represents

$$(2 * 10^2) + (2 * 10^1) + (1 * 10^0) = 221$$

Decimal values have ten numerals (0 to 9) to express how many of a particular power of ten is included in a number. In fact, the word *decimal* is derived from the word *ten*.

The binary number system works like the decimal system with two exceptions: Each position in a binary number represents a power of two, and the binary system uses only two numerals (0 and 1) to express whether a particular power of two value is included in a number.

Earlier I proved why the number 101 represents *one hundred and one*. Now look at why the binary number 101 represents the decimal value 5:

$$(1 * 2^2) + (0 * 2^1) + (1 * 2^0) = 5$$

In this example, one times two to the second power plus zero times two to the first power plus one times two to the zero power adds up to the decimal number five. So, the binary number 101 is the equivalent of 5. Figure 2-15 shows the binary numbers equivalent to the decimal numbers from 0 to 20. Notice the progression of numbers. What would be the next binary number?

Each position in a binary number represents an increasingly larger power of two (starting from 0) as you move from right to left. Each position can hold only a one or a zero. A binary number cannot hold other values, such as a decimal 4,321. In order to store this number as a binary number, you need to substitute the binary values represented in this decimal number into the binary number. Table 2-3 lists the first eight powers of two.

Binary	Decimal
00000000	0
00000001	1
00000010	2
00000011	3
00000100	4
00000101	5
00000110	6
00000111	7
00001000	8
00001001	9
00001010	10
00001011	11
00001100	12
00001101	13
00001110	14
00001111	15
00010000	16
00010001	17
00010010	18
00010011	19
00010100	20

Figure 2-15: Binary numbers in an 8-bit byte.

TABLE 2-3 POWERS OF TWO

Power of Two	Calculation	Decimal Equivalent
2^0	2 * 0	1
2^1	2 * 1	2
2^2	2 * 2	4
2^3	2 * 2 * 2	8
2^4	2 * 2 * 2 * 2	16
2^5	2 * 2 * 2 * 2 * 2	32
2^6	2 * 2 * 2 * 2 * 2 * 2	64
2^7	2 * 2 * 2 * 2 * 2 * 2 * 2	128

Converting decimal to binary

To convert the decimal number 222 to binary, you must determine which power of two values can be subtracted from the decimal number and a one placed into the power of two position for that value. Here is how it is done:

1. The largest power of two that is not greater than 222 is 128 (the next power of two value is 2^8, or 256). The binary number at this point is 10000000, which now includes a one to indicate the inclusion of the value of 2^7 or the decimal value 128.

2. Now subtract the value placed into the binary number (128) from the beginning number to find the number remaining to be converted: 222 − 128 = 94.

3. Next, the largest power of two that is not greater than 94 is 64 (see Table 2-3). The binary number now includes a one to indicate the inclusion of the 2^6 position (11000000). If you stopped now, your binary number represents the decimal value of 192. Find the remaining value: 94 − 64 = 30.

4. The largest binary value not greater than 30 is 16, or 2^4. The binary number is now 11010000 or the equivalent of a decimal 208. This particular number conversion does not use the 2^5 (32) position. Find the remaining value: 30 − 16 = 14.

5. The largest binary value that is less than or equal to 14 is 8, or 2^3. The binary number at this point is 11011000, which represents the decimal value of 216 (128 + 64 + 16 + 8). The remaining value is 14 − 8 = 6.

6. The largest binary value less than or equal to 6 is 4 (2^2). Placing a one in the third position of the binary number makes it now 11010100 or the equivalent of 220. The remaining value is 2.

7. To complete the conversion, turn on the binary value for 2 (2^1), which results in the binary number 11011110, which represents the decimal value of 222 (128 + 64 + 16 + 8 + 4 + 2).

To store the number 222 in the computer, 8 bits would be used to store the binary number 11011110. Remember that the computer can only store the binary values of 1 and 0. It can't store, work with, manipulate, add, or use any value not expressed as a binary number. There just isn't any way to store a 2, a 4, or a 9 in a single bit.

Counting up to 16: The hexadecimal system

Many of the addresses and configuration values on the PC are expressed as hexadecimal numbers. Hexadecimal means six and ten, or a base 16 number system.

Hex, as it is commonly called, uses a combination of 16 values: the decimal numbers 0 through 9 for the first ten values and the six letters A through F to represent the decimal values of 10 through 15. See Figure 2-16.

Hexadecimal Values	
Binary	Decimal
0001	1
0010	2
0011	3
0100	4
0101	5
0110	6
0111	7
1000	8
1001	9
1010	A
1011	B
1100	C
1101	D
1110	E
1111	F

Figure 2-16: The values of the hexadecimal number system.

Hexadecimal numbers use 4 bits, or a nibble, to store each digit. The *nibble* represents the binary values ranging from 2^0 in the rightmost position to 2^3 in the leftmost position. This allows the nibble to store the equivalent of a decimal 15, or the hexadecimal value F. Because of its larger base (base 16), hexadecimal is able to store values like 11 or 15 as a single character.

Our friendly number 101, which was one-hundred and one in decimal and five in binary, now represents the decimal value 257 when stored in hexadecimal. This is an excellent illustration of how much larger values can be stored in hexadecimal. Another example is that the hexadecimal value ABCDEF represents 11,259,375 in decimal.

Upgrading Processors

Processors go through many revisions (steppings) in their lifetimes, usually in response to very small and unpublicized bugs. Intel has been very good about recording this information (possibly in response to criticism over the original handling of the Pentium bugs), and its Web site (www.intel.com) is a tremendous resource for identification of processor stepping and possible bugs. To their credit, some of Intel's competitors have also put together good Web sites in support of their processors and include similar data.

Getting processor info

Here are some Web sites that you can use for information on microprocessors:

- ◆ Intel processors: www.intel.com

- ◆ AMD processors: www.amd.com

- ◆ VIA Cyrix processors: www.cyrix.com

- ◆ Legacy Cyrix processor (supported by National Semiconductor): e-mail to support@nsc.com

- ◆ General information on processors: www.geek.com

Upgrading processors

The most valuable first step to upgrading a computer's microprocessor is to find the motherboard's documentation to see whether it lists the processors that it supports. Many computer manufacturers, such as Gateway (www.gateway.com), use off-the-shelf motherboards from major manufacturers and usually offer upgrade information on their Web sites. Write down anything from the motherboard that looks like a model number before you go to a manufacturer's Web site. Additional information can be found on motherboard manufacturer sites.

UPGRADING A PRE-PENTIUM TO A PENTIUM-CLASS PROCESSOR

If you have a 486-class processor, the first step is to determine the type of socket used on your motherboard. Most likely the socket is a Socket 1, Socket 2, or Socket 3 mounting. The socket type is usually embossed on the ZIF handle or on the side of the mounting. However, before you take any other action, carefully examine the processor and its mounting to be absolutely sure what you have.

If you see an unoccupied row of pins around your processor (and the processor is in an upgrade or Overdrive type), then you have a 237- or 238-pin socket (Socket 3 or 2, respectively).

At one time Intel produced a Pentium Overdrive processor that was used to upgrade pre-Pentium 25 MHz and 50 MHz processors to 63 MHz and 33 MHz, and 66 MHz machines to 83 MHz. Unfortunately, it has been discontinued. So, unless you can find someone who still stocks it (item number BOXPODP5V83), you will need to go with a clone upgrade processor, such as Evergreen Technologies (www.evertech.com).

TIP Some companies package processors, instructions, processor removal tools, fans, BIOS upgrade utilities, and performance monitoring software together in a kit at reasonable prices. If you are new to processor upgrades, I recommend that you either visit your local computer supply store or contact one online and use an upgrade kit at least for the first few times you do a processor upgrade.

USING A KIT TO UPGRADE A 486 (OR BEFORE) PROCESSOR

Follow these steps to upgrade a processor with an upgrade kit:

TIP Way before you begin upgrading the processor in a PC—before even buying a new processor—I recommend that you visit the Web site or contact the manufacturer of the PC and the motherboard. They can provide you with information and guidance that can save you much frustration and possibly money as well.

1. The kit should include software to check the speed of the processor on a floppy disk or CD-ROM.

   Run this software to check the speed of the existing processor and write it down in your notes. It is an especially good idea for you to take notes all through this process. When in doubt, write it down.

2. If the kit includes a BIOS update, it doesn't necessarily mean you have to apply it.

   Check the BIOS or motherboard manufacturer's Web site for compatibility information of the new processor on this motherboard and BIOS. If an upgrade is required, verify that the one in the upgrade kit is the correct version – and if not, download the correct version and install it. I hope you've been writing all this down.

3. Upgrade the BIOS if necessary.

   See Chapter 4 for instructions on how to go about flashing your ROM BIOS. Write down any ID numbers you see during the Power-On Self-Test (POST) for later reference.

TIP

Identifying the name or model number on a motherboard can sometimes be difficult, if not impossible. Look for stickers or printing on the motherboard itself and ignore anything written on the components (chips, cables, and so on) installed on the motherboard.

If you find what you believe are the motherboard's identity numbers, visit either Motherboards.org (www.motherboards.org) or Wim's BIOS Page (www.wimsbios.com) for help identifying your motherboard. You can also use Wim's BIOS Page to identify your system using the BIOS version and numbers displayed during the boot process.

Another way to identify the manufacturer of your motherboard or system is to use the Federal Communications Commission (FCC) number (found on the motherboard) to look it up in the FCC-authorized product database (www.fcc.gov/oet/fccid).

4. Put on an electrostatic discharge (ESD) wrist strap or take other ESD preventive measures before proceeding any further.

   See Chapter 27 for more information on ESD and how to avoid it.

5. Open the system case.

   Even with a wrist strap on, use caution inside the system unit and ground yourself to the metal chassis as frequently as possible.

6. If your processor mounting socket is a Zero Insertion Force (ZIF) type socket, like that illustrated in Figure 2-17, unlock the lever and move it up and around to unbind the processor's pins.

   Grasp the lever next to the socket and lift it up and back until it is vertical. You might need to pull the lever away from the socket very slightly before lifting it up. This causes the top of the socket to shift and open the socket. On older motherboards, the lever might stick, possibly requiring a bit more pressure to get it open. Never yank or jerk the ZIF lever. If you break it off, you'll probably need a new motherboard.

7. If the mounting isn't a ZIF socket, use the processor removal tool — also called a *spoon* or a *fork* (however, not an actual spoon or fork, please!) — which is an L-shaped tool that should look something like a small pry bar. Gently pry one side of the processor up about one-quarter of an inch.

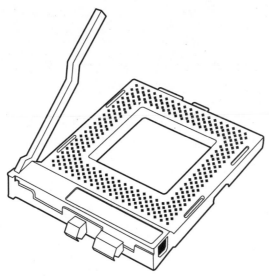

Figure 2-17: A ZIF-style socket.

Repeat this operation on each of the other three sides until you're able to grasp the edges of the processor lightly with your fingers and lift it out of the socket.

8. Holding the new processor lightly (just to remind you) by its edges using your fingertips, align the processor over the socket.

Because both the processor and the socket are square, you have to orient the processor so that its pins are lined up to fit into the correct holes. The processor will have some distinguishing characteristic to let you know where Pin 1 is (usually the lower-left corner of the processor). Look for one of the following marks on the processor: a dot in one corner; a notch in one corner; a bit of gold running diagonally from the underside of the chip; or on the underside of the processor, look for one of the corner pins to be inside of a gold square. Typically, the marking that you'll find is the numeral 1 or a notch in one order. As illustrated in Figure 2-17, some 486 motherboards have sockets with four rows of pins. These are intended for use by a Pentium Overdrive Processor (ODP). A 486 processor has only three rows of pins, so you need to use caution when inserting an ODP into a socket with four rows of holes. Some processors also have specially shaped pins that cannot be inserted into the wrong hole without damaging them.

9. Gently and with even force, press the processor's pins into place. When you first start, recheck to be sure that the pins are aligned.

   If the socket is a ZIF socket, you shouldn't need to force the processor into the socket. Remember that ZIF means *Zero Insertion Force,* which means little or no force needed to seat it in the socket. After it's pressed into place, lock the lever.

   If the socket is not a ZIF socket, you need to push the processor into place carefully to avoid damaging the processor. First set the pins just on the socket's holes. Then apply light pressure with your fingers by moving around the processor's surface and applying firm, even pressure. Don't rush, don't push too hard, and apply even pressure.

10. Check the motherboard documentation to see whether any voltage or clock speed settings need to be changed.

    If changes are needed, most likely they're affected through jumpers on the motherboard. Make these adjustments, if any, before the system is powered up.

11. Before closing up the system case, boot the system.

    If the system will not boot, check the POST error codes and make any adjustments needed. Wires, cables, or connectors were likely dislodged during the installation of the processor. If the system boots – so far, so good.

12. If the system has booted, test it using the CPU performance software that came with the kit.

    If the performance is less than you reasonably should expect, check the clock multiplier jumpers on your motherboard (see the motherboard's documentation for their location) and recheck whether you should have upgraded the BIOS for the new processor.

13. If all is well, replace the system case.

    Now is also an excellent time to perform any needed preventive maintenance inside the system unit. (See Chapter 27 for information on preventive care of the computer.)

Applying Overdrive to a Pentium processor

As with the pre-Pentium upgrades, I recommend using a kit for these upgrades. A number of Overdrive Pentium upgrades are available for Intel processors. Table 2-4 lists the upgrades that you're likely to need.

TABLE 2-4 INTEL OVERDRIVE UPGRADES

Original Pentium Speed	Overdrive Pentium Speed
75	150
90, 120, 150	180
100, 133	166 or 200 (Socket 7 only)
166	200

As before (see "Using a kit to upgrade a 486 (or before) processor" earlier in this chapter), read the motherboard's documentation before proceeding to determine whether jumper or BIOS changes are required before the processor will function.

Upgrading a Pentium Pro processor to Pentium II

Moving up from the Pentium Pro to the Pentium II is a simple matter of a drop-in upgrade. Because both processors use a ZIF socket, it is as easy as removing the Pentium Pro and installing the Pentium II. No other changes should be necessary. For more information, visit Intel's Web site (www.intel.com) or visit your local computer hardware vendor.

Upgrading to a faster version of the same processor

Except that you need to do all the things listed in each of the preceding upgrades, such as verifying your motherboard and BIOS and their compatibility to a faster processor, upgrading a processor to a faster (higher MHz rating) version of itself is fairly easy.

Processors within the same series use the same type of mounting, whether it be a socket or a slot (also referred to as a *slocket*). However, to avoid problems, verify that the upgrade processor that you wish to install actually does use the same mounting as the existing processor. The processor manufacturer's Web site is most likely the best place to get this information.

When upgrading to a newer version of a processor, be sure that you consider the stepping or revision number of the old and new processors. Steppings (Intel) and revision numbers (AMD and VIA) are used to indicate newer processor versions within a processor family. You wouldn't want to inadvertently replace your processor with what might actually be an older version.

Dealing with Processor-level Errors and Other Common Problems

This section contains some of the more common processor-related errors and problems that you might encounter along with some suggested solutions.

The PC locks up immediately after completing the POST

This can be a puzzling situation, I know. However, here are some ideas on how to deal with it.

- *The processor is likely overheating.*

   The fan attached to the processor might not be operating properly, or the heat sink is not properly attached. Remove and reattach either or both, applying thermal compound (thermal glue) as appropriate.

- *If this problem is encountered immediately after a processor upgrade, it could be the result of incorrect voltage settings on the motherboard.*

   Refer to the motherboard's documentation for how the voltage is set and correct accordingly.

- *The problem could also be the result of an incorrect processor clock multiplier.*

   This should only happen right after the processor has been upgraded. Check the motherboard and processor documentation to determine what the proper setting should be and adjust it.

The system functions erratically with several intermittent problems

You can safely assume that this is the result of the processor overheating. Here are some things to try when diagnosing this situation.

- *To verify your suspicions, run the PC for an hour and then open the system case (using ESD protection).*

   Carefully place your fingertip on the processor or its heat sink near where it attaches to the processor. If you cannot comfortably leave your finger there for more than one or two seconds, the processor is too hot, and adjustments are definitely needed.

- *The number one cause of processor problems is cooling . . . or the lack thereof.*

The first thing that you should check if you suspect that a PC's problems are the result of insufficient cooling is the processor's documentation or the manufacturer's Web site for cooling requirements and information. The newer Pentiums and clones require a constant operating temperature to operate properly. Be sure that you have the correct cooling devices (fans, heat sink, thermal lubricate, and so on) installed for the specific processor installed.

◆ *Another source of overheating is improper speed and configuration settings.*

After verifying that the processor is supported by the motherboard, check your motherboard documentation and verify all the jumper settings that affect the processor.

◆ *Too much voltage can cause the processor to overheat.*

Check the voltage requirements for the processor and adjust the system's settings appropriately.

◆ *Make sure that cables or other hardware aren't blocking the processor fan when the system case is closed or that something isn't lodged in the processor fan blades.*

The processor fan could also be worn out and need replacing, or the processor might need a bigger fan. If a processor fan is not in use, it could be time to install one.

◆ *Verify that the PC's cooling system, which the processor's cooling system is indirectly dependent on, is doing its job.*

The device lights are on and the fan operates, but the PC does not boot

When the PC is powered up, if you see the boot process flash the device lights (or if they stay on steadily) but the POST doesn't sound a beep code, several things could be causing the problem. Here are a couple of the more common causes.

◆ *If this happens immediately after a processor upgrade, it is very likely that the processor is not completely seated in its socket.*

Open the system case, using ESD protection, and verify the installation of the processor.

◆ *If the processor is installed properly, it just might be the processor itself.*

If you have a spare CPU of the same type (I know – oh, sure you do!), swap it out and reboot the system. If the system boots, it is the processor. If it still fails, the socket might be damaged, or the motherboard itself was damaged during the upgrade.

The processor is incorrectly identified during the boot process

This might or might not be a problem. Here's why:

♦ *There might not be a problem at all.*

 Some processors, especially early Pentium and late 486 clones, were identified by some BIOS as Pentiums.

♦ *It could be that the processor is a clone (AMD, Cyrix, or IDT) that was released after the BIOS version on the PC.*

 You might need to upgrade the BIOS. See Chapter 4 for information on how to upgrade the BIOS.

During the boot, the processor speed listed is incorrect

Actually, this isn't a processor problem. If you run into this situation, here are some things to consider.

♦ *The reported speed of the processor is reported from the BIOS or motherboard settings and not the processor itself.*

 Check the documentation of the motherboard to determine how to properly indicate the processor speed or upgrade the BIOS.

♦ *If the number you're referring to is the readout on the front of a pre-Pentium computer, it, too, is displaying the speed indicated in the BIOS or set by the clock rate jumper on the motherboard.*

 Check the documentation and adjust accordingly.

The ZIF socket will not open

If the ZIF (or LIF) socket won't release the processor's pins so that you can remove the processor, it can be very frustrating. Your first instinct should be to not break the ZIF handle off—then you *will* have problems!

♦ *This might sound like a no-brainer, but check to see whether anything is blocking the lever or holding it in place.*

♦ *Many ZIP sockets require you to pull the socket lever out away from the socket slightly before it can be lifted up to release the processor's pins.*

♦ *Never force the lever to the point that you can feel it beginning to bend or break.*

The lever could just be stuck. Use a gentle rocking motion, applying steadily increasing pressure to release the lever. Do not — at any cost — break off the lever or damage the socket because you'll need a new motherboard . . . and most likely another processor as well.

Dealing with Processor Bugs

In this section, I have included lists of some things that have been discovered on a few of the more popular processors. Many have fixes and have been fixed, but you never know when you might encounter a PC with a legacy processor to which no updates have been applied.

Addressing AMD bugs

AMD's processors are famously bug-free (as are the processors from Intel and VIA, as well). However, some problems, especially compatibility problems, have been identified. The primary compatibility problem has been between the NVIDIA 3-D graphics card and the AMD Irongate processor platform found in AMD's K6 and later processors. If you encounter a problem with the video on an AMD system, check out the AMD (www.amd.com) and NVIDIA (www.nvidia.com) Web sites for possible upgrades.

Coping with Cyrix bugs

The Cyrix processors have had a couple of problems in their lifecycles. Table 2-5 lists three of the biggest problems they've experienced.

TABLE 2-5 CYRIX PROCESSOR BUGS

Processor	Problem	Solution
5x86	The processor blacks out or functions erratically after running for longer than 20 minutes. This processor experiences serious problems with heat generation and must be well cooled.	Upgraded cooling systems are available to help solve this problem.

Continued

TABLE 2-5 CYRIX PROCESSOR BUGS *(Continued)*

Processor	Problem	Solution
6x86	The 6x86 processor is slow when running Windows NT 4.0.	Windows NT 4.0 includes instructions that switch off part of the system cache to prevent system crashes on the 6x86 (version 2.7). This results in about one-third less processor speed. If you experience this problem, Cyrix has a software patch that turns the cache back on.
	The processor and the system crash for no apparent reason.	Although this bug is one that nearly every user believes his system has, on the Cyrix 6x86, it's usually a result of the problem relating to system cache discussed in the preceding entry. Switch off the system cache and then repeat the conditions that caused the system to crash. If that doesn't solve the problem, you'll need to expand your troubleshooting.

Resolving Intel processor bugs

Intel is no different than the other manufacturers when it comes to bugs getting past their testing and quality control functions. Perhaps the most infamous of the Intel bugs was the Pentium floating-point division (FDIV) bug that plagued this processor when it was first released. Table 2-6 lists common bugs in Intel processors.

Processor versions are upgraded frequently to either add new features, add hardware support, or (gasp) fix bugs. Intel calls its processor upgrades *steppings,* and AMD and VIA call them *revision numbers.* Each manufacturer has a technical specification available on its Web site that details the updates included in each stepping or revision number.

Table 2-6 INTEL PROCESSOR BUGS

Processor	Problem	Solution
Pentium (60, 66, 75, 90, or 100 MHz)	The processor contains a floating-point flaw that affects its ability to accurately calculate some numbers.	You can verify that your processor has an FDIV problem using Intel's Processor Frequency ID Utility. You can access the Processor Frequency ID Utility at http://support.intel.com/support/processors/tools/frequencyid/. If your PC has this problem, Intel will replace it under their FDIV Pentium Replacement Program. For more information on this program, visit Intel's Web site for details at http://support.intel.com/support/processors/pentium/fdiv. Any Intel Pentium processor with 120 MHz or above does not have the FDIV flaw.
Pentium III	In some Pentium III processors, there is a bug that requires a computer to be powered on twice before the system will start.	This bug shows up in only around 2 percent of the PIII processors. If you have, or suspect that you have, one of the processors with this error, Intel has issued a recall for them. Details on the recall program are available at: ftp://download.intel.com/design/pentiumiii/specupdt/24445309.pdf.

Chapter 3

Chipsets and Controllers

IN THIS CHAPTER

I've included this chapter on chipsets to provide you some information and background on this essential component. Except in extremely rare cases, the chipset isn't a component that can be removed, replaced, or upgraded without changing the motherboard. However, its functions and services are so very important to the efficient operation of the PC that some coverage is needed. Read here for more on the following:

♦ Identifying the chipset in a PC (without opening the system case)

♦ Identifying the chipset in a PC (by opening the system case)

♦ Chipset memory caching limitations

♦ Identifying potential problems with a chipset

You won't find much in the way of troubleshooting in this chapter because in most cases, the problem lies with an incompatibility of a device driver (or perhaps the device itself), the chipset, microprocessor, or motherboard. Your choices are few: Change the device driver, the device, or the motherboard.

Munching on a Few Chipsets

Arguably, the motherboard is by far the most important component in a PC. What helps to make the motherboard so important is its chipset and associated controllers. A *chipset* is a group of devices combined into one or more integrated circuits (ICs). Chipsets provide a PC with much of its functionality, including its ability to take data in, display it, and move it about internally. A chipset controls the system bus structures and facilitates the movement of data and instructions between the CPU, cache memory, and internal and external peripheral devices. The system's chipset also defines the PC's possible feature set and peripherals, and plays a major role in its operating speeds.

A chipset, like the one shown in Figure 3-1, combines a group of functions that might have been on separate chips in earlier systems. A chipset provides the software and protocols necessary for the processor and other components of the PC to control or communicate with the devices installed on or attached to the motherboard. The instructions on the chipset are not very sophisticated and are only at the

63

most rudimentary level. In fact, most of the functions that occur between the chipset and any device are actually performed by the software driver reacting to the commands of the chipset.

Figure 3-1: The Intel 820E chipset.

Image courtesy of Intel Corporation.

A chipset controls the flow of bits (data, instructions, and control signals) over the motherboard's bus structures, including data and command transfers between the CPU, memory, and peripheral devices. A chipset also provides support for the expansion bus, where expansion and adapter cards are placed, and any power management features of the system.

Originally, a chipset consisted of several separate small single-purpose controllers. Each separate controller, which could consist of one or more discrete ICs, managed a single function, such as controlling the cache memory, handling interrupts, or managing the data bus. Present-day chipsets combine these controller functions and ICs into one or two larger, multi-function chips, like the Intel 820E shown in Figure 3-1.

Chipset chips are also referred to as *Application Specific Integration Circuits,* or *ASICs* (pronounced *ay*-six). However, not all ASICs are chipsets. Some are timers, memory controllers, bus controllers, or digital sound processors, or have other uses. The term *chipset* is also used by manufacturers of video graphics cards to indicate the function set on a video card, but don't confuse the two — one cannot be substituted for the other. (See Chapter 14 for more information on video cards and their chipsets.)

Much of the discussion about chipsets surrounds their support for device controllers and bus and interface structures, but another important characteristic of a chipset is that it dictates the maximum amount of random access memory (RAM) that its motherboard can support. On modern motherboards, this can be as low as 64 megabytes (MB) or as high as 32 gigabytes (GB). The chipset dictates most of the allowable characteristics of the memory that can be installed on a PC's motherboard.

Grouping chipsets

Chipsets are grouped by a number of distinguishing characteristics, such as the socket type of the processor, the generation of the processor, the controllers required, and the number and type of chips in the set.

A chipset can actually belong to more than one grouping based on its characteristics and features. The chipset that is compatible with any given motherboard has an exact fit to that system's characteristics.

The two major groupings used for chipsets are

◆ *Socket types:* One characteristic commonly used to group chipsets is the socket type of the processor. For example, Socket 7 chipsets are in one grouping, Socket 8 chipsets are in a second grouping, Socket 1 and 370 chipsets are in a third, and Slot A chipsets are in yet another. Chipsets for Intel processors fit nicely into this grouping scheme, but chipsets from other manufacturers, such as ALi Corporation, NVIDIA Technologies, Silicon Integrated Systems Corporation (SiS), or VIA Technologies, Inc., do not always fit into this grouping scheme. Chapter 2 has more information on the various processor mountings.

◆ *North Bridge and South Bridge:* The number of chips in the chipset is another characteristic used to group chipsets. Chipsets can consist of one, two, or more chips. The most common grouping is chipsets with two chips. The two-chip chipset contains a North Bridge and a South Bridge. However, manufacturers such as SiS and VIA produce mostly single chipsets today. Chipsets can contain as many as six chips.

TAKING THE NORTH BRIDGE

The *North Bridge* chip contains the major bus circuits that provide support and control for main memory, cache memory, the Peripheral Component Interconnect (PCI), and the Accelerated Graphics Port (AGP) buses. The North Bridge is typically a single chip (usually the larger IC in a chipset), but it can also consist of more than one chip itself.

The North Bridge also supplies the alpha designation and distinction of the entire chipset. For example, the chip *FW82439HX* is the North Bridge chip of the Intel 430HX chipset. The *HX* refers to the North Bridge in the chipset.

MOVING OVER TO THE SOUTH BRIDGE

The *South Bridge* includes controllers for peripheral devices and those controllers that are not a part of the PC's basic functions, such as the Integrated Device Electronics/AT Attachment (IDE/ATA) and Enhanced IDE (EIDE) controllers and the serial port controllers. A chipset family shares the South Bridge among all its variations and often between manufacturers as well. Which is to say, each chipset configuration in the Intel 430 chipset family has the same South Bridge. What varies from chipset to chipset within the 430 chipset family is the North Bridge. Got it? Well, maybe you will later in this chapter.

Figure 3-2 illustrates the relationship of the North Bridge and the South Bridge chips on a PC.

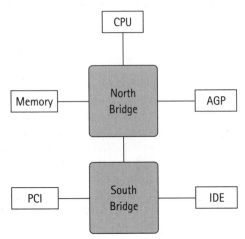

Figure 3-2: The relationship of a chipset's North Bridge and South Bridge.

Digging deeper into the chipset

In general terms, a chipset contains circuitry to provide controller functions and bus architecture support. Without going overboard, here is a brief overview of these chipset activities:

♦ *Controller chips:* The *controller functions* in a chipset control the transfer of data to and from peripheral devices by interfacing with the device controllers. Device controllers are typically single chips mounted directly on the motherboard or on an adapter card. Most motherboard designs include two or more controller chips outside of the chipset. In most cases, the keyboard controller and an input/output (I/O) controller (also known as the Super I/O chip) are mounted directly on the motherboard and supplement the controllers in the chipset. In addition, some video adapters, sound cards, network interface cards (NICs), and Small Computer System Interface (SCSI) adapters have their own built-in device controller chips.

♦ *Bus architectures:* Because they control the flow of data to and from peripheral devices, device controllers must be matched to the bus architecture of the motherboard. The motherboard's *bus architecture* is made up of traces, wires, connectors, and devices over which data and instructions travel around the PC. (See Chapter 1 for more information on bus architectures.) The bus structure connects device controllers on or attached to the motherboard to the CPU, memory, and I/O ports. Each of the bus architectures supported on a PC has its own bus controller chip function either incorporated into the chipset or mounted separately on the motherboard. Most of the newest motherboard designs include expansion slots for a variety of bus and interface structures, including PCI, the AT bus, and possibly SCSI.

In Case You're Curious: Chipset Controllers

The devices and controllers supported on a chipset are those common to the type of processor, motherboard, and PC that the chipset is designed to support. A few of the controllers and devices typically included in a chipset are

◆ *Memory controller:* This logic circuit controls the reading and writing of data to and from system memory (RAM). Other devices on the PC wishing to access memory must interface with the memory controller. This feature usually also includes error handling to provide for parity checking and *ECC* (error correction code) for every memory word.

◆ *EIDE controller:* Nearly all mid- to upper-range motherboards now include at least one Enhanced IDE (EIDE) connector for hard disks, floppy disks, CD-ROMs, DVDs, or other types of internal storage drives. The EIDE controller typically supports devices with ISA, ATA, and perhaps an ATA-33 or Ultra-DMA (UDMA) interface.

◆ *PCI bridge:* Like a network bridge that connects two dissimilar networks, this device logically connects the PCI expansion bus on the motherboard to the processor and other non-PCI devices.

◆ *Real-time clock (RTC):* This clock holds the date and time on your PC: that is, the date and time that displays on your monitor and is used to date stamp file activities. This should not be confused with the system clock that provides the timing signal for the processor and other devices.

◆ *Direct memory access (DMA) controllers:* The DMA controller manages the seven DMA channels available for use by Industry Standard Architecture (ISA)/ATA devices for most PCs. DMA channels are used by certain devices, such as floppy disk drives, sound cards, SCSI adapters, and some network adapters to move data into memory without the assistance of the CPU.

◆ *IrDA controller:* IrDA (Infrared Data Association) is the international organization that created the standards for short-range line-of-sight, point-to-point infrared devices, such as a keyboard, mouse, and network adapters. The IrDA port on your system is that small red window on the front or side of notebook and some desktop computers.

Continued

In Case You're Curious: Chipset Controllers *(Continued)*

◆ *Keyboard controller:* A chipset might include the keyboard controller, and many of the newer ones do. The *keyboard controller* is the interface between the keyboard and the processor. See the previous section for more information on this device.

◆ *PS/2 mouse controller:* When IBM introduced the PS/2 system, the controller for the mouse was included in the keyboard controller. This design has persisted; usually, wherever the keyboard controller is, so is the PS/2 mouse controller. This device provides the interface between the PS/2 mouse and the processor.

◆ *Secondary (Level 2) cache controller:* Secondary (L2) cache is located on the motherboard, a daughterboard, or (like on the Pentium Pro) in the processor package, and caches the primary memory (RAM), the hard disk, and the CD-ROM drives. The secondary cache controller controls the movement of data to and from the L2 cache and the processor.

◆ *CMOS SRAM:* The PC's configuration settings are stored in what is called the Complementary Metal-Oxide Semiconductor (CMOS) memory. The chipset contains the controller used to access and modify this special static random access memory (SRAM) area.

Although not technically a bus structure, you will see Accelerated Graphics Port (AGP) listed on most newer motherboard and chipset designs. The AGP interface is a 66–133 MHz interface structure (or higher on a Macintosh G4) that is typically combined with a 32-bit 33 MHz PCI bus to provide advanced video support and faster data transfers from system memory to video and graphics adapters.

Knowing Which Bus to Take

The following sections give overviews of many of the bus and interface structures supported by most of the popular chipsets.

AT bus

The AT bus is included on most chipsets primarily to provide support for expansion cards, such as network adapters, from older systems. The AT bus runs at 8 MHz and uses a 16-bit data path. It is commonly referred to as *Industry Standard Architecture (ISA)*.

The *Extended Industry Standard Architecture* (EISA) bus is another AT bus structure supported by many chipsets. EISA bus expansion slots have been included on some motherboards since the time of the 386 processor. EISA is a 32-bit bus but is also backward compatible to the AT and ISA buses.

Local bus

Because AT and ISA bus structures cannot keep up with the speeds required for high-resolution graphics and faster processors, many manufacturers now use local bus architectures. A *local bus* device, which provides for very fast data transfers, is local to the processor through a dedicated controller that bypasses the standard bus controller. PCI and Video Electronics Standards Association (VESA) local buses (VL-bus) are the most common of the local bus structures. Because Intel promotes PCI, it has become the de facto standard local bus structure for virtually all Pentium class computers.

SCSI bus

SCSI (pronounced *skuz*-zee) attaches peripheral devices to a PC through a dedicated controller card that's able to support a chain of devices over a dedicated interface structure and provides very fast data transfers. Very few PCs feature a SCSI interface as a standard. (The Apple Macintosh and some higher-end server-type computers do, however.) A SCSI host adapter is added to the PC through an expansion slot, typically a PCI or ISA slot.

USB and IEEE 1394

The Universal Serial Bus (USB) and the IEEE 1394 interfaces (such as Apple's FireWire and Texas Instrument's Lynx) are emerging standards for device connectors and interfaces. USB and 1394 are Plug and Play (PnP) architectures that allow users to add a wide range of peripheral devices to the PC without the need of an adapter board. These devices have their controllers built in, as do many SCSI devices. USB supports both low-speed devices, such as keyboards, mice, scanners, and printers, but newer standards also support many higher speed devices, such as scanners and digital still cameras. The 1394 interface is also known as the High Performance Serial Bus (HPSB) and provides support for devices requiring isochronous (real-time) support, such as digital video cameras.

IrDA and infrared

The Infrared Data Association (IrDA) has established standards for the use and interaction of infrared light beams as an interface for peripheral devices to a PC. *Infrared* or *IrDA connectors* are those little red plastic windows on your PC or notebook that can be used to connect a keyboard, mouse, and other specially equipped devices.

Bluetooth

Bluetooth, borne of the cellular phone industry, is a radio frequency (RF) technology that allows desktop and portable PCs, personal digital assistants (PDAs), and their peripherals to create a wireless personal area network (PAN) within a limited (30 meters) area.

Operating outside of the chipset

Typically, one or more device controller functions are kept outside of the chipset. The primary reason for excluding them from the chipset is their volume of activity — some controller functions are usually quite busy. Another reason for keeping them outside the chipset is that doing so provides better space economy on the chipset as well as on the motherboard. Here are some device controller chips that might be kept outside of the chipset:

◆ *Super I/O controller chip:* This discrete IC incorporates the functions that control the standard input/output devices and ports found on virtually every PC. Combining them on a special controller chip allows the motherboard and the system chipset to concentrate on other high-priority and unique functions. Included in the functions on a Super I/O chip are

- *Serial ports:* The universal asynchronous receiver/transmitter (UART) is used to drive the serial ports, and the control functions of data transfer are included in the Super I/O chip.

- *Parallel ports:* The functions that drive the parallel ports, including the various parallel port standards, Enhanced Parallel Port (EPP) and Enhanced Capabilities Port (ECP), are included in the Super I/O controller.

- *Floppy disk drives:* Because it is a very mature process, support for the floppy disk is included on the Super I/O chip.

- *Miscellaneous functions:* Newer versions of the Super I/O controller can also incorporate the keyboard controller's functions, the real-time clock, and perhaps the IDE hard disk controller, although this is more commonly found in the system chipset.

◆ *Keyboard controller:* The keyboard controller controls the transfer of data from the keyboard to the PC. The keyboard controller interacts with the controller located inside the keyboard over a serial link built into the connecting cable and connector. When data comes to the keyboard controller from the keyboard, the keyboard controller checks the parity of the data, places the data in a buffer, and then notifies the processor that keyboard data is in the buffer. A separate keyboard controller is common on most older PCs. On newer PCs, this function is either included in the chipset or included in the Super I/O chip.

The functions performed by the keyboard controller, or its equivalent, are

- *Keyboard control and translation:* When a key is pressed on the keyboard, a scan code is sent from the controller inside the keyboard to the PC's keyboard controller, which then signals the processor through IRQ1 (interrupt request 1). The keyboard controller then translates the scan code into the character it represents and places it on the bus to move it to the appropriate location in memory.

■ *Support for the PS/2 mouse:* On those systems that have an integrated PS/2 connector on the motherboard, the keyboard controller supports its functions. This port is most commonly used to connect a PS/2-style mouse.

■ *Access to the HMA:* Although the support for the High Memory Area (HMA) of system memory (RAM) is now incorporated into the system chipset on most newer PCs, access to this part of memory is controlled through the keyboard controller. See Chapter 6 for more information on the HMA.

◆ *Other device controllers:* Every peripheral device on a PC that needs to interact with the data bus or the processor must have a device controller. Peripheral devices generally have their controller chips either on an adapter card or built into their electronics. On older, pre-Pentium PCs, each device had its own adapter or shared a controller card. For example, it was common for the floppy disk and hard disk drives to share an I/O controller card.

In Case You're Curious — the Sequel: A List of Chipset Functions

The microprocessor is always faster than the PC's peripheral devices with which it must communicate. Because of this fact, designers have been forced to develop interfaces to serve as buffers between peripheral devices and the faster CPU. These buffers match up the speeds of the peripherals to the CPU and smooth out the timing of the PC's operations.

The very first PCs had an individual chip to control each of its peripheral or internal device functions, most of which are now embedded in chipsets, including

◆ *Math co-processor interface:* This chip controlled the flow of data between the processor and math co-processor.

◆ *Clock generator:* This chip controlled the timing of the PC's operations.

◆ *Bus controller chip:* This chip controlled the flow of data on the motherboard's buses.

◆ *DMA controller:* This chip controlled the processes that allowed peripheral devices to interact with memory without involving the processor.

◆ *Programmable Peripheral Interface (PPI):* This chip supervised some of the simpler peripheral devices.

◆ *Floppy disk controller (FDC):* This chip controlled the PC's diskette and tape drives.

◆ *CRT controller:* This chip facilitated the PC's display.

◆ *Universal asynchronous receiver/transmitter (UART):* This chip was used to send and receive synchronous serial data.

Getting to know the chipset

The characteristics of a chipset can be grouped into six categories: host, memory, interfaces, arbitration, South Bridge support, and power management. These characteristics define and differentiate one chipset from another. These characteristics are commonly included in the specifications for most chipsets. The characteristics defined in each of these categories are

♦ *Host:* The host processor to which the chipset is matched along with its bus voltage, usually Gunning Transceiver Logic Plus (GTL+) or Advanced Gunning Transceiver Logic Plus (AGTL+), and the number of processors the chipset will support.

♦ *Memory:* The characteristics of the dynamic random access memory (DRAM) support included in the chipset, including the DRAM refresh technique supported, the amount of memory supported (in megabits usually), the type of memory supported, and whether memory interleave, ECC, or parity is supported.

♦ *Interfaces:* The type of PCI interface implemented and whether the chipset is AGP-compliant supports integrated graphics, PIPE (pipelining), or side band addressing (SBA).

♦ *Arbitration:* The method used by the chipset to arbitrate between different bus speeds and interfaces. The two most common arbitration methods are Multi-Transaction Timer (MTT) and Dynamic Intelligent Arbiter (DIA).

♦ *South Bridge support:* All Intel chipsets and most of the chipsets for all other manufacturers are two processor sets. In these sets, the North Bridge is the main chip and handles CPU and memory interfaces among other tasks, and the South Bridge handles the USB and IDE interfaces, the real-time clock (RTC), and support for serial and parallel ports.

♦ *Power management:* All Intel chipsets support both the System Management Mode (SMM) and Advanced Configuration and Power Interface (ACPI) power management standards.

To view the information that is included for a given chipset, visit Intel's chipset Web site at `www.intel.com/design/chipsets/index.htm` for several examples.

Troubleshooting Chipset Problems

Because they are matched to the motherboard and processors, a chipset is very difficult to diagnose as the source of a performance problem. Instead, it is far more likely that another chip, adapter card, device, or function might have a conflict with the chipset and create a functional problem. Chipset manufacturers publish the software diagnostics tools that exist primarily for software developers working at the chipset level.

Some relatively good diagnostic packages are available that test the functions of the motherboard, including its buses, controllers, and interfaces, all of which are controlled by the chipset. One chipset issue problem that you might encounter is that the chipset could be the cause of a faulty or badly functioning PCI bus.

Here are a few of the software tools available that you can use to isolate problems:

- ◆ *AMIDiag from American Megatrends, Inc.* (www.amidiag.com): This software is a suite of PC diagnostic utilities for Windows and DOS systems.

- ◆ *Check✓It Professional Edition from Smith Micro Software* (www.smithmicro.com): This package performs a fast and thorough evaluation of a PC's configuration and performance. Although it is a bit pricey, it contains all the diagnostic software you'd ever need.

- ◆ *Micro-Scope from Micro 2000* (www.micro2000.com): This package is used by many technical schools to teach diagnostics on the motherboard. It features tests for virtually all buses, interfaces, and processors.

- ◆ *Ontrack SystemSuite from Ontrack Data International, Inc.* (www.ontrack.com): This is a comprehensive suite of PC utilities that includes PC diagnostics, data recovery, virus protection, and more.

- ◆ *PC Certify from PC Certify, Inc.* (www.pccertify.com): PC Certify (formerly Pc-Check) performs an extensive array of advanced diagnostics that allow you to pinpoint the source of both fixed and intermittent faults in all major hardware components.

- ◆ *PC Clinic from pcwiz, Inc.* (www.datadepo.com): PC Clinic is a family of menu-driven programs that combine systems information, diagnostics, utilities, and benchmark tests.

- ◆ *PC-Doctor from Watergate Software* (www.pc-doctor.com): PC-Doctor is a set of diagnostic and system information tools with over 250 test functions that provide a specific diagnostic for each part of the system's core technologies.

- ◆ *PC Pitstop from PC Pitshop, LLC* (www.pcpitstop.com): This site features a series of diagnostics and tests that are available over the Web that you can use to check out a PC's configuration or to track down a particular problem.

- ◆ *PC-Technician Pro from Windsor Technologies, Inc.* (www.windsortech.com): This is a comprehensive PC diagnostics package that is very popular among large corporate IT departments.

- ◆ *ToolStar Test from ProTech Diagnostics* (www.protechdiagnostics.com): This is a universal diagnostic program that uses its own operating system to test PC hardware on all versions of Pentium, AMD, and Cyrix processors and virtually all bus structures.

Identifying a chipset (without opening the case)

To identify the chipset on a particular PC, assuming that it's a Windows PC, use the following steps:

1. Access the Windows Control Panel and double-click the System icon.

   The System Properties window, as shown in Figure 3-3, opens.

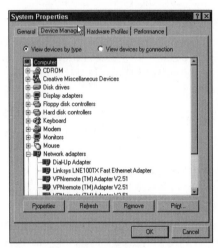

Figure 3-3: The System Properties window for a Windows system showing the Device Manager information.

2. Choose the Device Manager tab.

3. Expand the System Devices selection.

   The display in the window should look like that shown in Figure 3-4. Scan down the list. If your PC has an Intel processor, you should see at least two entries beginning with *Intel 82xxx* or the like. These chips should be the Processor to PCI and PCI to ISA bridge controllers and are the chips in your chipset.

The chipset entries in System Properties

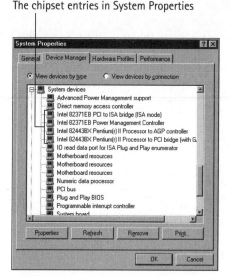

Figure 3-4: The System Properties window showing the System Devices information.

Identifying a chipset (by opening the case)

Another way to find out the chipset in use on a PC is to open the system case and locate the large square chips that are bigger than everything else on the motherboard (except the processor, of course). Nearly all chipsets can be identified by a white or yellow diagonal mark in the upper-left corner of the North Bridge or on a single-chip of a chipset. It really helps if you know the identity numbers of the chipset, but I know this isn't always possible. Remember that a chipset can have as few as one chip or as many as four separate chips.

Dealing with Pentium chipset problems

The 430TX (Triton III) and the 430VX are common chipsets in Pentium-class PCs. Like just about every chipset, these two have their problems. The following sections contain a list of the major issues with these chipsets.

CACHE LIMITATIONS

The TX and VX chipsets are from the time when 64MB was considered a lot of RAM. These chipsets are designed to cache only the first 64MB of RAM in L2 cache. More RAM can be added above 64MB, but it will not be cached and can cut the PC's performance in half. So unless you really need the additional RAM, you might be better off not to add it. Perhaps it's time to upgrade the PC or the motherboard and processor.

LIMITING MEMORY AS A WORKAROUND

Unfortunately, the chipset is part of the system board and cannot be replaced. Performance problems can be the result of more than 64MB on the PC. Windows 98 and Windows Me provide the ability to limit the amount of RAM that the system sees. Follow these steps:

1. Open the Run box from the Start menu and enter **MSCONFIG** in the Open text box.

   The System Configuration Utility window, shown in Figure 3-5, will open.

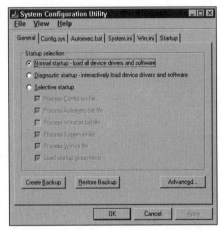

Figure 3-5: The System Configuration utility (MSCONFIG).

2. Click the Advanced button in the lower-right corner to display the Advanced Troubleshooting Settings window shown in Figure 3-6.

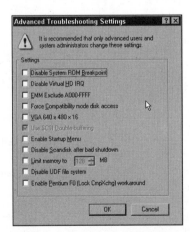

Figure 3-6: The Advanced Troubleshooting Settings dialog box of the System Configuration utility.

3. Mark the check box for Limit Memory To and set the scroll box value to 64MB.

RESOLVING MEMORY PROBLEMS ON OTHER PENTIUM CHIPSETS

Other Intel Pentium-class chipsets also have memory caching limits. The Triton I FX chipset is also limited to caching the first 64MB of RAM. The Mercury LX chipset is a little better in that it will cache 128MB of memory.

Identifying potential chipset problems

After you identify the chipset on a PC, the very best way to learn about problems with a chipset is to visit the manufacturer's Web site. Finding whether known problems exist with a chipset can save you a lot of diagnostic trouble.

Here are the Web sites of the major chipset manufacturers:

♦ Intel Corporation: www.intel.com

♦ NVIDIA: www.nvidia.com

♦ Silicon Integrated Systems Corp (SiS): www.sis.com.tw

♦ VIA Technologies: www.via.com.tw

For a complete list of chipset manufacturers, not all of whom manufacture PC chipsets, visit www.matrix-bios.nl/cmanad.html.

Listing the Intel Chipsets

Intel invented the chipset and has dominated the market since the days of the 486. About the only time that a competitor gains ground in the chipset market is when Intel decides to abandon a particular product. Intel dominates the market for a simple reason: Chipsets support processors and motherboards, and Intel dominates the processor market. Intel intimately knows its processors, so designing chipsets that support its processors is easy.

The following is a review of the major chipsets and chipset families that Intel has produced over the years.

486 chipsets

Because several styles of 486 systems exist, there were many different 486 chipsets. The two most common 486 chipsets were

♦ *420EX (Aries):* This chipset supported motherboards that combined the PCI and VL buses.

◆ *420TX (Saturn):* This 80486 chipset family supported systems through the 486 DX4 and most of the 486 overdrive processors adding power management support. The 420TX chipset was released in three revision levels numbered 1, 2, and 4, which was known as the Saturn II chipset.

Chipsets for the Pentium and beyond

Pentium chipsets were more closely in tune with the design of the processor than the 486 chipsets. Along with the Pentium processor, Intel developed the PCI bus and a chipset to support it. This chipset, which was exactly matched to the Pentium processor, became known as a *PCIset.*

The Intel chipsets are designated in numbered family series: the 420 for 486 chipsets, the 430 for Pentium chipsets, the 440 series for Pentium II, and the 450 series for Pentium Pro chipsets (along with the 440FX). The newer 460 and 800 series chipsets just being announced are designed to support the IA-64 (Intel Architecture–64 bits) processors, such as the Itanium, now emerging.

Here are some of the more common Intel Pentium and above chipsets:

◆ *430LX (Mercury):* The first Pentium chipset developed to support the 60 MHz and 66 MHz, 5 volt (v) processors. This chipset supported the PCI bus and up to 128MB of RAM.

◆ *430NX (Neptune):* This chipset was developed to support Intel's second generation of Pentium chips. It supported Pentium processors running at 90 MHz to 133 MHz and offered dual processors, 512MB of RAM, and 512K of L2 cache.

◆ *430FX (Triton I):* The first of the Triton chipsets, this chipset featured support for Extended Data Output (EDO) RAM, pipelined burst and synchronous cache, PnP, and PCI level 2.0. However, it supported only 128MB of RAM and did not support dual processors.

◆ *430MX (Mobile Triton):* This is a special chipset version designed for laptop, notebook, and other portable PCs.

◆ *430HX (Triton II):* This chipset, designed for business- and enterprise-level servers, supported 512MB of EDO RAM, dual CPUs, Uniscribe Script Processor (USP), and concurrent PCI buses.

◆ *430VX (Triton III):* The last of the Tritons, this chipset, developed for the home PC market, featured support for USB, SDRAM, and PCI interfaces.

◆ *430TX:* This chipset was adaptable for both desktop and mobile use and provided PCI, USB, DMA, and other interfaces.

◆ *440LX:* This AGPset, a chipset that features support for AGP interfaces, which was designed for the Pentium II, supports the LS-120 SuperDisk,

Ultra-DMA, AGP, USB, SDRAM, ECC RAM, and the PC97 power management specification. Figure 3-7 shows Intel's marketing image for this chipset.

Figure 3–7: The Intel 440LX AGPset and the Pentium II processor.

Image courtesy of Intel Corporation.

◆ *440LXR:* This chipset is a low-end version of the 440LX chipset.

◆ *440BX:* This chipset is another Pentium II chipset that supports 100 MHz bus, dual processors, IEEE 1394, and up to 1GB of RAM.

◆ *440GX:* Designed for midrange workstations, this AGPset, shown in Figure 3-8, supports dual CPUs and up to 2GB of SDRAM.

◆ *440FX (Natoma):* This chipset supports the Pentium II and the Pentium Pro processors with USB, EDO RAM, ECC memory, dual processors, and PCI.

◆ *450GX (Orion server):* The 450GX chipset and the 450KX share the same basic design with the GX version designed for use with the Pentium Pro processor with support for up to four processors and 8GB of RAM but only Fast Page Mode (FPM) memory.

◆ *450KX (Orion workstation):* The KX version of the 450 chipset is designed to support workstations with dual processors and 1GB of RAM.

◆ *450NX:* This chipset is designed to provide high-powered support for Xeon workstations and servers with up to four CPUs, 2MB of L2 cache, 8GB of EDO memory, and two 32-bit or one 64-bit PCI interface. Figure 3-9 shows the chips that make up this chipset.

Figure 3-8: The Intel 440GX AGPset, shown with a Pentium 4 processor.

Image courtesy of Intel Corporation.

Figure 3-9: The Intel 450NX chipset.

Image courtesy of Intel Corporation.

◆ *460GX (Merced):* This chipset, which is designed for very high-end servers and workstations with support for up to four CPUs and other high-performance features, is projected for use with the new high-powered Itanium processor.

◆ *810:* This chipset, which is based on the 440BX chipset and designed for value-priced PCs, includes support for integrated AGP 3-D graphics, MPEG-2, 100 MHz system bus, two USB ports, and 266 megabyte per second data bus speed between system memory and peripheral devices. The 810e chipset is an extended (that's what the *e* stands for) version of the 810 chipset, intended for home market and office PCs with added support for 133 MHz system bus and the ATA-66 interface. Figure 3-10 shows the 810 chipset.

Figure 3-10: The Intel 810 chipset.

Image courtesy of Intel Corporation.

◆ *815:* This chipset integrates an audio controller that uses the processor for integrated sound and modem support, and a graphics performance accelerator (GPA) for support of 2-D and 3-D graphics, and it will support the addition of an AGP 4X card. This chipset was developed for use in home and value PCs.

◆ *845:* This chipset family was designed exclusively for the Intel Pentium 4 processor to maximize the bandwidth of double data rate (DDR) 200/266 MHz or PC133 synchronous dynamic random access memory (SDRAM) on mainstream PCs.

◆ *850:* Designed for high-performance systems, this chipset provides for a 533 MHz system bus to the processor and 3.2GB of memory bus bandwidth to support the processing power of the Pentium 4 processor.

For more information on Intel Corporation's chipset products, visit www.intel.com.

Noting the Non-Intel Chipsets

Besides Intel, ALi (Acer Labs), Silicon Integrated Systems (SiS), NVIDIA Technologies, and VIA Technologies also manufacture Pentium-class chipsets. The chipsets of each of these manufacturers are covered in the sections that follow.

ALi

ALi (formerly Acer Laboratories, Inc.) manufactures chipsets for its AOpen motherboards. Its chipsets include

◆ *ALiMAGiK* is a core logic chipset with built-in support for the AMD Athlon and Duron processors with DDR PC1600/2100 and SDRAM 133 memory support and AMD's PowerNow technology.

◆ *M1651T ALADDiN Pro 5* supports most Slot 1 and Socket 370 processors, including the Intel Celeron, Pentium II, Pentium III, and the Pentium III mobile processor. This chipset is a single-chip solution that supports SDRAM 66/100/133 and DDR PC266 with 2.1GB of memory bandwidth.

◆ *M1671 ALADDiN P4* is designed for the Intel Pentium 4 processor. This chipset provides a high-performance interface for both SDRAM 100/133 and DDR 200/266/333 with 2.7GB of system memory bandwidth.

◆ *ALADDiN III* is comparable with the Intel 430VX chipset.

◆ *ALADDiN IV* is comparable with the Intel 430TX chipset.

◆ *ALADDiN V* is also known as the M1541 chipset, provides support for up to 100 MHz CPU bus speeds, and includes a high-performance RAM controller, a 64-bit ECC/parity memory bus interface, an AGP interface, and device controllers for IDE, USB, and PS/2, as well as a Super I/O controller.

For more information on ALi's chipset products, visit www.ali.com.tw.

SiS (Silicon Integrated Systems)

SiS (Silicon Integrated Systems) manufactures a single-chip chipset that combines the North Bridge and South Bridge into a single chip. SiS chipsets are available for nearly all processor mountings since the Socket 7 and feature a shared memory architecture and a Unified Memory Architecture (UMA) type of video adapter.

Popular SiS chipsets are

◆ *746:* This North Bridge chipset is designed for the AMD Socket A processors and features a high-performance memory controller, AGP interface, and the SiS *MuTIOL technology,* which is a media I/O technology with support for ATA 133, USB 2.0, and IEEE 1394 interfaces.

◆ *745:* This chipset integrates support for IEEE 1394 with DDR 333 bandwidth for the AMD Athlon XP processor.

◆ *740:* This chipset is an integrated graphic user interface (GUI) host and memory controller that supports high-quality 2-D/3-D graphics acceleration, including a Motion Picture Experts Group (MPEG) motion compensation system on AMD Socket A processors.

◆ *733/735:* These single-chip chipsets provide high performance at a lower price point for desktop PCs running AMD Socket A processors.

◆ *730S:* This single-chip chipset, which is shown in Figure 3-11, is designed to support the AMD Athlon Slot A/Socket A processor.

Figure 3-11: The Sis 730S single-chip chipset.

Image courtesy of Silicon Integrated Systems Corporation.

- *658:* This chipset features dual Rambus support, AGP 8X, and the SiS MuTIOL 1G technologies for the Intel Pentium 4 processor.

- *650/651:* These North Bridge chipsets are integrated GUI (IGUI) host memory controllers for the Intel Pentium 4 processor with a 2-D/3-D graphics engine, an AGP 4X interface, and MuTIOL.

- *648:* This chipset includes an AGP 8X controller for the Intel Pentium 4 processor.

- *645/645DX:* These chipsets, in addition to other features for the Intel Pentium 4 processor, provide support for DDR 333.

- *635/635T:* This single-chip chipset is a high-performance solution for desktop PCs at a lower price than Intel Slot 1 and Socket 370 processors — the Celeron and Pentium III.

- *630/630E/630S:* These single-chip chipsets are designed for Slot 1 and Socket 370 processors and feature an advanced 2-D/3-D GUI engine and a Super-South Bridge package.

- *600/620:* A two-chip chipset that integrates a high-performance host bus interface, a DRAM controller, an IDE controller, a PCI interface, a 2-D/3-D graphics accelerator, and a video playback accelerator for Slot 1 and Socket 370 processor-based systems.

- *540:* This single-chip chipset is designed for the AMD K6 processor mounted in a Super Socket 7 socket and features support for highly integrated PCI devices.

For more information on SiS' chipset products, visit www.sis.com.

NVIDIA Technologies

NVIDIA is a relatively new player in the chipset marketplace. It produces two chipsets within the nForce chipset family.

The nForce and nForce2 chipsets feature efficient memory processing, the Dynamic Adaptive Speculative Pre-processor to increase processor performance, and a high-performance I/O bus for the AMD Athlon processor. The nForce chipsets are available as either a discrete chipset that handles only chipset functions or as an integrated chipset that eliminates the need for a separate graphics card.

For more information on NVIDIA's nForce chipsets, visit www.nvidia.com.

VIA Technologies, Inc.

VIA Technologies, Inc. is the third-largest chipset manufacturer, after Intel and SiS. VIA produces chipsets to support processors with Slot 1, Socket 7, and Socket 370 systems. However, their more recent chipsets concentrate on the Cyrix (VIA) and AMD processors.

A few of the VIA chipsets are

- *Apollo KT333:* This chipset is the flagship of the VIA V-MAP chipset family designed to provide DDR 333 support to AMD Athlon XP and Duron processors.

- *Apollo P4X333:* This is a DDR 333 chipset designed for use with the Intel Pentium 4.

- *Apollo KT266A/P4X266A/Pro266:* These chipsets provide support for DDR 266 to AMD Athlon and Duron processors (KT266A) and the Intel Pentium 4 (P4X266A). The Pro version of this chipset is designed for use in multiple processor systems.

- *Apollo ProSavage KM266:* This is the first of VIA's chipsets with DDR support for AMD's Athlon and Duron processors.

- *Apollo KX266/KT266:* These single-chip chipsets are designed to provide support to the AMD Duron, Thunderbird, and Athlon processors. They feature an AGP 4X graphics bus, up to 2GB of RAM, a 200 MHz processor bus, and an ATA-66 IDE hard disk interface. The KM266 is shown in Figure 3-12.

- *Apollo PM601:* This single-chip chipset supports the Intel Pentium III processor and the Cyrix III processor and features advanced graphics, a scalable processor bus, a full set of integrated controllers, and several other advanced features.

◆ *Apollo MVP3:* This is a Super Socket 7 chipset that supports the AMD K6 and Cyrix MII processors with speeds up to 533 MHz and a flexible processor bus that scales from 66 to 100 MHz, advanced AGP graphics, power management, and other integrated features.

Figure 3-12: The VIA Apollo KM266 chipset.

Image courtesy of VIA Technologies, Inc.

Chapter 4

Booting and the BIOS

IN THIS CHAPTER

Way back before computers got their first operating systems, programmers had to write their own routines to input data and receive output. Each programmer had to include a routine in each program to read the input data source (usually punched cards) and to control the creation of output media (normally the printer). Eventually, it dawned on some very ingenious person that because just about every program wants to do input as well as move output to and from the peripheral devices attached to the computer, standardizing these functions – and including them in the system software library where they'd be available to everyone – might be an excellent idea. That way, efficient and error-free input and output functions are available to every program, eliminating at least one area of programming problems.

In this chapter, I cover the following:

◆ BIOS basics

◆ BIOS error beep codes

◆ System configuration

IN THE PRESENT-DAY COMPUTER, this same concept has advanced to the point that the PC even has a specialized set of instructions to tell it exactly which internal and peripheral devices are attached to it so that it can look for the input and output device drivers it needs to perform its basic input/output (I/O) tasks. These special instructions form the computer's *Basic Input/Output System* (for want of a better name) or, as it's more commonly known, its BIOS.

Getting to Know the BIOS

The BIOS performs three primary functions, all vital to the usefulness and function of the computer:

◆ *Boots the computer*

◆ *Verifies the information* provided to it about which internal and peripheral devices are supposed to be connected to the computer

◆ *Serves as the interface* between the hardware (attached devices) and the software (operating system, drivers, and applications)

The BIOS programs

The *BIOS* is a collection of software utilities and programs that can be invoked by the operating system or application software to perform a variety of hardware-related tasks. Although many operating systems now contain their own device-oriented programs for the sake of improved performance, the BIOS contains a program for just about every activity associated with accessing hardware, including the basics like reading and writing to the hard disk and moving data between devices.

BIOS manufacturers

Some of the larger BIOS manufacturers are Award, AMI (American Megatrends, Inc.), and Phoenix. All three manufacturers license their BIOS ROM to motherboard manufacturers and leave the support of the BIOS to the motherboard manufacturers. At one time, AMI was the sole provider of BIOS ROM chips to Intel, the market leader of motherboards. However, more than 80 percent of the motherboards on the market are Intel boards with a Phoenix BIOS. Award was bought by Phoenix in 1998, and Phoenix now markets the Award BIOS brand with the Phoenix name.

The BIOS in action

The instructions used to start up the PC and get its operating system loaded into memory and running are a part of the BIOS. The process of starting the PC is *booting* the computer, or the *boot sequence*. *Boot* does not refer to any part of kicking; it refers to the phrase "pulling one's self up by one's own bootstraps," or being able to start up by itself. When the PC boots up, the system BIOS is behind the scene causing and managing the actions taking place.

Although this might seem obvious, no PC can do anything at all without software. The computer's hardware is incapable of independent actions and must be given instructions to do anything. As I'm sure you're aware, *software* is really just a block of instructions that guide the hardware to perform specific activities.

The BIOS supplies your hardware with its first set of instructions when it's powered up, which your PC executes during its power-on or boot-up sequence until such time as the PC is able to fetch and execute instructions on its own.

Identifying the BIOS chip

When a PC is powered up, the processor is ready to function, but because no instructions are resident in its memory, the processor has nothing to do. The first instructions needed by the processor are those that direct the computer's start-up activities: the BIOS program. Because these instructions must be available to the processor each time that it starts up, they are stored on a ROM chip located on the motherboard, like the one in Figure 4-1.

Figure 4-1: A ROM chip on a PC motherboard.

Read This Only if You're Into BIOS Chips (Or Want to Know More about Them)

The instructions and data that make up the BIOS are permanently loaded to an integrated circuit (IC) or chip during manufacturing. This prevents tampering or an accidental change in the BIOS' data and routines. The following gives an overview of each type of chip on which a BIOS is stored.

◆ *Read only memory (ROM):* As its name implies, *ROM* is a type of memory chip that cannot be altered; it can only be read. ROM is *non-volatile,* which means that its contents are safely held even after a power source is removed. This makes it the ideal place to store system start-up instructions. Typically, the BIOS is stored on a ROM, which is why you hear the BIOS often referred to as the *ROM BIOS.*

◆ *Programmable read only memory (PROM):* A *PROM* is essentially a blank ROM chip that must be programmed with the data you want it to store. By using a ROM burner or ROM programmer, the chip can be loaded with any data that you desire. The ROM burner programs the PROM by inducing a high voltage (12 volt [v] compared with the 5v used for normal PROM operation). The higher voltage burns the memory location, turning the pre-existing binary 1 into a 0. This process is irreversible, so what you burn is what you get (WYBIWYG). You can't turn a 0 back into a 1. For this reason, you might hear PROM memory referred to as *OTP memory* (one time programmable memory).

Continued

Read This Only if You're Into BIOS Chips
(Or Want to Know More about Them) *(Continued)*

◆ *Erasable programmable read only memory (EPROM):* An *EPROM* (pronounced *ee*-prom) is a variation of the original PROM with an added feature — the data can be erased, and the chip can be reprogrammed. This means that the chip can be reused instead of being discarded when its contents are no longer valid. The EPROM chip looks identical to the PROM with the exception of a quartz crystal window on the top of the chip. The window is used to allow ultraviolet (UV) rays to access the chip's circuitry. The UV light causes a chemical reaction that erases the EPROM by turning the 0's back into 1's again. To prevent accidental erasure of the EPROM chip, a label tape is normally placed over the quartz crystal window.

◆ *Electronically erasable programmable read only memory (EEPROM):* An EEPROM (pronounced *ee-ee*-prom) is the standard type of BIOS chip on newer systems. An EEPROM chip can be reprogrammed like the EPROM, but unlike the EPROM, it doesn't need to be removed from the motherboard. An EEPROM can be updated through specialized software usually supplied by the BIOS or chip manufacturer from its Web site. The process of updating the BIOS EEPROM using software is known as *flashing*, which is why this chip is also commonly called *flash ROM*.

Flashing allows you to easily apply bug fixes or add new features to your system that might not have been available at the time your system was manufactured, such as the capability of booting to the CD-ROM drive. Improving the BIOS can also add new routines that improve your system's boot or overall performance.

◆ *Complementary Metal-Oxide Semiconductor (CMOS):* CMOS, also known as *non-volatile RAM (NVRAM)*, is used to store system configuration data. Although CMOS is technically a technology from which memory and IC chips are manufactured, it has become synonymous with the system configuration data.

The CMOS stores the PC's hardware configuration data as well as any changes made to the system concerning its hard drive parameters, peripheral settings, or any other BIOS settings. CMOS is also used to store the system clock or real-time clock (RTC) settings. Because it runs on about 1 millionth of an amp of electrical current, it can store configuration data for many years powered only by a low voltage dry cell or lithium battery.

From its ROM chip, the BIOS program is loaded into a specially reserved area in memory. Normally, this is the upper 64K of the first megabyte of system memory (memory addresses F000h to FFFFh). However, some BIOS programs use more than this 64K area. Processors always look for the BIOS to be available in the same memory location each time. The address (F000h) of this reserved area, the *jump address*, is the uniform standard among processor and BIOS producers. The processor gets its first instructions from this location, and the BIOS program begins executing. The BIOS program then begins the system boot sequence.

Several different BIOS programs are in a PC. In addition to the system BIOS program, there are also BIOS programs to control several of the peripheral devices added to the PC. For example, most video cards have their own BIOS that contain instructions for displaying video information. Hard disks and many SCSI adapters also have their own BIOS modules.

In older 16-bit computers, a technique called ROM shadowing is used to speed up the boot process because ROM chips have a very slow access speed (150 nanoseconds). *ROM shadowing* is a process that copies the ROM data into random access memory (RAM) and assigns the RAM the address originally assigned to the ROM. This allows the PC to ignore the ROM and work directly with the much faster RAM. RAM is discussed in detail in Chapter 6.

Newer 32- and 64-bit (or higher) PC systems use 32-bit drivers that are loaded into RAM during startup, bypassing the 16-bit ROM code during system startup.

Acting as the hardware intermediary

The BIOS relieves the computer's operating system and applications from needing to know the exact details about the hardware devices attached to the computer. Without the BIOS, each piece of software running on the PC would need to be updated for each PC as to where the hardware and drivers are located. This information would need to be updated each time that it changed, too. Because the BIOS manages this information for the computer, only the BIOS data must be updated when new devices are attached to the computer. As illustrated in Figure 4-2, the BIOS serves the needs of the processor (the hardware devices) as well as those of the software on the computer.

 The data that specifies the PC's hardware configuration is stored in the computer's CMOS memory. Originally, CMOS technology was used only for storing the system setup information. Although most circuits on the PC are now made using this technology, the name CMOS (*see*-moss) usually refers to the memory used to store the PC's hardware configuration data.

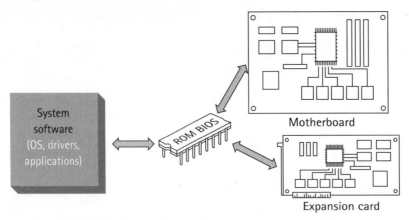

Figure 4-2: The BIOS acts as an intermediary between the parts of the computer.

When the PC is started up, the CMOS data is read and used as a checklist to ver-ify that the devices specified are in fact present and operating. After the hardware check is completed, the BIOS loads the operating system and passes control of the PC over to it. From that point on, the BIOS is available to accept requests for hard-ware assistance from device drivers and application programs and serve as an intermediary between them and the operating system.

Starting Up the PC

Although nearly all PCs are now shipped with their peripheral devices already installed and the system configuration and setup information already completed, you can view and alter this information if necessary. BIOS setup and configuration data is accessed through a start-up program that can be accessed each time the PC is booted. Typically, the system setup program is accessed by pressing Delete or the F1 key immediately after the BIOS program begins its processes.

BIOS activities

The most important activities performed by the BIOS are to start or boot the PC and to perform the Power-On Self-Test (POST). The next two sections detail the actions that take place during each of these activities.

SYSTEM BOOT SEQUENCE

The actual steps that are performed by the BIOS in its boot sequence vary slightly from manufacturer to manufacturer, but generally these are the steps performed during the system boot sequence:

1. When the PC is powered up, the internal power supply initializes.

   As I discuss later in Chapter 14, the PC's power supply does not immediately provide power to the rest of the computer. However, as soon as it determines that it can supply reliable power, its sends out a Power_Good signal that causes the chipset to issue a system reset signal to the processor.

2. The reset signal stimulates the processor to look for the jump address of the BIOS boot program at a hard-wired preset address.

   The jump address (normally address FFFF0h or the end of the system memory) contains the actual address of the BIOS boot program on the ROM BIOS chip.

3. The BIOS performs the POST process.

   Should any fatal errors be encountered, the appropriate beep codes are sounded, perhaps an error message is displayed, or the boot process stops.

4. If all is well with the POST (see "The POST Process" later in this chapter), the start-up process continues, and the system BIOS looks for the BIOS of the video card and starts it.

   That this part of the process is happening is evident by the fact that information about the video card is displayed on the display screen. This will typically precede information about the system BIOS itself.

5. The BIOS routines for any other hardware devices, such as storage devices, are started. Any device BIOS routines found are executed.

6. Information on the system BIOS is displayed on the monitor.

   This display usually includes information on the manufacturer and version of the BIOS program.

7. The BIOS begins a series of tests on the system, including the run-up of the amount of memory detected on the system.

   If errors are found at this point in the process, an error message is displayed on the screen rather than just the beep codes used prior to the monitor being available.

8. The system checks whether all the devices contained in the CMOS configuration data are present and functioning, including determining device speeds, access modes, and other parameters. The serial and parallel ports are also assigned their identities (COM1, COM2, LPT1, and so on).

   A message is displayed on the screen for each device found, configured, and tested.

9. If the BIOS program supports Plug and Play (PnP), any PnP devices detected are configured.

Although typically it goes by much too fast to read, the BIOS displays a message on the monitor for each device that it finds and configures.

10. If all is well, most BIOS programs display some form of summary data screen that details the PC as the BIOS sees it.

At this point, the system is verified and ready for use. Only one thing is missing. . . .

11. The BIOS looks in the CMOS data to determine which disk drive it should look to first for the operating system.

This data is contained in the boot sequence setting of the CMOS data. If the boot device is the hard disk, the BIOS looks for the master boot record; if it is a floppy disk, it looks at the first sector of the disk for the OS boot program. If the boot program is not found on the first device listed, the next device is searched and so on until the boot program is found. If no boot device is found, the boot sequence stops, and the error message No boot device available is displayed.

COLD BOOTS VERSUS WARM BOOTS

The boot sequence used after the PC is powered on from a powered-off state is called a *cold boot*. This refers to the fact that the PC is being started from a cold (or off) status. A *warm boot* is one in which the PC is already powered on and reset from using the Ctrl+Alt+Delete key combination or something similar. The primary difference between the cold boot and the warm boot is that the POST process is not performed on a warm boot.

THE POST PROCESS

After the BIOS is loaded to memory, it immediately begins the *POST* (Power-On Self-Test), which checks that all the system components and hardware listed in the system setup (CMOS) data are present and functioning properly. The POST is performed before the BIOS begins the start-up procedure for the computer.

The POST process is very fast and goes largely unnoticed unless there is a problem. Should there be a problem, the POST has no other means of notifying you than through the system speaker (which is technically a part of the motherboard) with beep tones. At the point that the POST is running, none of the hardware I/O functions are loaded, so the display or printer isn't available to let you know what's going wrong. Depending on the type of error, the POST routine will use a prescribed beep tone pattern to tell you exactly what type of problem it encountered. The beep codes are a like a POST Morse code, and the pattern (how many beeps and also how short or long each beep is) depends on the manufacturer of the BIOS. Most POST problems are fatal because the POST is verifying the essential system components.

BIOS BEEP CODES

Just about all BIOS programs will sound a single beep just before displaying the BIOS start-up screen. If the boot sequence continues successfully, the single beep means that no problems exist. If the boot sequence stops, the beep code sounded can be used to troubleshoot the hardware problems that caused the boot process to fail. You might need to cold boot the PC again to catch the beep code because often it will catch you by surprise the first time that it sounds.

Each BIOS producer has its own collection of POST error beep codes that it uses to alert you to a required hardware system failure that will prevent the POST and boot process from continuing. Four primary sets of beep codes are used on computers: IBM standard, AMI, Award, and Phoenix. Each BIOS beep code set uses a different sound pattern to indicate different problems. They involve short beeps, long beeps, and a varying number of beeps in a three- or four-beep series. These beep codes are listed in Tables 4-1, 4-2, 4-3, and 4-4.

TABLE 4-1 STANDARD IBM BIOS BEEP CODES

Beep Code	Meaning
No beep	Power supply or system board failure
1 short	POST is okay
2 short	POST error with error code display on screen
Repeating short beeps	Power supply or system board failure
1 long, 1 short	System board error
1 long, 2 short	Video display adapter failure
1 long, 3 short	EGA/VGA display adapter error
3 long	Keyboard error

TABLE 4-2 AMI BIOS BEEP CODES

Beep Code	Meaning
1 short	POST is okay
2 short	Memory failure
3 short	Memory/Parity failure
4 short	System timer failure
5 short	Motherboard failure

Continued

TABLE 4-2 AMI BIOS BEEP CODES *(Continued)*

Beep Code	Meaning
6 short	Keyboard controller failure
7 short	CPU failure
8 short	Video adapter failure
9 short	ROM BIOS checksum error
10 short	CMOS read/write error
11 short	Cache memory error
1 long, 3 short	Memory failure
1 long, 8 short	Video adapter failure

TABLE 4-3 AWARD BIOS BEEP CODES

Beep Code	Meaning
1 long	Memory error
1 long, 2 short	Video error
1 long, 3 short	Video failure
Continuous beeps	Memory or video failure

Actually, the codes listed in Table 4-3 are only examples of Award BIOS' codes. Award BIOS relied on the motherboard manufacturers to generate the beep codes used with its BIOS and shared its code with them to do so. Check with the manufacturer of a particular motherboard using Award BIOS to get a list of the beep codes in use.

The Phoenix BIOS POST error beep codes are more complex than the others, as shown in Table 4-4. When an error happens, four sets of beeps are sounded with a slight pause between each set. For example, the beep code that indicates a possible error in the BIOS ROM is 1-2-2-3, which would sound something like *beep,* pause, *beep-beep,* pause, *beep-beep,* pause, *beep-beep-beep.*

TABLE 4-4 PHOENIX BIOS BEEP CODES

Beep Codes	Meaning
1-1-3-1	Error initializing chipset registers with initial POST values; possible motherboard error
1-2-2-1	Motherboard error; initializing keyboard controller
1-2-2-3	BIOS ROM checksum error
1-2-3-1	System timer error
1-2-3-3	Motherboard error; initializing DMA controller
1-3-1-1	Motherboard error; memory refresh test
1-4-1-3	Motherboard error; CPU bus clock frequency test
1-4-2-1	CMOS RAM read/write failure
2-1-1-1	Error in setting initial CPU speed
3-1-1-1	Error in I/O bus or with serial or parallel ports
3-2-4-1	Power management failure; motherboard error
3-3-3-1	Failure writing to video adapter
4-2-4-1	Internal chipset error
4-3-4-3	Error initializing hard disk or loading operating system

---

BIOS start-up screen

Immediately after the BIOS loads the video BIOS, it displays its start-up screen, as shown in Figure 4-3.

Although this display varies by manufacturer, it generally contains the following information:

◆ *The name of the BIOS manufacturer and the version number of the BIOS.*

◆ *The release date or version date of the BIOS.* This is important because it's the key to the features included in the BIOS version.

◆ *The keyboard key used to access the BIOS setup program.* Typically, this is the Delete (Del) or a Function (F1 or F2) key, but it could also be a key combination, such as Ctrl+Esc.

◆ *A logo* from one or more of the following: the BIOS manufacturer, the PC manufacturer, or the motherboard manufacturer.

◆ *If the BIOS supports the Energy Star standard (the Green standard), an Energy Star logo is displayed.* Virtually all newer computers display this logo, but only those pre-Pentiums with an upgraded BIOS will.

◆ *At the end of the display (and in some cases, at the bottom of the screen), the serial number of the BIOS is displayed.* The serial number is specialized to indicate which motherboard, chipset, and BIOS version are in use. It also indicates which combinations of these components are compatible for the BIOS version. The BIOS manufacturer should have information on its Web site on the meaning of the serial number. Some (for example, AMI) have downloadable utility software to help you decode the serial number. An excellent site to visit for BIOS version and serial number information is Wim Bervoets' BIOS site (www.wimsbios.com).

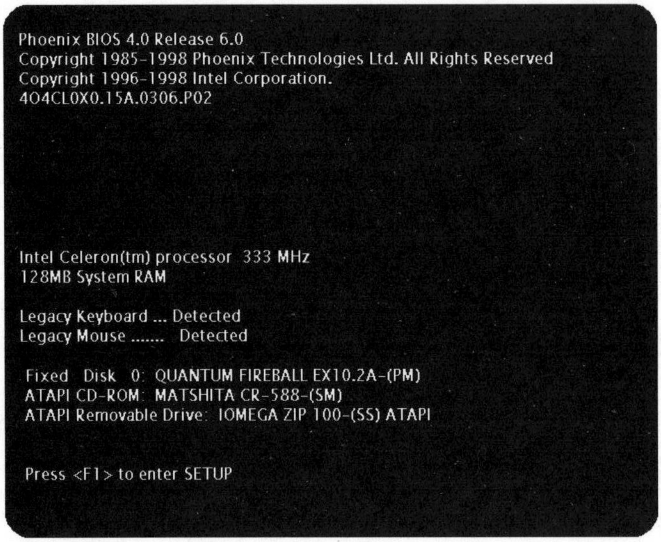

Figure 4-3: A sample start-up screen for a BIOS.

Configuring the System Setup

After the BIOS completes its work and right before it starts loading the operating system into memory, it displays a summary of the system configuration. Like everything to do with the BIOS, what displays depends on the manufacturer and version of the BIOS, but typically the following information is displayed:

◆ *Processor:* The type of microprocessor, such as Pentium, Pentium Pro, and so on, is displayed. Most of the newer BIOS versions recognize all Intel processors as well as those from Cyrix and AMD. However, some of the older BIOS versions might indicate processors from other manufacturers as a Pentium, but this is not an operational problem. Those processors that incorporate the System Management Mode (SMM) power management standard might be indicated as a Pentium-S.

◆ *Co-processor:* If a math co-processor or floating-point unit (FPU) is installed on the system, it will be indicated as *Installed.* Virtually every processor since the 386DX (with the exception of SX models of the 386 and 486 processors) has had an FPU integrated into it and will be indicated as *Integrated.*

◆ *Clock speed:* The clock speed of the processor in MHz is displayed. Sometimes this is displayed on the same line as the processor type.

◆ *Floppy disk drives:* If detected, the size and capacity of each floppy disk are displayed.

◆ *Hard disk and CD-ROM drives:* If the system includes IDE/ATA disk drives or ATAPI CD-ROM drives, the BIOS displays each of the drive types that it detected, including the primary master and slave drives and any secondary slaves and masters. The manufacturer, capacity, and access modes are displayed for each drive detected. At this point of the start-up process, the disk drives are designated physically as C: and D: regardless of the logical drive configuration of the disk drive.

◆ *Memory size:* The amount of memory in base, extended, and cache memory is displayed. The base memory (conventional memory) size will always be 640K. The amount of extended memory on the system minus the amount set aside for the BIOS is displayed. The BIOS does not report the amount of memory reserved for the upper memory block (UMB) that contains the BIOS itself. The cache size is displayed separately.

◆ *Memory type:* The type and configuration of the physical memory is displayed. This includes the number of memory banks or modules installed and the memory technology in use. For example, the display might indicate EDO DRAM at Bank 1 or FP: 0 was detected.

◆ *Video type:* Unless your PC is more than ten years old, the display type will be indicated as *VGA/EGA,* which really doesn't tell you anything other than that the video adapter was detected.

◆ *Serial ports:* The system resource address of any serial or COM ports detected is displayed. These addresses are usually 3F8h and 2F8h, which are the default I/O port addresses for COM1/COM3 and COM2/COM4, but there could be others.

◆ *Parallel ports:* The system resource address of any parallel ports detected is displayed. There is usually only one parallel port, and its I/O port address will normally be 378h (the default address for the LPT1 port), but it might also be 278h or 3BCh.

◆ *Plug and Play devices:* If any Plug and Play adapter cards are detected by the BIOS, it might display a description of each.

Setting the System Configuration

The hardware configuration of the PC is stored in the computer's CMOS memory. This data is managed through the BIOS' setup program. This section discusses how to access the setup program and each of the menu types it displays.

Setup program access

To gain access to the BIOS setup program, you press a designated key, usually displayed during the initial boot process. The keystrokes used to access the setup program for most of the popular BIOS are listed in Table 4-5.

TABLE 4-5 BIOS SETUP PROGRAM ACCESS KEYS

BIOS	Keystroke
AMI BIOS	Delete
Award BIOS	Delete or Ctrl+Alt+Esc
IBM Aptiva	F1
Compaq	F10
Phoenix BIOS	F2

The hardware configuration of a PC is stored in the CMOS memory. Exactly which data is stored depends on the type of PC and the BIOS in use. If you wish to see or modify the system setup data – the BIOS or CMOS configuration – press the key indicated immediately after the POST process has completed (usually the Delete or a function key, such as F1 or F2). After you press the indicated key, the BIOS setup program displays its configuration menu.

Setup program menu types

The BIOS setup program menu includes a number of submenus, each of which focuses on the configuration settings for a specific area of the configuration data. The following sections describe the primary setup program submenus and the settings that they list.

STANDARD SETTINGS

Two levels of configuration data are available on most newer computers: the standard configuration and advanced features. A typical BIOS has standard information on the initial menu, including the system clock, hard disk drives, the floppy drive, and the video adapter. The standard menu also lists other PC configuration information, such as the processor type, memory type and speed, and the amount and type of memory.

ADVANCED SETTINGS

Depending on the BIOS in use, you may see two advanced features menus listed by the startup program: advanced BIOS features and advanced chipset features. These advanced settings are specific to the motherboard, processor, and chipset in use. Although you might not find all the features in the following list on the advanced settings menu of every BIOS, here is a list of the most common options:

◆ *System BIOS Cacheable:* The system BIOS is cached to memory address F0000–FFFFFh, which results in faster performance.

◆ *Video BIOS Cacheable:* The video BIOS is cached to memory address C0000–7FFFh.

◆ *Video RAM Cacheable:* When this option is enabled, the caching of video RAM to memory address A0000–AFFFFh is allowed.

◆ *Auto Configuration:* When enabled, the default values of all chipset options are used.

◆ *DRAM Integrity Mode:* If your PC has error correcting code (ECC) memory, choose ECC; otherwise, set this option to No.

◆ *EDO DRAM Speed Selection:* If the system is using EDO DRAM, this option is used to set its access speed. The speed selected must match the actual speed of the system's EDO DRAM.

◆ *SDRAM CAS (Column Access Strobe) Latency Time:* If the system is using SDRAM (synchronous DRAM), this option sets the number of cycles between the SDRAM read command sample and when the controller reads sample data from the SDRAM.

◆ *SDRAM RAS (Row Access Strobe) Pre-charge Time:* This option sets the number of cycles to be allowed for a charge to accumulate in the RAS before the DRAM refreshes. If this time is too short, the DRAM is unable to fully refresh and might perhaps be unable to store data.

◆ *SDRAM RAS-to-CAS Delay:* This option is used to control the number of cycles between a Row Activate command and a read/write command.

◆ *SDRAM Pre-charge Control:* When this option is enabled, all CPU cycles sent to SDRAM signal an All Banks Pre-charge command.

◆ *Memory Hole at 15M–16M:* If this option is enabled, a 1MB block of empty RAM is created between the 15th and 16th MB of system RAM. This is used to allow some older software programs to run on systems with more than 16MB of RAM.

- *Plug and Play (PnP) Control:* Although the PnP settings are listed on a separate settings menu, on some BIOSes, such as the Award BIOS, PnP must be enabled through a setting found on the advanced BIOS features menu.

- *Passive Release:* This allows CPU to Peripheral Component Interconnect (PCI) access.

- *Delayed Transaction:* This enables support for PCI 2.1.

- *AGP Aperture Size:* This sets the size of the AGP aperture port, which is used for graphics memory.

- *CPU Warning Temperature:* This sets the high and low temperatures at which the environmental monitoring system on the system should trigger CPU temperature warnings.

- *Current CPU Temperature:* This displays the CPU's temperature, providing that the PC has an environmental monitoring system.

- *Shutdown Temperature:* If enabled, this setting causes the CPU to be shut down when either the high or low CPU Warning Temperature is reached.

- *CPU FAN Turn On Speed:* If the system has an environmental monitoring system, this option displays the speed of up to three internal fans.

- *IN0-IN6 (v):* If the PC has an environmental monitoring system, this feature displays the current voltage of up to seven lines (IN0 through IN6).

PLUG AND PLAY

Most new motherboards have options for Plug and Play (PnP) and PCI options, and a special menu might exist for these options in the system setup program, entitled PnP and PCI settings. If the BIOS supports PnP, which depends on the chipset in use, the features and options for it are also found in the advanced settings (see "Advanced settings" earlier in this chapter). The Plug and Play option in the advanced settings might need to be set off (No) or on (Yes) to match the capabilities of the operating system as well.

Some operating systems, such as Windows NT and 2000, are not themselves directly compatible with PnP, which means that the BIOS has to deal with any PnP device configurations. Setting the Plug and Play option to Yes causes the system to skip any BIOS-related PnP, thus leaving it to the operating system to perform, which speeds up the boot process. This menu is dependent on the motherboard chipset, and the options available will vary. A few of the more common options on this menu are

- *Used Memory Length:* This defines the size of the memory to be used as high memory.

- *Used Memory Base Address:* This sets a base memory address for use by any peripheral that requires high memory.

◆ *Assign IRQ for USB:* This option should be disabled if a USB controller is not in use; otherwise, it should be enabled.

◆ *PCI IRQ Activated By:* Some devices require that this option be changed to allow for edge-triggered interrupts.

 An *edge-triggered interrupt* is one that is activated either during the up (rising edge) or down (falling edge) cycles of a clock pulse, such as the timing cycles of the CPU (system) clock.

EXTENDED SYSTEM CONFIGURATION DATA

If the BIOS supports PnP, the CMOS is also used to store the *extended system configuration data* (ESCD), which stores the system resource assignments of PnP devices. ESCD also serves as a communications link between the BIOS and the operating system.

POWER MANAGEMENT

The *Power Management menu* contains the options used to control when the system will automatically power down using power conservation settings. The Advanced Configuration and Power Interface (ACPI), in use since 1998, is the power conservation standard applied to most PCs. The power management settings are configured in the Power Management Settings menu in most modern BIOS setup programs.

INTEGRATED PERIPHERALS

The peripherals controlled through the settings on this menu are integrated into the motherboard. The more common settings on this menu are

◆ *Base I/O Address:* Sets the system resource I/O address for the serial and parallel ports.

◆ *Interrupt:* Designates the system resource interrupt for each serial and parallel port.

◆ *Mode:* Sets the mode for the serial, parallel, and infrared ports on the motherboard.

◆ *Serial Port A and B:* A setting of Select Auto allows the system to assign the first available COM port. The Enable value sets the COM port designation and I/O address manually. This feature can also be used to disable the port for testing.

◆ *Parallel Port:* This option works like the serial port setting. The Select Auto option lets the system assign the available LPT port; the Enable option forces you to set the port address manually. The port can also be disabled.

◆ *Audio:* Enables or disables the audio system built into the motherboard.

◆ *Legacy USB Support:* Allows USB devices, such as keyboards or mice, to be activated without the device drivers being loaded.

IDE DEVICE SETUP AND AUTO-DETECTION

The IDE Configuration menu provides access to the IDE device configuration, including configuration for hard disk drives, CD-ROM drives, tape drives, and so forth. Here are many of the features found on this menu:

◆ *Auto Detect:* Enabling this feature, which is not available on all BIOS, causes any IDE devices (primary master, primary slave, and so forth) on the system to be automatically configured by the BIOS each time that the PC is booted.

◆ *IDE Controller:* Designates which of the IDE controllers are enabled – the primary, secondary, or both (default for multiple IDE devices).

◆ *Hard Disk Pre-Delay:* Normally this option is disabled, but the user can set disk pre-delays from 3–30 seconds.

IDE CONFIGURATION SUBMENUS

The IDE Configuration menu contains submenus for configuring the primary and slave IDE drives. The options found on these submenus are

◆ *Type:* Configures the type of IDE device installed on the system. The choices are Auto (default), ATAPI Removable, Other ATAPI, IDE Removable, CD-ROM, None, and User (user-defined).

◆ *Maximum Capacity:* The capacity of the hard disk.

◆ *Multi-Sector Transfers:* Sets the number of sectors per block in data transfers from the hard drive to memory.

◆ *LBA (Logical Block Addressing) Mode Control:* Enables or disables the use of Logical Block Addressing for hard disk drives larger than 528MB.

◆ *Transfer Mode:* Specifies the method to be used for moving data from one disk to the next. The choices are Standard, Fast PIO1, PIO2, PIO3, PIO4, FPIO 2/DMA1, and FPIO 4/DMA2.

SECURITY AND PASSWORDS

In the security menu, you find options for both a user password and a supervisor password. With the user password set, the PC is not allowed to boot until the proper password is entered. The supervisor password is used to protect the BIOS settings. Without the supervisor password, a user can't access the BIOS settings, but the system will boot.

If you set either the user or supervisor passwords, you *must remember* the passwords. If you forget the user password but remember the supervisor password, you can enter the BIOS setup and clear the password by pressing the Enter key when prompted. If you forget both passwords, you will be unable to boot your system without the user password or to get access to the BIOS without the supervisor password. Your only recourse is to open the PC and use the password-clear jumper, (see Figure 4-4), located on the motherboard.

Password-clear jumper

Figure 4-4: The password-clear jumper on a PC motherboard.

On most motherboards, this password-clear jumper is near either the lithium battery or the BIOS ROM chip. You can also clear the CMOS settings (including all advanced settings that you might have changed) as well as the passwords by removing the CMOS battery. (See Figure 4-5.) This is a good reason to keep a copy of the system setup written down and in a safe place.

Figure 4-5: The BIOS ROM battery on a PC motherboard.

Updating the BIOS

It's hard to draw the line between the old BIOS and the new BIOS, but on most of the older systems, if you wanted to upgrade the BIOS, it required a physical replacement. You had to physically remove the BIOS ROM chip and replace it with a new ROM chip that contained the newer BIOS version. This process had the potential for introducing new problems into your system, including electrostatic discharge (ESD), bent pins, damage to the motherboard, and more. Most people simply upgraded to a new PC to avoid this anxiety and any possible problems.

When the EEPROM began replacing the PROM and EPROM as the BIOS' vessel, with it came flash BIOS. Although some motherboard models still require a physical replacement of the BIOS PROM, most now support flash BIOS, which can be upgraded using special software.

Flashing dangers

After you begin flashing the BIOS ROM, you must complete the process. Otherwise, you'll probably end up with a corrupted and unusable BIOS. If for any reason the flashing process is interrupted – somebody trips over the power cord, or you experience a power failure – depending on where you are in the flashing process, the probability of a corrupted BIOS chip is high.

Another way to corrupt your flash BIOS is to load the wrong BIOS version onto the chip. The software provided to flash your BIOS might not include any security features to prevent this from happening. The flashing utilities from the larger BIOS companies, such as Award and AMI, include features that check the version of the flash file against the model of the motherboard and will let you know of any mismatch.

Should your BIOS become so corrupted that it will not boot, you could be stuck. In order to flash your BIOS ROM, you need to boot the PC – and until you repair the BIOS, you can't boot the PC. In spite of the dangers, the whole process of flashing the BIOS usually takes only a few seconds, and the risks of catastrophe actually striking are very low. But you should take no chances. Avoid flashing your BIOS in an electrical storm, be sure that your PC is protected against power surges or brownouts with an uninterruptible power supply (UPS), and check twice that you are flashing your BIOS with the current version.

Flashing security

With the convenience of flash BIOS comes the danger of accidental flashing. No harm is done if the BIOS is replaced with the same complete version. However, if the flashing operation is interrupted or for some reason an older or incompatible version is inadvertently (or maliciously) loaded, the effect might be the same as no BIOS at all – a system unable to start.

To prevent this from happening, most motherboards include a jumper block that can be set to disallow flash updates. In order to flash the BIOS ROM, you need to open the case and reset the flashing security jumper. If you use this feature and don't set it open and forget it, an accidental flashing cannot occur. Another very good reason to use the flashing security jumper is to prevent access from PC viruses that attempt to change flash BIOS code.

Applying the boot block

Because you run the risk of corrupting the BIOS in a flashing operation, many newer systems now have a boot block feature. This is similar to the switch in newer cars that will start the car when the battery is dead. The *boot block* is a 4K program that's included as part of the BIOS. This small program allows the system to recover from an incorrect or corrupted BIOS by restoring the BIOS from a special floppy disk or CD-ROM. If the motherboard supports it, this feature might need to be enabled through a jumper.

Gathering Repair and Maintenance Tools

A variety of tools are available for repair and maintenance of PC systems and peripherals. Some are physical – you hold them in your hand, like a pair of pliers, or they measure something – and some are diagnostic in nature.

Using hard tools

Here is a list of the tools that you need in order to work on BIOS-related problems:

- *Multimeter/ohmmeter:* A *multimeter* measures resistance, current, and voltage. An *ohmmeter* measures electrical resistance. These are essential tools for PC technicians and repairpersons. A wide variety of inexpensive multimeters, like that shown in Figure 4-6, are useful for in-depth testing and general electronic measurements. An ohmmeter is handy for checking for short circuits or open circuits.

- *BIOS POST Cards:* No, these aren't picture cards for you to mail to a friend wishing they were here. During the POST process, in addition to the beep codes sounded and error codes displayed on the screen, the BIOS sends an error code stream to a special memory location, usually address 80h. The BIOS POST card captures and displays the codes sent to this address so that you can locate exactly where the system is having problems. This can be extremely helpful when debugging very stubborn systems.

  The POST Card is installed in an ISA slot, as shown in Figure 4-7. When the PC is turned on, the POST Card displays information using the two alphanumeric/hex-type displays concerning POST error codes, the four power supply status indicators. The card is designed to withstand reasonable electrostatic abuse, and it is protected against reversal in an ISA bus slot and fused against defective motherboards that could damage it.

Figure 4-6: A digital multimeter.

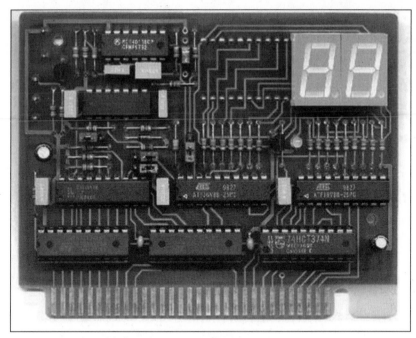

Figure 4-7: A BIOS POST Card displays POST error codes.

◆ *Test bed:* I recommend having an older system (but not too old – maybe one from the past two or three years) to use as a test bed for components. The test bed can be used to test an unknown device with other components that are known to work, which cuts down on guesswork and saves time. The cost of a simple PC for this purpose is minimal when considering the time that can be saved.

◆ *An ESD wrist strap:* This is more of a safety device than a tool, but using one will protect you and the systems and components on which you're working from electrostatic discharge (ESD). See Figure 4-8.

◆ *Needle-nose pliers:* These are very useful for grasping small items or removing and replacing jumpers on circuit boards.

◆ *A small flashlight:* Some things are impossible to read or find inside the PC case without a flashlight. The inside of a PC is dark and has many hiding places for dropped screws and small things you need to see, such as Pin 1 on a connector.

◆ *Tweezers:* Tweezers or a part retriever can be handy for picking up small items, like a lost jumper. A *retriever* is like a tiny set of retractable claws with a spring-loaded handle.

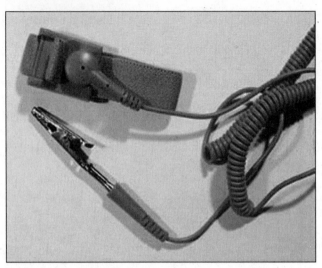

Figure 4-8: An ESD wrist strap.

Applying some soft tools

The use of diagnostic software tools can save you a great deal of time. Although they won't necessarily identify what is causing a problem, software tools often provide hints or other information about which components are working and which are not. Some software programs are free, some are included with the operating system, and other commercial products can be very expensive.

Here are a few commonly used software diagnostic tools that you might want to consider including in your troubleshooting kit:

◆ *Power-On Self-Test (POST):* Although this is the focus of this chapter, the POST can also provide you with good information on a PC when you're first starting your diagnostic procedure. Pay close attention to its audio and video messages.

◆ *Boot disk:* You should always have a boot disk on a floppy disk or CD-ROM that you can use to boot the PC in the event of a disk failure. I recommend that you include the MS-DOS commands FDISK, FORMAT, and MEM on this disk along with the operating system.

◆ *Microsoft Diagnostics:* This software utility, which has been around for a while, is also known as MSD.EXE. It is an MS-DOS utility that takes an inventory of the contents of a PC and displays them in a text-based format. It is a very useful tool for viewing the current configuration and system resource assignments of a system. MSD.EXE even displays the BIOS in use and the universal asynchronous receiver/transmitter (UART) chips that the serial ports are using. MSD.EXE is included with later versions of MS-DOS and can be downloaded from the Microsoft Knowledge Base at

http://support.microsoft.com/default.aspx?scid=KB;en-us;
122415&.

◆ `MEM.EXE`: This utility is built into nearly all versions of MS-DOS and
Windows. It displays details on the memory configuration and the current
contents of memory. A common command line is MEM /C /P.

◆ *The Windows 9x Device Manager:* When working with Windows 9*x* or
2000 systems, this is probably the most useful tool available for identifying system configuration and resource usage information. The Device
Manager, shown in Figure 4-9, is accessed through a Windows 9*x* Control
Panel's System icon and the Device Manager tab. On Windows 2000 systems, it is opened from the Control Panel's System icon and the Hardware
tab, where you'll find the Device Manager button.

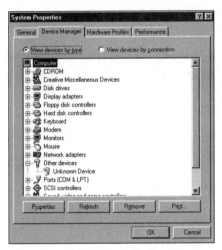

Figure 4-9: The Windows Device Manager.

◆ *Norton System Information:* This program, which is a part of Symantec's
Norton Utilities bundle, is very similar to MSD.EXE, but it provides more
detailed information about the components of the PC. It's really just an
information utility and not a true diagnostic utility. Find more about
Norton Utilities at www.norton.com.

◆ *Norton Diagnostics:* Another utility in the Norton Utilities suite, Norton
Diagnostics performs tests on the microprocessor, the motherboard, resource
allocations, and RAM to identify any existing problems or conflicts.

◆ *Microsoft ScanDisk and Norton Disk Doctor:* These programs, the former
an MS-DOS utility and the latter a Norton Utility member, check for hard
disk drive problems such as file system corruption and hard disk read
errors.

I also list some great software diagnostic programs in Chapter 1 that can be applied to track down a BIOS or configuration problem.

Dealing with BIOS and Boot Problems

This section contains some of the more common processor-related errors and problems that you might encounter along with some suggested solutions.

The system boots from the wrong disk

If you were trying to boot the PC from the floppy disk drive but it booted from the hard disk drive instead, you need to check out the BIOS settings using the following process:

1. Run the BIOS setup program and check the CMOS settings for the Boot Drive Sequence. If the floppy disk is not first, correct the settings and reboot.

   - If the boot sequence settings are correct, check whether the floppy disk drive is installed in the system configuration data. If not, enter its data and reboot.

   - If the BIOS data is correct, the floppy disk drive data connector or its power cable could be unplugged or improperly installed.

2. Open the case to check the cables, verifying that the data cable is properly installed with Pin 1 aligned correctly.

This process can be used to change the boot sequence so that any of the data drives (floppy, hard disk, or CD-ROM) will be used as the primary boot disk and to set the sequence in which you want the BIOS to check for the operating system.

An Invalid System Disk message displays

The BIOS diagnostic screen displays the message `Invalid System Disk` during the boot process.

1. Remove any data or non-boot floppy disks from the floppy disk drive.

2. Access the BIOS IDE Configuration data to check whether all hard disks are set to Auto Detect or that they have been manually set up and installed properly.

The hard disk is not detected during the boot

The BIOS does not detect the hard disk during the POST. The BIOS IDE configuration is set to Auto Detect and should be automatically detected when the system boots. The boot process stops at the point at which the disk should be found or displays an error that indicates no disk drive was detected.

1. Make sure that the jumpers on the hard disk drives are set to master (primary) or slave (secondary) appropriately.

2. The BIOS settings that enable auto-detection during the boot process could be incorrect.

   Recheck the IDE Configuration setting to ensure that it's set for Auto Detect.

3. If the IDE Configuration settings are okay, the problem is likely with the hard disk itself, its power connection, its connection to the hard disk controller card, or the motherboard.

   One way to test whether the hard disk controller can detect the hard disk itself is with the BIOS Auto Detect feature. If the disk cannot be auto detected, troubleshoot the controllers (see Chapter 8).

4. The hard disk drive might not be ready when the boot process is seeking it.

   If the disk isn't ready when the BIOS looks for it, it will appear to not exist to the system. Check the hard disk pre-delay in the IDE Configuration menu.

5. If all else fails, connect a hard disk drive that you know works into the controller to verify that the controller is good.

The boot has stopped, and the screen is blank

A beep code, other than a short single beep, is sounding, and the monitor is blank.

As listed in Tables 4-1 through 4-4 earlier in this chapter, beep codes indicate a system problem that is causing the POST process to stop before the video BIOS is available. Beep codes generally indicate a problem with a system component that is required for the POST to continue, such as the motherboard, video adapter, chipset, memory, and so on. The display is not functioning, so the only device available to signal you as to what the problem might be is audible tones (beeps) played through the system speaker.

A very common problem when you hear beep codes is that the video adapter card might not be seated in its expansion slot completely or properly.

USB problems

When you plug a USB device into the USB port, the device does not function and cannot be accessed. Check whether the Legacy USB feature in the Peripheral Configurations menu of the BIOS is set to Enable. If this feature is set to Disable, USB ports, USB mice, and keyboards will not function.

Forgotten BIOS passwords

Neither the supervisor nor user password work to allow the PC to boot or access the BIOS configuration data.

1. Reference the documentation for the PC's motherboard to determine the location of the password-clear jumper on the motherboard (refer to Figure 4-4).

2. After removing the PC case, remove the jumper to clear all the BIOS CMOS settings, including the supervisor and user passwords.

3. Reboot the PC, and then replace the jumper and the PC case.

4. Remove the CMOS battery (refer to Figure 4-5) and replace it after a few seconds.

   This will reset the BIOS CMOS settings to their default values.

   Remember that this also resets any values that might have been modified in the BIOS configurations settings. Keep a written record of the BIOS settings for just this situation.

When to flash the BIOS

How do you know when to flash the BIOS and then actually do it? To find out whether your BIOS should be updated, perform the following steps:

1. Find the version level of the BIOS loaded to BIOS EEPROM.

   The BIOS version is usually displayed during the boot sequence. When it appears on the screen, use the Pause key to stop the boot sequence (this doesn't work on all systems) and record the version information from the screen. To resume the boot, press any key.

On an ASUS (www.asus.com.tw) motherboard, here's how the version level is determined:

While the memory count is running up, watch for the line #401A0-*XXXX* (where the *XXXX* is the BIOS revision). This is usually on the third line from the top of the screen. A display of #401A0-0614 means that you have a BIOS revision level of 0614.

2. After you have the BIOS version, note the model of your motherboard, the PC model number, and the CPU type.

   Use this information to contact the motherboard manufacturer or visit its Web site to see whether a newer version of the BIOS is available. If several versions are available since your version, you need to update to the latest version only. It will incorporate all previous updates, as well.

   BIOS upgrades generally contain some or all of the following:

   ■ New BIOS features

   ■ Fixes for bugs and compatibility problems

   ■ Support for additional CPUs

If your PC is working without problems, don't flash your BIOS! Fixing a working system could result in a broken system.

To prepare for updating your BIOS, perform the following steps:

1. Copy down the existing BIOS settings so you'll be able to re-enter them after upgrading the BIOS.

   Any settings that have been altered will be lost as a result of the upgrade.

2. Be absolutely sure that you get the upgrade file from the motherboard manufacturer and not the ROM manufacturer.

   This shouldn't be a problem because the ROM manufacturer probably won't have BIOS upgrades for you to download anyway. You must contact the motherboard manufacturer to get the update files or download the correct EEPROM BIOS files from its Web site. Usually these files include the software used to install the upgrade as well.

3. Follow the manufacturer's installation instructions specifically.

   Not every BIOS upgrade is the same, but most follow the same general procedures.

How do you determine whether you can flash the BIOS on your motherboard? You need to determine three things about your system before you can even attempt to flash the BIOS:

1. Does your motherboard have a flash BIOS?

   Most newer motherboards have an EEPROM that can be flashed. Generally, if the motherboard has one of more PCI slots, it most likely also has a flash BIOS.

2. Does your motherboard revision support the BIOS revision that you wish to upgrade your BIOS to?

   The revision of the motherboard is printed very near the motherboard's model number, which is located somewhere near the CPU or the center of the motherboard.

3. Does your BIOS EEPROM chip support the BIOS revision level that you wish to upgrade to?

   Your motherboard manufacturer should list which chips are compatible with each BIOS revision. Also check whether the BIOS revision you wish to upgrade to supports PnP; otherwise, the PnP will not work.

After flashing the BIOS, the PC will not boot

You have painstakingly flashed the BIOS, but now the PC doesn't boot. The first thing to do is calm down! All is not lost. Some manufacturers have restore utilities and recovering routines included in the files that you downloaded. If this isn't the case with the manufacturer of your motherboard, simply call the manufacturer or visit its Web site to get instructions on how to obtain a fresh, working BIOS. There will definitely be a charge and some shipping to pay (more for rush orders), but after all — it's a lifesaver.

Chapter 5

Configuring System Resources

IN THIS CHAPTER

The inner workings of a PC – how the processor works with the other components of the computer – are not as magical as they might seem. What might appear to be smoke and mirrors is actually a well-coordinated series of actions and interactions that use a relatively small amount of the overall system's resources. When your application program needs a file or you wish to connect to the Internet, the processor seamlessly executes the required actions and provides the application with the data that it requests or displays the Web site that you seek.

In this chapter, I cover the following:

◆ Understanding and assigning system resources

◆ Resolving system resource conflicts

◆ Working with IRQ steering

HOW THE PC'S PROCESSOR AND COMPONENTS COMMUNICATE to facilitate these and other similar actions is a study of how, when, and why system resources are allocated and used.

Getting the CPU's Attention

The processor controls the activities of all the devices integrated into or attached to a PC's motherboard either directly or indirectly. Actually, these activities must be controlled from a single point or chaos would reign inside the system when the devices and services all compete for control of memory and the bus. The processor carries out the role of traffic cop by communicating commands, requests, and data directly to each device over communication facilities assigned specifically to each device. These communication facilities allow the processor to communicate with the PC's devices and the devices to pass requests and information back to the processor.

Requesting attention

To illustrate how this communication process takes place, imagine that every device installed inside the case, either connected to or mounted on the motherboard, is assigned a light bulb and an associated mailbox. Like a student in class who raises her hand to get the teacher's attention, a device must activate its light bulb to indicate when it needs the processor to do something for it. In the PC, some devices can take care of their own needs. But for the most part, peripheral devices and other hardware components need assistance from the processor for many actions, such as moving data to and from memory.

When an application program requests data from the hard disk drive, the hard disk's device driver works with the operating system and system Basic Input/Output System (BIOS) to instruct the processor that data is needed from the hard disk. To get the attention of the hard disk, it turns on the hard disk's light and puts a request for the data in the hard disk's mailbox. When the hard disk sees the light, it reads the request and moves the data into a buffer, turns on its light (see Step 1 in Figure 5-1), and puts a request in its mailbox asking the processor to move the data from its buffer into memory. When the processor can be interrupted, it turns off the light and performs the service requested. While this is going on, other devices probably turn on their lights as well (Step 2 in Figure 5-1).

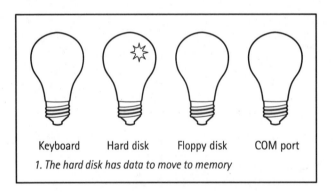

Keyboard   Hard disk   Floppy disk   COM port

1. The hard disk has data to move to memory

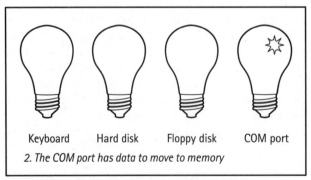

Keyboard   Hard disk   Floppy disk   COM port

2. The COM port has data to move to memory

Figure 5-1: Devices signal the processor that its services are needed with a mechanism similar to turning on a light.

Taking care of themselves

Some devices have the capability of performing the services normally requested of the processor for themselves. When these devices take care of their own needs, the processor is freed up to serve the requests of those devices that require assistance as well as all the other tasks that the processor must do. The majority of the tasks requested by peripheral devices of the process involve moving data in and out of memory. Devices that are able to directly access memory on their own without bothering the processor improve the performance of the entire PC.

Defining System Resources

As described in very general terms in the preceding section, a PC's system resources are a set of three mechanisms, which are used by the components of a PC to communicate with the processor. The three system resource mechanisms are

 ♦ *Interrupt request (IRQ):* This is the mechanism used by devices to request services from the CPU. An *IRQ* is a wire in the motherboard's bus on which a device sends a signal to the processor to get its attention. Sixteen IRQs are on all newer PCs (all PCs since the PC XT). Only ten of the IRQs are available for devices to use, with the remaining six reserved for system-level purposes. Although ten devices might seem like a goodly number of peripherals on any PC, there are often not enough to go around. See "Assigning interrupt requests" later in this section for more information.

 ♦ *Input/output (I/O) address:* This is the message box used by the processor and a device to pass information, such as memory addresses, to each other. Every device attached to a PC is assigned an I/O address. This resource is also called an *I/O port* or an *I/O base address.* See "Checking the mailbox" later in the chapter for more information.

 ♦ *Direct memory access (DMA):* A limited number of DMA channels are available to devices that have the ability to access memory directly without the assistance of the CPU. See "Directly accessing memory" later in the chapter for more information.

Many devices require only one of the system resources, which is typically an I/O address, but others require two and perhaps all three of the system resources. To view the system resources on your PC, access the System Information applet from the Accessories → Systems Tools menu (see Figure 5-2).

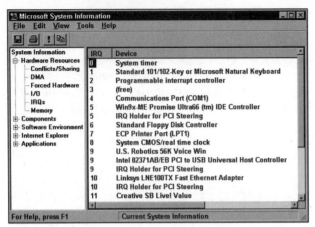

Figure 5-2: System resources on a Windows PC can be viewed through the System Information applet.

Assigning interrupt requests

A peripheral device communicates with the processor through an interrupt request (IRQ). A device sets an IRQ to get the processor's attention whenever it needs services that only the processor can perform. When the processor notices the IRQ, it interrupts its activities to service the request (which is where the term *interrupt request* comes from). IRQs are assigned to those devices that require assistance from the processor to handle data movement, data interpretation, error processing, and other tasks.

The 16 IRQs on a PC are actually two sets of 8 IRQs linked together. Of the 16 IRQs, 5 are set aside for use by internal system-level devices, and 1 is used as the link between the two IRQ sets, leaving only 10 available for assignments to I/O devices. Table 5-1 lists the standard default assignments of IRQs.

TABLE 5-1 TYPICAL IRQ ASSIGNMENTS

IRQ	Assignment
0	System timer
1	Standard keyboard
2	Programmable Interrupt Controller (PIC)
3	Serial ports 2 and 4 (COM2 and COM4)
4	Serial ports 1 and 3 (COM1 and COM3)
5	Standard sound card or LPT2

IRQ	Assignment
6	Floppy disk controller (FDC)
7	Parallel port (LPT1)
8	Complementary Metal-Oxide Semiconductor (CMOS) and real-time clock (RTC)
9	Hardware Motion Picture Experts Group (MPEG)
10	Modem audio
11	Video Graphics Array (VGA) video card
12	PS/2 mouse
13	Math co-processor/Numeric data processor
14	Primary Integrated Drive Electronics (IDE) controller
15	Secondary IDE controller

CONNECTING IRQS

An *IRQ* is an individual wire on the motherboard's system bus, and an IRQ wire is connected to every one of the expansion ports and slots on the motherboard. Regardless of which port, connector, or expansion slot an I/O adapter is placed into, it has access to the PC's IRQs, and an expansion slot can be assigned a particular IRQ line.

The particular IRQ used to support the adapter or device is determined by either the preset values of the device itself or those established in the BIOS setup configuration settings. Each specific hardware device can occupy only one IRQ, but an IRQ can be assigned to multiple devices.

After a device has been assigned an IRQ, the processor knows the device by its particular IRQ number. When a device sends an IRQ signal over the bus line, the number of the bus line identifies the device. When the processor has completed the requested task, it sends a clearing signal over the IRQ bus line, and the device knows that it may proceed.

IRQs have priorities that are set by the system to indicate which IRQ is to be handled first if two or more requests come in at the same time. The Programmable Interrupt Controller (PIC) manages priorities and other IRQ control issues.

MAKING MULTIPLE DEVICE ASSIGNMENTS

An IRQ can be assigned to multiple devices, but this can lead to problems if not managed properly. If two active devices share a single IRQ, the processor has no way of determining which of the two devices sent a request. In fact, the processor doesn't know whether more than one device is on an IRQ. The processor only knows that the device on an IRQ line has requested a service. When two active devices both contend for a single IRQ, conflicts are inevitable. In an extreme case, the danger exists that both devices could send a bus signal (which is voltage on the line) simultaneously, which could short the bus, the motherboard, or the device controller.

When two devices share an IRQ, such as COM ports (see Table 5-1), only one of the devices should be active at a time. In the early days of the mouse when most mice were serial devices, it was common for a mouse on COM3 and a modem on COM1 to share IRQ4. Only when both devices were in use did a problem surface. The resolution in this case is simple: Move one of the devices to either COM2 or COM4, thus avoiding new conflicts.

Today, a scanner or a Zip drive commonly shares IRQ7 with the LPT (parallel) port and a printer. The device drivers and operating systems know to compensate for some expected conflicts, but two active devices shouldn't share an IRQ.

Making IRQ assignments

Although no official standard controls IRQ assignments, IRQs are assigned to a device by using common practice and the de facto working standards currently in use by the computing industry. There has never been a set-in-stone standard for IRQ assignments, but processor, motherboard, chipset, and I/O adapter manufacturers have followed the lead of some of the larger motherboard and processor manufacturers (primarily Intel) on IRQ settings.

Table 5-2 compares the IRQ settings of the three primary bus structures that have been used in PCs. Notice that even Tables 5-1 and 5-2 differ slightly. Table 5-1 shows common IRQ settings used today, and Table 5-2 shows the default settings that were or are used on different bus structures.

TABLE 5-2 IRQ ASSIGNMENTS ON BUS STRUCTURES

IRQ	PC XT Bus	PC AT Bus	Pentium-class
0	System timer	System timer	System timer
1	Keyboard controller	Keyboard controller	Keyboard controller
2	8-bit available	Second IRQ controller	Second IRQ controller
3	COM2/COM4	COM2/COM4	COM2/COM4
4	COM1/COM3	COM1/COM3	COM1/COM3
5	Hard disk controller (HDC)	LPT2	Sound card
6	Floppy disk controller (FDC)	FDC	FDC
7	LPT1	LPT1	LPT1

IRQ	PC XT Bus	PC AT Bus	Pentium-class
8	Real-time clock (RTC)	RTC	RTC
9	NA	Available	Available
10	NA	Available	Available
11	NA	Available	Available
12	NA	PS/2 mouse	PS/2 mouse
13	NA	Math co-processor	Math co-processor
14	NA	HDC	Primary IDE controller
15	NA	Available	Secondary IDE controller

CONFIGURING IRQS

A device is configured for an IRQ setting with a variety of methods. Most expansion cards today use the Peripheral Component Interconnect (PCI) interface and are Plug and Play (PnP) compatible (more on this later in this section). PnP devices are automatically configured to the PC, including system resource settings, by the BIOS and operating system.

Legacy adapter and controller cards (those that are not PnP) are still around that use the Industry Standard Architecture (ISA), Enhanced ISA (EISA), and Video Electronics Standards Association (VESA) local-bus interfaces. These devices might require physical configuration to assign the system resource settings, including the IRQ. Physical configuration is usually done through jumpers or Dual Inline Packaging (DIP) switches on the expansion card itself.

Many older adapter cards, such as video adapters and network interface cards (NICs), use jumper blocks to configure IRQ settings. The position of the jumper, like those shown in Figure 5-3 on a NIC card, sets the card to use one of typically two alternative IRQ choices. Those adapter cards that are configured through jumpers are usually sold preset to a preferential setting but can be configured to one or more alternative settings through the jumper block.

Another means used to configure the system resources of an expansion card is a DIP switch. A *DIP switch,* a block of typically four, six, or eight switches (see Figure 5-4), is used to represent a binary value by moving the switches to on (open) or off (closed) positions. A card that is configured through DIP switch settings should have documentation that specifies the switch settings to use for the desired resource configuration.

Figure 5-3: A jumper is used on some adapter or controller cards to set the system resource settings.

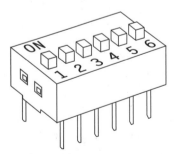

Figure 5-4: A DIP switch supplies a binary value based on the positions of its switches.

TIP Like cards configured with jumpers, the DIP switches should be in their default settings from the factory, but check the settings anyway — changing a switch inadvertently is very easy.

Another common means of configuring the system resource settings of an expansion card is using proprietary installation software supplied with the card on a diskette or CD-ROM. The disk might hold only a start-up program that downloads the installation software from the manufacturer's Web site. Thus, make sure that you have Internet access before purchasing a card that requires this type of setup. However, this approach ensures that latest system resource setting values and device drivers are being installed. Some installation software can adjust the IRQ assignment of its device to fit the existing system resource environment. However, you should always check the system resources assigned by a manufacturer's installation software after running it to avoid resource conflicts.

MANAGING BIOS SETTINGS

If automatic resource allocation is disabled in the PCI/PnP section of the BIOS configuration data, you can specify the IRQs and DMA channels that you want PnP to automatically assign to particular devices. For each IRQ or DMA channel, you can designate whether it's a PCI/PnP device (it's available to be assigned to PnP and PCI devices) or an ISA legacy device (not available for automatic assignment). PCI/PnP is the default type on all Pentium-class PCs.

TIP IRQs 1, 2, 6, 8, 9, and 13 are reserved or assigned by the system. The remainder can be designated for automatic or manual assignment. Let the IRQs default to PCI/PnP unless you have one or two particular IRQs that you wish to specifically reserve for legacy devices.

Working with PCI and IRQs

PCI devices share a common IRQ. Each port (slot) on the PCI bus has four interrupts of its own that are mapped to the single system IRQ using IRQ steering. The IRQ assigned to the PCI bus can be IRQ 9, 10, 11, or 12. The four interrupts on each PCI port are designated as PCI interrupt requests (PIRQs) A through D. In most cases, a PCI card takes PIRQ A.

IRQ steering prevents the system BIOS from assigning each PCI slot to a different IRQ, which avoids resource conflicts or a lack of resources for other devices. However, in order for IRQ steering to work correctly, the BIOS, chipset, PCI cards, and the software drivers must all support it. However, if IRQ conflicts occur between PCI devices, the PCI bus IRQ steering should be disabled so that you can determine exactly where the conflict is occurring.

IRQ steering is an operating system feature of the Windows system on versions beginning with the Windows 95 OSR2 (OEM) version.

Plugging and playing

Plug and Play (PnP) is a great feature for automatically detecting and configuring system resource assignments for new PC hardware. However, in order to work effectively, it must be supported by the PC's operating system, chipset, and BIOS.

PnP is not immune from IRQ conflicts. PnP can only assign those IRQs designated in the BIOS as being available for PCI/PnP use. A PnP BIOS looks at the system as only seeing PCI/PnP and legacy (ISA) devices.

PnP won't configure a legacy device. In cases where a PnP device requires a certain IRQ or when all IRQs are already in use, PnP cannot solve the problem by itself. PnP will add the hardware to the system but flag it in the Device Manager with either a yellow exclamation point or a red X to indicate that a problem exists. When this happens, check the resource information using the Windows System Information (refer to Figure 5-2) or Device Manager applets for any conflicts that have been created.

All PCI devices are PnP devices, but not all PnP devices are PCI devices.

Understanding the PIC

IRQs are handled by two dedicated integrated circuits called Programmable Interrupt Controllers (PICs). PIC circuits are integrated into the PC's chipset along with many other devices. (See Chapter 3 for more information on chipsets.) Each PIC controls eight IRQ lines. Figure 5-5 illustrates the general design of a PIC. PICs are so named because system components manufacturers can program the circuit so that each of its registers performs a particular function.

The IRQ lines have an Interrupt Mask Register (IMR) and two Interrupt Status Registers named PIC1 and PIC2. The IRQ enters the PIC through its IMR. The IMR determines whether the IRQ is masked (disabled); if so, the request is ignored. If the IRQ is not masked (enabled), the request is recorded in the Interrupt Request Register (IRR). The IRR holds the IRQ requests until they have been either processed or acknowledged, depending on what was requested. The Priority Resolver (PR) acts as a sort of traffic cop to ensure that the highest priority request is handled first.

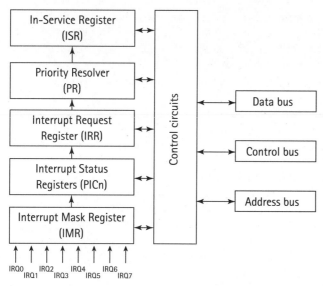

Figure 5-5: The circuitry of a Programmable Interrupt Controller.

Essentially, the lowest IRQs have the highest priority. When the IRQs are ready for processing, the processor is notified that requests are pending with a signal on its interrupt (INT) line. As soon as the processor completes its current task, it responds with an Interrupt Acknowledgement (INTA).

After the processor has acknowledged the INT query, the active IRQ is placed in the In-Service Register (ISR), which always holds the IRQ currently being processed. The status of the active IRQ is updated in the IRR and the applicable Interrupt Status Register. The address of the IRQ is sent to the processor, and the IRQ is serviced. When the requested activity is completed, the ISR tells the PIC that the IRQ has ended, and the ISR is cleared. The highest-priority pending IRQ in the IRR is then placed in the ISR, and the process repeats.

Checking the mailbox

As I explain earlier in this chapter, the processor and peripheral devices use a two-way mailbox to communicate with one another. The mailbox for each device is actually a small space in system memory, which is known by many names: the *I/O (input/output) address*, the *I/O port*, and the *I/O base address*. I/O address is the most commonly used name for this feature referencing the address in memory through which a device performs its input and output operations.

For example, when the processor has data to pass to the NIC, the address of the data is placed in the memory at the NIC's I/O address. Likewise, when the NIC gets data from the network that needs to be moved either to memory or a disk drive, the data is placed at the NIC's I/O address.

The size of the memory reserved for each device at its I/O address varies with the amount of data that the device passes in and out of the system. Not every device is assigned the same amount of space. The amount of space assigned to a device depends mostly on the bus architecture that it uses. Most devices are assigned 4, 8, or 16 bytes, but some devices use as little as 1 byte or as much as 64 bytes.

LOCATING THE I/O ADDRESSES

Literally thousands of available I/O areas are available, but conflicts do occur when multiple devices attempt to use the same I/O address or when devices have overlapping areas.

For example, NICs are commonly assigned the I/O address of 360h (the *h* indicates that the address is expressed as a hexadecimal number), and the default I/O address for LPT1 is 378h. If the NIC requires 32 bytes of I/O space, its ending address would be 37Fh, which creates an overlapping conflict with the parallel port. As long as no parallel devices are in use, that shouldn't be a problem. However, if an external device such as a printer is attached to the LPT1 port, the NIC might need to be assigned a different I/O address.

This approach to moving data is Memory-Mapped I/O. Each device is mapped to a specific location in memory (hence, the name). After a device has placed data in its I/O address area, it contacts the processor, typically with an IRQ, to let it know that the data is ready. Because the device is mapped to its memory area, the processor knows where in memory the device's I/O buffer is located.

DETAILING COMMON I/O ADDRESS ASSIGNMENTS

Although no formal standards exist to permanently set I/O address assignments, a generally accepted list of I/O address assignments is commonly used. Table 5-3 lists the most common default I/O address assignments used on PCs.

TABLE 5-3 COMMONLY USED I/O ADDRESS ASSIGNMENTS

I/O Address	Area Size (Bytes)	Assigned To
0000–000Fh	16	Slave DMA controller chip
0010–001Fh	16	System
0060–0063h	4	Keyboard
0064–0067h	4	PS/2 port
00C0–00DFh	32	Master DMA controller
0130–014Fh	32	Small Computer System Interface (SCSI) host adapter
01F0–01F7h	8	Primary IDE channel

I/O Address	Area Size (Bytes)	Assigned To
0200–0207h	8	Game port
0220–022Fh	16	Sound card
0270–0273h	4	PnP hardware
0278–027Fh	8	Parallel port (LPT2)
0280–028Fh	16	Liquid crystal display (LCD)
02E8–02EFh	8	Serial port - COM4
02F8–02FFh	8	Serial port - COM2
0300–031Fh	32	NICs
0320–032Fh	16	Legacy HDCs
0330–0331h	2	Musical Instrument Digital Interface (MIDI)
0360–036Fh	16	NICs (alternate)
0378–037Fh	8	Parallel port (LPT1)
03C0–03DFh	32	VGA video display adaptor
03E0–03E7h	8	PC card (PCMCIA) port controller
03E8–03EFh	8	Serial port - COM3
03F0–03F6h	8	Floppy disk drive interface
03F8–03FFh	8	Serial port - COM1
0533–0537h	4	Windows sound system
0678–067Fh	8	Enhanced Parallel Port (EPP)
0CF8–0CFBh	4	PCI data registers
FF00–FF07h	8	IDE bus mastering

I/O addresses are assigned in the area between address 0000h and FFFFh, which represents 65,536 bytes. Table 5-3 doesn't list every possible I/O address assignment. Several other I/O addresses are used for supplemental space for some devices and services, such as IDE bus mastering, serial ports, parallel ports, and IDE controllers.

AVOIDING I/O ADDRESS CONFLICTS

An I/O address is intended for a single device, and having multiple active devices sharing an I/O port can have disastrous results. Because the system is designed to be a one-on-one sort of thing, no identification is involved, which means that no possible way exists for the processor or a device to know which device a message is intended for or which device is sending data. You might encounter some legacy situations—such as on older parallel ports and ISA adapters, where more than one device is hard wired to a particular I/O address—but these situations are quickly disappearing. This happens when a legacy adapter card, which can be physically configured to only one of two I/O addresses, creates an I/O address collision with another legacy device.

ASSIGNING I/O ADDRESSES ON A WINDOWS SYSTEM

Like IRQs, I/O address assignments can be viewed on a Windows PC through the Device Manager or the System Information applet. Figure 5-6 shows the Computer Properties window with the I/O addresses resources displayed. This list displays the I/O addresses assigned to the PC's devices. You might see entries such as In use by unknown device or Alias to for devices requiring additional space.

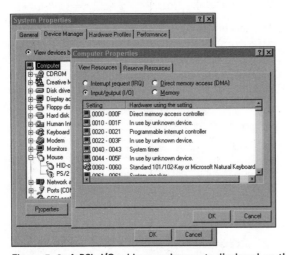

Figure 5-6: A PC's I/O address assignments displayed on the Computer Properties window of the Windows Device Manager.

You can also use the Device Manager to display the system resource assignments of an individual device (see Figure 5-7), including its I/O address. If a conflict exists for a device, it will have either a yellow exclamation point or a red X on the Device Manager tree. Any conflicts that exist can be resolved by assigning the device to a different I/O address. Remember that some system resources set aside for standard devices not found on every PC can be reassigned.

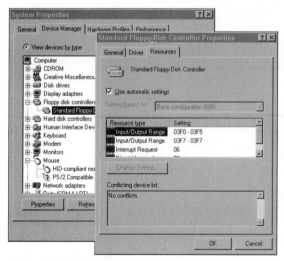

Figure 5-7: The Properties window of the FDC showing its
I/O address assignments.

Directly accessing memory

Direct memory access (DMA) allows non-PCI bus adapters and devices to access memory directly without assistance from the processor. Thus, a DMA device can move data in and out of random access memory (RAM) on its own. The processor normally controls all activities on the bus, but on most newer systems, the DMA controller is allowed to move data in and out of RAM while the processor takes care of other tasks. ISA cards and IDE/ATA interface devices have access to a PC's DMA channels.

 PCI and AGP (Accelerated Graphics Port) buses do not support DMA.

OPERATING WITH DMA

Without DMA, data is transferred from a peripheral device, such as a modem, to memory through the IRQ process. However, when a DMA device such as the floppy disk drive needs to transfer data, it requests assistance from the DMA controller. The DMA controller takes control of the system bus and acts as an intermediary between the DMA device and RAM, as illustrated in Figure 5-8. With the DMA controller controlling the system bus, data is transferred directly from the DMA device into memory. The DMA controller releases control of the bus when the data transfer is complete.

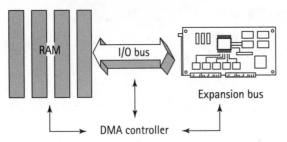

Figure 5-8: The components of a direct memory access
(DMA) channel.

DMA data transfers require fewer steps than those that use the IRQ process to
move data and eliminate the overhead of interrupt processing. When the processor
is interrupted, it must save its current state (what it was doing), process the interrupt, restore its state, and then resume what it was doing. Saving and restoring its
state requires numerous processor cycles. DMA devices help make the entire PC
more efficient.

IDENTIFYING DMA CHANNELS

DMA devices are assigned to DMA channels, another single-channel/device set of
system resources. Only in very limited instances can two DMA devices share a single DMA channel; and like an IRQ, they cannot both be active at the same time. Of
the eight DMA channels, channels 0 and 4 are reserved for use by the system, and
channel 2 is typically reserved for the floppy disk drive. If the PC includes an
Enhanced Capabilities Port (ECP) parallel port, another DMA channel (either DMA
channel 1 or 3) is reserved for it. Thus, a PC has either four or five DMA channels
available for assigning to ISA devices. Table 5-4 lists the DMA channels and the
devices most commonly assigned to each, and Figure 5-9 shows the DMA assignments on a Windows PC.

TABLE 5-4 DMA CHANNEL ASSIGNMENTS

DMA Channel	Common Device	Other Uses
0	Memory refresh	None
1	Sound card	SCSI host adapter, ECP port, NIC, voice modem
2	Floppy disk drive	Tape drive
3	Open	SCSI host adapter, ECP port, NIC, voice modem

DMA Channel	Common Device	Other Uses
4	Cascade to DMA 0–3	None
5	Sound card	SCSI host adapter, NIC
6	Open	Sound card, NIC
7	Open	Sound card, NIC

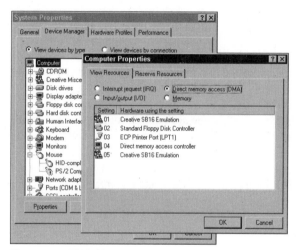

Figure 5-9: DMA Channel assignments shown in the Computer Properties window of the Windows Device Manager.

DMA MODES

Some IDE/ATA devices, such as a floppy disk drive, use two sets of DMA modes to transfer data. The modes are differentiated by the amount of data moved. Single-word DMA modes move one word (2 bytes or 16 bits) of data in each transfer with data transfer speeds ranging from 960 nanoseconds (ns) to as fast as 240 ns, or from 2.1 Mbps to 8.3 Mbps. A single-word DMA transfer must repeat the entire DMA transfer process for each two bytes of data. A multi-word DMA transfer transfers data in bursts of multiple words eliminating the overhead of transferring only two bytes at a time. Multi-word DMA modes move data at speeds between 480 ns (4.2 Mbps) in Mode 0 and 120 ns (16.7 Mbps) in Mode 3. Virtually all DMA modes on current PCs are multiword.

MASTERING THE BUS

Most ISA devices implement third-party DMA or conventional DMA, in which the DMA controller, located on the motherboard, manages the data transfer between a

DMA device and RAM (which are the first two parties of the transfer). *Third-party DMA* is an older implementation considered old and slow compared with first-party DMA.

A *first-party DMA* device has its own DMA controller built into the device. This allows the device itself to control the DMA data transfer directly. First-party DMA uses bus mastering to control the data transfer and does not require assistance from the motherboard's DMA controller.

Bus mastering means that the DMA device takes over the bus, becoming the bus' master. This allows the device and memory to transfer data without either the processor or the DMA controller. In order for an IDE/ATA device to implement bus mastering, its adapter must be installed in a PCI bus slot. The main benefit of bus mastering DMA is that it frees the processor to work on other tasks.

Using additional system resources

Some devices also require a block of memory in the upper memory area of RAM in addition to the space at the I/O address. This block of memory is used primarily for mapping a device's BIOS into memory or as a temporary holding area.

Memory address blocks are assigned during the system boot process. These memory blocks are not system resources in the sense of IRQs, I/O addresses, or DMA channels, but Windows lists them along with the system resources on the Computer Properties window (see Figure 5-10). Like system resources, memory addresses can create problems or conflicts if two devices overlap their memory blocks.

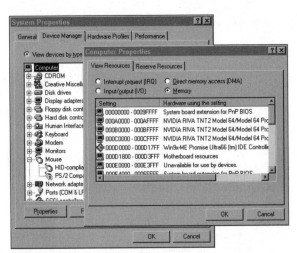

Figure 5-10: The Computer Properties window showing memory address assignments.

As illustrated in Figure 5-10, the devices that use memory address blocks are those devices that require their own device BIOS running in memory, such as PnP devices, Small Computer System Interface (SCSI) host adapters, bus controllers, processor-to-bus bridges, NICs with Wake-On-LAN technology, and other chipset and expansion card services.

Resolving Resource Conflicts

Resource conflicts don't just happen, and they normally show up after you've installed a new device. If your computer has any of the following symptoms, you very likely have a resource conflict:

◆ The PC locks up frequently for no apparent reason.

◆ The mouse operates erratically or not at all.

◆ The PC boots into Windows Safe Mode.

◆ You cannot format a floppy disk in the floppy disk drive.

◆ Anything printed on the printer is gibberish.

◆ The monitor displays distorted or strange images.

◆ The sound card either doesn't work or doesn't sound just right.

◆ Any existing device that was working before a new device was installed, especially a modem, suddenly stops working.

You should update your antivirus software and scan the PC just to verify that a virus is not causing the problem.

The Windows Device Manager is a good place to start when you think that you might have a system resource conflict. The Device Manager will indicate whether any of the installed devices have an issue with one of these three symbols: a blue *i*, a yellow exclamation point, or a red X. If a device has one of these symbols, you should investigate. Not much is wrong if all you have is a blue *i* symbol, but the yellow and red symbols indicate trouble and need to be resolved.

Avoiding resource problems when installing new hardware devices

Virtually every device installed in a PC expansion slot or directly to the motherboard requires system resources. The best way to avoid resource conflicts when installing new or replacement hardware is to install one device at a time and then test the system after each one. Don't install several new devices and then try to determine which is causing a resource conflict. Take the easy path: Add each device in a completely separate installation process.

Read the documentation that comes with a new device or component, especially the sections covering installation and troubleshooting. In the best case, a remedy already exists for a problem caused by the device. In the worst case, you'll probably find the telephone number of the technical support desk of the manufacturer.

Troubleshooting IRQs

All IRQ issues involve two devices assigned to the same IRQ. The solution is to reassign one of the devices to a new IRQ through the Device Manager or the BIOS settings or by changing an expansion card's jumper or DIP switch values.

IRQ 2 AND 9 CONFLICTS

A common IRQ problem is conflicts on IRQ 2 and 9. Originally, PCs had only eight IRQs, and when the second eight IRQs were added, the two sets were linked through IRQs 2 and 9 (on the upper group).

Video cards and other devices are occasionally assigned to IRQ 2, which can create conflict with any device installed on IRQ 9 if they're both active at the same time.

TWO DEVICES ON THE SAME IRQ

If two devices are installed to the same IRQ and they aren't used at the same time — such as a modem and a NIC (although this is a very strange pair of devices to share on an IRQ) — no problem should arise. However, a more common situation is to have devices installed on both COM2 (like a modem) and COM4 (like a serial mouse). If the mouse and the modem are used simultaneously, one or the other (or both) might not operate properly. This problem is common on a legacy system on which one or more devices are configured using proprietary installation software.

The most common (and just about only) problem that you can experience with IRQs is that two devices have been assigned to the same IRQ. The solution is to reassign one of the devices to a new IRQ by using the Device Manager, amending the BIOS settings, or by changing the card's jumper or DIP switch values.

Checking out IRQ settings

Not every PC has all the devices listed in Table 5-1. In fact, on any particular PC, the IRQs can be assigned differently. To find what the IRQ settings are on a Windows PC, use the following steps:

1. From the Windows desktop, right-click the My Computer icon.

   From the shortcut menu that appears, choose Properties to display the System Properties window, shown in Figures 5-6, 5-9, and 5-10.

2. Select the Device Manager tab, highlight the Computer entry, and then click the Properties button located at the bottom of the device window.

   This displays the Computer Properties window, shown in Figure 5-11.

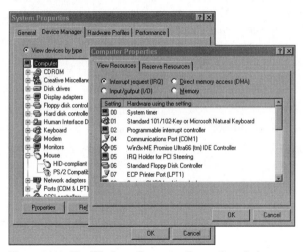

Figure 5–11: The Windows Computer Properties window.

3. Select the View Resources tab and mark the Interrupt Request (IRQ) radio button to display the IRQ assignments on your PC.

4. Compare the IRQ assignments of your PC with those in Table 5-1 (earlier in the chapter).

   Your IRQ settings should match those in Table 5-1 for the most part.

   Any exceptions are likely because of PnP devices or adjustments made to avoid conflicts. If you find differences, don't change your IRQ settings. Table 5-1 lists typical or default settings. They are by no means the only settings that will work.

You should always review the current IRQ settings before installing new hardware in the PC that requires an IRQ or any system resources. You should also review the documentation of the new device to determine the IRQ (and system resources) settings that it requires. If the device's default IRQ is available on the system, you should have no problem with the installation or the operation of the device. However, if that IRQ is not available, you might need to reassign the IRQ or to reconfigure the new device to an available IRQ.

Setting an IRQ with the Windows Device Manager

Use the Windows Device Manager to configure IRQs after a PnP device or a proprietary installation program has created a conflict by assigning a new device to an IRQ already in use by another device.

When you open the Device Manager, its default view lists the PC's devices by type (the general category of each device; refer to Figure 5-11). Clicking the + (plus sign) of a category expands the device category to show its devices.

If a problem exists with a device, it's indicated with one of three symbols:

◆ *A yellow circle with a black exclamation point:* This symbol before a device name indicates a possible resource conflict.

◆ *A red circle with a white X:* This symbol before a device name indicates that the device has been disabled, removed, or that Windows is unable to locate it. (Although the X technically is white, we geeks call it a "red X.")

◆ *A white circle with a blue lowercase i:* This information symbol before a device name indicates only that automatic settings are disabled and that the device was configured manually, possibly under software control. This is not necessarily a problem; this symbol is really just a reminder.

If you find a device conflict, the details of the problem are listed on the properties window for the device itself in the Conflicting Device List box at the bottom of the window. Figure 5-12 shows a device with no device conflicts, but if this device were having problems, the cause is probably a device driver issue.

To access the Properties window for any device, either highlight the device in the Device Manager tree and click the Properties button or right-click the device name in the tree and choose Properties from the pop-up menu that appears.

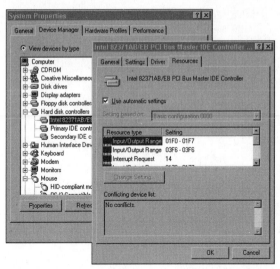

Figure 5-12: The Device Properties window showing no resource conflicts.

 TIP If you encounter an IRQ or I/O address conflict with a device, you might need to change its resource assignments. If required, follow the steps listed in "Changing a device's system resource settings" later in the chapter to change the resource settings for a hardware device on a Windows PC.

You might find that very few of your system resources can actually be changed — and that when you attempt to change a resource, an error message box pops up telling you that you cannot change the values of a resource. The primary reasons for this condition are

◆ *The device is a legacy device* and its resource settings are configured with jumpers or DIP switches on the adapter card.

◆ *The device is integrated* into the motherboard or chipset or mounted to the motherboard through a riser (daughter-) board with a preset resource setting.

◆ *The device cannot be configured to any of the available resources*, and resources must be freed.

Troubleshooting DMA channels

DMA channels are fairly straightforward to troubleshoot. A DMA device will use whatever channel is available to it, so what might look like a DMA channel problem (meaning that it's not an IRQ problem) might actually be either an I/O address or memory address issue.

If the device lists alternatives, first try choosing another I/O address or memory address for the device. If that fails, try using the Windows Troubleshooting utility before calling the manufacturer's technical support.

Changing a device's system resource settings

If you wish to change the IRQ settings of a device (providing that the system will allow you to do so), try using the following steps:

1. Open the Device Manager by right-clicking the My Computer icon and choosing Properties from the menu that appears.

2. Highlight the device that you wish to change and then click the Properties button.

3. From the device's Properties window that opens, choose the Resources tab.

   If no Resources tab appears, the device does not use system resources or does not have any alterable resources. In this case, you can skip the remainder of this process because obviously you can't change the system resource settings of this device.

4. Remove the check mark on the Use Automatic Settings check box.

5. Highlight the resource that you wish to choose and then click the Change Settings button.

   Figure 5-13 shows the Edit Input/Output Range dialog box that should display if the resource you have chosen can be changed. If the resource cannot be changed, a message box will display to tell you that a resource modification is not allowed.

6. After you change the value of the setting, verify that no conflicts show up in the Conflict Information box (bottom of the Edit Input/Output Range dialog box) before you click OK to affect the change.

7. Click OK to close the open Device Manager windows and then restart the system to completely verify that no problems exist.

TIP   If the system won't boot after making a system resource change, enter Windows Safe Mode and make any necessary adjustments to remove the resource problem. Read how in the upcoming section "Booting into Windows Safe Mode."

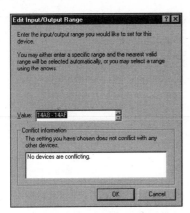

Figure 5-13: Use the Edit Input/Output Range
dialog box to change a system resource setting
in the Windows Device Manager.

Booting into Windows Safe Mode

To start the PC in Windows Safe Mode, press the F8 key when you see the first
Windows splash screen. The Startup menu will display. Choose Safe Mode from the
menu. Windows will start with only the essential device drivers.

Running Windows Troubleshooting

If the system resource problems cannot be resolved through the Device Manager, it
might be time for more serious troubleshooting. Boot the PC into Safe Mode (see
the preceding section); from the Safe Mode desktop, do the following:

1. Open the Control Panel and double-click the System icon.

2. From the window that opens, choose the Performance tab and then click
   the File System button from the Advanced Settings near the bottom of the
   window.

3. From the File System Properties window that displays (shown in Figure
   5-14), choose the Troubleshooting tab, which includes a list of system
   features that you can disable to narrow down the things that you must
   contend with when troubleshooting the system.

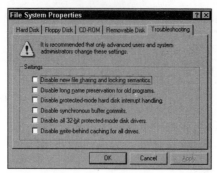

Figure 5-14: The Troubleshooting tab on the
File System Properties window.

4. Check every option in the Settings area and then attempt to reboot the PC
   into normal mode.

   If the PC does boot into normal mode, uncheck one item and restart the
   PC. Keep repeating this step – unchecking another item and restarting the
   PC – until it fails. You should be able to isolate the problem device.

   If the PC won't reboot into normal mode, reboot into Safe Mode. Use the
   Device Manager to disable every device (except those under System
   Devices) and then attempt to reboot into normal mode. If you can reboot,
   the issue is probably a bad or out-of-date device driver. Re-enable devices
   by type and restart the PC. You should eventually isolate the device group
   that has the problem device.

If the PC won't boot into Safe Mode, you need to begin physically removing
devices from the PC one at a time and restarting until the PC will boot, and
you've isolated the device causing the problem. After you isolate the problem
device, try putting the other devices back into the PC and rebooting. More
than one — or a combination of devices — could be causing the problem.

Decoding resource error codes in the Windows Device Manager

If a resource conflict exists and you're unsure as to the source of the problem, look
on the General tab of a device's Properties window. Figure 5-15 shows a device
with no problems, as shown by the This device is working properly message
in the Device Status field. If a problem did exist related to the device's system
resource settings, an error code and message would be included in the Device

Status field instead. Windows 98/Me/2000/XP PCs include a Solutions button that you can click to see suggestions for possible solutions.

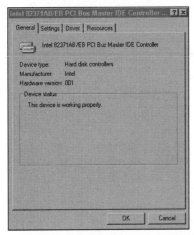

Figure 5-15: The Device Status field on the
General tab of a device's Properties window.

Of the many Device Manager error codes (around 35 and growing), most deal with device driver issues, but here are the ones that relate to resource conflicts:

◆ *Code 6:* Another device is already assigned the resources requested by a device. Change the new device's resource settings.

◆ *Code 9:* The BIOS is reporting the device's system resources incorrectly. It could be that you only need to remove the device from the Device Manager and let the system detect and install it. Or you might need to upgrade the BIOS on the PC.

◆ *Code 12:* No available resources exist of the type requested by a device. Another device must be removed, disabled, or its resources shared to install the new device.

◆ *Code 15:* The device is causing a resource conflict and must be reconfigured.

◆ *Code 16:* Windows cannot identify the resource needed by the device. You might need to fill in some missing resources on the device's Properties window. Follow the device documentation for the values that you should use.

◆ *Code 17:* A child device has been assigned a resource not assigned to the parent. Either use automatic settings or configure the device to be compatible with its parent.

◆ *Code 27:* Windows is unable to specify the resources for the device as configured. Check the documentation and make any necessary adjustments.

◆ *Code 29:* No resources were assigned to the device by the PC's BIOS. Most likely, the device needs to be enabled in the CMOS setup data.

◆ *Code 30:* The IRQ requested is already in use by a device that cannot share the IRQ. Change the IRQ setting for the device or find a more compatible device with which to share.

TIP

For a complete list of Device Manager error codes, check out Microsoft's Knowledge Base article Q125174 at `http://support.microsoft.com/default.aspx?scid=kb;en-us;125174`.

Dealing with IRQ steering

To check whether IRQ steering is enabled on your system, follow these steps:

1. Open the Windows Device Manager and click the plus sign to expand the System Devices device type.

NOTE

Some systems automatically implement bus mastering and IRQ steering and don't provide you with a means to alter this system.

2. Highlight the selection for PCI Bus and then click the Properties button.

3. Select the IRQ Steering tab to display the window shown in Figure 5-16.

4. To deselect IRQ steering, merely clear the Use IRQ Steering check box to deselect it and then reboot the system.

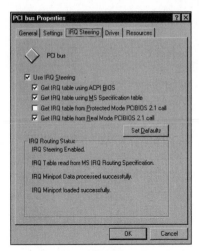

Figure 5-16: The IRQ Steering tab of
the PCI Bus Properties window.

In order for IRQ steering to be activated, the Use IRQ Steering check box must be marked. The other check boxes on this window tell IRQ Steering where it should look for its IRQ routing information:

◆ *ACPI (Advanced Configuration and Power Interface) BIOS:* Indicates the first IRQ routing table to use to program IRQ steering. *ACPI* is a power management specification that provides hardware status information to the operating system.

◆ *MS specification table:* Indicates that the MS (Microsoft) specification table is the second IRQ routing table to be used to program IRQ steering.

◆ *PCI BIOS 2.1 protected mode:* When marked, indicates that this routing table is to be used to program IRQ steering.

◆ *PCI BIOS 2.1 real mode:* Not checked by default; is selected only when a PCI device is not working properly. When checked, it specifies that this is the third IRQ routing table to be used to program IRQ steering.

If the system BIOS cannot configure a PCI device, try a different combination of options, including selecting the PCI BIOS 2.1 real mode. If the default selections don't work, you probably need to update the BIOS. One sure way to tell that you might need a BIOS update is that IRQ steering is causing the system to lock up or display `kernal32.dll` error messages.

Chapter 6

Memory

IN THIS CHAPTER

Memory refers to the electronic components of the PC that store data and instructions either temporarily or in various degrees of permanence. Technically, memory is any storage device on the computer, including the hard disk, floppy disks, ROM, RAM, and cache. However, in its more common usage and in this book, memory is the part of the computer's hardware used to hold data and instructions before and after they are passed to the CPU (the central processing unit or the microprocessor) for analysis and execution. The discussion in this chapter focuses on

- ◆ Random access memory (RAM)
- ◆ Various RAM technologies
- ◆ How the DOS/Windows operating systems allocate and manage memory

REMEMBER: You can never be too rich, too thin, or have too much memory.

Getting to Know RAM

RAM, which has become synonymous with the primary working storage (memory) of the PC, is referred to by several names, including main memory, system memory, and primary storage. Virtually every piece of data and every instruction processed or executed by the CPU are stored in RAM at one time or another.

RAM is random access because each memory location is individually addressed and can be accessed randomly and directly. The term *random access* was first used to differentiate internal core memories (little round doughnut-like iron bits) from external memory units, such as tape drives or other sequentially accessed devices, which had to be accessed sequentially and serially, front to back. RAM is organized to support access requests for data and instructions placed in randomly assigned locations.

The memory types that can be used as RAM vary from PC to PC depending on either the age of the system or how actively it has been upgraded. RAM and the memory used to create it are identified through a variety of characteristics. Perhaps the more important characteristics of memory are

- ◆ Volatility
- ◆ Synchronization

147

- ◆ Speed
- ◆ Technology
- ◆ Packaging

Differentiating volatility

The most distinguishing characteristic of the memory types used for RAM is its volatility. Up until the past year or so, the most common form of RAM was *dynamic RAM* (DRAM), which is volatile. *Volatile* RAM must have a continuous power source in order to store and hold data. When the power source is interrupted, DRAM is unable to retain any data or instructions that it is storing, which is where it gets its dynamic tag. Perhaps the largest drawback to DRAM is that it must be constantly refreshed (electrically recharged) because it can't hold its charge for very long. (More on this in a bit — see "Dealing with memory technologies" later in this chapter.)

On the other hand, *static RAM* (SRAM), which is rapidly gaining popularity, is created from non-volatile memory. *Non-volatile* memory is able to store its contents with little or no power supplied to it. Another benefit of SRAM is that unlike its volatile cousin, it doesn't need to be refreshed.

Getting synchronized or not

Data is moved across the memory bus by the memory controller either without being synchronized to the system clock or completely in time to the system clock's signals.

The most common form of DRAM, the type used in almost every PC since its beginnings until very recently, is *asynchronous DRAM*, which moves data without synchronizing the data movement to the system clock. Asynchronous DRAM is best used on systems with memory bus speeds lower than 66 megahertz (MHz).

The other type of memory is synchronous DRAM (SDRAM). As its name implies, *SDRAM* synchronizes its data movement to the system clock. Because it is faster than asynchronous DRAM (commonly referred to as just DRAM), SDRAM is better suited to higher speed memory buses, which is why it is showing up in the gigabit Pentium-class PCs.

Operating at RAM speed

The speed of a memory type is expressed as its *access speed*, which is the lowest possible time required for the memory to complete a read or write operation to memory.

RAM Measurements

RAM is measured in bytes. In what is being called the Communications Age, where speeds and capacities are measured in bits, the capacity of a PC's RAM is stated in bytes — actually megabytes (MB) or perhaps gigabytes (GB). Here are the most commonly used measurement units for RAM.

Unit	Size	Data Unit Stored
Bit	One binary digit	Binary 0 or 1
Byte	8 bits	One character
Word	16 to 64 bits	Use to store numeric values, including addresses
Kilobyte (K)	1,024 bytes	Memory sizing unit on pre-Pentium PCs
Megabyte (MB)	1,048,576 bytes	Memory sizing unit on Pentium-class PCs
Gigabyte (GB)	1,073,741,824 bytes	Memory sizing unit on servers and high-end PCs
Terabyte (TB)	1,099,511,627,776 bytes	Memory sizing on larger network or content servers
Petabyte (PB)	1,125,899,906,842,624 bytes	The next level of memory sizing to come

To put the units in this table into perspective, one byte holds a single alphabetic character (for example, A or a), one K holds approximately one page of double-spaced text, one MB holds a short novel (without illustrations), one GB should hold about 1,000 short novels (without illustrations), and so on.

Asynchronous DRAM is rated in *nanoseconds* (ns), or billionths of a second. Table 6-1 lists the various speeds of DRAM with the PC versions in which each speed has been used.

TABLE 6-1 ASYNCHRONOUS DRAM ACCESS SPEEDS

Memory Speed	Processor
150–100 ns	286 and earlier
80 ns	286–386
70 ns	286–Pentium-class
60 ns	486–Pentium-class
50 ns and lower	Pentium-class

Synchronous DRAM (SDRAM) is a lot faster than asynchronous DRAM, but the speeds can be a bit misleading. For example, SDRAM is rated with speeds of 12, 10, or 7 ns, but 12 ns SDRAM is not 4 times faster than 50 ns DRAM. Because SDRAM is tied to the system clock, its speed measures the time required to place a block of data onto the memory bus and doesn't include the time required to locate data in memory, which is a part of the access time used to rate asynchronous DRAM. At the core of SDRAM is DRAM, but because of the way it is engineered and controlled, SDRAM performs much faster.

When in doubt about which memory type to use, check the documentation of the motherboard. You can also find online guides provided by RAM manufacturers to help you match the bus speed of a system to the RAM speeds that will work. Table 6-2 lists the access speeds for most newer memories and the bus speeds with which each is compatible.

TABLE 6-2 BUS SPEEDS AND COMPATIBLE RAM SPEEDS

Bus Speed	RAM Access Speed
20 MHz	50 ns
25 MHz	40 ns
33 MHz	30 ns
50 MHz	20 ns
66 MHz	15 ns
100 MHz	10 ns
166 MHz	6 ns

TIP

When matching memory speeds to your motherboard's bus speeds, choose the memory that's the best possible fit. Using a slower memory speed slows the system down accordingly.

The part number on virtually all DRAM chips includes its speed appended to the end of the number. For example, a memory chip with a –50 (or possibly a –5) on the end of its part number is a 50 ns memory chip. SDRAM chips are marked with –12, –10, or –7, but be careful, some –70 DRAM is marked as –7, as is –7 SDRAM.

You might also run into SDRAM chips with a MHz rating in place of a nanosecond rating. For example, instead of a 12 ns rating, an SDRAM chip might be rated as 120 MHz. Actually, these two ratings are equivalent. One MHz represents one million cycles per second, which is the same as one-tenth of a nanosecond. Thus, 120 MHz equates to 12 nanoseconds.

NOTE

One word of caution when working with SDRAM rated in megahertz: The MHz rating of SDRAM does not represent the system bus speed to which it is compatible. For example, a 100 MHz (or 10 ns) SDRAM is not compatible with a 100 MHz system bus. Check the motherboard documentation for memory compatibilities.

Dealing with memory technologies

Several different RAM technologies and types are in use in PCs. The most common memory technologies, in general terms, are

- ◆ *DRAM (Asynchronous DRAM):* Pronounced *dee*-ram, this is the common RAM type used in desktop and laptop PCs. DRAM is inexpensive and can store a large number of bits on a single small chip. Each DRAM storage cell contains a capacitor, which holds one bit of data. A *capacitor* is an electronic component that stores an electric charge. In the DRAM cell, the capacitor holds either a positive or negative voltage value to indicate a 1 or 0 binary value. DRAM must be refreshed every two milliseconds by reading and writing the contents of every cell by a refresh logic circuit, whether the cell is in use or not. DRAM is the slowest type of memory, with clock speeds of around 50 ns or higher. **Remember:** Higher means slower.

- ◆ *SDRAM (Synchronous DRAM):* Pronounced *ess-dee*-ram, this type of RAM is found in many newer desktop and portable PCs. Like all forms of DRAM, SDRAM is dynamic and must be refreshed. However, it is the fastest form of DRAM.

♦ *SRAM (Static RAM):* Pronounced *ess*-ram, this memory technology is used primarily for PC cache memory and in PC Cards (PCMCIA). The primary differences between DRAM and SRAM are that SRAM is faster, more expensive, and requires more physical board space. However, another difference is that SRAM doesn't need to be refreshed. The primary use for SRAM is for Level 1 and 2 caching, often as onboard caching built into the microprocessor or motherboard.

♦ *VRAM (Video RAM):* Pronounced *vee*-ram, this is used exclusively for video and color graphics support. Video RAM is not technically a discrete memory technology exactly. Rather, it is memory placed on the video adapter to provide for better and faster graphics support. VRAM requires a feature called *dual-porting*, in which data is being written to VRAM by the system CPU at the same time that data is being simultaneously read from RAM by the video controller to refresh the display image. Here are a few of the video memory types in use:

  ■ *Video RAM (VRAM):* Not to be confused with the general VRAM, this VRAM (pronounced *vee*-ram) is DRAM that has been dual-ported and needs refreshing less often than ordinary DRAM. VRAM is a special type of DRAM that acts as a buffer (it's also called the *frame buffer*) between the CPU and the video display. You'll find more details on video systems in Chapter 14.

  ■ *Window RAM (WRAM):* This video memory type is also dual-ported, but because its contents can be accessed in blocks, it's faster than VRAM. *WRAM* (pronounced *double-you*-ram), which has absolutely nothing to do with any Microsoft operating system, is a high-performance video RAM type that's about 25 percent more efficient than standard VRAM.

  ■ *Synchronous Graphics RAM (SGRAM):* SGRAM is a single-ported, clock-synchronized video RAM that runs as much as four times faster than conventional DRAM memories. SGRAM (pronounced *ess-gee*-ram) uses a number of specialized instructions, such as its masked write and block write commands to combine what would be a series of instructions for other forms of VRAM to allow data to be handled more efficiently.

A bit more about DRAM

An increasing number of DRAM technologies have been developed to address the need for bigger and faster PC memory. In effect, each new DRAM technology is based at least in part on a preceding technology. The differences lie in their organization and access methods. Here are the more common of the DRAM technologies:

♦ *Fast Page Mode (FPM):* FPM DRAM, also known as non-EDO DRAM, is generally compatible with virtually all motherboards except those with a bus speeds over 66 MHz.

◆ *Extended Data Output (EDO):* This is the most common type of DRAM in use. It is slightly faster than FPM memory and is common in most Pentium and later PCs except those with bus speeds over 75 MHz.

◆ *Burst Extended Data Output (BEDO) DRAM:* This is EDO memory with pipelining technology that lets it transfer data from memory while accepting the next request. It bursts data over successive clock cycles and is found on PCs with clock speeds up to 66 MHz.

◆ *Enhanced DRAM (EDRAM):* This is a combination of SRAM and DRAM used for a Level 2 (L2) cache. The faster (15 ns) SRAM is packaged with slower (35 ns) DRAM.

◆ *PC100 SDRAM:* This is a special type of SDRAM designed to work with the Intel i440BX chipset over a 100 MHz bus speed.

◆ *Double Data Rate (DDR) SDRAM:* This SDRAM type is designed to operate on bus speeds of at least 200 MHz.

◆ *Enhanced SDRAM (ESDRAM):* ESDRAM is SDRAM with a small SRAM cache that lowers memory latency times and supports bus speeds up to 200 MHz.

◆ *Direct Rambus DRAM (DRDRAM):* This is a proprietary DRAM technology developed by Rambus, Inc. (www.rambus.com) and Intel that features RAM speeds up to 800 MHz.

◆ *Ferroelectric RAM (FRAM):* This RAM technology has the features of both DRAM and SRAM, which gives it the ability to save stored data when its power source is removed.

Packaging memory

I can safely say that all PC technicians revere the people who developed modern memory packaging. However, some technicians out there might wish that all memory were still sold and installed as discrete memory chips.

PC memories have evolved under the pressure to provide larger amounts of faster memory in the smallest space possible. This evolution has taken memory packaging out of the Dual Inline Packaging (DIP) days and into the day of the Dual Inline Memory Module (DIMM).

A memory chip or module, regardless of its packaging, has to be matched to the bus capacity of the motherboard over which data from memory to the CPU or peripheral devices flows. The bus capacity is stated in bits and represents how much data can flow in one clock cycle. The memory circuits on a motherboard are arranged to take advantage of the data bus' width and use the full data bus to transfer data.

DIP PACKAGING

In the beginning, DRAM chips were mounted on a PC motherboard as individual memory chips in a bank of chips or as a part of an integrated memory module that mounted in an expansion slot. Single memory chips are packaged in a DIP package, as illustrated in Figure 6-1. DIP memory chips are individually mounted into sockets in banks of four or more chips directly on the motherboard.

Figure 6-1: A Dual Inline Packaging chip has two inline rows of pins.

 TIP DIP memory chips are hard to come by these days, but if you're working on an older PC and need to add or replace its memory, be careful to match up any new or additional chips (in terms of speed and data bus width). You can add additional memory chips to the chips already in place or replace all the memory with newer chips. Fill up one bank (socket set) before moving on to the next.

On the motherboard, each arrangement of memory that provides an equal number of bits to match that of the data bus is a *memory bank*. A PC won't work if the memory installed in a memory bank doesn't match up to the data bus width. In fact, if a memory bank is not completely filled, the PC ignores it. It is especially important for the first memory bank (usually bank 0) to be completely filled because if it isn't, the PC won't detect any memory and fails in the Power-On Self-Test (POST) process.

 TIP The majority of motherboards (see Chapter 1) that take DIP memories include one or more memory banks. Fill the lowest numbered bank first and then proceed in sequence to the other banks.

SIMM

A *Single Inline Memory Module* (SIMM) consists of DRAM chips in special packaging (Small Outline J-lead [SOJ] or Thin, Small Outline Package [TSOP]) soldered on a small circuit board with either a 30- or 72-pin edge connector. The capacity of a SIMM can range from 1 to 128MB with chips mounted on either one or both sides of the board.

As illustrated in Figure 6-2, a SIMM is installed on the motherboard in a special socket designed to maximize the amount of memory that can be installed in a minimal space. The older 30-pin SIMMs must be installed in pairs to provide the correct amount of data bus width used by the memory bus. Each SIMM memory bank has two slots, and if legacy 30-pin SIMMs are in use, both slots must be filled before the next bank is populated. Newer SIMMs are 72-pin modules that provide up to 32 bits of data width, which means that a single 72-pin SIMM can be used to populate a memory bank.

Figure 6-2: A SIMM memory module mounted on a PC motherboard.

DIMM

An adaptation of the SIMM is the 168-pin *Dual Inline Memory Module* (DIMM), which has emerged as the memory standard for newer, larger 64-bit PCs. Matching a DIMM (see Figure 6-3) to a PC is slightly more complicated because they're available in different voltages (3.3 volt [v] and 5.0v) and either buffered or unbuffered. A smaller DIMM version is the *Small Outline DIMM* (SODIMM), which is used primarily in portable computers.

168-pin DIMM (5.375 x 1")

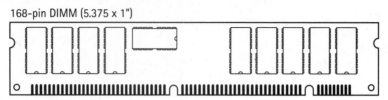

Figure 6–3: A DIMM memory module.

Pentium-class motherboards don't support the 30-pin SIMM because it would take eight of them to fill a memory bank, which would take up way too much space on the motherboard.

You can find the bus width and data capacities marked on a memory circuit or in its technical specifications. The memory size of a SIMM or DIMM is specified as *DWS* (depth, width, and speed), which should be similar to 16 x 64-60. This example notation indicates a DIMM with 16 million bits available for each of its 64 bits of width with a speed of 60 ns. The small *x* in the notation indicates that this example is 16 megabits *by* 64 bits in size.

GETTING DEEPER INTO MEMORY MODULES

The depth of the module is usually in millions, ranging from 1 to 32. Some older and smaller SIMMs use 256 and 512, but this is the exception and represents kilobits, not megabits. The width of the module is always in bits and is usually 8 or 9 (parity) for 30-pin SIMMs (or 32 for 256 or 512 kilobit SIMMs), 32 or 36 for 72-pin SIMMs, and 64 or 72 for 168-pin DIMMs.

The depth times the width yields the number of bits on the memory module. For example, a DIMM with a 16 x 64 notation has just over 1 billion bits (1,024,000,000). To compute the number of bytes of memory this represents, divide this number by 8 (8 bits to a byte). Thus, a 16 x 64-60 DIMM has 128,000,000 (128MB) of storage capacity. Table 6-3 lists the capacities for the more popular SIMM and DIMM modules.

What Is This Data Bus Width Stuff?

Each memory module is marked with its bit width, which indicates the number of bits that it can transfer simultaneously to the data bus. For example, a 30-pin SIMM has an 8-bit width; a 72-pin SIMM has a 32-bit width; and a 168-pin DIMM has a width of 64-bits.

Thus, on a system with a 32-bit data bus, either four 8-bit SIMMs (30-pin) or one 32-bit SIMM (72-pin) should be installed. This system couldn't handle even one 64-bit DIMM. If the memory module includes parity or error correction code (ECC; see "Detecting Memory Errors" elsewhere in the chapter), the memory bus is expanded by one bit.

Parity and ECC technologies add one bit for each eight bits in the bus width. An 8-bit SIMM that uses parity has a data width of 9 bits, and a 32-bit SIMM with parity has a data width of 36 bits. Parity bits are not transferred over the data bus, so they don't affect the match to the data bus. The following table lists the combinations of SIMMs and DIMMs that could be used for different data bus widths. The numbers under the 30-pin and 72-pin SIMM headings also represent the number of SIMMs required to populate a memory bank.

Bus Width	30-pin SIMM	72-pin SIMM	168-pin DIMM
8-bits	1	-	-
16-bits	2	-	-
32-bits	4	1	-
64-bits	-	2	1

TABLE 6-3 STORAGE CAPACITIES FOR COMMON SIMM AND DIMM MODULES

Module	Depth x Width (Megabits)	Capacity (MB)
30-pin SIMM (no parity)	1 x 2	1
	1 x 8	1
	2 x 8	2
	4 x 8	4
	16 x 8	16

Continued

TABLE 6–3 STORAGE CAPACITIES FOR COMMON SIMM AND DIMM MODULES
(Continued)

30-pin SIMM (parity)	1 x 3	1
	1 x 9	1
	2 x 9	2
	4 x 9	4
	16 x 9	16
72-pin SIMM (no parity)	1 x 32	4
	2 x 32	8
	4 x 32	16
	8 x 32	32
	16 x 32	64
72-pin SIMM (parity)	256K x 36	1
	512K x 36	2
	1 x 36	4
	2 x 36	8
	4 x 36	16
	8 x 36	32
	16 x 36	64
168-pin DIMM (no parity)	8 x 32	32
	4 x 64	32
	16 x 32	64
	8 x 64	64
	16 x 64	128
168-pin DIMM (parity)	4 x 72	32
	8 x 72	64
	16 x 72	128

Two metals are used for the pins and sockets of SIMMs and DIMMs: gold and tin. You'll find that SIMM modules are available in either gold or tin because older motherboards have gold SIMM sockets and newer boards have tin sockets. DIMMs use only gold for both its edge connectors and sockets.

Only memory modules with gold contacts should be installed in sockets with gold contacts, and a SIMM with tin contacts should only be placed in a tin socket. If you mix the two metals, it can cause a chemical reaction that can cause tin oxide to build up on the gold and create an unreliable electrical connection.

SODIMM

A special type of DIMM that is manufactured primarily for use in portable devices is the *Small Outline Dual Inline Memory Module* (SODIMM). This module is thinner and smaller overall than a standard DIMM and has only 144 pins.

In case you want to re-use some older 30-pin SIMMs on a motherboard that has only the newer 72-pin SIMM sockets, use an adapter board called a SIMM converter. This board plugs into the 72-pin socket and features two or more 30-pin sockets to receive your older SIMMs. You still have to get enough on the board to match the data bus width.

Detecting Memory Errors

DRAM memory includes one of two mechanisms to verify and maintain the integrity of the data stored in memory. The two methods used are parity and error correction code (ECC).

Playing with parity

Memory *parity* has been in use about as long as PCs have been around. Memory that implements parity adds an additional bit for every 8 bits of data. The extra parity bit provides a mechanism that is used to verify the data through one of two parity protocols:

◆ *Odd-parity:* This protocol validates that there are an odd number of 1 bits in a byte of data. If there is an even number of 1 bits, the parity bit is set on to force an odd number of bits.

◆ *Even-parity:* This parity protocol performs just like the odd-parity protocol, with the exception that the parity bit is used to force an even number of 1 bits, if necessary.

Table 6-4 shows the impact of the parity bit on SIMM and DIMM modules.

TABLE 6-4 MEMORY MODULE NON-PARITY AND PARITY BIT WIDTHS

Module Type	Memory Module	Non-parity Width	Parity Width
SIMM	30-pin	8 bits	9 bits
SIMM	72-pin	32 bits	36 bits
DIMM	168-pin	64 bits	72 bits

A *parity error* results when a byte doesn't have the appropriate number of 1 bits, either an even or odd number depending on the parity protocol in use. Unfortunately, the problems that can cause a memory parity error range from a one-time glitch to a much more severe problem like a faulty memory module.

Repeating and frequent memory parity errors are good indications of a faulty memory module.

The major shortcoming of memory parity is that it can only *detect* an error. Parity mechanisms don't have a means of identifying specifically where or what the error is; they can only detect that a possible error has occurred. All memory parity can report is that either the even or odd bit count was wrong.

Parity memory will work in a non-parity system with the extra bit being ignored. You can turn off parity checking on some systems in the BIOS setup.

Systems are available that use what is called *fake parity*, which makes every bit count come out correctly even or odd. Fake parity has the effect of turning off the parity checking.

Correcting memory errors

Another memory error detection protocol, *error correction code (ECC)*, is able to detect up to 4-bit memory errors and correct 1-bit memory errors. The discrepancy isn't as bad as it might sound. Four-bit errors in memory (which means that one-half of a byte is in error) are very rare. One-bit errors are much more common, and ECC corrects these without reporting the parity error. However, multiple-bit errors (which is to say 2-, 3-, or 4-bit errors) are reported as a memory parity error with no corrective action attempted.

 Because parity and ECC memory modules are more expensive than non-parity memory, non-parity memory is more commonly used. Non-parity memory is what you most likely think of as regular memory, with parity and ECC memories being the exception. Non-parity systems include about what their name implies for memory testing — nothing.

If your system has non-parity memory, you shouldn't mix in parity or ECC memory. If you do, expect a memory parity error as soon as the system boots unless you disable the parity/ECC settings in the BIOS setup configuration data.

What Is Virtual Memory?

Virtual memory is not memory at all. In fact, it's usually space on a hard disk drive. *Virtual memory* is a software-managed facility in a PC that allows you to address a portion of your hard disk as if it were an extension of system RAM. This is a very handy feature to have available if your PC suddenly runs out of RAM space. Virtual memory is included in this chapter only to acknowledge the word *memory* in its name. Virtual memory is covered in more detail in Chapter 7.

Logically Laying Out Memory

If you work with older PCs that run MS-DOS or PC-DOS (or any of the other DOS versions) or if you work on PCs that run Windows versions before Windows 2000, you should know how DOS and Windows logically categorize system memory.

DOS/Windows defines memory into four basic divisions, as shown in Figure 6-4 and described in Table 6-5.

TABLE 6-5 DOS/WINDOWS LOGICAL MEMORY LAYOUT

Memory Division	Description
Conventional memory	The first 640K of system memory. Used by standard DOS programs, device drivers, terminate-and-stay-residents (TSRs), and anything that runs on standard DOS.
Upper memory area	The remaining 384K of the first megabyte of memory, located immediately above conventional memory. Reserved for system device drivers and special uses like BIOS ROM shadowing. Also called *expanded* memory or *reserved* memory.
High memory area	The first 64K (less 16 bytes) after the first megabyte of memory. Used to store the startup (boot) utilities. The 16 bytes set aside hold the boot address for the CPU.
Extended memory	All memory above 1MB and after the high memory area. Used for programs and data.

Conventional memory

The first 640K of system memory (RAM) is reserved as conventional memory, as illustrated in Figure 6-4. The reason for the fixed 640K size is because early processors could not address more than 1MB of RAM, and IBM decided to reserve the upper 384K of the 1MB for the BIOS and its utilities, defaulting to 640K for the user and operating system.

Conventional memory contains operating system files, application programs, memory-resident and terminate-and-stay-resident (TSR) routines, and system-level device drivers.

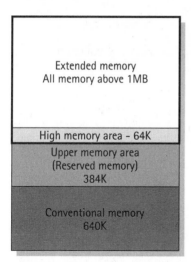

Figure 6-4: The DOS logical memory layout.

Upper memory area

The next 384K after conventional memory in the first megabyte of RAM is set aside for the upper memory area. Originally this area was allocated to such things as the system and adapter BIOS and video RAM. However, it didn't take long before developers, tired of the 640K limitation, reassigned this space as expanded memory and released special device drivers to facilitate its use, such as EMM386.EXE, which is an expanded memory services (EMS) driver. This program and the other expanded memory managers free up space in conventional memory by reallocating DOS drivers and memory-resident programs into unused spaces in the upper memory area.

EMM386.EXE is implemented by adding the following command lines to the CONFIG.SYS file in the DOS root directory:

```
DEVICE=C:\DOS\EMM386.EXE
DOS=UMB
```

UMB stands for *upper memory block* (see UMB in the last line in the above code), which is yet another name for the upper memory area.

If you don't want to start the expanded memory manager but you do want the ability to relocate drivers and TSRs to the upper memory area, then add the NOEMS (no EMS) option to the command:

```
DEVICE=C:\DOS\EMM386.EXE NOEMS
DOS=UMB
```

High Memory Area

The *High Memory Area (HMA)* is the first 64K of the extended memory area, as shown in Figure 6-4. To activate the use of this area for the operating system, include this statement in the CONFIG.SYS file:

```
DOS=HIGH
```

This statement allows the operating system to load a large portion of its code to the high memory area instead of to conventional memory. This frees up around 45K of conventional memory space for other software.

Extended memory

Extended memory is all memory after the first 1MB of RAM. However, there are limits to the amount of memory that can be in extended memory. Every PC has a maximum for how much total memory its hardware and operating system will support.

Extended memory is often confused with expanded memory. Remember that *expanded* memory (upper memory area) expands conventional memory to fill up the first 1MB of RAM, and *extended* memory extends RAM to its limit.

Understanding memory latency and burst mode access

Memory is arranged something like a spreadsheet in rows and columns. When a process requires something to be read from memory, first the row's identity is used, and then the starting column ID, and finally, the specific cells to be transferred.

MEMORY LATENCY

The time that it takes to find the row, the column, and then the starting cell takes longer for the first cell than the next one, two, or three cells. This additional amount of time is *memory latency*.

BURST MODE ACCESS

Memory accesses are generally done in sets (bursts) of four data segments, read in series from a starting cell location. The size of the data segment is determined by the width of the memory. This type of memory access is *burst mode access*. The time that it takes to access the first block of memory, which includes finding it, is not repeated, thus saving several clock cycles. Burst mode access is generally used in conjunction with L2 caching, which is sized to receive as many of these bursts as it can. If the data width of the memory is 32 bits, a 256-bit L2 cache could receive and buffer as many as two burst sets from memory.

Burst mode operations are usually stated with a notation (1-2-3-4) that indicates the number of clock cycles used in each of their four data transfers. This notation represents the number of clock cycles required for the first data transfer and each of its three subsequent transfers. For example, 4-1-1-1 indicates that four clock cycles are required to transfer the first data segment, but only one clock cycle is needed for each of the following three accesses. The whole transfer requires seven clock cycles. Without burst mode operations, each access would require 4 clock cycles for a total of 16 for the four segments.

Solving Memory Problems

To begin to solve memory problems on a PC, you first need to be sure that you have a memory problem. Both software and hardware diagnostic tools are available to test a PC's memory. Software tools check on the functionality of the memory, and the hardware tools check the reliability and structural integrity of the memory.

Applying software tools

Memory errors are often intermittent and difficult to diagnose. An essential tool in memory troubleshooting is a memory diagnostic program. Many programs are made for this purpose. Perhaps the simplest to use, not to mention the most popular, is the Power-On Self-Test (POST) program included in your PC's BIOS startup utilities.

The POST tests and counts all the memory that it detects and compares the result with previous POST results. If the latest POST memory count is different from the previous, a memory error is signaled with an audible beep or a text message alert. See Chapter 4 for detailed information on BIOS beep codes.

Unfortunately, the memory testing performed by the POST is not very thorough, so you might need to use memory diagnostic software. These programs are executed from a command prompt or from a boot disk. The tests can be run continuously for hours – or even days, if necessary – to find the source of an intermittent memory problem.

A few of the better memory test software packages are

♦ DocMemory from CSTInc. (www.simmtester.com)

♦ GoldMemory from Goldware CZ (www.goldmemory.cz)

♦ Memory+ from TFI Technology (www.tfi-technology.com)

For a list of software diagnostic and troubleshooting tools, visit the Google Web Directory at http://directory.google.com/Top/Computers/Software/Diagnostics/.

The limitation of both the POST and memory diagnostic software programs is that they are software programs limited to pass or fail judgments. These programs can't predict when a memory chip will fail or whether a chip is about to fail. These programs are limited to writing data to each memory location and then reading it back to test the read/write and parity and ECC functionality of the memory.

Using hardware tools

The best way to test memory is with a SIMM/DIMM tester. This device thoroughly tests a memory module at different speeds, voltages, and timing to indicate whether the memory is good or bad or for any indications that the memory might fail in the future. SIMM/DIMM testers are expensive, but if you're maintaining or repairing a group of PCs on a regular basis, this device can save you time (and money) in the end.

Diagnosing memory errors

Memory errors occur in large part because memory is an electronic storage device; the potential always exists to incorrectly return stored information. DRAM memory does occasionally experience memory errors. DRAM errors can be the result of the way that DRAM memory stores 1s and 0s in the form of electrical charges in small capacitors that must be continually refreshed to ensure that data is not lost. SDRAM is more reliable because it doesn't require the constant refreshing.

HARD AND SOFT ERRORS

The two most common memory errors are repeatable errors (also known as hard errors) and transient errors (also called soft errors). A *hard error* occurs when a memory module is defective; because of its physical flaw, the memory consistently returns the same erroneous results. For example, a memory cell might become damaged because of power surges or electrostatic discharge (ESD) and be stuck in a state that reads as a 1. This could cause parity errors or simply just return the wrong data.

A hard memory error can also be the result of a loose memory module, a system board defect, or a defective or blown memory chip. In most cases, hard errors are relatively easy to diagnose and fix because they are not intermittent. Hard errors are consistent and repeated, allowing you a better chance to isolate the source of the problem.

A transient error, or *soft error,* occurs when a bit provides the wrong data value one time — or intermittently — but otherwise continues to function correctly. Because these errors are moving targets, they are much harder to diagnose. In most cases, soft memory errors are usually the result of poor quality memory, motherboards, or ESD . . . and not necessarily the physical memory chip itself. The system timing could be too fast for the memory or vice versa. Or the stray radioactivity naturally present in the materials used in computer components is affecting the electromagnetic operation of a chip. Unlike a hard error, soft errors aren't consistent – but usually if you're patient enough, they do eventually repeat. However, how soon the error will repeat is anyone's guess: It could be in minutes or even years, so it's always better to diagnose the problem as best as you can.

Using a software tool or a memory tester are the best ways to detect as well as prevent memory errors. Be sure to match the tool to the task and especially to the error. Some software only detects one-bit errors, while others are able to detect multi-bit errors automatically. Still others (the *really* good ones) can detect – and better still, correct – memory problems.

DEALING WITH COMMON MEMORY ERRORS

Memory errors that show up during the boot process are usually caused by physical defects or installation problems with the RAM chips. These problems should be identified by the POST and signaled with beep codes or text messages. Memory errors that occur after the operating system has started running are identified with a range of error messages.

Some of the more common memory-related error messages are

- ◆ `Divide by zero error`: A divide operation attempted to use zero as the dividend, and an error has occurred. This means that some operation on the computer returned an erroneous value, there is a serious logic flaw is in a running program, or (more likely) this message is the result of an operation with a value too large to fit a register.

- ◆ `General protection fault`: A program in memory has been corrupted and has provided an erroneous memory address outside of its addressable space. This could be the result of a program flaw or a bad patch of memory. This message usually indicates that the offending program has been terminated. In many cases, this error is repeatable, but you will need to exactly reconstruct the load that was on the PC at the time of the error.

- ◆ `Fatal exception error`: An illegal instruction has been encountered, an invalid operation code was passed to the CPU, or data was attempted to be read from an erroneous memory location, typically from an address outside of the memory allocated to a function. However, faulty memory could be the cause; it's worth checking.

Checking memory

Before you begin testing memory, you must disable any write-back cache memory on the PC. (See Chapter 7 for more information on cache systems.) You can disable the write-back cache through the setup or advanced configuration menus of your BIOS program.

How memory testing programs work is that they write data to a memory location and then immediately read it back. If cache is left on, you're likely testing the cache rather than the memory. Disabling the write-back cache assures you that the test will be performed on the system memory and that the results will reflect the read/write performance of your PC's SIMMs or DIMMs.

After disabling the write-back cache, you can begin to troubleshoot the system memory. Follow these troubleshooting steps:

1. Restart the system.

   If a memory error is detected during the POST, a memory chip or module might be defective or improperly installed.

   If the POST doesn't detect a memory error, check the BIOS setup for the memory's speed in the timing parameters.

2. If the BIOS setup does provide a memory timing parameter, reset the memory speed to the BIOS or setup default values, which are usually the slowest of the available options.

   If you make any changes to the BIOS settings, save the changes and reboot the system. If the system successfully reboots, the source of the problem was an incorrect BIOS setting.

   If the POST still beeps or displays a memory error message, you probably have a bad SIMM or DIMM.

   Other possibilities are that a memory module is not installed or seated properly or the SIMM modules might not be installed in matching pairs.

3. Remove all but the first bank of memory modules and reboot the system.

   If you have a memory error at this point, you know that it's in the first bank of RAM.

4. Replace the memory in the first bank and reboot.

   If the system boots, continue adding the rest of the untested memory until you either run out of replaced memory or experience another failure. You might even want to reinstall the seemingly bad modules into another bank to see whether they've been miraculously healed during the testing.

   If you move or replace the memory modules and the system still won't boot, it's possible that the motherboard itself is bad. Unfortunately, the best way to verify whether the motherboard is faulty is to replace it and retest. (See Chapter 1 for more information on testing the motherboard.)

ENABLE THE WRITE-BACK CACHE

After testing your system and fixing your memory problems, be sure that you enable the write-back cache. This will avoid a slow running system that can have you chasing after wild geese.

MATCHING MEMORY

The speed of a system's existing memory can limit its ability to take faster memory. Avoid mixing memory speeds in the same computer; but if you must, follow these precautions:

◆ *Use identical memory in a bank:* You should only use the same type, speed, and technology of memory in a memory bank.

◆ *Put the slowest memory in the first bank:* Some BIOS systems have an auto-detection feature that determines the speed of the memory installed in bank 0. For example, if 50 ns memory is installed in bank 0 and 70 ns memory is installed in bank 1, the system will set the memory speed at 50 ns. This will definitely cause problems for the slower memory. **Solution:** Install the slower memory in bank 0.

Memory testing

If the memory errors show up after the operating system is running, you need to access the BIOS to disable the write-back cache and then reboot the system from a floppy disk that contains the memory testing application. Follow the instructions of the software to complete its tests.

If the test software finds an error, perform the memory checking steps described in the previous section. However, if the test software does not find a problem but you still get memory errors when you reboot, you might want to check with the motherboard or memory module manufacturer for updated software drivers, BIOS revisions, patches, or updates. If there are none, either whip out your handy SIMM or DIMM module tester or take your memory modules to a professional PC repair shop.

If you're still getting memory problems, test your power supply or the immediate physical environment of the PC for excess static, radio frequency interference (RFI), electromagnetic interference (EMI), or any other environmental factors that could be interfering with the operation of the PC.

Installing memory modules

Before beginning to install any new memory modules in your PC, especially if you plan to mix different types, sizes, or speeds of memory, you should take these precautions:

◆ Back up the hard disk drive.

◆ Work in a well-lighted and anti-static environment.

◆ Always wear a static strap.

◆ Keep memory modules in their protective packaging until you're ready to install them.

◆ Handle memory modules by their edges only and avoid touching a module's connectors.

INSTALLING A SIMM

When inserting a memory module, be sure to line up the notched end of the module with the matching end of the socket. A SIMM (see Figure 6-5) module is placed into the module slot on the motherboard using about a 45° angle sloping away from the back of the slot. When inserting a SIMM, line up its edge-connector pins with the connectors of the socket. With the module seated in place, lift the module gently until it clicks into place. The module should stand vertically in the socket.

Figure 6-5: A SIMM module is inserted at a 45° angle and then snapped into place vertically.

INSTALLING A DIMM

DIMMs are installed by aligning the notches on the module and pressing it straight down into the socket on the motherboard. The DIMM should snap into the socket's locking tabs.

If you encounter a socket that is keyed differently than the DIMM module you're trying to install, the new DIMM might not be the correct voltage (3.3v or 5v are the choices), or it might be buffered on a non-buffered system. Unlike a SIMM, DIMMs must be compatible with the motherboard. *Never force a DIMM into the socket.* Double-check the motherboard's specifications to make sure that you have the correct DIMMs. If the key of the socket doesn't match the DIMM, you probably have the wrong voltage or buffer type, and you must exchange it. Although DIMMs come in either 3.3v or 5v and buffered or unbuffered, the standard DIMM is 3.3v and the unbuffered type. Figure 6-6 shows a DIMM module installed on a motherboard.

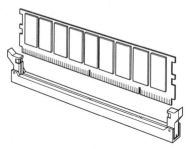

Figure 6-6: A DIMM module installed on a PC motherboard.

Installing memory, Part II

After adding memory to a PC, you might need to make changes to the BIOS configuration before the computer will recognize the new memory. You might even need to adjust jumpers or DIP switches on the motherboard to configure the system for the memory on some older systems. Newer systems automatically recognize the memory and make any necessary adjustments by themselves.

Removing memory modules

To remove a DIMM, release the locking tabs on the socket and pull the module straight up and out of the socket. **Remember:** SIMMs install at an angle, so a SIMM module is *removed* at an angle after the locking tabs are released. After the SIMM is at an angle in the socket, lift it up and out of the socket.

Calculating RAM size

The early PCs, such as the IBM PC XT and PC AT, supported 640K to 1MB of RAM. A multimedia computer today commonly has a gigabyte of RAM. How much RAM a computer needs has always been a guessing game; most technicians have a more-is-better philosophy.

How much RAM is right for a particular PC depends on a number of factors, not least of which is how the PC is to be used and what software will be running on it. Kingston Technology, a leading manufacturer of memory, has an online RAM calculator at www.kingston.com/tools/assessor/ that you can use to determine how much RAM a PC should have.

Chapter 7

Applying Cache Memory

IN THIS CHAPTER
On a PC, *cache* is fast computer memory used to store frequently used data or instructions. As you will see in this chapter, there is much more to it than that. In this chapter, I cover the following:

◆ How caching works

◆ Cache types

◆ Cache and its impact on memory

◆ How to add, map, install, and troubleshoot cache

ACTUALLY, THE TERM CACHE refers to any buffer storage used to improve computer performance by reducing its access times. A cache holds instructions and data likely to be needed for the processor's next operation. Caching copies frequently accessed data and instructions from either primary memory or disk (secondary) storage.

What Is Cache Memory?

As it applies to a PC, caching is referred to in two contexts:

◆ *Cache memory:* A smaller and faster storage placed between primary memory (RAM) and the CPU that copies and stores instructions and data from the primary memory for high-speed access by the CPU.

◆ *Disk cache:* A portion of primary memory or memory located on the disk controller card used to hold large blocks of frequently accessed data copied from a disk drive to eliminate slow disk access speeds.

As suggested by the title of this chapter, cache is also referred to as cache memory. *Cache memory* is a special type of high-speed, dynamic random access memory (static random access memory or SRAM; see Chapter 6) used to supply the instructions and data most frequently requested by the CPU. *SRAM,* which is made up of transistors, is used for cache memory because it doesn't require the frequent refreshing of dynamic random access memory (DRAM), which is made up of capacitors. Cache memory allows the CPU to work more efficiently because the data and instructions that it needs are served from high-speed cache memory, which allows the whole computer to run faster than if cache were not used at all.

Because SRAM, with access speeds as fast as 2 nanoseconds (ns) or faster, is quicker than DRAM, cache memory works at speeds closer to those of the CPU. Data and instructions stored in cache memory are transferred many times faster than those stored in the PC's main memory (RAM). It seems logical that because SRAM is so much faster than DRAM, it would be used for primary memory, thus eliminating the need for cache memory. Although this is logical, SRAM can cost as much as six times more than DRAM and take up much more space on the motherboard to store the same amount of data.

How Caching Works

In the PC, the processor is faster than the memory, which is in turn faster than the hard disk. As depicted in Figure 7-1, caching solves some of the speed issues by providing an intermediary buffer between a faster device (the processor or RAM) and a slower device (RAM or the hard disk).

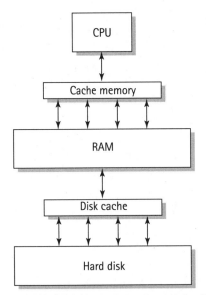

Figure 7-1: The memory cache and the disk cache help offset the speed differences of the devices in a PC.

Guessing right scores a hit

Caching operates on the principle called *locality of reference*, which presumes that the next data to be processed or the next instruction to be fetched by the CPU is the one immediately after the data or instruction just passed to the CPU. The effectiveness of cache memory is expressed as a *hit ratio*, which is calculated from the number of times that cache memory is successful in anticipating the data or instructions that the processor will want next. Each time that the caching system is correct, it is tallied as a *cache hit*.

As much of a gamble as caching may seem, it's actually very efficient and accurate. On average, cache memory systems have the exact data or instruction that the CPU wants next around 90 to 95 percent of the time. As I discuss in Chapter 5, when the CPU must access data or instructions from the PC's main memory, it requires several wait states to locate and transfer the data from RAM — provided that it's already in RAM. The efficiency of the cache memory system eliminates these wait cycles for the CPU, which makes the CPU and the entire PC more efficient.

Quenching the processor's thirst

Here's an analogy to help explain how a PC works without cache memory: Every time that you (the CPU) want a cold beverage to drink, you have to run down to the local supermarket (primary memory) and buy just one bottle (data). The PC's CPU must get data from memory, which might as well be clear across town because of the relative amount of time that it takes to locate and transfer the memory. In this example, adding a refrigerator close by — so that you can easily, readily, and quickly fetch a libation — is very much like adding cache memory to the system. No longer does the CPU need to access data directly from the across-town memory because what it needs is right at hand.

Cache even goes this example one better. Instead of storing only the next lone drink, it keeps the equivalent of a case of your favorite beverage on hand and cool, just waiting for your request, guessing that you'll want the same drink the next time that you ask. In this same manner, the cache controller retrieves a piece of data or an instruction from main memory, and it also gets the few chunks of data and the several subsequent instructions as well.

Here's a real-life example. When you open a document in a word processor or an electronic spreadsheet, the document often extends beyond the display. If each time you scrolled up or down or left or right, the data to be displayed had to be located in RAM and transferred to the display, your system would likely be slow to respond. Each movement of the screen requires the data and the instructions used to format or calculate it to be passed from RAM to the CPU to your application where the image is then passed to the video RAM. Cache memory eliminates the inherent delays in this process by storing the data most likely to be needed for your application program in a much faster memory source that exists solely to serve the data and instruction needs of the CPU.

Working internally and externally

The two general locations for cache memory on a PC are

◆ *Internal cache:* This is also called *primary* cache or *Level 1* (L1) cache. It is typically placed inside the CPU chip itself and ranges from 1K to 64K in size.

◆ *External cache:* This is also called *secondary* cache or *Level 2* (L2) cache. It is normally placed on the motherboard but can also be located in the CPU. External cache ranges in size from 64K to 1MB, but 256K and 512K are common cache sizes.

Although somewhat obvious, another distinction between the two placements for cache memory is that only external cache can be upgraded. L2 cache modules are plugged into special cache module mounts or cache memory expansion sockets, both of which are located on the motherboard. Increasing the amount of L1 (internal) cache on a PC requires that the CPU be replaced.

On older PCs, notably those with a 286 or 386 processor, the processor does not include internal cache, which means that any cache memory located on the motherboard is likely to be the primary cache. This cache, if it's present at all, probably has a fairly low capacity limit. If you're uncertain about adding cache to one of these systems, check with the motherboard manufacturer.

Sizing cache

Like most things on the PC, more is better when it comes to cache memory, but there are limits. The amount of cache on your PC can increase the overall speed of the system, but it can decrease it, too. At a point, keeping the cache filled begins eroding the performance gains of the cache memory.

As I describe earlier in this chapter, if one refrigerator provides a caching buffer that eliminates trips to the store for drinks, it seems logical that two refrigerators should save twice as much time. True, but only if you could carry two refrigerator's worth of drinks in one trip. If you have to make a second trip to the store to fill the second refrigerator, your time savings are drastically impacted. On some systems, adding too much L2 cache can have the same affect on performance. The first 256K of cache might improve the performance of a PC, but adding an additional 256K might not improve performance nearly as much – and can even reduce performance.

Having too much RAM?

The amount of RAM that your PC can cache is another important consideration of cache sizing. Nearly all Pentium and later PCs include caching for 64MB of RAM, but some aren't capable of caching any more than that. In fact, many of Intel's most popular chipsets, including the 430FX, 430VX, and 430TX, cannot cache more than 64MB of RAM. This is only an issue if you plan to add more primary memory to your PC than it is able to cache, which will likely result in reduced system performance. What happens is that all the memory in excess of the cache size limit is uncached. Requests for data stored in the uncached memory require more time, including the overhead time to first determine that the memory *is,* in fact, uncached.

Playing tag

Level 2 cache memory is divided into two parts: the data store and tag RAM.

◆ *Data store:* This is the area in L2 cache where the actual data is stored. The size of the data store sets the amount of data that the cache can actually hold.

◆ *Tag RAM:* The value stored in tag RAM is used to determine whether a cache search will result in a hit or a miss.

PCs typically have 256K of L2 cache (data store) and 8 bits of tag RAM. This combination is capable of caching 64MB of primary memory. In order to cache more memory, you must increase the size of the tag RAM. More bits of tag RAM are able to address larger memory addresses. Some motherboards allow additional tag RAM chips to be added, like the one shown in Figure 7-2, but this is still fairly rare. Most systems include the tag RAM in their chipset; and some, such as the Pentium Pro, include additional tag RAM that can allow the system to cache up to 4GB of RAM.

Figure 7-2: A tag RAM chip on a PC motherboard.

Cache bursting

Level 2 cache is made up of a series of cache blocks, or lines, each of which has 32 bytes. Data is transferred into and out of the cache one line (32 bytes or 256 bits) at a time. Typically, the data bus widths of most cached PCs are 64 bits wide, requiring four consecutive 64-bit transfers to move the 256-bit line.

When the processor requests data from RAM on a 32-bit system with no cache memory installed, it is provided with a *burst* containing the four consecutive 32-bit or 64-bit blocks. The number of clock cycles required to locate and transfer each block determines the timing of this transfer. The first block is located by its address, and the data is transferred. Each of the second, third, and fourth blocks are transferred from consecutive blocks, so no addressing or lookup is required. For example, the first block might require four cycles, and each of the other blocks, one cycle each. This is shown in the notation form of 4-1-1-1 to indicate the burst speed of the cache.

Cache misses

Some overhead is involved in checking whether the data requested is in the memory cache. If the data is not in the cache — a *cache miss* — some cycles have been expended looking for it even before it's requested from primary memory. If it normally takes 10 clock cycles to transfer a burst of data from RAM, it could actually take 12 cycles on a cache miss, thus slowing system performance.

A too-small L2 cache can aggravate this situation. A small cache translates into a low cache hit ratio, where too much data is being served from RAM after cache misses. Increasing the cache size doesn't increase the overhead of checking whether data is in the cache; thus, adding more L2 cache increases the chance that data is there, but no more overhead is suffered looking for it.

Sorting Out the Types of Cache Memory

Three types of cache memory are used on PC systems: asynchronous, synchronous, and pipelined burst. The primary differences among these cache memories are in their timing and their level of support from chipsets. More than anything else, which type of cache memory used on a PC is dictated by its chipset and motherboard.

The three types of cache memory in use are

- *Asynchronous:* This type of cache memory transfers data without regard to the system clock cycles.

- *Synchronous:* This type of cache memory is tied to the cycles of the system clock.

- *Pipelined burst:* This synchronous cache memory type transfers the blocks of a burst in an overlapping mode that allows them to be partially transferred at the same time.

Asynchronous cache

Asynchronous means that data is transferred without regard to the system clock cycles. This type of cache memory, which has been around the longest, is by far the slowest. Asynchronous cache (async) was common on 486 systems but hasn't been used much after that.

When the CPU requests data, the cache responds independently of the system clock timing on the memory bus, which is why it's relatively slow. Asynchronous cache memory also has problems with clock speeds above 33 MHz. In fact, at speeds of 66 MHz or higher, asynchronous cache actually requires around twice as long to transfer data than at slower clock speeds. At 33 MHz, asynchronous cache transfers data in a four-block burst at 2-1-1-1 (meaning two cycles to locate and transfer the first block and one cycle for each of the remaining three blocks), which is actually very good. However, at 66 MHz, async cache slows down to 3-2-2-2. This is the primary reason why it's not used on Pentium or later PCs.

Synchronous cache

Synchronous cache, also known as *synchronous burst cache*, transfers data to and from cache in sync with the cycles of the memory bus clock. This allows it to work at faster bus speeds unlike asynchronous cache. Synchronous cache does require that the speed of the cache memory matches the system bus and clock speeds to avoid caching problems, such as system crashes or lockups. However, synchronous cache also has some of the same problems as asynchronous cache at very high speeds, so it has largely been replaced by pipelined burst cache.

Pipelined burst cache

Pipelined burst (PLB) cache includes special circuitry that transfers the four data blocks in a burst at essentially the same time. The transfer of the second block begins before the transfer of the first block has completed. The analogy of the pipeline is that before the first gallon of water leaves the hose, the second gallon and subsequent gallons enter the hose for transport.

In terms of speed, PLB cache is actually slower on its first block than synchronous cache because of the overhead of setting up the "pipe." However, it is faster for the remaining blocks, averaging bursts of 3-1-1-1 on systems up to 100 MHz. Most Pentium level motherboards include pipelined burst cache.

Writing to cache

Cache write policies allow the system to keep data in cache in sync with the data in memory. If the system updates a certain block of data that's being held in cache memory, also updating the data stored in cache is needed. How this is done, meaning which write policy is used, can affect system performance. The two policy types used are

♦ *Write-back cache:* When memory locations mirrored in cache memory are updated, the system only writes its new data to the cache location affected. When the data is cleared from cache, the modified data is then written back to the appropriate location in system memory. This type of cache saves on write cycles to memory, which are time and cycle consuming. As you will see, write-back is better than write-through in most cases.

♦ *Write-through cache:* Updates to data currently held in cache are written to both cache and main memory at the same time. This caching policy is simpler to implement and ensures that the cache is never out of sync with main memory. However, it doesn't perform as well as a write-back caching policy.

Non-blocking cache

Many caching systems can handle only one request at a time, which can be a problem when the data requested by the CPU causes a cache miss. When this happens, the requested data must be transferred from memory, leaving the cache blocked while it waits for the transfer action to complete. A *non-blocking* (also called *transactional*) cache can set aside a request for data not in cache and work on other data requests while the missing data is transferred from main memory. Non-blocking cache is common for L2 cache on higher-end Pentium processors. For example, the Pentium II (and later) microprocessors support up to four non-blocking requests simultaneously using the Intel dual independent bus (DIB) architecture.

Caching Impacts on Memory

Most people believe that adding more or faster memory to a PC will increase its performance. However, the size of a PC's cache can neutralize any benefit of the faster memory. A PC with a large L1 and L2 cache serves the majority of its requests for data and instructions from its memory cache. If the cache system can accurately predict the CPU's next request from 90 to 95 percent of the time (which is incredibly about what it actually is), only 5 to 10 percent of such requests come from RAM. This is great system performance, but it can offset the impact of a faster memory. Adding a memory that's 100 percent faster than the old memory can result in only a gain of 5 to 10 percent in performance.

Mapping the Cache

Some Pentium-class systems split the L1 cache to store data and instructions in separate cache partitions. Among the characteristics that differentiate these caches are their mapping techniques. The mapping technique used by a cache sets a number of the functional features for the cache, including its hit ratio and transfer speed.

The three mapping techniques used with caching are

◆ *Direct mapped cache:* Most motherboard-mounted caches are of this type. A single cache line is used to address several memory locations in a direct address mapping. This approach is the least complex of the mapping techniques used in cache memory.

◆ *Fully associative cache:* Because a memory location can be referenced from any cache line, this mapping approach is very complex and applies complicated search techniques to locate a cache hit. It can be slow, but it provides the best hit ratios.

◆ *N-way set associative cache:* The cache is divided into sets with *n* cache lines each: typically two, four, eight, or more. This mapping technique is a combination of the direct mapped and fully associative cache mapping techniques but provides better hit ratios than direct mapped cache without the speed impact of a complicated search. Processor-based L1 caches commonly apply either a two-way or four-way set associative cache.

Adding Cache

Older cache systems use SRAM (static RAM) chips mounted directly on the motherboard in individual sockets, which means that in most cases, the cache memory can be replaced or upgraded. However, on most newer systems (virtually all Pentium-class PCs), cache memory is fixed (usually soldered) directly on the motherboard, if not embedded in the processor packaging. If your PC mounts its cache in sockets, you might be able to add additional SRAM to increase the cache's size. Some motherboards with soldered SRAM might also allow additional cache modules to be installed, which could also require a jumper setting to be changed. The size and type of SRAM chips that you can add are determined by the motherboard and chipset, so check your motherboard's documentation or visit its manufacturer's Web site.

A cache module commonly used to add cache to many later 486 and early Pentium systems (and some newer) is available in a packaging called *COAST* (Cache on a Stick), which is a cache module that looks something like the Single Inline Memory Module (SIMM) packaging used for RAM (see Figure 7-3). A COAST module is mounted on a motherboard in a special socket type called a *CELP* (card edge low profile). Some motherboards include only a CELP socket for mounting cache memory, and others allow COAST modules to be added to soldered cache chips.

One word of warning about COAST: No standard exists for CELP-mounted modules. Be sure to check your motherboard's documentation for compatibility before purchasing a COAST module for your system.

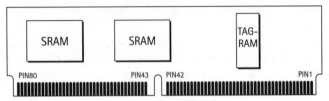

Figure 7-3: A Cache on a Stick (COAST) module.

Working with Cache

In a vast majority of cases, you wouldn't be adding cache memory to a PC. However, if you find it necessary, the guidelines in the following sections should provide you with some help.

Installing a cache module

First, review the motherboard's documentation or check with the PC manufacturer or vendor to determine whether the PC is able to expand its L2 cache. If no caching is installed and you wish to include caching, use the motherboard's specifications to select the correct SRAM chips of the COAST module.

Most newer motherboards don't have a cache slot when the cache module is installed. It is very common on motherboards to find cache sockets instead of a cache module slot or the CELP socket. To install a COAST module:

1. Place the motherboard on a flat, solid, clean, and static-free work surface.

   Place the motherboard so that it won't flex or bend when you press the caching module or chips into their sockets.

2. Before installing the module into the socket, first line it up with the socket to visually match the pins of the edge-connector to the socket connectors.

   Cache (COAST) modules are usually keyed, which means that they have a guide pin or relief feature on the leading edge of the connector that mates to a receptacle or slot on the socket to prevent being inserted into a socket incorrectly.

3. Place the module into the socket slot and press down gently but firmly until the module seats into the slot.

   If the module won't seat easily, try first gently pressing down on one end of the module and then the other end until it begins to set into the slot. The module is seated when the edge-connectors are most of the way into the socket and the module will not fit farther into the socket under firm pressure.

Troubleshooting problems after installing new cache

If you have a problem right after you've installed new or additional cache memory in a PC – perhaps the system won't boot or fails immediately after the POST – more than likely the problem is that you've installed the wrong cache for your motherboard and chipset.

On an existing system on which no changes have been made, a cache failure is extremely rare. Cache problems are generally the result of human intervention, such as the following:

♦ Removing, replacing, or adding the wrong type of cache memory modules to a PC

♦ Not setting the motherboard jumpers required to configure it properly

♦ Dislodging something while installing the cache

Here is a checklist of things to check if your PC fails after you have installed cache memory:

1. Before purchasing new cache memory – and definitely before installing it in your PC – check the motherboard's documentation or visit the manufacturer's Web site to verify the type and mounting of the cache that it supports.

2. If you've replaced the old cache modules or added new cache to the system, check the motherboard's documentation to see whether you need to change the settings of any jumpers.

   Newer PCs automatically adjust for new or additional cache, but some PCs configure the size or type of cache memory through jumper settings.

3. If you suspect that the cache is causing the problem, replace it with another cache module. If the problem goes away, you know that the original module was bad.

   This is probably the most foolproof troubleshooting step, provided that you have a spare cache module.

4. Disable the cache options in the PC's BIOS configuration data.

   These options are accessed through the BIOS setup program.

   If the problem goes away after disabling the cache settings, you need to continue checking to determine the source of the error.

5. After the PC has been powered on for a few minutes, if you can't hold your finger on the cache module for more than a few seconds because it's too hot, the cache module itself could be bad.

If the new module also gets too hot to touch after replacing the cache module, the motherboard is the likely problem. Re-verify that the cache is the right type for the motherboard; and if so, test the motherboard.

6. Ensure that you're using the correct cache memory type for your system.

   If not, immediately remove and replace it.

   Remember to check and change, if necessary, the cache memory options in the BIOS settings.

7. Verify that the cache is installed in its mounting correctly and that it's properly oriented and firmly seated in the socket or slot on the mother-board.

8. Check all drive and power supply connectors to see whether you accidentally unseated or dislodged one when installing the cache.

9. If you still cannot locate the problem, test the primary memory and check for any updated device drivers or software patches that have recently been installed.

   The problem could very well be coincidental and just happened to show up at this time.

Adding cache didn't improve system performance

It is a commonly held belief that adding more L2 cache will improve system performance. But what if you add more L2 cache (assuming that the installation is correct and uses the right type of cache memory), and the PC doesn't seem to be performing any better than it did before the cache was added?

If your PC already has 256KB of L2 cache and is already caching 90 percent or better of memory requests, the amount of improvement available is marginal, perhaps in the range of 5 to 10 percent. At the speed of the processor and SRAM, it's very unlikely that you will notice this slight improvement.

On the other hand, it could be that the cache isn't installed properly and isn't being recognized by the PC — and that's what is accounting for the lack of improvement.

Here are some steps that you can use to verify whether the cache is installed correctly:

1. Check the BIOS display during the boot to determine how much cache is detected and reported.

   If it's not the correct amount, check the cache modules to see whether they're the right type for the motherboard or whether they're installed correctly.

2. Check the motherboard's documentation to see whether adding cache memory, especially more cache memory, requires jumpers to be changed. Then check the BIOS data for settings that might need to be changed.

3. If everything looks okay and checks out, use benchmark software (before and after the installation of the cache memory) and then compare the results.

Even on the most efficient systems, you should see some improvement, no matter how small it might be.

The processor disables the cache

This problem is caused when a processor is installed on a PC, and the BIOS system is unable to properly recognize the processor.

1. Verify that the processor is properly seated in its socket.

If so, this problem can usually be fixed by upgrading the BIOS.

2. Contact the motherboard or BIOS' manufacturer to obtain a new BIOS ROM or flash BIOS upgrade file that supports the processor installed in the PC.

Determining why adding RAM slows down the PC

Some chipsets support the caching of over 64MB of primary memory. However, if the chipset, such as Intel's Triton II 430HX (which supports caching of up to 512MB of RAM), is installed on a motherboard with only 8 bits of tag RAM, the system is limited to 64MB of caching.

In order to cache more primary memory, more tag RAM must be added to those systems that can support the caching of more than 64MB of RAM. If the motherboard includes a chipset that supports higher levels of caching, it depends entirely on the motherboard as to whether additional tag RAM can be added. Check the motherboard's documentation for the location, type, and specification of the tag RAM chips that are supported.

 Even if you add tag RAM, the size of your L2 cache will still control how much actual RAM you are able to cache. These two elements must be balanced to each other.

Here are the steps that you should use to determine the problem caused by adding RAM to your system:

1. From the motherboard's documentation, check to see whether the motherboard supports and has the 11 bits of tag RAM installed needed to cache up to 512MB of RAM.

If the motherboard supports this much tag RAM but it's not installed, check with the motherboard manufacturer for the specification of the chip that will provide this capability. Be sure to match the capacity of the tag RAM to the L2 cache and primary memory of your system. You might need to add additional L2 cache.

2. If your motherboard supports the additional tag RAM, it should have a chip socket into which a second tag RAM chip can be installed.

   The motherboard's documentation or the manufacturer's Web site should list the tag RAM chips that are compatible with the chipset and cache memory as well as any jumpers that need to be changed.

   Motherboards that have CELP slots for COAST modules might accept the type of cache module that incorporates an extra tag RAM chip. If so, when you add the extra 256K of cache, you also add the extra tag RAM needed to cache more than 64MB of RAM. Not all COAST modules have tag RAM included on them.

Be very sure which modules are compatible with your motherboard and chipset. Remember that it isn't the extra cache that lets more memory be cached; it's actually the tag RAM that allows this to happen.

Your only recourse if you can't add additional tag RAM is to either live with only 64MB of cached RAM (regardless of how much RAM is on the PC) or to change out the motherboard with one that will allow you to increase the caching and with it improve your system's performance.

3. If the tag RAM needed to exceed 64MB is installed, the problem is in mismatched components, an improper configuration, or even the wrong components.

   Check the RAM and then the cache memory to find the possible causes for the slowdown. If RAM and cache memory check out, the cause is likely in the motherboard, its configuration, or an incompatibility of its components.

Enabling the internal (L1) cache

Virtually all microprocessors sold today include some amount of internal cache memory. A system's internal cache is enabled or disabled through the BIOS setup program and the BIOS configuration data. You really have no reason to disable internal cache unless you're trying to troubleshoot a caching problem.

1. Enter the BIOS setup area of your PC by using the key indicated by your BIOS during the boot process.

2. Check your BIOS settings to make sure that the internal cache is enabled and functioning.

   If for any reason you cannot enable the internal cache, you have a problem with hardware configuration (among the motherboard, chipset, and processor). If you disable the internal cache, you can expect the performance of the PC to degrade.

Enabling the external (L2) cache

External cache is located between the processor and a PC's primary memory. If your PC has L2 cache, it should be enabled. Like the L1 (internal) cache, L2 cache is also enabled through the BIOS settings. If you cannot enable the L2 cache, you have a problem with the PC's hardware configuration, either in the external cache itself or on the motherboard.

Part II

The System Case and Power Supply

Chapter 8

The System Case

IN THIS CHAPTER
The PC's case is largely taken for granted. It is definitely not high on the list of components that you deal with the most. However, in spite of the fact that the system case has only one or two active components – namely, the power supply and the front panel – it plays a major part in the overall operation of the PC.

In this chapter, I discuss

- The construction and purpose of the PC's case

- The components of the PC case

- Dealing with system case issues

- Installing a motherboard in a PC case

THE SYSTEM CASE consists of six major components. Each of these major components is covered in the sections that follow.

Dissecting the System Case

The six major components of the case are shown in Figure 8-1. These components, which I cover in depth in this chapter, are

- Power supply

- Cover

- Chassis

- Front panel

- Switches

- Drive bays

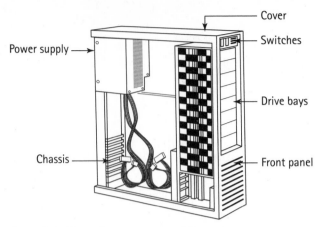

Power supply →

Chassis ——

Cover

Switches

Drive bays

Front panel

Figure 8-1: The major components of the system case.

Although not actually a physical component in the hardware sense, a very important part of a PC's case is its form factor. A case's *form factor* describes its shape, the way that its components fit together, and its size. Form factors apply to the case and the power supply and motherboard that fit into it. These three components must fit together to provide protection, power, cooling, safety, and of course, function. Therefore, it's very important that all three components have the same or compatible form factors.

Building the Case of the Case

The PC case does much more than just sit on the desk or floor holding the PC's parts or holding up the monitor, performing a number of very valuable functions that are for the most part taken for granted. The case also provides the aesthetics of the system; it provides the physical structure of the PC; and it provides protection and cooling to the electronic components and other devices mounted inside its covers. The PC's case isn't just another pretty face; it has a very important role to play in the overall function of the PC.

PC cases come in all sorts of sizes, shapes, colors, and animals; see those shown in Figure 8-2. The variances in size and shape are driven primarily by the form factor of the case, but increasingly, case designers are adding color, new plastic and metal materials, and even character faces to case designs in an attempt to make them less boring and more appealing to a wider audience. The cases shown in Figure 8-2 represent a wide variety of case types and form factors from a number of different case manufacturers.

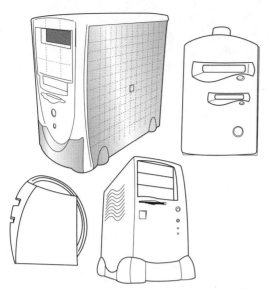

Figure 8-2: PC cases come in all sizes, shapes, and faces.

Sorting out the case components

As shown in Figure 8-2, not all system cases are the same size or shape, but they all contain virtually the same components and parts. Here is a list of the most common system components found inside the PC's case:

◆ *Chassis:* This is the skeletal framework that provides the structure, rigidity, and strength of the case; it also plays a major role in the cooling system of the case.

◆ *Cover:* The cover, along with the chassis, plays an important role in the cooling, protection, and structure of the PC.

◆ *Drive bays:* Beginning with the PC XT, disk drives with removable media have been mounted in the case so that they can be accessed on the front panel. Typically, the drive bays house 5.25" and 3.5" disk drives, such as floppy disks, CD-ROMs, DVDs, and removable hard drives.

◆ *Front panel:* In addition to providing the PC with its looks and placement of the power and reset switches, the front panel provides the user with information on the PC's status, is a means of physically securing the PC, and can be the starting point for removing the case's cover.

◆ *Power supply:* As you are undoubtedly aware, the power supply is a very important component of the PC in general and not just to the case. The power supply's primary job is to rectify (convert) AC power into DC power for use by the PC's internal electronics. However, it also houses and powers the main system cooling fan. Power supplies are not discussed in detail in this chapter other than to discuss how they fit in a case and their form factors. See Chapter 9 for more specific information on the power supply.

◆ *Switches:* Most newer systems have their two main switches (the power switch and the reset switch) on the front panel. If the power switch is not on the front panel, it's probably located either in the right-rear corner or near a corner on the back of the PC.

CHASSIS

Beneath the sheet metal or plastic exterior skin of a PC's case is a metal framework that provides the structural framework of the PC. Just like the interior of a building or the human skeleton, the PC's chassis (pronounced *chass*-ee) provides the frame on which all other parts of the PC mount, attach, or hang. As shown in Figure 8-3, the sheet metal of the chassis gives the PC its shape, size, rigidity, strength, and the location of its components.

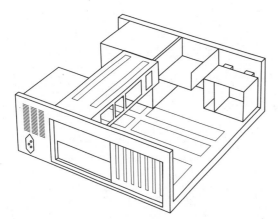

Figure 8-3: The chassis of a desktop PC.

CONSTRUCTION

The frame of the PC must be a rigid structure. Many of the components and devices in the PC cannot withstand being flexed, especially when they're operating. This is especially true of the motherboard. If the frame can twist and bend, the fragile electronic traces on the motherboard or other components could break, the motherboards mountings could slip or break, or expansion cards could be partially ejected from their slots — any of which could damage or destroy the motherboard or expansion cards. In these situations and many others, the rigidity and strength of the case's chassis is one of its key attributes. When evaluating a system case, assure yourself that a chassis' structural framework is constructed strongly and can protect the components mounted to and in it.

Not that you would usually know, but the frame of the PC chassis should be constructed from a heavy-gauge steel that's at least 18-gauge steel; 16-gauge steel is even better. Less-expensive cases might use lighter-gauge steel or aluminum. Nothing is wrong with a lighter metal or aluminum case, provided that the case is reinforced in key supporting locations with heavier-gauge steel. Be wary of bargain cases made of lightweight aluminum because these cases are much too pliable and can flex too much when being moved or lifted, causing the problems listed earlier.

TIP

The few pounds of the PC's total weight that you save by buying a lighter-weight case made of lighter-gauge metals are definitely not worth the potential for problems that a flexing or bending case can cause.

Something more to consider when choosing a case for a PC is its internal design and layout. Where the crossbeams are located in relationship to where the motherboard, power supply, disk drives, and other components mount can pose problems later when you're trying to repair or upgrade the PC.

COVER

Of the many ways to attach the cover to the chassis, the most common method is to use a few screws, but you'll also see *screwless* or *tool-less* systems where the case covers literally hang on the chassis by using keyholes or slide-and-lock features. However the cover attaches to the chassis, it's extremely important that it has a snug and secure fit.

The case's cover is engineered to provide the best possible airflow dynamics. It is also a key component of the radio frequency interference (RFI) and electromagnetic interference (EMI) protection designed into the system. If your PC is certified by the Federal Communications Commission (FCC) (and virtually all PCs are), the case was designed to be a major part of the radio frequency (RF) emissions control of the PC. One of the risks in having a cover that doesn't fit tightly and securely without gaps or loose parts is that it can emit RF signals and thus affect other devices near it. Sometimes, though, the problem with loose or badly fitting case parts can just be an annoying rattle from the escaping airflow breeze.

Many methods are used to attach the outer cover of the PC to the chassis. The most common is that the cover is attached with screws to the front, sides, and rear of the chassis. Rarely would you completely remove all sections of the PC's cover from the chassis. Normally, only the side (tower) or top (desktop) is removed to provide access inside the case. The following sections discuss the more common styles of covers and how they are attached and removed from the chassis.

LEGACY DESKTOPS

The desktop PC, an example of which is shown in Figure 8-4, is by far the most common of the case designs. There are desktop models for nearly every form factor (see "Factoring in the case form" later in this chapter), including the earliest PCs (such as the PC XT and the PC AT systems), the more common PCs (such as the Baby AT and ATX systems), and the newer LPX slimline systems. For the most part, older systems have a U-shaped piece that incorporates the covers for the top and sides of the PC. This piece is attached to the chassis with four or five screws to the rear panel. It is removed by either sliding it all the way back or forward off the PC or by sliding it back a bit and then lifting it straight up. The benefit of this cover design is its simplicity, but you must be careful when removing or replacing it that you don't snag power and data cables, expansion cards, or disk drives and dislodge or damage them.

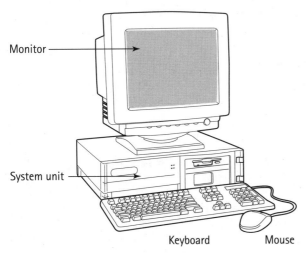

Figure 8–4: A desktop PC.

LEGACY TOWERS

Of the many types of tower cases (see Figure 8-5), the most common tower designs are typically the full-size AT, Baby AT, or ATX case. On these cases, the cover is a U-shaped piece with very long sides that fit down and over the frame of the tower's case. This cover is attached to the rear of the case with four to six screws. To remove this cover, the screws are removed; then the cover is either lifted straight up and off, or it slides back a bit and is then lifted up and off.

TOOL-LESS CASES

Many brand-name PCs feature a case that has one or two large knobby screws on the back panel of the case. This case design is called *tool-less* because you should be able to remove and replace the screw(s) with your fingers without a screwdriver or other tools. (See Figure 8-6.) The cover pieces are held firm by spring clips that apply pressure to chassis points to hold the cover pieces in place.

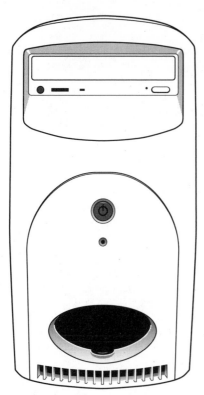

Figure 8-5: A PC in a mid-tower case design.

Figure 8-6: A tool-less case design is secured
with one or more large screws.

SCREWLESS CASES

This type of case cover features several individual cover pieces, generally one piece
to a side. The key to removing this type of case cover is to remove the locking panel
(usually the front panel) to unlock the remaining panels of the case. The front panel
is attached by a spring clip and is pulled up and lifted off one or more hook-like
tabs built into the chassis, as shown in Figure 8-7. After the front panel is removed,
the top is first removed (typically by lifting it straight up) and then the sides, one at
a time, if needed.

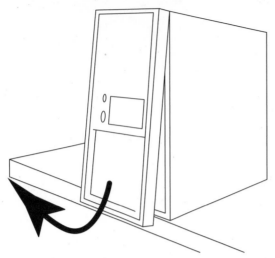

Figure 8-7: Removing the front panel of a screwless case.

Some screwless cases have a cut-in indentation at the bottom of the front panel that can be used to grasp the edge of the panel to pull it up. On others, where no such handhold is provided, you might need to use a small screwdriver or pry tool to pull the front panel up enough to gain a grasp of its edge.

 One minor drawback to a screwless case is that you have several case parts to track instead of just the one-piece desktop case.

RELEASE-BUTTON CASES

This case design, which is common on Compaq desktop models, is removed by pressing spring-release buttons located on the front or rear of the PC. After pressing the release buttons, the cover (which includes the front, rear, top, and sides of the cover) lifts straight off the case.

 A case with a similar design is called the *flip-top* case. This case design also uses release buttons to unlock the cover, but instead of the entire top lifting off, the top cover tips up like a top-loading washer. If you need to remove the entire case for some reason, strategically placed screws can be removed to release the entire cover.

FRONT-SCREW CASES

On this case design, the screws that hold the cover on the PC are located on the front panel and are usually hidden behind sliding tabs or a snap-on panel. Removing the screws (and possibly some on the rear panel as well) allows the case to be pulled forward and off the case.

Scanning the front panel

The primary purpose of the *front panel* (or *bezel)* is to cover up the front end of the chassis, but because it's the part that the user looks at most of the time, efforts have been made to make it useful and appealing.

Some PCs feature doors and snap-on panels to mask disk drives, the power and reset switches, and even the light-emitting diodes (LEDs) on the front of the PC. Typically, doors on the front panel are a characteristic of larger PCs and network servers. Figure 8-8 shows a WTX server with two doors: one for the removable drives and the other to cover the normal parts of the front panel. This computer also features a key lock for the doors to provide a small amount of security.

 See "Factoring in the case form" later in this chapter for information on the WTX, ATX, and other PC case form factors.

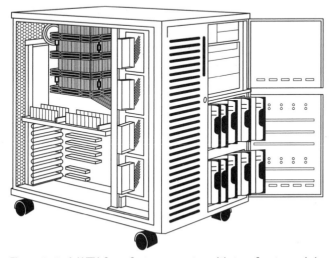

Figure 8-8: A WTX form factor computer with two front panel doors.

STATUS LEDS

Most PCs have LEDs on the front panel to show the status and activity of certain parts of the system. Typically, two LEDs are used: one that is lighted when the power is on, and one that indicates when the hard disk is being accessed. Other LEDs are visible on the front of the PC, but they are generally part of the disk drive installed in a drive bay. Very old PCs also have a Turbo LED that indicates that the system is in Turbo mode, which raises the processor speed of a PC. Turbo systems are generally obsolete now.

Here is a quick overview of the front panel's LEDs:

♦ *Hard drive LED:* When the disk drive is seeking, reading, or writing data, this red, orange, or amber LED is lighted and flashes. The speed with which the hard drive LED flashes is a good indicator of how busy your PC is. Typically, this LED is wired to the motherboard or the disk controller or adapter, which means that it reflects the activity of all disk drives on the PC.

♦ *Power LED:* This LED is typically green in color and is illuminated when the PC's power is on.

♦ *Turbo LED:* If present, this yellow LED indicates that the PC is in Turbo mode. The Turbo button was used on very early systems as a part of a backward compatibility strategy. There wasn't a lot of software available to begin with, and when the 8 MHz systems were released, many people had a fair investment in software that would run only in the older 4.77 MHz, or PC XT mode. Normal mode on these systems, 286 and 386 processors, was Turbo mode. However, when the Turbo button was released, two things happened: The PC processor was slowed to 4.77 MHz, and the Turbo LED was turned off.

FRONT-PANEL SWITCHES

Nearly all PCs now have at least one main switch (usually the power switch) on the front panel of the PC. Some older designs have two switches: the power switch and a reset switch. Figure 8-9 shows a PC front panel with its power switch.

POWER SWITCH   On older PCs, the power switch was a part of the power supply and extended through the case wall on the right-rear corner of the PC. More recently, the power switch is on the front panel.

On Baby AT systems and before, the power switch located on the front panel is not a switch in the sense of a physical on/off switch. It is actually a proxy switch that transfers a press on the front panel switch to the actual power supply switch located on the back of the front panel and wired directly to the power supply.

Newer systems, such as the ATX, NLX, and LPX form factors, have an actual power switch on the front panel, but instead of being wired to the power supply, the switch is now electronic and is actually connected to the motherboard. On these systems, you don't turn the computer on or off with the power switch; rather, pushing the power button sends a request to the motherboard to power off the PC.

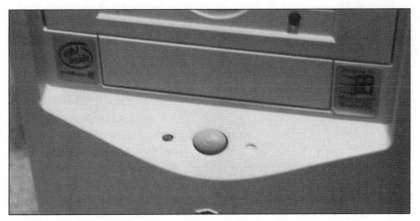

Figure 8-9: The power switch on a PC's front panel.

RESET BUTTON   Although disappearing from PCs largely to prevent accidental resets, the *reset switch*, also referred to as the *reset button*, performs a hardware reset when pressed. This provides the user with a means of restarting the PC should it halt and not respond to normal shutdown or restart commands. Using the reset button is better than powering the PC off and back on, which can sometimes result in POST or BIOS errors.

On some older PCs, the reset button was placed on the front panel and was easily accessed, which caused more than one unexpected system reset. Newer cases, if they feature a reset button, recess the button to prevent inadvertent resets from taking place. A few manufacturers have moved the reset button to the back of the PC, which is safer yet.

Some manufacturers, such as Gateway, don't include a reset button on their systems. Resetting the PC must be done via the keyboard (by pressing Ctrl+Alt+Del) or by using the operating system's restart process.

TURBO BUTTON   As I explain in the earlier section "Status LEDs," the Turbo button and its functions are now obsolete except on 286 and early 386 computers. If your front panel has a Turbo button, chances are that it's not connected to anything; to avoid any possible problems, you should never press it.

KEYLOCKS

Although not technically a switch, some cases have keylocks on their front panels. The two types of keylocks available on PC front panels are a front panel door lock and a keyboard lockout.

◆ *Front panel door lock:* If the front panel of your PC has one or more doors, it might also have a door lock either on the door or on the front panel. When the doors are closed and locked, curiosity seekers are prevented from accessing the drives behind the doors. However, because the doors are made of plastic and can be pried open easily, this feature should not be used or thought of as a means to secure the system.

♦ *Keyboard lockout:* When locked, this type of keylock sets a logical condition on the system that locks out the keyboard, thus preventing anyone from using the PC. When someone attempts to use the PC while this keylock is locked, an error message is displayed on the monitor that in effect says that the system is not available for use. While this keylock is locked, the PC will not boot. The keyboard lockout keylock was intended to be a first-level of security for PCs in large offices and work areas. The keys for a PC keylock are usually round, and many manufacturers use the same key for all their systems. Thus, the security that keylocks can provide is limited. Anyone with a screwdriver can open the case and disable the lock; and on some cases, you don't even need the screwdriver.

If your case has a keylock or a front-panel door lock, be sure that it also has keylock keys. Typically, you'll get two of each key. If you plan to use them, store one of the keys in a safe place so that if you lose the first one, you can still unlock your PC.

DRIVE BAYS

Since the PC AT, you have been able to decide the number and type of disk drives in your computer. As long as the power supply and cooling system would support them, you could add floppy disk drives, hard disk drives, CD-ROM drives, tape drives, and more to your PC.

Generally, drives are installed in the drive bays provided on virtually all PC case designs and form factors. Figure 8-10 shows a desktop computer with its drive bays exposed. This system, an ATX case, provides three 5.25" half-height drive bays, two 3.5" one-inch high drive bays, and two 3.5" drive bays hidden inside the case.

Originally, disk drives required a drive bay that was 3.5" in height. As technology was able to reduce the size of the overall drive, this height was cut in half, and now most of the drive bays available for 5.25" devices are less than 2 inches in height and are called *half-height.*

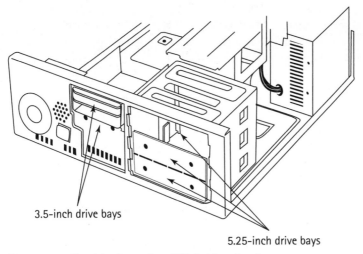

3.5-inch drive bays

5.25-inch drive bays

Figure 8-10: The drive bays of an ATX desktop chassis.

INTERNAL VERSUS EXTERNAL BAYS

As indicated in the previous paragraph, the two types of drive bays are external and internal:

- *External drive bays:* These drive bays are actually internal to the case and chassis, but they can be accessed externally, which is how they get their name. External drive bays are typically used for drives that have removable media, such as floppy disks, CD-ROM, DVD, tape drives, and the like.

- *Internal drive bays:* Internal bays are completely inside the system case and have no access from outside the chassis, as shown in Figure 8-11. These bays are designed for devices, primarily hard disk drives, with no need for external exposure. Simply put, internal drive bays are for hard disks.

Internal drive bays

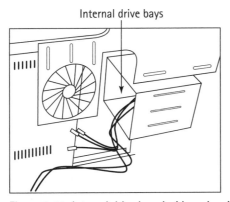

Figure 8-11: Internal drive bays inside a chassis.

TIP Internal devices can be installed in external bays. Before internal bays were common, hard disk drives were installed in the external bays (the only kind available), and a solid faceplate was put over the external opening of the bay to hide the drive.

MOUNTING RAILS

You have two methods to mount a device in a drive bay, whether internal or external. One way is with the use of drive rails, and the other is mounting the device directly to the walls of the drive bay.

♦ *Drive rails:* These two strips of metal are mounted to the sides of the disk drive. With the drive rails attached, a device is placed into the drive bay with the rails sliding into notches or facets on the sidewalls of the bay. The device is suspended from the rails, which are then secured to the walls of the bay.

♦ *Sidewall mounting:* This method, used in most newer cases, involves attaching the disk drive to the sidewalls of the drive bay. Screws are placed through holes in the sidewall that match the standard placement and spacing of pre-threaded holes on the sides of the disk drive. The drive is solidly attached to the chassis.

DRIVE CAGES

A newer feature on system cases is snap-in cages for internal drive bays, like those shown in Figure 8-11. To install a hard disk in an internal cage, you remove the cage, install the drive, and then snap the cage and drive assembly back into place. If you use a cage to install an internal drive, think ahead to the cables and connectors that might be added later and the process that will be needed to remove the drive for servicing.

STYLING THE CASE

The two basic styles of PC cases are the *tower case* and the *desktop case*. Figure 8-12 shows a family of PC cases that includes both tower and desktop styles. The tall, thin ones are the tower case style, and the flat, boxy one is the desktop case style. At one time, they were actually very much alike. In fact, the tower came about when people tried to save space by turning their desktop PCs on their sides. Today, these case styles are very distinctive with their internal designs, the way the case is attached, and the features that each supports.

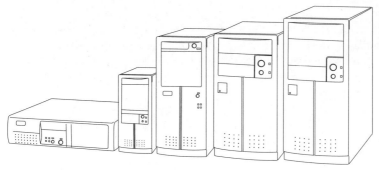

Figure 8-12: A family of PC cases.

TOWER VERSUS DESKTOP

Which case style is right for a particular setting really depends on how it is to be used – and frankly, the setting itself. Tower cases are designed to sit on the floor or large shelves. Desktops are designed to sit on desks, which is why they're called *desktops*. A tower case does free up desktop space, but if the space on the floor is limited, the case can be in the way, kicked, or knocked over. The desktop cases of today are a lot smaller (shorter and narrower) than they were when the PC was first moved off the desktop.

The two case styles really aren't interchangeable, despite the claims of the vendors selling conversion kits. Turning a desktop PC on its side changes the orientation of the removable media drives: namely the CD-ROM, DVD, and other such drives. If you wish to move from a desktop to a tower, or vice versa, I recommend that you purchase the appropriate case and convert the PC into the new case.

DESKTOP CASES

Although this case style is not as popular in recent years as it once was, desktop cases are still generally available from most PC manufacturers and resellers. Because it also doubles as the base for the PC's monitor, the desktop case is actually more space efficient than the mid-sized tower models. Some tower styles are small enough to sit on a desktop but cannot hold the monitor and thus end up using more space than a desktop unit would. In some situations, the desktop PC is better suited than a PC in a tower case, primarily where floor space is limited.

Until very recently, the desktop case style had been the unofficial standard for PC cases. The first PCs, the PC XT and PC AT, were desktop units. The desktop cases of today are smaller than those of the original PC AT and its clones. The common desktop form factor is the Baby AT and now the LPX low profile case, which is also known as the *pizza box case*. Newer slimline cases, such as the NLX (which was designed to replace the LPX), are becoming more popular.

TOWER CASES

In today's market, the tower case style is far more popular than the desktop case style mainly because a tower case can sit under a desk to free up workspace on the desk, thus providing more space than the desktop inside the case for upgrading the PC. Three of the more popular tower case sizes are the mini-tower, the mid-tower, and full-tower.

Variations on these sizes exist between manufacturers because no standard sizes are associated with these three case styles. Figure 8-13 shows a tower case family from one vendor. What one vendor calls a mini-tower, another might call a mini-mid-tower.

When buying a PC, first pick the brand that you wish to buy (if you have a preference) and then look at the form factor, sizes, and styles of cases available. With a tower case, the primary difference between models is usually the number of external drive bays and the size of the power supply. As the number of external bays increases, the case gets taller, and usually the power supply gets more powerful.

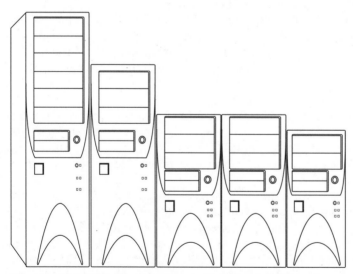

Figure 8-13: A family of computer cases showing a full AT tower on the left down to an ATX mini-tower on the right.

Here are the popular variations of the tower case style:

◆ *Full tower:* Full tower cases are the largest standard PC cases available. They offer the most of any case style in the way of expandability, typically having three to five external drive bays and a few internal bays as well (see Figure 8-14). A full tower case will normally have a high-end power supply under the assumption that the case will be filled with devices. This style of case is popular among high-end users and for servers.

Figure 8-14: A full tower case featuring external drive bays.

◆ *Mid-tower:* A mid-tower case is a slightly shorter version of the full tower case. This particular size seems to vary the most among manufacturers, but within a single manufacturer's line, it represents a good compromise of size and price. For example, the mid-tower case shown in Figure 8-15 provides external drive bays and can accommodate either ATX or full AT form factor system boards, which should be room enough for most applications.

◆ *Midi-tower:* This case style exists somewhere between the mid-tower and the mini-tower cases. By definition, a *midi-tower* is smaller than a mid-tower and larger than a mini-tower. However, what you will typically find advertised as a midi-tower is either a small mid-tower or a large mini-tower – or as available from one manufacturer, a mini-mid-tower. Regardless of the case's style name, if it fits your needs, it's the right one.

◆ *Mini-tower:* This case size is probably the currently most popular. It provides slightly more expansion capacity than desktop cases and is small enough to sit on a desktop next to the monitor. If you're considering converting a desktop case to a tower, this would be an excellent and economical choice because they run around $25 or less. Figure 8-16 shows a mini-tower case.

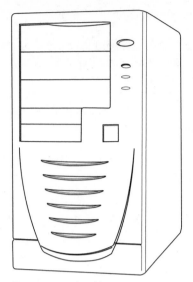

Figure 8-15: A mid-tower case.

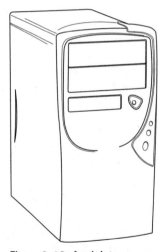

Figure 8-16: A mini-tower case.

RACKMOUNT CASES

Another type of case that has usage in special purpose or networking applications is the rackmount case. This case is designed to be attached to the rails of a rack-mount cabinet or a rackmount stand. Figure 8-17 shows a rackmount PC with its cover opened.

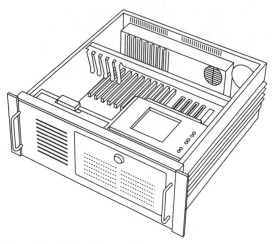

Figure 8-17: A rackmount PC case.

Factoring in the case form

The *form factor* of a PC case defines its style, size, shape, internal organization, and the components that are compatible with cases of that form factor. Computer form factors define a general standard for compatibility for the system case, the motherboard, the power supply, the placement of input/output (I/O) ports and connectors, and other factors.

The three most popular types of case form factors are the Baby AT, ATX, and NLX.

◆ *Baby AT:* Although virtually obsolete by today's standards, the Baby AT form factor still has a very large installed base from its popularity in past years.

◆ *ATX:* The ATX form factor is the de facto standard for motherboards, power supplies, and system cases. Virtually all Pentium-based systems use the ATX form factor.

◆ *NLX:* The NLX form factor, also called slimline form factor, is popular for mass-produced desktop systems.

Here is a quick look at some of the other form factors that have been used or are still in use for system cases:

◆ *PC XT:* This form factor was used on the original desktop PCs: the IBM PC and its successor, the PC XT. The case was made of heavy-gauge steel and had a U-shaped case that was fastened on the rear of the PC and was removed over the front of the case. The power supply had 130 watts (only 63.5 watts on the PC) and was located at the rear of the case with a power switch that protruded through a cutout on the case.

♦ *AT:* The IBM PC AT, although not much different on the outside than its predecessors, was quite different on the inside. The motherboard and power supply (which was much larger) were repositioned inside the case. The AT quickly became the standard form factor among manufacturers; all subsequent form factors, whether desktop or tower, are based in one way or another on the AT.

♦ *LPX:* Although never officially accepted as a standard form factor, LPX is the oldest of the low-profile form factors. Over the past ten years, it has been one of the most popular slimline form factors sold. Slimline cases are a little shorter than Baby AT or ATX cases. This is achieved by moving expansion cards to a riser board that mounts horizontally in the case instead of vertically, thereby saving inches of height.

♦ *Micro-ATX and Flex-ATX:* These two ATX-based form factors define specifications for smaller versions of the ATX motherboard. Micro-ATX and Flex-ATX do not define case form factors, but manufacturers are designing cases to take advantage of their smaller footprint. These form factors are intended for PCs targeted to the mass market and home users.

♦ *WTX:* The *W* stands for *workstation*, and the WTX is a form factor intended for high-performance workstations and servers. This form factor defines a modular case that features a motherboard that's twice the size of an ATX motherboard. A WTX case features space for high-capacity, redundant power supplies, removable panels for easy access to components, a large number of hard drive bays, and support for multiple cooling fans. Refer to Figure 8-8 for a WTX form factor computer.

For more information on PC form factors as they relate to motherboards and power supplies, see Chapters 1 and 9.

SYSTEM CASE FEATURES

When you buy a system case, like the one shown in Figure 8-18 without its covers, it will include some pre-installed components and features, which are usually the optional pieces that conform a generic case to fit a particular form factor and your particular requirements. Because several of the form factors are very close in their size and component placement, manufacturers make cases that can be used with a number of form factors. Applying such items as an I/O template, the appropriate power supply, and motherboard mounts turns the generic case into a custom case that's just right for your needs.

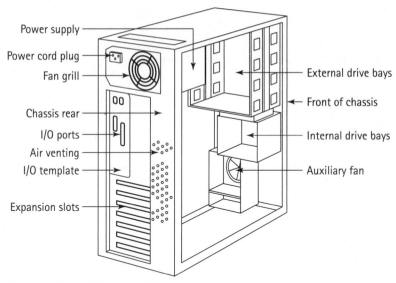

Power supply

Power cord plug

Fan grill

Chassis rear

I/O ports

Air venting

I/O template

Expansion slots

External drive bays

Front of chassis

Internal drive bays

Auxiliary fan

Figure 8-18: An ATX case and its components.

I/O TEMPLATES

Each motherboard form factor also defines the location and placement of the ports used for such input/output devices as the keyboard, mouse, printer, and others. For the most part, these ports are connected either directly or indirectly to the motherboard. Directly connected ports are physically mounted on the motherboard. The case must accommodate these ports with a hole in the right shape and place so that the port can be accessed through the case. Indirectly connected ports mount to the case and are attached to the motherboard with a cable. Either way, the case has to either be manufactured with the portholes already in place or provide an adapter for this purpose.

Older form factor cases, such as the PC XT, AT, Baby AT, and LPX, were manufactured with holes cut into the rear panel of the case to match a particular form factor. However, to make cases more flexible and allow them to service more than a single form factor, manufacturers devised I/O templates, which can be snapped into a case to provide the I/O port pattern desired. Figure 8-19 illustrates what the templates look like out of the box.

A current trend among case manufacturers is to leave a punch-out or knockout slug in the I/O ports on the I/O template (as shown in Figure 8-19) and the expansion slots. If you're not using a port or slot, you can leave the slug in place. However, be sure that you ask and understand how this affects the case cooling before assuming that it's a part of the overall case design.

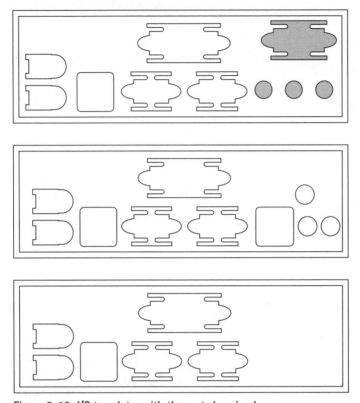

Figure 8-19: I/O templates with the port slugs in place.

Supplying power

Most (not all) system cases come with a power supply (see Figure 8-20) matched to its form factor. Power supplies are not a part of the case even though they're generally sold together as one assembly. When buying a PC case, be sure that a power supply appropriate for your application is included – or that a power supply is not included, as you wish. Many case manufacturers sell their cases à la carte, and you can select the options and power supply to meet your needs. See Chapter 9 for more information on power supplies.

Auxiliary fans

The main cooling fan in the PC is in the power supply, which is an important reason why you should match the power supply to the form factor of the motherboard and case, in that order. Many newer case form factors provide a location for an auxiliary or supplemental fan to help cool the inside of the PC. Typically, the location of the auxiliary fan, if available, is on the opposite front or back panel from the main cooling fan, as shown in Figure 8-21.

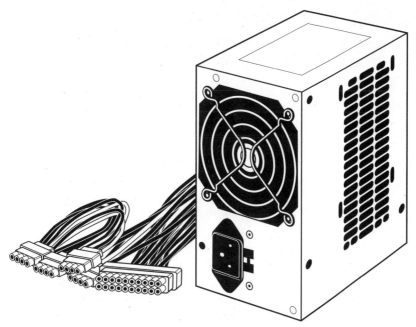

Figure 8-20: A power supply can be purchased separate from the system case.

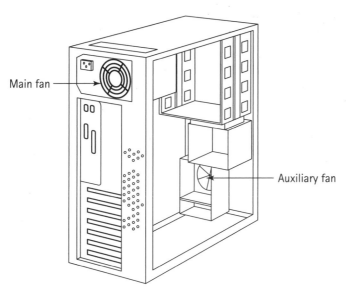

Figure 8-21: The locations of the main cooling fan and an auxiliary fan on an NLX case.

Lights, sound, and the connecting wires

The other components of a PC case are the LEDs, the system speaker, and the wiring that connects these two items, plus a few more, to the power supply and motherboard.

◆ *LEDs:* Most PC cases include at least two LEDs that are used as indicators for the power and hard disk. Although fairly uncommon today, some cases might have other LEDs for Turbo mode and the CPU's activity level.

◆ *Front panel wiring:* On the back of the front panel (near the system speaker, the LEDs, and the keylock) should be a small bundle of multi-colored wires that connect these items to the motherboard and perhaps each other. The LEDs should have two wires: one that's either black or white (ground) and one that's some other color (positive).

◆ *System speaker:* The system speaker isn't intended for stereo sound or to play your audio CDs. Rather, it's only meant to be a basic means of communication between the motherboard, BIOS, chipset, processor, and other system components and the user. About the best it can do is sound beep codes during the boot and other monotone sounds by some application software. The system speaker is normally mounted inside the case near or on the front panel. On a new case, it might be included loose (not pre-mounted), allowing you to place it where you wish.

Cooling vents

Although this might seem obvious, air must have a means to get into or out of the system case. Usually, the case should have a grouping of small vent holes, cuts, louvers, or the like. Because of its larger airflow, a bigger case cools the internal components better than a smaller case, but both must still have a way to vent the case. You can assume that any case you buy from a reputable manufacturer is engineered properly for cooling and ventilation.

 When assembling a system case and its components, be aware of where the vents are and take care not to block them.

Mounting the motherboard

If you're buying a new case, it should come with mounting hardware. These pieces normally come with the case and *not* the motherboard. Make sure that you have the appropriate mounting hardware, or your PC building project will come to a halt! The exact hardware included varies greatly and depends on what the manufacturer decided to include in the case, but you'll generally find some combination of the following:

◆ *Fixed mounting hardware:* Some cases already have their mounting hardware fixed (meaning soldered or welded) in place to match the mounting holes of a motherboard of the same form factor as the case. This is intended to save you time, but if you ever want to move to another form factor motherboard, you'll need a new case.

◆ *Metal standoffs:* Metal standoffs are rarely used because they're a bother to work with and they cost more than the plastic type. However, if your case has threaded holes in place of mounting slots, these brass hexagon spacers need to be used. The standoff has screw threads on one end and a threaded screw hole on the other end. The screw end is screwed into the case, and then the motherboard (along with some insulating Teflon, Delran, or paper washers) is attached to the other end with a screw. The washers are placed between the standoff and the motherboard and between the motherboard and the screw. This keeps the metal-edged mounting hole from contacting the screw and standoff and preventing it from shorting the board.

◆ *Plastic standoffs:* These small plastic parts are also called *spacers, risers,* and *sliders.* The standoffs used inside the case to mount the motherboard are typically small plastic legs (see Figure 8-22) that snap into the mounting holes on the motherboard and then slide into the mounting slots on the case. In addition to anchoring the motherboard in place, the standoffs keep the motherboard from contacting the system case and grounding or shorting itself.

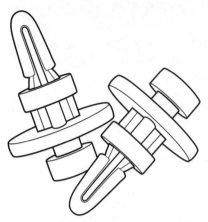

Figure 8-22: The plastic standoffs used to mount a motherboard in a PC case.

Dealing with Case Issues

Problems directly related to the case itself are rare, but when they do occur, they typically involve the fan, power supply, wiring, or improper installation of components or devices. The sections that follow deal with the problems and activities that you might encounter when working with a system case.

Preparing a case for a motherboard

If you're building a new PC from the ground (or from the case) up, you must first perform these steps to prepare the case to accept the motherboard.

1. Open the case by removing the cover piece that exposes the inside of the case.

   The case should come with a manual that has instructions and (hopefully) illustrations on how this is done.

2. The case should have one or more plastic bags of parts that you'll need to assemble the case and to mount other system components in the case.

   At minimum you should have

   - Mounting hardware for the motherboard – either plastic or metal standoffs or spacers.

   - Metal slot inserts that are used to close any unused expansions slots in the back of the case. These might already be installed.

   - Rubber feet for the bottom of the case, which might already be attached.

- Drive cages (if the case supports them) or drive rails.

- A power supply AC cord, if a power supply is included with the case. If not, you'll need to install one before installing any other components to the case.

3. Use compressed air to blow out any packing materials or dust in a new case.

4. Check the power supply for apparent damage, and then check the cables, fan, and its casing.

   Make sure that the voltage selector is set appropriately for your power source.

5. Install the feet, if they're not already installed.

   After the motherboard is installed, this step might not be as easy as it is now.

6. Install the slot inserts into the expansion slots.

   This step can wait until after the expansion slots are installed, if you prefer.

7. Install any auxiliary fans that you wish to use, if the case supports them.

8. If the case has a removable or swing out motherboard panel, remove it (see the case's documentation) so that you can install the motherboard to it outside of the case.

The front panel LEDs don't light up

If the front panel LEDs don't light up, the problem is probably that the front panel's LEDs aren't connected or have been connected incorrectly. The good news about connecting the front panel LEDs is that if you do it wrong, all that will happen is that they won't light up.

Front panel LEDs will have a ground wire. The ground wire is either a black or white wire attached to a one-pin push-on connector that's connected to the motherboard's LED ground connector, which should be marked on the mother-board. The positive wire is some other color (perhaps red, blue, or green) that's connected to the motherboard's LED connector. It, too, is a one-pin push-on connector. These connectors are usually located along the front or side edge of the mother-board. Check the motherboard's documentation for the location of these connectors if you cannot find them.

If the LEDs don't light up, try reversing the wires of the bad LED or exchanging the wires of two or more of the LEDS. Chances are that you'll find a combination that works.

No sound is coming from the system speaker

If no sound is coming from the system speaker, the speaker has probably not been connected to the motherboard or the connectors are plugged in incorrectly.

Like the LED wires covered in the previous section, the system speaker has two wires that connect to the motherboard with either a single 4-pin connector or two 1-pin connectors. If you get the connectors on backwards or off to one side or the other, the worst that can happen is that it just won't work. You won't damage the speaker by connecting it incorrectly.

Also, the speaker could be defective. If the wiring looks right and checks against the documentation, try using the speaker in a new PC or using a new speaker in this PC.

The reset button does not restart the PC

If the PC has a reset button, it should restart the PC when pressed. If nothing happens when you press this button, the wires that connect the reset button to the motherboard were probably not installed, were not installed properly, or have come loose – or you have a problem with the motherboard that you might just have to live with.

Check the motherboard's documentation to verify the location of the connector for the reset button's wiring and verify that it's properly connected.

The power on/off button does not work

If the power on/off button doesn't work, make sure you know which case, motherboard, and power supply form factors you have before you do very much to troubleshoot this problem. ATX form factor motherboards and power supplies pass live AC through to the on/off switches that are on the front panel, and getting these connections wrong can be dangerous to the motherboard and yourself.

Follow the instructions in the motherboard's documentation for connecting these switches or that in the case's documentation for the front-panel switches. An ATX power supply doesn't have a front-panel cable and might not have an on/off switch of its own. An ATX motherboard controls the power supply with a logic circuit that turns it on and off. The switch on the front panel sends a signal to the motherboard, which relays it the power supply. The ATX motherboard always has at least 5 volts of standby power on it, even when the power supply is off.

Setting the monitor on the system case halts the PC

If the PC freezes, reboots, or powers off whenever you set anything (especially the monitor) on top of the case, chances are that something is causing the motherboard to touch the case and short out, which should happen soon after the system boots, if it will boot. The weight of the monitor or other object is apparently too much for the case's structure, thus causing it to bend or flex.

Here's another possibility: In some weird way, the monitor (or whatever else you are putting on the case) is changing the airflow inside the system case and causing the processor or motherboard to overheat. The processor and chipset will shut down when they approach operating temperatures outside their normal ranges.

Check to see that the monitor is sitting squarely in the center of the case or over the main structural points of the case. Avoid setting the monitor off to one side or on a corner of the case.

Then try operating the system without the monitor on top of the case. If it works fine, the case just isn't strong enough to hold the monitor, especially if it's a 17" monitor or larger. If workspace is an issue, several monitor stands are available that function like bridges placed over the PC's system unit to hold up the monitor. You can also place the monitor on a swing arm mount that connects to the desk.

If the problem continues, investigate a cooling issue or perhaps a faulty power supply. Try rearranging the cables inside the case to open up some airflow or perhaps, if the case supports it, add an auxiliary fan.

Chapter 9

Powering Up the PC

IN THIS CHAPTER

Because a computer is an electrical device and digital logic circuits require a non-fluctuating direct current (DC), a switching power supply is used to convert an alternating current (AC) power source to the DC power that it needs. The electronic components of the PC, such as the processor and memory, require +3.3 volts (v) or +5v of DC power, and hard disk drives and other permanent storage devices need +12v DC.

To that end, this chapter includes information on the following:

◆ The physical construction and components of a PC power supply

◆ The electrical systems of a PC power supply

◆ Protecting the PC from external power problems

◆ Diagnosing and resolving common PC power supply issues

YOU DON'T HAVE TO BE AN ELECTRICIAN TO WORK ON COMPUTERS, but a good working knowledge of PC electrical systems, and especially its power supply, can save you time and energy (no pun intended) when trying to chase down an intermittent problem.

Understanding the Functions of the Power Supply

The primary functions of a PC power supply are cooling, rectification, filtering, regulation, isolation, power management, and voltage conversion. Here is an explanation of each of these functions:

◆ *Cooling:* The system fan, which controls the airflow through the system case, is located inside the power supply.

◆ *Rectification:* This function is directly involved with converting the AC power of the power source to the DC power needed by the PC's components.

◆ *Filtering:* Rectification usually introduces a ripple in the DC voltage, which filtering smoothes out.

221

♦ *Regulation:* Along with filtering, voltage regulation removes any line or load variations in the DC voltage produced by the power supply.

♦ *Isolation:* This separates the AC power supply from the converted, rectified, filtered, and regulated DC power.

♦ *Power management:* Most computers produced over the past few years have included energy-efficiency tools and power management functions that help reduce the amount of electrical power used by the PC.

♦ *Voltage conversion:* This function involves changing the 110v AC primary power source into the +12v and +5v DC used by many older systems and the +3.3v DC used by most newer computer. During the reign of the 80486, +3.3v processors were introduced and used voltage regulators on the motherboard to reduce the DC current to this level. However, power supplies that now provide +3.3v DC are common.

In those areas of the world where the power source is already a direct current, the power supply performs all the same tasks except rectification. Most power supplies have the ability to take either a 110v AC input or a 220v DC input and have a slide switch on the outside by the fan grill to select the power source voltage to which it is attached.

Producing good power

In addition to providing converted power to the motherboard and the other parts of the PC, the power supply sends a very important signal to the motherboard through its umbilical connection – the POWER_GOOD (or Pwr_OK on an ATX form factor power supply) signal.

Read more about form factors in Chapter 8.

When the PC is powered on, the power supply performs a self-test and checks whether the required voltages (in and out) are correct. If so, the POWER_GOOD signal line is set high (on) to indicate that the motherboard can rely on the power being supplied. If the signal is not set, the processor's timing chip (to which this signal line is attached) sends the processor a reset command that starts the Basic Input/Output System's (BIOS') initialization code.

The effect of the POWER_GOOD signal not being set is that the PC is trapped in a loop continuously calling the BIOS. In this situation, the power supply appears to be working, and some power is being supplied to the PC and its peripherals. The front panel lights might be on, the disk drives spinning, and the power supply fan running, but the BIOS will never reach the Power-On Self-Test (POST) process and will appear to be hung.

Turning power on and off

On ATX and NLX form factors and most of the other later form factors, the motherboard can turn the power supply on or off. This is done through the PS_ON (power supply on) signal that passes between the motherboard and the power supply. If your PC powers off when Windows is finished shutting down, you have this feature.

Another indicator that your power supply supports PS_ON is the use of momentary-on or always-on power switches that are connected to the motherboard in place of an exterior switch connected to the power supply. When this signal line is pulled to a low voltage signal, the +12v DC, +5v DC, +3.3v DC, –5v DC, and –12v DC power lines (see Figures 9-1 and 9-2) are turned on. When pulled to a high-voltage signal, or open-circuited, the DC output lines should no longer have current. The +5v DC output is always on as long as the power supply receives AC power. Because the ATL, NLX, LTX, and other form factor motherboards have some power running to them at all times, you always want to unplug the PC before working on it.

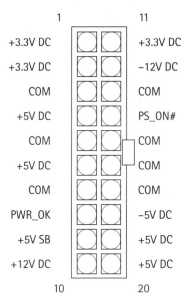

Figure 9-1: ATX/NLX power supply to motherboard connector and pinouts.

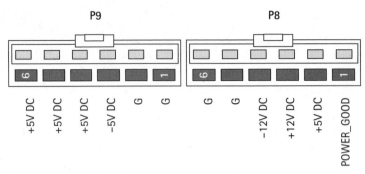

Figure 9-2: Baby AT-style power connectors and pinouts.

Figures 9-1 and 9-2 show the two most popular connector types used to supply power to the motherboard from the power supply. Figure 9-1 shows the connector used in the ATX and NLX form factors, and Figure 9-2 shows the two connectors used on the AT, Baby AT, and other AT-based forms. On each diagram, note the separate wires used to deliver different voltages for different parts of the PC.

Breaking down the power supply

A PC power supply is technically a switching power supply. A switching power supply uses a combination of high-frequency switching devices such as bipolar junction transistors (BJTs; also known as *normal transistors*), metallic oxide semiconductor field effect transistors (MOSFETs), insulated gate bipolar transistors, and Silicon Controlled Rectifier (SCR) thyristors to condition the converted power into pulsed waveform.

Here's a quick overview on what these electronic switching devices are:

♦ *Bipolar transistor:* An active semiconductor device that amplifies an electrical current.

♦ *Metal oxide semiconductor field effect transistor (MOSFET):* A transistor type that uses a layer of oxide as insulation between its conducting channel and gate terminal.

♦ *Silicon Controlled Rectifier:* A thyristor type designed specifically for unidirectional power switching and control.

♦ *Thyristor:* A semiconductor device that can be switched between off and on states. Thyristors are used for power switching applications.

Generally, you shouldn't work directly with the interior components of a power supply, but you might come across these terms when researching PC power supplies.

Converting the waveform

After the AC signal is rectified (see Figure 9-3), the output is a 150v–160v DC pulsed waveform current. At this point, a high-frequency transformer converts the pulsed waveform into the multiple output voltages needed by the PC, which are then rectified and filtered by a capacitor. A feedback signal controls the pulse frequency and width of the switching devices to maintain the proper voltage outputs.

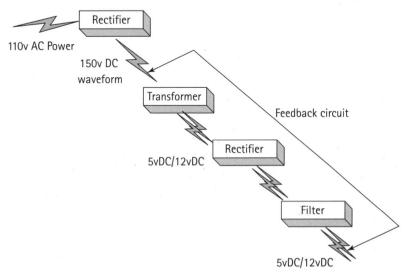

Figure 9-3: A simplified view of the power conversion process in a power supply.

Controlling the voltage

The PC power supply provides multiple voltage levels to the motherboard and connected peripherals, such as the disk drives. Each device and component in the PC is designed to operate on a certain vDC (volts of direct current) level, and the power supply rectifies the AC power input into these separate voltages. Here are the various voltages typically provided by a power supply:

- ◆ *+/-0 vDC:* Circuits with 0v (zero volts) DC provide the ground used to complete circuits with the other voltages on a PC. This is also referred to as the *common* or *earth ground.*

- ◆ *+2.8 vDC:* The latest voltage standard, which goes by no other name, is common on later Pentium-class motherboards beginning with the Pentium Pro with MMX, the AMD K6, and the Cyrix (VIA) 6x86L.

See Chapters 1 and 2 for more information on motherboards and processors, respectively.

♦ *+3.30 vDC:* Also called *standard voltage.* This voltage is common on the
ATX, NLX, and other newer form factors to provide power to Pentium
CPUs, memory, Accelerated Graphics Port (AGP) ports, and the other com-
ponents on the motherboard.

♦ *+3.38 vDC:* Also called *voltage reduced* (VR). Before the ATX form factor,
voltage regulators on the motherboard were used to reduce +5 vDC to
+3.38 vDC, which is why it is referred to as *reduced.*

♦ *+3.50 vDC/+3.52 vDC:* Also called *voltage reduced extended* (VRE). These
voltages are Intel adaptations of the VR standard.

♦ *+5 vDC:* Also called *system +5 volts.* Prior to the second generation of
Pentium processors, this was the primary voltage on the motherboard for
CPUs and most of their attached components. This is the standard voltage
on Baby AT power supplies and those preceding it. Most newer systems
now use +3.3 vDC.

♦ *–5 vDC:* This voltage level is now essentially obsolete. It was used on
some of the earliest PCs for floppy disk controllers and Industry Standard
Architecture (ISA) bus cards. For backward-compatibility purposes, most
power supplies still generate this voltage, but it mostly goes unused.

♦ *+12 vDC:* This voltage level is used to power devices directly connected to
the power supply, such as disk drive motors, the main cooling fan, and
other similar devices. Rarely is it used by the motherboard in a modern
PC; instead, it's passed onto the system bus slots for any cards that might
need it. Of course, drives are connected directly to the power supply
through their own connectors.

♦ *–12 vDC:* Like –5v, this voltage is a holdover from earlier systems, where
it was used on some serial ports. Most power supplies provide this voltage
for backward compatibility with older hardware.

Factoring power supply forms

Power supplies, like motherboards (see Chapter 1), are available in a variety of different form factors, typically matching the form factor of the motherboard and system case. With the exception of the early IBM PCs, most AT-class power supplies (which include the AT, Baby AT, ATX, and others) are roughly the same, differing only in their size and mounting requirements.

The size and shape of the system case has a direct bearing on the capabilities demanded of its power supply. Tower cases (see Chapter 8 for more information on system cases) are usually larger and require more watts of power output to run their hard drives, cooling systems, and accessories. Desktop or mini-tower cases are smaller overall and usually have fewer internal devices needing power, thus needing fewer watts of output from the power supply.

In general, a power supply's form factor refers to its general physical shape, fit, and size. A power supply's form factor must be the same as the system case and, in most instances, the same as the motherboard. Because the power supply is typically purchased as a part of the system case, matching the two is rarely an issue. Only when a power supply must be replaced does its form factor – and that of the case and motherboard – come up. However, newer designs of power supplies are compatible with more than one case form factor, and some cases can take any one of many power supply form factors. Take care to match the power requirements of the motherboard to the power supply, though.

Here is an overview of each of the form factors of the past and present:

◆ *PC XT:* The IBM PC and the IBM PC XT (extended technology) established the first form factor for power supplies as well as cases and motherboards. These desktop systems placed the power supply in the rear-right corner of the case, and an up-and-down toggle switch on the exterior of the power supply was used to power it on and off. The PC XT power supply was used in many early AT clones as well.

◆ *AT:* The power supply of the IBM PC AT (advanced technology; see Figure 9-4) was a little larger and had a slightly different shape and about three times the power wattage of the PC XT. The AT standard soon became the form factor of choice among clone manufacturers, who built a wide variety of AT-compatible systems. The AT form factor was the foundation of several form factors that followed.

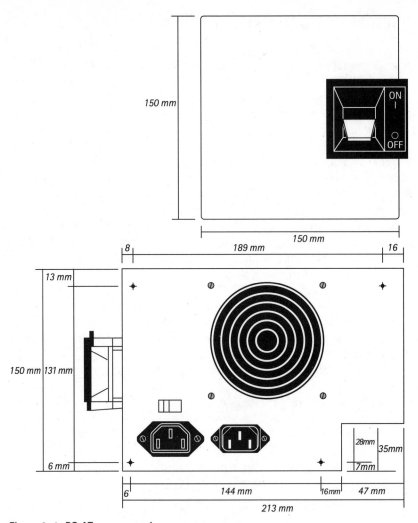

Figure 9-4: PC AT power supply.

♦ *Baby AT:* This form factor is a smaller version of the AT form factor. The Baby AT power supply, shown in Figure 9-5, is only 2" narrower, with the same height and depth. It is also compatible with the AT form factor in either tower or desktop case styles. The Baby AT, which sports the same motherboard and drive power connectors as the AT, was the most popular form factor for most of the late 1980s and early 1990s.

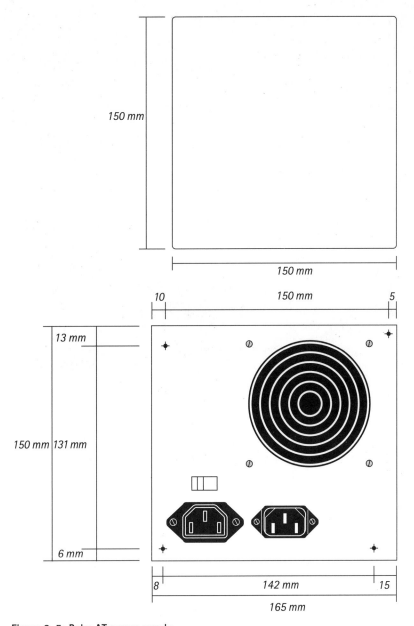

Figure 9–5: Baby AT power supply.

◆ *LPX:* Also known as the *slimline* or *PS/2* form factor, the LPX (low profile) power supply (see Figure 9-6) has a reduced height and general
dimension while maintaining the same power production, cooling ability,
and connectors as the Baby AT and AT. The LPX form factor has generally
replaced the Baby AT.

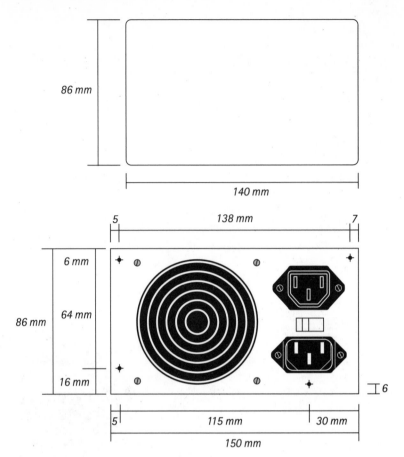

Figure 9-6: LPX (slimline) power supply.

◆ *ATX:* This form factor, introduced in 1995, was a major change over all previous form factors that were based on the PC XT and PC AT forms. The ATX form factor is generally considered the de facto standard for all PCs. On the outside, the ATX power supply (see Figure 9-7) is the same as the LPX power supply in size and where its cables and other components are placed. The most noticeable difference is the removal of the AC power pass-through outlet used for PC monitors on early form factors.

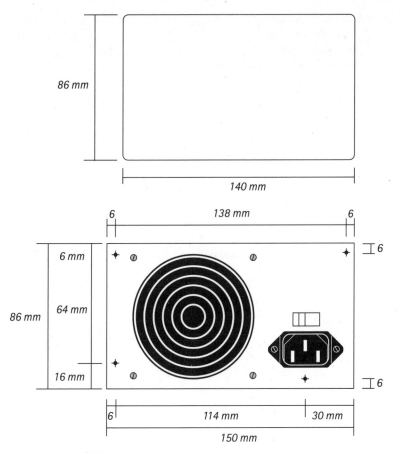

Figure 9-7: ATX/NLX power supply.

◆ *NLX:* The NLX form factor defines a motherboard and case design intended to replace the LPX form factor. Because it uses the same power supply as the ATX, the ATX power supply form factor is also referred to as the *ATX/NLX* form factor.

◆ *SFX:* This form factor, which is one of the few power supply-only form factors, was developed by Intel for use in the Micro-ATX and Flex-ATX form factors. Its acronym refers to its small form. Figure 9-8 shows a diagram of the SFX power supply.

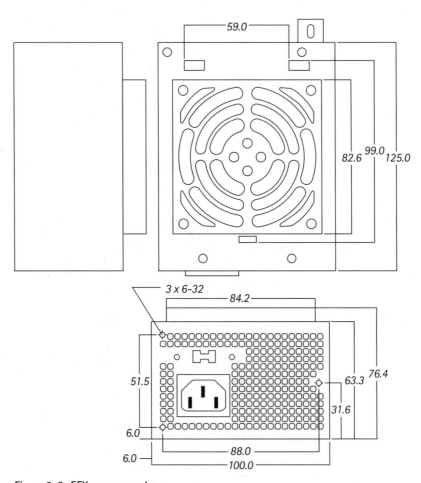

Figure 9-8: SFX power supply.

◆ *WTX:* The WTX form factor defines a form factor for motherboards, system cases, and power supplies for use in large workstations (which is where the *W* comes from) and servers. WTX is a modular design that locates parts of the PC into physical zones. The WTX power supply, shown in Figure 9-9, is larger and more powerful than most other power supplies. In addition to a range of power output options, it features two system cooling fans.

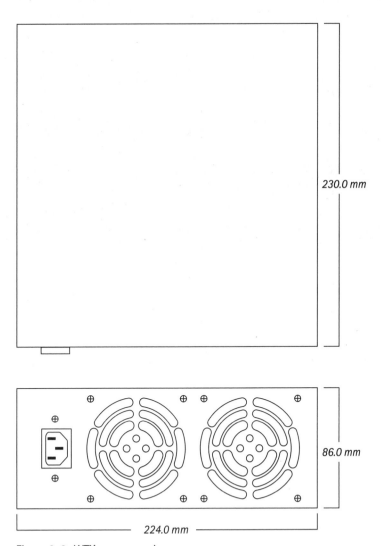

230.0 mm

86.0 mm

224.0 mm

Figure 9-9: WTX power supply.

Table 9-1 summarizes and compares the differences of the power supply form factors.

TABLE 9-1 POWER SUPPLY FORM FACTOR CHARACTERISTICS

Form Factor	Dimensions (W x D x H) in Inches	Case Style	Form Factors	Motherboard Connection
PC XT	8.8 x 5.7 x 4.8	Desktop	PC XT	AT
AT	8.5 x 6 x 6	Desktop or tower	AT	AT
Baby AT	6.6 x 6 x 6	Desktop or tower	Baby AT, AT	AT
LPX	6 x 5.6 x 3.4	Desktop	LPX, Baby AT, AT, ATX	AT
ATX/NLX	6 x 5.6 x 3.4	Desktop or tower	ATX, NLX	ATX
SFX	4 x 5 x 2.5	Desktop or tower	MicroATX, FlexATX, ATX, NLX	ATX
WTX	6 x 9.2 x 3.4 (single fan) 9 x 9.2 x 3.4 (double fan)	Tower	WTX	WTX

Table 9-2 lists the output voltages for each of the power supply form factors.

TABLE 9-2 POWER SUPPLY FORM FACTOR OUTPUT VOLTAGES

Form Factor	Output Voltage
PC XT	+/–12v, +/–5v
AT	+/–12v, +/–5v
Baby AT	+/–12v, +/–5v
LPX	+/–12v, +/–5v
ATX/NLX	+/–12v, +/–5v, +3.3v

Form Factor	Output Voltage
SPX	+/– 12v, +5v, +3.3v
WTX	+12v, +5v, +3.3v

Sorting out the ratings

On manufacturer's power supply specification lists, you're likely to find items such as operating range, frequency, efficiency, electromagnetic interference (EMI), output current, regulation, ripple percent, hold time, Power Good (PG) delay, agency approval, noise, and Mean Time Between Failures (MTBF). At the very least, the operating range (or power range), outputs, and safety approval (such as Underwriters' Laboratory [UL], Canadian UL [C-UL], or Technischer Uberwachungs-Verein [TUV]) should be listed. Some might also include their conformity with radio Federal Communications Commission (FCC) or the European Community for Electric and Electronic Equipment (CE) emissions standards.

The following are some definitions to help you understand what you find:

◆ *Agency approvals:* You should have a list of test and certification agencies for the power supply. This is your assurance that the power supply meets the safety, environmental, and regulatory requirements of your country or location. Some of these are the UL, Canadian Standards Association (CSA), TUV, and FCC. Among other tests, these companies and agencies rate and certify power supply designs, radio frequency (RF) and EMI emissions, environmental issues, and product safety.

◆ *Efficiency:* This is a ratio, expressed as a percentage, of how much output power is produced to the input power received.

◆ *EMI:* This lists the amount of electromagnetic noise generated by the power supply. The FCC puts limits on the amount of EMI that a power supply can produce.

◆ *Hold-up time:* This is the amount of time that output voltage continues to be provided following the loss of input voltage. This is an indication of the size of the power supply's capacitors and how much time you have until the uninterruptible power supply (UPS) takes over.

◆ *Line and load regulation: Line regulation* is the amount of change in the output voltage as it varies from the normal output voltage caused by fluctuations in the input voltage. *Load regulation* measures how output voltage changes as a percent of normal output voltage in respect to increases in output voltage load.

- *Mean Time Between Failures (MTBF):* This is generally an estimate based on the manufacturer's testing of how long the power supply will run before a failure. The larger this number is, the better.

- *Noise:* This is a rating in decibels (dB) of the actual noise that the power supply produces. Most of the noise produced from the power supply comes from the fan. Each 3 dB increment represents a 100 percent increase in the volume of the noise level.

- *Operating range:* This measures the minimum and maximum range of input voltages that the power supply can receive and still maintain an acceptable output voltage. A wide range denotes a power supply that can provide steady output even in areas with an unreliable or dirty power source.

- *Output current:* This is the maximum current in volts that the power supply can consistently produce and supply to the motherboard and the disk drives.

- *PG delay:* This is the amount of time that the power supply delays before sending the Power Good signal to the motherboard. This time is necessary to allow the power supply to warm up and start producing good DC power.

- *Ripple percent:* This is the amount of variance in the DC output levels because of incomplete rectification and filtering of the AC power input.

Protecting the PC

The power supply accounts for nearly one-third of the problems on a PC. This doesn't include the problems caused by the power supply that cannot be directly attributed to it, such as electronic components that are damaged over time by a faulty power supply. What causes the most problems with a power supply is the AC power source, which is generally an unreliable, noisy, and fluctuating electrical source.

Identifying electrical evils

A number of bad things are associated with AC power, most of which your PC can be protected against. You should be aware of these common electrical problems, listed here by severity (at least in my opinion):

- *Spike:* An electrical *spike* is an unexpected, (usually) short-duration, high-voltage event on the AC power line. A spike can be caused by a variety of events, such as lightning strikes, generator switchovers, power pole incidents (a car hitting one, for example), or large electrical motors on the same power source. The safeguard against an electrical spike is a surge suppressor or a UPS that includes surge suppression.

◆ *Power surge:* A *power surge (over-voltage)* is a high-voltage situation that raises the voltage above normal levels much like a spike but for a longer period of time. Often, it's a spike followed by a slow tapering of the power level back to normal. A large nearby electrical user can cause the power level on the source lines to surge or drop if that user suddenly cuts its power consumption. Although not as instantly damaging as a spike, surges can cause component failures, nonetheless. A surge suppressor or a UPS, which absorbs the increase in power, is good protection against a power surge.

◆ *Noise:* EMI and RFI are the two primary causes of line noise on the AC power line. Power cables can act as an antenna and pick up disruptive signals emitting from computer monitors, fluorescent lighting, electrical motors, radio transmitters, and natural phenomena, such as lightning. Avoid placing any device that causes an interruption or static on an amplitude modulation (AM) radio on the same electrical circuit as a PC. Some surge filters also include noise filters, but unless you're using a line conditioner, a UPS is your best bet to filter out line noise.

◆ *Blackout:* A *blackout* is a total loss of power. It can last anywhere from a split second to many days. If your power supply's Hold Up Time is greater than the amount of time that you're without power, you'll probably only notice a momentary flickering or dimming of your screen. The average Hold Up Time is around $\frac{1}{20}$ of a second. Anything longer than that, and your PC will probably reboot itself. The best defense against a blackout is a UPS.

◆ *Brownout:* A *brownout* is the opposite of a spike, except that a brownout can last for some time. If the voltage lingers too long below the nominal point, the result can be the same as a blackout or worse. Brownouts can destroy components by causing a power supply to draw too much current to make up for the low voltage. A UPS can protect against a brownout by making up the difference between the low voltage level and what is the normal voltage level.

Suppressing the surge

Many of the power strips and plug strips on the market, like the one shown in Figure 9-10, also contain surge suppressors (also know as *surge protectors*). The active component in a surge suppressor is a metallic oxide varistor (MOV) that reacts to over-voltage situations and diverts (or shunts) the power to a grounding circuit.

Surge suppressors are rated by the amount of electrical power that they can divert. The measurement unit is *Joules,* which measures the amount of electricity that the suppressor can absorb and not pass through. An MOV is essentially a one-shot device, much like a fuse. If an MOV is triggered by a power surge, its life (and usefulness) is over. And in most cases, you cannot tell whether it's been triggered.

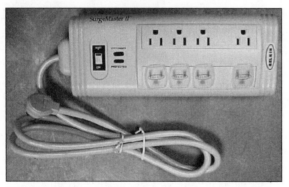

Figure 9-10: A plug strip that includes a surge suppressor.

Some power strips include a lighted fuse in series with the MOV that should also blow when a surge takes out the MOV. Sometimes the lighted fuse blows with a smaller surge, leaving the MOV to handle the next large surge or group of smaller surges. On the other hand, the fuse can be strong enough to withstand a small surge that might be strong enough to wear down the MOV. It might not take all that many small surges to knock out the MOV, while the fused light shines on.

Some surge suppressors have more advanced surge interception technology such as gas discharge tubes and pellet arrestors, which are a little slower to react, but these types of suppression devices can be used more than once.

UPS-scaling protection

A *UPS* is a large battery and battery charger that provides a PC or server with protection against short-term power outages, surges, spikes, and brownouts. A UPS monitors its input voltage (AC power), and when the voltage level deviates more than a certain percentage from normal, switches electrical service from its battery. The DC battery power stored in the UPS is passed through an inverter to create an AC supply for the PC (which immediately converts it back to DC power). Figure 9-11 shows the back panel of the type of UPS commonly found in an office setting.

The best UPSes supply power to the PC when needed in a smooth wave, which is probably better than the original AC source. Less-expensive UPSes can provide the power in a square wave, which can contain potentially harmful frequencies that can damage sensitive equipment. However, note this compromise between the expensive and the inexpensive: namely, UPS units that produce a wave made up of several small square wave steps. Some unfavorable frequency harmonics still exist — but a lot fewer. When buying a UPS, be sure that you're aware of the type of wave output that it provides.

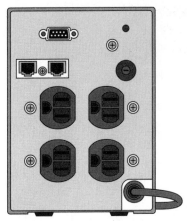

Figure 9-11: The back panel of an APC SU620Net
uninterruptible power supply (UPS).

CATEGORIZING UPS DEVICES

UPS units are available in two general categories based on how they store and provide electrical power. The two categories are

◆ *Standby UPS:* This type of UPS generally does nothing more than provide a battery backup to the PC connected to it as a safeguard against a power failure (blackout) or a low-voltage event (brownout). In standby mode, the UPS draws off a small amount of power to charge its battery and passes unfiltered AC power on to the PC. In the event of a blackout, the standby UPS provides the PC with an AC power source. The switchover does take some time, which increases the importance of the PC power supply's hold-out time. If the hold-out is long enough to cover the switchover time, you shouldn't have any serious problems. One of the downsides to most standby units is that any large surges, spikes, or low-voltage events will most likely be passed through the UPS to the PC.

◆ *Online (or inline) UPS:* An *online (inline) UPS* provides power to a PC through an AC power service provided from the UPS' battery and a power inverter that converts the battery's DC power to AC power. The UPS' battery is constantly being recharged from an AC power source through an input inverter. An online UPS requires no switchover because the UPS absorbs any events, such as spikes and blackouts, on the AC power line. An extended brownout would begin discharging the UPS' battery, which would eventually fail without the AC power being restored. Essentially, the PC runs on AC produced by the battery, and the battery is being constantly kept charged while there is input power. Figure 9-12 shows a large inline UPS that would be used to protect one or more servers on a network.

Figure 9-12: A rackmount UPS used for network servers.

UPS CHARACTERISTICS

Here is a list of characteristics that you should keep in mind when choosing a UPS:

◆ *Simple or interactive displays or warnings:* Even the least-expensive UPS on the market tries to give a warning near the end of its charge. Low-end (meaning low-price) UPSes sound a beep at given battery charge levels, but it's up to you to guess how much of the battery's charge remains. A better UPS has light-emitting diode (LED) gauges to show the current level of charge, as well as how much is being demanded, to allow you to make an educated guess as to how much time you have to shut down your system before the battery is dead. The best UPSes display an estimate in minutes and seconds on their control panel based on the current battery level and draw rate.

◆ *Warning mechanisms:* A UPS designed to support a single computer will generally have a serial "heartbeat" cable that's attached to a serial (COM) port on the PC. The UPS generates a regular signal that's monitored by a background process running on the PC. If the UPS fails to signal – in other words, misses too many heartbeats – the monitoring software (typically supplied by the UPS' manufacturer or part of the PC's operating system) tries to gracefully shut down the PC.

A UPS that features monitoring is very important to use with servers that cache a lot of data in memory instead of on a hard disk to speed data access times. In this case, if the power suddenly fails, all the cached data would be lost if it couldn't be saved to disk before a shutdown or sync request.

A newer UPS is as likely to use a USB cable as the serial cable. The heartbeat signal can also be broadcast over a network from a UPS that supports multiple servers. The UPS monitor checks incoming Transmission Control Protocol/Internet Protocol (TCP/IP) messages and sorts out the information coming from its UPS. The downside to this is if the server loses communication with the UPS (pulled cable, bad hub, and so on), the server might shut down even though power is available.

◆ *Software interfaces:* The software monitor that interacts with the UPS in real time (see previous bullet) is typically supplied by the manufacturer of the UPS. At minimum, these software programs monitor the heartbeat signal sent by the UPS to indicate that power is still available. If the UPS stops sending the signal, the software begins the process to perform a system shutdown. Advanced systems are available that display console messages, send an e-mail, or dial a pager to notify the system administrator. These systems also usually include support for remote status checking.

◆ *Line conditioners and alarm systems:* A true *line conditioner* (also known as a *power conditioner*) filters the incoming power to isolate line noise and keep voltage levels normal. It isolates the input power source from the output power in a transformer stage. A line conditioner can't protect against a power outage, but it can smooth out any intermittent under- and over-voltage (surge and spike) events that occur on the input source. When the input power becomes unreliable, a line conditioner (and most UPS units for that matter) sends up an alarm if it detects that there are more problems on the line than it can handle.

Working with Power Supplies

Whether diagnosing, troubleshooting, or repairing a power supply, the very first thing that you must understand about working on a power supply is that you should never – repeat, **never** – open the power supply case and work inside the unit.

 The amount of electrical voltage stored in the capacitor of the power supply is more than enough to hurt you — or perhaps worse. And if that isn't enough reason, you could accidentally damage the internal components of the power supply, which could in turn destroy the motherboard, disk drives, and other electrical parts of a PC.

However, you can use a number of processes to isolate power supply problems. In the following sections, I detail the processes used for the most common power-supply-related problems on a PC.

Gathering the tools

Here is a list of tools that you need, followed by some general troubleshooting steps used when working with power supplies:

◆ Diagonal cutters

◆ Screwdrivers (including Torx bits)

◆ Needle-nose pliers

◆ Multimeter or digital voltage meter (DVM)

◆ An AC power monitor that plugs into a wall outlet (such as Tasco)

◆ Soldering iron

◆ Cable ties

◆ Continuity tester

◆ Variac (variable power supply)

Notice that an electrostatic discharge (ESD) wrist strap is missing from this list. The power supply has a big nasty capacitor in it that you really don't want to ground through your body. But you weren't planning to open up the power supply, anyway, were you (hint, hint)? If the power supply is bad, it's generally inexpensive to replace the whole thing. Those big, bright warning labels aren't there for decoration. Read them and heed their warnings.

Deciding when to troubleshoot a power supply

The power supply is obviously a very important component of the PC, but did you know that it's also the one most likely to fail? Day in and day out, it suffers the slings and arrows of mean and nasty electrical power, sacrificing itself for the good of your computer. A recent study shows that on average, the common workstation or desktop PC suffers over 120 power events every month. Not surprisingly, it can develop problems.

Three conditions require that you check out or troubleshoot the power supply:

◆ *Upgrading the system:* You're planning a big upgrade (new motherboard, new hard drive, DVD, and the works) and you're worried that your power supply could be too weak to handle the new load.

When upgrading, remember that a power supply is rated by its power output in watts. You can get from 100- to 600-watt power supplies to fit the common form factors (ATX and LTX). Unless you're planning to build a superserver with quad Pentium Xeons, a DVD, an internal tape drive, and four or five internal Small Computer System Interface (SCSI) drives (in which case you'll need to look into the WTX form factor), a power supply rated between 230–350 watts works well for most average systems.

♦ *Intermittent problems:* If to no avail, you've tried everything that you can to track down an intermittent problem on the motherboard without isolating the problem, the power supply might be the real culprit if the problem is at all related to a power issue.

How can you tell whether the power supply is going bad? These telltale signs can tip you off that the power supply is on its way to failure: overheating, occasional boot failures or errors, frequent parity errors, noisy operation, or mild electrical shocks when you touch the case.

If you ever receive a shock other than ESD when you touch the case, you have power supply problems of the first magnitude. Replace the power supply immediately!

♦ *Catastrophic problems:* If smoke is coming out of the power supply or off the motherboard, the power supply has probably gone awry and needs to be replaced. If the system fan has stopped turning, you absolutely need to replace the power supply. You should also test the motherboard with a new power supply and also be on watch for parity errors, system lockups that become more frequent, and disk read and peripheral input/output (I/O) errors. These are signs of damaged motherboard components beginning to fail.

Isolating the power supply as a source of a problem

Here are some steps that you should use any time that you suspect that the power supply is the source of a PC problem:

1. First, determine that the problem isn't something as trivial as a blown fuse caused by a legitimate overload.

Be sure to remove the source of the overload before beginning work.

2. Try to classify the problem by when it occurs and what it affects. The categories that you might use are a BIOS, boot, or startup problem; an input power-related problem; an output power-related problem; excessive noise, ripple, or other power conversion errors; or a catastrophic failure that poses a danger to the system or the operator (especially the technician).

3. Based on the form factor, determine what the proper output voltages should be and measure the output of the appropriate pins.

Read the documentation for your power supply. Some power supplies cannot have their electrical load removed (meaning that they must stay connected to the motherboard or disk drives) without causing damage to the power supply. AT power supplies and earlier form factors are generally safe to remove, but check the documentation anyway.

Ruling out the power supply

If the general steps listed in the previous section don't solve or identify a problem with the power supply – or if they prove inconclusive – the problem could still be the power supply even when the problem shows up elsewhere. You can safely bet that when an electrical power problem exists on the PC (regardless of where it shows up), the power supply is involved in the cause in some way.

One of the quickest and easiest ways to troubleshoot a computer power supply is to put your hand in front of the cooling fan. If you don't feel any air passing into or out of the fan, chances are that the power supply is bad. One exception to this test is that an ATX form factor motherboard might have a bad PS_ON switch.

The most effective way to absolutely, positively tell whether a power supply is the cause of a problem is to swap it out. If the problem is solved after you install a replacement power supply, there you are. However, if the new power supply doesn't solve the problem, the problem lies elsewhere. Don't jump to the conclusion that the old power supply is vindicated. Before you decide to put the old power supply back in its PC or put it on the shelf as a ready spare, try putting it in another system to see whether it works there. Unfortunately, some problems that can be caused by a power supply with a low-level or intermittent problem can take days, weeks, or months to show up.

If the computer case is still under warranty, you don't have to send the entire computer case back just to return a faulty power supply. The computer case has at least four or five major components, and the power supply is one of two electrical parts (the other is the front panel) that can be Dead on Arrival

(DOA). Most manufacturers or resellers will likely want to replace the faulty part rather than the entire system case. Shipping back only the power supply will also save you money on the shipping charges.

Diagnosing POST power problems

You can run into situations that require you to know the symptoms that indicate a power supply problem. Here are a few of the leading symptoms that indicate an ailing power supply:

- ◆ The power light on the front panel is off.
- ◆ The power supply fan isn't operating.
- ◆ The computer either sounds a continuous beep or doesn't beep at all.
- ◆ The computer sounds a repeating short beep.
- ◆ The computer displays either a POST error in the 020–029 series (Power Good signal error) or a parity error.

Nothing happens when the power switch is turned on

If you switch on a PC and nothing happens (meaning no lights, beeps, and so on), here are some steps that you can use to determine whether the power supply is the problem:

1. Check to see whether the PC's power cord is plugged into an AC power outlet on a surge protector or a UPS and into the PC.

2. Check the surge suppressor switch to see whether it's on and working properly. If it appears that no AC power is being provided, move the plug to a different outlet. If no power is available on more than one outlet, check the building's circuit breakers.

3. If power is available at the wall plug, either the power supply's switch is bad, or the power supply itself has completely failed.

   In either case, you should replace the power supply.

The fan isn't spinning

The fan is a very important part of the cooling system designed into the case and motherboard form factor. If it's not spinning, something is wrong – and if not replaced, this could cause serious damage to the PC.

Never insert anything like a screwdriver blade into the fan to turn the blades in an attempt to make it go. There is a serious shock hazard inside the power supply.

Use compressed air to clean around the spindle of the fan, blowing the air through the fan grill that's located on the outside of the case. Before you do this, remove the system case cover and perhaps even take the unit outside, depending on how dirty it is. If nothing is obviously impeding the fan from spinning, immediately replace the power supply.

 Do not open the power supply to replace the fan because of the electrical shock danger that lurks inside the power supply.

The PC doesn't boot and has no sign of power

If the PC doesn't boot and shows no sign of power, here are some things to check:

1. Check whether the outlet (such as the surge suppressor, UPS, or wall outlet) into which the PC is plugged has power. If it does, check that the cord is seated tightly and snuggly at the PC end and plugged in all the way on the outlet end.

2. Disconnect everything from the back of the computer except the power and then boot the computer. If the PC boots, add back one connector at a time, rebooting after each one is added, until the PC fails to boot.

   If the PC fails to boot after a certain device is added, switch your focus to that device because the problem (this time) isn't the power supply.

   If the problem seems to have gone away after you reconnect all the devices to the PC, the problem was probably a loose connection – or something else that you should be looking for as an intermittent occurrence.

3. Obviously, if the computer won't boot or power up with just the power cord attached, you should replace the power supply.

   As you'll find, the easiest way to solve a power supply problem, especially pesky ones that are hard to pin down, is to replace the power supply and not waste your time trying to track down a specific problem that will cause you to replace the power supply anyway.

An ATX system doesn't work when the power is turned on

An *ATX power supply* is soft-switched through the power supply switch on the motherboard and the functions in the system BIOS. An ATX power supply also requires a load to operate, and connecting it to the motherboard supplies a part of that load. Thus, if you install an ATX power supply in a system, don't expect it to work until you connect it to a motherboard that also has a microprocessor, memory, and a video card installed on it.

If you install an ATX power supply and it fails to power up, the problem could lie in the motherboard, processor, memory, or video card — or not.

The ATX power supply, which is not compatible in Baby AT cases, allows for *soft-switching* — controlling the power on and off functions under motherboard control. The ATX power supply uses a one-piece connector that's keyed to fit in only one way, which prevents the possibility of frying the motherboard as well as possibly injuring yourself. The power supply also eliminates the need for a motherboard voltage regulator by providing *split voltage,* which is a range of voltages, usually 12v, 5v, and 3.3v, to the motherboard.

Setting the input voltage selector switch

If you're located in North America (Canada, United States, and Mexico), your voltage selector (usually located on the back of the power supply near the fan grill) should be set to 110–115v. If you're located in Europe or another country outside of North America, the voltage selector switch should probably be set to 220–230v.

If your computer is a laptop, notebook, or other portable computer manufactured in the past few years, it probably has a built-in voltage detector that automatically switches the voltage setting for you.

Because the vast majority of cases and power supplies are manufactured outside of North America, the power supply was probably tested with a 220v setting. If this setting isn't reset for 110v for use in North America, when you first plug in a PC right out of the box, it will appear to be DOA because of a dead power supply. Before you use any PC right out of the box — except notebook computers — first check the voltage selector switch to make sure that it's set for the right voltage.

Testing power supply peripheral connectors with a DVM

If you keep a PC for any time at all, you'll probably need to replace the power supply at some point. Here are the steps used to test the power leads going to the peripheral devices:

1. Turn off the PC.

   If the PC is an AT or earlier form factor, it should remain connected to the wall outlet. However, if it's an ATX or later, unplug it from the wall outlet.

ATX motherboards are always on and carry enough juice to power up the PC. Therefore, unplugging these systems before placing metal objects, such as screwdrivers, inside the case is a good idea.

2. Remove the system case covers, watching for any grounding wires attached to the case.

   If you have one or more of these wires, leave them attached if possible.

3. Set your DVM or multimeter to read DC volts in the range higher than 12v.

4. Locate a power supply connector (see Figure 9-13), either an unused one or by disconnecting one from the floppy disk or CD-ROM.

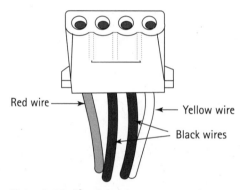

Red wire ──────→   ←── Yellow wire
                                   Black wires

Figure 9-13: A peripheral power connector.

You use this connector to perform a test on the power supply. The pinning that you will need for the test is listed in Table 9-3.

5. Power on the PC.

6. Insert the black probe of the DVM (it should have two probes: a black and a red) into the power connector on one of the two black wires in the center two holes. See Figures 9-13 and 9-14.

7. With the black probe in place, touch the red probe to the connector on the red wire of the power connector.

   You should get a reading of +5v DC.

8. Touch the red probe to the connector on the yellow wire of the power connector.

   You should get a reading of +12v DC.

9. If either or both of the readings in Steps 7 and 8 are wrong, retest.

   If neither test gives a reading, replace the power supply.

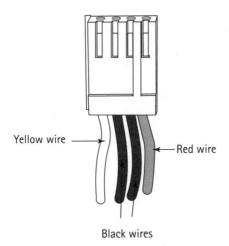

Yellow wire ⟶   ⟵ Red wire

Black wires

Figure 9-14: The floppy drive power connector.

TABLE 9-3 POWER SUPPLY CONNECTOR PINOUTS

Pin	Signal	Color
4	+5v DC	Red
3	Ground	Black
2	Ground	Black
1	+12v DC	Yellow

Correctly sizing a UPS

A UPS is rated in volt-amps (VA) and can range from 200VA to greater than 5000VA. With a UPS, you definitely get what you pay for. The higher the volt-amps, the more powerful the UPS is – and in direct proportion, the higher the price tag will be.

The VA rating of a UPS is the amount of VA that the UPS can supply for a five-minute period. A UPS with a 500VA rating can deliver 500VA for five minutes. This assumes that the UPS has a load equal to its rating. If the load on a 500VA UPS were only 250VA, the UPS would be able to supply power for 20 minutes.

Before picking the UPS for your PC, you should determine the amount of VA that it needs to continue running for as long as you need it. Fifteen minutes is generally considered ample time to shut down a system properly without a loss of data. Remember that the more VA a UPS is rated for, the more it will cost. You can certainly find a UPS to power your PC for an hour, but the cost will be very high.

Use the following calculation to determine about how long you have before your UPS is exhausted:

```
(Max. amp draw x 120) + (Power supply (in watts) x 1.4) = Total Volt Amps Required
```

Here is what the terms included in the above formula mean:

◆ *Maximum amp draw x 120:* This calculates the total amps of all the devices in or attached to the PC to be powered by the UPS, including the internal devices (such as the hard disk, CD-ROM, and the like) and the external devices (such as the monitor or modem).

◆ *Power supply (in watts) x 1.4:* This calculates the watts rating of your computer's power supply.

After you calculate the total VA required, how much of the UPS' reserve power that you wish to draw has a direct bearing on how long it can supply power to your system:

◆ *Full draw:* Drawing as many volt-amps as the UPS' rating should provide you with about seven minutes of power.

◆ *Half draw:* Placing a load on the UPS at about one-half its rating provides about 20 minutes of power.

For example, if the total volt-amps required by a PC is 350 and the UPS' rating is 700VA, the UPS should supply power for at least 15 minutes and perhaps as long as 20 minutes.

Table 9-4 lists the VA draw for several common peripheral devices. The manufacturer or reseller of your PC should be able to tell you the VA requirements of your entire system. You can also try checking Web sites of the manufacturers of each of the major components of the PC.

TABLE 9-4 COMMON VA USAGE

Device or Component	VA Usage
CD-ROM	20–25
Small expansion card	5
Large expansion card	10–15
3.5" floppy drive	5

Device or Component	VA Usage
Pentium II processor	38
Motherboard	20–35

Taking preventive measures

Things that you can do to lengthen the life of a power supply include many environmental, hardware-related, and common sense activities:

♦ The better the environment is for the PC, the better it will perform, just like for its human operator. Run the computer in a cool, moderately humid environment. The cooler the air entering the fan, the better. The power supply produces heat like all other transformers. Use an air-conditioned room if possible.

♦ Either reduce the amount of dust and smoke in the air around the computer or plan to clean the inside of the system case and fan often. Blow the dust bunnies off the fan and power supply grills frequently with compressed air. It can't hurt to do the same for the inside of the case occasionally, either.

♦ Use a surge protector – or better yet, a true line conditioner – and by all means, a UPS.

Part III

Storage Devices

Chapter 10

Working with Hard Disks

IN THIS CHAPTER

Originally, PCs didn't have hard disk drives, but it's now hard to imagine a PC without one. Virtually every PC sold over the last eight or more years has had at least one hard disk drive.

Primary storage is the PC's main memory or RAM (see Chapter 6 for more information about memory) and serves as the PC's active storage that temporarily stores data and instructions while they're in use by the system. The hard disk (along with the floppy disk and CD-ROM) is a *secondary storage* device that provides permanent storage for the user's data, programs, and other objects, even after the power goes off. In this chapter, I discuss

- ◆ How a hard disk is organized
- ◆ The parts of a hard disk
- ◆ How a disk accepts, reads, and writes data
- ◆ How to partition, format, and install a hard disk

THE HARD DISK is by far the most commonly used form of secondary storage. The future of disk storage definitely includes the hard disk drive, although not perhaps in the form that you know today.

Studying the Hard Disk Drive

The hard disk used in virtually all PCs is derived from mainframe fixed disks of the 1960s/1970s and the early Winchester drives, which were introduced in the 1980s and provided a prototype for today's hard disks. The technology used to record data on a hard disk has remained essentially the same as that used on the early drives, although the size of the drive is quite smaller, its speeds are much faster, and the capacity is very much larger.

 Because the floppy disk came first, hard drives were given the moniker *hard* to differentiate them from floppy disks.

Organizing data on a disk drive

Hard disks (and floppy disks) organize media into logical divisions: cylinders, tracks, sectors, and clusters. This organization, along the servo system on the disk (see "Servo systems" later in this chapter), is the foundation of the addressing system used to locate, store, and retrieve data on the disk.

The basic organization elements on hard and floppy disks are

♦ *Tracks:* A floppy disk has around 80 tracks, and a hard disk can have 1,000 tracks or more. Figure 10-1 illustrates how disk tracks are concentric bands that complete one circumference of the disk. The first track on a disk, typically track 0, is on the outside edge of the disk.

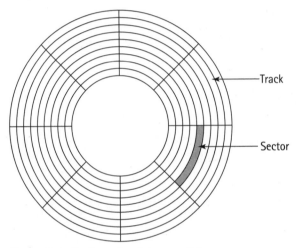

Figure 10-1: Tracks and sectors on a disk.

♦ *Sectors:* Disks are divided into cross-sections that intersect across all tracks, as illustrated in Figure 10-1. The result is that each track is broken into a number of addressable pieces, called sectors. A *sector* is 512 bytes in length; a hard disk has from 100 to 300 sectors per track, and a floppy disk from 9 to 18 sectors per track. Sectoring creates addressable elements on a track, including its starting point.

♦ *Cylinders:* All the tracks with the same number on all the *platters* (the flat round metallic disks located inside the hard disk) of a hard disk drive create a logical entity called a *cylinder.* The read/write heads of a disk move in unison and are all over the same track number on each disk platter. A hard disk with three platters, as illustrated in Figure 10-2, has six disk surfaces and six track 52s, which logically create cylinder 52. Cylinders are not used on floppy disks.

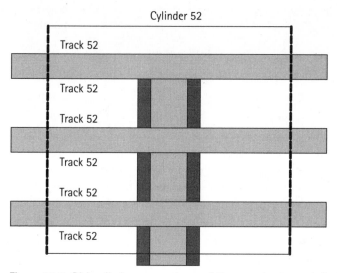

Cylinder 52

Track 52

Track 52

Track 52

Track 52

Track 52

Track 52

Figure 10-2: Disk cylinders are made up of the same tracks on each platter.

◆ *Clusters: Clusters* are logical groupings of disk sectors used by operating systems to track and transfer data to and from the disk. Typically, a cluster comprises around 64 sectors, but the total capacity of the disk drive and the operating system determine the number of sectors in a cluster on any particular PC. Operating systems that use clusters as the basic transfer unit operate in *block mode.*

Reviewing disk capacities

Disk drive capacities are stated in megabytes (millions of bytes; MB) and gigabytes (billions of bytes; GB), but drives with terabyte (trillions of bytes; TB) capacity are beginning to appear. Table 10-1 lists the common data capacity measurements used with disk drives.

TABLE 10-1 DATA CAPACITY MEASUREMENTS

Measurement	Abbreviation	Capacity
Kilobyte	K	One thousand bytes
Megabyte	MB	One million bytes
Gigabyte	GB	One billion bytes
Terabyte	TB	One trillion bytes

Continued

Tᴀʙʟᴇ 10-1 DATA CAPACITY MEASUREMENTS *(Continued)*

Measurement	Abbreviation	Capacity
Petabyte	PB	One quadrillion bytes
Exabyte	EB	One quintillion bytes

 Most hard disk drives available today are in the 1 to 40GB range and come in many different types and styles. However, they use the same basic components, are constructed essentially the same way, and operate the same. Where they differ is in their storage capacities and speeds, how they encode the data, and the interface used to communicate with the PC.

Looking inside the disk drive

A typical hard disk has the following major components (see Figure 10-3):

- ◆ Disk platters
- ◆ Spindle and spindle motor
- ◆ Storage media
- ◆ Read/write heads
- ◆ Head actuators
- ◆ Air filter
- ◆ Logic and controller boards
- ◆ Connectors and jumpers

Differentiating Logical and Physical Entities

When discussing disk drives, the term *logical* is used quite often, usually in a context that's not all that logical at all. A *logical* entity is one that's created logically, meaning *with software*. For example, when a disk is formatted (see "Formatting a hard disk drive" later in the chapter"), system software logically creates the tracks, sectors, cylinders, and so on that are used to address the disk. These entities don't physically exist; that is, they're not hard etched into the recording media permanently. Hope that helps.

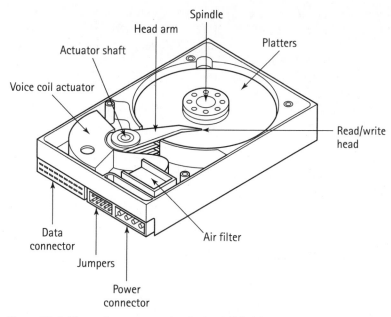

Figure 10-3: The major components of a hard disk drive.

With the exception of the connectors and jumpers and the controller board, all the other components on this list are inside the metal enclosure of the disk drive, called the Head Disk Assembly (HDA). The *HDA* is a sealed unit that is never opened outside of the factory.

DISK PLATTERS

Platters, the primary components of a hard disk drive, are where data stored in the hard disk is recorded. Hard disk platters are made from two primary materials: aluminum alloy and a glass-ceramic composite. Aluminum alloy has been used for hard disk platters almost from the beginning because it provides strength in a light-weight material. However, aluminum platters expand and flex when heated, which can resort in misreads and corrupted data. Consequently, a glass-ceramic material is now used for most disk platters.

Glass-ceramic platters only need to be about half the thickness of an aluminum disk to have the same rigidity. Glass disks do not expand nor contract as the temperature changes, which means the hard disk is more reliable. As the size of disk drives continues to shrink while the amount of data is increasing, all hard disks will probably be manufactured with glass-ceramic platters. Many of the top hard disk manufacturers already use glass composite materials, including Seagate, Toshiba, and Maxtor.

PC hard drives have between one and ten platters, with the majority using two platters to store data. The smaller form factor hard disks use either one or two platters. The number of platters used is controlled by the overall size of the disk drive. The form factor of the hard disk drive is derived from the diameter of its platters. However, the form factor can also represent the size of the drive bay into which the drive can be installed.

The common hard disk form factors with the platter sizes in each are listed in Table 10-2.

TABLE 10-2 COMMON PC HARD DISK DRIVE FORM FACTORS

Form Factor	Platter Size
5.25"	5.12" (130 millimeters [mm])
2.5"	2.5" (63.5 mm)
3.5"	3.74" (95 mm)
1.8"	1.8" (45.7 mm)

 The 3.5" form factor drive is the most popular of the disk drives listed in Table 10-2 and has been for some years now. Prior to that, the 5.25" drive was used in most desktop and tower-style PCs. The 2.5" drive and 1.8" drives are popular in notebook computers because of their size and weight.

Platters are mounted to a spindle inside the HDA (see Figure 10-4). The platters are separated with disk spacers that keep them evenly spaced and provide the space needed for the read/write heads to access the data on each side of the platter. Each surface of the platter is polished and covered with a very thin layer of magnetic material that is used to hold the electromagnetic charge representing the data stored on the disk.

SPINDLE MOTOR

As I discuss in the preceding section, the platters are mounted to the disk spindle, as illustrated in Figure 10-4. The spindle (and the platters mounted to it) is rotated by the spindle motor at speeds of 3,600, 4,800, 5,400, and 7,200 revolutions per minute (rpm). Many newer hard disk drives have rotational speeds of 10,000 or 15,000 rpm. The spindle motor is a direct-drive motor mounted to the bottom on the spindle assembly.

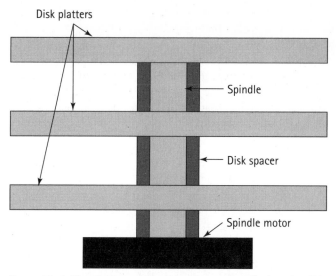

Disk platters

Spindle

Disk spacer

Spindle motor

Figure 10-4: The platters of the disk drive are attached to the disk spindle.

The spindle motor, shown in Figure 10-5, is connected directly to the spindle. No belts or gears are used in this mechanism in order to eliminate noise and vibration that could cause read/write problems on the platters. Two types of spindle motors are used in hard disk drives: in-hub motors that are placed inside the HDA and bottom-mount motors that are placed outside the HDA. The spindle disk motor, which is a brushless and sensorless DC motor, is designed to prevent oil or dust from contaminating the sealed dust-free environment inside the HDA. Special seals are placed in the spindle drive assembly to prevent the lubricating oil that can turn into a mist from the spindle motor's high rotation rates from getting inside the HDA. The spindle motor is obviously a vital part of the disk drive's operation, but because of its speeds and constant use, many hard disk failures are the result of a spindle motor failure.

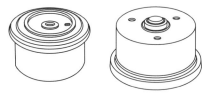

Figure 10-5: Views of a spindle motor.

STORAGE MEDIA

Data is stored on a hard disk (or a floppy disk) by using electromagnetic principles (see "Recording data on the disk" later in this chapter) that are used to alter the particles of the disk media placed on each side of a disk platter. The quality of the storage media can directly affect the performance of the disk drive.

The two types of media used on hard disk platters are

◆ *Oxide media:* The type of media used on older disk drives, *oxide media* are relatively soft materials that are easily damaged by a head crash (when the read/write head strikes the disk's surface). The primary ingredient in oxide media is ferrous oxide (iron rust).

◆ *Thin-film media:* This is the media used on virtually all disk drives manufactured today. *Thin-film media* is an extremely thin layer of metals that is plated on disk platters by using a process similar to plating the chrome on your car. Thin-film media is harder and thinner, allowing stronger magnetic fields to be stored in smaller areas.

READ/WRITE HEADS

The hard disk's read/write heads are constructed with a magnetic core that's wrapped by one or more electrical wires through which an electrical current is passed in one direction or the other to change the polarity of the magnetic field emanating from the core. As the read/write head passes over the magnetic media, the polarity of the core is changed as needed to change the value stored in a certain location on the platter's magnetic media (see "Storage media" earlier in this chapter for more information on the magnetic media on the disk platter).

Each side of a disk platter has magnetic media to store data and at least one read/write head. Figure 10-6 illustrates a disk drive with two disk platters or four read/write heads (one for each platter surface). The read/write head for each surface is connected to an actuator mechanism that moves the read/write heads in and out together, moving between the inside edge near the spindle to the outside edge of the platter. When the read/write head over the top platter (or disk 0) is over track 29, all the other read/write heads are also over track 29 on the other platter surfaces. While the read/write heads are moved around the disk surfaces, only one head is active at a time.

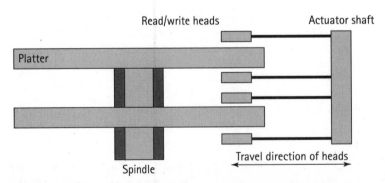

Figure 10-6: Each platter has a read/write head for each of its sides.

What's New in Read/Write Head Technology?

The four types of read/write heads that have been or are currently used in hard disk drives are

- ◆ **Ferrite heads:** This is the oldest, biggest, and heaviest of the magnetic head designs. Because of its size, it uses a larger floating height to guard against contacting the disk surface. Ferrite heads use an iron-oxide core that's wrapped with an electromagnetic coil, which is energized to create a magnetic field.

- ◆ **Metal-in-Gap (MIG):** This type of read/write head is an enhanced version of the ferrite head. Additional metal is added to the head on the leading and trailing edges of the head gap that allows it to ignore nearby fields and focus only on the fields beneath the head.

- ◆ **Thin-film (TF):** This type of read/write head is manufactured from semiconductor material (see Chapter 2) and is used in small form factor high-capacity drives. They are light and much more accurate than the ferrite heads and operate much closer to the disk surface.

- ◆ **Magneto-resistive (MR):** This type of head is used in most 3.5" disk drives with a capacity over 1GB as the read head. Disk drives with MR heads typically also have a TF head for writing data.

HEAD ACTUATORS

A *head actuator* positions the hard disk's read/write heads by extending and retracting the heads over the platters. The two types of actuators used on modern hard disk drives are stepper motor and voice coil actuators. These two types of actuators are very different. A *stepper motor* actuator is slow, sensitive to temperature changes, and less reliable than a voice coil actuator. A *voice coil* actuator is fast, unaffected by temperature changes, and extremely reliable. Despite their deficiencies, stepper motor actuators are less expensive, which makes them desirable to some manufacturers. The type of actuator used in a disk drive speaks volumes about the drive's performance, reliability, and cost.

A stepper motor is an electrical motor that moves in a series of steps. The motor cannot stop between steps and must advance from one step to the next to operate. On a disk drive that uses a stepper motor actuator to move the read/write heads, the stepper motor is located outside the HDA and connects to the head arm gang through a sealed hole in the HDA case. The stepper motor connects to the read/write heads with either a flexible steel band wrapped around the actuator motor's spindle or through a rack-and-pinion gearing arrangement. The steps of the actuator motor coincide with the tracks on the disk. To move the read/write head's ten tracks, the stepper motor must rotate ten steps. The biggest problem with this approach is that the head actuator arms can drift slightly off their original positions. A stepper motor actuator uses a blind location system, which means that the disk heads must rely solely on the stepper motor to place them correctly over the track to be accessed.

Comparatively, nearly all disk drives with capacities above 80MB (which is just about all currently manufactured disk drives) use a voice coil actuator. The technology used to create its core mechanism is very similar to the voice coil of an audio speaker. The voice coil in a hard disk drive is an electromagnetic coil attached to the ends of the arms on which the read/write heads are located. As the voice coil is energized, it produces an electromagnetic field that, depending on the flow direction of the electricity used to energize it, either attracts or repulses a stationary magnet that's located opposite the voice coil actuator. As the voice coil moves away from or closer to the stationary magnet, the read/write heads are extended or retracted.

A voice coil actuator doesn't move in steps like the stepper motor actuator. Instead, it relies on a feedback system, called a *servo*, to position the heads over a particular location on the disk. The servo, which is a block of data stored on the disk, lets the actuator know exactly where its heads are on the disk. Unlike the blind location system of the stepper motor, a voice coil actuator receives feedback signals from the servo that guides it exactly to the correct location.

Virtually all voice coil systems in use today use rotary voice coil actuators. This actuator system attaches its voice coil to an actuator arm that's mounted like a pivot. As the coil moves to or from the stationary magnet, the head arm rotates in and out, moving the read/write heads over the disk. The one problem that develops with a rotary voice coil is that as the heads are moved deeper into the disk (closer to the spindle), they tilt slightly. This tilt of the heads creates a problem with the alignment of the heads to the disk, also known as an *azimuth* problem. Azimuth issues are typically dealt with by not allowing data to be stored on the center part of the disk.

SERVO SYSTEMS

Servo systems are special coding stored on a formatted disk to help the read/write head actuator mechanism position the heads precisely over a specific location on the disk (see Figure 10-7). This special coding is called *gray code,* and it's placed on the disk when it is manufactured. Gray code, which identifies each track – and in some cases, each sector on the disk – cannot be overwritten, and its area is set aside and isn't included in the disk's total data capacity.

AIR FILTERS

Two air filters – a recirculating filter and a barometric or breather filter – are permanently sealed inside the HDA. The HDA does not pull in outside air and circulate it. The recirculating filter traps any media particles that are knocked off the platters by the read/write heads or any particles trapped in the HDA during manufacturing.

However, because the HDA isn't airtight or watertight, outside air can get inside and cause problems. A vent and a breather filter on the HDA allow the air pressure inside the HDA to be equalized for barometric pressure changes, such as the change between the factory in China at near sea level and the PC's final destination at an office in Denver at 5,000 feet above sea level. As the altitude changes, air is pulled in or vented out through the breather filter until the internal and external air pressures are equal. This is important to create the air pressure used to float the heads.

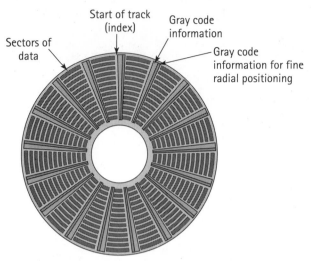

Figure 10-7: Gray code is inserted on the disk to provide feedback to the read/write head actuators.

LOGIC/CONTROLLER BOARDS

Hard disk drives have a *logic board,* also called the *controller board,* which controls the functions of the drive's read/write mechanisms as well as supports the interface of the drive, typically either Integrated Drive Electronics/AT Attachment (IDE/ATA) or Small Computer System Interface (SCSI). The logic board contains the microprocessor that executes the firmware stored on the hard disk drive to perform device control, data conversion, interface, and command queuing activities of the hard disk drive.

CONNECTORS AND JUMPERS

Hard disk drives use a standard five-pin power connector from a PC power supply to receive 5 volts (v) and 12v of direct current (DC) power. The logic board and other circuitry of the disk drive use 5v, and the spindle motor and head actuator use 12v.

Many hard disk drive units have a grounding tab that can be connected to the PC's chassis to create a positive ground. Disk drives that are mounted directly to the metal of a drive bay don't need to take this extra step, but for a hard disk installed in a plastic or fiberglass mounting, connecting the grounding tab to the PC's chassis is a good idea. Electrical ground problems show up as read and write errors.

Hard disk drives use jumpers for a couple of different purposes. IDE/ATA disks use jumpers to configure the master/slave configuration of a disk on a shared interface. SCSI disks use jumpers to set the unique SCSI ID of the drive.

Figure 10-8 shows two of the three general types of connectors found on most disk systems: data and power.

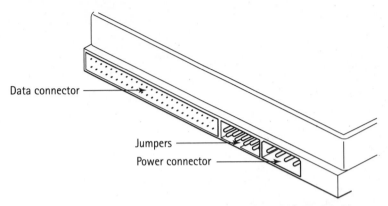

Data connector

Jumpers

Power connector

Figure 10-8: The connectors and jumpers on a standard IDE/ATA disk drive.

The data connector carries both the data and command signals to and from the controller board and central processing unit (CPU). Most current disk drives, which are primarily SCSI and IDE/ATA drives, use only a single 40-pin data cable. The IDE interface supports up to 2 disk drives on a single cable, an Enhanced IDE (EIDE) interface supports up to 4 disk drives on an interface, and the SCSI interface allows up to 7 or 15 drives on the same interface cable, depending on the SCSI standard in use. Special adapters and controllers are available to extend the number of drives that can share an interface. For example, a special EIDE controller is available that allows 8 EIDE devices to share an IDE controller.

An excellent site to look up hard disk terms is Western Digital Corporation's Hard Disk Glossary Web site at www.wdc.com/company/glossary.asp.

Reading and writing the disk

As the read/write head passes over the platter in a write operation, its polarity changes the orientation of the magnetic particles of the disk's media (see "Storage media" earlier in this chapter) to represent an electrical value, either a binary 1 or 0. As the polarity of the head is changed, the electrical value of the disk's media also changes. The polarity of the read/write head is changed by reversing the direction of the electrical flow in the wire wrapped around the head's core, which influences the storage media, and data is written to the disk. To read data from the disk, the read/write head only needs to detect the polarity of the storage media's store electrical value.

On new, formatted, or erased disks, the particles in each magnetic field are randomly assigned, which makes the disk appear blank to the read/write heads. When the particles in a field are aligned in one direction or another, the read/write head recognizes them as having a value representing a binary digit.

The disk's read/write heads float over a platter's surface on a cushion of air. When the disk drive is operating, the high-speed rotation of the disk platters creates air pressure that pushes the read/write heads away from the disk surfaces. Springs in the read/write head's actuator arm provide resistance that keeps the head floating above the disk's surface at a constant height of three to five microinches (millionths of an inch). This space is the *floating height* or the *head gap*. When the disk drive is not operating and the platters are not turning, the springs force the heads onto the surface of the disk, but only after they have been retracted to a safe parking zone. Disk drives have a *landing zone,* located beyond the inside edge of a disk's recording area, where the head can be safely parked. Virtually all disks automatically park their heads when the power is turned off.

Recording data on the disk

Magnetic flux is used to record data on the disk's media. *Flux* refers to the process used to align the particles in a single magnetic field in a single direction. The read/write head reverses its polarity back and forth to change the particle alignment of each field on the disk, called *flux reversal.* The read/write head uses a series of flux reversals to alter the particles in a bit cell, which is a cluster of magnetic particles that represents a single binary digit (bit).

As illustrated in Figure 10-9, the read/write head acts as a flux voltage detector. Each time that the head detects a flux transition, it sends a voltage pulse. A *flux transition* is a change from a positive charge to a negative charge, or from negative to positive. If no transition is detected, no pulse is sent.

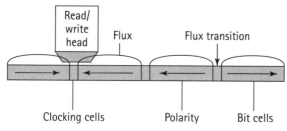

Figure 10-9: The read/write head senses the flux transition of the disk's media to store data on the disk.

A component called an encoder/decoder (*endec* for short) converts the voltage pulse signals into binary data and binary data into flux transitions. When the read/write head performs a write operation, the endec creates a signal pattern to be stored on the disk. During a read operation, the endec interprets the voltage pulses and converts them to binary data.

Read/write operations use a clock signal to ensure that all the electronic devices involved remain synchronized. Each data signal is preceded with a clock signal that's used by the read/write head and the endec to ensure that they're working on the same clock signal. If they get out of sync, they use the clock signals to resynchronize themselves. Clock cells are also stored on the disk media between bit cells. The clock signals also help the endec to determine the data value being stored or retrieved. Remember that a voltage pulse is sent for a flux transition. Two clock cells in a row indicate that no transition was detected.

Encoding data onto the disk

The different read/write head and storage media technologies (see "Storage media" earlier in the chapter) directly affect how densely the data cells can be placed on the disk media, which translates to the amount of data that can be stored on the disk. Data can be encoded or arranged in a bit cell by using different schemes, which are called *encoding methods*. Several encoding methods are used with hard disk drives, and each read/write head and storage media combination uses the encoding method that minimizes the number of flux transitions required to store a maximum amount of data.

The three primary encoding methods used on hard disk drives are

♦ *Frequency modulation (FM):* This encoding scheme simply records a binary 1 or 0 as a different polarity. FM was one of the earliest encoding methods used for disk drives; and although it was very popular through the late 1970s, it's not used on new disk drives.

♦ *Modified frequency modulation (MFM):* This encoding method is still used on all floppy disks and a few hard disks as well. MFM reduces the number of flux transitions required to store data, using clock cells only to separate the 0 bits (for which the read/write head does not generate a voltage pulse). MFM stores about twice as much data with the same number of flux transitions as the FM encoding method. MFM enabled high-density floppy disk media.

♦ *Run length limited (RLL):* This is the most commonly used encoding method. RLL produces higher densities by spacing the 1 bits farther apart and specially encoding bit cell groups so that they can be accessed together. RLL introduced data compression techniques, and virtually all current disk drives (IDE/ATA, SCSI, and so on) use some form of RLL encoding.

Interfacing to the disk

The processor and hard disk drives communicate by using one of several transfer interface standards. Hard disk drives are manufactured to work in virtually any PC system, and interface standards help ensure that the hard disk is compatible with a PC's motherboard and processor. Exactly which interface a disk drive uses is defined in its device controller and drive electronics.

ST506/412 INTERFACE

The first widely adopted disk interface standard was the ST506/412 interface developed by Seagate Technologies in the early 1980s for its 5MB (ST506) and 10MB (ST412) disk drives. It was universally adopted because it used standard cables to connect any compatible drive to an ST506/412-compatible adapter. This interface is now obsolete except in older systems still in use.

ESDI

The *Enhanced Small Disk Interface (ESDI)* standard introduced a number of innovations, such as adding the endec into the HDA. ESDI drives were used on high-end systems from brand-name manufacturers in the late 1980s, but this interface is largely obsolete except on a few high-end proprietary systems.

IDE/ATA INTERFACE

The *IDE/ATA (Integrated Drive Electronics/AT Attachment)* interface is the most popular hard disk interface used for PC systems. Because most current design motherboards include at least one IDE/ATA interface connector, these devices can be connected directly to the motherboard — or in cases where the motherboard doesn't include an onboard connector, to a pass-through IDE/ATA board. If you do need to add a separate IDE/ATA adapter card in a motherboard PCI expansion slot, the card also includes support for a floppy drive, a game port, perhaps a serial port, and more.

 IDE and *ATA* are interchangeable names for essentially the same technology. *IDE* defines a disk drive type that incorporates the disk controller functions into the hard disk drive, and *ATA* defines the interface used to communicate to the PC.

The standard IDE/ATA interface supports up to two devices. In addition to hard disk drives, IDE/ATA also supports CD-ROM, DVD, and tape drives by using the compatible *ATAPI* (AT Attachment Packet Interface). *EIDE*, also called *ATA-2*, is an upgraded version of IDE that increases the capacity of the interface to four devices — and with special interface adapters, an EIDE channel can support up to eight drives.

SCSI

The *Small Computer System Interface* (SCSI) is a system standard made up of a collection of interface standards that includes a wide range of peripheral devices, including hard disks, tape drives, optical drives, CD-ROMs, and disk arrays. Several SCSI devices can connect to a single SCSI host controller over a common interface, called a SCSI *bus* or SCSI *chain*. Figure 10-10 illustrates a simple SCSI chain.

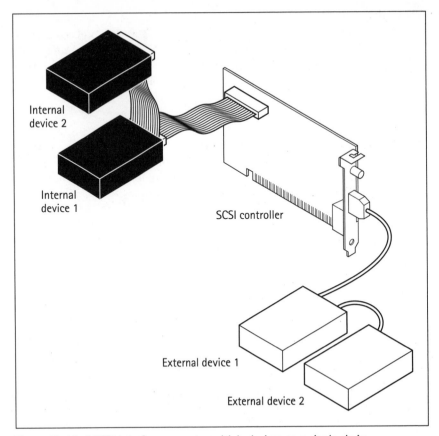

Figure 10-10: A SCSI interface supports multiple devices on a single chain.

The device controller card for each SCSI device is built into each device, but each device must communicate with the SCSI host adapter. To uniquely identify each device so that the host adapter can direct data traffic appropriately, each device is assigned a unique ID number. The SCSI host controller and a device use this ID number in all communications. To prevent messages and data blocks sent over the SCSI bus from bouncing back onto the bus, the SCSI bus must be terminated at each end.

THE FIBRE CHANNEL INTERFACE

The *Fibre Channel-Arbitrated Loop* (FC-AL), or fibre channel interface, is used primarily in very large network disk arrays. The FC-AL interface has built-in data recovery and fault-tolerant components. Fault-tolerant fibre channel disks are more expensive than other types of disk drives, including SCSI devices.

Fault-tolerant systems have built-in mechanisms and protocols to combat the effects of a device failure. Fault-tolerant (also called *high-availability*) systems can withstand the loss of a server, hard disk, power supply, network adapter, and other mission-critical components on a system.

FC-AL uses fiber optic cables to connect up to 127 devices that can be up to 10 kilometers apart on a single interface channel. FC-AL devices can also be *hot swapped*, meaning that they can be inserted and removed without interfering with the operation of the system.

Transferring data

The most commonly used data transfer protocols used to transfer data between the hard disk drive and memory are

◆ *Programmed I/O (PIO):* This is the data transfer protocol used by nearly all older disk drives that relied on the PC's processor to execute the instructions needed to move data from the disk to the PC's memory.

◆ *Direct memory access (DMA):* This protocol transfers data directly between the hard disk and RAM without involving the PC's CPU in the transfer. The DMA device's built-in processor completely manages the transfer between the disk and memory. All IDE/ATA hard disks support DMA transfers. DMA is also common on floppy disks, tape drives, and sound cards.

Addressing data

Data is addressed on a hard disk by using one of two methods:

◆ *Cylinder-head-sector (CHS):* IDE/ATA drives use this data-addressing scheme that locates data on a hard disk drive by its cylinder, head, and sector. The *cylinder* refers to the track, the *head* indicates the platter surface, and the *sector* is within the track. For example, a data file could have the addressing of cylinder 27, head 4, and sector 33, which pinpoints the data at track 27 on the top side of the third platter (the first platter is accessed by head 0) and sector 33 on the track. See "Organizing data on a disk drive" earlier in this chapter for information on cylinders, tracks, and sectors.

◆ *Logical Block Addressing (LBA):* LBA assigns each sector on the disk a logical block number (logical block address). A data file is addressed by its LBA location, which is associated with a CHS-type location address. SCSI and EIDE disk drives use LBA addressing.

 The number of cylinders, heads, and sectors configured for the hard disk in a particular PC can be found in the PC's BIOS setup configuration data.

Using RAID

Redundant Array of Independent (or Inexpensive) Disks (RAID) is a high-availability technique used to create a fault-tolerant environment that protects the data stored on disk from the failure of a disk drive. RAID systems store mirrored copies of data files on separate disks or spread data over several disk drives in stripes. RAID technology is not frequently implemented on standalone PCs or small networks. RAID, usually because of its cost and overhead, is reserved for larger enterprise-level networks.

HARDWARE VERSUS SOFTWARE RAID

RAID can be applied to a system either through hardware or software RAID. Each has its advantages and disadvantages, so it can be simply a matter of preference.

◆ *Hardware RAID:* An independent RAID controller, which is either an external device or an expansion card, manages the RAID system independently of the computer and its operating system, which see the RAID disk array as a single disk device.

◆ *Software RAID:* Software RAID is implemented as either a part of or an add-on to the operating system and doesn't require the cost or bother of a RAID controller device. Typically, software RAID has better performance than hardware RAID. Software RAID is available on most server-level operating systems (such as Windows NT/2000 or Linux).

HOT SWAP AND FAULT TOLERANCE

One of the primary benefits of a RAID system (either hardware or software) is that it allows the use of hot-swap drives, which can be removed or installed while the system is running.

Fault tolerance, the ability for a system to automatically overcome system failures on its own, is the primary reason why you would implement a RAID system. However, not all RAID specifications provide the same level of fault tolerance, so you should know which RAID type is in use before you feel too comfortable. For example, RAID 0 doesn't provide any fault tolerance (see the next section for more information on the RAID types), but RAID 5 offers full fault tolerance, at least until a device fails. The data can still be accessed, but fault tolerance is lost until the data array is rebuilt.

DISK STRIPING AND MIRRORING

The two primary data storage methods used in RAID are disk striping and disk mirroring:

◆ *Disk striping:* This method writes data files across several disks in stripes, which speeds up I/O operations; as one stripe is being written or read, the next stripe can be staged on another disk drive. Except for systems using

RAID 0 (which doesn't allow for rebuilding lost data), if there is a disk failure, the lost data can be rebuilt by using information from other disks.

◆ *Disk mirroring:* This method involves creating a duplicate file that is stored on a separate hard drive.

 Disk striping and mirroring are not mutually exclusive storage methods. Several RAID standards implement various combinations of these two methods. You'll also see disk striping and mirroring referred to as *data striping* and *mirroring* in some sources.

Many RAID levels or implementations exist, but only four RAID levels are commonly used: 0, 1, 3, and 5.

◆ *RAID 0 (disk striping):* Disk striping does not provide any redundancy. If a disk drive fails, the data stripes written to it are lost. RAID 0 doesn't provide fault tolerance or data recovery and is used mostly as a way to speed up disk access on database applications and the like. However, when RAID 0 is used, data protection and integrity issues must be applied externally.

◆ *RAID 1 (disk mirroring):* Although it doubles the amount of disk space needed to store the same data, RAID 1 is very popular because it provides complete data redundancy.

◆ *RAID 3 (disk striping with fault tolerance):* RAID 3 adds parity and error correction code (ECC) to RAID 0. The parity information is maintained on a separate disk and can be used to reconstruct the data if a hard disk drive fails. RAID 3 uses at least three hard disk drives: two for the data stripes and one for the parity information.

◆ *RAID 5 (disk striping with fault tolerance):* RAID 5, like RAID 3, uses at least three hard disks but stores data stripes on all disk drives along with stripes of the parity information. This adds fault tolerance to all aspects of the RAID configuration.

◆ *RAID 0+1 and 1+0 (disk striping and mirroring):* Two other RAID variations that are gaining popularity are RAID 0+1 (also known as RAID 01; striping plus mirroring) and RAID 1+0 (also known as RAID 10; mirroring plus striping). These two implementations use the best of both RAID features to provide highly reliable disk arrays.

Solving Hard Disk Issues

The hard disk is a black or white device: It either works or it doesn't. In fact, many supposed hard disk problems are actually power, memory, or interface issues. However, a few events do occur from time to time where the hard disk must be checked out – or at least ruled out as a problem. In the following sections, I detail the steps or processes that you use to solve the most common hard disk issues and problems.

Choosing a hard disk drive by using performance metrics

Gilster's Law on Choosing the Right Hard Disk (or any other peripheral device) is "You never can tell, and it all depends." Seriously, what might be the best hard disk for any given situation really depends on the situation. In most situations, the price and capacity of the disk are usually the most heavily weighted factors, but a number of performance metrics and indicators are included in the specifications of most disk drives that can be used to choose the best disk drive to meet your requirements.

The most common performance specifications are

- *Seek time: Seek time* measures the time that it takes the head actuator to move the read/write heads from one track to the next in milliseconds (ms). However, seek time does not include the time required to move to a specific data location. *Average seek time,* which is a commonly used term to compare the performance of different drives, is calculated from the drive's seek times for a number of randomly located requests. Nearly all quality disk drives have an average seek time between 8 to 14 ms.

- *Access time: Access time* measures the time required to position the read/write heads over a particular track and to find the sector containing a particular data location. Access time adds *latency,* or rotational delay, to the seek time to calculate the total time required for the disk to position the read/write head over a specific data location. Latency is measured in milliseconds and is generally around one-half the time required for the disk to make a single revolution. At 10,000 rpm, latency is around 3 ms. While the rotational speed of the drive increases, the latency time decreases proportionately.

- *Data transfer rate:* This is the amount of data that can be moved between the disk and the PC's main memory (RAM) in one second, measured in megabytes per second. A higher data transfer rate, which means more data transferred per second, translates to less time that a user must wait for a program to load or a document to be opened. Today's hard disks support transfer rates from 5 to 70 megabytes per second.

◆ *Data access time (QBench): QBench time* combines the access time with the data transfer rate to produce an indicator that rates a disk drive's overall performance. QBench is a specification developed by Quantam Corporation (www.quantum.com), which also provides the QBench benchmarking tool that is widely used as a standard for drive performance measurement and comparison.

◆ *Disk capacity:* Disk drives typically have two capacity ratings: unformatted and formatted. The formatted capacity is usually the most important of the two because it states the usable disk space on the drive.

◆ *Areal density:* A disk's *areal density* is an indicator of its storage capacity. Areal density is calculated by multiplying a disk's bits per inch (bpi) by the total number of tracks on the disk, which yields the number of bits (typically megabits or gigabits) per square inch. An area density of around 1.5 gigabits per square inch is common on most newer disk drives.

Preparing a hard disk drive for use

The two major steps to preparing a disk drive to receive an operating system and to store data are partitioning and formatting. The following projects detail the steps used to complete each of these steps.

PARTITIONING THE HARD DISK

When you partition a hard disk drive, you can

◆ Divide the disk into logical sub-drives that are assigned a different drive letter, such as C:, D:, and E:, and can be separately addressed

◆ Load multiple operating systems on the same disk, such as Windows 98 and Linux, with each operating system in its own partition

◆ Support multiple file systems, such as NT File System (NTFS) and FAT32, on the same disk drive

◆ Separate data files from application files on different partitions to speed up data backups

Partitioning a hard disk can improve the disk's efficiency and overcome an operating system's sizing issues. For example, Windows sizes disk clusters proportionately to the size of the partition. A bigger partition can result in bigger clusters, which translates to numerous, small unused spaces on the disk. Strategically reducing the partition sizes or creating many smaller partitions reduces cluster sizes to better match the data.

A disk can have more than one partition, but some operating systems limit each partition size. Thus, on some systems, larger disks must be divided into smaller partitions. DOS, Windows 3.*x*, or early releases of Windows 95 don't support partition sizes larger than 2GB. This means that to use the entire disk drive, a disk larger than 2GB must be divided into two or more partitions. Later versions of Windows (98, NT, 2000, and XP) allow you to create partitions up to 4TB (2GB being the norm), depending on the Windows version and the file system in use.

A hard disk can be divided into two types of partitions:

♦ *Primary partitions:* A primary partition is created to hold an operating system and is typically the partition used to boot the PC. A hard disk can be divided into as many as four primary partitions, but only one primary partition can be active (set as the system partition) at a time. Another type of primary partition is the boot partition, which stores the operating system's files, such as the Windows folders.

♦ *Extended partitions:* An extended partition can be divided into as many as 23 logical sub-partitions. Each logical partition can be assigned its own drive identity, such as D:, E:, or F:, and used for any purpose other than as the active partition.

USING FDISK TO PARTITION A HARD DISK

The DOS command FDISK is the most commonly used utility for partitioning a hard disk drive. It is typically included on a DOS boot disk that also includes the DOS FORMAT command and is used to partition and format the hard disk during system setup.

To use the FDISK command, use these steps:

1. At a DOS command line prompt, enter the command FDISK.

   If you are on a PC with a hard disk drive larger than 512MB, a dialog box message is displayed (see Figure 10-11). This dialog box contains a message advising you that you can enable large disk support and warning you of the consequences of doing so.

2. Press the Enter key to accept the default value of Yes (Y, which accepts large disk support) or enter an N (for No) and then press the Enter key.

   The FDISK menu displays (see Figure 10-12).

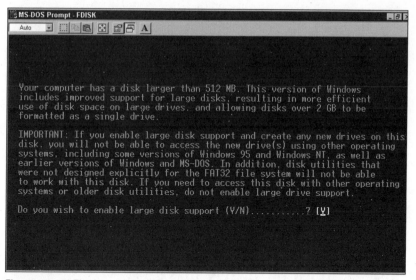

Figure 10-11: The large disk support message is displayed by FDISK on PCs with large hard disk drives.

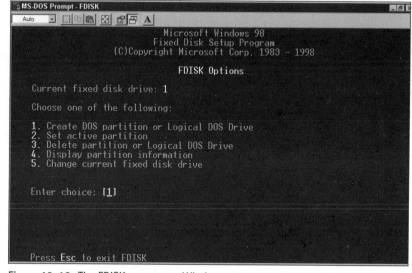

Figure 10-12: The FDISK menu on a Windows 98 system.

3. Use menu choice 1 to create partitions on the disk, one at a time.

   Another menu appears with three options:

   a. To create a primary DOS partition (meaning a system partition)

   b. To create an extended partition

   c. To create logical partitions within an extended partition

   If you're partitioning a new drive, choose the first option.

   You can create one large partition for the entire disk, which is commonly done. Or if you have a plan for how the disk is to be divided (by using percentages to divide the disk into primary and extended partitions), you would use options a, b, and c accordingly. If you do create more than one primary partition, you need to activate the one that you wish to use as a system partition.

Formatting a hard disk drive

Before the partition or partitions on a hard disk drive can receive the operating system or be used to store data, they must be high-level formatted. Although the majority of new PCs now come from the factory with the operating system installed, a hard disk might be repartitioned and formatted when a new hard disk drive is installed, when the operating system is upgraded, or for many other reasons. A disk drive must be physically formatted (low-level format), partitioned, and logically formatted (high-level format) before it can store data.

The two formatting levels that are performed on a hard disk drive, regardless of whether it's an IDE/ATA or SCSI, are low-level formatting and high-level formatting.

◆ *Low-level formatting:* A *low-level format* is a destructive scan of the disk intended to find any defects in the recording media. The location of any defect found is recorded as unusable to avoid data problems. I recommend that you don't low-level format an IDE/ATA disk drive in the field, and here's why: IDE/ATA drives cost less than other drives because they use zone recording. Because the inner (closer to the spindle) tracks have a shorter circumference than the outer tracks, the drives, regardless of whether they use Enhanced Small Disk Interface (ESDI), run length limited (RLL), or modified frequency modulation (MFM), record at their maximum density on inner tracks. IDE/ATA drives use several zones and put more data on the outer tracks, which allows the IDE/ATA drives to store more data than older drive types. Low-level formatting destroys the zone recording in use and consequently wastes several megabytes of storage space.

A low-level format should not be done on an IDE/ATA or SCSI hard disk out-side of the factory. If a drive ever needs low-level formatting, you should con-tact the manufacturer to obtain the necessary software.

◆ *High-level formatting: High-level formatting* is used to prepare disk parti-tions to receive the operating system and to store data files. The high-level format prepares the disk's partitions by creating a root directory and the File Allocation Table (FAT). The *FAT* is used to record the location and relationships of files and directories on the disk. When you format a hard disk that contains data files, the FAT is reconstructed, removing all refer-ences of the existing files.

I have heard from many readers who challenge me on the notion that you should never low-level format an IDE/ATA or SCSI hard disk in the field. Yes, software and utilities are available that will low-level format a hard disk drive nicely, and I have used them to low-level format a drive once or twice. However, my best advice is still not to do it.

To format a hard disk drive on most PCs, you have two choices:

1. Use the DOS FORMAT command at a DOS command line prompt. The com-mand used should be in this form:

```
FORMAT X:
```

In this command, X: is replaced by the drive letter of the partition that you wish to format. The active primary partition is usually the C: drive.

2. With the following steps, use the Windows Explorer to format an existing partition for reuse:

   a. Right-click the drive letter in the left pane of the Windows Explorer window of the drive that you wish to format to display a shortcut menu (see Figure 10-13).

   b. Choose Format from the shortcut menu that appears.

   The formatting dialog box will display. Windows will not allow you to format the C: drive from Windows Explorer.

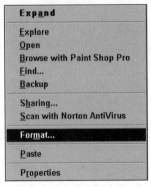

Figure 10-13: The Windows Explorer drive shortcut menu includes the option used to format a disk.

Installing a new hard drive

Follow these steps to install a new hard disk in a PC system case:

1. If you're upgrading to a new and larger hard disk drive or adding a second (or higher) disk drive, first create a full backup of the disk drive being replaced.

2. Enter the BIOS setup program (by pressing the key indicated on the PC's startup screen) and document the settings that affect the disk drives. See "Configuring the BIOS for a hard disk" later in this chapter for more information on this part of the task.

 I always recommend having a complete written record of the Startup program's configuration data.

3. Create a bootable floppy disk by using the following command at a DOS command line prompt:

```
FORMAT A: /S
```

If you have a blank, formatted disk, you can also execute the following command from a DOS command line prompt or in the Open dialog box that appears after choosing Start→Run:

```
SYS A:
```

Or you can use Windows Explorer to format a disk and select the Copy System Files option in the Format Disk dialog box.

4. If the new hard disk drive is in addition to an existing disk drive, decide which drive is to be configured as the master and which as the slave.

   Check the drive's documentation for the correct jumper settings and make the necessary changes on the new disk drive. Most disk drives are pre-configured at the factory as a master. If the new drive is to be a slave, set the jumper accordingly. If the disk drives are SCSI drives, you need to set the device ID jumpers; SCSI devices do not use a master/slave configuration. Also check the SCSI bus and the position of the new disk on the bus to verify that the disk drive is not required to provide termination.

5. Shut down the PC, turn off the power switch, unplug the PC's power cord from its AC power source, and put on an electrostatic discharge (ESD) strap.

6. Remove the system case cover, watching for snagged data cables and power connectors.

7. Create a diagram of the placement of the hard disk's cables, studying the orientation of the hard disk drive's data (ribbon) cable and power cable.

8. Remove the cables from the old drive (even if you're not replacing it).

When removing cables from the old drive, don't jerk any of the cables. Use steady, firm pressure to pull the cable connectors apart. Use a rocking motion (side-to-side) to remove them if necessary. Never flex the connectors up and down.

9. If you're replacing the existing hard disk drive, remove its mounting screws and save them for the new drive.

   Paper cups or an egg carton are good for keeping the screws organized.

   If you're adding the new drive in addition to the existing drive, make sure that you have mounting screws available. If you need to remove any expansion cards to get to the hard disk, draw a diagram of their placement and their cable orientations, if any, before you remove any card anchor screws.

10. If you're replacing the existing drive, remove it from the drive bay.

    Unless the drive is damaged and not usable in the future, protect it in antistatic material.

11. If you're adding a drive to the PC, remove the existing drive and verify that its device configuration jumpers are appropriately set to the configuration that you wish to use.

12. Install the new disk drive in a drive bay, anchoring it to the drive bay's walls with mounting screws.

   You might need to attach the data and power connection before anchoring the drive in place.

13. Reinstall the cables on the existing drive, if needed, making sure to align the red or blue edge of the data cable to pin 1 on the disk drive's connector and the connector on the adapter card or motherboard.

14. Replace the cover, connect the PC to its power source, and boot the PC by using the floppy boot disk.

15. Prepare the disks by partitioning and formatting as needed (see "Preparing a hard disk drive for use" earlier in this chapter). Verify that the BIOS is correct for the new disk (if added in addition to an existing disk) and that its interface is enabled.

Configuring the BIOS for a hard disk

When installing a hard disk drive in a PC, you need to verify the BIOS settings to ensure that the drive parameters are set correctly. In most cases, the PC has built-in support for IDE/ATA hard disk drives, but to be sure that the BIOS knows the characteristics of the hard disk and how to interact with it, you should check these settings.

   Virtually every BIOS includes two sets of disk drive parameters for IDE/ATA drives: one for the primary channel's master drive and one for the primary slave.

 System BIOS settings aren't required for SCSI disk drives. SCSI disks are controlled through the host adapter and its BIOS.

HARD DISK AUTODETECTION

Most BIOSes also support hard disk auto detection. The BIOS polls each hard disk in the system to learn its configuration and specification data using either dynamic or manual IDE auto detection. Virtually all newer BIOSes can be set to Auto or Manual depending on your preference.

   ◆ *Dynamic IDE auto detection:* One of the BIOS' hard disk drive configuration settings is Auto Detect, which allows the BIOS to automatically interrogate the disk drives and set the appropriate settings each time that the PC is booted.

   ◆ *Manual IDE auto detection:* Set for manual auto detection, the BIOS will scan the IDE/ATA channels and set the hard disk parameters according to the information that it receives. You must save these resulting settings to make them permanent. The downside of the manual approach is that if you change a disk drive, you have to remember to reset the parameters.

HARD DISK BIOS SETTINGS

If you must set each of the hard disk's BIOS settings individually, the following list includes the settings that you must affect:

- *Type:* This entry is a carry-forward from the days when hard disks were assigned numeric type codes (typically from 1–47). The entries that you can enter for a disk drive's type are

  - *Defined disk drive types:* Older, legacy hard disk drives (those in the 40–100MB range) have a drive type number assigned to them. If you insist on not using auto detection, study the manufacturer's documentation for the drive type, which will be from 1 to 45, 46, or 47, depending on the BIOS.

  - *User defined types:* The user option (which is either the word *User* or the last number in the defined types list of the BIOS) allows you to specify each of the hard disk's settings, which I still don't recommend unless you feel that you absolutely have to do this.

- *Auto Detect:* Your choices are either Auto or Manual – and guess which one I recommend!

- *CD-ROM:* When enabled, this setting indicates that a CD-ROM device is occupying a particular IDE/ATA device position.

- *Disabled/None:* This setting indicates that no disk drive is installed in a particular IDE/ATA device position.

- *Size:* This setting indicates the disk capacity, typically in megabytes. On most BIOSes, this value is calculated from other settings by using this formula:

```
Size = (Heads*Cylinders*Sectors*512[sector size])/1,000,000
```

- *Cylinders:* This is the number of physical or logical cylinders (tracks) on each disk platter. Newer BIOSes use a calculation to set the number of logical cylinders on the disk. This calculation is done to reconfigure the drive logically to get around the 504MB restriction of some operating systems. For example, a 3.1GB drive with 6,136 cylinders, 16 heads, and 63 sectors is logically configured to have 767 cylinders, 128 heads, and 63 sectors. Some BIOSes record the nominal characteristics of the drive and perform internal translation, especially when Logical Block Addressing (LBA) is in use.

- *Heads:* This setting indicates the number of read/write heads used by the disk drive, which can be either the number of physical heads (on older disk drives) or the number of logical heads (on newer systems, typically 16).

◆ *Sectors:* This setting indicates the number of sectors per disk track. Each sector is 512 bytes, and on older drives will typically be 17. However, on newer disk drives that apply zone recording, this value is normally set to 63 (the highest value that can be recorded in this field), and the BIOS uses internal translation to adjust the number of sectors on each zone.

◆ *Write precompensation:* On virtually all IDE/ATA and SCSI disk drives, this value is largely ignored. It exists only for use by older disk drives that require an offset of a certain number of tracks to write to the disk.

◆ *Landing zone:* Another legacy parameter, this setting specifies the cylinder number used to park the hard disk read/write heads when the power is turned off. Virtually all disk drives made in the past six years have a reserved and set-aside location for the head landing zone and ignore this value.

◆ *Translation mode:* The setting in this parameter tells the BIOS which addressing or translation mode is to be used for large hard disk drives. The most common values you can use in this field are

   ■ *Auto:* This is my personal choice and the one that I recommend to you. This value tells the BIOS to automatically detect and set the configuration settings for the hard disk drives on the PC.

   ■ *Block:* This setting tells the BIOS to transfer data from or to the hard disk in block mode, which means as much as 16 or 32 sectors at a time. However, verify that a hard disk is block-mode compatible before using this setting.

   ■ *Normal or cylinder-head-sector (CHS):* This is the normal or standard setting for IDE/ATA drives with less than 504MB capacity. Data is addressed on the disk using its CHS location.

   ■ *Large:* Also referred to as Extended CHS (ECHS), this addressing mode uses CHS addressing and works with systems with less than 1,024 cylinders, which is why it is essentially obsolete and not recommended for use with modern hard disk drives.

   ■ *Logical Block Addressing (LBA):* Each sector on the disk is assigned a serialized integer ID, which is then used to address the disk.

◆ *Programmed Input/Output (PIO) mode:* IDE/ATA drives can be set to transfer data using one of two transfer modes:

   ■ *Direct memory access (DMA):* If the disk drive is a DMA device, choose this setting.

   ■ *PIO:* Five PIO modes are available for use, ranging from 0 (slowest) to 4 (fastest). Nearly all newer hard disk drives using PIO support the faster PIO modes. Use the highest PIO value that the disk drive supports.

♦ *32-bit Transfer Mode:* On those disk drives that support 32-bit transfers between the CPU and the PCI bus, enabling this setting should result in a slight performance increase.

Troubleshooting a hard disk drive

Here are a variety of problems (and the troubleshooting steps used to solve them) that can show up after a new hard disk is installed in a PC.

1. If the PC won't boot, check the following:

   a. If you have only one disk drive, make sure that it's configured as a master. This isn't a problem on most systems with only one disk drive, but on some, a single drive must be configured as a master.

   b. If you have two drives on a single IDE/ATA channel, check the jumpers on the drives to verify that one is a master and one is a slave. Two of one or the other will not work. If the drives are from different manufacturers, check their Web sites for possible compatibility alerts.

   c. Check the power connection on each disk drive to make sure that the connectors are snuggly fitting and that there are no bent or broken pins. If you suspect that the power connector is the problem, try using a different power connector from the power supply.

   d. Verify that the red or blue edge of the data cable is aligned to pin 1. Typically this connector is *keyed* (a locking or guiding feature is built into the connector and port). Also verify that the connector is not off by one row of pins up or across.

   e. You might need to partition and format the hard disk. If you get a drive C: boot failure even after formatting the C: drive and copying the system files to it, you could have a corrupted boot sector. Boot with the floppy boot disk and copy the system file to the C: (SYS C:). If the drive continues to have problems, try a different hard disk drive to see whether the device interface is the problem. If so, acquire a new adapter card. If the new drive works, the problem is the original disk drive itself.

   f. Use the Windows Device Manager to verify that the hard disk drives of the primary and secondary device controllers don't have system resource conflicts.

2. If the system does boot but you're having problems, check out the following.

   a. If a large disk drive (over 500MB) is only recognized by the BIOS as a 500MB drive, you need to update your BIOS.

   b. If you're getting disk read/write errors when running applications, run the Windows utility ScanDisk to check for disk media problems. On

Windows 2000 or XP systems, you should run the Chkdsk utility to check for errors on the disk. You might also want to run the Disk Defragmenter utility as well. If you continue to have problems reading or writing the disk, you could repartition and reformat it or simply replace it.

c. Just about any operational problem with a hard disk drive is the result of three things: bad configuration, improper installation, and improper maintenance. Problems caused by any one of these areas can show up immediately or later. If you begin to develop disk read and write errors, recheck the physical installation (and especially that the connectors are properly fitted) and the Complementary Metal-Oxide Semiconductor (CMOS) setup data. Check the configuration jumpers on IDE/ATA devices and the device ID and termination jumpers on SCSI devices. Regularly scan the disk for viruses, use ScanDisk at least once a week, and run Disk Defragmenter at least once a month.

 On Windows systems, you can find ScanDisk, Disk Defragmenter, and Chkdsk (Windows 2000 or XP) by choosing Start → Accessories → System Tools on a Windows system.

Chapter 11

Hard Disk Interfaces

IN THIS CHAPTER

Choosing which hard disk interface is best for a particular PC has more to do with how the PC will be used than wishing to install the latest and greatest technology in every PC that you support.

Not every PC needs to have an elaborate disk drive arrangement, such as a Redundant Array of Independent Disks (RAID) or a fibre channel connection to a network attached storage (NAS) array. In fact, virtually any PC that isn't a network server of some sort needs only a simple hard disk interface. In this chapter, I cover the following:

- ◆ Interfacing IDE/ATA hard disk drives

- ◆ Understanding hard disk translation and addressing modes

- ◆ Interfacing SCSI hard disk and other drive types

- ◆ Troubleshooting hard disk issues

THIS CHAPTER COVERS THE DISK DRIVE INTERFACES that you would encounter in the typical standalone or networked PC. I don't include server and network-related disk interfacing.

Interfacing an IDE/ATA Hard Disk

On most PCs, the motherboard and chipset establish which hard disk interface(s) are supported and available for use. In a typical system, the hard disk interface of choice is the Integrated Drive Electronics (IDE), which is also called the AT Attachment (ATA) interface. In fact, the abbreviations *IDE* and *ATA* are used virtually interchangeably these days — so much so that I refer to them together as the IDE/ATA interface.

Reviewing hard disk interface characteristics

When choosing a hard disk interface, or just understanding the one already installed on a PC, a variety of characteristics must be considered. However, the four primary characteristics of a hard disk interface are

◆ Bus compatibility

◆ Cost

◆ Disk drive support

◆ Performance

These characteristics are discussed in the sections that follow.

SYSTEM BUS COMPATIBILITY

A Pentium-class PC uses the Peripheral Component Interconnect (PCI) bus architecture for its system bus but can still also provide support for the older Industry Standard Architecture (ISA) bus. Most legacy systems use the Video Electronics Standards Association (VESA) local bus (VL-bus) in combination with the ISA bus to support hard disk drives.

The system bus interconnects the memory, processor, and other primary components of the PC, including the hard disk drive.

See Chapter 1 for more information on bus structures.

The PCI bus, which has a standard data speed of 33 MHz on Pentium-class PCs, provides the high-speed local bus required by today's hard disk drives. Some older PCI systems run at 25 or 30 MHz and might not be able to support newer hard drives. In fact, some new disk drives require faster versions of PCI and IDE/ATA.

Early Pentium (and before) PCs used a discrete hard disk controller/interface card that was inserted into one of the available PCI expansion slots on the motherboard. If you're using Small Computer System Interface (SCSI) disk drives or wish to install an upgraded disk drive interface, such as Ultra direct memory access (DMA), the controller board must be added to even the newest PCs in a PCI expansion slot. Ensure that the hard disk drive you're interfacing is compatible with the add-in controller card before booting the system.

Most newer motherboard designs now provide one or (most commonly) two IDE/ATA channels and connectors built onto the motherboard.

INTERFACE COST

Most third-party hard disk controller boards, which add support for hard disk features and interface modes not natively supported by the motherboard and chipset, are not expensive. However, if the standard IDE/ATA interface built into the system satisfies the user's need and the functional requirements of the PC, you don't need to spend the money.

Ultra DMA and SCSI add-in controller/interface boards typically cost between $35 and $250, depending on the brand and the features included and supported.

DISK DRIVE SUPPORT

Most generic hard disk controller/interface boards support a wide range of hard disk drives – as long as the specification set of the hard disk drive is compatible with that of the controller card. However, many proprietary cards are not recommended for hard disk drives outside the manufacturer's product lines.

DISK DRIVE INTERFACE PERFORMANCE

The purpose of the hard disk interface is to provide for the efficient transfer of data between the hard disk itself and the rest of the PC system. However, the speed of the disk drive interface is limited to the performance of the hard disk drive. A very fast hard disk drive interface won't make up for a hard disk drive that is slower than the interface. In fact, upgrading the hard disk drive interface without changing the hard disk drive can create new problems from incompatibility.

If the hard disk drive doesn't read access data fast enough for the interface, any improvement from a faster interface will be on data already transferred into the disk drive's internal buffer and won't show up as an overall performance improvement.

Read any claims from interface vendors with caution and some cynicism. Claims that a new and improved (meaning faster speed) interface will drastically improve your data transfer speeds are generally false. Not many IDE/ATA disk drives can completely keep up with even a 66 MHz interface. Thus, upgrading the interface alone to 100 MHz won't provide much performance improvement.

Using an IDE/ATA interface

By far the most common hard disk drive interface in use is the IDE/ATA, largely because of its relative simplicity, compatibility, and availability.

One of the better features of IDE/ATA is that each of its *channels* (the path over which data is transferred) is able to support up to two IDE/ATA devices. An IDE/ATA channel isn't limited to only hard disk drives. An IDE/ATA channel is also able, in most cases, to support AT Attachment Packet Interface (ATAPI) tape drives, CD-ROMs, and DVD devices.

 Most IDE/ATA (including Enhanced IDE [EIDE]) channels also support ATAPI devices, such as a tape drive, CD-ROM, or DVD. ATAPI provides an IDE/ATA channel with additional commands that allow it to communicate with drives other than hard disk drives provided that they're supported in the system BIOS.

On a system with more than one IDE/ATA channel (usually two to four), each channel is an independently configured device. Table 11-1 lists the four standard IDE/ATA channels and the system resources that each is typically assigned in a common configuration.

TABLE 11-1 SYSTEM RESOURCE ALLOCATIONS FOR IDE/ATA CHANNELS

Channel	IRQ	I/O Address (Master/Slave)	Usage
Primary	14	1F0–1F7h/3F6–3F7h	IDE0 on PCs with an IDE/ATA interface
Secondary	15 or 10	170–177h/376–377h	IDE1 on PCs with two IDE/ATA channels; typically used for ATAPI drives
Tertiary	11 or 12	1E8–1EFh/3EE–3EFh	Not commonly used and can cause some software issues
Quarternary	10 or 11	168–16Fh/36E–36Fh	Very rare; can cause software issues

Don't sweat it that the I/O address of a slave device on a primary IDE/ATA channel overlaps that of a floppy disk controller. Manufacturers are aware of this and adjust for it.

Recent developments, such as Ultra DMA controller expansion cards and the use of PCI steering, now allow IDE/ATA channels to share a single IRQ.

PRIMARY AND SECONDARY CHANNELS

Nearly all newer motherboards include support for two IDE/ATA channels with two IDE/ATA connectors included on the motherboard itself. On most systems, interrupt requests (IRQs) 14 and 15 are reserved for the primary and secondary IDE/ATA channels, and virtually all expansion cards avoid the IRQs and input/output (I/O) addresses assigned to them. The exception to this is a SCSI host controller card, but a system using both interfaces is unusual.

Many legacy Pentium motherboards and chipsets, although providing two IDE/ATA channels, didn't always provide the same support on both channels. On these systems, the primary channel supported the faster Programmed I/O (PIO) modes (see "PIO modes" later in this chapter), but the secondary channel supported only slower PIO modes and was intended for older hard disk drives and ATAPI devices. Fortunately, this IDE/ATA configuration is now in the past.

TERTIARY AND QUARTERNARY CHANNELS

The primary issue of including a third or fourth IDE/ATA channel is that when other non-IDE/ATA devices (such as sound cards, network interface cards, and PS/2 mouse units) are added to a PC, they can be assigned automatically to some of the same system resources that you'd assign to the additional channels. In addition, the use of a tertiary or quarternary IDE/ATA channel can create some issues for operating systems and application software hard-coded to the primary and secondary channels.

The best way to add a third or fourth IDE/ATA channel to a PC is to use a PCI IDE/ATA channel adapter card. In fact, adding a four-channel IDE/ATA controller card and disabling the primary and secondary system channels actually frees up an IRQ.

Many sound cards, especially Sound Blaster cards from the 1990s, can be configured to add a tertiary IDE/ATA channel. This practice began back when CD-ROM drives were attached through a sound card and a proprietary non-IDE/ATA interface. This is not the best way to add an additional IDE/ATA channel because typically the sound card is installed in an ISA slot, which means that the tertiary IDE/ATA channel is also running through the ISA bus.

PIO MODES

IDE/ATA devices that use one or more Programmed I/O (PIO) modes to transfer data require the system processor to be involved in the transfer between the system and the hard disk drive. PIO was the only data transfer method used until the mid-1990s.

PIO is defined into five separate modes (see Table 11-2). The first three PIO modes were defined in the original ATA standards, and the later two are defined in the ATA-2 standard (among others).

TABLE 11-2 PROGRAMMED I/O (PIO) MODES

PIO Mode	Cycle Time	Maximum Data Transfer Rate
0	600 nanoseconds (ns)	2.2 megabytes per second
1	383 ns	5.2 megabytes per second
2	240 ns	8.3 megabytes per second
3	180 ns	11.1 megabytes per second
4	120 ns	16.7 megabytes per second

 If you encounter PIO mode 5 when studying motherboards, understand that this proposed standard was never implemented, although some motherboard manufacturers did show some early support for it.

DMA MODES

As hard disk drive performance improved, it became apparent that a better and faster data transfer interface than PIO had to be developed. The most obvious way was to remove the CPU from the process and make the overall system more productive. This thinking led to the development of direct memory access interface modes.

Direct memory access (DMA) is a generic term that refers to interfaces that allow a peripheral device to transfer data directly into or from system memory without the processor's involvement. Conventional DMA, which was originally implemented on ISA channels for sound cards and floppy disk interfaces, is separate from the DMA modes defined for use on the IDE/ATA interface.

IDE/ATA DMA uses two sets of modes: single-word and multiword. Table 11-3 lists the characteristics of the various DMA modes, as defined in the ATA standards. *Single-word* DMA modes transfer data in a word (2 bytes or 16 bits), which matches the width of the IDE/ATA channel. The problem with single-word DMA mode is that it sets up and transfers each word as a separate transfer. *Multiword* DMA modes eliminate the overhead of setting up and transferring each word by streaming multiple words of data as a single transfer.

TABLE 11-3 ATA DMA MODES

DMA Mode	Cycle Time	Maximum Transfer Rate
Single-word 0	960 ns	2.1 megabytes per second
Single-word 1	480 ns	4.2 megabytes per second
Single-word 2	240 ns	8.3 megabytes per second
Multiword 0	480 ns	4.2 megabytes per second
Multiword 1	150 ns	13.3 megabytes per second
Multiword 2	120 ns	16.7 megabytes per second

 Multiword DMA interfaces, defined by the ATA-2 standard, have now replaced the older (and slower) single-word DMA modes (which are actually now obsolete) on today's hard disk drives.

FIRST-PARTY DMA

The two different types of DMA transfers are conventional DMA (also called *third-party* DMA) and first-party DMA (the kind used on hard disk drives).

Third-party DMA defines three parties in a data transfer from a peripheral device: the external DMA controller (party of the first part), the peripheral device (party of the second part), and the system memory (party of the third part). Conventional DMA controllers haven't really changed much over the years. They are still largely ISA devices, which are no longer used as a hard disk transfer interface.

First-party DMA and multiword DMA modes use the high-speed PCI bus; the peripheral device controls the transfer of data to and from system memory on its own, without the need of an external DMA controller involved, freeing up the CPU for other tasks. This process is also referred to as *bus mastering* because the peripheral device is the master of the PCI bus during the data transfer to memory, and first-party DMA is more commonly known as *bus mastering DMA*.

ULTRA DMA MODES

The next development in hard disk data transfer was the development of Ultra DMA modes, which improve the efficiency of the data transfer interface. Most of the components of the IDE/ATA interface are limited in terms of how fast they can carry data without serious problems from signaling problems and interference. Prior to Ultra DMA, one data transfer occurred on each clock cycle – on the rising or strobe edge of the clock signal. Ultra DMA transfers data on both the rising and falling edges of the clock signals, using a process called *double transition clocking*. Double transition clocking effectively doubles the data rate at any clock speed.

Ultra DMA also adds a cyclical redundancy checking (CRC) process to the data transfer to improve data integrity in its high-speed transfers. The sending device (for instance, the hard disk drive) calculates the CRC code that is sent along with the data. The receiving device (system memory) performs the same calculation and compares its code with that included with the data. If the two codes are different, it is assumed that the data was corrupted in transit, and a request is sent to the sending device to resend that data block. If frequent CRC errors are detected, the system has the option to move to a slower Ultra DMA mode or to disable Ultra DMA operations altogether.

Three Ultra DMA modes were specified in the ATA/ATAPI-4 standard with data transfer speeds up to 33 megabytes per second. Since then, two additional Ultra DMA modes have been defined with interface speeds now up to 100 megabytes per second. Table 11-4 lists the characteristics of the Ultra DMA modes in use.

TABLE 11-4 ULTRA DMA MODES

Ultra DMA Mode	Cycle Time	Maximum Transfer Speed
0	240 ns	16.7 megabytes per second
1	160 ns	25.0 megabytes per second
2	120 ns	33.3 megabytes per second
3	90 ns	44.4 megabytes per second
4	60 ns	66.7 megabytes per second
5	40 ns	100.0 megabytes per second

Modes 0 and 1 haven't been used in hard disk drive interfaces and were defined primarily for backward compatibility. Most of today's hard drives implement Ultra DMA mode 5.

Hard disk drives that support Ultra DMA are typically labeled as Ultra ATA/nn, where the *nn* represents the data transfer speed of the interface in use. For example, an Ultra DMA mode 5 system is commonly labeled as Ultra ATA/100.

To actually implement Ultra DMA on a PC, several system features and components must be present:

♦ *80-conductor cable:* Ultra DMA modes 3, 4, and 5 require an 80-wire cable. If a 40-conductor cable (the standard IDE/ATA cable) is in use, the interface will disable transfer speeds of 66 MHz or higher.

♦ *Hard disk controller:* The controller in use must be compatible with the Ultra DMA interface.

♦ *Hard disk drive:* The hard disk drive must be Ultra DMA compatible, and the appropriate Ultra DMA mode must be enabled.

♦ *Operating system:* The BIOS and the operating system must be Ultra DMA compatible.

Configuring an IDE/ATA interface

On a newer PC with only a single hard disk drive, configuring an IDE/ATA interface is relatively easy. Adding a second hard disk drive to the interface isn't much harder; in fact, it might be easier. However, complications appear when adding older hard disk drives, adding a third or fourth disk drive, installing hard disks and ATAPI devices on the same channel, or enabling advanced transfer protocols such as bus mastering DMA.

Perhaps the most difficult part of working with transfer protocols such as Ultra DMA is the 80-conductor cable. The 40-pin standard IDE/ATA cable was hard enough to get properly installed, and the 80-pin Ultra DMA cable only adds to the difficulty.

ALIGNING AN IDE/ATA DATA CABLE

The pin 1 edge of an IDE/ATA data cable, whether it's 40- or 80-conductor, is marked with either a red or blue stripe. If the cable is installed improperly – for example, upside down – you will definitely get beep codes and error messages when you boot the PC – typically something like the hard disk drive is missing.

 See Chapter 4 for more information on the BIOS beep codes and error messages.

The IDE/ATA connector on the motherboard or controller card should also be marked with a 1 to indicate the location of socket 1 in the connector. Carefully align the cable's socket 1 to the connector's pin 1 (matching up all the other pins and sockets) and push the cable connector into the controller's connector. Most of the time, the controller or motherboard connector is also *keyed;* that is, it has a physical feature meant to prevent it from being connected incorrectly. Figure 11-1 shows two IDE/ATA connectors on a typical Pentium-class motherboard.

Figure 11-1: IDE/ATA connectors on a motherboard.

CONFIGURING IDE/ATA

Before you start the actual configuration of the interface, you must decide how you wish to configure the devices to be attached to the interface.

1. On a typical system these days, with one hard disk drive and an ATAPI CD-ROM, the hard disk is normally configured as the master drive on the primary IDE/ATA channel and the CD-ROM drive as the master on the secondary channel. Mixing these two drives on a single channel (with the disk as the master and the CD-ROM as the slave) is not recommended. Remember that the channel will default to the slowest interface that supports both devices. This configuration also allows for a second hard disk drive to be added and perhaps a second CD-ROM or DVD drive as well.

2. After you decide on the device configurations, make any necessary jumper changes on the devices.

See Chapter 10 for information on hard disk drive jumper settings.

3. Configure the motherboard for the IDE/ATA interface. Motherboards use either jumpers or BIOS settings to configure an IDE/ATA interface. If you're not sure whether your motherboard has jumpers, check the motherboard's documentation, which you should do anyway.

4. Follow the manufacturer's procedures to enable the IDE/ATA interface required to support each channel.

5. Enable the BIOS setup data setting for AutoDetect, which allows the system to configure the IDE/ATA devices automatically.

If the motherboard has jumpers, they are typically labeled with a *JP* code, such as JP10. You should also know that some motherboards use a *J* code, such as J12, for labeling pin connectors, so make sure that you know which one you're working with.

Considering EIDE

Enhanced IDE (EIDE) is a standard for a high performance hard disk interface that was developed by Western Digital for use with its hard disk drives. EIDE supports two IDE (actually IDE/ATA) channels and up to four devices. The IDE/ATA interface supported on virtually all Pentium-class motherboards since the mid-1990s is an EIDE-level interface.

Working with SCSI

Small Computer System Interface (SCSI; pronounced *skuz*-zee) controllers are built into SCSI devices, such as hard disk drives, tape drives, CD-ROMs, and more. The SCSI bus is capable of connecting many devices, both internal and external, to a single SCSI controller on a common SCSI bus interface. Several different SCSI standards are available that use a variety of different connectors. Table 11-5 lists the connectors used internally and externally for each of the various SCSI standards in use. Figures 11-2 and 11-3 illustrate the connectors referenced in the table.

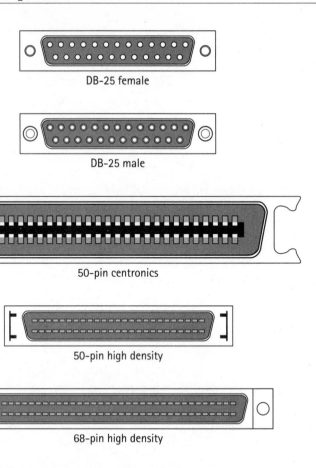

DB-25 female

DB-25 male

50-pin centronics

50-pin high density

68-pin high density

68-pin very high density

Figure 11-2: External SCSI connectors.

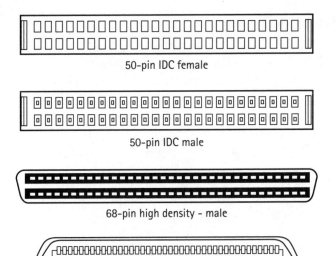

50-pin IDC female

50-pin IDC male

68-pin high density - male

80-pin SCSI SCA connector

Figure 11–3: Internal SCSI connectors.

TABLE 11–5 SCSI STANDARDS AND THEIR CONNECTORS

SCSI Standard	External Connector	Internal Connector
SCSI–1	50-pin Centronics	50-pin insulation displacement connector (IDC)
SCSI–2	50-pin high density	50-pin IDC
Ultra SCSI	50-pin high density	50-pin IDC
Fast SCSI	50-pin high density	50-pin IDC
Wide SCSI	68-pin high density	68-pin high density
Fast Wide SCSI	68-pin high density	68-pin high density
Ultra SCSI–3	68-pin high density	68-pin high density
Ultra2 SCSI–3	68-pin very high density	68-pin high density

Connecting with SCA

Single connector attachment (SCA) connectors are designed to simplify hard drive connections for hot-swappable hard disk drives, such as those used in a RAID system. The SCA standard combines a Wide SCSI connector and a hard drive power connection into a single, compact 80-pin adapter, like the one shown in Figure 11-4.

Figure 11-4: A single connector attachment (SCA) adapter combines a SCSI connector with a power connection.

Differentiating SCSI voltages

SCSI connectors must support the voltage differential of the SCSI standard in use. When buying cables for a SCSI bus or a SCSI device, make sure that you match the voltage differential of the SCSI standard in use.

The *voltage differential*, also called the *signaling* type, affects the total length of the SCSI chain. Here are the signaling types used on a SCSI bus:

◆ *Single-ended (SE):* Supports a terminated SCSI bus chain not longer than 3 to 6 meters.

◆ *High-voltage Differential (HVD):* Allows for a SCSI chain of up to 25 meters.

◆ *Low-voltage Differential (LVD):* A less-costly signaling method that supports an overall distance of only 12 meters.

Connecting SCSI

When selecting a SCSI host adapter, one of the first decisions to be made is the type of host adapter that you want. A variety of SCSI host adapters are available that vary widely in their cost and features. Generally, low-end adapters are designed specifically to provide access to external and non-hard disk drive SCSI devices, such as a scanner or CD-RW drive. High-end SCSI adapters have more capabilities and deliver better performance for hard disk drives.

The characteristic that best differentiates SCSI host adapters is the expansion bus for which the expansion card is designed. Although SCSI host adapters have been made for virtually all popular I/O buses, PCI and ISA are the most common today.

Because ISA is limited to not more than about 8 megabytes per second, which would limit the performance of the SCSI channel, it's typically a poor choice. Thus, a PCI SCSI host adapter is really the only choice. Even standard PCI can limit the performance of the later SCSI standards available, so higher-end SCSI standards, such as Ultra160, require 64-bit PCI and the newer PCI-X bus, which support over 200 megabytes per second and up to 1 gigabyte per second, respectively. Another reason to use PCI to support a SCSI host adapter is PCI's support for bus mastering.

Higher-performance PCI cards, which are typically 64-bit devices, are backward compatible with 32-bit PCI and will fit into a standard PCI slot.

Configuring a SCSI hard disk drive

Unlike an IDE/ATA hard disk controller, the SCSI bus is not configured nor supported by the system BIOS. The boot ROM on the SCSI host adapter provides support for the SCSI drive along with any operating system-specific device drivers provided with the SCSI system or a third-party vendor.

As long as the PCI bus is enabled and there are no system resource conflicts with the host adapter, the SCSI system should essentially support itself. However, you must provide or verify a small bit of configuration data and a few settings:

◆ Host adapter type

◆ Host adapter number

◆ Target ID of the hard disk controller

◆ Logical unit number (LUN) of the hard disk drive

Each device on a SCSI bus must have a unique SCSI bus ID assigned to it, including the host adapter. Each SCSI peripheral device has a built-in controller, and the device controller is what the ID number identifies. Up to 8 controllers can be installed on a SCSI 1 bus with IDs from 0 to 7. On a SCSI 2 bus, up to 16 controllers can be installed with IDs from 0 to 15. The host adapter is typically assigned ID 7 in either standard.

SCSI devices can be installed on the bus in any order, but each must have a unique controller ID. A device's ID is typically set via a jumper, Dual Inline Packaging (DIP) switch, or thumb-wheel on the device itself. Check the host adapter and SCSI device's documentation for the appropriate setting procedure.

Hard Disk Interface Terminology

Here are a few of the terms that you should know to effectively support hard disk drive interfaces:

- ◆ *Fibre channel (FC):* Although it has other applications, one of its uses is as a disk drive interface that supports up to 400 megabytes per second in full-duplex, half-duplex, or dual loop configurations. Typically, FC is implemented on a continuous arbitrated loop (Fibre Channel-Arbitrated Loop [FC-AL]) and can support up to 127 discrete storage devices or host systems without switching in high-end storage area networks (SANs).

- ◆ *Parallel ATA (ATA):* This industry standard, generally referred to as just *ATA,* defines a command and register set for the disk drive interface to the PC. ATA is the current hard disk interface standard and is implemented in several direct attached storage (DAS) and network attached storage (NAS) systems.

- ◆ *Parallel Small Computer System Interface (SCSI):* Commonly referred to as *SCSI,* this is a shared bus technology used to connect internal and external devices to a PC or server.

- ◆ *Serial ATA (SATA):* This is one of the very latest disk interface technologies that were designed to replace parallel ATA. SATA supports data transfer rates from 150 to 300 megabytes per second.

- ◆ *Serial attached SCSI (SAS):* This standard is under development as an improvement over parallel SCSI. As currently defined, SAS will support up to 128 devices on a single SCSI channel with speeds up to 300 megabytes per second.

Troubleshooting Disk Interface Issues

After it's configured and operating, not really much can or will go wrong with an IDE/ATA or SCSI disk drive interface. More commonly, a disk drive problem is physical (referring to the cables or power connections) or something power-related or logical. However, you can certainly check some things as a part of diagnosing a hard disk problem. The following sections include the most common things to troubleshoot.

Clearing out unnecessary connections

For general performance considerations, you might check for the following:

1. If they're not in use or needed by the PC, disable the IDE/ATA functions on any sound or multimedia cards. Check the manufacturer's documentation for the location and procedure to do so.

2. Install new IDE/ATA devices on the motherboard IDE/ATA channels, if available, a multifunction I/O controller, or hard disk controller card. If any existing controllers have available space, use them in place of the IDE/ATA cards packaged with IDE/ATA devices.

Every IDE/ATA device must be assigned a unique set of system resources, regardless of the number of IDE/ATA connectors available on a PC. In most cases, if two IDE/ATA controllers share an I/O address or an IRQ, the system will lock up.

Installing more than one device on an IDE/ATA channel

If you wish to configure more than one IDE/ATA device on a single channel, here are some considerations:

◆ *Two hard disk drives:* Place these devices on IDE0 (primary) with the boot disk as the master and the other as the slave.

◆ *Hard disk drive and CD-ROM:* Although this is not generally recommended, if you need to mix these devices on the same IDE/ATA channel, make sure that the hard disk is the master and the CD-ROM is the slave.

◆ *CD-ROM and tape drive:* Place these devices on IDE1 (secondary) with the CD-ROM as the master and the tape drive as the slave.

◆ *Other IDE/ATA device with either a CD-ROM or tape drive:* Place these devices on IDE1 (secondary) with the CD-ROM as the master and the other device as the slave, or the other device as the master and the tape drive as the slave.

You probably shouldn't mix an IDE/ATA hard disk drive and a tape drive on the same IDE/ATA channel. If you do, you risk data corruption on the channel.

Isolating IDE/ATA interface problems

IDE/ATA hard disk drive problems have a number of possible causes:

◆ A newly installed hard disk is improperly configured.

◆ The hard disk drive configuration information in the BIOS setup is incorrect.

◆ A virus is present on the hard disk drive.

◆ The data cable on the hard disk drive is not properly installed or is damaged.

◆ A system resource conflict exists with the hard disk controller and another device (most likely newly installed).

◆ The disk drive's partitions are corrupted or have been deleted.

◆ On a Pentium-class PC, the boot sector on the hard disk is write protected.

The basic troubleshooting process for a hard disk error is

1. Boot the system from a clean boot disk.

   The problem could be a resource conflict or a setting in the `autoexec.bat` or `config.sys` files.

2. Check the hard disk drive's configuration in the Complementary Metal-Oxide Semiconductor (CMOS) settings.

   If the drive is not properly identified or specified, the system typically won't boot up.

3. Run an antivirus program to scan the hard disk drive and memory.

4. Check the power and data cable connections to the hard disk drive and to the motherboard connectors or a multifunction I/O controller card.

5. Check the motherboard's documentation to verify that the appropriate jumpers are set to enable IDE/ATA support.

Improving the performance of a slow hard disk drive on a Windows 9*x* system

If an IDE/ATA hard disk drive is performing slowly on Windows 9*x* systems, the system might be in MS-DOS compatibility mode. This can happen when the hard disk controller isn't properly initialized when Windows 9*x* was started. When this condition occurs, a `NOIDE` entry is created in the registry, which tells Windows not to attempt to initialize the protected-mode driver required by the IDE/ATA controller to serialize between primary and secondary IDE/ATA channels.

Always back up the registry files before making any edits to the registry. See "Backing up (and restoring) the Windows registry" later in this chapter.

To change the drive compatibility mode settings, use the following steps:

1. Choose Start → Run.

2. In the Run dialog box that appears, enter **regedit** and then click OK to display the Registry Editor applet.

   The Registry Editor has two panels: The left-hand panel contains the registry key tree, and the right-hand panel displays the contents of each key selected.

3. Expand the HKEY_LOCAL_MACHINE key and locate the System/CurrentControlSet/Services/VxD/IOS folder by expanding each successive folder until the contents of the IOS folder appear in the right-hand panel.

4. In the Setting (right-hand) panel, find the NoIDE setting, if any, and delete it.

5. Exit the Registry Editor to save the changes, if any, and reboot the system.

 You might also want to scan the hard disk drive for a virus. A virus that modifies the Master Boot Record (MBR) can shift the disk drive to MS-DOS compatibility mode. To repair the MBR, boot into MS-DOS mode and run `fdisk /mbr`.

Backing up (and restoring) the Windows registry

Any time that you plan to make changes to the information stored in the registry of a Windows system, you should create a backup of the registry, just to be safe. A corrupt registry can keep a PC from starting up — never a fun thing.

To create a backup of the registry, follow these steps:

1. Choose Start → Run and enter **regedit** in the Open text box.

   This displays the Registry Editor.

2. On the Menu bar, choose Registry and then choose Export registry from the menu list to open a new window that asks you to name the exported registry file and to choose its destination folder.

3. Click the X in the corner of the applet to close the Registry Editor.

Your registry backup will be exported and stored using the name that you provided in the location that you selected.

If you ever need to restore a previous registry version, open the Registry Editor (Step #1 in the preceding steps) and choose Import from the Registry menu list. However, I strongly recommend that you back up the current (though suspect) version of the registry before restoring a previous one.

Chapter 12

Floppy Disks and Removable Storage Devices

IN THIS CHAPTER

The floppy disk, which has been obsolete for at least five years, still hangs on and can still be found in most PC systems and even new systems being sold today. Rumor has had the floppy disk dying off to be replaced by Zip/Jaz disks, SuperDisks, and other removable storage media. In this chapter, I cover the following:

- ◆ Reviewing the construction and operation of a floppy disk drive

- ◆ Using other removable storage devices

- ◆ Maintaining a floppy disk drive

- ◆ Troubleshooting and resolving floppy disk drive issues

THE FUTURE OF THE FLOPPY DISK DRIVE is allegedly becoming less secure with each wave of new technology. However, in spite of its projected imminent demise, it is still around long after newer technologies were supposed to have replaced it.

Understanding the Floppy Disk Drive

The floppy disk drive continues to be included in even the newest PC systems, years after it was to have been made obsolete by newer and better types of storage devices. The floppy disk has had a variety of sizes over its lifetime, including the 8", 5.25", and 3.5" disks, the latter of which has been the most popular size for about ten years now. Figure 12-1 illustrates the features of the 3.5" diskette.

Floppy disk drive construction

The floppy disk drive is an internal device that is mounted into an open drive bay of the system case. Although it is an internal device, its bezel (its front plate) extends through the drive bay opening and the case.

A 3.5" floppy disk drive is about the same size as most newer hard disk drives. Newer cases mount the diskette in a smaller drive bay or require an adapter kit to

mount it into a full-sized drive bay. If your system is old enough to have a 5.25"
drive, it is most likely a half-height drive (about 1.75 inches in height) and fits into
a full-sized drive bay.

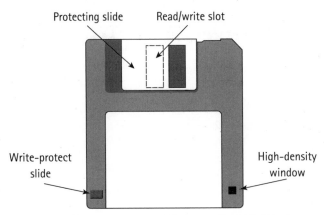

Figure 12-1: The components and features of a 3.5" diskette.

The floppy disk drive is made up of numerous components, which are similar in
name and function to those of a hard disk drive. Here are the primary components
of the floppy disk drive:

- ◆ *Connectors:* A floppy disk drive uses two connecters to connect to the system: a data connector that connects the drive to the floppy disk controller
  (FDC) and a power connector that supplies DC power from the power supply. Most floppy disk data cables, like the one shown in Figure 12-2, connect either one or two floppy disk drives to the FDC. On the rare system
  that connects two floppy disk drives, Drive A is connected to the cable
  above (after) the twist in the cable, and Drive B is connected below
  (before) the twist. Depending on the manufacturer and model, the floppy
  disk drive uses either a power supply connector like the one used for the
  hard disk drive or a smaller flat connector. Virtually all power supply
  form factors include at least one power connector for a floppy disk drive.

- ◆ *Head actuator:* Most floppy disks have 80 tracks per side, and the head
  actuator, which is powered by a stepper motor, moves the read/write
  heads from track to track. The stepper motor has a stop for each track on
  the disk. If the head develops alignment (azimuth) problems, it's cheaper
  to replace the disk drive than to realign the heads.

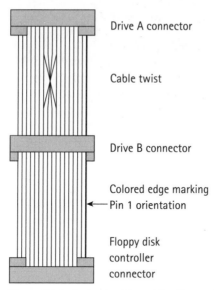

Drive A connector

Cable twist

Drive B connector

Colored edge marking
← Pin 1 orientation

Floppy disk
controller
connector

Figure 12-2: A standard two-drive floppy disk data cable.

♦ *Read/write heads:* The process used by a floppy disk drive to read from or write to the disk media is very much like that used with a hard disk drive. An electromagnetic field aligns the media particles to store electrical values that represent binary data. However, because the floppy disk media has a lower areal density, its read/write heads don't need to be as sensitive as the heads used on a hard disk. The read/write heads of a floppy disk, typically one for each side of the disk, access the media through a slot in the disk's outer jacket. The heads move in a straight line up and back over the slot to access the disk's tracks.

Areal density measures the number of bits per square inch on a disk's media and is calculated by multiplying the number of bits per inch times the number of tracks per inch. A larger areal density indicates that a disk uses more bits per inch to store data.

♦ *Media:* Except on PCs more than ten years old, virtually all floppy disk drives are designed to use 3.5" diskettes (refer to Figure 12-1). The 3.5" disk was developed to overcome the fragility of the 5.25" disk that preceded it and to provide a smaller, better-protected disk. The 3.5" diskette features a rigid outer jacket, a sturdy metal slide to protect the read/write slot, and a sliding window switch that write-protects the disk. A floppy disk has between 70 to 150 tracks compared with the thousands of tracks on a hard disk.

◆ *Spindle motor:* When you insert a floppy disk into a drive, a clamping mechanism that's attached to the spindle motor locks the disk into a fixed position. The spindle motor rotates the disk inside its jacket and under the read/write heads. The speed of the spindle motor is tied to the physical size of the disk, but for the 3.5" disk, the spindle motor rotates the disk at 300 revolutions per minute (rpm). This very slow rotation speed adds to the latency and data transfer speeds of the disk, but it also keeps the contact heads from wearing out the disk.

Maintaining head alignment

The read/write heads in a floppy disk drive are controlled by stepper motors that extend and retract the heads in steps that correspond to the tracks (see Figure 12-3) on the disk media. The stepper motors are controlled by signals generated by the FDC, which is included in the system's chipset, in the Super I/O chip, or on an FDC or multidisk expansion card.

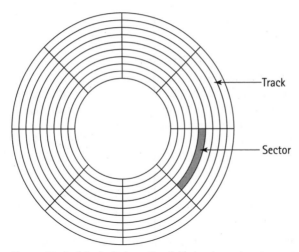

Figure 12-3: A logical view of a disk's tracks and sectors.

When you power up a PC, the floppy disk's read/write heads are automatically positioned over track 0, which is the first track on the disk. Most floppy disk drives include a sensor that indicates when the heads are over track 0. As data is either read or written to the disk media, the stepper motor moves the head positioner in or out one track for each step signal received from the FDC.

The floppy disk drive and its read/write heads have no clue where the heads are exactly positioned. It is assumed that because the heads began over track 0, the movements in or out from that point are accurately positioning the heads over the correct track. In contrast, a hard disk drive, which uses servo systems, is constantly monitoring and correcting (when needed) the exact position of its read/write heads.

A floppy disk drive has no feedback mechanisms to indicate whether it's properly aligned over the intended track location. Because of its built-in feedback mechanisms, a hard disk drive system is referred to as a *closed-loop system;* and because it lacks a feedback system, a floppy disk drive is an *open-loop system.*

RADIAL MISALIGNMENT

If the track 0 sensor isn't properly adjusted, the read/write heads could have a false starting position, which would be reflected in the misalignment of the read/write heads over the tracks on the disk.

Because the positioning mechanism in a floppy disk drive uses a stepper function that moves the read/write heads in even step increments across the disk media, the track 0 sensor and the read/write heads must be properly aligned to ensure that data is stored and retrieved reliably. The floppy disk might not be the sexiest device on the PC, but when you need it, you definitely want it to work right.

The read/write head positioner can become misaligned to the point that the heads aren't completely positioned over a track, which results in a condition called *radial misalignment.* In this situation, when the head tries to read or write data, the electromagnetic signal of the data might be greatly reduced, or interference might be detected from nearby tracks. These conditions can result in a bad data read or write or an incomplete erasure of the data.

Remember that diskettes are portable. Trying to port data between two floppy disk drives that might have misaligned heads (especially if they're misaligned in opposite directions) can result in one drive not being able to read the other drive's data.

 Some high-capacity floppy disk drives are available that employ servo systems to position the read/write heads. These drives are relatively expensive compared with the common variety of floppy disk drives.

AZIMUTH

Azimuth refers to the rotational alignment of the read/write heads. Floppy disk read/write heads can also become misaligned by being slightly rotated right or left on their axis (azimuth). Don't misunderstand: As the read/write heads are moved out over the tracks on the disk media, the head positioner rotates the heads very slightly to keep them in alignment to the curvature of the disk tracks. The azimuth alignment is set at the factory and should never change. If the drive becomes damaged or badly worn, the azimuth could become misaligned.

Aligning a floppy disk drive

Two sets of alignment parameters control the reliable operation of a floppy disk drive: read/write head alignments and drive operation alignments.

READ/WRITE HEAD ALIGNMENT

A floppy disk drive uses three primary read/write head alignment parameters that should be verified and maintained:

◆ *Radial head alignment:* Perhaps the most important of the three alignment parameters, this parameter reflects the position of the read/write heads over any specific track location. As much as they are taken for granted, even a mere 600-millionths of an inch misalignment will put a floppy disk drive out of specification and likely cause read/write problems. Figure 12-4 illustrates the proper and improper radial alignment of the read/write heads.

Proper radial and azimuth alignment

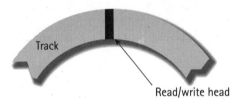

Radial misalignment

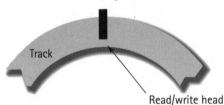

Figure 12–4: The upper illustration shows the proper radial alignment for a floppy disk's read/write heads, and the lower illustration shows an example of improper radial alignment.

◆ *Azimuth head alignment:* Although occurring much less frequently than radial misalignment, azimuth misalignment can be just as serious. Azimuth alignment refers to the angle of the read/write heads to their vertical axis. Azimuth is measured in minutes (fractions of degrees), which reflects its sensitivity. Even a few minutes of misalignment can cause serious read/write problems. Figure 12-5 shows an example of azimuth misalignment.

Figure 12-5: An exaggerated illustration of the azimuth misalignment of a floppy disk's read/write head.

◆ *Index timing alignment:* Floppy disk drives include an *index sensor,* which is a mechanism that sends out a signal each time that the disk rotates to let the drive know the starting point of each track. If the index sensor becomes misaligned, the starting point of every track is misaligned. In this situation, the data written before the sensor became misaligned might become unreachable. Fortunately, most of today's soft-sectored disk formats no longer rely on this alignment or the index sensor being perfectly aligned. So, unless the index sensor has failed completely, index-timing problems seldom occur.

DRIVE ALIGNMENT

In addition to read/write head alignments, a few other adjustments should be maintained in a floppy disk drive to ensure its reliable operation. The primary adjustments are described in the following list:

◆ *Head positioner linearity:* Because the spacing of the tracks on the disk media should be constant, the drive's radial alignment must be maintained across the entire disk. The ability of the drive's head positioner to retain its radial alignment across all tracks is, therefore, equally as important. A drive that has proper radial alignment on one track but improper alignment on another track can cause a read failure of a diskette moved to another PC.

◆ *Index timing:* This is the standardized angle between the index sensor and the read/write heads and is typically a physical adjustment made to the drive's index sensor.

◆ *Index skew:* This adjustment controls the drive's ability to maintain constant index timing across all tracks on the media. If the index timing is good on track 0 but bad on track 96, the drive has an index-skew problem. This problem is caused by a misalignment of the head positioner mechanism and can affect the drive's azimuth if not brought back into specification.

◆ *Spindle eccentricity:* The tracks on a diskette should have the same fixed distance from the diskette's center while it rotates. A drive that has an eccentricity problem – a slight wobble while it rotates – varies the radial alignment along a track while it moves under the read/write heads. This situation can result in some tracks being readable and others being unreadable.

◆ *Spindle speed:* This drive parameter indicates how many revolutions the drive is spinning the diskette, either in revolutions per minute or milliseconds per revolution. The drive should spin a diskette constantly at the correct speed. If the drive is spinning too slowly or too fast, the FDC can't work in sync with the drive.

◆ *Track 0 sensor alignment:* Because the FDC relies on the track 0 sensor to accurately mark the beginning point of the read/write heads, if the sensor is out of adjustment, the reference point for every track on the disk is changed. Therefore, the proper adjustment and alignment of the track 0 sensor is critical.

Misalignment causes

There are probably as many causes for a floppy disk drive becoming misaligned as there are vendors, models, and designs of floppy disk drives. Some common causes for misalignment are

◆ *Damage:* When diskettes are improperly inserted into a disk drive, or when pencils, paper clips, or other foreign objects are used to clean the drive, the read/write heads or the head positioning system can be bent or damaged. Perhaps the damage isn't enough to cause the drive to fail completely, but the damage could be significant enough to misalign several vital adjustments or cause a problem that surfaces some time in the future.

◆ *Dirt:* Because a floppy disk drive has a big open slot and diskettes are not always cared for in the most sterile manner, flotsam, jetsam, and other debris make their way inside the drive. This debris can speed up the wear of the drive and even change how its sensors and other mechanisms work.

◆ *Wear and tear:* The wear on the drive's components from the constant movement of the head positioner system can eventually cause the radial alignment to become out of adjustment.

 All floppy disk drives will eventually wear out, become misaligned, or fail. To lengthen the life of a floppy disk drive, use good-quality disk drives and high-quality (meaning name-brand) diskettes, and keep the drive clean and properly maintained.

Building a Better Floppy Disk

Although it might be the most common of the removable media drives, the floppy disk drive has several would-be replacement systems available on the market. In fact, at one time, it was believed that the 100MB Zip drive (described in the following section) would be the natural replacement for the floppy disk drive. However, with the growing popularity of the CD-ROM, many software publishers began releasing their software products on CDs in place of floppy diskettes, and the need and opportunity to replace the floppy disk drive never came about.

What did happen was that many types of "super disks" emerged, including the Iomega Zip and Jaz drives and the Imation LS-120 SuperDisk. With their expanded capacities, as compared with the 1.44MB capacity of the 3.5" floppy disk, the new forms of removable media are a much better choice for storing large files and creating hard-disk system backups on home and workstation PCs. The more popular removable media drives, both internal and external, are discussed in the following sections.

Zipping and jazzing along

A Zip disk, which shouldn't be confused with a Zip file (a file created with WinZip software that contains compressed versions of one or more other files), is physically a little larger than a floppy disk but can currently store 100, 250, or 750MB of data. Figure 12-6 shows Iomega Corporation's 250MB Zip external drive. The larger 750MB capacity Zip disk makes it an excellent alternative to CD-R or tape. For more information on Iomega's products, visit www.iomega.com.

Figure 12-6: The Iomega 250 Zip drive and disk.

Photo courtesy of Iomega Corporation.

THE ZIP DISK VERSUS THE FLOPPY DISK

What differentiates a Zip disk from a floppy disk is the type of magnetic coating used on the Zip disk. To keep costs down, both for manufacturing and for the consumer, floppy disks use a fairly low-quality magnetic material to coat the storage media. A Zip disk uses a high-quality material that allows the read/write heads of a Zip disk drive to be much smaller than those of a floppy disk drive. The read/write heads on a Zip disk are about ten times smaller than the heads on a floppy drive, allowing the Zip drive to store data signals more closely together.

Another feature that allows the Zip drive to store and retrieve more data is that it uses a head positioning mechanism that's very similar to that used in a hard disk drive. A Zip disk stores data on literally thousands of tracks per inch and optimizes the use of space on the disk media.

THE JAZ DISK

The Iomega Jaz (pronounced like the word *jazz*) disk, which is actually a cartridge, is very much like a mini hard disk. Each Jaz cartridge has several disk media platters that are housed in a plastic case. The Jaz drive provides the read/write heads and the spindle drive mechanism that spins the platters past the heads.

Storing on a SuperDisk

A product that competes with the Iomega Zip disk is the SuperDisk from Imation Corporation (www.imation.com). The SuperDisk has the same physical size and shape as the 3.5" floppy disk, but because of its storage capacity, the SuperDisk requires a special disk drive.

The SuperDisk stores as much as 120MB, which is roughly the capacity of 85 floppy disks. Although the SuperDisk drive supports standard diskettes, standard floppy drives do not support SuperDisk diskettes.

Whereas Zip and Jaz drive models are available for both internal and external mounting on a PC, the SuperDisk drive is primarily an internal device.

 Another removable media used for many of the same purposes as the Zip and SuperDisk is the rewritable CD or CD-RW. See Chapter 13 for more information on CD drives.

Working with removable hard disks

One way to use removable media is to install a docking kit that includes a drive bay bracket and a special bezel that allows you to insert and remove an actual hard disk drive.

Why, you ask, would you want to be able to remove the hard disk drive from a PC? Well, perhaps the best reason is security, but using a removable drive as a backup is often the reason as well. I recommend using a hard disk of the same type and capacity to completely back up or mirror the primary drive on a system. However, if you leave the backup drive in the PC, the same forces that could destroy the primary drive are likely to destroy the backup as well.

Universal Serial Bus (USB) technology has facilitated the use of completely external and portable hard disk drives. Portable hard disk drives, which have all the same internal workings of the stationary, installed-inside-the-case disk drives, can be quickly and easily added or removed from a system without the need to interrupt the system or its user. One example is the 20GB Pockey drive (see Figure 12-7) from Pocketec (www.pocketec.net).

Figure 12-7: The 20GB Pockey drive is one example of a removable hard disk drive.
Photo courtesy of Pocketec.

Another way that an external hard disk drive can connect to the PC is through its Personal Computer Memory Card International Association (PCMCIA) or PC Card interface. The hard disk controller (HDC) is embedded in the PC Card that is inserted in the card slot, and the disk drive itself is a standard-sized external disk drive.

Another hard disk drive type that uses the PC Card slot is the microdrive, like the one shown in Figure 12-8. Microdrive hard disk drives are PC Cards that can add additional hard disk capacity to a notebook, palmtop, or other portable computing or graphics devices. Microdrives use the CompactFlash (flash memory) technology to store as much as 1GB of storage to a portable device. Not much bigger than a quarter, these drives pack a lot of storage into a compact area.

Figure 12-8: This microdrive hard disk drive provides up to 1GB of removable hard disk capacity to portable devices.

Plugging in a USB drive

A recent development in external removable media is the USB Pen drive, which gets its name from its packaging. The outer case of a pen drive, as shown in Figure 12-9, looks something like an ink pen, complete with pocket clip. The top part of the case removes to expose the USB port connector that plugs into a USB port on a PC.

Pen drives, which use flash memory technology to store data, are available from a variety of manufacturers.

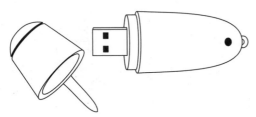

Figure 12-9: Although very small, a USB pen drive can store up to 1GB of data.

Dealing with Removable Media Issues

Removable media is not without its issues. Because the media is removable, it's bound to have problems, but in general, these devices tend to be mostly trouble-free. However, some things can and do go wrong occasionally.

The following sections deal with the more common problems or actions required to keep removable media devices running properly.

Troubleshooting a floppy disk drive

Regardless of whether the floppy disk is a newly installed device or an existing drive, problems with the floppy disk drive are usually caused by one of the following conditions:

- ◆ A newly installed floppy disk drive isn't properly connected to the FDC or the power supply. Verify that the A: drive is above (after) the cable twist, and the B: drive, if installed, is below (before) the cable twist. The A: drive cannot connect to the B: position.

- ◆ The floppy disk drive is not enabled or set up correctly in the BIOS configuration data. Make sure that the device settings are appropriate for the drive, which is normally a 1.44MB, 3.5" drive.

See Chapter 4 for more information on BIOS and its configuration data settings.

♦ The system resource assignments of the floppy disk drive are conflicting with another device. If you've recently installed a new device, such as a tape drive or another floppy disk, remove it to see whether the problem is resolved. If so, either reinstall the device so that it doesn't conflict with the floppy or remove the floppy disk drive.

♦ The wrong version of the floppy disk drive device driver is in use.

♦ The diskette in the drive is bad, unformatted, or write protected. This is the most common cause of floppy disk problems. Replace the diskette, format it, or change the write-protect slide.

♦ The floppy disk drive (most likely the read/write heads) has gone bad, and the drive needs to be replaced.

Cleaning a floppy disk drive

Data is read and written to a floppy disk by the read/write heads directly contacting the media, which causes the heads to pick up bits of the recording media (which, like on a hard disk, is a magnetic metal oxide material) and any dirt or debris that has found its way inside the disk. This problem is compounded by the fact that the PC's cooling system forces air to flow through the drive, which carries dust, smoke, and other debris.

You should clean the floppy disk's read/write heads periodically . . . but not too often. In most cases, when the head begins to read or write to the disk media, it brushes aside any large bits of debris, but dust and other fine particles can collect on the head and damage it. The heads shouldn't be cleaned too often because the cleaning process can also wear them out.

Wait a minute! How can cleaning the read/write heads wear them out? Floppy disk cleaning disks only clean the read/write heads and work by rubbing (scraping) the read/write heads to clean them. Cleaning the drive too often can eventually wear out the drive's heads.

Keeping the entire drive clean requires a simple preventive maintenance routine. (Cleaning disks does nothing to clean the drive's mechanical parts.) The use of long-stemmed swabs and a mild cleaning solution can help to keep the interior of the drive clean. See Chapter 27 for more information on cleaning a floppy disk drive.

Maintaining a floppy disk's alignment

The best way to maintain the adjustment and alignment of a floppy disk drive is to use some of the same tools used by floppy disk manufacturers. Many vendors produce diskette and software products to test and adjust the critical alignments of a floppy disk, such as Accurite Technologies' Analog Alignment Diskette (AAD), which includes a set of test procedures and patterns commonly used by service and repair technicians to measure the various alignments of the disk drive. For more information, visit the Accurite Technologies Web site at www.accurite.com.

Formatting a floppy disk

A floppy disk, regardless of its size or density, must be formatted before it can receive and store data. Formatting performs two tasks, in two separate steps of the same process:

◆ *Low-level formatting:* Creates the organization structures on the disk, including the tracks and reference points for the sectors on each track

◆ *High-level formatting:* Adds the logical structures, including the File Allocation Table (FAT) and the root directory

You can purchase disks that are already formatted everywhere, including drugstores, supermarkets, discount clubs, and even computer supply stores. Preformatted diskettes might not work with every floppy disk drive and might need to be reformatted before you can use them. Formatting is also used to completely erase a diskette for future use.

Setting up a removable hard disk drive

If you want to add a removable hard disk drive to a PC, the following sections describe the materials and configuration steps that you should use.

ASSEMBLING THE COMPONENTS

To install a removable hard disk system on a PC, you need the following components:

◆ *Hard disk:* Okay, this might sound obvious, but just in case, you'll need at least one AT Attachment/Integrated Drive Electronics (ATA/IDE) or Small Computer System Interface (SCSI) hard disk drive.

◆ *Drive bay:* Perhaps this is the first thing that you should check. You'll need to have a 5.25" drive bay available on the system case. Otherwise, you might need to also change the system case or opt for an external device altogether.

- ◆ *Disk tray/docking bay:* A removable hard disk kit typically includes a removable hard disk tray (which is mounted on the hard disk drive) and a docking bay (which is installed in the case drive bay). Be sure that you get a docking bay that supports the drive interface type you plan to use (ATA/IDE or SCSI).

- ◆ *Data connector:* You need to have an available data connector on the ATA/IDE controller or controller card or the SCSI host adapter, as appropriate, and a power connector.

INSTALLING THE REMOVABLE DRIVE

Installing the removable hard disk system isn't particularly hard, and if you've ever installed an internal CD-ROM or hard disk drive, you know the drill. Here are the steps to complete the installation:

1. Slide the docking bay into the open 5.25" drive bay on the system case and secure it in place with the screws that came with it.

   Of course, you need to remove the system covers and the drive-bay bezel filler before you begin.

2. Connect the appropriate data and power connectors to the back of the docking station.

3. Set the appropriate master/slave level on the disk drive.

4. Connect the data and power connectors in the tray assembly to the hard disk drive.

5. Attach the removable tray assembly to the hard disk as directed in the documentation of the tray assembly.

6. You should now be ready to slide the disk drive (in the removable tray assembly) into the docking bay and connect the tray assembly connector into that of the docking station. Be sure to close the locking handle to hold the drive assembly securely in place.

You should only insert or remove the hard disk drive from the PC when the system is shut down and the power is off. Adding the docking bay does not automatically make the drive hot-swappable, which allows you to remove and replace the drive while the PC is running.

Chapter 13

CD-ROM and DVD

IN THIS CHAPTER

Like the cassette tape, the CD-ROM (Compact Disc–Read Only Memory) wasn't originally developed for use on a PC, but it has been adapted for this purpose very nicely. In fact, it has become the de facto standard for software product releases in a very short time.

Compared with its predecessor (the floppy disk), the CD-ROM has enormous storage capacity and is a little more durable and generally easier to use. On the PC, CD-ROMs really took off when the CD-ROM drive became commonplace on standard PC models. CDs are commonly used to distribute music, software, multimedia, databases, books, encyclopedias, mailing lists, and more to PC users. In this chapter, I detail the following:

- ◆ Installing an internal IDE/ATAPI CD-ROM drive
- ◆ Installing a DVD drive
- ◆ Installing a SCSI CD-ROM drive
- ◆ Adding CD-ROM support to a boot disk
- ◆ Troubleshooting an IDE/ATA/ATAPI CD-ROM drive
- ◆ Troubleshooting a SCSI CD-ROM drive
- ◆ Troubleshooting IDE CD-ROM master and slave conflicts
- ◆ Improving the performance of a CD-ROM drive
- ◆ Troubleshooting CD-ROM sound problems

CD-ROM DRIVES are now sold as standard equipment on virtually all PCs, including notebook PCs, although many higher-end PCs now feature a DVD-ROM drive instead (more on DVDs later in the chapter).

Grasping the Technology of Discs

The PC CD-ROM drive uses the same compact disc (CD) technology used for audio CDs. In fact, the physical media (see Figure 13-1) used to record data, programs, music, and multimedia on a CD-ROM for use with a PC is exactly the same as that used to record Creed, Garth, and Herbie Hancock.

When Is a Disk a Disc?

Many experts insist that the platters inside the hard disk are *discs*, and you'll see them referred to with that spelling in different publications and Web sites. Essentially, the two spellings (*disk* versus *disc*) are now interchangeable, but there are still those diehards who insist on the disc spelling. The CD-ROM and DVD folks insist that *disc* is reserved for optical disks. Whatever. Either spelling is fine — a disk is a disc is a disk — and the *disk* spelling is used most often.

Figure 13-1: A CD can be used to record music for audio playback or as a data source on a PC.

Formatting CD-ROMs

CD technology includes a variety of formats and applications, although most aren't designed for use on a PC. The two most common formats that are used on the PC are one for music CDs and one for data CDs.

Somewhat like the formatting used on hard and floppy disk drives, a CD's format is the pattern and method used to record its contents. In general, a CD is recorded in a spiraling pattern, in contrast to the circular track pattern used on a floppy or hard disk or a cassette tape. However, like the other secondary storage media, information is placed between the files on a CD to identify a file's beginning, end, size, and content type to the CD player.

COLORING THE BOOKS

The formats used to record a CD for use with a PC are

◆ *Compact Disc-Digital Audio (CD-DA):* The first standard CD format was developed for audio content (music and other recorded sounds). Royal Phillips Electronics Company and Sony Corporation developed CD-DA as the first standard for recording CDs. The specification of *CD-DA* is commonly referred to as the *Red Book,* and CD-DA is known as *Red Book audio.* Red Book defines the technical specifications for CD-DA, including the number and spacing of tracks on the disk, the number of minutes of contents, the data transfer (playback) rate, the error correction methods used to correct for minor sound errors, the format of the digital audio, and the physical specifications for compact discs, including the media's size. Although this standard is now more than 20 years old, it is still in use today for audio CDs.

CD standards are defined in a series of books that are designated by different colors, such as the Red Book, Yellow Book, and White Book.

◆ *CD-Read Only Memory (CD-ROM):* The CD's large data capacity makes it attractive to software developers, database compilers, and multimedia producers. The *CD-ROM*, as the CD was designated for use with the PC, has a capacity of 650 million bytes (MB) of data. The first CD-ROMs also used the 150 Kbps single-speed transfer rates used by audio CDs, which established the transfer rate as being relative to the CD-DA transfer rate. CD drives on PCs are still rated using a multiple of the CD-DA transfer rate. The CD-DA transfer rate is designated as 1X (one times). Modern CD-ROM drives are boasting 40X transfer rates, meaning that they transfer data from the CD at 40 times faster than the CD-DA standard of 150 Kbps.

To provide for data addressing on a CD, the Yellow Book standard was developed from the Red Book and specifies how data is stored on a CD-ROM. The *Yellow Book* designated two content sectors and recording modes to be used to store computer data (Mode 1) and compressed audio, video, graphic, or multimedia data (Mode 2). A Yellow Book CD can store both types of data content by using Mode 1 sectors to store computer data (such as programs and files) and Mode 2 sectors to store compressed multimedia content.

◆ *CD-ROM Extended Architecture (CD-ROM XA):* This adaptation of the Yellow Book (CD-ROM) format allows CD-ROM Mode 1 and Mode 2 sectors to be interleaved (mixed) on the disc. *CD-ROM XA* allows different types of data, music, programming, and graphics to be intermixed and stored on the same CD. Accessing a CD-ROM XA disc requires a CD-ROM drive certified for the CD-ROM XA format. A CD-ROM XA drive contains a hardware codec (compressor/decompressor) to deal with the compressed audio and video typically found on a CD-ROM XA disc.

◆ *CD-Interactive (CD-I):* This CD-ROM format is designed especially for multimedia producers. *CD-I* discs hold text, graphics, audio, and video in a single disc format. Special hardware was used to connect CD-I players to television screens for playback. CD-I, like the CD-ROM XA, is a derivative of the Yellow Book, but CD-I uses a proprietary and unique formatting.

◆ *Bridge CD:* This format standard, known as the *White Book*, bridges the CD-ROM XA and the CD-I formats and is compatible with either format interchangeably. CD-I discs work in CD-ROM XA drives, and CD-ROM XA discs work in CD-I drives. Examples of a bridge CD are

- *Video CD (VCD):* This format stores compressed video using a standard that's also defined in the White Book. VCDs use the Motion Picture Experts Group (MPEG) compression algorithms to store 74 minutes of full-motion video in the same space used by CD-DA audio. Playing a video CD requires a video CD-compatible CD-ROM drive or a video CD player. The compression algorithm used for VCD doesn't produce a high-quality video, and this format is giving way to the DVD.

- *Photo CD:* The photo CD standard, developed by Philips (but this time with Kodak), holds photographs in a digital form. The photo CD standard is defined in the *Orange Book* that also defines the CD-Recordable (CD-R) format, which I describe in the next section. A Photo CD uses CD-ROM Mode 2 formatting to store photographic images on a CD. The Photo CD is a Bridge CD that can be read by a CD-I drive or player.

RECORDABLE CD

The CD formats covered to this point have been read-only discs to which data cannot be stored or modified after manufacturing. Orange Book formats also allow users to take advantage of the large storage space on a CD and provide methods to allow data to be written to special CD media via special CD drives.

Two types of CD-R processes are used to record data to a CD:

◆ *Magneto Optical (MO):* More commonly known as CD-RW (Read/Write) discs, an MO disc can be written to, read, modified, and written to again.

◆ *WORM (Write Once/Read Many):* This is a CD-R disc that can have data or music written to it — but only once. Data written to a WORM disc is permanently recorded and cannot be erased or modified, and the disc itself cannot be written to a second time.

Dissecting CD media: Pulling apart the layers

A CD, like other forms of PC data storage, stores data in digital form. However, whereas hard disks, floppy disks, and memory store data in electromechanical forms, data is recorded on a CD with a more physical recording method. A look at how a CD is made is the first step to understanding how data is recorded to it.

A CD starts out as a slice of polycarbonate substrate with a diameter of about 4.75 inches that's 1.2 millimeters (about .05 inches) thick. A metal stamp, with the reverse image of a finished disc, is used to master (stamp) indentations into the substrate — a process called *mastering*. After it's mastered, the disc substrate has a pattern of pits and flats — *lands* — on its surface. Figure 13-2 illustrates the mastered substrate in a CD assembly.

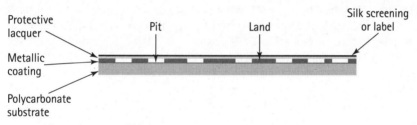

Figure 13-2: The layers of a CD.

Figure 13-2 illustrates the make up of a single-session disc. At the core of the disc is the substrate surface, with its pits and lands, which is overlaid with a shiny, reflective silver or aluminum coating. This shiny coating has a very important role in the ability of the drive to read the data stored on the CD. A clear plastic cover is placed over this. The CD's label or silk-screening is applied to the clear plastic cover.

Reading the CD

A CD-ROM drive works somewhat like a floppy disk drive. (See Chapter 12 for more information on floppy disks.) The difference is that in place of a read/write head to sense electromagnetic flux on the magnetic disk media, a CD disc spins while a laser beam sweeps over the lands and pits. The beam reflects to a sensor that senses whether the data in a certain location is a one or a zero.

As the laser beam sweeps across the disc surface, if it hits a *land* (the flat surface of the disc), the beam is reflected by the shiny metal coating and detected by a sensor as a binary zero. Should the beam hit a *pit* (tiny dents in the media), the beam is deflected and is not detected by the sensor. This takes place very quickly, with the beam shining on thousands of pits and lands per second.

Another difference between a floppy disk and a CD is that the CD is recorded on a single, long spiraling track instead of the floppy disk's circular track. This spiral track is about three miles long on a CD-DA disc and is the equivalent of about 16,000 tracks on a hard disk platter.

Recording data on a CD

Data is recorded on the CD's substrate core, which is located directly beneath the CD's label. The laser is beamed from the bottom of the CD directly through the clear portions of the substrate, which are about 1 millimeter (mm) thick. A CD can have minor scratches and still be read just fine. As long as the scratches don't interfere with the laser striking the substrate or reflecting back to the sensors – and the substrate is intact and undamaged – the disc should be readable. However, if the scratches are deep enough (1 mm or more) or smudges on the disc are thick enough, the disc would be unreadable.

The first sector on the CD is located at 0 minutes, 2 seconds, and 0 hundredths of a second (00:02:00) or 600 blocks into the CD's spiral track. A CD uses blocks of 512 bytes, which means that a minute of data uses 18,000 blocks and that there are 300 blocks in a second of data and 600 in the first two seconds. This also means that the first block in the first sector (Logical Block 0) is at 00:02:00 as well.

A CD-R disc is manufactured essentially the same as a CD-ROM disc but with some slight variations. In place of the substrate is a layer of organic dye over which is placed a reflective gold-colored metallic coating. Over this is the protective lacquer layer, just like on a CD-ROM. A CD-RW (magnetic optical) disc contains a layer of a special metal alloy, over which is placed the reflective gold-colored metallic coating and protective lacquer layer.

Writing to a CD

Data is recorded on a CD-R WORM disc by changing the reflective properties of the organic dye. After they're changed, the properties of the dye cannot be changed back. The light properties of the metal alloy used in the CD-RW (also known as a CD-MO) are changed to store a data bit, but the properties can be reset to their original values to rewrite the disc.

The newest form of CD-RW is the *CD-E* or *CD-Erasable*. This disc uses a technology called *phase change* to record or erase data stored on the disc. A CD-E uses a layer of silver alloy and different laser energy levels and temperatures to record, read, and erase data from the disc. Data is recorded on and erased from the silver alloy substrate by using a higher temperature than is used to read the disc. The higher energy and temperature crystallize the silver alloy, which changes its reflective properties.

Installing and Operating a CD-ROM Drive

A CD drive (any type of PC CD drive, including CD-R, CD-RW, and CD-E) typically fits in a PC's 5.25" half-height drive bay. A drive or a drive bay with a height of 1.75 inches is considered a half-height device or bay, which is the standard on virtually all newer PC cases.

CD-ROM drives have a sheet metal enclosure that surrounds the drive, and screw holes are tapped into the sides of the enclosure that allow for mounting it directly into a standard drive bay.

On some older PCs, a CD-ROM, as well as a hard or floppy disk drive, is mounted in the PC bay with mounting rails that attach to the sides of the drive and then slide into the drive bay. Another option is an external CD-ROM drive connected via a Small Computer System Interface (SCSI) adapter.

Looking into the read head assembly

The CD-ROM's laser, which is produced by an infrared laser diode, is aimed at a reflecting mirror in the read head assembly and not directly at the CD itself. The read head moves along the CD's spiral track just above the surface of the disc. The light beam from the laser reflects off the mirror to a lens that focuses the light on a specific point, where the light is reflected back from the disc's metallic layer.

The reflected light (the intensity of which depends on whether it's being reflected from a land or a pit on the disc substrate) is passed through a series of collectors, mirrors, and lenses that focus the reflected light and send it to a photo detector. The photo detector converts the light into an electrical signal. The CD-ROM rarely has read errors except when the laser is obstructed, a mirror becomes dusty, or some foreign object gets on the disc. If the CD-ROM disc and the mirrors are clean, very little can go wrong.

Because the CD-ROM disc spins, the components that read the disc don't require much movement. The read head assembly adjusts its position side to side to move along the spiraling track. The CD-ROM, unlike the DVD (Digital Versatile Disc), is a one-sided media with all its data recorded on the substrate. The CD-ROM drive requires only one read head and head assembly.

The read head is guided over the disc on a set of rails which position the head on the outermost edge of the disc on one end and stop it near the CD's hub ring on the other. A small motor integrated into the read head mechanism controls the positioning of the read head over the disc.

CONSTANT ROTATION

The CD-ROM disc rotates on a spindle that spins the disc at variable speeds. The speed of the disc's rotation depends on the part of the disc being read. A hard disk drive spins at the same speed regardless of the position of the read/write heads, which uses a constant spin speed — constant angular velocity (CAV). CAV ensures that every spin takes the same amount of time.

CAV is necessary because the inside tracks of a hard or floppy disk are much shorter than its outside tracks. When a disk drive's read/write heads are over the outside tracks, the disk travels a longer linear path than it does with inside tracks. This phenomenon is measured as linear velocity, which is higher for outside tracks and shorter for inside tracks — and it is never constant across an entire disk. To compensate, many newer hard disk drives now use *zoned bit recording* to place more data on the outside tracks and less on inside tracks.

VARIABLE ROTATION

A CD-ROM drive adjusts the speed of the spindle motor using constant linear velocity (CLV) to keep the linear velocity of the disc constant. The spindle turns slower when the read head is near the outside edge of the CD and turns faster when the read head moves toward the hub ring. CLV ensures that the same amount of data passes under the read head at any point. Early CD-ROM drives operated at about 210 to 539 revolutions per minute (rpm) and a standard data transfer rate of 150 Kbps, or one time (1X) the CD-DA standard rate. As the electronics in CD-ROM drives have improved, the spindle motor is now capable of faster spindle speeds, which translate to increased transfer rates.

CLV is used on CD-ROM drives with transfer speeds of 12X or slower. Newer CD-ROM drives use CAV and now vary the transfer rate to synchronize with the linear velocity of the disc. On CD-ROM drives with speed ratings higher than 12X, the transfer speed rating (13X, 24X, 32X, 72X) represents the best possible data transfer rate of the drive, usually for data located nearest the outside edge. For example, a CAV drive claiming an 80X transfer rate can't transfer data at that speed over the entire CD.

Loading the disc

The disc loading mechanism is the physical way that a CD is loaded into the CD-ROM drive. Three distinct ways are used to load a CD:

◆ *Tray loading:* The most common loading mechanism in use, the tray-loading method uses a plastic horizontal tray that opens and closes with gears inside the drive (see Figure 13-3). Pressing the eject button on the CD-ROM drive activates the gears and servos that extend the tray out of the drive. The CD is placed in the portion of the tray designed to hold the disc; and with either a gentle push on the tray or by pressing the eject button, the tray is pulled back into the drive.

Figure 13-3: A tray-loading CD-ROM drive with its tray extended.

On some older PC cases, the CD-ROM drive is installed vertically. These drives use tabs that extend and retract to hold or release the disc when the tray closes and opens.

◆ *Caddy:* A CD caddy, like those shown in Figure 13-4, is a small plastic case that's something like a CD jewel case. The caddy is hinged on one side and opens so that a disc can be placed inside. The caddy has a sliding metal cover on its bottom that slides out of the way when the caddy is inserted into the CD drive. With the sliding cover open, the laser can access the disc. When the CD is inserted into the caddy and placed inside the drive, the effect is very much like the action of a 3.5" floppy disk.

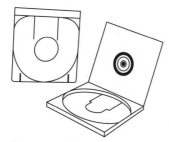

Figure 13-4: A CD caddy is used on some models of CD-ROM drives.

◆ *Front loading:* This method is very common on automobile CD players and Macintosh computers, but it's not very common on PCs.

Connecting to audio output and controls

Early CD-ROM drives included playback controls used to play and listen to audio CDs on the front of the drive. Most current CD-ROM drives have eliminated audio controls and rely on audio playback software, such as the Windows CD Player, Windows Media Player, the Real Audio Player, or others like the WinAmp player, to control the playing of an audio CD. Figure 13-5 shows the audio playback controls of the Windows Media Player.

 At one time, many CD-ROM drives also included a $1/8$-inch headphone jack. On later CD drives, headphone jacks are found only on some CD-RW drives. More commonly now, the headphone jack is on the sound card to be used.

The Media Player playback controls

Figure 13-5: The audio playback controls on the Windows Media Player can be used to control the playback of an audio CD.

LOCATING THE CONNECTORS AND JUMPERS

The jumpers and cable connections on a CD-ROM drive are very similar to those found on a hard disk drive. CD-ROM drive manufacturers have standardized the location and use of the jumpers and connectors. The jumpers and connectors are always located at the back of the CD-ROM drive, as shown in Figure 13-6.

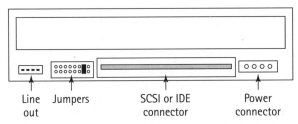

| Line out | Jumpers | SCSI or IDE connector | Power connector |

Figure 13-6: The connectors and jumpers on the back of a CD-ROM drive.

A 4-pin Molex-style connector is used to connect to the power supply. The data and other connections or jumpers on the drive are dependent on the type of interface in use. The two most popular interfaces are the Integrated Drive Electronics/AT

Attachment Packet Interface (IDE/ATAPI) and the SCSI. An ATAPI drive uses a standard 40-pin data cable and connector and jumpers to set the drive as either the master or slave device on its channel. A SCSI drive, depending on whether it's an internal or external device and the SCSI mode in use, typically uses either a 50-pin or 68-pin connector. A SCSI device must have a device ID configured, which is done through jumpers on the device. If the device is the last on the SCSI bus, it must also be terminated. (See Chapter 11 for more information on the SCSI interface.)

ATAPI is an interface between the PC and the CD-ROM drive that adds the commands used to control a CD-ROM (or DVD or tape drive) to the standard IDE/ATA interface. *SCSI* is an interface type that allows the PC to communicate directly with peripheral hardware, including disk drives, tape drives, CD-ROM drives, and more. The two interfaces (IDE/ATA and SCSI) are not compatible, however.

CONNECTING THE AUDIO CABLE

A CD-ROM also has a thin audio connector that's used to connect it to a sound card (see Figure 13-7). The audio connector is either a three- or four-wire cable that sends the CD's audio output directly to the sound card so it can be recorded on the PC or played back on the PC's speakers.

Figure 13-7: The CD audio connector cable used to connect the CD-ROM drive to a sound card.

Stacking in multiple discs

The most common CD-ROM drives can only load a single CD at a time. However, some drives can load two, four, six, or more discs. The primary benefit of a multi-CD drive is that it allows you to access multiple discs, although still only one at a time, without having to physically remove and replace the discs in the drive. The discs that you use frequently can remain in the CD-ROM drive until they're needed.

A single disc CD-ROM drive is mapped to the PC with a single drive letter, usually E: or something close to that. However, a multiple-disc CD-ROM drive is mapped to the PC with a drive letter for each disc that it's capable of loading. Multiple disc drives also require special software device drivers to give you access to each disc independently.

Dealing with Digital Versatile/Video Disc (DVD)

The DVD began life back in the early 1990s as a compromise between two proposed formats: the Multimedia CD (MMCD) and the Super Density Disk (SDD). Many higher-end PCs now include a DVD drive (see Figure 13-8) as an option, but it has little use on standard data input/output (I/O) function on a PC except to read standard CD-ROMs, to which DVD drives are backward compatible.

Figure 13-8: A tower PC with DVD drive and disc.

A DVD can store the equivalent of 17GB of data, which is about 25 times more than a standard PC CD-ROM. Through the use of MPEG and Dolby compression technologies, a DVD can store hours of high-quality audio-visual content, such as a full-length movie along with other supporting content. Although still waiting to replace the CD-DA format, a DVD-Audio disc can hold up to 400 minutes of 2-channel stereo sound or 74 minutes of 6-channel sound.

DVD formats

The read mechanism on a DVD is very similar to that used in the CD. The primary difference is that the DVD uses a dual focus pick-up to read the disc. A DVD is the same size physically as a CD-ROM, but the formatting on a DVD is considerably different than the formatting on a CD. Table 13-1 compares the formatting of a DVD-Audio disc with a CD-DA disc.

Table 13-1 COMPARISON OF DVD AND CD FORMATTING

Feature	DVD-Audio	CD
Capacity	4.7GB	640MB
Recording time	200 minutes	74 minutes
Transfer rate	9.6 Mbps	1.4 Mbps
Maximum sampling rate	192 kHz	44.1 kHz

Sorting out DVD standards

A number of DVD types are available:

◆ *DVD-ROM:* The type of DVD drive typically installed in a PC.

◆ *DVD-R (Recordable):* A WORM-type disc that can record up to 3.95GB. DVD-R is recorded using the same dye-layer technology as the CD-R.

◆ *DVD-Video:* A read-only DVD disc that has the capacity to hold around 133 minutes of full-motion video. DVD-Video is most commonly used for full-length movies.

◆ *DVD-RAM:* Looks like a big diskette more than a CD-ROM and is a rewritable form of DVD. A DVD-RAM has a capacity of 4.7GB per side and is available in both single-sided and double-sided versions. A DVD-RAM drive will also read virtually all DVD-Video and DVD-ROM media as well as all types of CD media.

◆ *DVD-R/W (Read/Write):* Competing technology for the DVD-RAM that also holds 4.7GB per side and can be rewritten more than 1,000 times.

Dealing with CD-ROM and DVD Issues

By and large, most PC systems come with CD-ROM or DVD drives already installed, but a good number of users want their existing systems upgraded with either new or faster drives. The following sections outline the steps used to install a CD-ROM or DVD drive and deal with their problems.

Installing an internal IDE/ATAPI CD-ROM drive

Before opening the PC's case to install the drive, a few precautions and preparations are necessary. Make sure you do, have, or take the following actions and items before starting the installation:

1. Have a Phillips screwdriver and possibly a slotted screwdriver as well (for cases with slotted screws).

2. Back up the PC's hard disk drive.

   Anytime you open the case, back up the hard disk. You might also want to use this opportunity to clean out the inside of the case with a can of compressed air.

3. Have a boot disk that boots the system to a DOS command line prompt.

4. Check the Basic Input/Output System (BIOS) configuration information for the PC to determine the configuration assigned to all existing IDE/ATA devices, noting which are masters and which are slaves, as well as the channel to which each is attached.

5. Have an electrostatic discharge (ESD) wrist, heel, or ankle strap or place the PC on an antistatic mat.

   Using both an EDS strap and an antistatic mat is always better.

6. Have documentation for the CD-ROM drive and the motherboard or IDE/ATA adapter card (for wherever the IDE/ATA cables are attached).

7. Turn off the PC with its power switch and remove the power cord from the power supply. Also power off and disconnect all peripheral devices connected to the PC.

Follow these steps to install the drive:

1. Remove the PC's case cover.

   If you need to slide the case to remove it, do so carefully so that you don't snag or nick any interior cables. The ones that you're most likely to ding are the power cables.

2. Use a PC vacuum or a can of compressed air to clean up any dust or debris.

   You should always take the opportunity to clean out the inside of the case any time that you remove the case cover. Make sure that you wear eye protection when using compressed air.

3. Study the case's available half-height drive bays and choose the one that's most accessible and the one that's least likely to require you to move

other drives to accommodate cabling and fit. If the case has a bay cover on the bay that you choose, remove it by removing the screws holding it to the case or by snapping it out.

4. Examine the IDE/ATA arrangement already installed in the PC.

   If the PC has only one hard disk drive, it's probably an IDE/ATA drive, which is good. The flat ribbon cable that's about two inches wide and connects the disk drive either to the motherboard or to an adapter card is the IDE/ATA data cable.

5. Check how many IDE/ATA connectors are available on the motherboard or the adapter card.

   Check the documentation of the motherboard or adapter card if you are unsure of their location. On the motherboard, the connectors should look like those in Figure 13-9.

Figure 13-9: IDE/ATA connectors on a PC motherboard.

If you have an available IDE connector on the motherboard or adapter card, you can use it to install your CD-ROM. You might need to purchase an IDE cable to do so because very few CD-ROM kits include an IDE/ATAPI data cable. However, if you have no empty IDE connectors, you must connect the CD-ROM drive to an existing cable.

One more thing that you should verify is the type of interface that the CD-ROM drive uses. You must match the interface to the cable (ATA-33 or ATA-66 or something else).

The cable used by the floppy disk drive *is not* an IDE/ATA cable. Don't try to use this cable for installing a CD-ROM drive, even if it does have an available connector on it. It could damage the floppy drive, the CD-ROM drive, and the motherboard.

If you're connecting the CD-ROM drive to an existing compatible cable, there should be an available connector about midway between the disk drive and the adapter connection.

6. After you find the connector, verify your choice of location for the CD-ROM drive.

   You might need to swap some drives around to be able to reach the CD-ROM drive with the connector without putting strain on the cable or the hard disk drive's connector.

7. Before installing the drive in its bay, you must check and set the master/slave jumpers.

   Refer to the CD-ROM drive's documentation for the proper jumper placement for the configuration that you're assigning the drive. Figure 13-10 shows the jumpers of an IDE/ATA device.

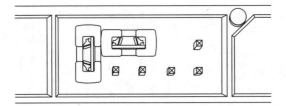

Figure 13-10: The master/slave jumpers of an IDE/ATA device.

You must know the master/slave configuration of each existing IDE/ATA device installed in the PC. In most cases, the PC has only one IDE device — the hard disk drive — and it should be set to master. If so, set the jumper of the CD-ROM drive to slave, which should be its default setting from the factory. If the hard disk drive's jumper is not set to master, you should set it as well. If you don't have access to the hard disk's documentation, visit the manufacturer's Web site for this setting.

Figure 13-11 illustrates the common positions for the jumpers on an IDE/ATA device. The Cable Select (CSEL) position is used on only some devices and eliminates the master/slave problems. A special cable determines the master device from its position on the cable, in much the same way as floppy drives.

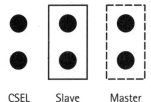

CSEL   Slave   Master

Figure 13-11: The device configuration jumpers on an IDE/ATA device.

8. Remove the CD-ROM drive from its packaging and slide it into the drive bay that you've chosen from the front of the PC.

Push it in about halfway and then check whether the power cable and data cable will reach. If so, connect them; if not, keep pushing the drive in a bit at a time and checking the cables for reach. As soon as the cables can be connected to the drive, do so. Sometimes connecting the cables on the drive after it's been pushed all the way back into position in the bay is very hard.

The cables involved in this step are the ribbon data cable and the power connector from the power supply. The connectors on these two cables are keyed to fit only one way.

 TIP On a ribbon-type data cable, Pin 1 is indicated by the red or blue stripe down the edge of the cable.

9. Attach the digital audio (DA) cable to the back of the CD-ROM drive and to the appropriate lead on the sound card.

Refer to the CD-ROM drive's documentation for the correct settings and connections.

10. Insert and tighten the screws that attached through the side of the drive bay to hold the CD-ROM drive in place. Check for loose cables or wires hanging down between the sides of the drive and the bay before tightening the screws completely.

11. Recheck the fit of all connectors and cables on the devices in the immediate area to make sure that you haven't accidentally dislodged them.

    You might want to take this opportunity to check the connectors and chips on the motherboard for fit as well.

12. Replace the case cover and secure its screws. Reconnect the device connectors and the PC's power cord. Turn on the peripheral devices and cold-start the PC, watching carefully for any Power-On Self-Test (POST) or boot problems.

13. If the CD-ROM drive requires a special device driver, use the Add New Hardware icon on the Windows Control Panel to install it.

Installing a DVD drive

Installing a DVD-ROM drive in a PC uses essentially the same process as used to install a CD-ROM drive (see the preceding section). A DVD drive does have a couple of extra steps to be performed, though.

A DVD drive usually comes in an installation kit that includes an ATAPI/EIDE DVD drive, an MPEG II decoder card, the cables needed to connect the drive, and usually a CD (or DVD) with some software and drivers. If the DVD drive uses software decompression, it won't have an MPEG card, but understand that software decompression doesn't perform as well as the hardware kind.

The additional step required for installing a DVD drive is that the MPEG decoder card is installed in a Peripheral Component Interconnect (PCI) expansion slot and connected to the sound card with a DA cable – and perhaps to the video card as well. The PCI decoder card is a Plug and Play (PnP) device, but you will be prompted for the device drivers. Use the Have Disk option and insert the CD that came with the drive.

Installing a SCSI CD-ROM drive

A SCSI CD-ROM drive has two jumper settings that must be made to the disk drive beyond those done in an IDE/ATA drive installation. The two settings are

♦ *SCSI device ID:* Each SCSI device must be configured with a unique device ID number. Device numbers are assigned using a jumper on the SCSI device.

♦ *Termination:* Many new SCSI devices build in a termination capability right on the device itself that can be set through a jumper. If the CD-ROM drive is the last device on the SCSI bus, it needs to terminate the bus. If the CD-ROM doesn't include termination, a terminator block (likely the one previously used) is moved after the new device. You should also check to make sure that the device preceding the CD-ROM doesn't need to have a termination jumper changed.

Here are two ways to avoid duplicating a SCSI ID number already in use on the SCSI bus. The first is to use a utility available from most SCSI manufacturers that reports the IDs in use and which devices are using which numbers. The EZSCSI utility from Adaptec (www.adaptec.com) is one example of this utility. The second way is to look at the jumpers of the other SCSI devices to see what IDs they're set to use. Some SCSI host adapters report this information during the boot process as well.

Beyond these steps, the process is very close to that used to install an IDE CD-ROM drive. Just be sure that you match the SCSI standard of the host controller with that of the SCSI CD-ROM drive.

Adding CD-ROM support to a boot disk

When you create a boot disk with the DOS command FORMAT A: /S, the start-up files of the operating system and the COMMAND.COM command line interpreter are placed on the diskette. If you wish to have any other functions, such as FORMAT, FDISK, or EDIT, they must be copied to the disk after it's formatted. The same is true if you wish to have access to the CD-ROM after you boot a system using the boot disk.

1. To add CD-ROM access to a DOS boot disk, you must first create a
   CONFIG.SYS file on the boot disk, using the EDIT command or the
   Windows Notepad utility. The CONFIG.SYS file must have a line to start
   the HIMEM.SYS extended memory device driver, which is

   DEVICE=C:\WINDOWS\COMMAND\HIMEM.SYS

   After this command, enter the following:

   DEVICE =A:\<filename of device driver> /D:MSCD001

   The device driver's filename should be something like NEC_BM.SYS or
   something close to that.

If you don't know the name of the device driver, open the Windows Device Manager from the My Computer folder and find the CD-ROM drive on the components tree. Right-click the CD-ROM entry and then choose Properties to find the device driver's filename. Close and save the CONFIG.SYS file. Make sure that you copy the device driver file onto the boot disk.

2. Create an AUTOEXEC.BAT file on the boot disk. Using either EDIT or the Windows Notepad utility, create the file with the following entry:

```
C:\WINDOWS\COMMAND\ MSCDEX /X:MSCD001 /V
```

3. Close and save the AUTOEXEC.BAT file.

   Your boot disk is now ready to provide access to the CD-ROM if you need to completely restore the operating system or take any other emergency measures.

Troubleshooting an IDE/ATA/ATAPI CD-ROM drive

You don't have that many physical things to check on an IDE CD-ROM drive when it begins performing badly or not at all. Here is a list of the things that you should check out to troubleshoot an IDE CD-ROM drive:

♦ *Problem:* The CD-ROM/DVD drive light is on all the time — or the tray is extended or retracted when the system starts — but the device does not respond.

   Solution: The problem is likely with the cabling.

   Do this: With proper ESD protection, remove the case cover and check the cables on the CD-ROM drive to make sure they're correctly oriented and snuggly connected.

 A common error is to connect the 40-pin data cable either one row off or shift one or two pins to the side — or completely reversed. These connectors are keyed to prevent this, but it still happens. Remember that the 40-pin data cable has a red or blue stripe down the edge on which pin 1 is located.

♦ *Problem:* No lights show at all, and the system doesn't see the device (it doesn't show up in the Device Manager list).

   Solution: The CD-ROM drive probably doesn't have a power connection. It could be that there was not one to use, and it was forgotten.

   Do this: If you have no available power connections, purchase a power cable Y splitter and share power with another device, preferably one that's not often used at the same time as the CD-ROM drive.

◆ *Problem:* If the CD-ROM drive isn't configured appropriately as a master or slave device on the IDE/ATA channel, it might not be detected by the system.

Solution: Check the device configuration jumper to make sure that the drive is properly set to master, slave, or CSEL (as is appropriate for the channel).

Do this: Every IDE device must be configured to one of these settings. CSEL isn't very common and requires a special cable, so the device typically must be either a master or a slave. Each channel (most Pentium-class motherboards support two IDE/ATA channels) can have only one master and one slave device unless it's an EIDE (Extended IDE) channel, in which case it can have one master and three slaves. If the CD-ROM is the only device on its channel or connected to an IDE adapter card, it should be set as a secondary master. Otherwise, it is either a primary or secondary slave.

◆ *Problem:* The IDE cable is longer than 18 inches.

Solution: IDE cables longer than 18 inches can cause problems for some IDE/ATA devices.

Do this: Try a shorter cable to see whether that's the problem. Devices that support the ATA66 and ATA100 interface standards use a special 80-wire/40-pin cable. Make sure that you have the correct cable for the device and controller that you're connecting.

Here are some other things to check:

◆ Check the BIOS settings to be sure that the IDE channel controller is enabled and that the drive type selector for the IDE channel is set to its auto-select choice, which is usually AUTO.

◆ Open the Windows Device Manager or start the System Information applet to check for hardware conflicts or device driver problems.

If you see a yellow exclamation point or a red X next to the CD-ROM entry in the Device Manager, investigate further. Or start the System Information applet from the Accessories → System Tools menus and look in the CD-ROM or Problem Devices folders. Figure 13-12 shows the System Information window.

◆ Check to be sure that another device, such as a Zip or Jaz drive, has not been assigned the same drive letter.

◆ If you get the error `Drive is not accessible or device is not ready` when you try to read from the CD, the CD tray is probably not completely closed or the CD isn't centered in the tray.

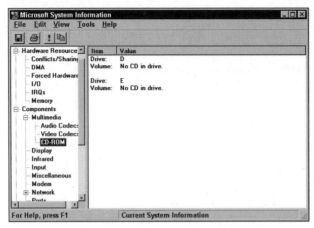

Figure 13-12: The Microsoft System Information applet can be used to identify device problems.

Troubleshooting a SCSI CD-ROM drive

The two things that you should check first on a SCSI CD-ROM drive that isn't responding as it should are the same two things that I emphasize during the installation process: termination and SCSI ID. To troubleshoot a SCSI CD-ROM drive, use these steps:

1. Check to make sure that the drive is properly terminating the SCSI bus.

   Perhaps you're using the wrong kind of termination for the signaling mode of the system. Some systems require active termination, but some older systems still support passive termination. Verify the type of termination that should be in use. If the device itself supplies the termination through a jumper setting, verify that the setting is correct.

2. Recheck the SCSI ID numbers assigned to the devices on the bus and eliminate any duplication.

3. Check the SCSI cable for loose connections or broken or damaged connectors.

4. Test another SCSI device on the same bus to verify that it's working.

   If not, the problem could be with the host adapter, that too many devices are installed on the bus, or that the bus is too long.

Troubleshooting IDE CD-ROM master and slave conflicts

The following are some steps that you can use to check out why a CD-ROM drive is not responding in a situation where you're unsure that the correct master/slave configuration has been made.

1. Check the CD-ROM's documentation to determine whether your CD-ROM drive won't work if it's the only device on an IDE/ATA channel set as a slave.

   Some CD-ROM drives have no problem with being a slave as the only device on a channel. Check the CD-ROM's documentation to determine whether this is the case for your drive. If this information isn't in the documentation, contact the manufacturer.

2. When you add a second drive on an IDE channel, you might need to reconfigure the drive that was already on the channel.

   Some drives have two master-level settings: master, and master with slave. It could be that the device won't work with another device on the same channel unless it's configured to a sharing mode. On the same note, if you remove one of the two drives on an IDE channel, you might need to reconfigure the remaining device to work alone.

3. Some hard disk drives won't work with a CD-ROM attached to the IDE channel as a slave.

   Call it hardware snobbery or what you like, but in these cases, you'll need to move the CD-ROM drive to another channel.

Improving the performance of a CD-ROM drive

Here is a list of things that can improve the performance of a CD-ROM drive in terms of speed, throughput, and avoiding minor problems.

◆ *Direct Memory Access (DMA):* This is supported by many newer CD-ROM drives and can be used to lighten the load of the processor. To enable DMA on a CD-ROM drive, perform these steps:

   1. Right-click the My Computer icon on the Windows Desktop, choose Properties to display the System Properties window, and then select the Device Manager tab.

   2. Select the CD-ROM drive from the Computer Components list and then click the Properties button to display the CD-ROM drive's properties.

   3. Select the Settings tab on the CD-ROM drive's Properties window, mark the check box next to the DMA option, click OK to apply the change, and then click OK again to close the other windows.

   4. Restart the PC.

      After the system is back up, check the DMA setting to see whether it's still selected. If so, the CD-ROM drive does support DMA and should speed up just a bit. If not, the drive doesn't support DMA . . . but it was worth a try!

◆ *Auto Insert Notification:* Turning off the Auto Insert Notification option, which is on by default, stops the system from launching the support software for the CD's contents whenever a new CD is loaded.

For example, each time when you place a music CD in the tray and load it, the CD Player automatically starts up. If you don't wish to run this software, you must stop it and close it. To avoid this problem, you can turn off the option that causes this to happen.

1. To do so, choose the System icon from the Windows Control Panel and then select the Device Manager tab.

2. Double-click the CD-ROM device entry to open the Properties window and then select the Settings tab.

3. Deselect (clear) the check box for Auto Insert Notification and then click OK.

Restart the system.

Troubleshooting CD-ROM Sound Problems

The obvious thing to check when the CD is playing but you hear no sound is whether the speaker is turned off. Double-click the speaker symbol in the task bar tray to open the Play Control window. Slide the volume button up the scale on the Play Control slider (on the left-hand side of the box). If there is still no sound, make sure that the sound is not muted on any of the other sound choices in this window (see Figure 13-13).

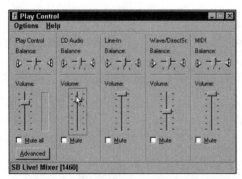

Figure 13-13: The Windows Play Control window is used to adjust the sound volume for each of the various sound players on the PC.

VOLUME PROBLEMS

If the Play Control settings aren't the problem, here are some things to try:

1. If the sound volume is turned up but you still have no sound, open the PC's case and check that the CD-ROM drive is connected to the sound card with a DA cable.

2. Check the documentation of the sound card to ensure that no additional settings need to be made to the sound card to enable a certain CD-ROM drive brand or model.

If you can listen to a CD via the headphone jack on the CD-ROM drive's front panel but you can't hear its sound through the speakers attached to the sound card, the DA cable is definitely missing or misconnected.

SOUND QUALITY PROBLEMS

If the sound quality produced by a CD-ROM drive is very poor, the problem is usually not the CD-ROM drive. It could be any one of a variety of problems, including not enough RAM, bad speakers, a poor speaker connection, or even a bad CD.

However, you can check one setting to perhaps improve this situation:

1. Right-click the My Computer icon on the Windows Desktop and choose Properties from the menu that appears. Select the Performance tab and click the File System button to open the File System Properties dialog box shown in Figure 13-14.

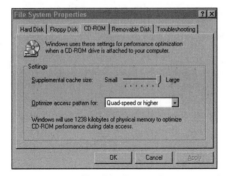

Figure 13-14: The File System Properties window is used to set the performance enhancing or limiting settings for several hardware devices on the PC.

2. Choose the CD-ROM tab and then set the Supplemental Cache Size slider to Large and the Optimize Access Pattern For option to Quad Speed or Higher.

This last value is only valid on CD-ROMs with transfer speeds of 4X (Quad Speed) or higher.

 Another option that you have to speed up a CD-ROM drive is to install a CD-ROM caching program, such as Symantec's Speedrive, Circuit System's CD Quick Cache, or CD Speedster from Syncronys. However, a faster drive is probably the best way to speed up CDs.

Part IV

Sight and Sound Systems

Chapter 14

Video Systems

The outputs of a PC are geared to two human senses: sight and sound. This chapter provides information and background on video systems and their installation, configuration, and troubleshooting, and a bit about how they work.

In its most basic form, a PC's video system provides a connection between the monitor and the PC. However, the video system is really so much more than just a connecting device. The PC's video system controls how images appear on the monitor, where they are placed, and how well the user can see them. All the data destined for the monitor travels through the video system, which converts the binary data supplied by the CPU into the text, graphics, and images displayed on the monitor. In this chapter, I cover the following:

A PC'S VIDEO SYSTEM, also called the *video controller* or *video adapter,* can be an expansion card (with numerous choices between types and capabilities) or it can be built into the motherboard. In any case, without its video, the PC would be definitely limited in the services and utility that it could provide its user.

Checking Out How Video Systems Work

The images displayed on a PC's monitor are generated as digital data by software (such as the operating system, like Windows or Linux) or an application program (such as Microsoft Word, Adobe PhotoShop, or *Slime Fighters from Hell*). The software generates instructions to the PC telling it exactly how each frame of video output should look. The CPU and the video controller then share the work to generate the image displayed by the monitor. Creating the display involves a lot more geometry than most people care to know, but don't worry—I won't put you through that.

Chapter 16 provides information on sound systems and sound cards.

Generating the image

The instructions generated by the operating system or application software are sent to the CPU and video controller, which work together to create images by putting *pixels* (picture elements) together to form text or 2-D images or tiny triangles (a great many tiny triangles, actually) for 3-D graphics. The images formed by using pixels or triangles, which are themselves made up of pixels, are generated in two phases:

◆ *Transform and lighting:* In the transform and lighting phase, the PC figures out how to assemble the pixels and triangles to create the image desired by the application software—the *transform* part of the process. Any lighting effects are then included in the graphics instructions and are applied to the tips of the triangles *(vertices)*—the *lighting* process.

◆ *Set-up:* During the set-up phase, the video card plots out exactly where the monitor should place each piece of the image. This involves another very math-intensive process. Next, the digital graphics data is passed through the hardware triangle setup, a feature of the video controller, which prepares the data for display.

On some systems, transform and lighting data is processed by the CPU. On others, the video controller processes it, in which case all the graphics-related information generated by the application software is sent to the video card.

Dividing up the work

If you're playing a video game and one of the scenes shifts to the right, the game software sends out instructions defining what color and how bright each pixel in the display should be to regenerate the displayed image. However, this doesn't mean that the software waits for movement to send out instructions. The display information is updated not less than 30 times a second—typically around 70 times per second – to eliminate screen flicker and to facilitate the onscreen animation to move smoothly.

Newer, more robust video cards now handle both the transform/lighting and the set-up phases with the CPU simply routing the graphics information from the application to the video card. This frees the CPU to perform other tasks, such as the physics or calculations related to the software's logic, resulting in a more efficient overall operation of the PC. Less-powerful or legacy video cards rely on the CPU to perform the transform and lighting phases and typically perform only the set-up phase themselves. This puts a drain on the CPU, resulting in less-efficient performance of the whole PC.

The processes used to generate 3-D graphics images are somewhat more involved than to generate 2-D graphics, thus using considerably more computing resources. This is why most 3-D graphics cards handle the whole job.

To create a 2-D (two-dimensional) image, the information that must be provided by the generating software for each pixel in use is: its color, brightness, and X (horizontal) and Y (vertical) coordinates (the two dimensions).

However, a 3-D image has a third dimension: depth. To create 3-D images, the video card must track all pixels and triangles up and down and side to side on the monitor in addition to ones which are in the foreground and background of the images. Also, the video controller must also manage the technologies used to improve image quality, all of which consume considerable resources, adding to the reasons why the graphics controller should handle the entire job.

Creating pathways

Regardless of which device handles the transform and lighting phase, the CPU and video controller communicate using one of two (or both) bus structures: the Accelerated Graphics Port (AGP) bus or the Peripheral Component Interconnect (PCI) bus. See "Interfacing the video system" later in the chapter for more information on these bus structures.

The typical video card has a component that could very well be the most important part of this entire process – the random access memory (RAM) digital-to-analog converter (RAMDAC). Although this device sounds like a character in a very bad science fiction movie, a *RAMDAC* converts the digital data stored in the video card's RAM into the analog signal used by the monitor to create images on the screen.

Reviewing the video standards

Video display standards have evolved right along with monitor, CPU, and memory technology. The following sections provide a brief overview of each of the standards that have been or are still in use on PCs.

MONOCHROME STANDARDS

Way back when, the Monochrome Display Adapter (MDA) displayed only text on monochrome (one-color) monitors. The Monochrome Graphics Adapter (MGA) that combined graphics and text for display on a monochrome monitor soon followed using a technology developed by Hercules Computer Technology.

 The abbreviation *MGA* is now used by Matrox Graphics, Inc. to represent its Matrox Graphics Accelerator. If you see MGA used in current literature, including this chapter, it probably refers to the Matrox technology and not the older monochrome technology.

COLOR GRAPHICS

The Color Graphics Adapter (CGA), developed by IBM, was the first graphics adapter standard that included a range of colors (that is, other than shades of a single color). CGA could display up to 16 colors but was capable of displaying only 2 colors at its highest resolution of 640 x 200 (640 pixels horizontally by 200 pixels vertically).

IBM also developed the next graphics standard released, the Enhanced Graphics Adapter (EGA), which increased resolution to 640 x 350 with up to 64 colors. About this time, the Multicolor Graphics Array (MCGA) also came along, but it was soon replaced by the Video Graphics Array (VGA) standard.

VIDEO GRAPHICS

In 1987, IBM developed the VGA standard that increased the number of displayed colors from 256 to a palette of 262,144 colors using a resolution of 640 x 480. Even today, VGA remains the default standard for many operating systems, including Windows.

Most of the video graphics standards that followed the VGA are grouped and labeled under the umbrella of Super Video Graphics Array (SVGA). Actually, an actual SVGA standard, developed by Video Electronics Standards Association (VESA), includes just about all video graphics standards with better resolution or more colors than VGA. However, many similar or adapted standards are so close to VESA's SVGA that they're all grouped together.

The general SVGA standard supports a color palette with over 16 million colors available and a range of screen resolutions, including 800 x 600; 1024 x 768; 1280 x 1024; 1600 x 1200; and a few even higher. Not all models of SVGA boards, depending on the manufacturer, can display all 16 million colors or support all SVGA resolutions.

Table 14-1 lists the more popular video graphics standards in use today.

The Colors column in Table 14-1 represents the number of colors that can be displayed on a video controller with minimum video memory. As more memory and capability are present on the video card, the number of colors and effects can increase.

TABLE 14-1 PC VIDEO GRAPHICS STANDARDS

Video Standard	Minimum Resolution(s)	Colors
Video Graphics Array (VGA)	640 x 480	16
	320 x 200	256
Super VGA (SVGA)	800 x 600	16
	1024 x 768	256
	1280 x 1024	256
	1600 x 1200	256

 The video or graphics cards on the market today (primarily SVGA cards) are less tied to video standards than they are to increasing the capabilities of the video controller to process all the graphic information and produce better images. In general, they're all priced somewhere between $100 and $400; they have double data rate (DDR) DRAM, synchronous DRAM (SDRAM), or DDR SDRAM, and probably either sport an Open GL or Direct3D application program interface (API) used by the video card to produce 3-D graphics.

Mastering the bus

Bus mastering allows the video card to control the PC's system bus and transfer data into and out of system RAM directly without the assistance of the CPU. This improves the performance of certain video operations that use RAM for calculations, such as 3-D acceleration.

Controlling the video card

The logic circuits that control the functions of the video card are grouped together as the video card's chipset, which is also called the *graphics chip*, the *accelerator*, or the *video co-processor*. Much like the functions performed by the system chipset on the PC's motherboard, the video chipset supports the functions performed by the graphics processing unit (GPU), as well as the interfaces, data transfers, and compatibility of the card. (For more on GPUs, read the upcoming section "Processing the video.")

Some video card manufacturers manufacture their own video chipsets, such as Matrox and 3dfx, who design and build their cards from start to finish. Others use chipsets manufactured by other companies, such as Diamond Multimedia and others.

When buying a video card, know the capabilities of the video chipset because it holds the key to the card's performance, capabilities, and compatibility. You need to match the video card to the needs of the system into which it will be inserted and the monitor that it will drive.

An important feature of the video chipset is the refresh rate of the video card. A higher refresh rate means less flicker on the screen, which translates to less eyestrain for the user. A good video chipset should provide a refresh rate of at least 75 hertz (Hz). However, the refresh rate must be balanced to the resolution settings. Using a higher resolution setting will result in a lower refresh rate and vice versa.

A refresh rate of 75 Hz or higher is required by the VESA standard to qualify for its flicker-free logo. Refresh rates decline with higher resolution settings because when the number of pixels to be refreshed increases, the ability of the monitor to refresh them all slows down. For example, the Hitachi SuperScan 750 series monitors have a default setting of 100 Hz, but its higher resolutions (up to 1600 x 1200) are reduced to as low as 75 Hz.

Riding the video bus

Over the years, video systems have improved from the monochrome video bus of the early PCs to the 3-D color high-resolution systems of today. Most of today's PCs support video through either a PCI or AGP bus connector. The PCI bus is independent of the processor, which makes for fast video. The AGP bus offers a higher bandwidth — and with it, higher frame rates. It has a direct line to RAM, which allows it to better prepare 3-D images and textures.

Video BIOS

The video basic input/output system (BIOS) is very much like the functions of the system BIOS. It provides an interface between the PC, its BIOS, operating system, and application programs to the video hardware. The issues that affect the video card at the BIOS level are video interfaces, system resource requirements, and video drivers.

Interfacing the video system

A large amount of information is moved about on the video system between the video card and the PC's CPU and RAM. The pathway over which this data travels is the video system interface that connects the GPU and video RAM to the PC. Because of the amount of data to be transferred, the video system interface requires more bandwidth than any other peripheral device on the PC.

One common mistake made by users is that the number of bits used on the video card is also the number of bits required in the video system interface. But a 64-bit or 128-bit video card only uses this bandwidth internally on the video card between its components. The width in bits of the interface to the CPU and memory is either 16-bits (Industry Standard Architecture/Extended Industry Standard Architecture [ISA/EISA] cards) or 32-bits (VESA local bus [VL-bus], PCI, or AGP).

The two most popular video system interfaces in use today are the PCI and AGP buses. (See Figure 14-1 for the location of PCI and AGP ports on a motherboard.)

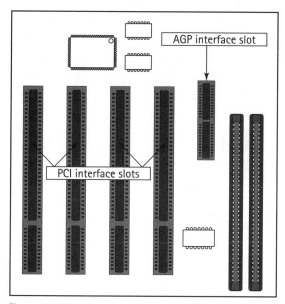

Figure 14-1: A motherboard with PCI and AGP interface slots.

◆ *Peripheral Component Interconnect (PCI):* Support for the PCI interface bus is included in the system chipset on all Pentium-class computers. PCI is commonly used for 2-D graphics cards, sound cards, network interface cards, and other expansion cards that attach directly to the motherboard. Of course, a PCI card slot is required.

♦ *AGP (Accelerated Graphics Port):* This interface was designed specifically for use as a video system interface. AGP, which runs twice as fast as the PCI interface, creates a high-speed link between the video card and the PC's processor. The AGP interface is also directly linked to the PC's system memory, which makes it possible for 3-D images to be stored in main memory and 2-D systems to use system RAM for some calculations. All AGP video cards require the motherboard to have an AGP slot.

However, the AGP interface is fast replacing the PCI interface as the interface of choice for video cards because of its faster transfer rates. In fact, AGP has evolved into several standard versions, each noting its multiple of the original standard. For example, AGP 1X has a data transfer rate of 266 Mbps (compared with PCI's 133 Mbps), AGP 2X supports 533 Mbps, and AGP 4X transfers data at 1.07 Gbps.

Video and system resources

Unlike most internally mounted peripheral devices, video cards don't use much in the way of system resources. Not all video cards use an interrupt request (IRQ). Those video cards that do use an IRQ use one of the pairs set aside for PCI devices (IRQ11 and IRQ12). All VGA-compatible video cards, which are virtually all of them, use the same I/O addresses (3B0-3BBh and 3C0-3DFh). Manufacturers of other types of expansion cards avoid these addresses, which eliminate conflicts during installation.

Video device drivers

The device driver for the video card translates the images generated by an application program into instructions that the GPU can use. Whereas the software might consider the display as a collection of pixels, the GPU sees it as a series of line and shape drawings. The graphics driver software's job is to convert between the application's vision and that of the graphics processor.

Typically, separate graphics drivers are used for each resolution and color depth combination, which is why the video system can perform differently on different resolution and color depth settings. The same can be true of the different drivers used on different operating systems for a video card. Video drivers are frequently updated, so if optimum video performance is your thing, check the manufacturer's Web site frequently.

The RAMDAC

The RAM digital-to-analog converter (RAMDAC) solves the simple problem that the PC and video card are digital and the monitor is an analog device. The information stored in the video memory is digital data that must be converted into an analog signal before it can be used by the monitor to create the display image.

The RAMDAC reads data from the video memory, converts it to an analog signal wave, and then sends it over the connecting cable (the one connected to the back of the PC) to the monitor. The RAMDAC has a direct effect on the quality of the screen's image, how often the screen is refreshed, the color palette used, and the resolution and color depth used in the display.

There is a digital-to-analog converter (DAC) for each of the three primary colors (red, green, and blue) that are used together to create the right color mix for each pixel. The speed of the RAMDAC has a lot to do with how well it can support the quality of the display. A fast RAMDAC has a rating between 300 megahertz (MHz) to 350 MHz; but only a year ago, 150 MHz was fast.

Accelerating 3-D graphics

The three-dimensional images displayed on computer monitors are actually *surface modeling,* or creating the illusion of 3-D objects on a 2-D surface.

Surface modeling represents 3-D objects by using a mesh of polygons, typically triangles, to create images with their outside edges. If enough triangles can be used to create an image, even the curved surfaces can be made to look smooth on the PC's display. A variety of geometric descriptions are used to define each triangle, including its *vertices* (corners), *vertex normals* (which side points out and which is inside to create shading), reflection characteristics of its surface, the coordinates of the viewer's perspective, the location and intensity of a light source, the location and orientation of the display plane, and more.

With this information available, the GPU and graphics chipset renders the 3-D image onto the 2-D screen. To create the 3-D look, mathematical equations calculate the tracing through a scene, determine any light reflections and light sources, place some objects in view and obscure others, and make distant objects smaller and darker *(depth cueing)*. Obviously, the 3-D process is very complicated, involving a tremendous number of calculations, regardless of the complexity of the scene displayed. If shading is added to the process, the number of computations required is doubled.

To speed up the process, all the computations are made on the video card by the GPU, and the chipset and the graphics program (the one running on the PC) are written in a standard 3-D graphics language, such as OpenGL. The graphics program might also use an application program interface (API) that provides a library of standard graphic commands that can be passed to the graphics processor. Graphics APIs allow the game or application to remain compatible to all versions of a 3-D card.

Taking a Look at Video Card Operations

A *video card* is virtually a separate computer mounted inside the PC to handle video graphics reproduction on the monitor. It has its own processor, BIOS, memory, chipset, and connectors, all of which are focused at processing graphics images for display.

Processing the video

On most older video cards, the PC's processor serves as the system's GPU and performs the geometric and mathematical calculations used to complete the transform and lighting phases. The system CPU sends the raw screen image to the video controller's *frame buffer*, where the video card reads it and performs the setup phase.

The video cards that include a GPU can process the graphics information through the transform and lighting phases with only some assistance from the system processor. The video controller's GPU processes the graphics information as much as ten times faster than the system CPU primarily because that's all it does.

On newer video and graphics cards, the system CPU passes video tasks on to the video card GPU using the AGP or PCI bus. The GPU extracts the drawing instructions from the stream of data generated by an application to produce the image requested.

The GPU works with its video driver firmware to produce the data needed for the setup phase. The processes performed by the GPU include: bitmap transfers and painting; window resizing and repositioning; line drawing; font scaling; and polygon creation. This data is then written to the video frame buffer for use in the setup phase.

Working with video memory

A certain amount of memory is needed to hold the graphics information being passed to the setup phase from the transform and lighting phase of the video graphics process. Exactly how much memory is needed is directly related to the amount of information being passed, the resolution of the monitor, and the number of graphic dimensions being generated. For example, a monochrome text display on an MDA monitor required less than 2K of space, but today's 3-D high-resolution displays might need as much as 64MB.

As the video standards and capabilities evolved, the need to place memory on the video card became apparent. The 2K of memory needed by the MDA display was carved out of system memory — actually, from the upper memory area. Remember that for monochrome text graphics, the PC's CPU did most of the processing for the display, which meant that working out of main memory was convenient — and, at the time, less expensive than putting RAM on the video card.

On most current systems, video memory (or video RAM, if you prefer) is now located on the video or graphics controller card. As the need for video memory increased from kilobytes to megabytes and as the video controller began taking on more of the processing, conveniently locating video memory on the video card itself made more sense.

The AGP technology allows the video GPU to use a small amount of the system RAM for scratchpad memory to make calculations, but the frame buffer is located in the video RAM on the video card. The AGP approach to RAM provides flexibility without affecting the video system's performance.

In some less-expensive home PC's, some of the video processing functions are included on the motherboard, and a portion of the system RAM is used for the frame buffer. This approach to video memory is called *unified memory architecture,* which means that the system RAM is used to support video as well. This results in eliminating the need for a separate video card and its cost. However, these systems always have a lower-quality video system compared with those supported directly by a video card with its own video RAM.

Resolving the resolution

The primary factor affecting how much video RAM should be included on the video card is the monitor's resolution. Each of the pixels on the monitor's display requires a certain amount of data to encode exactly how the pixel is to appear. For example, nearly 6MB of data are needed to generate a true color image using 1600 x 1200 resolution (1,920,000 pixels) on a monitor.

Resolution is the number of pixels used to display an image. Although the size of the display (15", 17", and so on) has some bearing on the number of pixels available, display detail improves with the more pixels that are used.

A monitor using 640 x 480 resolution uses 307,200 pixels to create the image that it displays. The same monitor set to a resolution of 1280 x 960 now uses 1,228,800 pixels in the same display space.

As the pixel count increases, the size of the pixel and the amount of space around it also decrease. On a Windows system, try using the Settings tab of the Display Properties to change the display resolution. As the resolution increases, the detail in the display also increases while its size decreases.

Adjusting for the aspect ratio

Another defining measurement of the video display is its *aspect ratio,* which is the ratio of horizontal pixels to vertical pixels in use. The standard aspect ratio is 4:3 (4 to 3), which is commonly used for 640 x 480, 800 x 600, and 1024 x 768. The aspect ratio helps the monitor and graphics software define onscreen shapes and graphics, such as making a circle appear round.

Diving into color depth

Another important factor in determining the amount of video RAM needed on a system is the monitor's color depth. The *color depth* represents the number of individual colors that each pixel on the screen can display. Color depth is always expressed as the number of bits used to describe each color in the color set. The common color depth settings are 8-bit, 16-bit, 24-bit, and 32-bit color. Figure 14-2 shows the settings available on a Windows 98 PC and its monitor.

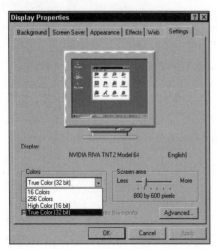

Figure 14–2: The color depth settings available on a Windows PC.

The number of bits used for the color depth determines the number of colors that can be displayed. For example, 8-bit color uses eight bits to number each of the colors. In binary numbers, the range of numbers is 00000000 to 11111111 – or, in decimal, the range of 0 to 255, or 256 colors. A particular color depth can describe (or number) as many as the largest binary number that can be represented by the number of bits of the color depth plus 1. This means that a 16-bit color depth can display 65,536 colors (or $2^{15} + 1$), the 24-bit color depth has 16.7 million colors that each pixel could conceivably display, and 32-bit color supports over 4 billion colors.

Depending on the PC, video card, and monitor, a 24-bit or 32-bit color depth is designated as a True Color setting.

The human eye cannot distinguish more than 16 million colors. Above that, the human eye typically has difficulty discerning the colors of two adjacent pixels.

Connecting to external A/V devices

Beyond the standard output ports for the monitor, some video cards come with additional output ports, which are used to connect the video card to a TV, VCR, or projector.

Generally, these extra video output ports are either composite or S-Video. *Composite video,* the most common type of output port on video cards, supports good image quality on most TVs and VCRs. *S-Video* is a high-quality display interface that provides better color and resolution than composite video.

Other miscellaneous output ports and interfaces can be included on some video cards. Here are a few of the most common ones:

◆ *Virtual reality (VR) goggles:* This type of port supports video for VR goggles or can be used to produce a display with increased depth on a standard monitor.

◆ *DVD:* Digital Versatile Disc (DVD) drives need special video interfaces, and many of the newer high-end video cards come with ports to support DVD drives or MPEG-2 decoder card interfaces.

◆ *TV tuner:* This port allows the computer to receive video streams from a TV, VCR, laserdisc, or TV antenna.

◆ *Scan Line Interleaving (SLI):* This interface enables two 3-D acceleration cards to share the load of generating the displayed image by dividing the screen between the two cards.

Determining How Much Video Memory You Need

Although most video cards on the market today come with between 8–32MB of video RAM, high-end cards are available with as much as 64MB and higher. Some folks think that 64MB is far more than is needed, but others — especially the 3-D crowd — think that even that might not be enough. The latest video card releases include as much as 128MB or video memory, which is likely to become the new standard in the not-too-distant future.

Calculating 2-D video RAM requirements

To figure the amount of video RAM needed for a particular system, perform the following calculation:

```
Resolution * (Color Depth / 8) = Video RAM required
```

Dividing the color depth by eight converts the calculation of the resolution times the color depth into bytes, which is the common measurement for RAM.

If you plan on using 24-bit color depth on a monitor with 1024 x 768 resolution, the calculation for the minimum amount of video RAM that you need is

```
1024 * 768 = 786,432 (pixels in the resolution)
24 / 8 = 3 (bytes in the color depth)
786,432 * 3 = 2,359,296 (bytes of video RAM needed)
```

So, for 1024 x 768 using 24-bit color depth, the video card must have at least 2.4MB of video RAM.

For a monitor with 1600 x 1200 resolution on which you want to display 32-bit color depth, the graphics card needs about 8MB:

```
1600 * 1200 = 1,920,000 (pixels of resolution)
32 / 8 = 4 (bytes of color depth)
1,920,000 * 4 = 7,680,000 (bytes of video RAM required)
```

These preceding sample calculations (brought to you by the video RAM manufacturers of the world) compute the video RAM requirements for generating 2-D images. Table 14-2 lists the amount of video RAM required by several common graphics settings.

TABLE 14-2 COMMON 2-D VIDEO RAM REQUIREMENTS

Resolution	Color Depth	VRAM Required
640 x 480	8-bit	307K
1024 x 768	16-bit	1.57MB
1024 x 768	24-bit	2.36MB
1600 x 1200	24-bit	5.76MB
1600 x 1200	32-bit	7.68MB

Figuring 3-D video RAM requirements

Video cards that support 3-D graphics require more video RAM than 2-D cards even on the same resolution. In addition to 2-D (down and across), a third dimension of depth (*the Z-plane* — which has nothing at all to do with Fantasy Island) is added. Real 3-D cards use three buffers (width [x dimension], height [y dimension], and depth [z dimension]) to hold the graphics data: a front buffer, a back buffer, and a Z-buffer (so called because it buffers the Z-plane). This is why a 2-D video card with 4MB of video RAM can support a 1600 x 1200 16-bit display but can only support a 3-D game with an 800 x 600 16-bit setting. The Z-buffer consumes enough of the available RAM to require the resolution to be reduced.

The front and back buffers are set to the size required by the color depth, and the Z-buffer uses 16-bits (or 2 bytes). To calculate the amount of video RAM needed to support a 3-D display, use this calculation:

```
Resolution * ((Color Depth (in bytes) * 2) + 2) = 3D video RAM requirements
```

For a 1024 x 768 resolution using 16-bit color, the calculation is

```
1024 * 768 = 786,432 (pixels of resolution)
16 / 8 = 2 (color depth in bytes)
2 * 2 + 2 = 6 (buffers required in bytes)
786,432 * 6 = 4,718,592 (video RAM required for 3D graphics)
```

The result of this calculation is that more RAM is required to support a video card with 4MB of RAM (even if it is a 3-D card) using 1024 x 768 resolution with a 16-bit 3-D display.

Sorting Out the Video RAM Technologies

The memory located on a video card is also called the *frame buffer* because it holds the graphic instructions about each frame to be displayed. On older systems, the frame buffer is managed by the system CPU and is located in system memory. However, by placing memory on the video card, the frame buffer can be carved out of the video RAM and be managed by the video GPU.

Video RAM (VRAM) serves two purposes on the video card: One, it acts as a buffer between the CPU and data bus and the monitor; and two, it's the work area used by the video processor and chipset to perform the calculations used to formulate the graphics image as an analog signal for the monitor.

VRAM is a bit different than the RAM used as primary memory on the PC. It is usually *dual ported,* meaning that it can be written to simultaneously while being read. This allows the CPU to write to VRAM while the monitor is reading it. A new type of video RAM that's becoming very popular on high-end graphics packages is Rambus memory, which operates much faster than other forms of VRAM.

A variety of memory technologies have been and are being used as video RAM on video cards. The most common RAM technologies used for video RAM are

♦ *Dynamic Random Access Memory (DRAM):* This is the same RAM used on early PCs. Extended Data Output (EDO) DRAM has largely replaced DRAM on the PC for main memory, but other types of DRAM are still used for video RAM.

◆ *EDO DRAM:* EDO DRAM provides a higher bandwidth than standard DRAM and manages read/write cycles more efficiently.

◆ *Video RAM (VRAM):* VRAM, not to be confused with the generic term *video RAM,* is dual ported (it can be written to and read from at the same time). VRAM is a special type of DRAM that doesn't need to be refreshed as often as standard DRAM.

◆ *Windows RAM (WRAM):* This video RAM used on Matrox video cards is dual ported and runs a bit faster than VRAM. The Windows name is unique to the function of this memory and has nothing to do with any Microsoft products.

◆ *Synchronous DRAM (SDRAM):* SDRAM is very much like EDO DRAM, except that it's synchronized to the video card's GPU and chipset, which allows it to run faster. SDRAM is a single-ported memory technology that's very common on video cards.

◆ *Multi-bank DRAM (MDRAM):* MDRAM is a newer memory type that is divided into 32K banks that can be accessed independently. MDRAM also offers the advantages of interleaving, true memory sizing, and better memory performance. Interleaving allows memory accesses to overall memory banks. MDRAM can be sized exactly to the amount of video RAM needed to support a particular display type.

◆ *Double Data Rate SDRAM (DDR SDRAM):* DDR SDRAM doubles the data rate of standard SDRAM to produce faster data transfers. DDR memories are becoming more commonplace on video cards, especially 3-D video accelerators.

◆ *Synchronous Graphics RAM (SGRAM):* This improvement on SDRAM supports block writes and write-per-bit, which yield better graphics performance. SGRAM, a single-ported memory technology, is found only on video cards with chipsets that support these features, such as many Matrox video cards.

◆ *Double Data Rate SGRAM (DDR SGRAM):* DDR SGRAM is showing up on the very latest cards. It doubles the data rate of SGRAM and offers better performance.

◆ *Direct Rambus DRAM (RDRAM):* This newer, general-purpose memory type, also used on video cards, includes bus mastering and a dedicated channel between memory devices. RDRAM runs about 20 times faster than conventional DRAM.

See Chapter 6 for more information on memory technologies.

The earliest video RAM was standard DRAM, which requires constant electrical refreshing to hold its contents. DRAM didn't work well for video RAM because while it's being refreshed, it cannot be accessed, which meant that video performance suffered.

Installing Video Cards and Solving Video Problems

For the most part, installing a video card involves little more than using a screwdriver to remove and replace the screw that anchors the card into the motherboard and case slot.

As far as diagnostics go, the diskette or CD-ROM included with the graphics card (primarily to provide the device driver) sometimes includes a proprietary diagnostics utility as well. Otherwise, very little is available in the way of software designed to specifically troubleshoot or diagnose video card problems, especially 3-D graphics cards.

Because most of the components on a video card are mounted directly on its circuit board (with the exception of its RAM perhaps), when the video card is malfunctioning (and it's usually very apparent), it might just be time for a new card. Be sure to fill out and send in your warranty cards and also use care when installing or removing this card, treating it very much like you would a motherboard.

Here are some common problems and how to resolve them.

Nothing displays on the monitor

If nothing displays on your monitor, first check the obvious:

◆ Is the monitor plugged into a power source?

◆ Is the monitor switched on?

◆ Is the monitor connected to the proper connection on the back of the PC?

If you really want to eliminate the monitor as a suspect (or confirm that it is the problem), try connecting another monitor (one that you know works) to the PC. If you have video display with the new monitor, the original monitor could be bad. However, if the second monitor also doesn't work, the problem is probably not the monitor.

If the monitor is not the culprit, check the following:

1. If you hear three short beep tones (or something similar, depending on your BIOS) when you boot the system and nothing displays on the monitor, you can generally surmise that you have a problem with the video system.

Perhaps the video card isn't installed properly, the slot in which the video card is installed could be bad, there is a BIOS set-up issue for the interface bus, or (more common) the video card is defective.

2. Open up the system case and reseat the video card.

3. Check the expansion slot for bent tines or corrosion and check the motherboard traces around the slot for problems, such as burn spots, scrapes, or dripped solder.

4. Reboot the system.

5. If the problem persists, try installing the video card in another slot (of the same bus) on the same PC. If that fails, try installing the video card in another PC.

   If the card fails in the new system, it's time to get a new video card. If the video card works in either the new slot or PC, you might have a bad expansion slot on the motherboard. Hopefully it's not the AGP slot because that means you either need to switch to a PCI video card or get a new motherboard.

The display is scrambled

If the display looks like the picture on a badly adjusted TV set, the video refresh rate is probably not set correctly. This is definitely the problem if the display is okay through the boot cycle but then fritzes out when the operating system starts up.

To clear up the video on a Windows system, try the following steps:

1. Boot into Windows Safe Mode.

See Chapter 27 for information on how to start a Windows system in Safe Mode.

2. After Windows starts and the desktop shows the words Safe Mode in each corner of the display, right-click any empty part of the desktop display to open its shortcut menu.

3. From the desktop shortcut menu that appears, select Properties to open the Display Properties window.

4. From the Display Properties window that appears, select the Settings tab and then click the Advanced button at the bottom of the display.

5. From the Adapter tab, choose a Refresh Rate setting (located near the middle of the window).

Figure 14-3 shows the Properties window for the video card. If the refresh rate isn't set to Optimal or Adapter Default, check the documentation of the video card and monitor for the best rate to use. Typically, it's around 70 or 72 Hz. After clicking all the necessary OKs, restart the PC.

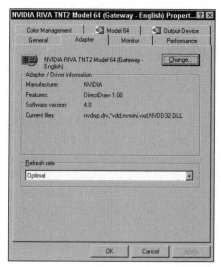

Figure 14-3: The Adapter tab of the Display Properties window.

The display is fuzzy or blurry

A fuzzy or blurry display could be caused by a problem with the refresh rate setting. See the previous section "The display is scrambled" for how to make sure the refresh rate is optimized. But if the refresh rate is set as it should be, you've had your eyes checked recently, and things are still out of focus, try this:

1. Adjust the brightness and contrast settings on the monitor.

   The problem is probably the settings on the monitor itself, not the video card.

2. If the problem persists, the monitor might be defective.

The video card settings aren't listed in the Windows display settings

If you try to change the desktop settings in Windows to reflect a new video card but only 640 x 480 and 16 colors are available, the video card's software drivers are probably not installed or need to be reinstalled.

1. To check which video device drivers are installed, open the Device Manager and select the video display adapters option.

   If the video card is a PCI card, you might need to drill down to it through the Plug and Play devices first and then through the PCI bus entries. (It might be listed as Standard VGA.)

2. To install the device drivers, use the disk or CD-ROM that came with the video card. Use the Add Hardware icon from the Control Panel to rerun the video card installation and to add the video device drivers.

   Be sure to click the Have Disk button when asked for the location of the drivers and then insert the disk when prompted.

 On older Windows systems (Windows 9x and before), you should avoid using the driver from the Windows library if you have a driver disk from the manufacturer. These Windows drivers are typically out-of-date and might not always support all the features in newer versions of the hardware. However, on newer systems (Windows 2000 or Windows XP), the drivers in the Windows driver library have generally been tested thoroughly with the operating system and are digitally signed to work with it.

Installing a new video card

To install a new video card, follow this process:

1. Follow appropriate electrostatic discharge (ESD) safeguards to protect your video card, the PC, and yourself. Leave the card in its anti-static packaging until you are ready to install it.

2. Remove the old video card both physically and logically from the system.

   Note: Before you open the system case, delete the card from the Windows Device Manager and track down and remove its device drivers.

3. Verify the adapter interfaces available on your PC.

   Hopefully before you bought the card, you determined the adapter interfaces available on your PC. If you plan to use a PCI interface, be sure that the card is a PCI card; if you plan to use an AGP slot, you should have an AGP card.

Motherboards with a Pentium II processor or higher usually have an AGP port for use by video cards only. You must also be running at least the Windows 95 OSR2 version. The fact that your PC has an AGP port most likely means that you can install or upgrade to an AGP card.

4. Insert the new video card.

   a. Assuming that the case is open, remove the video card from its anti-static package.

   b. Hold it only by its ends and, avoiding contact with its components or edge connectors, align the card's edge connectors to the appropriate slot with the metal mounting bracket fitting into the open slot in the case.

   c. With your fingers spaced evenly across the top of the card, press down firmly to seat the card in the slot.

   d. Align the mounting bracket with the screw hole in the case and attach it with a screw.

5. Use an available connector to connect the card to the power supply.

   Some video cards, and especially AGP cards, have a power supply connector. Check the card's documentation if you're unsure which power supply connector to use, if required.

6. After the card is installed and ready to go, install the device drivers.

   Typically, the video card comes with an auto-run CD-ROM that begins its installation routines when you close the CD tray.

   See "The video card settings aren't listed in the Windows display settings," earlier in this chapter, for instructions on installing software drivers.

7. After the video drivers and any other utility software for your video system are installed, restart the PC.

   If you have problems, review "The video card settings aren't listed in the Windows display settings," earlier in this chapter, and "Troubleshooting the video card," which follows next.

Troubleshooting the video card

If you're unsure of the problem on a video or graphics card, use the following general troubleshooting steps to try to isolate the problem.

TIP

Most video card manufacturers have technical support available as Frequently Asked Questions (FAQs) on their Web sites. The documentation that came with the card might also have a troubleshooting guide in it.

1. Make sure that the video card is firmly seated in the appropriate bus slot.

   Chances are slim that you have a PCI card in an AGP slot or vice versa. They shouldn't fit in each other's slot — and if forced into the wrong slot type, the card is probably no longer good to use.

2. If the card requires it, verify that the card is properly connected to the power supply through one of the power supply's connectors.

   Most video cards that require power use the same type of power supply connector (Molex) used by a hard disk drive.

3. Verify that the video card hasn't been assigned system resources that had already been assigned to another or conflicting device.

   Typically, video cards aren't assigned IRQs, but check anyway — the card that you're troubleshooting might just be one of the ones that is.

4. Verify that the device drivers are installed.

   You might want to reinstall the device drivers before taking any other more drastic measures. See "Installing a new video card" earlier in the chapter.

5. Check the documentation of the video card.

   Many cards have specific requirements for the BIOS settings of the PC. If this is the case, reboot the PC and access the BIOS' configuration data by pressing the specific key (typically F1, F2, or Del) during the boot sequence to enter the Complementary Metal-Oxide Semiconductor (CMOS) setup. Verify that the BIOS settings are correct for the video card. In many cases, the Hidden Refresh, Byte Merge, Video BIOS shadow and cache RAM, VGA Palette Snoop, and DAC Snoop might need to be disabled. If you change any of the CMOS settings, be sure to save them before exiting.

6. If the previous steps don't solve or isolate the problem, call technical support at the video card manufacturer or check with the reseller.

Replacing integrated video support with a video card

Review "Installing a new video card" earlier in the chapter for some generic steps to use to replace an existing video or graphics card. This project adds to that one with steps on converting from an integrated video card to an expansion card.

1. Completely uninstall the previous video card's drivers and switch over to the Standard VGA Display Driver for Windows.

   The display might be bad until a few more adjustments are made.

2. Disconnect any cables attached to the card and remove the card by grasping it by the upper corners and pulling firmly upward.

   OR

   If the PC has an integrated video card (the video controller is built into the motherboard's chipset), disable it before installing the new card.

   Check the documentation of the motherboard and chipset for instructions on how this adapter is disabled. You might need to change a jumper or disable a port in the BIOS configuration data.

3. Follow the steps listed earlier in "Installing a new video card."

Determining the type of video card in a PC

One way to find out the type of video card installed in a PC is to use the DOS debug utility, shown in Figure 14-4, which is included with virtually all versions of Windows.

1. Open an MS-DOS prompt or command line.

2. Type **debug** and press Enter.

   A dash prompt displays.

3. Enter **d c000:0010**, as shown in Figure 14-4.

4. After the first block of data is displayed, look at the text translation of binary data on the right side of the display.

   If the video card data is not shown, type **d** and press Enter to display the next block of memory.

5. The video data should appear in either the first or second blocks.

Figure 14-4: Use the `debug` command to display the video controller information on a Windows PC.

Upgrading the RAM on a video card

The video RAM on many newer video cards can be upgraded to increase its speed, color palette, and the performance of its graphics.

1. Video RAM must be matched to the video card and to its bus structure (PCI, AGP, ISA).

   If you're unsure of the video card, see "Determining the type of video card in a PC," earlier in this chapter.

2. Verify the amount of memory already installed on the card by the manufacturer and how much you can add.

   You should be able to get this from the card's documentation or from the manufacturer's Web site. You might need to call the technical support number of the manufacturer. If you really want to upgrade the video RAM on the video card, you need to know these facts. Typically, you should add memory in 2MB increments but follow the advice of the manufacturer on this.

3. You must remove the video card from the PC to add video RAM to it.

   Be sure that you're working on a flat surface that is ESD protected.

4. Follow the instructions in the video card's documentation or on the manufacturer's Web site for how new memory chips are installed on the card.

   If none are available, use the following generic steps.

5. Locate the mounting on the card for the memory chip and align the edges and dots, pushing the memory chip into place, and making sure that the chip is firmly in place and will not fall off.

   The mounting should have four toothed edges that align with four dots on the corners of the memory chip.

6. Verify that the new video RAM is recognized by the system by checking the BIOS configuration data. Reboot the system (you need to anyway) and enter the BIOS setup utility. From the Startup menu, select Devices and I/O Ports, and from its menu, choose Video Setup.

   The amount of video RAM recognized by the PC is listed. If the amount is not the new total, check the installation of the video RAM on the card and verify that the card is installed correctly.

Selecting higher resolutions

If the video card doesn't have enough RAM to support a higher-level resolution or color depth, it's likely that they are disabled on the Windows Display Settings window. In order to provide access to capabilities that the video card has within its specifications, you might need to add more memory.

Verify with the manufacturer how much additional video RAM can be added to the card and then follow the steps in "Upgrading the RAM on a video card" earlier.

To calculate the amount of RAM needed to support the resolution and color depth you desire, use the calculations shown in "Determining How Much Video Memory You Need" earlier in the chapter.

Video cards all have a processor or chipset on the card. The onboard processor generates some or all of the image to be displayed on the monitor. How much of the video load the video card's processor and chipset carry depends on the age of a video card or how much it cost.

Older cards use the frame buffer technology in which the video card is tasked with displaying only one video frame at a time and the CPU (the one inside the PC) actually creates each video frame.

The next step up for video processors is graphics acceleration. In fact, some video cards are called graphics accelerators. On this type of video card, the video processor performs the routine tasks associated with generating graphics images under the guidance of the system CPU. This type of video card processing is the most common in PCs.

On newer high-end video cards, the onboard processor and chipset have the complete responsibility for generating all displayed graphics, which leaves the CPU free to do other tasks.

Video processors are divided into two categories:

♦ *2-D:* This is the type of graphics used by most of the standard applications, such as word processing and spreadsheets, and many multimedia applications, such as PowerPoint and CorelDraw. This is the minimum level of graphics on a PC.

◆ *3-D:* This is the graphics type used by games and 3-D rendering and drawing software. Unfortunately, 3-D graphics and the processor commands used to generate them are not standardized. As a result, some 3-D programs and games might not work with every video card.

Configuring BIOS settings for better AGP performance

A common video performance problem on PCs with an Accelerated Graphics Port (AGP) video card is the card having higher capabilities than the BIOS is configured to support.

To possibly improve the performance of the AGP video system, check the BIOS' AGP Capability setting. If it's not already at 4x, set it for that value. Many BIOSes default to 1x, which severely constrains the transfer power of the AGP video card.

Chapter 15

Monitors and Displays

IN THIS CHAPTER
Without a video display device of some type, the personal computer wouldn't be a very helpful tool. Monitors and displays provide the user with a view to the PC and its applications. A monitor is the source of information and entertainment for the PC user. Whether a CRT or LCD produces the display, its purpose remains the same – to display the visual temporary output of the PC.

There would be no What You See Is What You Get (WYSIWYG) on a PC without some form of display (to see what it is that you do get). PCs are limited to producing outputs that can be handled by human senses; to this point, technology is limited to sight and sound. Given a choice, users still prefer sight over sound. Although much can be accomplished on a PC with no sound output, very little could get done without the ability to see the PC's output. In this chapter, you'll find coverage on the following:

◆ Performing preventive maintenance for a monitor

◆ Resolving monitor problems

◆ Changing color depth and resolution

◆ Setting and maintaining the refresh rate

◆ Proper disposing of a CRT monitor

THIS CHAPTER PROVIDES some basic background on CRTs and LCD displays. You won't find much in the way of troubleshooting or problem-solving because a vast majority of the problems that arise on a monitor are either handled through the monitor's adjustment controls or require the services of a monitor repair facility.

Looking into CRTs and LCDs

The two general categories of PC visual display peripheral devices are the CRT and the LCD. A *cathode ray tube* (CRT) looks and works very much like a standard, conventional television set (without the remote control, of course). On the other hand, *liquid crystal displays* (LCDs) are flat-panel devices that are stand-alone monitors, attached to portable PCs, or hung on the wall. The CRT (shown in Figure 15-1) is largely a desktop or tabletop device, but an LCD (shown in Figure 15-2) can either sit on a desk or be portable, like the personal digital assistant (PDA) in Figure 15-3.

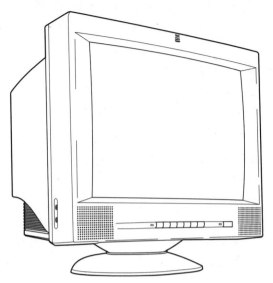

Figure 15-1: A PC desktop monitor.

An LCD display is really an adaptation of the CRT display, but because it uses completely different technology, it is differentiated from the CRT monitor. In the following sections, I discuss both in some detail. However, the video card controls much of the capabilities of the PC's monitor.

Figure 15-2: A flat-panel PC display.

Figure 15-3: A handheld personal digital assistant.

Photo Courtesy of Handspring Visor.

Chapter 14 provides more information on the features and functions of video cards.

Reviewing PC monitors

Despite the fact that PC technology is advancing as fast as it is, the monitor is about the only part of a PC that can be considered a long-term investment. A PC monitor is about the only PC component that actually holds its value over time and has a lasting durability. Good-quality monitors last for years and can be used with several generations of PC systems. A number of things should be considered when making the decision about investing in a PC monitor, including the following:

◆ *Cost:* Cost can be a major consideration when selecting a new monitor. A monitor budget of less than $400 won't be sufficient for an LCD display, at least not until those prices come down a bit more. However, if cost isn't a factor, the choices and comparisons are virtually unlimited.

◆ *Size:* A monitor's size has a lot to do with its capability, but more importantly, it affects your working comfort. As is true with many things – and especially with monitors – bigger is better. Many experts recommend that given today's technology, the minimum CRT monitor size should be 17 inches or an LCD monitor should have a resolution of at least 1024 x 768.

◆ *Type:* Although you'll find feature and cost variations within each monitor type, your choice boils down to between the traditional and conventional CRT display and the state-of-the-art (and expensive) digital flat-panel LCD.

CRT DISPLAYS

Until very recently, standard PC system packages featured only CRT displays. However, newer systems are being offered with flat-panel LCD displays (more on this in the upcoming section "Flat-panel displays"). As prices for LCD displays continue to drop, experts believe that the CRT could soon be replaced as the standard monitor by LCD displays on standard PC packages, with a CRT display available only as an option. However, recall that the floppy disk was to have been obsolete over five years ago.

CRT displays have some advantages over LCD displays. A CRT is bright, well-lit, economical, and produces excellent color and graphic qualities. CRTs use the same common and well-developed technology found in conventional (*not* high-definition TV, or HDTV) television sets. The manufacturing process is well defined, and CRT costs are comparatively low.

A *CRT* is a funnel-shaped glass tube that uses an electron gun to excite (light up) dots of phosphorous material on the back of the CRT's display glass. The CRT's display contains literally millions of phosphorous dots. Together, the glowing phosphors form images that show through the display glass for the user to see. The display glass is slightly curved, which is why the display is bright and easily viewed at an angle.

Larger screen sizes and higher visual standards continue to make the CRT the visual display of choice for many PC users. Some detail on how the CRT creates its display is discussed later in the section "Operating the Display."

FLAT-PANEL DISPLAYS

The answer to the bulk problem of a PC monitor on a desk or worktable with limited space is a flat-panel (LCD) monitor. The major benefit, among others, of a flat-panel monitor is its size, which really means its depth. A typical CRT display, especially the larger displays in use today, are 15 inches or more from front to back, which can take up a considerable amount of valuable real estate on a desktop. Comparatively, a flat-panel LCD display is typically only a few inches deep, including its base. This makes it perfect for small desks, cubicles, or in places where a large CRT monitor could negatively affect the aesthetics or decor, such as a reception desk or the like. Some new style systems even integrate the PC and monitor into a single flat-panel package that's only a few inches thick front to back.

FLAT-SCREEN VERSUS FLAT-PANEL

Many people confuse the terms *flat-screen* and *flat-panel*. *Flat-panel* monitors use LCD displays to reproduce images on a screen. A *flat-screen* display is a type of CRT that has a flat glass screen as opposed to the more standard, curved glass screen found on the normal, everyday CRT.

On conventional CRTs, the front glass panel is like a section cut out of a ball — curved both horizontally and vertically. Curving the face of the CRT places each phosphor dot the same distance from the electron beam. So-called flat screens have a flat glass front on the CRT in an effort to be easier on the viewer's eyes. However, because the electrons that are illuminating the phosphor must travel farther to reach the top, bottom, and side edges of the screen, the image along the edges of the screen can be fuzzy and distorted.

Some CRTs, such as Sony's Trinitron and Mitsubishi's Diamondtron tubes, offer a compromise to the flat screen with a screen that's more like a section out of a cylinder — curved horizontally and flatter vertically. Another alternative to the flat screen is CRTs with screens that are curved more like a section cut from a bigger ball with the center of this bigger piece used to make the CRT's screen appear to be flat to the viewer. The focus on the electron beam has also been improved so that it can travel longer distances accurately. Another attempt to solve the distortion problems of the flat-screen display has been to place a special glass plate over the CRT to optically remove the distortion near the screen's edges. The LCD display, which is naturally flat, avoids these problems by illuminating each pixel equally and without an electron gun, thus eliminating the need for a curved screen or any optical effects.

Drawing up dots and pixels

The images displayed on a PC's monitor are created by a pattern of phosphor dots arranged in much the same way that a photograph is reproduced in a newspaper. The halftone dots of the newspaper are shaded lighter or darker, and the reader's eyes and brain form a visual image from them. A CRT creates an image by illuminating the phosphor dots on the back of its screen.

MONOCHROME MONITORS

A *monochrome* (single color) monitor has phosphor of only one color. Text characters are formed very much the same as characters on a dot-matrix printer, as illustrated in Figure 15-4. Although this illustration is exaggerated a bit, the concept is accurate. Earlier CRT monitors and video display standards define text character capabilities in terms of the size of the grid used to define a text character, very much like how a

Measuring the Viewable Size

For some reason (probably a marketing reason), the sizes used for CRT monitors are overstated anywhere from one to two inches. On the other hand, an LCD display's size is actually the size of the display area. So be careful when comparing the *viewable area* — the part of the screen where images are displayed — on these two types of monitors.

CRT display sizes

The most popular CRT monitor sizes on the market today are 15, 17, 19, and 21 inch. These sizes are the monitor's *nominal size,* which is measured diagonally from the bottom-right corner to the top-left corner, case and all (as illustrated here).

CRT monitor cases have a front *bezel* (the plastic around the edge of the display) that covers up a small portion of the CRT's screen to hold it in place. The bezel cuts down the area of the CRT that can be viewed by as much as a full inch all the way around the edge of the monitor. Most CRT monitor manufacturers now list the viewable size of the monitor along with the monitor's nominal size.

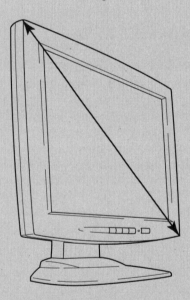

The viewable size of a 17-inch CRT display is actually a bit less than 16 inches. When comparing monitors, compare viewable areas rather than nominal screen sizes because not all monitors have the same size bezels. Many smaller monitors can be better values when you compare the price-per-inch of the monitor's viewable area. The following table lists the average nominal and viewable screen sizes for CRT and LCD monitors.

Nominal Size	CRT Viewable Size	LCD Viewable Size
14"	13.2"	14"
15"	13.8"	15"
17"	15.9"	17"
19"	18"	19"
21"	19.8"	21"

LCD display sizes

As illustrated in the table above, LCD flat-panel monitors can provide a better bargain on a per-viewable-inch basis. The nominal size of an LCD display is the same as its viewable area as opposed to the 1-inch or more margin of error used by CRT manufacturers.

The display size for an LCD monitor is accurate because only the display area is measured diagonally. A 15-inch LCD display is usually 15 inches, diagonally measured. And as shown in the table above, smaller LCD displays offer about the same display area as larger CRT monitors.

dot-matrix printer is specified. When the CRT's phosphor dots are illuminated, the text or graphic image appears as a single color on a contrasting background. Typically, the background is black, and the display color is green, amber, or white.

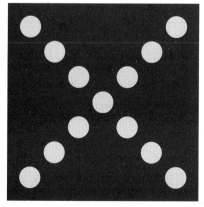

Figure 15–4: A text character formed on a monochrome CRT.

COLOR MONITORS

A color CRT has millions of phosphor dots on the display screen. One-third of the dots are red; one-third of the dots are green; and one-third of the dots are blue. The dots are arranged so that a dot of each color can be combined to create a triangular element called a *triad*, as shown in Figure 15-5. More commonly, the triad is called a *picture element*, or a *pixel* for short.

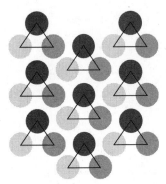

Figure 15-5: Pixels are formed from triangles of phosphor dots.

A color CRT actually has three electron guns, one for each color in the pixel. The *electron beam*, which is the combined beams of the three electron guns, lights up the phosphors of each pixel. The intensity of the beam used to illuminate each dot creates color and shading combinations that define the image displayed on the screen. The electron beam sweeps over the pixels from side to side, one row at a time, to create or refresh the displayed image.

LCD displays are of two different types: passive matrix and active matrix. A *passive matrix* display has a layer of LCD elements on a grid (matrix) of wires. When current is applied to the wire intersections, the pixels block the light, and the area appears dark. A passive matrix refreshes the display by applying current to the pixels at a fixed refresh rate. *Active matrix* displays control each LCD element individually with transistors that continually refresh each pixel. Find more on both of these LCD display types later in the section "Categorizing LCDs."

Resolving resolution

The number of pixels on a display, whether CRT or LCD, determines the amount of detail that can be used to create an image. More pixels in the display increase the image quality that a monitor produces. The number of pixels in a display represents its *resolution.*

A monitor's resolution is expressed as the number of pixels on each row and the number of pixel rows on the display. For example, a display with 640 x 480 resolution (read as *640 by 480*) has 640 pixels on each horizontal row and 480 vertical rows of pixels on the display. This monitor uses 307,200 (640 times 480) pixels to create its displayed images. Table 15-1 shows the resolutions most commonly supported by today's monitors.

TABLE 15-1 MONITOR RESOLUTIONS

Resolution	Total Pixels Used
640 x 480	307,200
800 x 600	480,000
1024 x 768	786,432
1280 x 1024	1,310,720
1600 x 1200	1,920,000

 Larger monitors, such as 19- or 21-inch, have trouble displaying smaller resolutions. And most smaller monitors, such as 14- or 15-inch, cannot produce higher resolutions with very good image quality. Match the monitor and its resolution to your needs.

Resolution is essentially a real estate issue. Most larger monitors natively support higher resolutions but can also support lower resolutions by using fewer pixels or a smaller area of the screen to produce the display. LCD displays have fixed resolutions for the most part; if you use another resolution higher or lower than its native resolution, the image quality will suffer. Depending on the resolution in use, CRTs can enlarge or reduce images easily without too much image quality loss, but typically LCD panels have some trouble doing so.

Because of their construction, LCD displays have natural resolutions set by the number of pixels on each line of the display. Often an LCD display must reduce the display area to reproduce images in lower resolutions. For example, a 12.1" LCD monitor (800 x 600 resolution) has 800 pixels on each row of its display. If the resolution is changed to 640 x 480, it's not possible to evenly represent 640 pixels with 800 pixels and produce clear text or images. Thus, the display image area is reduced to 10.4" for the 640 x 480 image. However, because an LCD displays natural resolution and screens get larger, lower resolutions become much easier to reproduce in the standard display area.

Table 15-2 shows how LCD displays adjust for resolutions other than their natural resolution. In the table, *Small* means that the display area is reduced, *Full* indicates the natural resolution, and *Linear* means that the user must scroll up and down and left and right to see all the displayed image.

TABLE 15-2 LCD RESOLUTIONS

Natural Resolution	640 x 480	800 x 600	1024 x 768
640 x 480	Full	Linear	Linear
800 x 600	Small	Full	Linear
1024 x 768	Small	Small	Full

Applying an aspect ratio

The *aspect ratio* of a monitor is the relationship of its height (in pixels) to its width (in pixels). On most of the commonly used CRT resolutions, the aspect ratio is 4:3, which is by far the most common. The aspect ratio helps software determine how to place images on the screen in relationship to each other as well as to help circles look round (not elliptical) and squares look square (not rectangular).

Relating monitor size to resolution

The physical size of the monitor has a lot to do with the resolutions that the monitor can support. As the space available to hold more pixels increases, so does the monitor's ability to handle higher resolutions. Another factor in this equation is the age of the monitor. Most newer monitors can display higher resolutions than many older and larger monitors.

Higher resolutions require smaller pixels, and when applied on a smaller monitor, can require a magnifying glass to read the screen. A 15-inch monitor can support 1280 x 1024 resolution, but it might never actually be used. In fact, the highest resolution available on any monitor smaller than a 19-inch monitor might also never be used.

Developing color depth

Another very important characteristic of a monitor is its *color depth,* which is the maximum number of colors that it can display. The color depth is represented as the number of bits required to hold the maximum number of colors in the color depth as a binary number. For example, an 8-bit color depth has a maximum of 256 colors because that's the highest binary value that can be expressed in 8 bits. In binary numbers, the range of numbers available in 8 bits is 00000000 to 11111111, or the range in decimal numbers of 0 to 255, which represents 256 different colors.

Table 15-3 lists the number of colors associated with each of the commonly used color depths.

TABLE 15-3 COLOR DEPTHS

Color Depth (In Bits)	Colors Available	Common Name
1	2	Monochrome
4	16	Video Graphics Array (VGA) standard
8	256	256-color
16	65,536	High color
18	262,144	LCD color
24	16,777,216	True Color (24-bit)
32	4,294,967,296	True Color (32-bit)

Depending on the PC, video card, and monitor, either 24-bit or 32-bit is typically designated as the True Color setting. The number of colors that 32-bit color (popular with 3-D video accelerator systems) can develop is perhaps overkill. The human eye cannot distinguish beyond 16 million or so colors. Above that, the eye has difficulty distinguishing the color differences of two adjacent pixels.

Refreshing rates

Another key characteristic of a monitor is its *refresh rate*, which is the number of times per second that the screen can be entirely redrawn. The refresh rate is also a function of the video card and indicates how many times per second that the data used to refresh the display is sent to the monitor.

The phosphor dots on the CRT's screen begin to fade almost immediately, so the electron beam must sweep back over each pixel multiple times per second to keep the display sharp and bright. A low refresh rate can make the CRT screen flicker and also cause eye fatigue and possibly headaches. Most of the current monitors support refresh rates around 75 hertz (Hz) or faster. Because of how they work, LCDs aren't rated with a refresh rate and don't have refresh rate issues. Because of this, LCDs can provide stable images at 60 Hz, and sometimes lower, rates.

Hertz is a measurement of electronic cycles per second for an event or on a device. For example, if a monitor has a refresh rate of 75 Hz, the screen is completely refreshed 75 times per second.

Connecting the display

Another major difference between CRT and LCD displays is that a CRT is an analog device and an LCD is a digital device. CRTs, even those with a digital connection, use an electrical wave to create the display, which means that the PC's digital signal must be converted into an analog signal. This is done either on the video card or in the monitor by a digital-to-analog converter (DAC). The video card sends the digital information generated by an application program to its DAC, which converts the signal into an analog wave and sends it over the connecting cable to the monitor. Even if the CRT has a digital interface, the signal must still be converted to analog.

A flat-panel LCD monitor connected to a standard DAC video card must reprocess the analog signal through its analog-to-digital converter (ADC), which can lead to image degradation. Analog and digital flat-panel monitors are available. To use a digital flat-panel LCD monitor, the video card must be capable of producing digital output.

Controlling the monitor

Most CRT-style monitors have a control panel on the front or side so that its brightness, contrast, focus, and screen size or shape can be adjusted as needed. Some have separate knobs for each adjustable feature, and others have a single control knob or wheel. Virtually all new monitors, LCD and CRT, have an onscreen display (OSD) that allows users to see onscreen the results of their adjustments.

Focus controls on a CRT adjust the convergence of the electron beams on pixels. The three beams can become misconverged or out of alignment, which can cause a blurry or fuzzy image. The CRT's size and shape adjustments are used to fix *barreling* (when the sides of the display bow outward), *pin-cushioning* (when the sides bow inward), and *rotation* (when the top or bottom of the display is not level).

Although they don't have misconvergence problems, LCD monitors can have display and focus problems. A flat-panel monitor has adjustments to synchronize it to the video card. LCD monitors are set to standard VGA timings at the factory, but a particular PC and video card might use a slightly different timing, which can result in a distorted or blurry display. To correct this, LCD monitors have adjustments for the Frequency/Clock and Focus/Phase settings.

Working within the standards

Video display standards are developed more to define the capabilities of video cards than they are for monitors. However, by listing the video standards to which the monitor is compatible, its capabilities in terms of color depth and resolution are automatically defined.

What differentiates one video display standard from another are the resolutions that it supports; how it creates text characters; whether it's color or monochrome; and its color depth, color palette, refresh rate, scan rates, and bandwidth. Table 15-4 lists the resolutions and color depths of the VGA and Super VGA (SVGA) video standards, the two most commonly used today.

TABLE 15-4 VIDEO STANDARDS

Standard	Name	Resolution(s)	Color Depth
VGA	Video Graphics Array	640 x 480	16
		320 x 200	256
SVGA	Super VGA	800 x 600	16
		1024 x 768	256
		1280 x 1024	256
		1600 x 1200	256

Reviewing older video standards

Over the years, several video display standards have been used. Here are a few of the more popular ones:

◆ *Monochrome Display Adapter (MDA):* This was the original text-only standard for monochrome monitors.

◆ *Monochrome Graphics Adapter (MGA):* Also called *Hercules Graphics,* this integrated graphics standard primarily displayed text on a monochrome monitor.

◆ *Color Graphics Adapter (CGA):* This was the first color graphics standard. It provided a 16-color palette on a 640 x 200 resolution.

◆ *Enhanced Graphics Adapter (EGA):* EGA improved on the text and graphics capabilities of CGA and offered a 64-color palette.

◆ *Video Graphics Array (VGA):* VGA is the de facto graphics standard for all monitors, video cards, and most software. As shown in Table 15-4, it supports a range of resolutions and color depths, but 640 x 480 is considered the VGA standard.

◆ *Super VGA (SVGA):* This comprises essentially all the graphic standards above VGA, but it is typically associated with 800 x 600.

Working with Today's Standards

The VGA display standard is considered the base standard for video display systems today. Virtually all current monitors and video cards support the VGA standard. It is the default standard for Windows and almost all other operating systems as well as device drivers that interact directly with the video system.

Most monitors on the market today claim to be at least SVGA compatible. That is, they have some capabilities that are higher than the VGA standard, including resolution and color depth. The same holds true for UVGA and XGA, which are more marketing identities than they are video standards. The Video Electronics Standards Association (VESA) has recently defined the VESA SVGA standard in an attempt to standardize the standards above VGA.

Of these video display standards, only VGA and SVGA are in common use today. The others were part of the video standard evolution with each new standard improving on the last. Other video display standards are in use, such as Extended Graphics Array (XGA) and Ultra VGA (UVGA), which are loosely defined standards that vary from manufacturer to manufacturer.

Driving video

In general, the video card processes the graphics data produced by software running on the PC and prepares it for use by the monitor by converting it from digital data to an analog signal. The video card also sends out the data needed by the monitor to refresh the image or renew it as it changes.

Video cards, graphics cards, and accelerator cards are all names for the adapter card inside the PC that is responsible for generating the signals that tell the monitor what to display. The relationship between the video card and the monitor should be carefully matched. These two devices must be compatible in terms of the signal used to communicate to the monitor, the type of connector used to connect them together, the video display standards that they support, and their speed.

For more information on video cards, see Chapter 14.

Operating the Display

The CRT is the biggest and most expensive part of a conventional PC monitor. The primary element of the CRT, as illustrated in Figure 15-6, is the electron gun that shoots a beam of three electron streams on the display screen, which is lined with millions of tiny phosphorous dots. The phosphor dots glow when struck by the electrons.

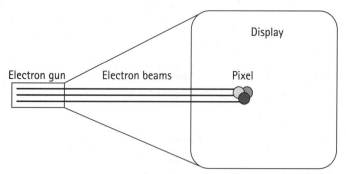

Figure 15-6: The elements of a CRT.

Three phosphor dots are grouped together to form a pixel (picture element). In each pixel (see Figure 15-7), one dot is red, one is green, and one is blue. How much intensity is used to light each dot of the pixel determines the color that your eye sees in the pixel. The blending of these three colors is the basis of *red/green/blue (RGB) color,* which is the color display standard used in all monitors.

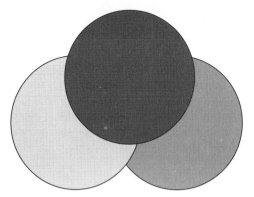

Figure 15-7: A pixel consists of three phosphor dots: one red, one green, and one blue.

When the monitor receives an analog wave from the video card's DAC with instructions for the image to be displayed, it's translated into the color and intensity of each dot in every pixel. As illustrated in Figure 15-8, the electron beam sweeps across and down the CRT's display area, illuminating the pixels to produce or refresh the image. The electron beam moves left to right over the top row of pixels; then, at the end of the row, the beam returns to the start of the next row and scans it left to right, and so forth. At the bottom of the screen, the sweep moves back to the beginning of the top row and begins again. The intensity of the electron beam, which controls the color and brightness of each pixel on the screen, is adjusted as it moves across the screen to paint the display's image.

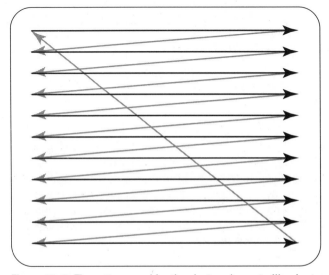

Figure 15-8: The pattern used by the electron beam to illuminate the CRT's phosphorous material.

On a color monitor, the electron beam is made up of three electron streams from three separate electron guns, one for each color in the pixel. The streams are arranged to match the standard arrangement of the dots in the pixels. By changing the intensity of the streams, the closely grouped dots appear to the human eye to produce a certain color. Its color depth sets the number of colors the monitor can produce, but the VGA standard is 256 colors. However, most of today's monitors are SVGA and are capable of displaying over 16 million colors.

Refreshing the display

One pass of the entire display by the electron beam requires only a small fraction of a second. However, the phosphor begins to loose its glow almost as fast and must be refreshed constantly. Most monitors refresh the display between 60 and 75 times per second. A CRT's refresh rate is expressed in Hz (per cycles per second), and common refresh rates for CRT monitors (and video cards) are 60 to 85 Hz.

Interleaving divides the screen into two (or more) passes by refreshing every other row as it sweeps down the display. On one pass, it refreshes the odd-numbered rows; on its second pass, it refreshes the even-numbered rows. When you consider that most CRTs have at least 600 rows of pixels and that 300 of the rows are refreshed in each pass, the screen has an even balance of refreshed pixels. Without interleaving, the top of the screen fades when the bottom is being refreshed, which causes the image to appear to flicker.

Masking the display

Because the electron beam moves so quickly, it's difficult for it to be very precise. A CRT includes one of two different types of guides to prevent the beam from lighting up the wrong phosphor materials and producing the wrong colors: either a shadow mask or an aperture grill.

SHADOW MASK

The *shadow mask* is a very fine screen that's mounted between the electron gun and the pixels. The shadow mask, illustrated in Figure 15-9, has openings that permit each beam to hit only where it should. Any phosphor material in its shadow is masked and will not be illuminated. The holes in the mask are aligned to match perfectly with the pixels on the screen.

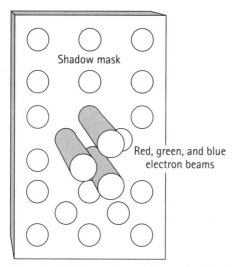

Shadow mask

Red, green, and blue electron beams

Figure 15-9: The shadow mask prevents the electron beam from straying off target.

APERTURE GRILL

The alternative to the shadow mask method is the aperture grill, illustrated in Figure 15-10. On an *aperture grill* display, pixels are masked into vertical stripes between fine metal wires, which are held in place by thin wires that run horizontally across the display. The vertical wires perform the same function as the shadow mask and keep the electron beam from illuminating the wrong parts of the phosphor. Two popular types of CRTs that use this method are the Sony Trinitron and the Mitsubishi Diamondtron, which are used in many of the more popular monitor brands.

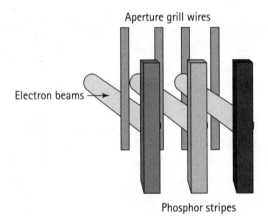

Figure 15-10: The aperture grill divides the display into vertical stripes.

Aperture grill monitors have some advantages over those that use shadow mask CRTs. The advantages include a brighter picture; a sharper image; and because the front of the tube is flat vertically, less glare and less distortion. However, because the vertical wires used to mask the phosphor tend to vibrate (especially in larger monitors), thin wires are placed horizontally across them to hold them in place and dampen the vibrations. This results in very faint lines across the screen where the horizontal wires run.

DOT PITCH AND STRIPE PITCH

The distance in millimeters (mm) between two phosphor dots of the same color on the display is the *dot pitch* (see Figure 15-11). This is an indication of the spacing of the pixels on the screen. A monitor with a low dot pitch produces better images than one with a higher dot pitch. Even the smallest difference in dot pitch shows up on the screen, especially on larger monitors. Current monitors offer dot pitch distances in the range of .24 mm to .31 mm, with .28 mm being the most common.

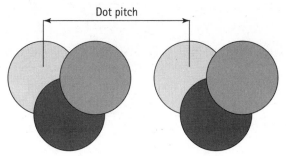

Figure 15-11: Dot pitch measures the distance between two dots of the same color.

Stripe pitch is used on aperture grill monitors to indicate the distance between two stripes of the same color. Common stripe pitch distances are about the same as current dot pitch distances – from .24 mm to .32 mm.

SCAN RATES

How fast a CRT is able to complete its sweep left to right and complete the refresh of the entire screen is an indicator of its brightness and image sharpness. The quicker the screen can be refreshed, the less likely the parts of the display will fade before they can be refreshed again.

The horizontal and vertical scan rates of a CRT are used to indicate these speeds. The horizontal scan rate indicates in kHz or the number (in increments of one hundred) of left-to-right sweeps made by the electron gun to refresh the pixels on a single row. The vertical scan rate indicates how fast the electron gun completes a scan of the entire display area. Table 15-5 lists the scan rates for the more commonly used CRT resolutions. Remember that it takes 100 kilohertz to make one hertz.

TABLE 15-5 TYPICAL CRT SCAN RATES

Resolution	Horizontal Scan Rate	Vertical Scan Rate
640 x 480	31.5–43 kHz	60–85 Hz
800 x 600	32–54 kHz	50–85 Hz
1024 x 768	48–80 kHz	60–100 Hz
1280 x 1024	52–80 kHz	50–75 Hz

Integrating Monitors

New systems are being introduced seemingly daily that integrate the PC into the case of a flat-panel monitor. These PCs integrate the motherboard, disk drive, CD-ROM, and sometimes a floppy disk drive into the housing of a flat-panel monitor. In effect, these devices are the equivalent of a notebook computer on a stand with a very large flat-panel display. They are the ultimate in desktop space efficiency with the keyboard having the largest footprint of the system. The PC's desktop *footprint* is literally its footprint — the space taken up by the foot on the monitor's stand.

These systems vary in features and price and generally offer a fair to good configuration in terms of RAM and disk space. However, because of their tight packaging, there isn't much room for expansion cards, disk drives, or other internal devices. Any additional peripheral devices must be added through a Universal Serial Bus (USB) or an Institute of Electrical and Electronics Engineers (IEEE) 1394 (FireWire) connector.

Moving from digital to analog

In contrast to the rest of the PC, the monitor has evolved from digital to analog. For a while, monitors were digital devices, but when the demand grew for more than 64 colors, monitors became analog devices. Using an analog signal allows the CRT to develop more colors and shades from the three primary colors red, green, and blue.

Theoretically, an analog signal can represent an unlimited number of colors and shades. However, standard analog color is limited to 256 color variations for each of the 65,536 colors (16-bit color). This creates over 16 million colors that can be encoded in an analog signal. Virtually all monitors in use today are analog monitors.

Figuring Out Flat-Panel Displays

The primary difference between a flat-panel monitor and a CRT monitor is how the displayed image is formed on the screen. However, it's very hard to ignore the fact that a flat-panel monitor is only a couple of inches deep compared with a CRT that could be 18 inches deep or more. For the most part, flat-panel monitors are LCDs.

Lighting up an LCD

Liquid crystal displays are very common and are used in many products, including wristwatches, microwave ovens, CD players, and PC monitors. In fact, virtually all PC flat-panel monitors and portable computers sold today have an LCD screen. LCD is popular because it's thinner, lighter, and requires less power than other types of displays, especially the CRT.

LIQUID CRYSTAL

Liquid crystal, a material that exists somewhere between a solid and a liquid, is created by applying heat to a suitable substance to change it from a solid into a liquid crystal form. Because they are formed from heat, liquid crystals are sensitive to temperature changes. This is what makes them perfect for thermometers, mood rings, and PC monitors. This is also the reason why the LCD display on a notebook computer might not work well immediately after being exposed to cold or heat for any length of time.

Computer displays are made from *twisted nematic* (TN) crystals, which are rod-shaped crystals that are twisted lengthwise. When a current of electricity is applied to a TN crystal, it untwists in a predictable way. If enough electricity is applied, the TN crystal completely untwists and becomes flat. The predictability of how the TN crystal reacts to the electricity and thus untwists is the property that most appeals to LCD display manufacturers.

TN crystals are placed on layers of polarized glass filters. Without any electricity applied to the liquid crystal, light passes through the first glass filter to the last one because the twisted crystal is narrow and does not block the light. When electricity is applied, the TN crystals untwist and block the path of the light, thus creating a darkened area on the display.

LIQUID CRYSTAL DISPLAYS

An *LCD display* is made up of layers of different materials, all of which play a part in using light to create an image on the display. Figure 15-12 illustrates the layers that make up a common-plane LCD. From bottom to top, the layers are

- ◆ *Mirror:* The back of the LCD for reflecting light

- ◆ *Polarizing film:* A piece of polarizing glass

- ◆ *Electrode:* The common transparent electrode plane for the assembly

- ◆ *Liquid crystal:* TN liquid crystal placed between the two electrodes

- ◆ *Electrode:* A layer of glass with one or more smaller electrodes attached that define the static display

- ◆ *Polarizing film:* A layer of polarized glass placed at a right angle to the other polarized layer

As long as no current is flowing through the LCD, any light entering the front (which would be the top in Figure 15-12) passes through to the mirror and is reflected back out. When electricity is applied to the electrodes, the liquid crystals between them untwist and block the light from passing through. The result is that the liquid crystal in the areas between the electrodes that were energized now block the light and create a darkened area on the screen.

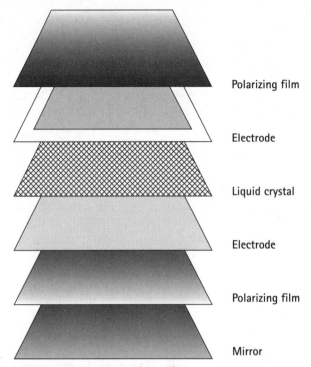

Polarizing film

Electrode

Liquid crystal

Electrode

Polarizing film

Mirror

Figure 15-12: The layers of an LCD.

In a simple LCD, like that on a wristwatch or handheld game, the top layer of electrodes provides the sections of the numerals or objects to be displayed. When these electrodes are energized in a pattern, the liquid crystal untwists to block the light source, the affected screen areas darken, and the viewer sees numbers or shapes. Figure 15-13 shows how seven electrodes are used to display numerals. When the electrode sections are energized, the corresponding portion of the display is darkened and numbers form, as illustrated in Figure 15-14.

Figure 15-13: The pattern of electrodes used to produce a numeral on an LCD.

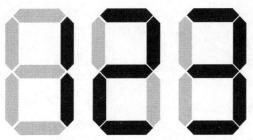

Figure 15-14: Examples of numerals displayed on an LCD.

LCD LIGHTING

An LCD uses one of two light source types: reflective and transmissive. A *reflective* LCD reflects only the light that enters through its polarized filters from its environment. In a well-lighted room or in sunlight, there is usually enough light to see the display. *Transmissive* LCDs, used in portable computers and flat-panel monitors, incorporate lighting elements to backlight the display. Typically, built-in fluorescent tubes located around the edges of the display and sometimes behind the LCD provide the lighting.

Categorizing LCDs

The three different types of LCDs used in various devices are common-plane, passive matrix, and active matrix.

COMMON-PLANE LCD

Common-plane LCDs aren't used for PC displays but rather in watches, handheld games, and microwaves, where the same numbers or objects are displayed repeatedly.

PASSIVE MATRIX LCD

A *passive matrix* LCD has pixels, like a CRT, instead of electrodes. However, its operating principles are the same that are used in a common-plane LCD. A grid organized in rows and columns is used to energize the pixels, which are located at the intersections of the rows and columns. Integrated circuits control the rows and columns to ensure that a charge sent over the grid gets to the specific pixel that it was intended to activate. The grid's rows and columns are on separate layers of a transparent conductive material that sandwich a layer of liquid crystal. A layer of polarizing film is added to the top and bottom substrates of the sandwich.

A pixel is energized when an electrical charge is sent down the appropriate column on one substrate, and a grounding charge is sent over the appropriate row on the other substrate. The two charges converge at the pixel located at the intersection of the row and column and cause the pixel's liquid crystal to untwist and block the light source and darken the pixel.

Another Passive Matrix Application

An application of passive matrix LCD technology is the portable stylus-based computer, also known as the personal digital assistant (PDA) or palmtop computer. Although these computers might have a keyboard, commands and data are typically entered through the screen via a special non-writing pen or stylus. The display is covered by a protective, plastic covering; beneath the display is a wire grid that recognizes the movements of the stylus. The wire grid records the movements of the pen over the grid's intersections, which is similar to the technology behind touch-screens.

A passive matrix LCD has its disadvantages. Its refresh speed (the *response time*) is slow, and the grid delivers electricity imprecisely to specific pixels. This latter problem can affect nearby pixels and create a fuzzy image or create contrast problems.

A passive matrix display uses one of two types of liquid crystal:

◆ *Twisted nematic (TN):* TN liquid crystal has a 90° twist and is used in low-cost displays. It produces a black on gray or silver background. TN liquid crystal is used primarily on consumer electronics and appliances.

◆ *Supertwisted nematic (STN):* Although its name sounds a bit like your wacky brother-in-law, *STN* is the type of liquid crystal found on a portable or handheld PC or a PDA. It is made with either a 180° or a 270° twist, which gives it a much wider range of motion, making it more tolerant against any energy radiating from nearby pixels and allowing it to provide more steps of color shadings. STN is used in both monochrome and color displays.

 Although not a type of liquid crystal, *dual-scan STN* (DSTN) is a process used in some LCDs to double the number of lines refreshed and to cut the time to refresh the display in half. This is accomplished by dividing the LCD into two equal halves that are scanned simultaneously.

ACTIVE MATRIX LCD

The pixels on an active matrix LCD use thin-film transistors (TFTs), which is why this type of LCD is often called a *TFT display*. *TFTs* are switching transistors and capacitors etched in a matrix pattern on a glass substrate that forms one of the layers of the active matrix LCD. Each pixel consists of three TFTs, one for each of the

RGB colors, which can add up to quite a few transistors in the display. For example, a VGA 640 x 480 color display uses 921,600 transistors; comparatively, a 1024 x 768 UVGA color display uses 2,359,296 transistors, all of which are etched into the substrate glass. If a transistor is defective, it creates a bad pixel. TFT displays commonly have at least a few bad pixels.

An active matrix LCD addresses its pixels somewhat like a passive matrix. However, when one row is addressed on the active matrix display, all the other rows are switched off, and the charge is sent down the appropriate column. Because only the addressed row is active, just the pixel at the intersection of the active row and column is affected. The TFT's capacitor holds the energy used to charge the pixel until the next refresh cycle.

The color of the pixel is provided by color filters that lay over the areas controlled by the pixel's three TFTs. Colors are created by the amount of light allowed to pass through the filters by each of the TFTs, which are controlled by the intensity of the charge sent to them by the image control circuits.

As illustrated in Figure 15-15, the TFT's control how much the liquid crystal elements open (untwist) to block the light passing through the color filters. In the situation shown in Figure 15-15, a small amount of the light source is being allowed to pass through the red filter along with a wide open blue, but no light is being passed through the green filter. Controlling the amount of electricity that flows to the pixel manages the action of the liquid crystal and the amount of light allowed to pass through the color filters. By controlling the light, active matrix screens are able to display 256 levels of color brightness per pixel.

Comparing Viewing Angles

A display's viewing angle measures how far above, below, and (more importantly) to the side of the display that images on the screen can be accurately viewed. The following table compares the viewing angles of the two LCD displays with a CRT. The figure here illustrates the relative differences of the viewing angles of these displays.

Display Type	Viewing Angle
Passive matrix LCD	49–100°
Active matrix LCD	90–120°
CRT	120–180°

Continued

Comparing Viewing Angles *(Continued)*

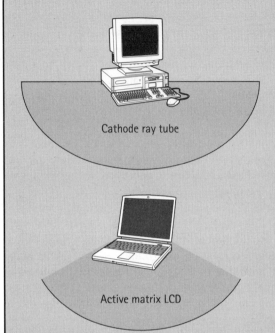

Cathode ray tube

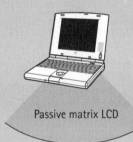

Active matrix LCD

Passive matrix LCD

The curvature of the screen has a lot to do with a display's viewing angle, but next on the list is the amount of contrast in the displayed image. An active matrix (TFT) display has deeper color, clarity, and contrast over a passive matrix display. In the eye of the viewer, LCD displays begin to lose their picture quality as the angle of view increases because less of the display's light (image) is able to reach the viewer. Obviously, the viewing angle champion is the conventional CRT. However, a flat-screen CRT might have a much lower viewing angle.

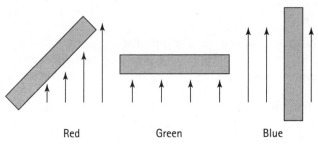

Figure 15-15: Controlling the color in an active matrix LCD.

Powering the Display

Monitors don't run off the PC's power supply, even if they are plugged into the back of the PC power supply. Plugging a monitor into the back of the PC's power supply is the same as getting AC power straight from a wall outlet. The plug on the back of the power supply is an AC power pass-through plug. A PC's monitor uses more power than all the other components of the PC added together. And because of how it works, several power issues exist on monitors that don't exist on a PC or its power supply.

Managing power

In an effort to reduce the tremendous amount of energy being consumed by monitors in active mode, governments and industry organizations have developed initiatives to reduce the amount of power consumed by PC monitors in general but especially when they're idle.

The U.S. Environmental Protection Agency (EPA) has the Energy Star program that certifies monitors and personal computers that meet a guideline for reduced energy consumption. This program certifies monitors that use less than 30 watts of power in all power modes and reduce their power consumption by 99 percent when in sleep or suspended mode. Most PCs sold today meet this standard, and you'll see the Energy Star logo displayed on the monitor during the boot sequence on these PCs.

Virtually all monitors on the market today are also compliant with VESA's Display Power Management System (DPMS) protocol. *DPMS* is used to power down parts of the monitor and PC after they've been idle for a certain period of time. DPMS is a Basic Input/Output System- (BIOS) supported protocol that can be enabled in the Complementary Metal-Oxide Semiconductor (CMOS) settings of the PC.

Degaussing the screen

The internal components of a CRT can become magnetized over time. If they do, it can have a negative affect on the quality of the image produced by the monitor. If the CRT becomes overly magnetized, color blotches can appear on the screen near the edges and in the corners. A CRT can be magnetized in lots of ways, including setting stereo speakers or other forms of magnets too close to the monitor (which can also distort the display), bumping the monitor very hard, or moving the monitor so that it's positioned over a PC's power supply.

The cure for magnetization of the CRT is *degaussing*. This term is derived from the word *gauss,* which is a measure of magnetic force. Most better monitors have built-in degaussing circuits that neutralize the CRT's magnetization through a coil of wire inside the monitor. The degaussing circuit is activated by either a manual switch or automatically through the monitor's controls.

On monitors with a manual degauss switch, pressing the switch activates a circuit that attempts to neutralize the CRT's magnetization. The degauss process involves some clicking and buzzing and takes only a few minutes to complete its cycles.

Occasionally degaussing a monitor is a good idea, but avoid pushing the degauss button repeatedly — once is typically enough to restore the monitor's color and sharpness. Overly degaussing a monitor can damage its degauss circuits.

Most newer monitors do an automatic degauss when they're powered up, which is the static buzz and click that you hear when the monitor is powered up. If the built-in degaussing circuits of the CRT don't clear up the magnetization problem, the monitor should be taken to a repair shop for manual degaussing with a special degaussing tool.

Maintaining a Monitor

The life span of a PC monitor, given fairly regular preventive maintenance and care, should be about five years. As I mention earlier, the monitor is the one part of the PC that holds its value because the price of a monitor today is about what it was two to three years ago on a price-per-feature basis. As long as the monitor is still doing its job, why replace it? Usually monitors are purchased in tandem with the PC, staying paired as long as both work. However, if the processor dies, the monitor can be used with a different system.

The user — and most technicians, for that matter — should never attempt to repair a monitor for circuitry or electrical problems. Only the manufacturer or an authorized repair shop should repair any monitor, whether CRT or LCD. Before you authorize any repairs, however, compare the cost estimate of the repair with that of purchasing a new monitor. In most situations, the cost to repair a monitor is relatively inexpensive, but if the monitor needs a new CRT or LCD, buying a new monitor could be a better investment.

Keeping safe

Rule number one: Never — repeat, *never* — open the monitor's case. All repairs that require opening or removing the monitor's case should be performed at a repair shop that's properly equipped to work on monitors.

Rule number two: Should you choose to risk your life by ignoring rule number one and open the monitor's case to work on it, absolutely *do not wear an ESD wrist strap.* If you do, you become the grounding circuit for all stored and static electricity in the monitor.

 Never attempt to work inside the monitor's case. So what if you have to buy a new monitor? You have to decide whether your life is worth saving two or three hundred dollars.

Another safety issue, although somewhat controversial, is the potential harm from electromagnetic monitor emissions.

ELECTRICAL SHOCK
The reason for the above warnings and gloom-and-doom (which cannot be emphasized enough) is that inside the monitor is a very large *capacitor,* which is an electronic device that holds power and uses it to regulate the power stream that it receives. Remember that the monitor isn't powered by the PC's power supply; it's plugged directly into an AC outlet. The monitor has a power supply much like the one in the PC itself. In this power supply is a large capacitor that stores enough electrical power to cause you very serious harm, even when the monitor is off and unplugged. The capacitor has a capacity of around 1,000 microfarads to absorb power spikes and fill in low-voltage events.

ELECTROMAGNETIC EMISSIONS
A CRT emits small amounts of Very Low Frequency (VLF) and Extremely Low Frequency (ELF) electromagnetic radiation, and a debate is ongoing as to whether this radiation is harmful to PC users. VLF and ELF aren't lethal emissions like an X-ray or a gamma ray, but many experts believe that they could be harmful after extended exposure periods.

Most of the CRT's radiation is emitted from its back and sides, with a very small amount emanating from the screen. The radiation doesn't carry far and is usually totally gone a few feet from the monitor. As a precaution, users should sit at an arm's length from the monitor screen to protect their eyes as well as to put themselves a relatively safe distance from the radiation emissions. Spacing monitors with a few feet of open space on their back and sides should keep everyone safe.

The debate on radiation emissions is that prolonged exposure can cause cancer, leukemia, and pregnancy complications, including miscarriage and birth defects. Nothing has been proven conclusively on whether this is fact or fear yet, but it is always better to err on the safe side. In fact, the Swedish government has created an organization to develop monitor standards that safeguard against monitor emissions. If you wish to purchase a monitor that conforms to these standards or check whether your existing monitor conforms, look for a TCO (which stands for the Swedish words that mean *The Swedish Confederation of Professional Employees*) certification. There have been four versions of these standards since its inception in 1991, with the latest being TCO, '99. TCO '0x is now pending.

Performing preventive maintenance

The life of a monitor can be extended with a regular program of preventive maintenance. Here are some things you can do to prevent overheating and magnetization, as well as some cleaning tips. Most of these tips apply to CRT monitors but can also be applied to an LCD display. For an LCD monitor, check its documentation for cleaning and care tips. In these and all other maintenance activities on PCs, let common sense be your guide.

◆ *Keep a free space buffer of a few feet in each direction around a CRT monitor.* This helps its cooling system to work efficiently as well as protect other users from radiation emissions.

◆ *Never stack anything on top of the monitor or closely around it.* Blocking the monitor's airflow will shorten the life of the CRT by causing it to overheat. The CRT is the most expensive part of the monitor to replace. Never place any form of magnetic media (diskettes, tapes, and so on) on top of the monitor . . . unless you wish to erase them. Remember that a very large magnet and lots of electromagnetic forces are inside the case.

◆ *Never place heavy items on the monitor's top.* This can cause the case to crack or at least flex and cause something inside the case to short.

◆ *Keep the monitor (and PC) at a distance from heat sources, damp environments, magnets (including those in standard PC or stereo speakers), motors, or areas in which static electricity is a problem.* Magnets can affect the quality of the display.

Okay, so some monitors come with side-mounting speakers. Typically, these speakers have been constructed with special magnetic shielding to prevent any electromagnetic interference with the monitor.

♦ *Use the power cord supplied with the monitor.* This cord is usually especially designed to handle your monitor's voltage. If you misplace it, obtain a replacement from the manufacturer or a dealer for that brand of monitor. *Hint:* Don't confuse the PC's power cord with the monitor's cord when moving the system.

♦ *The monitor's case should only be cleaned with a damp, lint-free cloth.* Always unplug the monitor before cleaning it or using any water-based cleaning solutions on it. The monitor's screen can be cleaned with the same cloth and with a little diluted glass cleaner. Don't spray any liquids on the screen; instead, spray the cleaner on the cloth and then wipe the screen clean. Always be sure to wipe the screen completely dry. Avoid strong degreasers or ammonia-based cleaners because they can affect the screen's glass and even the colors of the display.

♦ *Keep the monitor on its original base/foot.* The stand that shipped with the monitor is actually engineered as a part of the cooling system. If you remove it and set the monitor on its case bottom, you run the risk of blocking the air vents on the bottom of the case. The monitor needs to sit up a bit to allow proper airflow for the cooling system.

♦ *Avoid touching the screen with your hands.* Oil and dirt from your hands are very hard to remove from the screen.

The monitor is blank or has no picture

A variety of problems can cause the monitor to be blank or dark or appear to be dead. Use the following steps to debug this problem:

1. Verify that the monitor is connected to a power source and is receiving power.

   Most newer monitors have a small light on their front that indicates when the power is on.

2. Verify that the monitor is connected to the PC's video card and that the connection is snug.

   If the screen is white or gray (instead of black) and you hear a buzzing or high-pitched whine coming from the monitor, the monitor is probably not connected to the video card.

Check the connection at the monitor end if the monitor uses a two-end video cable. Check the pins in the cable connectors for bent or broken pins before reconnecting them.

3. Check that the brightness and contrast controls haven't been turned all the way up, which results in a dark screen.

If these two controls are okay, check a few of the other controls, such as the geometry settings (height, width, and trapezoidal shape and location), because some combinations of settings will also darken the display. Use the monitor's documentation to locate and use the monitor's adjusting controls.

4. Reboot the PC, listening for beep codes and watching for error messages from the POST.

If a single beep sounds and the PC seems to be continuing with the boot, the problem is most likely in the monitor. Otherwise, the problem might be that the boot is hanging up before the video BIOS and device drivers were loaded. Verify with your system BIOS or motherboard documentation what the beep code is for video adapter problems and listen carefully for that or another beep code indicating a hardware problem.

See Chapter 4 for more information on the system BIOS and its beep codes.

5. Replace the monitor with a known-good monitor.

If the display appears, the original monitor is bad. Otherwise, replace the video card and continue troubleshooting.

The monitor has display but isn't functioning properly

This is probably a device driver problem, a video card problem, or a failing monitor. Use the steps in the preceding section to troubleshoot the latter two but only after following the steps here to check the configuration of the monitor on the PC:

1. Verify the monitor's settings from the Windows Device Manager: Right-click My Computer and then choose Properties → System Properties → Hardware Tab → Device Manager.

2. Drill down through the device tree to find the video card (graphics adapter). Highlight the video card's device entry and then click the

Properties button (on Windows 2000 or Windows XP, just double-click the device name).

On the device's Properties window that opens, verify the driver and the system resources assigned to the video card. Resolve any resource conflicts.

 See Chapter 5 for more information on resolving resource conflicts.

3. Check the video card's manufacturer for any updates or newer device drivers and install them.

   Manufacturers' Web sites are a good place to start.

4. If all is well, make sure that the monitor is listed in the Windows system settings. Right-click the desktop in an open space; from the menu that appears, choose Properties to open the Display Properties window. (The Display icon on the Control Panel also opens this window.) Select the Settings tab and click the Advanced button there to open the video card Properties window, shown in Figure 15-16.

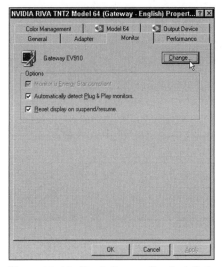

Figure 15-16: Check the monitor installed on the video card's Properties window.

5. Choose the Monitor tab. If the monitor listed is not the type in use, click the Change button (upper-right side of the window) to open the Update Device Driver Wizard (shown in Figure 15-17), which will guide you through the installation of the proper device driver.

If a disk came with the monitor, have it handy to use. When asked to choose a driver, click the Have Disk button.

Figure 15-17: The Windows Update Device Driver Wizard.

The monitor doesn't power on

If the monitor's power indicator light on its front bezel is lighted, the problem is probably not a power source problem. Use the steps in the earlier section "The monitor is blank or has no picture" to verify that the source of the problem is not elsewhere. If that doesn't find the problem, check the monitor on a different PC to verify that the video card isn't the problem. Otherwise, the monitor might have internal power or circuitry issues, requiring a trip to the repair shop.

To check the power, use the following steps:

1. Push the monitor's power button on and off a few times to make sure that the button isn't just stuck.

If the monitor powers up, you'll hear the static buzz and clicking associated with the automatic degauss and other start-up steps performed by the monitor.

2. If the power button isn't the problem, check that the power cord is snugly seated in its connector.

The power cord on many monitors is a specially designed cord. Check the documentation to see whether the monitor uses a special power cord and how it is identified. If needed, verify that the correct cable is in use.

3. Check the fuse on the back of the monitor.

   It probably looks like a small black knob with the word *Fuse* on the cap. If the fuse is bad (the element inside the fuse is broken or burnt), replace it. You can get replacement fuses at most computer or electronics shops. If the fuse frequently needs replacing, you have an internal electrical problem, and the monitor should go to the repair shop.

4. If the monitor is an older EGA (or older) monitor, it might be plugged directly into the back of the power supply. If this is the case, the PC must be powered up before the monitor will have power.

   The power supply pass-through plug could be defective.

5. If the monitor is plugged into a power strip, make sure that it's switched on and working.

   Plug the monitor into another AC source to verify the power source.

Changing the color depth or resolution

To change the color depth (bit depth) or resolution settings for the monitor on a Windows PC or notebook computer, use the following steps:

1. Right-click in an empty space on the desktop to display the menu shown in Figure 15-18.

Figure 15-18: The Windows desktop pop-up menu.

2. Choose Properties to open the Display Properties window shown in Figure 15-19.

3. Select the Settings tab.

   Toward the bottom of the Settings tab are two side-by-side settings that control the color depth (Colors) and the screen resolution (Screen Area), as shown in Figure 15-20.

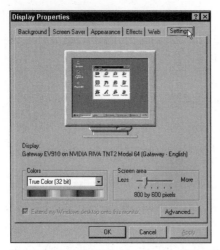

Figure 15–19: The Windows Display Properties window.

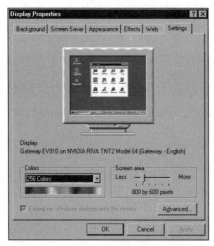

Figure 15–20: The Colors and Screen Area settings on
the Display Properties Settings window.

4. Change the Screen Area setting to its lowest value (move the slider all the way to the left).

   It should be 640 x 480.

5. From the Colors drop-down list, change the color depth to 256 Colors (8-bit).

   These settings are the VGA standard settings.

6. Click the Apply button and do not restart the system when asked.

   Unless these settings were how your monitor was set to begin with, the displayed image should be constructed of much larger elements and might not all fit onto the display.

7. Reopen the Display Properties window, change the resolution (Screen Area) and color depth (Colors) to the highest settings available, and then accept the settings without restarting your PC.

   The display should be much more detailed, and all the elements should be much smaller than under VGA standard settings.

8. Reset the Display Properties to their original settings unless you prefer their new values. Otherwise, just click OK to apply the new settings.

Setting the refresh rate

To set the refresh rate on your monitor or to check its setting, do the following:

1. Follow the steps used in the preceding section to display the Display Properties window.

2. Click the Advanced button to display the Properties window for the video adapter in your PC.

3. From the Adapter tab, select the Refresh rate from a list box located in the middle of the window.

Most monitors have a range of refresh rates that they support. The monitor's documentation should recommend its best refresh rate setting. On most Windows 9x, Me, 2000, or XP PCs, the refresh rate should be set to Optimal.

Recovering from an incorrect refresh rate

If you change the refresh rate and the result is a distorted or blurry image, reboot your PC into Windows Safe Mode and reset the refresh rate using the steps in the preceding project.

See Chapter 27 for the process used to boot a PC into Safe Mode.

The monitor goes blank and shuts off when idle

If your monitor goes blank and shuts off when idle, the monitor has its energy-saving settings activated. Use the following steps to adjust or turn off these features:

1. Open the Display Properties window by right-clicking the desktop in an open area and choosing Properties from the menu that appears.

2. From the Display Properties window that appears, choose the Screen Saver tab.

   If your monitor contains energy-saving features, the lower quarter of the window has an area with the Energy Star logo and a Settings button, as shown in Figure 15-21.

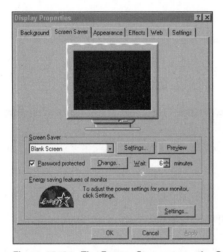

Figure 15-21: The Energy Star area on the Screen Saver tab.

3. Click the Settings button to open the Power Management Properties window, shown in Figure 15-22.

   From this window, you can set the period of inactivity for each of the devices included in the energy-saving controls. The times available are in the list boxes for each device.

   To save a new custom energy configuration, use the Save As function. Selecting Never from the menus turns off the energy-savings feature for a device.

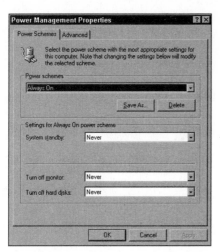

Figure 15-22: The Power Management Properties window is used to set the energy-savings parameters of the monitor.

Disposing of a CRT monitor

As much as 70 percent of a CRT's components contain lead, which is why CRTs come under the Land Disposal Ban Program of the Resource Conservation and Recovery Act (RCRA). This law requires CRTs to be disposed of using a very prescriptive procedure. You can't just throw them in the dumpster or the landfill. According to the RCRA regulations, a CRT must be dismantled, crushed, and encapsulated in cement to be disposed of properly. Because this isn't something that you should do yourself (even if you could), salvage companies exist that specialize in CRT and computer disposals and will do so for a small fee. By the way, this law covers TV sets as well.

Chapter 16

Audio and Image Capture Devices

IN THIS CHAPTER

Not long ago, the only sounds coming from a PC, aside from a noisy fan or hard drive, emanated from its tiny, tinny system speaker mounted somewhere inside the case. This PC speaker was intended primarily to emit beeps, squawks, and whistles to alert the user of diagnostic Power-On Self-Test (POST) messages and error and other operating system alerts.

Today's sound systems, which have expanded the audio world of the PC near high fidelity, are standard equipment on new PCs. The audio or sound system of today's PC range in complexity from simple playback devices for games and system sounds all the way to full-fledged Digital Audio Workstations (DAW), which are used in professional audio and video production and post-production work. In this chapter, I cover the following:

- Resolving sound system problems

- Dealing with CD audio issues

- Connecting a CD-ROM or DVD to a sound card

- Solving system resource conflicts

- Connecting a scanner to your PC

- Downloading images from a digital camera

WITH THE ADVANCEMENT OF THE SOUND RECORDING and reproduction capabilities of the PC, along with the advancement of its video and multiple media playback capabilities, the PC is finally beginning to fulfill the promise of a true multimedia device. This chapter explores the components of the PC sound system and looks at a few of the devices used to capture and import video images into the PC.

Examining the PC Sound System

Just like that fancy component stereo system that you've always wanted, the PC's sound system is made up of a number of different pieces. Each of the sound system components, which I discuss in the following sections, performs a certain function in the sound capture and playback abilities of the PC.

417

Audio Software Publishers

Some of the better-known audio software publishers include

- ◆ **Cakewalk:** www.cakewalk.com
- ◆ **Microsoft:** www.microsoft.com/windows/windowsmedia
- ◆ **Nullsoft:** www.winamp.com
- ◆ **RealNetworks:** www.real.com
- ◆ **Sonic Foundry:** www.sonicfoundry.com
- ◆ **Steinberg:** www.steinberg.net
- ◆ **Waves:** www.waves.com

The primary components of a PC sound system are the following:

- ◆ *Amplifier:* After digital audio has been converted into an audible signal, it has to be amplified before it can be played back on speakers. Most sound cards include a weak amplifier capable of driving a set of headphones or small passive (unpowered) PC speakers. Many PC speaker systems integrate an amplifier into one or both of the speaker enclosures, taking the burden of amplification off the sound card. With the correct cabling, the signal from a sound card can be routed to any stereo or home theater system, creating the possibility of true audiophile-quality sound from a PC. In a DAW configuration, the signal is often routed through a mixing console before it's amplified.

- ◆ *Audio software:* With the exception of the basic playback controls on the front of some CD-ROM drives, most PC audio operations are controlled by software. Microsoft's Windows family of operating systems, as well as many distributions of Linux, include basic tools for recording, playing, and mixing audio from different sources. Advanced tools for recording and manipulating digital audio are available from a variety of vendors.

- ◆ *Magnetic shielding:* Dedicated PC speaker systems differ from conventional home-stereo speakers in an important way: Because they are typically placed fairly close to the computer monitor, PC speakers must be magnetically shielded to avoid distorting the image on the screen and ultimately damaging the monitor. Therefore, caution should be used when configuring a PC audio system with components not specifically designed for PC audio.

◆ *Sound card:* The sound card combines into a single unit all of the inputs, outputs, and signal processors (digital-to-analog converter [DAC] and analog-to-digital converter [ADC]) required to convert audio information to and from digital form. Traditionally packaged as an Industry Standard Architecture (ISA) or Peripheral Component Interconnect (PCI) adapter card, there has been a recent trend toward mounting an integrated audio chip directly on the motherboard, thus eliminating the need for a separate device to handle audio.

◆ *Speakers:* PC speakers come in a wide range of configurations, from small passive systems powered by the sound card's headphone output to active (amplified) 3-way and surround systems that would rival many home theaters. Some computer monitors have integrated speakers either incorporated into the bezel or designed to snap on and off the sides of the monitor.

A recent development in PC audio is the Universal Serial Bus (USB) speaker system. USB speaker systems don't require a separate sound card. Digital audio is sent directly to the speakers via the USB cable, and all signal processing is done within the speaker enclosure itself, external to the PC. This has a few advantages, including reducing the potential for audible interference (hum or static) from other PC components. One disadvantage of USB speakers is that they don't provide a way to connect to the analog output of a CD-ROM or DVD player. (See "Connecting a CD-ROM or DVD to a sound card" later in this chapter.)

Taking a Closer Listen to Sound Cards

The sound card combines the components required to transfer sound into and out of a PC, including the following:

◆ *Analog inputs:* Most sound cards have separate line-level and mic-level inputs. *Line-level inputs* are designed to either accept a signal from an electronic source (such as a CD player or tape deck) or direct input from a musical instrument (like a synthesizer). *Mic-level inputs* are designed to accept the much lower voltage signal generated by a microphone or an unamplified electric guitar. Professional sound cards for DAW applications often have one or more stereo pairs of analog inputs for recording multiple channels simultaneously. The most common type of connector for analog input is a standard ⅛" phone jack identical to those found on a portable stereo. More specialized sound cards might include left and right stereo RCA (you know, RCA as in RCA-Victor) jacks or ¼" phone jacks in order to be more compatible with professional studio gear.

- *Analog outputs:* Two analog outputs are frequently found on a sound card. One's a small amplifier, capable of driving a pair of headphones or passive speakers, powers one that's often identified as *Phones Out/Speaker Out.* Another, usually called *Line Out,* is designed to send a line-level signal to an input such as that found on a home stereo receiver. Professional sound cards for DAW applications commonly have one or more stereo pairs of analog outputs for playing back multiple channels simultaneously. As with the inputs, ⅛" phone jacks are most common, but some cards use RCA or ¼" phone jacks.

- *Analog-to-digital converter (ADC):* The *ADC* converts analog audio information, such as a voice or a musical instrument, into digital data that can be stored and edited on a PC.

- *Digital input/output (I/O):* Once found only on high-end professional sound cards, digital interfaces are beginning to show up on consumer sound cards as well. Digital I/O makes it possible to transfer data to and from digital devices such as MiniDisc and Digital Audio Tape (DAT) machines without ever leaving the digital domain. This eliminates the potential for signal degradation that accompanies the use of a DAC or ADC. The most common types of digital interfaces found on sound cards are Sony/Philips Digital Interface (S/P-DIF) and Audio Engineering Society/European Broadcasting Union (AES/EBU).

- *Digital Signal Processor (DSP):* Another feature formerly found only on high-end sound cards, DSPs are finding their way to less expensive cards as well. DSPs can serve a variety of functions, but the goal is always the same: to reduce the burden on the computer's CPU when processing audio. Among the tasks performed by DSP chips are *resampling* (which reduces the size of the audio file without reducing the sound quality) and digital effects (such as reverb and echo).

- *Digital-to-analog converter (DAC):* The *DAC* converts audio data stored on a hard drive or other medium into audible information that can be played back on speakers or headphones.

- *Game/Musical Instrument Digital Interface (MIDI) port:* This versatile connector found on many sound cards is most often used for game controllers such as joysticks or gamepads. With a special cable, this port can be connected to any external MIDI device in order to send and receive MIDI data. Most sound card MIDI interfaces are designed to emulate the MPU-401 interface developed by Roland.

♦ *Synthesizer:* Some of the sounds produced by a sound card are generated by the card itself using a synthesizer chip. Unlike digital audio, which resides on a hard drive or other storage medium until it's sent through the DAC, the sound card's synthesizer responds to MIDI messages, which tell it what sounds to play, at what frequency, and for what duration. An external MIDI device, as well as the PC, can control the synthesizer. Synthesizer chips vary widely in capabilities and sound quality. Many newer sound cards incorporate a process called *Wavetable Synthesis* to produce a higher quality sound. Wavetable Synthesis uses digital samples of actual instruments in place of synthesized sounds.

Capturing Sound

The sound card input used to capture audio differs depending upon the source. If the source is an electronic device like a CD player, stereo receiver, or synthesizer, a line-level input is used. Although most sound cards use ⅛" phone jacks for their inputs, very few other devices use these jacks, so a special cable or adapter is usually required (readily available at any electronics supply store). In most cases, the appropriate cable for recording from home stereo sources is one with left and right male RCA plugs on one end and a single stereo male ⅛" phone plug on the other end. Many synthesizers use ¼" phone jacks, so the appropriate cable would have left and right male ¼" phone plugs on one end and a single stereo male ⅛" phone plug on the other end.

If the source is a live sound like a voice or an acoustic musical instrument, a microphone needs to be connected to a mic-level input on the sound card. Inexpensive PC microphones are designed with ⅛" phone plugs to connect directly to the mic input of most sound cards. Higher-end microphones typically have ¼" phone plugs or XLR connectors (multipoint plugs used with professional audio equipment), so they require an adapter or specialized cable to connect to a ⅛" phone jack.

If the source is a device with digital I/O (such as a MiniDisc or DAT machine) and the sound card also has digital I/O, the proper cabling varies depending upon what type of ports are available. When cabling between digital devices, use cables specifically designed for digital data. S/P-DIF cables, for example, look almost identical to standard RCA audio cables, but their construction is quite different. The same is true for AES/EBU cables, which look like standard XLR microphone cables but are in fact very different underneath the wrapper.

After the connections are made, the rest of the operation takes place within the software. A wide variation in the capabilities and controls is found in audio software. At the most basic level, to record a sound, you click a Record button and start making noise. But here are a number of considerations to address when capturing audio to a PC:

♦ *Input level:* If a sound is recorded at too quiet of a level, playing it back at an adequate volume can produce a noisy result. Conversely, recording a sound at too high of a level can result in *clipping,* which means literally cutting off the peaks of the digital audio waveform, thus producing distortion. Most audio capture programs provide visual cues to let you know the loudness of the input and whether it's close to clipping.

◆ *File size:* One of the first things that many people notice when they start capturing audio is how quickly the hard drive fills up. Audio files can be enormous, particularly if the sound is captured at a CD-quality sample rate and resolution. For instance, just ten seconds of stereo sound recorded at 44.1 kilohertz (kHz) and 16 bits (referred to as *CD-quality*) will use approximately 2MB of hard disk space. If disk space is an issue, consider whether the material being recorded needs to be reproduced at such high quality. Also consider whether it can be stored as a mono file rather than stereo, thereby cutting the file size in half.

◆ *File type:* Although you can choose from a bewildering array of audio file types, the most common audio capture format in Windows systems is the WAV file. Even if the ultimate format for the file will be something other than WAV, the WAV format provides the most flexibility in terms of editing and conversion to other file types. In fact, many audio capture applications will only capture to WAV files, but a growing number will also capture MPEG formats as well.

◆ *Sample rate:* Expressed in kHz, the *sample rate* refers to the number of samples taken from the audio input per second. As I mention above, 44.1 kHz is the sample rate used by a CD and will produce good results for most applications. Audio recorded for professional applications might be sampled at a higher rate to increase fidelity and provide more headroom for audio editing. Lower sample rates use less disk space at the cost of audio quality. The maximum and minimum sample rates available are subject to the limitations of both the sound card and the software being used.

◆ *Sample resolution:* Expressed in bits, *sample resolution* refers to the size of the samples taken. CD audio is stored at a resolution of 16 bits. Sample resolution involves the same trade-offs with regard to file size and sound quality that apply to sample rate.

TIP

Digital Audio Extraction (DAE) is a method of capturing data from an audio CD without leaving the digital domain. DAE differs from other audio capture methods in that it doesn't require the use of a sound card. With DAE, you can make an exact copy of an audio CD without introducing any signal loss inherent in digital-to-analog conversion. Most new CD-ROM drives support DAE (check with the manufacturer). In addition to a CD-ROM drive that supports DAE, special software is also required. DAE tools are frequently bundled with CD writing software and with MP3 creation suites. DAE output is typically stored in the form of a WAV file.

Microsoft Windows includes a basic mixer for adjusting the volume level of various sound events. Some games, for instance, send different audio events to separate channels on the sound card: speech and digital audio to the WAV channel, CD music to the CD audio channel, and synthesizer output to the MIDI channel. The relative volume of these different sound sources can be balanced using the Windows mixer, accessed via the yellow speaker icon in the taskbar notification tray. Many sound cards are bundled with an enhanced mixer application that duplicates the functions of the Windows mixer and adds features specific to that card's capabilities.

Differentiating Sound File Formats (Or Which Sound File Does What)

A variety of audio file types can be recorded or played back through a PC sound system. Typically, a different type of audio file is indicated by each of the various file extensions, which is how most audio file formats are known.

The most common PC audio file formats are

◆ **AIFF:** Audio Interchange File Format (AIFF) is the Macintosh equivalent of Windows' WAV format and can be played back on newer versions of the Windows Media Player.

◆ **AAC:** The MPEG compression standard expected to succeed MP3, Advanced Audio Coding (AAC) is another name for MPEG-2, not to be confused with MP2.

◆ **AU:** AU (short for audio) is the audio file standard on Unix systems. PC users might encounter AU files on Internet sites. Most Web browsers have built-in AU support, and newer versions of the Windows Media Player will also play back AU files.

◆ **MID:** Files with the MID extension are not digital audio files at all but instead contain MIDI data. MIDI can be thought of as a language or a standard for sharing information about musical events, such as the pitch and duration of a note, between multiple devices. How a PC handles MID files depends on the system's configuration. Often MID files are routed to the sound card's onboard synthesizer, which in turn generates the corresponding sounds. MID files can also be played back on an external device attached to the sound card's game/MIDI port. Windows Media Player will launch MID files, but dedicated MIDI sequencing software is required to create and edit MIDI music.

Continued

Differentiating Sound File Formats (Or Which Sound File Does What) *(Continued)*

◆ **MP2:** Also known as MPEG-1 Layer 2 (an earlier MPEG compression format that produces lower quality results than MP3), these files can be played back with any MP3 player.

◆ **MP3:** Short for MPEG-1 Layer 3, MP3 is an audio compression standard developed by the Motion Picture Experts Group (MPEG). Audio compression is a means of reducing the size of WAV files to make them more portable and to take up less storage space. MP3 compression has become popular in recent years because file sizes can be reduced dramatically while retaining most of the original WAV file's audio quality. For example, a 50MB WAV file stored at 44.1 kHz and 16 bits can be reduced to around 5MB and maintain a sound quality comparable with that of a CD. Less compression results in larger file sizes but also higher sound quality. The portability of MP3 has led to an explosion of music trading on the Internet and considerable controversy surrounding the potential for copyright infringement. MP3 files require specialized software for playback, and a number of free MP3 applications are available on the Internet. MP3 files are also sometimes available as streaming content on Internet sites, meaning that the file doesn't need to be copied to the local system before it can be played. Streaming audio is commonly handled by Web browser plug-ins.

◆ **RA or RAM:** Both abbreviations refer to Real Audio files, which is a streaming audio format developed by Real Networks. The quality of Real Audio files varies with the speed of the Internet connection. Real Audio files targeted for high-bandwidth connections such as digital subscriber line (DSL) or T1 can approach CD quality, and files designed for modem downloads are similar to the quality of an AM radio signal. Real Audio files require a dedicated Real Audio player or browser plug-in for playback.

◆ **WAV:** WAV (Windows Audio/Video) is the Windows audio standard. Recording and playback support is built into the operating system. Double-clicking a WAV file launches a Windows applet by default unless a third-party program has been associated with WAV files.

◆ **WMF:** Windows Media File is Microsoft's answer to Real Audio. Like Real Audio, WMF sound quality is bandwidth dependent. WMF files can be played back on Windows Media Player.

Interfacing CD-ROM and DVD Devices

CD audio is unique among PC audio formats in that the computer doesn't process the output from an audio CD. Instead, both CD-ROM and DVD drives send CD audio directly to the sound card via a specialized cable. Although it might appear that the computer is processing CD audio because volume levels can be adjusted with a software mixer, all that's truly being controlled is the sound card's output level. In most cases, digital audio from a CD is converted to analog by a DAC on the CD-ROM or DVD drive itself. Less commonly, a digital output on the CD-ROM or DVD drive is cabled to a digital input on the sound card to allow the card's DAC to handle the conversion. Although digital outputs on CD-ROM and DVD drives are fairly common, digital CD audio inputs on sound cards are still somewhat rare.

Cabling between a CD-ROM or DVD drive and a sound card is generally straightforward, especially if the drive shipped with its own audio cable (and most do). The analog output is always located at the rear of the drive, often to the left of the Integrated Drive Electronics (IDE) or Small Computer System Interface (SCSI) connector, and is typically well marked.

Working with older CD drives or those shipped without an audio cable (also called a *pig-tail cable*) can be a bit more complicated because no single standard exists for cabling between a CD-ROM or DVD drive and a sound card. Different sound card and drive manufacturers often use proprietary connector types, creating a situation in which, for example, a Panasonic-to-Sound Blaster or a Sony-to-Pro Audio Spectrum cable might be required.

Fortunately, inexpensive (less than $10) universal CD to sound card cables are available in a wide variety of formats to support connectors for almost any combination of manufacturers and can be found at many computer superstores and online PC hardware vendors.

Scanning Image Capture Devices

The objectives of image capture are not unlike those of audio capture. In both cases, the purpose is to convert analog information such as a photograph or a human voice into digital data that can be stored and edited on a computer. Although not yet as universal as PC sound systems, image capture devices have increased in popularity with the rise of the Internet and have quickly become essential tools for developing visual content for Web pages.

Capturing an image with a scanner

Scanners are devices used for capturing still images by using a light source that reflects off the image being captured. Information about the reflected image is digitized and sent to image capture software, such as Photoshop or Paint Shop Pro, where it can be stored, edited, and printed.

Scanners are available in a wide variety of configurations, which can be categorized according to imaging method, how the scanner interfaces with the PC, and how the original image is delivered to the scanner.

IMAGING METHOD

The three primary imaging methods used on PC scanners are

◆ *Charge-coupled device (CCD):* CCD scanners make up the vast majority of general-purpose scanners found in homes and offices. A *CCD* is a small solid-state sensor that converts light into an electric charge, which in turn is converted into data that can be stored on a computer. Thousands of CCDs are arranged into an array that scans the entire surface of the image. A larger number of CCDs in the array translates into a higher maximum resolution for scanned images.

◆ *Photomultiplier tube (PMT):* This type of scanner uses a vacuum tube to convert light reflected from an image into an electrical signal that is amplified before ultimately being sent to the PC. PMT scanners are typically more expensive and more difficult to use than their CCD counterparts and are reserved for high-end applications that can take advantage of their wider dynamic range.

◆ *Multi-pass versus single-pass: Multi-pass scanners* collect color data by using three passes of the light source and CCD array over the surface of the image. A single scan requires one pass each for red, green, and blue information. When the three passes are completed, the information gathered is combined to make a full color image. The drawbacks of this method are fairly obvious. In addition to the time that it takes to make three passes, image quality can suffer from tiny inaccuracies in the alignment of the three sets of data used to create a composite image. These problems are eliminated with the advent of *single-pass scanners,* which collect all color data at one time. The result is usually a faster scan with less potential for image distortion than a multi-pass scan.

PC INTERFACES

With the exception of USB, serial interfaces (those using DB-9 or DB-25 connectors) aren't typically used for interfacing a scanner to a PC. However, most of the remaining common interface types include the following:

- *Parallel:* A *parallel interfaced scanner* connects to the PC's parallel port over a standard DB-25 cable. Most parallel scanners include a pass-through connector to allow a printer to share the same port. An advantage of parallel scanners is that they don't involve the additional expense and trouble of a SCSI adapter, but there is usually a trade-off in slower speed. In addition, some printers and other parallel devices such as Zip drives can have problems with a scanner's pass-through port.

- *Small Computer System Interface (SCSI): SCSI scanners* are either designed to work with standard SCSI interfaces from manufacturers such as Adaptec, or they ship with their own, sometimes proprietary, adapter cards. SCSI scanners are often faster than their parallel counterparts, but overall cost can be higher, especially when the price of the SCSI adapter is figured in. And because a SCSI adapter is required, installing a SCSI scanner can be more difficult than installing a parallel scanner.

- *Universal Serial Bus (USB):* USB scanners eliminate most of the problems with SCSI and parallel scanners. Speeds are comparable with many SCSI scanners, typically with a lower price and a simpler installation. Obviously, USB scanners are only appropriate for operating systems that support USB. All recent versions of Windows (98, 2000, and XP) support USB out of the box. Patches are available that will allow Windows 95 to work with many USB devices. Some USB devices, including some scanners, will not work in Windows 95 even if the patches for USB support have been applied.

IMAGE CAPTURE METHODS

Like everything else on the PC, a variety of ways are used to scan the original document and capture its image. Although the flatbed scanner is by far the most commonly used method, others out there in use include

- *Drum:* Drum scanners are photomechanical transfer (PMT) scanners, which require the original to be mounted to a transparent cylindrical spinning drum in order to capture an image. Drum scanners are typically used to capture or transmit graphics or photos and are not used with home systems.

- *Flatbed:* Flatbed scanners have become the most popular type of scanner because of their flexibility and ease of use. The material to be scanned is placed on a flat glass surface, and the light source and CCD array pass underneath it. The dimensions of scanner beds vary significantly. For example, many flatbed scanners are unable to scan an entire legal-sized page in a single pass. Therefore, a scanner should be chosen with some consideration of the size of the material likely to be scanned. A flatbed scanner can be used to capture photos, graphics, or other images.

◆ *Handheld:* This type of scanner must be moved across the surface of the original by hand. Because they are often narrower than a typical page, more than one scan could be necessary to capture a full-page image. When this is the case, the multiple scans must be "stitched" together in software before the image is complete. Handheld scanners are typically used to scan images, text documents, and secret files (like in the movies) from sources that are bound or not suitable for other types of scanners.

◆ *Sheet-fed:* Operating much like a copy or fax machine, sheet-fed scanners use rollers to move an image past the light source and CCD array. Some sheet-feeders can automatically feed one page after another, making it possible to scan multiple images in a single event. The obvious disadvantage of sheet-fed scanners is that they can only accept loose pages and aren't useful for scanning books, magazines, or rigid objects. This is the technology used in those multi-function printer/scanner/copier devices offered by most printer manufacturers. Sheet-fed scanners are primarily used to scan documents. Many newer flatbed scanners offer an optional sheet-feed attachment that allows the flatbed scanner to also server as a sheet-fed scanner.

Catching the action

The term *video capture* can be somewhat misleading because it implies that all video capture devices capture moving images. Many video capture devices do capture full-motion video, but many others, such as the popular Snappy from Play Inc., capture only still images, just as a scanner does.

Video capture devices, then, are devices that use video cameras or VCRs as a source for capturing still or moving images. In addition to whether moving images can be captured, video capture devices can also be categorized according to how they attach to the PC, whether they accept a digital signal, and the type of compression used.

INTERNAL VERSUS EXTERNAL

Video capture devices typically connect to the PC in one of three ways: an adapter card (usually PCI), an external parallel interface, or an external USB interface. The distinction between internal and external video capture devices can be blurred by the fact that many capture cards use a *breakout box,* which is a separate piece of hardware that attaches to the rear of the card and contains all the connectors for interfacing with the input device (video camera, VCR). Some video cards also double as video capture devices, with varying capabilities.

DIGITAL VERSUS ANALOG

Some video capture devices accept only an analog signal, like that from a traditional camcorder or VCR, using Composite or S-Video inputs. Digital video capture devices use high-speed IEEE 1394 (also known as *FireWire*) interfaces to transfer data directly from digital video cameras. Some capture devices include a combination of digital and analog inputs.

Image-Editing Software

Like a digitized sound, a visual image must be sent to software before it can be manipulated and stored. Scanners come bundled with software for controlling the scanning process and typically include some basic tools for image editing. Advanced tools for image editing are available from a number of publishers, including

- ◆ **Adobe:** www.adobe.com

- ◆ **Corel:** www.corel.com

- ◆ **Jasc:** www.jasc.com

- ◆ **Ulead:** www.ulead.com

- ◆ **Xara:** www.xara.com

CODEC

Digital video, like digital audio, is huge and can require a ton of disk space to store. One second of uncompressed, full-motion video and audio captured at 24-bit, 640 x 480 resolution takes up approximately 30MB of disk space. Because of this, all video capture devices use one or more methods of compression. Special circuits or devices, called *codecs* (*c*ompression/*dec*ompression), reduce the amount of storage space required.

The compression method used has a direct bearing on which applications the captured video is compatible with, so the compression scheme should be chosen carefully.

The most common codec compression methods used by video capture devices are

- ◆ *Digital video (DV):* This is the compression method used by digital video cameras, which perform their own compression during recording. DV capture cards connect to digital cameras over an IEEE 1394 interface, which transfers digital video at very high speeds with no signal loss. DV is not scaleable, meaning that screen size and data rate (the number of megabytes per second of playback) cannot be adjusted.

- ◆ *DivX:* DivX is the name given a newer software codec based on the MPEG-4 compression scheme. MPEG-4 is a newer standard for high-quality video compression. DivX, also called MP3 for video, uses only about 15 percent of the space required by earlier standards. DivX is being used for streaming video over the Internet as well as DVD video. DivX was developed by an open source group called Project Mayo (www.projectmayo.com).

◆ *Motion Video - Joint Photographic Experts Group (MJPEG):* This motion video compression method is based on the still image compression method developed by the Joint Photographic Experts Group (JPEG). MJPEG (pronounced em-*jay*-peg) is optimized for transfer to and from videotape but is less appropriate for multimedia and Internet applications because it requires specialized hardware for playback. Image quality is high but can vary with the amount of compression.

◆ *Motion Picture Experts Group-1 (MPEG-1):* This is one of two common video compression methods developed by the Motion Picture Experts Group (MPEG). MPEG-1 is ideal for multimedia and Internet video because playback is software based, and file sizes can be reduced dramatically while maintaining a good image quality.

◆ *MPEG-2:* This compression method is used with video capture devices. MPEG-2 improves upon MPEG-1 in a number of ways, including supporting resolutions up to four times higher. MPEG-2 compression is scaleable, so it can be used for multimedia or Web-based applications all the way up to broadcast quality video at higher data rates (which, of course, translates to larger file sizes).

◆ *MPEG-4:* The latest MPEG compression scheme is in use with digital television and is beginning to be used for Web-based interactive graphics and multimedia.

 No, I didn't leave out MPEG-3. This standard name was not used to avoid confusion with MPEG-1 Layer 3, which is commonly referred to as MPEG-3.

Digitizing an image

Generally, sound and image capture methods are designed to capture or reproduce an original as faithfully as possible. If captured correctly, a digitized sound is virtually identical to the original. Similarly, a printed copy of a scanned page and the original, sitting side by side, can be impossible to distinguish from each other. However, a manually operated digitizing device is unique in that its function is to create something that did not exist before.

Digitizers, also called *digitizing tablets, drawing tablets,* or just *tablets,* are drawing tools designed to capture the movements of the operator's hand. Their operation is similar to that of a mouse, but there is a significant difference between the type of information that a mouse generates and the data that's sent to the computer by a digitizer.

The information generated by a mouse is always relative to the position of the cursor on the screen. If you draw a line with a mouse and then pick up the mouse and move it to a different position on the desk, the input will continue from the last position of the cursor. However, with a digitizer, each position on the tablet corresponds with a specific position on the screen. This makes it possible to accurately trace an existing drawing or to create original drawings such as architectural designs that must correspond to very precise dimensions.

A digitizer accomplishes this with two main components: an electronic tablet, and one of two types of drawing devices.

♦ *Pen:* Also called a *stylus,* a *pen* is held like an ordinary pen and is used to draw directly on the tablet, thus creating a corresponding drawing on the PC.

♦ *Puck:* Also called a *cursor,* a *puck* closely resembles a mouse and is used in much the same way. A small window with crosshairs makes the puck ideal for very precise tracing of existing drawings.

In both cases, the tablet detects the exact position of the drawing device and sends X and Y coordinates to the PC. Both pens and pucks are available in either corded or cordless configurations. Many digitizers include software that allows the pen or puck to duplicate the functions of an ordinary mouse.

Like scanners, digitizers connect to the PC in a variety of ways. Many digitizers use a proprietary controller card, either ISA or PCI, which must be installed before the tablet can be operated. There is no standardization among the types of cables used between these proprietary interfaces and the tablet, so the manufacturer must be contacted for replacements if necessary. Another common interface for digitizers is the serial port. Although one end of the connecting cable uses a standard DB-9 or DB-25 connector, the other end is designed specifically to connect to the tablet. Again, the manufacturer can provide information about replacement cables. Some newer digitizers connect to the PC through the system's USB port by using a standard cable.

Problem-solving Audio and Video Capture Device Issues

The first step in troubleshooting any audio/visual device is to make sure that the most recent drivers are installed on the system. Fierce competition among hardware developers has created a situation in which devices are released to the public as quickly as possible, often before all the bugs have been worked out of the drivers. Even if a device is fresh off the shelf, a newer driver than the one in the box is probably already available.

TIP   The Internet has become an indispensable tool for PC technicians looking for the latest drivers for the equipment that they're troubleshooting. See the sidebar "Sources for Audio/Visual Drivers and Tools" for a list of URLs for major audio/visual hardware manufacturers, pointing directly to the driver download area wherever possible.

Installing a sound card

Installing a sound card is very much like installing any other type of expansion card. You need to apply the same safety considerations that I discuss in Chapter 23.

Here is a review of the general considerations that you must use to install a sound card:

1. Power down the system before opening the case, checking that no lights are illuminated on the front of the case and that no fans are spinning.

   On ATX systems, you might have to press and hold the power button for several seconds before it turns off.

2. Always use an anti-static wrist strap when working inside the PC to prevent damage from electrostatic discharge (ESD).

3. Avoid using magnetized screwdrivers while working inside the PC.

4. To avoid damage, use caution not to contact the surface of the Printed Circuit Board (PCB) on the motherboard or other adapter cards with your tools.

5. Before closing the case, check to see that all expansion cards, RAM modules, and cable connections are still firmly in place.

The following sections discuss the specific steps used to install sound cards for each of the major interface bus structures.

ISA SOUND CARDS

Like other ISA expansion cards, ISA sound cards usually require manual configuration of resources such as port address, direct memory access (DMA), and interrupt request (IRQ). These values are typically set with a series of jumpers on the card. Some cards require a combination of jumper settings and lines in the AUTOEXEC.BAT and/or CONFIG.SYS files.

ISA sound cards can be especially complicated to configure because they often use a separate set of values for different functions. For example, some sound cards require a separate port address, DMA, and IRQ for general use, another set of values for Sound Blaster emulation, and a third set of values for MPU-401 (the de facto standard for MIDI interfaces) emulation. That's several resources to configure for a single expansion card!

As you can see, there is no universal set of steps for configuring an ISA sound card. The only way to know exactly what values need to be assigned and how to assign them is to refer to the manufacturer's documentation. If the manual for the card is unavailable, many sound card manufacturers publish installation guides on their Web sites.

SOUND BLASTER

Creative Labs' *Sound Blaster* (along with its many variations) was one of the first sound cards to gain widespread use among PC gamers and multimedia enthusiasts. As a result, many game and multimedia publishers began developing titles with audio content specifically designed to work with the Sound Blaster.

A number of these titles rely upon the SET BLASTER environment variable in AUTOEXEC.BAT to determine how to route sound data. Unfortunately, manufacturers of sound cards with Sound Blaster emulation often omitted the SET BLASTER variable from their installation routines. In many cases, this meant that there would be no sound even if Sound Blaster emulation had been implemented correctly.

A typical SET BLASTER line looks like this:

```
SET BLASTER=A220 I5 D1 T6 P330
```

where A is the port address, I is the IRQ, D is the DMA channel, T identifies the type of Sound Blaster being emulated, and P is the MIDI port address.

PCI SOUND CARDS

Many of the difficulties associated with configuring an ISA sound card are eliminated with PCI sound cards. Although a number of resources still need to be assigned, this is typically accomplished by the Plug and Play (PnP) Basic Input/Output System (BIOS) in conjunction with a PnP-operating system such as Windows 95, 98, or 2000. In most cases, resources, such as IRQ and DMA, cannot be assigned manually.

A few conditions must be met before a PCI card can be installed:

◆ First, and most obviously, there must be an available PCI slot.

◆ Many older motherboards use an earlier revision of the PCI BIOS that might not be compatible with newer sound cards. Check with the motherboard manufacturer if you have an older PCI motherboard and aren't certain that the PCI BIOS revision might be less than version 2.1.

◆ Motherboard manufacturers commonly develop system BIOS updates after the motherboard is released. Sometimes these updates are designed to address issues, such as PnP device enumeration, that can affect whether a card is successfully installed. Check with your motherboard manufacturer to see whether any critical BIOS updates are available. Always use caution when upgrading a system BIOS.

See Chapter 4 for more details about BIOS upgrades.

A typical PCI sound card installation goes as follows:

1. Insert the card into an available PCI slot.

2. Power on the system.

3. When the operating system prompts you for an installation disk, insert the manufacturer's driver disk and point to the directory specified in the manufacturer's documentation.

Although Windows 98/2000/XP includes drivers for a handful of PCI sound cards, in most cases, you should use the manufacturer's device drivers to ensure that the sound card is configured correctly. If a driver disk is unavailable, drivers can often be found on the manufacturer's Web site. Frequently a manufacturer will release updated drivers that include features or bug fixes not found on the original installation disk, so it's always good practice to check the Web site for updates.

Sources for Audio/Visual Drivers and Tools

Here is a list of companies that provide driver software and a few sound system support tools for sound cards, scanners, digitizers, and video capture devices:

Sound cards

◆ **Aztech:** www.aztech.com/support.htm

◆ **Creative Labs:** www.americas.creative.com/support/

◆ **Diamond Multimedia (SONICblue):** www.diamondmm.com

◆ **ESS Technology** (ESS supplies audio chips to motherboard and sound card manufacturers. They provide generic drivers that work with many, but not all, of the third-party products that use their chips): www.esstech.com/techsupp/drivers.shtm

◆ **SIIG:** www.siig.com/drivers/

- ◆ **Turtle Beach:** www.turtlebeach.com/site/support/ftp.asp

- ◆ **Yamaha:** www.yamaha.com/ycaservice/group003/fgrop003.htm

Scanners

- ◆ **Agfa:** support.agfa.com/support

- ◆ **Canon:** www.usa.canon.com/html/cprSupportDetail.jsp?navfrom=DrivD

- ◆ **Epson:** support.epson.com/filelibrary.html

- ◆ **Fujitsu:** www.fcpa.com/download/

- ◆ **Hewlett-Packard:** www.hp.com/cposupport/software.html

- ◆ **Microtek:** www.support.microtek.com/~admin/

- ◆ **Mustek:** www.mustek.com/Imaging/drivers/driverindex.htm

- ◆ **Ricoh:** www.ricoh-usa.com/download/?usa

- ◆ **Umax:** www.umax.com/download/

- ◆ **Visioneer:** www.visioneer.com/support/drivers.stm

Digitizers

- ◆ **Acecad:** www.acecad.com/support.html

- ◆ **Altek:** www.altek.com/drivers.htm

- ◆ **Calcomp and Summagraphics:** www.gtcocalcomp.com/support.htm

- ◆ **Numonics:** www.interactivewhiteboards.com/drivers.htm

- ◆ **Wacom:** www.wacom.com/productsupport/index.cfm

Video capture

- ◆ **ADS:** www.adstech.com/support.asp

- ◆ **ATI:** www.ati.com/support/

- ◆ **Dazzle:** www.dazzle.com/support/updates.html

- ◆ **Iomega:** www.iomega.com/software/

- ◆ **Matrox:** www.matrox.com/mga/support/drivers/

- ◆ **Pinnacle:** www.pinnaclesys.com/support/

- ◆ **Sigma:** www.sigmadesigns.com/support.htm

When all else fails, you might want to look for the driver that you need at www.driverguide.com.

Dealing with common sound card problems

Here are a number of common problems that can be experienced with a sound card installed in a PC system:

♦ *Distorted recordings:* If recordings made with the sound card sound fuzzy or distorted, the input volume was probably set too high. Most audio capture programs use input meters to give the user a graphical depiction of the input level. Typically these meters will turn red if input levels are too high. Many of these applications include an audition mode that makes it possible to set input levels without actually recording. Distortion can also occur when recording with a microphone if the source is either too close to the microphone or is too loud.

♦ *No CD audio:* Assuming that the CD audio channel on the mixer is turned up, the most likely reason for no CD audio is that the drive and the sound card are improperly cabled.

♦ *No MIDI music:* Assuming that the MIDI channel on the mixer is turned up, MIDI data could be routed to the wrong destination. The Multimedia applet in Windows Control Panel makes it possible to route MIDI data to either the sound card's internal synthesizer or to the game/MIDI port to control an external device. Obviously, if there is no external device and MIDI data is sent to the game/MIDI port, there will be no sound.

♦ *No sound:* If you know that you have a working sound card but you have no sound, check every point along the signal path, starting with the master volume control in Windows. Make sure that the mixer channel for the sound source (CD audio, WAV, MIDI) is turned up. If the volume is set correctly, check the connection between the sound card and the speakers, making sure that the correct output is used. If the speakers are passive, make certain that they're plugged into an amplified output, usually Phones Out/Speaker Out. If the speakers are active, make sure that they're switched on and that the volume control on the speakers themselves is set correctly. If you still have no sound, try attaching another set of speakers or headphones. Many PC speakers are cheaply made and are frequently the first part of a sound system to fail.

♦ *Stuttering playback:* If a brief segment of sound stutters or repeats the same sound sample over and over again, you probably have an interrupt conflict with another device. Use the Windows Device Manager to determine what devices are conflicting. If the sound card allows you to set the IRQ manually, try a different setting. Many PCI sound cards don't allow manually setting resources, but you might be able to change the IRQ assigned to a PCI device within the system BIOS (consult the motherboard documentation). You might also be able to change the interrupt assigned to the sound card by putting it into another slot. If necessary, try changing the IRQ for the device that the sound card is conflicting with.

◆ *Skipping playback:* If digital audio within a game or multimedia title skips or sounds choppy, particularly when accompanied by full-motion video, the system might simply not be powerful enough to keep up. If the software allows it, try reducing the resolution of the video. If the sound improves when video is played at a lower resolution, a CPU upgrade and/or a faster video card would probably improve performance at higher resolutions.

Connecting a CD-ROM or DVD to a sound card

Connecting the cable between a CD-ROM or DVD drive and a sound card involves working inside the PC case, so the usual precautions should be observed. A sound card typically has a number of connectors on its surface, each serving a different function. There might even be more than one CD audio connector to increase compatibility with different drives and cables, but it's only necessary to use one. Other connectors include modem, auxiliary, and PC speaker interfaces, any one of which can easily be mistaken for the CD audio connector.

TIP If the connectors on the sound card aren't clearly labeled, consult the manufacturer's documentation. The drive might have a digital output next to the analog output on the back of the drive, but these are usually well marked. The connector for the drive's digital output is usually very different from the analog connector, so it's unlikely that the cable can be attached to the wrong output.

Many CD audio cables are keyed to prevent inserting them incorrectly. If the cable isn't keyed, often it's marked to correspond with markings on the drive and sound card indicating the pin-outs for the left and right audio channels. If an unkeyed cable is inserted with the right and left channels swapped, it won't damage the drive or sound card, but CD audio channels will be reversed so that the left channel is heard from the right speaker and vice versa.

If the drive manufacturer's audio cable is unavailable, the easiest solution is to obtain a universal audio cable with multiple connectors for most types of drives and sound cards unless a specific part number for the cable can be found.

Resolving system resource conflicts

System resource conflicts, as I discuss in Chapter 5, are a common source of problems with audio/visual hardware. PnP, PCI, and USB devices are much less susceptible to resource conflicts than their ISA counterparts. However, when a conflict does appear on one of these newer devices, there is often no simple solution because resources usually cannot be assigned manually. A well-behaved PnP device won't claim a resource that's already in use elsewhere in the system. An exception to this is found in the case of PCI chipsets that support *IRQ steering,* a process that allows multiple PCI devices to share a single interrupt.

Because of IRQ steering, seeing two devices in Windows' Device Manager using the same interrupt does not necessarily indicate a problem. In rare instances, however, two PCI devices assigned the same interrupt will conflict with each other, causing system lock-ups when an audio or video file is played back.

In many cases, the IRQ for a PCI device can be changed in the system BIOS by assigning a fixed interrupt to a given slot. Sometimes simply moving a PCI device to another slot will force the system to assign a different, possibly less-problematic, IRQ. In other cases, you might need to disable IRQ steering altogether. Typically this is accomplished through the BIOS, the Device Manager, or both. Consult the motherboard manufacturer's documentation for information about BIOS settings.

To disable IRQ steering in Device Manager, open the System Devices branch and double-click the PCI Bus icon. On the IRQ Steering tab, clear (disable) the Use IRQ Steering check box. Note that disabling IRQ steering means that there must be an available interrupt for every device on the system because interrupts will no longer be shared.

Connecting a scanner to a PC

Most SCSI and USB scanner connections are trouble free, assuming that the SCSI card or USB interface has been correctly installed and is recognized by the operating system. However, a few potential problems are associated with parallel scanners, many of them related to the pass-through parallel port. Some parallel devices perform erratically or not at all when connected to a pass-through port.

 TIP Be careful when using certain scanners with Windows XP, especially if the system has been upgraded from Windows 98 or Me. Windows prefers Windows Image Acquisition (WIA) drivers over Independent Hardware Vendor (IHV) drivers. You might need to uninstall the vendor's IHV drivers and install the Microsoft digitally signed WIA drivers.

CONNECTING A PARALLEL SCANNER

Two hardware solutions for connecting a parallel scanner to your PC are available:

◆ *Switch box:* Using a manually switched parallel port switch box allows two parallel devices to attach to a single parallel port without the use of a pass-through. Note that only one device has use of the port at a time. This can create problems for devices that must be initialized when the system boots, including some scanners. Active (meaning automatic) switch boxes are available (and relatively more expensive) that allow multiple devices to be connected and to access the channel seemingly simultaneously.

◆ *A second parallel port:* Adding an additional parallel port is subject to all the considerations that I discuss at length in Chapter 10. Traditional ISA parallel cards use the standard resources for parallel ports: A port set for LPT2 would use an address of 278 and IRQ5. Therefore, those resources must be available if an ISA parallel card is to be installed. Newer PCI parallel cards often can overcome those restrictions and can even share an interrupt on a system with IRQ steering.

USING THE BEST PARALLEL OPTION

Many scanner manufacturers either recommend or require a bidirectional parallel port for use with their parallel scanners. Most parallel ports found on Pentium-class and newer motherboards are bidirectional, but it might be necessary to enable bidirectional communication in the system BIOS. Consult the motherboard manufacturer's documentation for specific settings. Windows will usually detect bidirectional ports automatically, but this can be confirmed by checking Device Manager to see whether the port is listed as bidirectional, Enhanced Parallel Port (EPP), Enhanced Capabilities Port (ECP), or EPP/ECP, all of which are bidirectional modes. In addition, scanners that require a bidirectional port often require an IEEE 1284 cable in order to take full advantage of the port's capabilities. Parallel port issues are discussed in Chapter 24.

Downloading images from a digital camera

Digital cameras differ from the other audio/visual devices discussed in this chapter in that they do most of their work without the aid of a computer. Like traditional cameras, digital cameras are portable devices used to capture images in the field. Unlike traditional cameras, however, "developing" a picture involves dumping the camera's memory into a computer, where images are then stored and can be edited.

Digital cameras come bundled with software for transferring data from the camera to the PC. Physical connections between the camera and the PC are usually straightforward via a cable (provided with the camera) that runs from the camera either to a serial port or a USB port on the PC. Assuming that the ports are correctly recognized by the operating system, all that's required is to configure the software for the specific port being used.

In the case of a camera attached to the serial port, the software typically defaults to COM1, which is fine unless another device such as a mouse or a personal digital assistant (PDA) is already using that port. If the camera is attached to COM2, the software must be configured to download from that port. If problems persist, make certain that COM2 has been enabled in the BIOS and correctly detected in Device Manager. An unused COM2 is commonly disabled in the BIOS in order to free up resources for other devices.

Part V

Printers

Chapter 17

Impact and Inkjet Printers

IN THIS CHAPTER
A PC is almost always directly or indirectly connected to a printer of some type. In fact, a high number of PC systems are now sold in a package that includes at least an inkjet printer as a standard part of the package.

Like the PC's monitor, and perhaps even more so, the printer has become an absolute necessity to users. When the printer doesn't work (or seemingly doesn't work), users are typically on the line immediately needing you to rush right down to figure out why something that worked just fine yesterday is now not producing reams of paper with valuable information printed on them. You, as the PC technician guru, are expected to have printers (and all else) back online and spewing forth documents in no time. To this end, this chapter (and the next) provides some background into printers, their characteristics, operation, and some troubleshooting and diagnostics tips. Read here to discover the following:

- ◆ Diagnosing common printer problems

- ◆ Connecting a printer to a PC

- ◆ Setting up a printer in Windows

- ◆ Using a switchbox with a printer

- ◆ Connecting to a network

- ◆ Safeguarding a printer

- ◆ Troubleshooting dot matrix printers

- ◆ Troubleshooting inkjet printers

I'M CONFIDENT that I've hit the major problems and issues that you should encounter, but I can't say I've covered every condition that your users will throw at you. Some things are just beyond my clairvoyant abilities.

Examining Printer Characteristics

The general characteristics of a printer are essentially the same for all printer types. The following sections describe each of the major characteristics used to define the capabilities of a printer.

Differentiating type qualities

The type quality standard with which printers are compared is the typewriter and daisy wheel printer. These devices print whole characters by striking a solid, raised form against an ink-impregnated ribbon to impact and mark upon the paper. *Type quality* is primarily used to describe the type capabilities of dot matrix printers but can be applied to other printers as well.

The type qualities most commonly used to describe a printer's print are

◆ *Draft quality:* A low-quality print in which the dots or print elements used to form the characters are individually visible on the page. Figure 17-1 illustrates a draft-quality character in comparison with other type qualities. Low-end inkjet and dot matrix printers produce draft quality type.

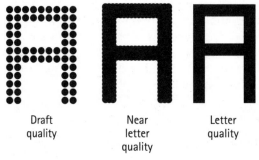

Draft
quality

Near
letter
quality

Letter
quality

Figure 17-1: Examples of draft, NLQ, and letter quality print types.

◆ *Near letter quality (NLQ):* This type quality is somewhere between letter and draft type qualities. This type quality is considered better than draft quality but not good enough to be considered letter quality because the dots or elements used to form the characters are partially visible. Printing the character twice with a second pass slightly offset from the first produces an NLQ character. The results would look something like the middle example in Figure 17-1. Inkjets and dot matrix printers that print at 150 dots per inch (dpi) use NLQ as their type quality default.

Dots per inch (dpi) is a print quality measurement used on inkjets and dot matrix printers. It measures the number of print pixels (picture elements) per linear inch used to create the printed image. For example, a 300 dpi printer prints 300 pixels per inch or 90,000 pixels per square inch.

◆ *Letter quality (LQ):* This is the best type quality that an impact printer can produce. A printer with a letter quality rating is able to produce characters that appear to have been created by a typewriter or a solid character form. Daisy wheel, high-end inkjet, dot matrix, thermal, and laser printers produce LQ type. Letter quality print requires a printer capable of producing 300 dpi. Letter quality characters appear to be solid without any gaps appearing, like the far-right example shown in Figure 17-1.

Print speed

A printer's speed is measured in either the number of characters per second (cps) or pages per minute (ppm) that the printer can produce. However, these two measurements are rarely used together. *Characters per second* is used with printers that form characters one at a time, such as daisy wheel and dot matrix printers. *Pages per minute* is used for inkjet and laser printers that produce entire pages without printing each individual character separately. Larger printers, such as line printers used with mainframe computers (which print an entire line at once) are rated by a lines per minute (lpm) print speed.

Daisy wheel printers are by far the slowest of the impact printers, with a top print speed around 30 cps. Line printers are the fastest at 3,000 printed lpm, or the equivalent of about 6,600 cps. Dot matrix printers print up to 500 cps; inkjet printers produce from 2 to 10 ppm; and laser printers (see Chapter 18) range from 4 to 20 ppm. A laser printer with a print speed of 6 ppm has the equivalent speed of around 40 cps in letter quality. The quality of the print and whether it's color or black and white have a direct effect on the speed of a printer.

Impact versus non-impact

Dot matrix, daisy wheel, and line printers are classified as *impact printers* because they make contact with the paper while they print. These printers use a striking mechanism to bang an inked ribbon onto the paper to create a character or graphic. Impact printers are typically slower and noisier than non-impact printers but are better for continuous or multipart forms.

Inkjet, thermal, and laser printers are *non-impact printers*. These printers don't make a forced contact with the paper; instead, they use non-impact methods such as ink spray, thermal-chemical reaction, and xerography, respectively, to produce characters and documents.

Text and graphics

Those printers that have a locked-in character set, such as daisy wheel and line printers, are limited to a specific set of characters, which are usually only alphabetic characters, numbers, and special characters. Because of this, they can't produce graphics. Special printers, called *plotters,* use a combination of inkjet technology and the X/Y coordinates of the drawing elements to create drawings for use in engineering and other technical areas. Laser printers, inkjets, and many dot matrix printers are capable of merging text and graphics into a single document.

Fonts and typefaces

A *font* or *typeface* is the style and design of the characters a printer prints, such as Times New Roman, Courier, and Ariel. Figure 17-2 shows a sampling of some of the more common fonts.

This is Times New Roman font
This is Courier font
This is Bookman font
This is Lucida font
This is Garamond font
This is Arial font
This is Script font

Figure 17-2: Samples of common fonts.

Word processing and graphics software offer literally thousands of font styles and typefaces. However, not every printer is capable of printing every font available.

For example, a different wheel must be used in a daisy wheel printer for each font. To change the font, the daisy wheel must be changed. Most dot matrix printers offer between 2 and 16 hard fonts (fonts that are built into the printer's firmware). However, many printers allow for soft fonts (logical fonts added from a disk or software) to be added and managed by the printer's device drivers. Laser and inkjet printers are able to produce just about any font that the PC can generate because they treat the document as a graphics image. The issue on these printers is often printer memory and not fonts.

Print styles

Fonts can be modified with print styles. A print *style* is applied to emphasize a character, word, title, and so on. Figure 17-3 shows samples of the five standard print styles. The styles used with most fonts are

- *Natural:* This is the natural typeface of the font.

- *Boldface:* **This print style darkens the type.**

- *Italics: This print style normally tilts the typeface slightly to the right.*

- *Underline:* This print style places a horizontal line beneath the type.

- *Strikethrough:* ~~This print style places a horizontal line through the center of the type.~~

This is a natural typeface

This is a bold typeface

This is an italic typeface

This is an underline typeface

~~This is a strikethrough typeface~~

Figure 17-3: Common print styles used to modify a font.

Print size

Another feature of a font is its *scalability,* which is its ability to be printed in different character sizes. Font size is measured in points (pts). A point is $\frac{1}{72}$ of an inch; conversely, there are 72 points to an inch. Figure 17-4 shows a comparison of different point sizes for the Times New Roman font.

This is 8 point font size

This is 10 point font size

This is 12 point font size

This is 18 point font size

This is 24 point font size

This is 36 point font size

Figure 17-4: A comparison of font point sizes.

Fonts fall into one of two classifications:

◆ *Bitmapped: Bitmapped* fonts form characters with patterns of dots. Each particular bitmapped font (Times New Roman, Courier, and so on) specifies a dot pattern to be used for each letter, number, and special character; print style (bold or italic, for example); and type size (10 pt, 12 pt, and so on). Bitmapped fonts are stored in a font file that contains the predefined character patterns for each point size. If more point sizes are added to a bitmapped font, the font file requires more disk space.

◆ *Scalable: Scalable* fonts are defined as a base font (a kind of starting point), which outlines the basic font typeface and design and contains a mathematical formula that's used to generate the character in a requested point size or print style. Variations of a font are generated from the base whenever a point size other than the base is needed. TrueType and PostScript fonts are examples of scalable fonts.

Printer standards

Printers connect to PCs most commonly through a parallel port and use a standard protocol to communicate. A *protocol* defines the rules used by two devices when communicating. The Institute of Electrical and Electronics Engineers (IEEE) standardized parallel port protocols as the IEEE 1284 standards. The IEEE 1284 standards are

◆ *Standard Parallel Port (SPP):* A parallel port standard that allows data to travel only from the computer to the printer.

◆ *Enhanced Parallel Port (EPP):* A parallel port standard that allows data to flow in both directions but only one way at a time (half-duplex). When not receiving a print file, the printer can send signals to the processor indicating that it's out of paper, to open its cover, and other conditions.

◆ *Enhanced Capabilities Port (ECP):* The parallel port protocols that allow bidirectional simultaneous (full-duplex) communications between the printer and the PC over special IEEE 1284-compliant cables. EPP cables are bidirectional but do not support ECP communications.

Printer controls

Most PC printers have a set of buttons located on a front panel (see Figure 17-5) that is used to control the activities or change the configuration of the printer. Nearly all printers have buttons for at least online/offline, and older printers have *line feed* (to advance the paper a single line) and *form feed* (to advance the paper one page).

When a printer is online, it receives printing instructions from a computer that indicate the character to print along with the line and form feed commands. Others have buttons to cycle through a configuration menu or to select a font or point size. Many printers also include a small liquid crystal display (LCD) screen, shown in Figure 17-5, on which the printer's status and activity of the printer is displayed as well as menu and option choices during configuration.

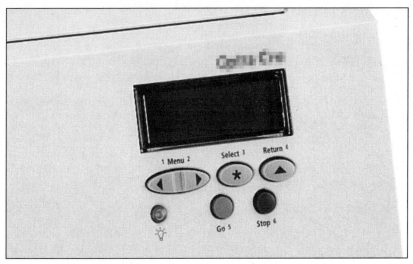

Figure 17-5: An example of a printer's control panel.

Dealing with Dot Matrix Printers

Because the daisy wheel printer is generally obsolete today, I begin a review of the various printer types with the dot matrix printer. The dot matrix printer uses a matrix of pins in its printhead to create text and limited graphics with a pattern of dots.

The dot matrix printer is much faster and quieter than a daisy wheel printer, but it's still considered somewhat noisy. Dot matrix printers incorporate tractor-feed mechanisms to feed continuous-form paper and documents.

In the beginning

The Centronics Corporation produced many of the first popular dot matrix printers for the early Apple computers. The cable connector that Centronics chose for use on its printers was a distinctive 36-pin connector that featured pins arranged on a center bar (see Figure 17-6). The Centronics connector was actually developed by the Ampenol Corporation, but because of the early popularity of Centronics printers, it is commonly referred to as the Centronics connector.

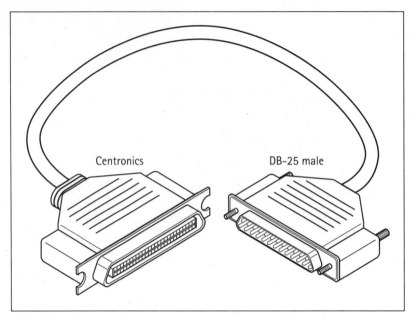

Figure 17-6: A standard printer cable has a 36-pin Centronics connector on the printer end and a DB-25 connector on the computer end.

The dot matrix today

The dot matrix printer, like the one in Figure 17-7, has been largely replaced by inkjet and laser printers in the home and small office environments. However, the dot matrix printer continues to provide a service and fills a market niche. Because it is an impact printer that strikes hard enough to print through several layers of carbon copies and because it can feed multipart continuous forms, the dot matrix printer is still commonly used for many office and industrial applications.

Dot matrix printers, which are common in pharmacies, receiving docks, and warehouses, are used for many administrative tasks, including printing mailing labels, cash register tapes, and automatic teller machine (ATM) receipts. Several manufacturers still offer full lines of dot matrix printers, including IBM, Epson, Oki Data, and Lexmark.

Dot matrix printers are available in two standard physical widths: narrow and wide. A narrow-width dot matrix printer is usually limited to 80 columns and is typically used only for letter-size paper and forms.

A wide-width dot matrix printer can print 132 columns or more. This type of dot matrix printer is typically used as a general printer. Wide-width dot matrix printers can be adjusted down to narrow widths to accommodate narrower paper sizes.

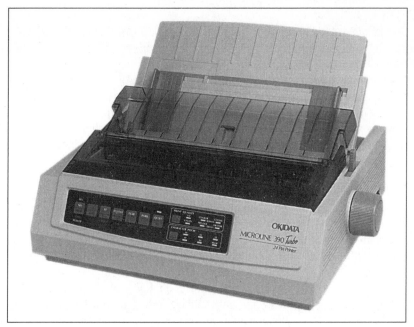

Figure 17-7: A dot matrix printer.

Photo courtesy of Oki Data Americas, Inc.

Printing with a dot matrix printer

Compared with inkjet and laser printers, the operations of the dot matrix printer are fairly simple. However, to print data on a dot matrix printer does involve quite a few steps, many of which are also used with all other printer types. The following sections describe the processes used to print on a dot matrix printer.

PRINT PROCESS

The printing process for any type of printer always begins with the PC and its software. Typically, an application program such as a word processor (like Microsoft Word or Corel WordPerfect), a graphics package (like Adobe Illustrator or Photoshop), or a desktop publishing package (like Microsoft Publisher or Adobe PageMaker) generates a print-image file, which can be anything from a plain text document to a complex full-color photograph. The application communicates to the operating system that it would like to send its file to the printer. The operating system places the print file in the system print queue (line), where it awaits the availability of the printer. When the printer is available, the operating system and the printer's device driver begin transferring the print file to the printer, which involves translating the print file into commands and information that the printer can interpret into a printed document or image.

PRINT QUEUE

After a user sends a document to the printer, the application in use communicates to the PC's operating system and the printer's device drivers to create a file that contains print commands and codes that are used by the printer to create the document. The commands included in this file are those needed to produce the letters, numbers, special characters, graphics, print styles, and other document effects, such as tabs, line feeds, page feeds, and so forth. This file is placed in the system's print *queue,* which is a buffer that holds print files waiting to be sent to a printer. When the printer is available, the file is sent to the printer. Otherwise, the print file is held until the printer is available and no other print files are in the queue ahead of it.

PRINT BUFFER

When a print file is transferred to a dot matrix printer, it is stored in the printer's print buffer. The print buffer is needed because the PC transfers data to the printer much faster than the printer is able to print it. The print buffer receives the print file and releases the PC to perform other tasks. Without a print buffer, the PC would have to wait while the printer processed each line of the print file and printed the data. Early PC printers either had no print buffer or had a very small one. This meant that the PC and the printer were both tied up until the print job completed.

Dot matrix print buffers typically hold between 8 and 60 kilobytes (K) of data, depending on the age, manufacturer, and model of the printer. Dot matrix printers with enhanced graphics or extended font capabilities tend to have larger print buffers. The size of a dot matrix printer's print buffer is commonly listed right along with its print speed as one of its major features, and more is always better.

PRINTER AND PC COMMUNICATIONS

Although this isn't specific to just dot matrix printers, I want to discuss the dialog that goes on between a printer and a PC to print a file.

Often the size of the print file exceeds the capacity of the print buffer. When the print buffer is full, it sends a command to the PC to stop sending data. Typically, this is a transmission off (XOFF) command. As the printer empties the print buffer and more space is available, the printer notifies the PC that it can resume sending the file with a transmission on (XON) command. This dialog continues until the entire file is transferred. After the file is completely transferred to the printer, the computer disengages and moves on to other tasks while the printer finishes printing the file.

FORMING A CHARACTER

The printer's processor reads the instructions for one line of print from the print buffer and translates it into the dot patterns needed to print each character on the line. The printer's processor also decides the best travel direction for the printhead to print the line: whether the head should travel left-to-right or right-to-left. The processor also controls the movement of the paper, advancing it a single line or to the top of the next page, or even feeding an entire page.

As illustrated in Figure 17-1 earlier in the chapter, a dot matrix printer forms its characters with a pattern of dots. Characters are formed in stages depending on the number of pins in the printhead, which is commonly either 9 or 24. A *9-pin print-head,* in which the pins are arranged in a single column (see Figure 17-8), forms characters by printing the appropriate dots in a series of connecting columns. The 9-pin dot matrix printers are capable of only draft quality print and are commonly used for forms.

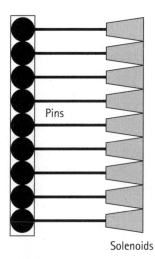

Figure 17-8: The arrangement of the pins in a 9-pin dot matrix printhead.

A 24-pin printer is used in high-end dot matrix applications. Whereas the 9-pin dot matrix printer has a single row of 9 pins, the 24-pin dot matrix printer has two rows of 12 pins. The three extra pins per row allow the 24-pin printer to produce a higher quality character, which is why 24-pin dot matrix printers are referred to as LQ printers.

Most dot matrix printer manufacturers use the Epson model naming convention to indicate the type and quality of their printers. If the model name includes an *X*, such as LX 300, the printer has 9 pins. If the model name includes a *Q*, such as LQ 500, the printer has 24 pins.

THE PRINTHEAD

The *printhead,* the most important part of the dot matrix printer, forms the characters and prints them on the page. The major components in the printhead, as illustrated in Figure 17-8, are the solenoids and pins, along with a permanent magnet and the wire coils and springs of each pin.

Inside the printhead is a large permanent magnet that holds the pins away from the front of the printhead. On the shaft of each pin is a spring that pushes against the pull of the magnet and a wire coil. When the wire coil is charged, its electromagnetic force neutralizes that of the magnet, and the spring pushes the pin forward to strike the ribbon and place a dot on the paper. When power is removed from the wire coil, the magnet counteracts the spring and retracts the pin.

The friction of the moving parts of the printhead and the constant energizing and de-energizing of the wire coils create heat. A dot matrix printhead gets very hot when it is printing, which is why most have a heat sink either attached or designed into their housing. The tines of the heat sink provide multiple surfaces to cool the printhead.

PRINT SPEEDS AND RESOLUTIONS

The speed of dot matrix printers has increased dramatically over the past few years to the point that their speeds now range from as low as 200 cps to 1,200 and 1,400 cps. At the same time, the resolution of a dot matrix printer has also increased. Early dot matrix printers supported only 10 dpi, but they now offer resolutions of 360 dpi and higher. However, a typical dot matrix printer is more likely to support around 75 dpi printing for NLQ print.

Moving up to color dot matrix printers

Some dot matrix printers require the addition of a color kit, but most color dot matrix printers have a built-in color capability. On the low end, changing the ribbon and choosing a different print mode through the control panel transform the printer from a monochrome printer to a color printer.

High-end dot matrix color printers include color functions in their firmware, including the ability to produce thousands of colors using only the colors included in its ribbon. In addition to its firmware, the color functions of a dot matrix printer are controlled by the printer's device drivers that handle the translation of a color image into the commands needed to produce it on paper. The ribbon of a color dot matrix printer is divided horizontally into two to four color stripes. The print mechanism shifts the ribbon up and down to place the correct color in front of the printhead as needed.

Printing with Inkjet Printers

Inkjet printers (see Figure 17-9) create printed images by spraying small droplets of very quick-drying ink through tiny nozzles (jets) onto the paper. The documents produced by an inkjet printer are typically better quality documents than can be produced on a dot matrix printer. Inkjet printers are also less expensive and usually physically smaller than most laser printers, which appeal to home and small office users. However, inkjet printers are slower than laser printers; have a reputation for occasionally smearing, bleeding, or running the ink on the page; and can have page feed problems. In spite of these problems, the inkjet printer has become very popular with home and small office users because it produces good quality printing at a reasonable price.

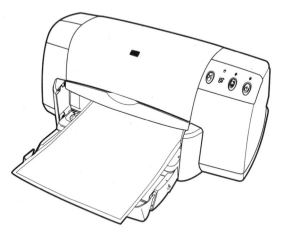

Figure 17-9: An inkjet printer.

Inkjet technologies

Inkjet printing uses small droplets of ink to print text and graphics on paper. An inkjet printhead has dozens of nozzles through which ink is jetted (fired) onto the paper. The two general types of inkjet technologies used are continuous flow and drop-on-demand. *Drop-on-demand* inkjet printing has two forms: piezoelectric and thermal.

CONTINUOUS FLOW PRINTERS

Continuous flow inkjet technology isn't used in PC printers. In this inkjet technology, the ink flows continuously through the printhead, but not all the ink is put on the paper. Ink droplets are passed through a variable charge chamber where they are selectively given an electrical charge. Only the droplets selected by the timing mechanism for use in creating the printed image are charged. All the droplets then flow over a deflector plate that fires the charged droplets onto the paper and deflects the uncharged droplets back into the ink supply to be reused. The printhead of a continuous flow inkjet printer is fixed in place. Instead, the paper is moved back and forth under the print head. This prevents the ink from being splashed about, which would happen if the head were moved.

DROP-ON-DEMAND PRINTERS

Piezoelectric is one of two inkjet approaches. As the printhead moves over the paper, a piezoelectric crystal in each nozzle is charged with electricity, which makes the crystal expand. As the crystal expands, it fires a droplet of ink out of the nozzle (which is smaller than a human hair) with enough force to strike the paper. Piezoelectric inkjet printers can change the size of the droplet put on the paper by changing the amount of electricity applied to the crystal and altering the rate and amount of its expansion. A larger electrical charge causes more expansion in the crystal and forces more ink from the nozzle.

The other type of drop-on-demand inkjet printer is the thermal inkjet. The *thermal* process involves heating the ink in the ink channel between the ink reservoir and the printhead's nozzles. Heating the ink creates a bubble that forces the ink out of the nozzle just like the piezoelectric crystal. Only about a third of the ink is actually heated; and at full speed, the ink increases in temperature only to around 30° Celsius (or about 86° Fahrenheit).

Thermal inkjets are the most common type in use with models produced by Hewlett-Packard, Lexmark, and Canon, which are the companies that also hold nearly all the thermal inkjet patents.

Halftoning

The first step of the inkjet print process is called *halftoning,* which is the same technique used to print monochrome photographs in newspapers. If you look very closely at a standard (black-and-white) newspaper picture, you can see thousands of small dots of various halftone shades of gray and black. Your eye and brain blend the dots to form an image.

To print an image in halftones, the page is first divided into an arrangement of cells. Each cell is a matrix of dots, as shown in Figure 17-10. A solid black cell has all its dots printed, and a white.cell has no printed dots. Printing only some of the dots in the cell produces a shade of gray on the page. Understandably, lighter grays have fewer printed dots, and darker grays have more printed dots. For example, a 25 percent grayscale has one-in-four of a cell's dots printed black; a 50 percent grayscale has half its dots printed.

The number of dots in a cell, which is set by the printer's resolution, determines the number of grayscale shades available. A cell made up of 4 dots x 4 dots can produce 16 (4 x 4) shades of gray plus white (no dots in the grid). An 8 x 8 cell is capable of 64 shades of gray plus white. The halftone cells are then applied across and down the page like tiles to create an image.

Printing in color

The output from the halftoning process is a bitmapped version of the image to be printed. In addition to the bitmap image of the document, the file can also contain additional bits for color text or images. An additional bit is included for each of the four cyan/magenta/yellow/black (CMYK) colors to indicate which color is on or off for each dot. The printer's device drivers compress the bitmap image file to minimize the amount of data transmitted to the printer.

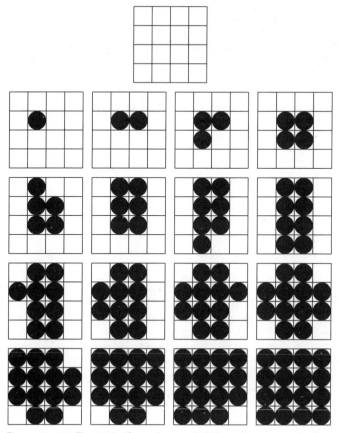

Figure 17-10: The 17 halftone dot possibilities using a 4 x 4 halftone cell.

An inkjet printer doesn't print an entire line of text in one pass; it can take many passes to complete one line of 12 pt text. The controller interprets the data from the bitmap file for one pass of the printhead. When a certain color is called for, a signal is sent to the printhead to fire the nozzles for that color when the printhead passes over the correct dots on the printed line. When the printhead passes over the exact spot on the print line that calls for a certain color, the nozzles for that color either heat up or the piezoelectric crystals fire for precisely the right amount of time and precisely place the amount of ink called for in the image file sent from the application program.

The printing process used by inkjet printers involves spraying drops of ink that are about one million times smaller than a small drop of water through nozzles that are thinner than a strand of human hair.

COLOR CONVERSION

Converting the colors from the red/green/blue (RGB) color scheme used inside the computer to the CMYK color scheme of the printer is the challenge of printing an application-generated or scanned color image on a color inkjet printer. Humans see *colors,* which are actually the combination of different light wavelengths. As color wavelengths are added or subtracted, different colors are created.

An image displayed on the monitor in RGB color image must be converted to CMYK colors before it can be printed. The RGB color scheme, which uses up to 24 bits to specify each pixel of an image, depends on the *radiance* (wavelengths) of the RGB dots of each pixel to blend and create its colors. This additive approach to color creates a spectrum that ranges from black (the absence of color wavelengths) to white (the presence of all color wavelengths).

On the other hand, paper is reflective and produces color through a subtractive process. A fresh sheet of paper appears white because it includes all color wavelengths. When color is printed on paper, the ink absorbs color wavelengths from the paper to create a color. Each of the CMYK colors absorbs different wavelengths, and when used in combination, absorbs enough wavelengths to create a wide array of colors. For example, cyan (blue) ink absorbs red wavelengths and produces greenish-blue colors. Magenta (red) ink absorbs green wavelengths and creates reddish-blue colors. Yellow absorbs blue wavelengths to create yellowish-red colors. Black ink absorbs all color wavelengths.

To convert from the RGB color scheme to the CMYK color scheme, a *Color Lookup Table (CLUT)* is used. The binary RGB code for a color is looked up in the CLUT, and its corresponding CMYK binary code is used. Often the colors of an image are different on the monitor than on paper because it's impossible to exactly match RGB colors with CMYK colors.

COLOR PROFILES

In order to have your What You See Is What You Get (WYSIWYG – pronounced *whiz*-ee-wig) image printed in exactly the same colors shown on your display requires the application of color profiles, which are also called device profiles. *Color profiles* allow for the accurate translation of colors from one device to another.

The International Color Consortium (ICC) was organized in 1993 to develop color management system standards that are industry wide, vendor neutral, and cross platform. Without the use of a color profile, or what's called a color management system (CMS), your WYS won't be your WYG. A *CMS* is a set of software tools that reconcile the different colors between scanners, monitors, and printers to ensure that the original colors are retained throughout the printing and imaging processes and that the colors displayed on your monitor are the same colors that are printed in your document.

Most browsers, graphics and image software, and operating systems (Windows and Mac OS) have standard color profiles included. If you wish, you can also download and install other color profiles from software publishers and imaging hardware manufacturers. For a sampling of available color profiles, visit Integrated Color Solutions' ProfileCity Web site at www.icscolor.com.

COLOR HALFTONING

Whereas monochrome halftoning creates the image to be printed using cells that produce shades of gray, color halftoning is able to produce a wide range of colors with only four ink colors. Color halftoning works very much like monochrome halftoning except that a separate halftone layer is created for each color. Four halftone layers are created: one for each color with a dot anywhere that color is used. When the layers are logically superimposed on the printed page, the actual colors of the image emerge.

The challenge of the halftone process is to hide the dots used to create an image and present a smooth blending of colors that creates a realistic-looking image to the viewer. This requires very sophisticated software (which is why color qualities vary by manufacturer) and a process that allows the viewer's eye to smooth the dot patterns on the page. This is accomplished by one of two halftoning methods: ordered dithering or image diffusion. Most inkjet printers use image diffusion as their halftoning method because it creates more uniform dot patterns. However, some manufacturers (most notably Lexmark) offer both halftone methods and allow the user to choose which to use on a given project.

ORDERED DITHERING

Ordered dithering creates the transition from one color to another by evenly spacing pixels of each color along the common edge of the two colors (see the middle sample in Figure 17-11). This method, which is faster to create than image diffusion, is used on professional-level graphics that require more accurate color representations.

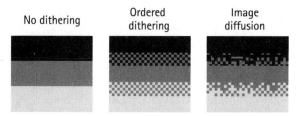

Figure 17-11: Samples of an image section showing no dithering, ordered dithering, and image diffusion.

Like monochrome halftoning, ordered dithering divides each color plane into cells. Each cell uses a separate pattern of dots depending on the size of the cell. The number of pixels in a cell is a function of the print resolution of the printer, but the more dots in the cells, the more shades of a color that can be represented.

A threshold matrix is applied that allows only the cells in certain locations to be printed and blocks other cells from being printed. This screening creates the dithering (or transition) for each color. A separate threshold matrix is used for each color layer. Remember that each layer of the color halftone represents only a single color and that the ordered dithering from one color to the next is handled partially on each color's layer.

The *threshold* is actually a file with binary values that are used to determine whether a color should print for a particular cell. Each cell has a binary value that indicates the dots that are to receive color. The threshold matrix has a corresponding binary value for each cell. The two binary values for each cell are compared; if the value in the halftone cell is greater than that in the threshold matrix, the cell is printed. If the threshold's value is equal to or greater than that of the halftone cell, the cell is not printed.

IMAGE DIFFUSION

Image diffusion, also called *diffuse dithering* and *error diffusion,* is the technique used by virtually all inkjet printers. This process treats each dot in the image as if it could be printed in one of 255 shades of a color or grayscale, despite the fact that an inkjet printer is only capable of printing the dot in one of its four colors. For discussion purposes, assume the color being printed is black, which has a value of 255 (no dot, or white space, has a value of 0).

The image diffusion process determines a grayscale color value for each dot in the image. It then calculates an error value that represents the difference of what will actually be printed at the dot's location (either a dot or no dot) and the grayscale value that it determined for that location.

For example, the printer driver determines that a dot should have a grayscale value of 128, but no dot is to be printed. The error for that dot would be 128 – 0, or 128. If a dot *were* to be printed at that location, the error would be 128 – 255 for an error of –127. The error values are used to diffuse the color of the adjacent dots. If the error is a negative number, black dots are less likely to be printed in adjacent pixels. If the error is positive, black dots are more likely to be printed in the adjacent cells. The final determination depends on the error diffusion applied to the neighboring dots. The overall result is an averaging of the color in neighboring cells and a more subtle color change. See the example on the right in Figure 17-11.

Inkjet cartridges

Monochrome inkjet printers have only a single ink cartridge. Comparatively, color inkjet printers typically have two cartridges — one black and one tri-color (CMY). The black cartridge is separate because the vast majority of printing done on an inkjet is text or line drawings done only in black. One of the downsides to having cyan, magenta, and yellow in the same cartridge is that when one color runs out, regardless of how much ink remains of the other colors, the cartridge needs to be replaced if you wish to use all the colors in the printer's palette. Newer color inkjet printers feature ink cartridges with a replaceable ink tank for each of the CMY colors, which helps to address this problem.

Some newer color inkjet printers now use separate ink cartridges for cyan, magenta, yellow, and black, which can save money if you print a lot of the colors in which each is used or just a lot of any one of these colors.

Virtually all inkjet cartridges have a built-in printhead, which guarantees a fresh printhead each time you install a new cartridge. The printhead has either 64 or 128 microjets through which the ink is fired to the paper. The printhead also contains built-in resistors on the flexible circuits located on the front of the cartridge. These resistors do wear out in time and can cause slanted or wavy print. When this happens, the cartridge should be replaced.

Printer drivers

The workhorse of the inkjet printing process is the software device driver that converts RGB to CMYK, performs the calculations in halftoning operations, and manages the flow of the print file from the PC to the printer. The *printer driver* controls the applications and hardware with which the printer will work and manages the communications between the printer and the computer to keep the printing process flowing smoothly.

A printer's device driver is usually included with the printer on a diskette or CD-ROM. Newer or updated versions of device drivers are constantly being made available as well as updated Basic Input/Output System (BIOS) and firmware for some printers. These updates are typically found on the manufacturer's Web site. Many manufacturers now have alert systems that notify you via e-mail or fax when new drivers are available.

Heating Up a Thermal Printer

A *thermal printer* uses a heating element that writes by causing a chemical change on specially treated paper. Two types of thermal printers are available:

- ◆ *Direct thermal:* This thermal printer uses heat to change the chemical coating that has been directly applied to the thermal printer paper.

- ◆ *Thermal transfer:* This thermal printer includes a ribbon or carrier that applies a thermally reactive chemical to the paper while it's fed to the printing mechanism.

The primary part of the print mechanism of a thermal printer is a stylus tip that heats up when electricity flows through it. This tip, called a *resistance,* is very small and heats up and cools down in a fraction of a second. A thermal printer moves the heated tip over the treated thermal paper to create text. A real advantage to thermal printers is that they are virtually silent in operation.

Thermal printers are typically used in specialized applications, such as server stations in restaurants, where their lack of noise is a plus. They are also used on many cash registers and have been popular for portable printers for notebooks and other portable PCs.

Among the downsides to thermal printers are

◆ *Burn danger:* After operating for a time, they get hot, which can burn anyone needing to load more paper.

◆ *Paper expense:* Thermal paper is chemically treated and expressly made for use in a thermal printer, which means it can't be used in other types of printers.

◆ *Handling requirements:* Thermal paper must be loaded very carefully into the printer. If the paper isn't loaded just right, any creases or wrinkles in the paper will come out as black streaks on the printed document.

◆ *Exposure to light or heat:* Thermal prints can't be exposed to bright light or sunlight because parts of or the entire document will turn black.

Printing All in a Line

Larger systems (such as mainframes) that print thousands of pages of reports, checks, or billing statements daily are *line printers*. The name indicates that an entire line of text is printed in one strike. These printers are usually capable of printing 132 to 168 characters per line. At each character position is a print chain that contains each of the characters in the printer's font set. As each line is formed, the chain at each character position is rotated to the proper character, and the line is struck through the ribbon to the paper. The character positions are then reset, and the next line is printed.

Diagnosing Common Printer Problems

Printer problems can originate from either the printer or the PC. Use the following steps to diagnose common printer problems on either the printer or the PC:

On the printer

1. Verify that the printer is powered on.

   The printer's front panel should have a power LED. If the power LED is not lighted, flip the printer's on/off (1/0) button to its on (1) position. If the power does not come on, verify that the printer is connected to a power source. If the power source is a plug strip or surge suppressor, verify that it has power or that its fuse is not blown.

2. Verify that the printer is online.

   On the printer's front panel, there should also be an LED indicating whether the printer is online. If this LED is not lighted, press the Online button on the front panel to place the printer online with the PC. If the button doesn't light, you have three possibilities: The printer is not powered up, the LED is burned out, or the printer is not connected to the PC.

3. Verify that the printer is connected to the PC (or network).

   A cable should connect the printer to the PC. This cable should be like the one shown earlier in Figure 17-6 with the Centronics connector on the printer end and the DB-25 end connected to a parallel port on the PC. If the printer is properly connected and the cable isn't faulty, the printer's online indicator should light. You should also verify that the cable is the right one for the parallel port protocol in use. If an Enhanced Capabilities Port (ECP) protocol is in use, verify that the cable is IEEE 1284-ECP compatible.

4. Look for error messages displaying on the printer's LCD panel (if it has one).

   Unfortunately, dot matrix and inkjet printers don't provide the very best diagnostic and error messages, but if these printers have a printing error, the error is typically fairly obvious and easily isolated.

5. Try resetting the printer.

   The printer could have a print job stuck in its memory that it's unable to process for some unknown reason. Try powering off the printer, waiting a few seconds, and then powering it back up.

On the PC

1. Check for error dialog boxes.

   On a Windows PC, print errors are displayed in a dialog box, like the one shown in Figure 17-12.

   Typically, if a printer error message is displayed, the problem is likely with the printer itself.

Figure 17-12: A Windows PC error message box displays when a printer is out of paper.

2. Check the network printer connection.

   If the printer is a network printer, a common error message is that the PC can't find the network. The most common cure for this is to reboot the PC and resend the print file.

Connecting a printer to a PC

Most PC printers connect through a parallel port, which is usually designated as LPT1. A PC can have more than one parallel port, but most systems usually have only one. The connectors most commonly used to connect a printer directly to a PC are

♦ *25-pin DB (data bus) female connector:* The LPT/parallel port on the back of a PC is usually a 25-pin female connector, shown in Figure 17-13, into which a 25-pin male DB connector (see Figure 17-14) on the PC end of the printer cable is connected. Most PCs only have a single LPT port that is mounted on the motherboard or an expansion card.

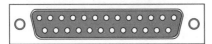

DB-25 female

Figure 17-13: DB-25 female connector.

♦ *36-pin Centronics:* This is the most common connector for the printer end of a printer cable. This connector, shown in Figure 17-14, is also the default for the Hewlett-Packard–Interface Bus (HP-IB) used to connect Hewlett-Packard printers. The PC end of the cable is normally a 25-pin male connector.

♦ *Universal Serial Bus (USB):* Some of the latest printers offer a USB connection in addition to the standard parallel connector. If the parallel port is already in use by a scanner or Zip drive, the USB port allows the printer to be connected to the PC without using the parallel port or any additional system resources. Older printers can be connected via a USB connection, as shown in Figure 17-15, by using a USB-to-parallel adapter cable that has a Centronics connector on the printer end and a USB connector on the PC end.

♦ *Infrared (IR) or Infrared Data Association (IrDA):* Adapters are available that connect a parallel printer to a PC through its IrDA connection, which frees the parallel port on the PC for other uses. A number of small hand-held-size printers are available for use with notebooks and personal digital assistants (PDAs) with an IrDA connection.

Parallel cables have distance limitations. Older Centronics cables should not be more than 15' in length: Between 9' and 12' is best. Newer IEEE 1284 cables can extend up to 30' in length, and some 50' high-end cables are available as well. Typically, if you need to be more than 10' away from a printer, connect into a network or move the printer or PC closer.

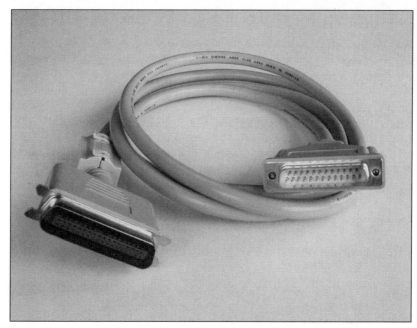

Figure 17-14: Centronics 36-pin connector and DB-25 male connector on a printer cable.

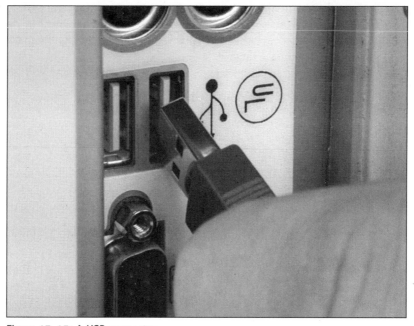

Figure 17-15: A USB connector.

Setting up a printer on a Windows PC

Setting up a printer on a Windows system is virtually the same for every type of printer. However, you should always follow the setup instructions and always use the device drivers that come with the printer. Windows 9x, Windows NT, and Windows 2000 each carry a remarkable number of printer drivers with them. However, to be absolutely certain that you have the very latest driver for the PC's operating system, visit the manufacturer's Web site. Some printers come with a separate printer driver included on a diskette or a CD-ROM.

To add a printer to a Windows PC, use the Printers function found in the Control Panel or from the Settings option of the Start menu. In either case, the Printers dialog box displays the Add Printer Wizard.

The following steps detail the process used to add a printer to a Windows computer:

1. From the Windows desktop, click the Start button to display the Start menu. Access the Settings menu and choose the Printers option.

    Alternatively, you can double-click the My Computer icon to display the My Computer folder. Open the Control Panel and choose the Printers icon.

2. With the Printers folder open, click the Add Printer icon (see Figure 17-16) to start the Add Printer Wizard, shown in Figure 17-17.

    If the printer being added isn't listed in the supported printers list, use the diskette or CD-ROM that came with the printer to supply the device driver by clicking the Have Disk button when prompted. In fact, even if the printer is listed, use the disk if you have it.

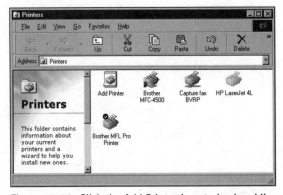

Figure 17–16: Click the Add Printer icon to begin adding a printer.

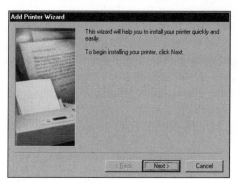

Figure 17-17: The Add Printer Wizard.

After the printer driver loads, an icon for the new printer will display in the Printers folder. You might want to open the Properties windows for this printer to make any print control adjustments that you desire.

3. Set the default printer. If the PC is a standalone system with only one printer, when the printer is configured, it will automatically be set as the default printer. However, if the PC is connected to a network and has access to more than one printer, you should designate one of the printers as the default printer. To do this, right-click the printer that you wish to set as the default and then choose the Set as Default option in the pop-up menu that appears.

Using a switchbox

A *switchbox*, either manual or automatic, can be used to connect more than one non-laser printer or any other parallel device or devices to a single parallel port. You can also use a switchbox to allow multiple PCs to share a single printer. A dial designates which PC or device is to be connected to the primary device of the switchbox. Switchboxes are also called *A/B switches* because the devices attached are labeled as A, B, C, and so on. An automatic switchbox senses activity on a line and automatically switches to that line.

In general, a laser printer should not be connected to a switchbox, especially newer laser printers. Laser printers are highly interactive with the printer and have very high voltage requirements. You should also consider the issue of electrical noise. Taking the laser printer online and offline by changing the active location, either manually or automatically, can interrupt device driver commands and create electrical noise spikes that could possibly damage the laser printer or the PC's parallel port.

Safeguarding a printer

Here are a number of common sense procedures and a few more technical ones that you can use to keep a printer working and reliable:

◆ *Cleaning:* Clean dot matrix or other impact printers regularly with a vacuum or blow them out with compressed air.

◆ *Conditioning:* Use a flexible wire brush or rubber-conditioning product to clean and maintain the paper transport of an inkjet printer.

◆ *Paper:* Always use the type and weights of paper recommended by the manufacturer for the printer and never use paper heavier than the recommended maximum weight. This will help avoid print feed and paper path jams. Some printers prefer laser printer paper that's finished on one side. Check your printer's documentation.

◆ *Power protection:* Plug inkjet, dot matrix, and other non-laser printers into a surge protector or uninterruptible power supply (UPS).

Troubleshooting inkjet printers

Inkjet printers are relatively error-free, with the exception of a few ink smears and paper jams. In fact, most of the problems that the printer itself can have are nearly the same as those listed in the previous project for dot matrix printers. Instead of ribbon problems though, the inkjet can have cartridge problems. Here are the more common cartridge problems:

◆ *The printer goes through the motions without printing:* If the print cartridge moves from side to side like it's printing but the paper is blank, the problem is either a clogged or an empty ink cartridge. If the cartridge isn't empty, the problem is most likely clogged nozzles on the inkjet. This is far more likely to happen on a monochrome inkjet printer. Gently wipe the cartridge's nozzles with a soft lint-free cloth (one that you don't mind staining for life). Never use a facial tissue for this job because it can leave behind more lint than you're trying to remove.

◆ *One color does not print:* If one color won't print, either the color has run out (time to replace the cartridge) or the nozzles for that color are clogged. As required, replace the cartridge, replace the color cylinder (if the printer is so equipped), or clean the cartridge (see the preceding bullet).

◆ *The printer cartridge light on the printer is flashing:* If you see this light flashing, something is wrong with the cartridge, and it should be reseated (or in the worst case, replaced). It could be that the resistors on the printhead are damaged. See the earlier section "Inkjet cartridges" for more on resistors. Another possible cause of this problem is that the hinged cover of the printer isn't completely shut.

- *The paper is feeding slightly askew:* The print feed rollers could be dirty, or part of the paper feed mechanism might be broken. Clean the feed rollers with a cotton swab and denatured alcohol. If the feed mechanism is broken or defective, you have just discovered why inkjet printers are considered disposable technology.

- *Colors are misaligned and text is not aligned to graphics:* When you install new ink cartridges, always take the time to align the printer's print-heads. This process aligns the cartridge carriages and adjusts the positions of the nozzles so that ink that should be placed on top of other ink to create a color is exactly where it needs to be and not slightly off to one side.

Troubleshooting dot matrix printers

Dot matrix printers, for all their moving parts, really don't have a lot of problems. However, here are some of the more common problems and some possible causes to investigate:

- *No power:* If the printer isn't getting power, check the obvious (power switch on, power cord, and so on). However, the problem could also be caused by the printer's power supply or a failure with the printhead motor. If the power light is on but the printer won't work, check whether the case is open. If the printer is on and online, check that the printer cable connection is solid. You can also check the printer cable itself to ensure that it's properly connected to the PC, or for any breaks, pet tooth marks, or other damage.

- *The paper won't feed:* If paper won't properly feed into the printer, you probably have an obstruction in the paper path or the alignment guides are released. If the forms tractor or *platen* (the black round rubber thing that moves the paper through the printer) won't push or pull paper through the printer, you might have a broken or stretched belt, a bad platen motor, or perhaps a defective forms tractor.

- *Ribbon won't feed:* If the ribbon is stuck in one place, it might be time to replace the ribbon, the belt on the ribbon feed could be defective, or one of the ribbon gears could be broken.

- *Print is bad:* If the same part of each letter is missing or you see an errant line across an entire printed line, a pin has been bent, the printhead is defective, or the cable that pulls the printhead across the platen has stretched or is about to break.

Chapter 18

Laser Printers

IN THIS CHAPTER

At one time, only the most wealthy (or spendthrift-y) of companies could afford a laser printer for general use. However, technology and competition are helping to drive down the cost (especially the effective cost) of laser printers. Affordability and network-ability help even small businesses justify their acquisition and operating costs.

The generic term *laser printer* has grown to include not only printers that actually use a laser in their printing process but typically also those printers that use light-emitting diode (LED) or liquid crystal display (LCD) technologies in their printing processes. To discover more about laser printers, take a look at this chapter, which covers the following:

◆ A review of laser printer operations

◆ A look inside the laser printer at its components and functions

◆ How to troubleshoot a laser printer

◆ Techniques to resolve laser printer print problems

BEYOND REMOVING A JAM or cleaning it, truly being able to repair a laser printer requires some specialized training, akin to what's needed to repair a copy machine. However, a PC technician can do a few things to keep a laser printer operational. This chapter provides information on the processes that you can use to perform top-level maintenance and diagnostic activities on laser printers.

Looking into Laser Printers

A laser printer, like the one shown in Figure 18-1, uses the same electrophotographic (EP) process used in a photocopier. A laser printer produces a printed document by using a focused beam of laser light and a rotating mirror to reproduce the image of a document as an electrostatic charge on a photosensitive drum. *Toner* (the so-called "ink" of the laser printer) is added, and the charge on the drum attracts and holds it in the image of the document. A sheet of paper, fed in from the paper supply and electrostatically charged, is rolled over the drum and picks up the toner. Heat is then applied to the toner to fuse it with the paper. The document is completed and placed on the output rack of the printer.

Figure 18-1: A mid-range laser printer.

A laser printer is a page printer, producing a finished page on each cycle. This is in contrast to the other types of printers that print single characters (daisy wheel and dot matrix) or all or part of a line of print (line printer and inkjet) on each cycle. (See Chapter 17 for more on these types of printers.)

A laser printer prints the text and graphics of one full page simultaneously. As a cut-sheet printer, its paper supply is a stack of individual sheets of paper. It cannot handle multipart forms or any type of continuous forms. The processes used to form the page to be printed are essentially the same as used for the inkjet printer, with some minor differences, which I explain later in the section "Caring for a laser printer."

Laser printing technologies

Laser printers use three different printing processes to produce a printed page. Each of the technologies in use is directly attributable to one or more laser printer or photocopier manufacturer(s):

- *Electrophotographic (EP):* The *EP process* is the printing process used by virtually all laser printers. Its characteristics are the use of a laser beam to produce an electrostatic charge and a dry toner to create the printed image.

- *Light-emitting diode (LED):* An *LED printer* uses an array of around 2,500 light-emitting diodes (like very small light bulbs) in place of a laser as the light source used to condition the photosensitive drum.

- *Liquid crystal display (LCD): LCD printers* use light shone through an LCD panel in place of the laser to condition the photosensitive drum. See Chapter 15 for more information on how liquid crystal works.

ELECTROPHOTOGRAPHIC PROCESS (EP)

The *electrophotographic process (EP)* used in laser printers has its roots in the dry photocopy method xerography. Closely aligned with the Xerox Corporation, the word *xerography* roughly translates to *dry writing* and is the name for a photo-copying process used in nearly all laser printers and all dry photocopiers.

Xerography is ideal for the laser printer because it requires no liquid inks or special paper (such as those used with a thermal copier). This process relies on the fact that some substances become electrically charged when exposed to a light source. Here is a general overview of the EP printing process:

1. The printer's drum, which is made from selenium or another photosensitive (responsive to light) material, is electrically charged.

2. The laser printer uses the print image and the associated print instructions generated by application software on the PC to create a logical image of a document.

   This image is then used to guide the laser using mirrors to electrically discharge the print drum where no text or graphics are to appear on the finished document.

3. Negatively charged toner is sprayed on the drum and adheres to the parts of the drum, which is still electrically charged, creating the desired document in a reverse image on the drum.

4. A sheet of paper is fed from the paper supply and is positively charged.

5. The paper is then fed closely past the drum and toner.

6. The charge on the paper attracts the toner onto the paper; the paper and toner are fed through heated rollers that literally melt (fuse) the toner onto the paper.

If multiple copies of the same document are being printed, additional toner is added to the drum, and another sheet of paper is charged, passed by the drum, and fused. If only one copy is being printed of the page, any remaining toner is removed from the drum, the drum is recharged, and the process begins again.

The EP laser printing process can be organized into six separate phases, as follows:

◆ *Conditioning:* The entire drum is uniformly charged to −600 volts (v) by the primary corona wire (also known as the *main corona*) located inside the toner cartridge.

◆ *Writing:* The laser printer's controller uses a laser beam and one or more mirrors to create the image of the page on the drum. The laser beam is turned on and off to created a series of small dots on the drum to match the document to be printed. Where the light of the laser contacts the photosensitive drum, the charge at that spot is reduced to about −100v.

After the entire image of the document has been transferred to the drum, the controller starts a sheet feeding through the printer, stopping it at the registration rollers.

♦ *Developing:* Inside the developing roller, which is also located inside the toner cartridge, is a magnet that attracts the iron particles in the toner. While the developing roller rotates by the drum, the toner is attracted to the areas of the drum that have been exposed by the laser, creating a mirror image of the document on the drum.

♦ *Transferring:* The back of the paper sheet is given a positive charge. As the paper passes the drum, the negatively charged toner is attracted from the drum onto the paper. The paper now has the image of the document on it, but the toner, held in place by simple magnetism, is not bonded to it.

♦ *Fusing:* The fusing rollers apply heat and pressure to the toner, melting and pressing it into the paper to create a permanent bond. The fusing rollers are covered with Teflon and a light silicon oil to keep the paper and toner from sticking to them.

♦ *Cleaning:* Before the next page is started, the drum is swept free of any lingering toner with a rubber blade, and a fluorescent lamp removes any electrical charge remaining on the drum. Any toner removed in this step is not reused but is put into a used-toner compartment on the cartridge.

LED PRINTING

An LED printer uses the same printing phases as a laser printer. However, an LED printer replaces the laser and mirrors of the laser printer with a bank of light-emitting diodes (LEDs). The number of LEDs in the light source is directly related to the resolution of the printer. Because LEDs are both tiny and very bright, one LED can be used for each dot in the printer's resolution. For example, a printer rated at 600 dots per inch (dpi) has 600 LEDs in each inch of its light source. When the drum rotates past the light source, the LEDs are used to discharge the dots that form a single row of dots in the image.

LCD PRINTING

An LCD printer uses the same printing phases as the laser and LED printers. The difference is that an LCD printer uses light passing through a liquid crystal display (LCD) panel to discharge the drum. These printers are also called *LCD shutter printers* because of how the liquid crystal elements work.

See Chapter 15 for more information on LCD technologies.

A liquid crystal pixel is used for each dot on one pixel row of the drum. If a printer is rated for 1,200 dpi, 1,200 liquid crystal pixels are used in each inch of the light source. As the drum rotates past the light source, the crystals are opened and closed to discharge the drum for each line of pixels in the document's image.

Color laser printing

Monochrome laser printers use the same halftoning techniques as the monochrome inkjet printer. The difference is that a laser printer forms the document on the print drum all at once before it's printed as opposed to a series of printhead passes.

 See Chapter 17 for more information on monochrome inkjet printing techniques.

The *Raster Image Processor* (RIP), which is part of the printer's internal control circuitry, translates the print commands sent from the PC into the cells that make up the image to be printed. The RIP computes the position of each cell and dot on the page and creates an image of the document in the printer's memory, where one bit of memory corresponds to each dot position of the image. The controller then directs the laser (or LED or LCD) to create the dot pattern on the drum. In a laser printer, the laser beam is focused on a multisided mirror that rotates to direct the beam onto the drum. Wherever the beam touches the drum represents a dot in the image. LED and LCD printers turn their light sources on and off for each of the dot positions on the drum.

The number of dots in use to create printed pages varies with price and manufacturer. Laser printers commonly offer resolutions of 400 to 1,200 dpi, with 600 dpi commonly seen. Heavy-duty workgroup laser printers can offer up to 2,400 dpi, but these are normally outside the price range of most home or small office users. A 600 dpi laser printer offering standard paper widths (8.5") uses over 5,000 dots in each row on the drum.

A color laser printer has two page per minute (ppm) ratings: one for monochrome and one for color. The difference is because the laser printer forms the image for each of its colors separately. The color ppm rating will always be the slower of the two. A laser printer might have a 16 ppm rating for monochrome but only 3 ppm for printing color documents.

For each of the cyan/magenta/yellow/black (CMYK) colors used in a document, a complete print cycle must be completed. This means that for each of the four colors, the drum is written, the correct color toner is applied, the partial image is transferred to the paper, the excess color toner is removed, and the process repeats for the next color. The paper can make as many as four passes around the drum: that is, one trip for each color layer. The fusing process is performed only once on the page after the toner for all the colors has been transferred. A variation of this process is Hewlett-Packard's *one-pass* system that applies each layer of toner to the drum before the full-color buildup is transferred to the paper. For each color in the image, the drum completes a complete cycle (except that there is only one conditioning phase). After all the colors are added to the drum, the paper passes the drum for a single transfer phase.

Building up the image

The challenge of color laser printing is creating millions of colors and shades using only the four CMYK colors. To do this, two primary color printing methods are used in color laser printing:

◆ *Bi-level:* In this basic color printing method, no control is provided for the intensity of a color. Each color dot is either on or off with no in-between shading.

Dithering, which I explain in Chapter 17, is used to create transitions between colors.

◆ *Multi-level:* Multi-level color printers have the ability to adjust the intensity of each dot to produce 256 shades of each color (256 shades of cyan, 256 shades of magenta, and so on) and then mix the 256 shades of each color to produce a total of over 16 millions colors that can be printed. This ability eliminates the need for dithering to produce the transition from one solid color to the next.

Nearly all color laser printers use the fusing process to blend colors. One color dot is placed on top of another color dot and blended into the final color by the heat of the fusing phase. Some printers can control how much toner is placed on a dot by controlling how long the laser is allowed to strike the drum. The length of time that the laser strikes the drum results in a larger or smaller dot. A bigger dot collects more toner during developing, and a smaller dot collects less toner.

Inside the Laser Printer

The components inside a laser printer, although a bit different and given slightly different names by the different manufacturers, are all essentially the same between models. At least, they have the same basic functions. Knowing which component does what can save you time and your user money by avoiding the unnecessary replacement of the wrong components.

The primary components of a laser printer are used to drive the six printing phases I describe in the earlier section "Electrophotographic process (EP)." The primary components of a laser printer (illustrated in Figure 18-2) are the following:

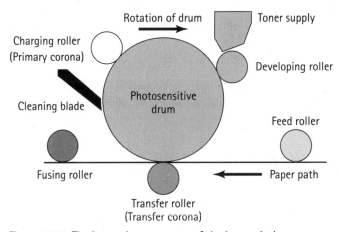

Figure 18-2: The internal components of the laser printing process.

◆ *Controller:* The *controller* is the laser printer's motherboard. It handles the communications with the PC, houses the memory in the printer, and controls the formation of the printed page. The printer's memory is located on the controller board. A laser printer's memory can be expanded; adding memory allows the printer to reproduce larger documents, higher resolution graphics, and additional soft fonts.

◆ *DC power supply:* This is the laser printer's electronic components direct current (DC) power. For example, the printer's logic circuits use +/–5 vDC (volts direct current) and the paper transport motors require +24 vDC. The laser printer's DC power supply also houses the main cooling fan.

◆ *Drum:* The photosensitive *drum,* which is made of selenium or another light-sensitive material, is located inside the toner cartridge on most laser printers. However, some larger systems have fixed drums.

◆ *Fusing rollers:* The toner is fused permanently to the page with pressure and heat by the fusing rollers. The temperature of the fusing rollers is between 165–180° Celsius (or 330–350° Fahrenheit).

TIP

The fuser — not the laser — is why the pages coming out of a laser printer are hot.

- ♦ *High-voltage power supply:* The EP process uses very high voltage to charge the drum and to transfer and hold the toner on paper. The high-voltage power supply converts alternating current (AC) into the higher voltages used in the printer.

- ♦ *Paper transport:* A laser printer has at least four sets of rubberized rollers (each with its own motor) used to move paper through the printer: feed (paper pick-up), registration, fuser, and exit rollers. The rollers are rubberized to grip the paper and grip with only the pressure needed to move paper to the process.

NOTE

Most printer problems occur in the paper transport system, particularly the paper feed rollers.

- ♦ *Primary corona:* Also called the *main corona* or the *primary grid,* this component forms an electrical field that uniformly charges the photosensitive drum to –600v during the conditioning phase.

- ♦ *Transfer corona:* This component supplies a charge to the back of the paper that pulls the toner from the drum onto the front of the paper. When the paper exits the transfer corona area, a static charge eliminator strip reduces the charge on the paper so that it won't stick to the drum. Not all printers use a transfer corona; some use a transfer roller instead.

The toner cartridge

On most laser printers, a removable cartridge supplies the printer with several valuable parts of the printing process. Typically, a toner cartridge (shown in Figure 18-3) contains the following components:

- ♦ *Photosensitive drum:* Perhaps the major component of a laser printer

- ♦ *Primary corona wire:* Conditions the drum

- ♦ *Developing roller:* Deposits toner on the drum

- ♦ *Toner:* The dry ink (if you will) of the EP process

Including these components in the toner cartridge provides the printer with a fresh drum each time the toner cartridge is changed.

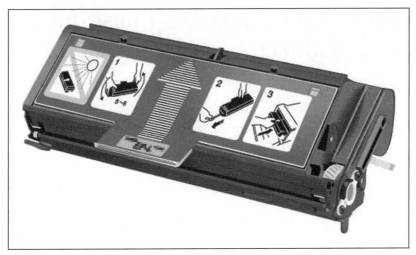

Figure 18-3: A laser printer toner cartridge.

Because older laser printers and photocopiers have a fixed print drum, they commonly experience scratches and grooves on the drum that are caused by paper bits, staples, or other foreign bodies that fall into the printer. These problems are far less common on printers with the print drum sealed inside a cartridge.

Toner

Toner, the dry granulated ink used in a laser printer, is made from the following ingredients (listed by declining amount used):

- ◆ *Plastic:* Each toner particle is coated with an outer layer of styrene plastic or a blend of styrene and acrylic plastics. The plastic melts in the fusing phase to bond to the paper.

- ◆ *Iron:* Toner particles contain as much as 40 percent *ferrous oxide,* which is a magnetic iron material. During the print process, toner is negatively charged so that it will be attracted to the drum and paper to form a document image.

- ◆ *Silica:* Silica is a very fine sand-like material that prevents the toner from clumping.

- ◆ *Charge dye:* This special dye helps control the amount of electrostatic charge that the toner can hold.

- ◆ *Wax:* When the wax melts during the fusing phase, it helps the toner flow and blend.

- ◆ *Carbon black:* This is added to black toner to deepen the color.

Maintaining and Troubleshooting a Laser Printer

As I explain earlier in this chapter, unless you are specially trained to repair and maintain a laser printer, you should only attempt the most basic of troubleshooting and repair on one. The voltages inside a laser computer, along with the heat, are things that you shouldn't be messing around with.

However, the following sections do include some steps and processes that you can use to take care of and to make minor repairs on a laser printer.

Caring for a laser printer

Laser printers have special needs when it comes to maintenance. The following sections contain tips to help you care for a laser printer.

TONER SPILLS

Toner cartridges are typically sealed units that require you to remove a strip, tape, or tab before installing them in a laser printer.

Toner incidents are rare, but if you ever spill toner either inside or outside the printer, **don't** use a standard vacuum cleaner to clean it up. Because toner comprises very fine particles of iron and plastic, trying to vacuum it will result in it seeping through the walls of most vacuum bags and getting into the motor where it will melt and clog up the works. Special vacuums and vacuum bags are made for dealing with toner.

Never rinse toner off your skin with hot or even warm water. Hot water can cause toner to fuse to your skin. Wipe off as much toner as you can with a dry paper towel or soft cloth. Then rinse your skin with cold water and finish up by washing with soap and cold water.

Usually packed with a new toner cartridge is a cleaning brush or large plastic wand with a cotton pad that can be used to clean the transfer corona wire. You should clean the corona wires each time that you change a cartridge but only after the printer has cooled down. Be gentle when cleaning these wires because they are breakable.

OZONE

During the print process, a laser printer produces ozone gas. Most laser printers have an ozone filter that captures the ozone gas as well as toner dust and paper dust.

The ozone filter should be replaced or at least cleaned in accordance with the manufacturer's instructions, which are usually included in the owner's manual for the printer.

Spare filters are usually shipped with the printer. If not, contact the manufacturer or vendor to get spare ozone filters.

MIRRORS

Inside the laser printer are two or more multi-sided mirrors that are used to reflect the laser onto the drum. Periodically clean these mirrors with a clean, lint-free cloth.

When cleaning printer mirrors, be sure that the power is off and that the unit is unplugged. **Never ever,** repeat, **never** look directly at the laser — it could harm your eyes. Along this line, **never** operate the printer with its covers off. (Most printers will not power up with a cover open, anyway.)

FUSER PADS AND ROLLERS

The fuser cleaning pad (that cleans the fusing roller after it presses the melted toner onto the paper) and the fusing roller can become dirty and begin to leave unwanted toner blobs on the paper. Check the fuser cleaning pad and the fuser rollers regularly and clean them as necessary. If the fuser rollers become too dirty to properly clean, check with the manufacturer for a replacement fuser roller kit.

Be careful around the fuser part of a laser printer. Typically covered for your safety, the fuser roller can get very hot when printing. Wait at least one hour for the laser to cool down before you begin cleaning in the fuser area.

Perhaps the best way to clean the fuser cleaning pad and the fuser roller — after they've cooled — is with either the fuser cleaning wand included with the printer or a cotton swab and a bit of isopropyl alcohol. Don't soak the area with alcohol because an alcohol fire could start if the fuser area is still hot.

> **TIP** Avoid touching any of the rollers in a laser printer with your fingers or hands. The oil on your skin (it's there whether you know it or not) can contaminate the rollers, especially warm rollers, and reduce the friction needed for the rollers to move the paper along its path.

Connecting a printer to a network

With the cost of a high-quality, high-volume laser printer, its best and most efficient use is likely as a workgroup printer attached to a network. You should share an expensive resource, such as a high-end color laser printer, among several PCs by placing the printer on a local area network (LAN). Printers to be shared over a network can be purchased network-ready or can be easily adapted for connecting to a network.

Network-ready printers have an internal network adapter into which an RJ-45 network connector can be inserted. A printer that's not network ready can be attached to a network through a network printer interface such as Hewlett-Packard's JetDirect. These devices can be used to connect one or more printers to the network. A printer connects to a network interface device through its parallel port. The network interface device provides the network adapter that interfaces the printer to the network. Figure 18-4 illustrates both a network-ready printer connected directly to the network and another printer that's not network ready connected with a network interface device.

It isn't absolutely necessary to directly connect a printer to a network in order for network users to share it. A printer connected to a networked PC via a USB or parallel connection can be shared with other users by configuring it as a sharable device through the Windows File and Print Sharing service.

Safeguarding a printer

Here are a number of common sense procedures (and a few more technical ones) that you can use to keep a printer working and reliable:

◆ *Cleaning:* If you wish to vacuum out a laser printer, be sure that you use only a toner vacuum and dust bag specially made for this task. The toner can really gum up the works of a regular vacuum cleaner.

◆ *Paper:* Always use the type and weights of paper recommended by the manufacturer for the printer and never use paper heavier than the recommended maximum weight. This will help avoid print feed and paper path jams. Some printers prefer laser printer paper that's finished on one side. Check your printer's documentation.

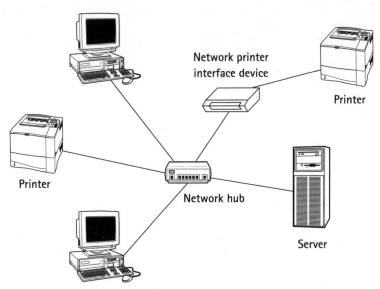

Figure 18-4: Many users can share a printer over a network.

◆ *Power protection:* You should never plug a laser printer into a conventional uninterruptible power supply (UPS). Laser printers draw a tremendous amount of power at startup, and few UPS units have enough power to handle the demand. If you use a UPS for your laser printer, be sure that the UPS can handle the peak loading (peak power requirements) of the laser printer.

◆ *Safety:* Never put anything inside a laser printer to try to clear the paper path while it's running, and always wait until the fusing area has cooled down before working in that area of a laser printer. The fusing area uses high heat to melt the toner and stays hot for some time afterward.

Part VI

Keyboards and Pointing Devices

Chapter 19

Keyboards

IN THIS CHAPTER
In this chapter, I cover the following keyboard-related topics:

◆ Troubleshooting the keyboard

◆ Solving keyboard boot sequence problems

◆ Setting keyboard controls on a Windows PC

◆ Setting the accessibility options on a Windows PC

◆ Configuring the Basic Input/Output System (BIOS) settings of a keyboard

◆ Performing preventive maintenance on a keyboard

A KEYBOARD, which is the most commonly used input device, allows users to communicate with a PC through keystrokes that represent data and commands. Every PC includes a keyboard in its standard package.

Looking Technically at Keyboards

Despite its many variations and styles, a keyboard, like the one shown in Figure 19-1, has been standardized to use the same basic keyboard layout, attach to a PC with standard connectors, and be interchangeable between manufacturers.

Figure 19-1: A typical PC keyboard.

The layout of a PC keyboard – the alphabetic, numeric, and special character keys – can vary by continent (North America or Europe), country (France), or language (Chinese). However, with a few minor exceptions, virtually all English language keyboards are the same. The keys on a typical keyboard can be grouped into functional groups, as illustrated in Figure 19-2:

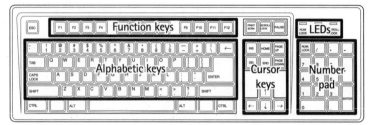

Figure 19–2: The major key groupings on a keyboard.

♦ *Alphabetic keys:* The alphabetic keys form the main body of the keyboard and the row of numbers and special characters above them. These keys typically have the same layout as on a QWERTY-layout typewriter.

♦ *Cursor keys:* Found only on keyboards with more than 100 keys, this group of keys, which is located to the right of the alphabetic keys, has two smaller groups: the cursor control keys and the cursor command keys.

♦ *Number pad keys:* All PC keyboards have a number pad in one form or another. On older 83- and 84-key keyboards, the number pad is placed alongside the alphabetic keys. Newer keyboards, with 101, 104, and 105 keys, place the number pad on the extreme right-hand side. The standard number pad has 10 number keys and keys for the four arithmetic functions (add, subtract, divide, and multiply). By toggling off the Num Lock key, the number pad can also be used as a cursor control pad.

♦ *Function keys:* A keyboard with less than 100 keys usually has only 8 function keys that are located in two rows on the left-hand side of the keyboard. Newer keyboards typically have a single row of 12 function keys that are placed across the very top of a keyboard.

Alphabetic keys

These keys make up the main area of the keyboard. The specific keys included in this area are

♦ *Alphabetic keys:* There is a key for each of the 26 English language alphabet characters of A through Z. The default is for a lowercase character, but pressing and holding the Shift key or pressing the Caps Lock key and then pressing the character key can generate an uppercase letter.

♦ *Special characters and punctuation:* These keys, which are located along the right side of the alphabetic keys, are the following: \ (backslash), | (vertical bar), / (forward slash), ? (question mark), . (period/dot), > (greater than), , (comma), < (less than), ; (semi-colon), : (colon), ' (single quote/apostrophe), " (double-quote), [(open/left bracket), { (open/left brace),] (close/right bracket), and } (close/right brace). These keys are paired on keys as lowercase keys and uppercase keys that are selected through the Shift/Caps Lock key.

♦ *Action keys:* This group of keys contains the primary action key of the keyboard — the Enter key — and two key subgroups: the character selection keys and the command action keys.

  ▪ *Enter key:* This might be the most-used key on the keyboard and is generally the largest. The Enter key is used to end a command, text line, or an entry in an application, as well as serve as a trigger or other action button in a game.

  ▪ *Character selection keys:* The character selection keys are the two (right and left) Shift keys, the Caps Lock key, and the Backspace key. The Shift keys toggle an alphabetic, numeric, punctuation, or special character key between its lowercase and uppercase choices. The Caps Lock key locks the alphabetic keys into their uppercase characters. The Backspace key erases a character by replacing it with the character or white space that follows it.

  ▪ *Command action keys:* These keys include the two (right and left) Control (Ctrl) keys, the Escape (Esc) key, and the two (right and left) Alternate Control (Alt) keys. The Ctrl and Alt keys are used mostly to create key combinations with alphabetic, numeric, and function keys for actions or commands to software programs.

♦ *White space keys: White space* is any empty space on a page either between characters, words, lines, or paragraphs. The keys that create white space are the spacebar and Tab keys. Pressing the spacebar produces one character of white space per keystroke, and pressing the Tab key defaults to $1/2$" of white space. The value of the Tab key — that is, the length of space that it creates — can be adjusted in most word processing applications.

♦ *Number/Special character keys:* The 12 or 13 keys in the row across the top of the alphabetic keys contain 24 or 26 different numbers and special characters. Half of these values can be typed in the key's unshifted mode and the remaining half by using the Shift key. The number keys (1–9 and 0) are standard on all keyboards, but the special characters located on these keys vary by region. The special character keys, most of which are accessed with the Shift key, are: ~ (tilde), ` (accent grave), ! (exclamation point), @ (each at sign), # (pound or number sign), $ (dollar sign), % (percent sign), ˆ (caret), & (ampersand), * (asterisk), ((opening/left parenthesis),) (closing/right parenthesis), - (dash/hyphen), _ (underscore), = (equal sign), and + (plus sign).

Toggle keys and locks

The Shift, Control, and Alt keys are *toggle keys,* which are keys that are used to toggle another key between two or more values. On most keys, the two values that a key represents are a *default* value (the value of the key when no toggle key is used to modify its value) and an *alternate* value (selected when a toggle key is pressed). For example, pressing the A key without pressing the Shift key produces the lowercase character *a* (assuming that the Caps Lock key is not locked), which is the key's default value. Pressing and holding the Shift key and then pressing the A key produces the uppercase character *A,* or the key's alternate value. Pressing and holding the Shift key toggles any alphabetic key to its uppercase or alternate value. The toggle value is only in effect while a toggle key is being pressed. When the key is released, the value reverts to its default.

Locking keys, which are the Caps Lock, Num Lock, and Scroll Lock keys, also toggle between two actions or values. However, unlike the Shift, Control, and Alt keys, they must be pressed a second time to release the toggle. Locking keys work something like an on/off button on a monitor. When the button is pressed, the monitor is powered on and stays on until the button is pressed again to power the monitor off. When the Caps Lock key is pressed, it has the same effect as pressing the Shift key permanently. The Caps Lock key only affects the alphabetic characters, which are shifted to uppercase as their default values. In fact, if you use the Shift key after the Caps Lock key is pressed, the shifted value will be a lowercase character. The Num Lock key toggles on and off the number pad, alternating it into a cursor control pad. The Scroll Lock key enables and disables software control for the scrolling of the display.

Repeating keystrokes

Many keyboards and operating systems allow you to repeat a key (virtually forever) by merely holding it down. This is *typematic key function.* You can set the typematic settings for a keyboard via the Windows Control Panel's Keyboard icon (which open the Keyboard Properties window, as shown in Figure 19-3) by choosing Start → Settings → Control Panel.

Cursor keys

Keyboards with 101 or more keys include a separate group of cursor control keys than those on the alternate positions of the number pad keys. The Num Lock key can be used to toggle the number pad into a cursor control pad. On the 101-key design and the keyboard designs that followed it, two small sets of keys are included to provide for cursor movement and control. Located between the alphabetic keys and the number pad, one is a set of four dedicated cursor *(arrow)* keys and the other a six-key set of cursor action *(navigation)* keys.

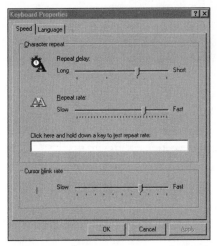

Figure 19-3: Control the repeat of repeating keys here.

These groups of keys comprise

◆ *Cursor control (arrow) keys:* These four directional keys, which are supported by virtually all software, are used to move the cursor left, up, down, or right on the screen. A large percentage of PC game software uses these keys to move characters through scenes by assigning each key to a point of the compass (up is north, down is south, right is east, and left is west). Some higher-end keyboards add an additional four keys that are used to move the cursor in diagonal directions between the directions of the four standard keys.

◆ *Cursor command/navigation keys:* This is a group of six keys located immediately above the cursor control keys, just to the right of the alphabetic keys. These keys duplicate the six cursor commands and control functions of keys located in the number pad. These keys allow the number pad to remain in use while the cursor is being manipulated. The keys included in this group are Insert, Delete, Home, End, Page Up (PgUp), and Page Down (PgDn).

  ■ *Insert:* This key is a locking key that toggles software between insert and replace modes. *Insert mode,* which is the default mode for most word processing systems, inserts characters at the point indicated by the cursor. *Replace mode,* also called *type-over mode,* replaces any existing characters with characters being entered.

  ■ *Delete:* Although the function of this key is typically controlled by software, it is generally used to erase a single character to the right of the cursor or to delete a selected object.

- *Home* and *End:* In most applications, the Home key is used to position the cursor at the beginning of a text line; and its opposite, the End key, is used to move the cursor to the end of a text line. When used with the Control key, pressing the Home key moves the cursor to the beginning of a document and pressing the End key moves the cursor to the end or bottom of a document.

- *Page Up* and *Page Down:* These two keys are used to scroll the screen up or down to the previous or next page, respectively. One page in this context is the amount of a document that the screen can display.

The number pad

Although every one of the number pad's keys is duplicated somewhere on a keyboard, these keys were added as a standard feature of PC keyboards to aid in the entry of numeric data. The layout of the number pad, shown in Figure 19-4, duplicates the keys on a ten-key calculator, adding machine, or keypunch machine. For the many users who must enter large volumes of numeric data, the numeric keypad is an absolute necessity.

The keys on the number pad are

- *Num Lock:* This locking key toggles and locks the number pad between its function as a number pad and its cursor control function. The state (on or off) of the Num Lock key is assigned during the boot sequence and can be set in the PC's BIOS settings. Virtually all PCs lock the Num Lock key on during the boot.

- *Arithmetic operators:* The keys for the four standard arithmetic operators, / (divide), * (multiply), – (subtract), and + (add) are included around the upper edge and side of the number pad.

- *Number/cursor keys:* When the Num Lock key is toggled on (and the Num Lock light-emitting diode [LED] is lighted), the ten number keys type the digits 0–9. When the Num Lock key is toggled off (the LED is off), these keys are now cursor control keys, including keys for diagonal movement.

- *Insert/Delete:* These two keys are the zero and decimal point of the number pad when it is in number mode, but in cursor control mode, they duplicate the actions of the Insert key and the Delete key.

- *Enter:* The number pad includes an Enter key so that the end of a number or entry can be marked without leaving the number pad.

Figure 19-4: The number pad on a standard keyboard.

Function keys

The top row of all newer keyboards contains 12 function (F) keys that are controlled strictly by software and have no default functions of their own. Some software applications make extensive use of the function keys, such as Corel's WordPerfect and the MS-DOS operating system. For example, on the MS-DOS (and Windows) command line, pressing the F3 key is used to repeat the last line entered. In WordPerfect, pressing F7 exits the program, and pressing the Shift key and the F7 keys together prints a document.

In virtually all Windows applications, pressing the F1 key is used to open the Help system.

The earliest PCs had ten function keys on the left side of the keyboard arranged in two columns of five keys. When the enhanced (101-key) keyboards were introduced, the function keys expanded to 12 keys and were placed on the top edge of the keyboard partly to make room for the cursor keys.

Special-purpose keys

You'll find a few special purpose keys on the standard keyboard. For the most part, users rarely or never use these keys because they aren't supported by all software — and even when they are, the need for their functions aren't frequently required. These keys are

♦ *Esc:* The Escape (Esc) key is typically enabled as either an exit or cancellation key by most software. It is used to either cancel a command or to exit an application, such as its use in Windows to close a context menu. It can also be used in combination with other keys to create a special key value, such as with the Control key to access the BIOS settings of a PC.

♦ *Print Screen/SysRq:* The Print Screen (Print Scrn) key is used on an MS-DOS system to send the contents of the display to the printer. On a Windows PC, the Print Screen key sends the contents of the display to the Windows Clipboard. Figure 19-5 shows a screen capture generated by the Print Screen key in the Windows Clipboard Viewer. The System Request (SysRq) mode of this key has no real function on most PCs unless the PC is emulating an IBM terminal connected to a mainframe computer — and then only if the terminal emulation software supports it.

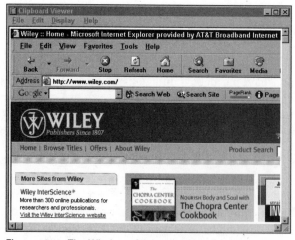

Figure 19-5: The Windows Clipboard Viewer showing a screen captured by pressing the Print Screen key.

◆ *Scroll Lock:* Originally, when this key was pressed, it would pause the text display scrolling on the display screen, and pressing it again would release the pause and allow the display to resume its scrolling. However, this key is now available only if it's supported by software (and most of today's software does not) for whatever purpose the software wishes to assign to it.

◆ *Pause/Break:* If this key has been enabled by software, its default mode (Pause) freezes the display or pauses the action of an application program. The Control key toggles this key in the same manner as how the Shift key is used with other keys. When used with the Control key, it interrupts or halts some software programs, primarily MS-DOS commands and applications.

Windows menu keys

The difference between a 101-key and a 104-key keyboard are three Windows-specific keys that provide shortcuts to Windows menus. Figure 19-6 shows the two keys on the right of the spacebar; the third Windows-specific key is found to the left of the spacebar.

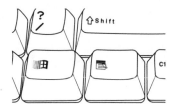

Figure 19-6: The two Windows keys to the right of the spacebar are used to display the Windows Start menu and the current context menu.

◆ *Windows keys:* These keys, which are marked with a flying Window symbol, pop up the Windows Start menu when pressed. However, when used in combination with other keys, they perform the equivalent of several keystrokes to display menus, start applets, or open windows.

◆ *Context Menu key:* This lone key is located on the right side of the spacebar between the Windows key and the Control key. Pressing the Context Menu key performs the same action as right-clicking the display to pop up a context menu for the current application.

Sizing Up Keyboard Form Factors

The PC keyboard has evolved from its beginning on the first PCs where it was not much more than a typewriter keyboard attached to a PC to the sophisticated multi-function input device of today.

Enhanced keyboards

In 1986, IBM released its last PC AT model (Model 339) that included what IBM called an *enhanced* keyboard. This 101-key keyboard continues to be the de facto standard for all newer systems. The 17 keys that were added to the 84-key keyboard that preceded this keyboard are dedicated cursor control keys, multiply and divide keys on the number pad, Control and Alt keys on the right side of the spacebar, and two more function keys.

The 101-key keyboard has variations in virtually all non-English speaking regions of the world. The variations of the keyboard from one region to the next are primarily that the keys on the keyboard are moved or replaced. For example, the top row of keys on an English-language keyboard begins with the QWERTY keys (Q, W, E, R, T, and Y). In France and other countries, the top row of keys comprises AZERTY (A, Z, E, R, T, and Y) with other characters also rearranged.

Windows keyboards

The current standard for keyboard layout is the Windows keyboard that features 104 keys. The three keys added to the 101-key design are the Windows and Context Menu keys that I discuss in the earlier section "Windows menu keys."

Natural keyboards

In an attempt to relieve repetitive stress injuries (such as carpal tunnel syndrome) that can be caused by the position of a user's hands and wrists when using a standard keyboard, manufacturers have developed keyboard designs that reshape the keyboard so that the user's hands and wrists are in a more natural position. These popular keyboards, like the one in Figure 19-7, are *natural* or *ergonomic* keyboards.

Portable PC keyboards

The keyboard of a notebook computer with the same number of keys must be smaller than a normal keyboard just to fit inside the portable PC's case. To accomplish this feat, the arrangement, layout, and even function of the keys must be altered slightly, resulting in a keyboard that is small with the keys more closely placed and a non-standard layout that locates the cursor control and number pad keys either in the alphabetic keyboard or as alternate values on other keys. Many notebook PCs include a special Function (Fn) key that is used like a Shift or Control key to modify Function keys to control display, sound, and other input/output (I/O) actions of the PC.

Figure 19-7: A natural, ergonomic-style keyboard.

Figure 19-8 shows a sample keyboard of a notebook PC. Notebook PCs with larger displays have more room for the keyboard. A notebook PC with a 12-inch display has a fairly limited space for a keyboard dictated by the PC's overall size. However, a notebook with a 15-inch display, like the one in Figure 19-8, has more overall size to accommodate the keyboard and provide for a better arrangement of the keys. Notice the touchpad at the bottom of the keyboard in Figure 19-8. See Chapter 20 for more information on touchpads and other pointing devices.

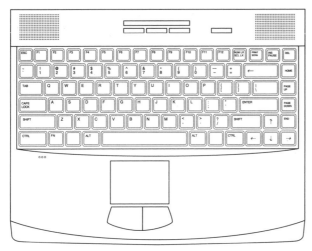

Figure 19-8: The keyboard on a notebook PC.

Notebook PCs also provide PS/2 and Universal Serial Bus (USB) ports that can be used for an external standard keyboard and mouse. An external number pad can also be added to compensate for the lack of a dedicated number pad on virtually all portable PCs.

In the Beginning: Early Keyboards

The very first PC keyboards, those of the IBM PC and PC XT, had 83 keys (over 20 keys fewer than most current keyboards). The IBM PC keyboard, which established the design basis for all future PC keyboards, established some enduring characteristics, including that it was a separate device from the PC; it had 10 software-controlled function keys; and it included a 10-key number/cursor control pad. The PC AT keyboard had 84 keys (it added the System Request key) but improved on the spacing of the keys, enlarged the Shift and Enter keys, and added the three LED indicators for the Caps Lock, Num Lock, and Scroll Lock keys.

Miscellaneous keyboard styles

Several so-called "Internet" keyboards are available that include buttons preprogrammed to connect to the Internet, open a browser, or check e-mail. Multimedia keyboards include audio controls, such as the sound volume and CD controls (play, stop, pause, previous, next, and others), as illustrated in Figure 19-9. Several new designs have buttons to perform the same actions as the buttons on a mouse, and some have a mouse, trackball, or touchpad built right into the keyboard on the style of a portable PC. And outside of North America, these keyboards also have power management buttons as well.

Figure 19-9: A multimedia keyboard.

Photo courtesy of Belkin Components.

Digging into Keyboard Technology

Beneath each key on the keyboard is a *keyswitch,* which closes a circuit or creates a change in an electrical field when its keycap is pressed. Each key on the keyboard is a combination of a *keycap* (which provides a surface for fingers) and a *keyswitch* (which registers the keystroke). Here is a simplification of the events that occur when a key is pressed on a keyboard:

1. All the keys of the keyboard are either attached to or are a part of a grid or matrix that is constantly being scanned by the keyboard's built-in processor. When a key is pressed, the keyswitch contacts the grid and is detected by the keyboard processor, which then assigns a scan code to the keystroke data based on its grid position. The keys, as indicated by the keycaps, remain in the same positions at all times. The A key is always the A key, allowing the processor to remember the scan code, which represents only a key's grid position and not the character printed on its keycap.

2. The keyboard processor clocks the scan code to the PC's keyboard interface. The keyboard processor sends the scan code data over a serial line in the keyboard's interface cable along with clock signals that are sent over the clocking line of the cable. The clocking data helps the PC know when keystroke data begins and ends.

3. After the keyboard interface receives the keystroke data, it starts the keyboard service routine that converts the scan code data and the keyboard status byte (which indicates whether the Shift, Control, or Alt keys are in use) into the two-byte key code that is put into the keyboard buffer.

4. The key code indicates the American Standard Code for Information Interchange (ASCII) code of the character. The keystroke's ASCII code is passed to the application.

Make and break codes

Two different codes are actually used to indicate the beginning and ending of a keystroke. When the keyboard processor detects that a key has been pressed, a *make code* is sent to the PC; and when the key is released, a *break code* is sent. Each key location on the grid has a unique pair of make and break codes, which are used by the PC to determine both the character or value associated with the keystroke and whether the keystroke is beginning or ending. If a key is held down, the keyboard controller sends a scan code for each scan of the keyboard until the key is released. This is how you can repeat a key simply by holding it down. Table 19-1 lists a few of the scan codes of most 101-key and 104-key keyboards.

TABLE 19-1 SAMPLE MAKE AND BREAK CODES

Key	Make Code	Break Code
1	16	F0 16
0	45	F0 45
Backspace	66	F0 66
Q	15	F0 15
A	1C	F0 1C
Enter	5A	F0 5A
Right Shift	59	F0 59
Left Control	14	F0 14
Space	29	F0 29
Escape	76	F0 76
F1	05	F0 05
Num Lock	77	F0 77
Insert	E0 70	E0 F0 70
Page Up	E0 7D	E0 F0 7D
Delete	E0 71	E0 F0 71
Up arrow	E0 75	E0 F0 75
Print Screen	E0 12 E0 7C	E0 F0 7C E0 F0 12

To type an uppercase A, for example, the following actions take place:

1. The right Shift key is pressed and held, which causes the make code for the right Shift key (59) to be sent to the keyboard interface.

2. The A key is pressed, and the A key's make code (1C) is sent.

3. The A key is released, and the A key's break code (F0 1C) is sent.

4. The right Shift key is released, which causes the right Shift key's break code (F0 59) to be sent to the keyboard interface.

When the keyboard interface receives the break code, it translates the make code into its ASCII equivalent and stores it in the keyboard buffer in RAM. Scan codes and ASCII codes are represented as hexadecimal values. For more information on hexadecimal values, see Chapter 2. A few of the ASCII values used with PC keyboards are listed in Table 19-2.

TABLE 19-2 PC ASCII CODES

Character	Hexadecimal
Space	20
!	21
"	22
0	30
1	31
2	32
=	3D
>	3E
?	3F
A	41
B	42
C	43
H	48
I	49
J	4A
a	61
b	62
c	63

Keyswitches

The keyswitches used in a PC keyboard are typically one of two general types: contact or capacitive switches. Most users cannot tell the difference between these two switch types or their variations, but there are differences among the various types.

CONTACT KEYSWITCHES

For a contact keyswitch to complete a circuit, two parts of the switch must make contact. The two types of contact keyswitches commonly used in PC keyboards are

◆ *Foam and foil keyswitch:* The core of this keyswitch is a foam pad that has a piece of foil on its underside. When the key is pressed, a plunger presses the foam pad and its foil into contact with a pair of copper contacts on the keyboard's circuit board.

◆ *Rubber dome keyswitch:* The core of this keyswitch is a small rounded dome of rubber that has a pad of carbon material on its underside. When the key is pressed, a plunger presses down on the rubber that collapses under the pressure, and the carbon contacts the circuit board to complete the circuit. This type of keyswitch is the most common type used in current keyboards.

CAPACITIVE KEYSWITCHES

Capacitive keyswitches operate on the general capacitance principles of a capacitor. A *capacitor* stores an electrical charge between two metal plates, and the energy in the charge is its capacitance. As the plates move closer together or farther apart, the capacitance changes. The change in the capacitance signals that a keystroke has occurred.

A capacitive keyswitch has a plunger on which a metal plate is attached at the bottom. At the bottom of the switch and beneath the plunger is another metal plate. When the plunger is pressed, the space between the plates is reduced (or increased in some designs) to create a change in the capacitance of the switch. The keyboard controller's circuitry detects the change in capacitance, and a keystroke is generated.

Keyboard controller

The *keyboard controller* consists of a microprocessor and a read only memory (ROM) chip that holds the keyboard processor's instructions. The keyboard controller constantly scans the keyboard grid, which is typically a circuit board beneath the keys. Any keystrokes detected are translated into scan codes and transmitted to the PC.

Keyboard cable

The keyboard's *interface cable* is a four-wire cable that carries the signals sent between the PC and the keyboard: data, clocking, ground, and power. The cable has four plastic-coated copper wires around which a metal grounding sheath is placed. The wire bundle is covered with a thick plastic or rubber outer sheath. The cable is usually four to six feet in length and is typically a straight cable, although coiled cables are also common. If the keyboard requires additional length, a keyboard cable extension can be used to extend it.

Keyboard connectors

Keyboards attach to a PC through one of five connector types:

◆ *5-pin DIN connector:* Also known as the *AT connector,* this connector has been used since the very first PCs. Deutsche Industrie Norm (DIN) is a German standards organization that developed the round connector style used on this and the 6-pin version of this connector. Only four of the five pins in this connector are used: clocking (pin 1), data (pin 2), ground (pin 4), and +5 volt (v) of power (pin 5).

◆ *6-pin mini-DIN (PS/2) connector:* This DIN connector is smaller than the 5-pin AT connector and uses four of its six pins for data (pin 1), ground (pin 3), +5v of power (pin 4), and clocking (pin 5). This connector, now the standard for virtually all cabled keyboards, is also called the *PS/2 connector* because it was first introduced with the IBM PS/2 computers. Figure 19-10 shows this connector.

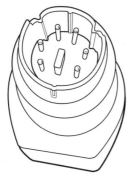

Figure 19–10: A 6-pin mini-DIN (PS/2) connector is standard on most PC keyboards.

◆ *Universal Serial Bus (USB) connector:* The USB connector, shown in Figure 19-11, is becoming a common connector for keyboards (and mice). This connector is useful when a notebook computer has only one PS/2 port and both an external keyboard and a mouse are to be connected.

◆ *Infrared Data Association (IrDA) connector:* Several keyboard styles are available with an infrared (IR) cordless interface for use with desktop and notebook PCs that support the IrDA standard interface, which is that small red plastic window on the front, side, or back of the PC. IR devices require a direct, unobstructed, line of sight between the transmitter and receiver to work properly.

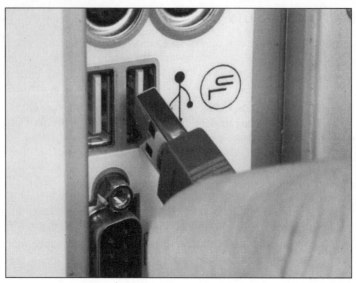

Figure 19-11: A USB connector and port.

◆ *Radio frequency (RF) connection:* Radio frequency (RF) is the most common form of cordless connection used to connect a keyboard (or mouse) to a PC. Unlike IR devices, an RF device doesn't need a line of sight to work. An RF keyboard communicates to the PC through a transceiver that attaches through either a PS/2 or USB port.

Troubleshooting the Keyboard

Keyboards are considered throwaway technology. They can be repaired, but the time, expense, and risk of introducing other problems usually mandates just replacing a problem keyboard. However, before the keyboard is blamed for a problem that might actually be on the motherboard, the following steps should be performed:

1. Power off the computer.

2. Unplug the keyboard connector from the motherboard.

3. Power on the computer.

4. Use a digital multimeter to check the voltages of the connector pins.

   If all the connector's voltages are in range – which is normally in the range of +2v to +5.5v, depending on the pin – the problem is probably in the motherboard's keyboard interface circuits. The keyboard's documentation should list the specific voltage for each pin in the connector.

5. If the voltages in the connector check out, connect a known-good keyboard and reboot the system.

   If the new keyboard also fails to work, the problem is likely on the motherboard or its connector. Before replacing the motherboard because of a bad keyboard port, consider a USB keyboard if a USB port is available.

 You should never install a PS/2 connector in a port while the PC is powered up because it could damage the bus circuitry on the motherboard. If the new keyboard works, the original keyboard is bad.

Solving keyboard boot sequence problems

Keyboard-related problems, which are extremely rare, are usually detected during the Power-On Self-Test (POST) process. If the POST should detect a keyboard problem, a beep code is sounded. Remember that the beep codes are unique to the BIOS on a PC, so check the documentation of the motherboard or BIOS or visit the BIOS manufacturer's Web site for the beep code set in use. If the keyboard error is detected after the POST completes, a boot error message with an error code in the 300–399 number range is displayed.

The most common keyboard boot error is a keystroke detected during the POST. This could be the result of a stuck key, an accidentally pressed key, someone leaning on the keyboard, or a book laying on the keyboard. The remedy is simple: Clear the problem and reboot the computer.

Setting keyboard controls on a Windows PC

On Windows 9*x* and NT PCs, the Keyboard Properties options (choose Start → Settings → Control Panel) include some settings that can be used to adjust and set the language set of the keyboard as well as a few performance levels. Click the Keyboard icon to open the Keyboard Properties window, which has two tabs:

◆ *Speed tab:* This tab contains the typematic settings for the keyboard, which include the amount of time between repeated characters, how quickly a character repeats when you hold down a key on the keyboard, and how fast the cursor blinks on the display. These speed settings are each controlled by a slider that sets the rate between long and short or slow and fast, as applicable. For most folks, the default settings are usually okay.

◆ *Language:* This tab is used to set the language of the keyboard. To see the list of available languages (including the eight versions of English) that Windows supports by default, click the Add button. If you wish to add a different language, you'll need the Windows CD or a disk with the appropriate keyboard device driver. If you wish to have multiple languages available on a system, you can enable them here and assign shortcut keys so that you can easily switch between them. If you want an indicator in the system tray, that option is also available.

On a Windows 2000 or Windows XP PC, the Keyboard Properties window has three tabs:

◆ *Speed:* This tab contains the same settings and performs the same functions as the Speed tab on any Windows system.

◆ *Input Locales:* The settings on this tab allow you to control input locales and to configure the keyboard.

◆ *Hardware:* This tab is used to troubleshoot and configure keyboard device properties.

Setting the accessibility options on a Windows PC

Windows includes the Accessibility Properties (via the Control Panel) to help make a PC easier for people with physical limitations to use. As shown in Figure 19-12, the options indicated by the tabs on the Accessibility Properties window allow the keyboard, display, sound system, and mouse to have customized settings to meet the particular needs of challenged users.

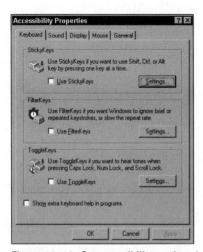

Figure 19-12: Set accessibility options here.

The Keyboard tab contains the following options:

♦ *StickyKeys:* This feature converts the Shift, Control, and Alt keys into locking keys that stay toggled until they are pressed again. This allows someone able to press only a single key at a time to complete key combinations, such as Control+Alt+Delete or Ctrl+Shift+F7.

♦ *FilterKeys:* Recognizing that some users might not be able to release a key as quickly as would normally be required without repeating the key, this option works like the opposite of the typematic features.

♦ *ToggleKeys:* This feature enables or disables an audible tone that sounds when any locking key is pressed. This option is the sound equivalent of the LEDs illuminating on the keyboard.

Configuring the BIOS settings of a keyboard

The BIOS contains a number of settings that can affect the operation of the keyboard. Here are the most important ones to check:

♦ *Halt On/Halt on Errors:* This option tells the BIOS whether it should stop and display error messages when a certain error is detected during the POST or boot. This is important for systems that might not have a keyboard attached when booted, such as a server. The All Errors but Keyboard setting instructs the BIOS to continue to boot if the only error is a bad or a missing keyboard.

♦ *Keyboard Present:* This BIOS configuration setting is a very specific indication as to whether a keyboard is attached to the system (Yes) or not (No).

♦ *Typematic Delay:* Although this can also be set in Windows, this value (in milliseconds) can also be set in the BIOS data.

♦ *Typematic Rate:* This option can also be set via the Keyboard Properties of the Windows system or from the BIOS (in characters per second).

♦ *USB Legacy Support:* This option is not on every BIOS; but on those that support it, it allows a USB keyboard to be used.

Chapter 27 includes information on the preventive care and maintenance of keyboards.

Chapter 20

Mice and Other Pointing Devices

IN THIS CHAPTER
In this chapter, I cover the following mouse/pointing device topics:

◆ Cleaning a dirty mouse

◆ Installing a mouse

◆ Troubleshooting an optomechanical mouse

◆ Configuring a mouse on a Windows PC

◆ Installing a joystick

THE PC MOUSE is a natural, intuitive, and inexpensive pointing device that has become a standard part of the PC's hardware. Introduced by Microsoft but popularized by the Apple Macintosh, the PC mouse really gained popularity after Windows and its graphic user interface (GUI) were released. Virtually every PC sold today includes a mouse as standard equipment.

Catching Up on the Mouse

The three types of mouse units used with PCs are

◆ *Mechanical mouse:* This type of mouse was used with early Macintosh and PC GUI systems. In a mechanical mouse, moving a rubber ball causes a pair of wheels to spin. Sensors detect the movement of the wheels, and signals are sent to the PC.

◆ *Optomechanical mouse:* This type of mouse uses light-emitting diodes (LEDs) to sense mouse movements. This is the most commonly used type of mouse.

◆ *Optical mouse:* This type of mouse has no moving parts, and the mechanical devices (balls, rollers, and wheels) are replaced with an optical scanning system that detects the movement of the mouse over virtually any surface.

509

Standard mouse

If such a thing as a standard mouse exists, it's the 2- or 3-button roller ball mouse that's basically not all that much different functionally than the mouse developed at the Xerox Stanford Palo Alto Research Park (SPARC) by Douglas Engelbardt back in the 1960s.

This type of mouse, which is shown in Figure 20-1, is still the most commonly used type of mouse for PCs.

Figure 20-1: A PC mouse.

Wheel mouse

The wheel mouse, shown in Figure 20-2, gets its name from a finger wheel that's usually placed between its buttons and can be used to scroll the display. The wheel allows the user to scroll forward and backward through a document in place of clicking a window's scroll bar or using the Page Up and Page Down keys or buttons or the cursor control arrow keys.

Figure 20-2: An example of a wheel mouse.

Optical mouse

The optical mouse replaces the mouse ball with optical sensors that track the movement of the mouse over whatever surface it passes over. The bottom of an optical mouse is shown in Figure 20-3. Older optical mice required a highly reflective mousepad with a printed grid that was used to detect movement. This mouse did eliminate the mouse ball and its inherent problems, but it was slow — and if the mousepad were lost, the mouse couldn't work.

A newer optical mouse captures images of the surface under the mouse at more than 1,500 images per second. A Digital Signal Processor (DSP) inside the mouse analyzes and compares the images to detect even the slightest movement of the mouse. This optical mouse design works on virtually any flat surface and doesn't need a mousepad, although one can be used. However, some surfaces don't work well with an optical mouse, such as glass, mirrors, or smooth shiny, solid-color surfaces that lack detail. On these surfaces, it might not hurt to actually use a wooden mousepad!

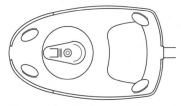

Figure 20-3: The bottom of an optical mouse.

The biggest advantage that an optical mouse has over a conventional mouse is that it doesn't need to be cleaned internally. An optical mouse has no moving parts and thus doesn't pick up the dust and dirt that plague a mouse with a ball. Manufacturers also claim that optical mice are 33 percent faster and more accurate than optomechanical mice.

Inside the mouse

Because the optomechanical mouse is the most popular design in use, this discussion of how the mouse works focuses on this type of mouse. A mouse translates the motion of the user's hand into electrical signals that the PC uses to track a pointer across the monitor's display. To capture the motion of the user's hand, an optomechanical mouse uses seven primary components:

◆ *Ball:* The rubber ball is the largest and certainly most important part of the mouse. When the user grasps the mouse and moves it over a mousepad, the ball rolls inside the mouse, which is key to detecting the motion.

◆ *Rollers:* Two rollers are in contact with the ball. As the ball rolls inside the mouse, the two rollers track its rotation side to side and up and back.

◆ *Roller shafts:* The two rollers are each connected to optical encoding disks by a roller shaft.

◆ *Optical encoding disk:* The movement of the ball causes the rollers to spin, which in turn spins the shafts and the optical encoding disks attached to them. Each disk has 36 holes along its edge.

◆ *Infrared LED and sensor:* On one side of each optical encoding disk is a light-emitting diode (LED) that shines an infrared (IR) light beam on the part of the disk where the holes are located. On the opposite side of the disk is an IR sensor. As the disk turns, the solid areas between the holes break up the IR beam so that the IR sensor sees pulses of light. The rate and duration of the light pulses translate to the speed and distance of the mouse's travel. Figure 20-4 illustrates the placement of the infrared LED and sensor to the optical encoding disk.

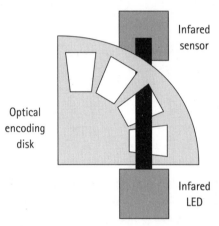

Infared sensor

Optical encoding disk

Infared LED

Figure 20-4: As the mouse moves, the holes and solids of the optical encoding disk create light pulses that translate into cursor movement on the screen.

◆ *Processor:* Inside the mouse is a processor that converts the light pulses into binary data that represents the motion of the mouse, which is sent to the PC's interface.

◆ *Buttons:* The mouse also has one, two, or three (or more) buttons that the user can use to indicate actions to the PC. As the user clicks the buttons (connected to small switches) to select an object or start a program, the processor converts the clicks into binary data that's sent to the PC. Windows systems most commonly use two-button mice; Macintosh systems have gotten by very nicely with a single mouse button; and many Unix and Linux applications make use of a third (middle) mouse button.

Other devices are used in place of a mouse, such as a joystick, and you can read more about them in "Examining Other Pointing Devices" later in the chapter.

Putting it all together

Here's how all this works together: Assume a mouse has a ball that's 21 millimeters (mm) in diameter and optical encoding disks with 36 holes. When the user moves the mouse 1 inch (25.4 mm), the ball rotates slightly more than once, and the rollers cause the disks to spin a little more than one complete revolution, matching the movement of the ball. This results in the sensor detecting about 40 light pulses, and the PC is sent 40 bits of data to indicate the mouse's movement.

Each optical encoding disk actually has two sets of LEDs and sensors: one on the left side of the disk and one on the right. Having two sets of LEDs and sensors enables the processor to detect the direction of the disk's rotation. Although not shown in Figure 20-5, there is also a small plastic window placed between each LED and disk to aim the LED's IR light beam. The plastic windows on each side of a disk are set at slightly different heights, which forces the sensors to see the light pulses at different times.

Figure 20-5 illustrates how the sensors see the light beams. As the disk rotates, the IR beams are in view through the disk's holes at slightly different times. The processor is able to determine the mouse's direction by the beam that's detected first.

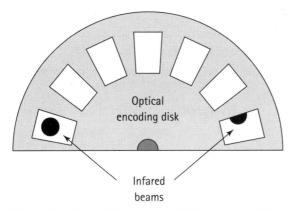

Figure 20-5: One of the mouse's LED beams is set slightly higher than the other to help detect the mouse's travel direction.

Connecting a Mouse

The three most common types of connections used by PC mouse units are the PS/2 (mini-Deutsche Industrie Norm [DIN]), Universal Serial Bus (USB), and cordless (infrared [IR] or radio frequency [RF]) connections.

PS/2 and serial

The most common connector for PC mice is the 6-pin mini-DIN (PS/2) connector. Early mouse units used a DB-9 serial connector (which is still available) to connect a mouse to a serial port. Newer PC systems typically include PS/2 connectors for the keyboard and mouse, which has lead to the serial mouse all but disappearing.

The mouse connects and communicates to the PC through the PS/2 connector with four pins. The communications technique used by the mouse is the same as used by the keyboard. Data is sent along with clocking signals that tell the PC when each piece of data begins and ends. The four pins of the connector carry +5 volts (v) of power (pin 2), clocking signals (pin 4), a grounding circuit (pin 5), and data signals (pin 6). A mouse uses the +5v of power for its processor and IR LEDs.

USB mouse

Other popular connectors for a mouse are USB, infrared (IrDA), and RF connections. The USB connector, which is hot swappable, gives the user an additional option, especially on portable PCs that have only one PS/2 connector. A device is *hot swappable* when it can be plugged in while the PC is running and does not require the system to be reset.

PS/2 and serial devices should not be connected while the system is running because it could damage the device or the interface circuitry.

Cordless mouse

Cordless mice used either an IR light beam or an RF receiver to connect and communicate with a PC. Many newer PCs include an Infrared Data Association (IrDA) or RF receiver, but both can be added as external devices through a PS/2 or USB port. A corded mouse gets its power over its cable, but a cordless mouse, which has no power connection, runs on a pair of AAA batteries.

IR connections are *line of sight,* which means they must have a clear, unobstructed view between the mouse and the receiver. They also don't operate well beyond a few feet of the receiver. On the other hand, a radio frequency connection doesn't require a clear line of sight, which means that the signal can get around any obstacles blocking its line of sight to the receiver. However, the RF device must also be within a few feet of the receiver.

Data interface

Whenever the user moves the mouse or clicks a mouse button, the mouse sends a three-byte data packet to the PC. The first byte of the mouse's data packet contains the following:

1. One bit for each of the right and left mouse buttons to indicate whether a button was clicked (0 = not clicked; 1 = clicked).

2. A 2-bit packet ID (01).

3. One bit for each of the X and Y axes to indicate the direction of the mouse's movement (0 = negative [backward/left]; 1 = positive [forward/right]).

4. One bit for each of the X and Y axes to indicate that the speed of the mouse was faster than 255 pulses in 0.025 seconds.

The second and third bytes contain the number of pulses detected by the X axis (side to side) and Y axis (up and back) sensors since the last packet was sent, respectively. These counts indicate the speed of the mouse in either or both directions.

The packet is sent to the PC over the data line of the connector as a serial data transmission with clocking signals used to indicate when each bit begins and ends. Eleven bits are sent by the mouse to the PC for each byte that it transmits, which includes 1 start bit, the 8 data bits, 1 parity bit, and 1 stop bit. The standard PS/2 mouse sends data at a rate of 1,200 bits per second, which translates to about 40 packets sent to the PC to report the mouse's status each second. Although this is fast enough for most situations and applications, extremely fast movement of the mouse can overwhelm the mouse's ability to report it accurately.

Examining Other Pointing Devices

Of the many of types of pointing devices, the four that have some popularity beyond the mouse are the touchpad, the trackball, the glidepoint, and the joystick.

Touchpads

Touchpads are becoming very common on notebook computers. A *touchpad*, like the one shown in Figure 20-6, is a fixed place, small, flat, square, or rectangular surface on which the user touches, slides, or taps a finger to guide the cursor on the display, select objects, and run programs. A touchpad is able to duplicate all the actions of a mouse.

Figure 20-6: A touchpad integrated into a notebook PC.

A touchpad uses a two-layer grid of electrodes to apply the principle of coupling capacitance. This grid includes an upper layer of electrodes placed vertically and a lower layer of horizontally placed electrodes. When the user's finger passes over a pair (one horizontal and one vertical) of electrodes, an integrated circuit (IC) attached to the grid detects the changes in the grid's capacitance, and data is sent to the PC via essentially the same technique used by a mouse and keyboard. Like an optical mouse, the touchpad has no moving parts and doesn't require cleaning other than that given to the keyboard to which it is attached. Touchpads are most common on notebook PCs, but they are also being integrated into desktop keyboards as well. An external touchpad can be added to a PC via its PS/2 port.

A digitizing tablet, like the one in Figure 20-7, works on the same principle as a touchpad but is typically used with a drawing stylus to create vector art or engineering objects.

Trackballs

A *trackball,* which is essentially an upside-down mouse, has two or more buttons like a mouse, but its ball is on top. The ball is manipulated with either a thumb or finger to move the cursor on the screen. Because only the ball moves, a trackball device requires less space on the desktop. A trackball is typically attached to a PC with a cord and uses the same technology as an optomechanical mouse to communicate movement to the PC over a PS/2 or USB connection.

Figure 20-7: A digitizing tablet.

Glidepoint mouse

A *glidepoint mouse,* which is common to many notebook PCs, is the pivoting rubber-tipped device located between the G and the H keys that looks like an eraser tip. A glidepoint mouse, like the one shown in Figure 20-8, works like a very small joystick but acts like a mouse on the screen. The benefit of the glidepoint technology is that it allows the user to leave his or her hands on the keyboard for mousing actions. The downside is that you have to get used to using your thumbs to do your mouse clicks.

Joysticks

Joysticks are used primarily with game software on a PC. The joystick device consists of a handle connected to a pivoting mechanism that allows it to move in any direction around a center point. Sensors inside the device detect the movement of the handle on an X or a Y axis and send data signals to an adapter card. A software device driver interprets the data and translates them to actions on the screen. Most joysticks attach to a game port on a game, video, or sound card installed in an expansion slot on the motherboard, but newer models also support a USB connection as well.

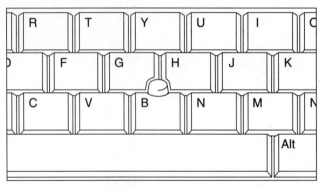

Figure 20-8: A glidepoint mouse in a notebook computer keyboard.

Installing a Mouse

The steps used to install each type of mouse vary in their degree of difficulty. The following projects describe the processes used to install a serial mouse, a PS/2 mouse, and a USB mouse.

Installing a serial mouse

A serial mouse connects to the PC with a female DB-9 (9-pin) connector, and nearly all newer PCs (and many older ones) have a 9-pin serial port available. Some PCs have only a 25-pin serial connection; if a serial mouse is the only option and this is the only type of serial port available, a 25-pin-to-9-pin adapter can be used to connect the mouse to the 25-pin port.

When installing a serial mouse, first check whether a COM port is available. On systems with both a 25-pin and a 9-pin serial port, the smaller port is often COM2 or COM3, depending on whether an internal modem is installed. Any operating problems that might happen after the mouse is installed could very well be an interrupt request (IRQ) or input/output (I/O) address conflict.

A primary difference between a PS/2 mouse and a serial mouse is that a PS/2 mouse gets its power from a wire in the connector. This is not the case with a serial mouse. You shouldn't connect a serial or PS/2 mouse to a PC with its power on because it could damage the mouse or the interface circuit or both.

A serial mouse can also be installed into a PS/2 port with a special serial-to-mini-DIN adapter. Some adapters allow a PS/2 mouse to be installed on a serial port. However, you need to understand that because of the electrical differences between the serial and the PS/2 devices, these adapters don't always work as well as they should. Many newer mouse units are actually combination mice that come with both connectors or the adapter to convert its default plug for the other connection.

Fortunately, connecting the mouse to the port is the hard part of this process. All Windows versions have built-in mouse device drivers for virtually every type of mouse, and most mouse units are Plug and Play (PnP). After you install the new mouse and reboot the system, Windows should recognize it and complete its installation by loading the appropriate device driver.

Installing a mouse manually

If Windows doesn't recognize the serial mouse, use the following steps to install it:

1. Before you start the system, examine the serial port on the PC for bent or broken pins.

   If not pushed straight on, a female connector (like that on the mouse) can bend or break pins in the serial port.

2. When you reboot the system, enter the Basic Input/Output System (BIOS) configuration data to verify that the COM port that you're trying to use is not disabled.

   If it is disabled, enable it, save the configuration data, and continue with the boot sequence. The system might not see the mouse. If not, continue with the following steps.

3. Because you don't have a mouse, you must use keyboard commands to recover:

   - Press a Windows key to display the Start menu and then press the up-arrow key to choose Run. In the Open box of the Run window, enter **CONTROL.EXE** or use the Browse button (tab to it) to find this program in your Windows folder. CONTROL.EXE is the Control Panel.

   - Tab over to the Add New Hardware icon and then press Enter.

   - From the wizard that appears, choose the options that allow Windows to search for new hardware. This typically involves pressing Enter three times to move through the wizard.

     Windows should first respond that it found the serial mouse. You then choose the options that allow Windows to complete the installation.

4. Restart the PC.

   The mouse should work.

Installing a PS/2 mouse

The PS/2 mouse is the de facto standard for all PC systems. The PS/2 mouse is installed identically to a serial mouse with two exceptions: A PS/2 mouse typically uses IRQ12 instead of a COM port IRQ, which reduces the potential for resource conflicts. Also, the PS/2 interface is powered and should not be connected to a running system because it could damage the mouse and the motherboard.

A PS/2 mouse is a PnP device for which Windows should load a device driver. If you encounter any problems, make sure that they're not rooted with the mouse itself before you start tearing into the system. Use a spare mouse (one that you know works) to verify the problem. If you have resource conflicts, see the preceding section or see Chapter 5 for more information.

Installing a USB mouse

Here is the installation instruction for a USB mouse: Plug it in. Because USB devices are hot swappable, they're instantly recognized by the system, and all necessary drivers are automatically installed.

Troubleshooting an Optomechanical Mouse

The problems of a mouse are limited to only a few things that can go wrong. If the mouse is having problems, check the following:

1. If the mouse rolls over the mousepad smoothly but the cursor on the screen moves erratically or jerks, the problem is probably that the mouse is dirty and needs to be cleaned.

   When dirt accumulates on the ball or the interior rollers, they slip when rotated against one another, forcing the other components out of sync and showing up as jerky cursor motion.

2. If a clean mouse still exhibits erratic motion, the mouse or its cable is probably damaged, or the ball is damaged or won't grip the underlying surface.

   The mousepad might be too hard or smooth for the mouse to gain a grip. Softer materials work better for optomechanical mice.

3. If the mouse is a serial mouse and works okay, but the PC freezes when you try to use the modem, the problem is a classic IRQ resource conflict.

   Both devices — the mouse on COM1 and the modem on COM3 — are trying to use IRQ4 at the same time. The modem should work fine as long as you don't use the mouse, and the mouse should work fine as long as you don't use the modem. If the two devices share the same interrupt, they can't be used simultaneously. The solution is to change the mouse to IRQ12 or another available IRQ.

4. If the mouse is a PS/2 mouse that doesn't work at all, check whether its connector is installed in the keyboard socket, which is directly connected to the keyboard interface circuitry on many motherboards and will not support the mouse.

Configuring a Mouse on a Windows PC

The Mouse Properties window (choose Start → Settings → Control Panel → Mouse) allows the user to set performance settings for the mouse. The Mouse Properties window, shown in Figure 20-9, has three tabs that contain the following:

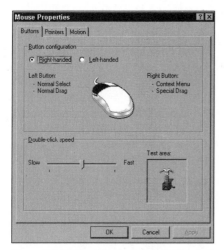

Figure 20-9: The Windows Mouse Properties window.

◆ *Buttons:* This tab contains options to set the mouse to either a right-handed (default) or left-handed device and to specify the actions associated with each button on a two-button mouse. Also on this tab is a slider control that sets the speed of the double-click action (how fast you must click and then click again).

◆ *Pointers:* From a variety of pointer schemes, here you choose the type of pointer that you wish to associate with a number of system activities. You can use a custom scheme if you have the appropriate file.

◆ *Motion:* This tab has two settings that are very important to how the mouse moves around the screen. The Speed setting sets the ratio of how far the mouse must actually move to move the pointer on the screen. If this setting is set to Fast, then small movements by the mouse result in large movements of the pointer on the screen. If the setting is set to Slow, a long movement by the mouse moves the cursor only slightly. Most users use the default setting, which is about in the middle. This tab also includes a setting to add a trailing image tail on the mouse pointer on the screen. This helps some people keep the mouse pointer in view when moving over some backgrounds.

On Windows 2000 or Windows XP systems, you should find a fourth tab entitled Hardware, which is used to examine and troubleshoot the mouse's properties.

Installing a Joystick

A joystick connects to a game port, which is also called a Musical Instrument Digital Interface (MIDI). Virtually every PC has a game port included either on its video adapter or its sound card. For most users, a PC's standard game port works well enough, but for power gamers, it might be better to install a speed-adjustable game card with a dedicated game port.

1. If the Windows system did not detect the joystick after connecting it, use the Add New Hardware icon (via the Control Panel) to add it or the game adapter card.

A joystick must be recognized by the system before it can be configured.

2. Because you can have only one active game port on a PC, you might need to disable the existing game port.

   Check the documentation of the card on which it is mounted or use the Game Controllers icon via the Control Panel to access the Game Controllers (Gaming Controls in Windows 2000 and XP) window, shown in Figure 20-10. This window is used to add and remove game controllers to the system. Windows 9.x systems include most of the software device drivers needed for basic joysticks. Advanced or 3-D joysticks might require a proprietary driver that should come with the device.

3. Calibrate the joystick.

   a. Open the Game Controllers window from the Control Panel, choose the Advanced Tab, find the joystick in the list, and double-click it.

   The display should show you that the joystick has an OK status.

   b. Click the Properties button.

Figure 20-10: The Windows Game Controllers window.

 TIP   Calibration adjusts the mechanical and electrical alignment of the joystick.

c. In the Properties window that appears, click the Calibrate button and perform the steps as instructed to calibrate the joystick. After you complete all the calibration steps, click the Test button to check the joystick's calibration. If it's not properly set, redo the calibration steps.

If a message displays during the calibration process indicating that the joystick isn't properly connected, you might have selected the wrong device driver from the Advanced tab list. Typically, this means that the joystick that you selected has more axes than the driver or Windows is able to detect. First check that the physical connection of the joystick on the game port is good by retesting the joystick with another driver. To test the connection, select a 2-axis, 2-button joystick, which is a default option (much like setting the monitor to Video Graphics Array [VGA] to troubleshoot it).

The problem could be a system resource conflict or that the joystick driver is defaulting to an incorrect I/O address value. A game port doesn't use an IRQ but rather uses a default I/O address of 0201 (or 0200 to 0207 for a PnP device). Use Device Manager to check these settings. See Chapter 5 for more information on checking system resources.

Cleaning a Dirty Mouse

Most mouse problems are related to cleaning problems and can be resolved with a cotton swab, some denatured alcohol, and perhaps a soft-bristle toothbrush.

Cleaning an optomechanical mouse

The mouse's ball can pick up lint, dust, and other debris from the mousepad, especially one that's heavily textured or painted. Because of this, the mouse should be cleaned regularly.

1. Power off the PC and disconnect the mouse.

   Disconnecting the mouse isn't required, but it can make the job much easier.

2. After you turn the mouse over to expose the bottom and find the ring that holds the ball inside the mouse, turn that ring counter-clockwise and remove the ball from the mouse.

   Don't try to dig the ball out; just turn the mouse over and let the ball fall out into your hand. Avoid squeezing or compressing the ball while holding it.

3. Dampen a lint-free cloth with water or the alcohol and gently rub the ball.

   When the ball has been completely wiped, let it air-dry.

 Don't use solvents or harsh cleaners on a mouse ball because they can leave the mouse ball out-of-round or flat-spotted on one or more sides.

4. Use the swab and alcohol to clean the rollers or contacts inside the ball cage.

   If the rollers have a dark buildup, gently scrape away the dirt with a small blade, being careful not to cut or score the roller.

5. Use compressed air to blow any dust out of the ball cage and the interior of the mouse.

6. Replace the ball in the mouse; then replace and turn the retaining ring clockwise to lock the ball in place.

Cleaning an optical mouse

Because the optical mouse has no moving parts (other than the user's hand), very little is involved when cleaning it. On the bottom of the optical mouse is a set of pads (feet) that are used to raise the mouse above the mousing surface and for the mouse to glide. If the pads aren't cleaned regularly, the user might need to use more effort to move the mouse around. Use a toothbrush to clean the pads and a soft cloth to wipe the underside of the mouse.

Part VII

Communications and Networking

Chapter 21

Dialup Networking

IN THIS CHAPTER

A *modem* (*mod*ulator/*dem*odulator) converts (modulates) the digital data of a PC into analog data to be sent over the Plain Old Telephone System (POTS) lines of the telephone service. Although many offices and businesses are now connected to outside communications through their networks, I would venture to guess that most homes and very small businesses still connect to the outside digital world through a modem.

Like problems with a printer or a monitor, modem problems can be cause for extreme anxiety in a user. Knowing what can go wrong and how to fix it are especially important parts of a PC technician's bag of tricks. This chapter provides you with information on the most common modem issues and their resolutions:

- ◆ Connecting a modem to a PC

- ◆ Configuring a modem on a Windows system

- ◆ Using error codes to troubleshoot a dialup problem

- ◆ Connecting to other connection services

A MODEM CONVERTS the digital data of a PC to the analog voice signals used on the standard telephone system and vice versa. For purposes of this book, it isn't really all that important exactly how this happens. Rather, I focus on how a modem attaches to a PC, what can go wrong after it's attached, and what you can do to resolve any problems or issues that are important.

Connecting a Modem

Most newer PCs include an internal modem as a standard feature. However, many users still prefer to use external modems . . . so that they can see the lights flashing and know that something's happening, I guess. In either case, sometimes you need to replace a modem or install a new one.

A modem is typically installed in a PC as an internal component – an expansion bus slot on the motherboard. External modems are connected to the PC through either a serial or Universal Serial Bus (USB) port.

Configuring a modem

Most newer internal modems don't require much in the way of physical configuration, if any. However, some older modem models use either Dual Inline Packaging (DIP) switches or jumpers, or both, to set their configuration, including transmission speed, stop bits, parity, or the designation of which COM (serial) port is to be used. Most newer modems are configured almost completely by the PC's operating system through its Plug and Play (PnP) support.

EXTERNAL MODEMS

If you're connecting an external modem, which is attached to either a serial or USB port, you might need to set its configuration through a bank of DIP switches located on the exterior of the modem's case. DIP switches are more common on external serial modems than they are on USB modems.

Most of today's modems (both internal and external) are typically configured by using proprietary installation and configuration software, normally found on a CD or a diskette included in the modem's packaging.

About the only concern involved with connecting an external modem to the PC is the cable.

♦ *Serial modems:* The serial cable used to connect an external modem to a PC is a *null modem cable.* If one isn't included with the modem, you can purchase one at nearly all computer supply stores. Tables 21-1 through 21-5 list the pin assignments and pinouts for serial null modem cables (DB-25, DB-9, and DB-25 to DB-9) if you want to make one up yourself.

♦ *USB modems:* If you're installing a USB modem, all that's required is for you to connect the USB cable between the modem and an available USB port.

 In most cases, the only configuration issues that you might have with an external modem are possible system resource conflicts — and usually only conflicts with its interrupt request (IRQ) assignment, if any.

TABLE 21-1 DB-25 PIN ASSIGNMENTS

Pin #	Code	Function
2	TD	Transmit data
3	RD	Receive data
4	RTS	Request to send

Pin #	Code	Function
5	CTS	Clear to send
6	DSR	Data set ready
7	SG	Signal ground
8	DCD	Data carrier detect
20	DTR	Data terminal ready
22	RING	Ring indicator

TABLE 21-2 DB-9 PIN ASSIGNMENTS

Pin #	Code	Function
1	DCD	Data carrier detect
2	RD	Receive data
3	TD	Transmit data
4	DTR	Data terminal ready
5	SG	Signal ground
6	DSR	Data set ready
7	RTS	Request to send
8	CTS	Clear to send
9	RING	Ring indicator

TABLE 21-3 DB-25-to-DB-25 NULL MODEM CABLE PINOUTS

Connector A Pin #	Connector B Pin #
2	3
3	2
4	5

Continued

TABLE 21-3 DB-25-to-DB-25 NULL MODEM CABLE PINOUTS *(Continued)*

Connector A Pin #	Connector B Pin #
5	4
6	20
7	7
8	20
20	6 and 8

TABLE 21-4 DB-9-to-DB-9 NULL MODEM CABLE PINOUTS

Connector A Pin #	Connector B Pin #
1	4
2	3
3	2
4	1 and 6
5	5
6	4
7	8
8	7

TABLE 21-5 DB-25-to-DB-9 NULL MODEM CABLE PINOUTS

DB-25	DB-9
2	2
3	3
4	8
5	7

DB-25	DB-9
6	4
7	5
8	4
20	6 and 1

Only eight pins are used in a null modem cable.

INTERNAL MODEMS

Because nearly all newer internal modems are PnP devices, between the BIOS and the operating system, they should be detected and configured automatically. However, on a PC with a large number of peripherals already installed, PnP can potentially create system resource conflicts, especially on the serial COM ports.

So even if you allow PnP to configure a new modem, you should check the resulting system resource assignments, especially IRQ and input/output (I/O) ports, for possible conflicts.

Working on a Windows system

On Windows systems, a modem is configured through its Install New Modem Wizard, shown in Figure 21-1, which guides you through the identification and configuration processes for a new modem. Even if the modem came with an installation CD or diskette, be sure that you use it to install the device drivers via the Have Disk button when prompted from the install wizard because drivers that are included with Windows might be even more out of date than the ones on the media itself.

Always check the modem manufacturer's Web site for updated modem drivers compatible with the operating system that you're using. Hardware purchased from a store — especially hardware purchased online — could've been sitting on a shelf or in a warehouse for some time ... and the drivers packaged with it could be out of date.

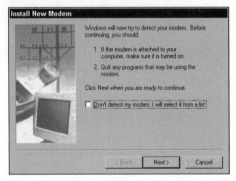

Figure 21-1: Use the Windows Install New Modem
Wizard to add a new modem to a Windows system.

Installing and configuring an internal modem on a Windows system is typically a hands-off affair except for the part where you must physically install the modem inside the case. After the modem expansion card is installed in either a Peripheral Component Interconnect (PCI) or an Industry Standard Architecture (ISA) slot, reboot the PC to let the operating system detect the new hardware and guide you through the configuration steps.

Configuring a modem connection in Windows 9x

Virtually every PC comes with an internal modem installed as part of its standard equipment. However, you might need to upgrade a PC by installing an internal modem or by replacing a faulty or out-of-date modem. After the modem is physically installed, use the following steps to configure the modem on a Windows PC:

1. Open the My Computer window (double-click its icon on your desktop) to determine whether Dial-up Networking (DUN) is installed.

   If it is, there should be a folder entitled (guess what) Dial-Up Networking.

   If not, add this service from the Windows distribution CD by using the Add/Remove Program applet from the Control Panel.

2. Double-click the Dial-up Networking icon and then double-click the Make New Connection icon to start the Make New Connection Wizard.

   If the wizard indicates that the modem isn't detected, let Windows try again to detect the modem.

3. Set up the dialing (and connection) information asked for by the wizard, including the phone number to be dialed by the modem, and then click the Finish button to close the wizard.

4. From the Control Panel, click the Network icon and choose the Identification tab from the Network dialog box that opens. Give the computer a name, a workgroup, and a description.

Entering this information updates the device information database and requires a system restart.

5. From the Control Panel, click the Network icon, this time choosing the Configuration tab from the Network dialog box that opens (see Figure 21-2), and then click the Add button.

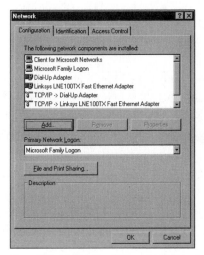

Figure 21-2: Use the Network window to configure a Windows PC to a network.

6. From the Select Network Component Type dialog box (see Figure 21-3) that displays next, highlight the Protocol list entry and then click the Add button to display the Select Network Protocol dialog box (see Figure 21-4).

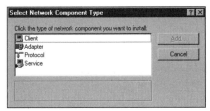

Figure 21-3: Use the Select Network Component Type dialog box to choose the network component to be configured.

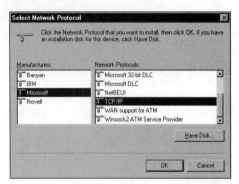

Figure 21-4: Use the Select Network Protocol window to add new dialup or network protocols to a Windows PC.

7. Highlight the listing for Microsoft (under the Manufacturers heading). Then highlight TCP/IP in the right pane (Network Protocols), click OK to return to the Network window, and click OK again to exit the window.

8. From the My Computer window, double-click the Dial-Up Networking folder.

9. Right-click the icon of the new connection and choose Properties from the menu that appears.

10. Select the Server Types tab (see Figure 21-5) and then click the TCP/IP Settings button to open the TCP/IP Settings dialog box (see Figure 21-6).

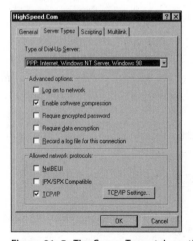

Figure 21-5: The Server Types tab on the Dial-up Networking dialog box.

The settings on this box should be verified with the Internet service provider (ISP) or the network administrator, depending on the use of the modem and the network to which the PC is connecting. However, except for the IP addresses, which are unique to each ISP or network, the settings shown in Figure 21-6 are fairly typical.

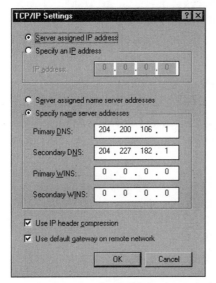

Figure 21-6: Use the TCP/IP Settings window to configure the network settings of a dialup or LAN connection.

11. Click OK to apply the settings.

    The PC must be restarted.

Configuring a dialup connection in Windows 2000 and XP

Like all other system-level functions, you must log in as an administrator to configure a modem's dialup connection in Windows 2000 and Windows XP. To set up the dialup connection for a particular location, use the following steps:

1. On the Windows desktop, right-click the My Computer icon and choose Properties from the pop-up menu that appears.

2. In the Properties window, choose the Network Identification tab and click the Properties button. If a Computer Name is not already assigned, enter one (using the local naming convention; if there is none, go for it) and click the More button to continue to the next screen.

3. Most ISP services prefer that you choose the Automatically Detect option, but if the ISP or remote location requires it and has supplied one, enter a Primary domain name system (DNS) suffix for this computer.

4. Click OK within each succeeding dialog box until you exit the Properties window and return to the desktop.

5. Right-click the My Network Places icon (on the desktop) and choose Properties from the pop-up menu that displays.

6. Double-click the Make New Connection icon to start up the Network Connection Wizard; after it displays, click Next.

7. Choose the Dial-Up to the Internet option (assuming that's what you're doing) and then click Next.

8. Choose the I Want to Set Up My Internet Connection Manually option (normally the third choice) and then click Next.

9. Choose the I Connect through a Phone Line and a Modem option and then click Next.

10. Enter the area code and phone number of the remote site (the ISP's dial-in number), enter the country/region name and code, and then choose the Use Area Code and Dialing Rules options, if applicable.

11. Click the Advanced button and choose the Addresses tab on the next display.

    Again, you need to know whether the ISP (or remote site) wishes for you to choose the Always or the Detect option under the DNS Server area. If the Always Use the Following is required, enter the DNS address (or addresses) provided and then click OK.

12. Click Next, enter the username and password of the PC owner (provided that you wish to save this information and not require the user to enter it each time when dialing up this particular destination), and then click Next again.

13. Assign this connection a name and then click Next.

14. If an Internet Mail client is loaded to the PC, the Connection Wizard will detect it and ask whether you wish to set up an Internet Mail account.

    If this connection is to an ISP, you can typically mark No and proceed by clicking Next.

15. If you wish to connect to the remote site after finishing the configuration, select the To Connect to the Internet Immediately check box and then click Finish.

You might need to disable call waiting on the telephone line. Otherwise, if left enabled, an incoming call can break the dial-up connection. To disable call waiting, choose the appropriate options (*70) in the My Location properties in the Dialing Rules dialog box.

Working on a Linux system

Because not all PCs in the world run Windows, I've included an overview of the process used to configure a modem on a Linux system.

The serial ports on a Linux PC are designated as ttyS0 and ttyS1 (there could be more) and normally correspond with COM1 and COM2, and so on. Each of the ttyS*n* ports has its own set of system resources (IRQ, I/O port, and so on) pre-assigned. However, you can change them by using the Linux command setserial. Pick a serial port on the PC, attach your null modem cable, and restart the PC.

Don't connect any serial or parallel cables to the PC while it's running because you could damage the system or the interface circuits.

Most Linux releases automatically detect and configure the serial port and the modem when it starts up. If the modem is Linux compatible (and many modems are), a CD-ROM or diskette included in the package will make the necessary adjustments to the startup files.

Two commands that might prove useful when working with a Linux system and a modem are

◆ isapnp: This program is used to configure PnP devices installed on the ISA expansion bus, including internal modems. The isapnp program finds all ISA PnP devices and displays your options for configuring them.

◆ wvdialconf filename: This command identifies which of a PC's serial ports have a modem attached to it and creates a wvdial program for it. The wvdial command is used to simplify dialing out through the modem by using the Point-to-Point Protocol (PPP). The filename parameter designates the name that you wish the command to assign to the configuration file that it creates.

Installing device drivers

Different modem models can differ in the functions supported by their device drivers. Essentially, these are the two general types of modems, as defined by the functions of their device drivers:

◆ *Standard modem:* A standard modem, internal or external, can be PnP or legacy. Standard modems are operating system neutral and use generic device drivers.

◆ *Windows modem:* A Windows modem is an internal PnP device that requires a device driver provided by or developed for the Windows operating system to function properly.

As long as you have the proper device driver for your system's modem, it will work fine. If you're not sure what type of modem you have, consult the documentation that came with the PC or the modem or visit the manufacturers' (both the operating system and the modem manufacturer) Web sites.

Commanding the modem

Virtually all PC-compatible modems use the Hayes Standard AT command set to establish the internal settings and to control the function of the modem. The AT commands give you the ability to control the modem's functions and settings directly through a modem interface from the PC or by using a command script that's sent to the modem each time that the PC is booted or the modem is accessed.

Driver Signing

With Windows XP, Microsoft is making a bigger deal of device drivers being tested and accepted as Windows XP compatible — something MS calls *driver signing* or *code signing.*

In its crusade to improve the quality of device drivers, Microsoft began digitally signing drivers for Windows 98 and has continued doing so through the Windows XP version. A digitally signed driver has been tested and passed by the Windows Hardware Quality Labs (WHQL).

A digitally signed driver has a catalog (CAT) file that contains the WHQL digital signature and an information (INF) file that references the CAT file, the digitally signed device driver, and a set of operating system policies that control whether an unsigned driver can be installed.

The abbreviation *AT* is derived from *attention*, which is used to precede each of the modem action commands in the AT command set.

Table 21-6 includes a few of the more commonly used AT commands. Remember that in actual use, each command is preceded with AT. For example, if you must dial 9 to get an outside line and you wish the dial program to pause a bit to wait for the second (outside) dial tone, the AT command string used to dial a phone number using touch-tone dialing is

AT DT 9,555-1212

TABLE 21-6 AT COMMANDS

Command	Action
A0	Answer incoming call
A/	Repeat last command
DT XXX-XXXX	Dial the telephone number using touch-tone dialing
DP XXX-XXXX	Dial the telephone number using pulse (rotary) dialing
H	On hook (hang up)
L	Speaker loudness (volume)
M	Mute (speaker off)
Z	Reset the modem to default settings
&X	Advanced configuration commands, where X is a command letter

Establishing a Dialup Connection

The most common use of a modem today is to connect to the Internet. The modem is connected to a telephone line with an RJ-11 connection on the modem. Figure 21-7 shows an RJ-11 connector, which is just like the connector used on nearly all phones.

Figure 21-7: Use an RJ-11 connector to
connect a modem to a telephone line.

Making the call

On Windows PCs, a modem is controlled through either the Dial-up Networking
(DUN) applet (on Windows 9.x, Me, and NT) or the Network Connections icon
(Windows 2000 and XP). These functions include a built-in dialer that is automatically activated each time that an application requiring a connection through a
modem is opened, such as a Web browser, an e-mail client, or a file transfer agent.
The dialer sends the appropriate AT command string to the modem, which dials the
target phone number and then makes and manages the connection.

The telephone portion of the dialup action is the same used to place a call to
anyone. The number is dialed, the phone company does its thing, and the remote
number rings.

At this point, the modem at the other end (if properly configured) takes over and
answers the call. However, before data can be exchanged between the two modems
(and the PCs to which they are attached), the local and remote modems must establish the connection using a process called a *handshake*. The handshake process is
the one that produces those strange sounding static, garble, bing, and bong noises
after the remote location answers the call.

The *handshake* process involves the exchange of a series of signals between the
two modems that negotiates the data speed and format to be used. In effect, the
handshaking process establishes the communications session that remains open
until one of the modems disconnects.

Dialup networking uses PPP to send packets over the Public Switched Telephone
Network (PSTN). PPP inserts the data to be sent into a PPP packet and carries it over
the transmission line to the remote modem. At the receiving end, the original data is
removed from the PPP packet and passed to the remote computer for processing.

Establishing a dialup connection

Windows (and most other operating systems for that matter) and virtually all
modems use a seven-step process to negotiate and establish a connection between
a V.90 modem and a remote network. Of course, each step presents a completely
new opportunity for something to go wrong. In each of the steps, if something does
go wrong, an appropriate error code and message is displayed (see "Using error
codes to identify a dialup problem" later in this chapter). If everything works as it
should, the following occurs:

1. *Modem availability check:* Windows interrogates the COM port to which the modem has been associated in the modem setup to see whether the port and the modem are available. If the modem is available, Windows passes the dial command string to the modem.

2. *Modem initialization:* A modem executes two sets of commands (and a possible third set) to initialize itself. The first set consists of the commands embedded in the modem's firmware. The modem's device driver provides the second set of commands. If any extra instructions have been entered into the Windows Modem Properties settings, such as start-up strings and so on, they are executed last.

3. *Modem dialing:* After the modem has completed its initialization commands, it accepts the dialing command, tests for a dial tone, and dials the phone number in the dialing command. A failure at this point is typically caused because no dial tone was detected.

4. *Call routing:* This step is performed completely under the control of the telephone company (telco) and its PSTN. If a telephone system validates the number dialed by the modem, the call is routed through the PSTN by using the telco's routing rules. If the number dialed is for a remote modem and it's not busy, the call is completed.

5. *Connection negotiation:* After the call is answered by the remote modem, the source modem begins the process of negotiating the connection, including the protocol, speed, data format, and so forth.

6. *Authentication:* After the connection is negotiated and "nailed up" (telco lingo), the remote network access server (NAS) demands that the dialing system identify itself and prove that it should be granted access to the remote network. Typically, a username and password are used to verify the connecting user or network for authorization to gain access.

7. *Protocol session:* The remaining step in completing the connection is to establish the protocol that will manage the transfer of data across the connection. In most cases, the Point-to-Point Protocol (PPP), a member of the TCP/IP protocol suite, is used to move data across a dialup modem connection. Both modems must agree on the protocol in use.

Dealing with Dialup Issues

After a modem is properly installed and configured, not all that much can go wrong. Typically, a dialup problem is usually caused by a phone number that has changed; the remote site's modem being off; or in the case of an ISP, technical difficulties.

However, a few things can be checked out when dialup problems occur. In this section, troubleshooting, diagnosing, and the steps taken to resolve some of the more common problems and issues are detailed.

Troubleshooting a failed connection

To troubleshoot a modem that fails to connect to a remote modem or fails to establish a connection, check the following:

◆ *Dial tone:* The sound produced by the modem allows you to track the progress of the connection during the handshake process. The first sound is normally the dial tone on the phone line. If you don't hear a dial tone, you have a problem with the wall jack connection, where the phone line is connected to the modem, or with the phone line itself. Most dialer software displays an error message when no dial tone is detected.

◆ *Modem:* If the remote modem answers and the handshake process begins but fails to establish a connection, one of the modems is probably not configured properly. In most cases, the modems adjust themselves for speed, but the character length, start and stop bits, and possibly speed configurations need to be checked.

◆ *Protocols:* If the connection is established by the modems but no data is being transmitted and the connection is broken off after a few seconds, the problem is likely protocol related. This is a common problem of newly installed modems. The TCP/IP or PPP protocols have not been properly configured. Verify that the protocols are enabled and that the proper bindings are set for the protocols.

◆ *Remote response:* The remote NAS or modem is possibly down or having problems. Call the ISP to check.

◆ *Telephone company:* As suburbs have grown around large cities, the telephone companies have not always been able to keep up. On occasion, phone lines have enough static or crosstalk to cause the modem to disconnect. If the modem disconnects soon after completing the connection and transferring data, or if the line is exceptionally slow, the line noise on the phone line is a likely culprit.

Using error codes to identify a dialup problem

Errors can occur at any point in the dialup process. Each of the seven steps (see "Establishing a dialup connection" earlier in the chapter) has its own unique set of problems that can happen to stop the dialup connection from being successfully set up. Table 21-7 lists the most common errors and their associated error codes and messages that can happen each step of the way.

TABLE 21-7 DIALUP PROCESS ERROR CODES

Phase	Problem	Error Code	Resolution
1. Modem availability check	Modem in use	602 (Port open)	Restart system
	Modem not installed	633 (Port unavailable)	Re-install modem
		666 (Device not ready)	Re-install modem/Check for resource conflicts
2. Modem initialization	Internal command error	630 (Hardware failure)	Restart modem/Contact modem vendor for assistance
	Modem driver command error	630 (Hardware error)	Re-install or update device driver
	Extra settings command error	630 (Hardware error)	Edit initialization commands in Modem Properties window
3. Modem dialing	Phone line not connected to modem	680 (No dial tone)	Connect phone line to modem
	Phone line busy	680 (No dial tone)	Clear phone line
4. Call routing	Invalid phone number	629 (Remote disconnect)	Verify dialed number
	Call cannot be routed	676 (Line busy)	Verify dialed number and retry/Contact telephone company
	Line busy	676 (Line busy)	Wait 5 minutes and retry
	Call cannot be routed	678 (No answer)	Verify dialed number and retry/Contact telephone company
5. Connection negotiation	Modem disconnected during connection negotiation	629 (Remote disconnect)	Verify telephone number and timeout settings in Windows

Continued

TABLE 21-7 DIALUP PROCESS ERROR CODES *(Continued)*

Phase	Problem	Error Code	Resolution
	Modem disconnected during connection negotiation	645 (Authentication error)	Verify username and password
	Modem protocol not recognized or supported (KFlex versus V.90)	650 (Server not responding)	Switch modem protocol or replace modem
	Incompatible protocols	678 (No answer)	Verify protocol with remote site
6. Authentication	Incorrect authentication information	635 (Unknown user)	Verify username and password
	Incorrect authentication information	645 (Internal authentication error)	Verify username and password
	Incorrect authentication information	691 (Authentication error)	Verify username and password
	Authentication timeout	629 (Remote disconnect)	NAS timeout/Verify username and password
	Protocol timeout	718 (PPP timeout)	Verify protocol configuration
7. Protocol session	Connection settings invalid	629 (Remote disconnect)	Verify dialup properties and settings
	TCP/IP not installed	731 (Protocol not configured)	Complete TCP/IP configuration
	Networking components corrupt	720 (PPP not configured)	Complete PPP configuration
	TCP/IP stack corrupt	731 (Protocol not configured)	Complete PPP configuration

ERROR 602

Error code 602 indicates that some application already has the port open and the modem in use, such as a fax, telephony, or other telephone line–related service. Commonly fax software has the modem in use waiting for an incoming call. Some other causes could be

♦ *Modem driver:* The modem's device driver is corrupted.

♦ *Modem in use:* Another program has the modem in use or tied up.

♦ *Modem memory:* The memory in the modem has been corrupted.

To resolve this problem, restart the PC and do a diagnostic test on the COM port to which the modem is attached. If the modem tests okay, try connecting again. If you get the same error code, delete the modem configuration and reinstall.

 TIP Other possibilities are that the modem is connected to the wrong COM port, or a resource conflict exists on the COM port on which it is installed. In either case, reinstall the modem configuration.

ERROR 629

The three different kinds of 629 errors occur when the remote computer disconnects the port during dialing and after authentication. The most common causes for this error are

♦ *Authentication error:* An invalid username and password has caused the connection to time out.

♦ *Disconnect setting too low:* The Disconnect if Not Connected Within setting is set too low.

♦ *Incompatible connection:* The modem is attempting to make a connection with an incompatible modem (V.90 versus KFlex).

♦ *Invalid Dial-up Networking (DUN) settings:* The DUN configuration settings are bad or corrupted.

♦ *Invalid number:* The DUN is dialing an invalid phone number, which might coincidently be a modem.

♦ *Modem driver:* The modem's device driver is out of date or corrupted.

REMOTE COMPUTER DISCONNECTING THE PORT   If the remote computer is disconnecting the port, the modem's device driver is probably bad, out of date, or corrupted. Update the modem driver from the manufacturer's Web site.

ERROR 629 DURING DIALING   If the 629 error occurs while the dialing status is being displayed on the connection box, verify the number being dialed. Or if the remote site is an ISP with which a new account has just been created, wait a couple of hours and try again. Check the Disconnect if Not Connected Within setting and ensure that it's at least 60 seconds. If you still have no luck, you might try disabling the V.90 protocol on the modem. If all else fails, you might need to completely reconfigure the networking settings on the PC. For information on solving this problem, search the Microsoft Knowledge Base for *error 629* information.

ERROR 629 WHEN AUTHENTICATION FAILS   First, make sure that a valid number is being dialed. That could save a lot of trouble right there. If that's not the problem, search the Microsoft Knowledge Base for *error 629* information.

ERROR 629 AFTER AUTHENTICATION SUCCEEDS   If Windows Internet Name Service (WINS) is enabled on the dialing PC, disable its value in the TCP/IP properties of the Network dialog box (access from the Control Panel). If WINS is disabled, enable it. Try the connection again. However, if changing the WINS setting doesn't solve the problem, try this:

1. After backing up the registry files, use `regedit` or `regedit32` (execute from the Start → Run) to remove the `Hkey_Current_User\RemoteAccess` registry key.

2. Create and configure a new DUN connection for the remote site.

3. Configure the Internet Options from the Control Panel to use the new DUN connection and then retry the connection.

ERROR 633

This error is common with WinModems. If the modem diagnostics are clear and the modem is listed as an active device, but you get an error saying that no modem is installed or configured, check the following:

◆ *Dial-up Networking (DUN) settings:* The settings for the modem in the DUN configuration are bad or missing.

◆ *Modem driver:* The modem's device driver is corrupted.

◆ *Modem memory:* The modem's memory has been corrupted.

◆ `telephon.ini:` The Windows `telephon.ini` file is bad.

Try performing the following to resolve this error:

1. Remove the `telephon.ini` file from the Windows directory. Choose Start → Run and run `tapiini.exe` there to re-create it.

2. Power off the PC and the modem.

3. Power the modem up and then the PC (in that order).

4. Run diagnostics on the modem's COM port.

   If the modem continues to fail, either the modem or the device driver is bad and should be reinstalled or replaced (starting with the device driver, of course).

   If the modem tests okay, you know that the modem itself is fine.

5. Back up the Windows Registry and use `regedit` or `regedt32` to remove the `Hkey_Current_User\Remote Access` key.

6. Re-create the modem and its DUN connection and then configure the Internet Options from the Control Panel to use the new connection.

7. Attempt to reconnect.

ERROR 630

This error indicates a problem with the modem itself. Its most common causes are the following:

◆ *Modem initialization:* An error exists in a modem initialization string that either you or the user entered.

◆ *Modem damage:* The modem has been physically damaged.

◆ *Modem driver:* The modem's device driver is bad.

◆ *Modem memory:* The modem's memory is corrupted.

To resolve this error, try this:

1. Power off the PC and the modem.

2. Power the modem up and then the PC (in that order).

3. Perform diagnostics testing on the modem's COM port.

   If the modem doesn't respond, remove the modem from the Modems folder (access through the Modems icon of the Control Panel) and redo Steps 1 and 2.

4. If the modem tests okay, delete any `AT` command strings that might have been entered in the Extra Settings section from the Modems icon (Control Panel) and the DUN connection for the modem.

5. After verifying that the DUN connection is configured to the correct modem or removing and re-adding the connection, retest the connection.

6. Set the Internet Options via the Control Panel to use the corrected DUN connection and retry the connection.

7. If the 630 error persists, something is physically wrong with the modem.

   You might have overlooked an incorrect cable connection or have a faulty connector.

ERROR 635

Perhaps the most common error condition that users encounter, this error results strictly from the entry of an erroneous username and password combination — provided that the access phone number was valid to begin with.

ERROR 645

This error typically results from a conflict in the internal (on the user's PC) protocols being used to authenticate and manage the connection. To resolve this condition, try these steps:

1. Verify that the Network icon (Control Panel) shows only the Client for Microsoft Network, Dial-Up Adapter, and TCP/IP as being active. Remove any other services listed.

2. Cycle the WINS resolution value.

   If WINS is already disabled, enable it and click OK on the error message that you should get — but then change the setting back to disabled and restart the PC.

3. Retry the connection.

   This should correct the problem in most cases. However, if the problem persists, continue on to the next step.

4. If the PC is a standalone unit, delete any *.PWL files and remove all active network components (services and protocols) via the Network icon (Control Panel).

   Don't restart the PC just yet.

5. Complete the process using the steps listed earlier for the "Error 629 during dialing" error condition.

ERROR 650

This error typically indicates that the remote system (such as the ISP's network access server) cannot understand the data being transmitted by the source modem. In most cases, the Microsoft Family Logon being active and a problem with a KFlex, X2, or V.90 protocol is the cause of this error condition.

To resolve this problem

1. Ensure the access phone number is good.

2. Verify that only the Client for Microsoft Networks, the Dial-Up adapter, and TCP/IP are active on the Network icon of the Control Panel.

3. Cycle the WINS resolution value.

   If WINS is already disabled, enable it and click OK on the error message that you should get — but then change the setting back to disabled.

4. Restart the PC.

5. Depending on the modem:

   - *On a 56K, KFlex, or X2 modem:* Connect to the manufacturer's update site using the V.34 modem protocol and download the files needed to update the modem.

   - *On a V.90 modem:* Disable KFlex or X2 and try again. If this fails, you might need to use V.34 to update the modem.

6. Retry the connection.

ERROR 676

Beyond the obvious reasons why a line-busy error is returned (the called number is busy), here are a few of the most common:

◆ *Bad phone number:* The number being dialed is not a valid telephone number or was entered into the settings incorrectly.

◆ *Central office (CO) issues:* The telco's CO could not complete the call as dialed because its circuits were busy, which normally results in either an operator intercept (a recording) or a fast busy tone.

◆ *Misapplied settings:* The dialing instructions might indicate that a 9 or a *70 should be dialed when this is not the case on the line in use.

◆ *Point of presence (POP) issues:* The building's POP doesn't support enough lines to facilitate the call at this time.

To resolve this problem, here are some things to try:

1. Verify the phone number to be dialed.

   You should try dialing the number from a regular handset to verify that you are truly dialing a valid modem line number.

2. Check the settings in the DUN connection and dialing instructions to disable the *70 function and remove (or add) any numbers that don't need to be (or must be) dialed to get an outside line.

3. If the POP is too busy, try shifting the dial time into a period when the phone system isn't so busy.

ERROR 678

If you get this error, there was no answer on the remote end of the call. If the number is a valid modem phone number, try the steps listed for Error 676. This error can also occur because of a failed connect negotiation (handshake) between the modems, typically caused by one or both modems having out-of-date firmware.

If you think the latter is the problem, disable the 56K protocols on the modem and connect to the vendor's update site by using a V.34 connection.

You might also want to mark the Cancel the Call if Not Connected Within check box on the Connection tab of the Modem Properties window (via the Modem icon of the Control Panel) to either deselect this option or make sure that its value is 60 seconds or more.

ERROR 680

You either have a dial tone or you don't; it's just that simple. The most common cause of this error condition is that the phone line isn't connected to the modem. However, here are a few other remotely possible causes:

◆ *Voice messaging:* Some modems don't recognize the stuttering dial tone used to signal that voice messages are pending.

◆ *Modem error:* The modem might have lost its ability to detect the dial tone, which could also indicate other modem problems (but not always).

To resolve this problem, try these steps:

1. Verify that the phone line is snugly connected into both the wall jack and the modem.

2. Verify that the phone line is connected into the line jack on the modem and not the phone jack.

   If the line is connected as it should be, try moving the line to the other jack because the jacks could be mislabeled.

3. Remove any line splitters or surge protectors from the phone line.

4. Test the line by plugging it into a handset.

   If you have no dial tone on the line, you'll need to contact the telco to have the problem resolved. The phone line also might be in use by another party.

5. If there is a service on the phone line that affects the sound of the dial tone (voice messaging, for example), add **S6=3** (instructs the modem to wait three seconds before attempting to detect a dial tone) to the modem initialization string in the Extra Settings area (via the Modem icon of the Control Panel).

6. If all else fails, try entering an X3 command in the initialization string to tell the modem to ignore any error codes returned when it attempts to detect a dial tone.

Otherwise, if it still doesn't work, replace the modem.

ERROR 691

In virtually every instance, this error condition is caused by the entry of an invalid username and password. However, it could also be the result of line noise or interference on the line. If the access phone number in use is valid, try using the corrective steps listed for "Error 629 when authentication fails" earlier in this section.

ERROR 718

This error condition indicates that the ISP or remote site is down for maintenance, its NAS has failed, or for some reason, the dial-in POP is malfunctioning. The best solution is to wait and try again later.

The problem could also be the TCP/IP settings on the user's PC, but typically the problem is with the remote site.

◆ *Windows 9x, Me, 2000, or XP systems:* Check the DUN information for correctness, power down the PC and restart it, and try the connection again. If that fails, check with the remote site or the ISP. Use the process listed for "Error 629 during dialing" (earlier in the chapter) if the problem persists after the ISP swears that it's up and running.

◆ *Windows NT systems:* Try using a Generic Login Script by selecting the setting Run After Connecting in the Phonebook Entry Properties.

ERROR 720/731

These errors are caused by some problem in the protocol configuration on the dialing PC. Reconfigure the TCP/IP configuration by using the procedure listed for "Error 629 when authentication fails" earlier in the chapter.

Making Other Phone Connections

A dialup modem isn't the only type of service available to connect a local PC to a remote site. In fact, it isn't even the only one offered by the phone company. The phone company offers at least two other types of remote connection services to homes and small businesses: digital subscriber line (DSL) and the Integrated Service Digital Network (ISDN).

Connecting with DSL

A *digital subscriber line* (DSL) transmits high-speed data over a standard telephone line with data transmission speeds that vary with the type of DSL service installed. DSL data speeds range from 128 Kbps (ISDN over DSL [IDSL]) to over 2.0 Mbps (Symmetrical DSL [SDSL]), with 1.5 Mbps commonly available.

DSL service uses existing telephone lines to carry incoming and outgoing data. In most cases, DSL requires that copper wire be in use for the entire connection from your house to the telco's central office. Because of the limitations in its technologies, DSL service is only available to residences and businesses that are located a relatively short distance from the CO, as the wire runs. For example, the distance limitation could be as low as 12,000 linear feet but not much more than 20,000 linear feet.

The most common type of DSL service is Asymmetrical DSL (ADSL), which is the most commonly offered service for home and small office users. ADSL transmits and receives asymmetrically, using a higher speed for downloads and a lower speed for uploads.

SDSL transmits and receives symmetrically, using the same speed for both uploads and downloads. SDSL is typically used more for business and high-end users who require higher bandwidth.

The customer premise equipment (CPE) used to terminate the line at the user's building for ADSL is typically an external DSL modem or DSL bridge. The DSL modem is attached to a PC by using a twisted pair cable and an RJ-45 connector to a network interface card (NIC) installed in the PC. The DSL modem, which can also be an internal device, bridges the incoming data from the phone line into a format usable by the NIC and PC and vice versa.

An SDSL line uses either a bridge or a router for its CPE. A router allows several PCs to share the higher SDSL bandwidth.

 A typical ADSL installation, which at one time required an additional telephone line, is now installed on the existing phone line to a home or business. This is accomplished using a technique called *line-sharing,* which uses a splitter (filter) to allow a single telephone line to support both voice and data transmissions.

Connecting to ISDN

Integrated Service Digital Network (ISDN) is another remote communications service over telephone lines that can be purchased from the telephone company or a wide variety of resellers.

Two types of ISDN services are available: Basic Rate Interface (BRI) and Primary Rate Interface (PRI). *BRI* is typically used for home or small office Internet connections, and *PRI* is most commonly used to provide high bandwidth connections for voice and data in larger companies and telecommunications providers. At the user PC level, if ISDN is in use, I'm almost certain it will be BRI service.

BRI ISDN is single-line service that connects to a PC through a terminal adapter, which feeds digital data from the PC directly to the ISDN line with no digital-to-analog conversion required.

BRI service carries data over two bearer channels (B channels) and control signals over a single digital channel (a D channel). Each B channel carries 64 Kbps, and the two B channels combine to carry 128 Kbps. The D channel has a bandwidth of 16 Kbps, so altogether the ISDN line has the capacity of 144 Kbps.

Connecting with a cable modem

Another alternative to a dialup modem for accessing the Internet is with a cable modem that shares the line connected to the cable TV system. Nearly all homes have cable TV lines already in place. Thus, this service, where available, is fairly easy to get.

The Internet service provided over the cable system is very similar to ADSL service with faster downloads and slower uploads. The CPE for cable Internet access is a modem that's usually an external device.

A cable modem allows you to get high-speed Internet access without tying up your phone line, and you can watch TV while surfing the Internet. A signal splitter is used to separate the data and television signals.

Chapter 22

Networking the PC

IN THIS CHAPTER

These days, a personal computer, whether in a home, office, or a large corporation, is (probably) attached to a network in one form or another. PCs in corporate settings are typically attached to a local area network (LAN) and most likely to a wide area network (WAN) as well. PCs in a small office might be interconnected on a peer-to-peer network, and a home PC probably connects to the Internet with either a dial-up connection over the Public Switched Telephone Network (PSTN) or some form of always-on broadband connection.

This chapter deals more with general networking and the issues associated with connecting a PC to a network, regardless of the medium used to make that connection. I cover the following topics:

- ◆ Displaying the Media Access Code (MAC) address of a Windows PC

- ◆ Displaying the Internet Protocol (IP) address of a PC

- ◆ Troubleshooting a modem that fails to establish a connection

- ◆ Configuring a modem connection

- ◆ Installing and configuring a network interface card (NIC)

- ◆ Troubleshooting a NIC connection

- ◆ What to do when the computer hangs when the NIC's device drivers are loaded

- ◆ What to do when the Wake on LAN (WOL) feature supported by the NIC isn't working

BECAUSE A PC IS COMMONLY CONNECTED to some form of a network, a focus on networking and how to connect a PC to a network should be part of your repertoire.

Networking Basics

A *network* comprises two or more computers connected by a communications line for the purpose of sharing resources. Figure 22-1 illustrates a basic network used to connect two PCs so that they can share a printer and a modem. The sharable resources on a network are files, data, hardware (such as printers, modems,

CD-ROM drives), and other peripherals. The communications line can be a cable directly connecting PCs through their parallel or serial ports or to their NICs.

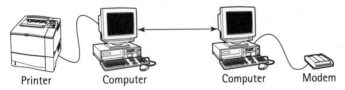

Printer   Computer   Computer   Modem

Figure 22-1: A very simple network structure.

Thus, two computers that are connected to each other by a cable between their NICs are able to share their attached hardware as well as their data from a very basic and small network — but a network, nonetheless. Most networks are more complicated than this, but regardless of how sophisticated the network becomes, it really exists only to allow networked devices to share or be shared.

Differentiating network types

The different levels and types of networks are classified by their size and the scope of the area that they encompass. The most common classifications for networks are the following:

- *Personal area network (PAN):* A *personal area network* is one set up to support the peripherals and devices of a single user. A PAN is typically created from a single PC and a variety of peripheral devices (such as a printer, scanner, mouse, keyboard, and so on) that connect to the PC with some form of wireless connection, such as infrared (IR) or radio frequency (RF) signals.

- *Local area network (LAN):* A *LAN* is typically an arrangement of PCs in a relatively small area, such as a single office or building.

- *Campus area network (CAN):* Campus area networks are a type of LAN that extends to include PCs and other devices in buildings within an office park or campus setting. The buildings in a CAN are connected by cable or perhaps even a wireless network.

- *Wide area network (WAN):* A *WAN* interconnects two or more LANs over a large geographical area. The *Internet,* which gets its name from the concept of internetworking or the interconnection of networks, is actually a very large WAN. However, a network that connects a company's Dallas office LAN to the LAN at its headquarters in Seattle is a more typical WAN.

◆ *Metropolitan area network (MAN):* A *MAN* is a variation of a WAN that interconnects LANs and PCs within a specific geographical area, such as a city or a cluster of campuses or office parks. Several cities, including Cleveland, Chicago, and Spokane, have established MANs to provide connectivity to the Internet for their downtown businesses and citizens.

Structuring a network

A network can be as simple as two PCs or as complex as a thousand PCs connected together throughout the world. The needs of the users should be what drive the structure of any network; depending on those needs, the network can be very simple or quite complex. The two basic network structures are

◆ *Peer-to-peer (peer-based) networks:* Two or more computers directly connected to one another for the sole purpose of directly sharing data and hardware resources. The very simple network shown in Figure 22-1 illustrates a peer-to-peer network. A cable directly connects these two PCs, and their users are able to grant permission to the other users to access files on their hard disks or CD-ROM drives as well as printers and other hardware. A peer-based network doesn't have a central administrator; rather, the users are responsible for setting permissions to allow other network users access to their PC.

A peer-to-peer network is also practically limited to a maximum of ten PCs. With more than ten PCs, the administration of the permissions becomes so complex that a central administrator is required, and the network activity that must be passed from one PC to the next becomes so heavy that a central server is more efficient.

◆ *Server-based (client/server) networks:* A network of computers and peripherals connected to at least one centralized computer. The central computer is called a *server* because it services requests for data, software, and hardware resources from the network users. The PCs attached to the network are *clients* in this network model. Servers process requests for network resources and services from network clients. A client/server network typically has a central administrator who manages the permissions and access to the resources of the network. This structure is used for the majority of LANs and virtually all WANs and other network types that connect over a WAN.

Actually, any PC on the network can be a server much the same that any PC can be a client. In fact, on a peer-based network, the PCs alternate between being clients and servers. They are clients when they request a file or a service from another PC, and they are servers when they provide a file or service to another PC.

For example, Joe has a new laser printer attached to his PC, and he has granted permission to Rose to use it. When Rose sends print files to Joe's printer, Rose's PC is the client, and Joe's PC is the server (a print service, actually). On server-based networks, the centralized server processes a variety of service requests from the client PCs on the network, as illustrated in Figure 22-2. Typically, on a larger network, clients are clients, and servers are servers.

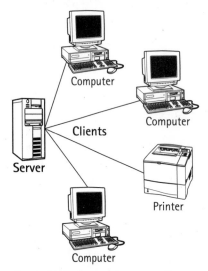

Figure 22-2: A server processes the requests for network services from network clients.

Identifying network components

Served-based networks, the most common implementation of a LAN, are constructed from servers, workstations (clients) and other nodes (such as printers, modems, and so on), a network operating system (NOS), connectivity devices, and the cabling or media used to interconnect it all. A network can actually have many of each of these components, but it must have at least one server and one workstation to be considered a network.

Each of these components is essential to a network's efficient operation overall. Here is an overview of the role played by each of the major network components:

◆ *Cable or media:* The most common form of network is one that connects its nodes via a cable. The most commonly used cable types are coaxial, copper twisted pair, and fiber optic. However, a network can be created without a physical cable, and wireless network technology can be used to connect network elements.

◆ *Client/workstation:* This is a PC connected to a network that makes requests to the network for common services and centrally stored data. Clients or workstations are also called *nodes.*

♦ *Connectivity devices:* These devices, which include hubs, bridges, switches, routers, and the like, are used to connect or cluster one or more workstations to the network and its resources. As I discuss later in the chapter (see "Speaking Network"), each of the various network connectivity devices provides its own type of network services.

♦ *Node:* A network *node* is any addressable networked device, including workstations, peripheral devices, and network connectivity devices. A workstation is a node, but not all nodes are workstations. Some nodes are printers, routers, modems, and so forth.

♦ *Server:* A *server* is a network computer from which clients (workstations and nodes) request files, printing, communications, and other services. Servers can perform a single service, such as a file server, print server, application server, or Web server. A server can also become a client that must request services that it does not provide itself.

Serving the network

A *server* is a networked computer set up to service the resource needs of the network's workstations (clients). A network can actually have a number of different servers with each performing a single function on behalf of the network. On a majority of networks, only one computer is designated as a server, and it performs a variety of services for the network. Table 22-1 lists the most common types of servers implemented on a network.

 A server isn't specifically a piece of hardware. A server is actually software used to provide a specific service to or process specific requests made by network clients. A single hardware server can support many different software servers.

TABLE 22-1 NETWORK SERVERS

Server Type	Function/Purpose
Application server	Shares common application software, eliminating the need for the software to be installed on each workstation
Communications server	Handles common communications functions, such as e-mail, fax, dialup modem, or Internet services

Continued

TABLE 22-1 NETWORK SERVERS *(Continued)*

Server Type	Function/Purpose
Database server	Manages the common database, handling all data storage, database management, and requests for data
Fax server	Provides centralized access to fax and data transfer services to network clients
File server	Stores common network files and users' data files
Print server	Manages network printers, print queues, and printing of user documents
Web server	Provides access to the Web site of a local network

Cabling Up a Network

Assuming that the network is not a wireless network, copper or glass cabling is used to carry data signals across the network. Copper and glass are both relatively inexpensive and abundant, but more importantly, they are excellent conductors of electricity and light, respectively.

 A *conductor* is a material through which energy, either electricity or light, can easily pass through.

Cabling types

Three standard cable types are commonly used on wired networks: coaxial, twisted pair, and fiber optic. Twisted pair cable is the most commonly used network medium, but fiber optic and coaxial cable each have situations for which they are better suited. The following sections provide an overview of the more commonly used cable types.

COAXIAL (COAX) CABLE

The type of coaxial cable used for networking is similar to the coax cable used to connect your TV set to the cable TV outlet. Actually, two coax cable types are used in networks: thin and thick. Thin coax (also called *thinnet* and *thin wire*) is still commonly used in many networking environments, such as where a longer cable run is required than twisted pair cable can support without additional equipment (see "Cabling characteristics" later in this chapter). Thick coax (also called *thicknet, thick wire,* and *yellow wire*) is rarely used today in LAN situations.

As shown in Figure 22-3, coaxial cable is constructed with a single, solid copper wire core surrounded by an insulator made of plastic or Teflon material. A braided metal shielding layer (and in some cables, another metal foil layer) covers the insulator, and a plastic sheath wrapper covers the cable. The metal shielding layers act to increase the cable's resistance to electromagnetic interference (EMI) and radio frequency interference (RFI) signals. The connector shown in Figure 22-3 is a Bayonet Neill-Concelman (BNC) connector, which is the common connector for coaxial cable.

Figure 22-3: A thin coaxial cable showing its components and a BNC-style connector.

TWISTED COPPER PAIR

Twisted pair cable is available in two types: unshielded twisted pair (UTP) and shielded twisted pair (STP). UTP (see Figure 22-4) is less resistant to EMI and RFI noise than STP, but it's less expensive and easier to work with because it's more flexible than coaxial cable. UTP is very similar to the wiring used to connect your telephone. STP is the cable media of choice in certain situations where EMI and RFI are a problem or the wire must be installed near other electrical components.

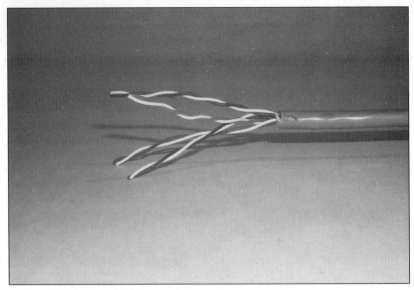

Figure 22-4: Unshielded twisted pair network cable.

As shown in Figure 22-5, each wire pair of STP cable is wrapped with a grounded copper or foil wrapper that shields each pair of wire from electrical noise and other interference. The shielding makes STP more expensive than UTP, which is the primary reason why UTP is more popular. However, STP supports higher transmission speeds and can carry signals over longer distances. See "Twisted pair wire," later in this chapter, for more information on UTP and STP cables.

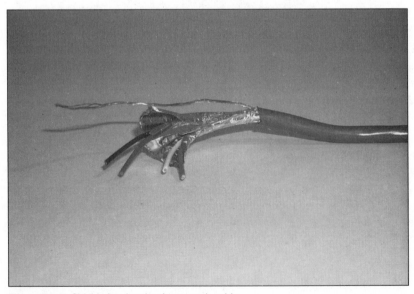

Figure 22-5: Shielded twisted pair network cable.

UTP cable uses an RJ-45 connector, shown in Figure 22-6, which is very much like the RJ-11 connector used on your telephone. The differences between an RJ-11 and an RJ-45 are the number of wire pairs that each connects (RJ-11 accommodates two pairs, and an RJ-45 accommodates four pairs) and their physical size (the RJ-45 is larger overall).

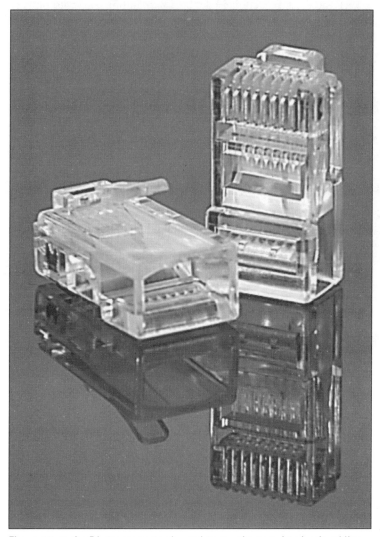

Figure 22-6: An RJ-45 connector is used to terminate twisted pair cabling.

FIBER OPTIC
In fiber optic cable, glass fibers carry modulated pulses of light to represent digital data signals. Light travels through a fiber optic cable much faster than electrical

impulses through a copper cable, which is why fiber optic cable is used for the long line portion of WANs and carrying signals between cities.

A fiber optic cable carries data in the form of modulated pulses of light. To simulate how data travels through a fiber optic cable, you would need to turn a flashlight on and off around two million times in a second. The core of fiber optic cable consists of two (or more) extremely thin strands of glass. Glass cladding covers each strand, helping to keep the light in the strand. Light is carried one way only on each strand because you cannot send light in two directions simultaneously on a single strand. The two core strands carry light either up or down the cable run. A plastic outer jacket covers the cable. Figure 22-7 shows the makeup of a fiber optic cable.

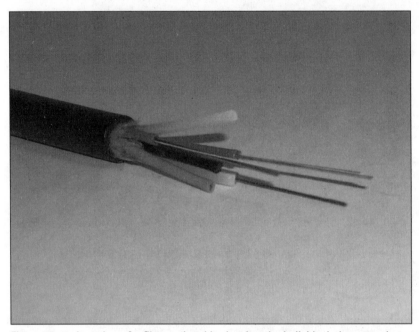

Figure 22-7: A section of a fiber optic cable showing the individual glass strands of the cable.

Because it uses light and not electrical signals, fiber optic cable is not susceptible to electromagnetic or radio frequency interference, which gives it incredibly long attenuation and maximum segment lengths. Network backbones commonly use fiber optic cable.

Cabling characteristics

The most commonly used network cable is UTP. In some situations, however, UTP isn't the best choice. Each type of cable has characteristics that make it appropriate for a given networking situation. Here are the cable characteristics that should be considered when making a cable choice:

◆ *Bandwidth:* This is the amount of data that a cable can transmit in a second, measured in kilobits or megabits. Most copper cabling is nominally rated at 10 Mbps, or ten million bits per second.

◆ *Maximum segment length:* Each type of cable has a distance at which a transmitted signal begins to weaken and must be re-energized to prevent data loss. This natural tendency of transmitted signals over a physical medium is *attenuation.* The maximum segment length, expressed in meters, represents the distance at which attenuation begins to affect the quality of the data signal. In other words, this is the maximum distance between two network nodes for a particular type of cable.

◆ *Maximum number of nodes per segment:* When a node is added to a network cable, its attenuation distance is reduced. This works something like what happens when you punch holes in a water hose: Each hole reduces the water pressure in the hose, and eventually, no water reaches the end of the hose. To guard against a reduction in its bandwidth and data loss, each type of cable limits the number of nodes that can be supported on its maximum segment length.

◆ *Resistance to interference:* Each type of cable resists EMI and RFI in varying degrees. EMI and RFI are caused by electric motors, fluorescent light fixtures, and other electrically noisy devices located near the network cable. As the construction of the cable and its covering varies, so does its resistance to EMI and RFI signals.

Table 22-2 lists the characteristics of thin and thick coaxial cable, unshielded and shielded twisted pair cable, and fiber optic cable.

TABLE 22-2 COMMON NETWORK CABLE CHARACTERISTICS

Cable Type	Bandwidth	Maximum Segment Length	Maximum Nodes/Segment	Resistance to Interference
Thin coaxial	10 Mbps	185 meters	30	Good
Thick coaxial	10 Mbps	500 meters	100	Better
UTP	10–100 Mbps	100 meters	1,024	Poor
STP	16–1,000 Mbps	100 meters	1,024	Fair to good
Fiber optic	100–10,000 Mbps	2,000 meters	No limit	Best

TWISTED PAIR WIRE

Because it provides the most installation flexibility and ease of maintenance of the cable options, unshielded twisted pair (UTP) cabling is by far the most common cable type used on LANs. The Electronics Industries Association (EIA) and the Telecommunications Industries Association (TIA) define UTP cable by five cable categories — each of which is referred to as a *Cat* — that are used on data networks:

- *Cat 3:* 4-pair (8-wire) cable that supports bandwidth up to 10 Mbps — the minimum standard for 10BaseT networks.

- *Cat 4:* 4-pair cable commonly used in 16 Mbps token ring networks.

- *Cat 5:* 4-pair cable that supports 100 Mbps and higher bandwidth. Cat 5 cable is commonly used for 100BaseT networks. UTP cable for most networks is commonly Cat 5.

- *Cat 6:* 4-pair cable that supports 1000BaseT and other high-speed networking applications.

- *Cat 7:* 4-pair shielded (STP) or screened (ScTP) twisted pair cable designed to support 10000BaseT networking. This is an evolving standard, so don't be surprised if you can't find any.

The specification called *NEXT* (Near End Cross Talk) is a higher performance level for Cat 5 cabling that allows a Cat 5 cable to be used as a replacement for 25-pair communications cable.

Understanding the IEEE cable designations

The Institute of Electrical and Electronics Engineers (IEEE) 802.3 (Ethernet) networking standards designate each of the approved cable media with a coding that describes its approved specifications and performance characteristics. The most common designation is 10BaseT cable, which is essentially Cat 3 UTP wire. Other common designations are 10Base5 for thick coax; 10Base2 for thin coax; and 10BaseF and 100BaseF for fiber optic cable.

The *Institute of Electrical and Electronics Engineers* (IEEE) is an international engineering trade and standards organization. IEEE is pronounced *eye-triple-eee.*

The *10Base* or *100Base* part of this code indicates that the cable is capable of supporting 10 Mbps or 100 Mbps bandwidth on a baseband (digital) signal. On the coax cable, the *5* and *2* indicate the maximum segment length of 500 meters and 200 meters of the two cable types, respectively. The number *200* is used for 10Base2 because it's easier to remember than 185, which is its actual maximum segment length. The *T* in 10BaseT refers to twisted pair cable, and fiber optic cable is designated with an *F*.

The common designations for Ethernet cable are the following:

♦ *10Base2:* 10 Mbps Ethernet implemented on thin coaxial cable

♦ *10Base5:* 10 Mbps Ethernet implemented on thick coaxial cable

♦ *10BaseT:* 10 Mbps Ethernet implemented on UTP cable

♦ *100BaseT:* A 2-pair wire implementation, along with 100BaseTX, of *Fast Ethernet,* which is a 100Mbps Ethernet system

♦ *100BaseTX:* Another name for the 2-pair wire version of Fast Ethernet (100BaseT)

♦ *100BaseT4:* A 4-pair wire implementation of Fast Ethernet

♦ *100BaseFX:* Fast Ethernet using two-strand fiber optic cable

♦ *100BaseVG:* A 100 Mbps standard over Cat 3 cable

♦ *1000BaseTX:* Gigabit Ethernet networking implemented on Cat 6 cabling

♦ *1000BaseF:* Gigabit Ethernet networking implemented on a fiber optic backbone

♦ *10000BaseT/F:* Ten Gigabit Ethernet networking cable supported by either Cat 7 or fiber optic cable

Broadband versus Baseband

Baseband networks use only one channel to support digital transmissions. This type of network signaling uses twisted pair cabling. Most LANs are baseband networks.

Broadband networks use analog signaling over a wide range of frequencies. This type of network is unusual, but many cable companies now offer high-speed Internet network access over broadband systems.

Speaking Network

Networking virtually has a language all its own. When troubleshooting common network problems, you might encounter one or more of the following terms:

◆ *Bridge:* This device is used to connect two different LANs or network segments to create what appears to be one network. A bridge intelligently sends network messages to the network segment by using information that it gathers about the MAC addresses of the nodes sending messages through it.

◆ *Gateway:* This is a combination of hardware and software that enables two networks using different transmission protocols to communicate with one another. Gateways are implemented in three primary forms:

   ■ *Address gateway:* Connects networks that use different addressing schemes, such as connecting a Microsoft Windows network to a Novell NetWare network.

   ■ *Format gateway:* Used to connect networks that use different data format schemes, such as a network using the American Standard Code for Information Interchange (ASCII) and another using Extended Binary-Coded Decimal Interchange Code (EBCDIC). This type of gateway is used to connect a PC to a mainframe computer.

   ■ *Protocol gateway:* The most common type of gateway. A protocol gateway connects networks using different communications protocols, such as a router connecting a LAN to the Internet (WAN).

◆ *Hub:* As illustrated in Figure 22-8, a hub connects PCs, workstations, and peripheral devices to a network. Network devices are connected directly to the hub that is in turn connected to the network backbone. Hubs are commonly used on Ethernet twisted pair networks, especially 10BaseT and 100BaseT configurations. A typical hub is configured with 8, 16, or 24 ports.

◆ *Repeater:* A *repeater* is used to extend the maximum segment length of network cabling, to eliminate attenuation, and to regenerate a cable's signal, allowing the signal to reach its destination.

◆ *Router:* A *router* is used to send network messages across the network via the most efficient path available, which it determines from the destination of the network message. A router can also be used to control broadcast storms on a network. When a network node doesn't know the address of a particular workstation or node, it broadcasts a message to the entire network. When too many workstations send broadcast messages, a broadcast storm results.

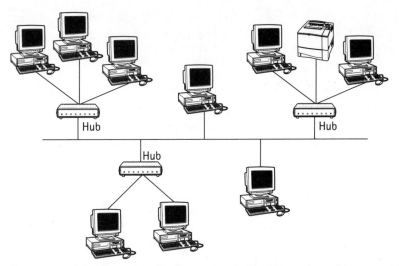

Figure 22-8: A hub is used to distribute network signals to nodes and to connect the nodes to the network backbone.

♦ *Segment:* A *segment* is a discrete portion of a network, usually represented by a single run of cable, a group of workstations, or even a local area network in a WAN. A *cable segment* is a single run of cable with terminators at each end. Typically, a network segment is located on one side of a bridge or router.

♦ *Switch:* A *switch* is used to connect network segments together to form a single network or a larger network segment.

Working without a Wire

Instead of using of physical cable media to interconnect workstations and nodes to a network, a wireless network uses radio frequency (RF) devices to transmit and receive data.

A wireless RF connection can be used to connect one or more workstations to a conventional wired network, or it can be used as the backbone of an entire network, thus forming a wireless local area network (WLAN; pronounced *double-you-lan)*. A WLAN is very flexible and can overcome building or area problems that make installing a cable impractical.

A wireless network is formed in clusters around a device called an access point (AP), much like how a 10BaseT network is formed around a hub. The wireless AP serves as a master station for any wireless network adapters within its broadcast area. The AP transmits and receives data to and from the 802.11 Peripheral Component Interconnect (PCI) and Personal Computer Memory Card International Association (PCMCIA) cards either permanently in its area or those that are just passing through. An AP can be mounted on a tabletop or wall, in a cabinet, or even on a ceiling, but typically the AP is connected to a conventional network backbone with standard network cabling.

802.11 Networks

The IEEE 802.11 standard, commonly called the wireless fidelity (WI-FI) standard, defines wireless networking. Wireless network adapters used to connect a PC or portable computer to a WLAN are 802.11 cards (see Figure 22-9). Devices manufactured to this standard are interoperable with devices from other manufacturers.

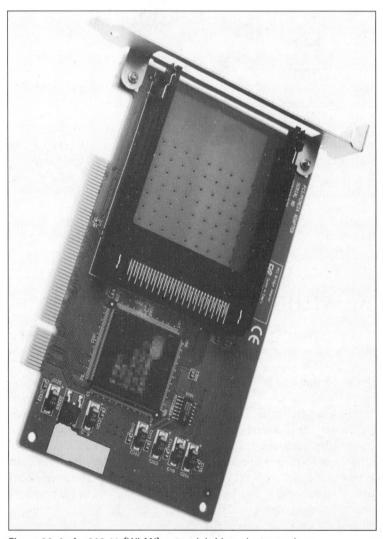

Figure 22-9: An 802.11 (WLAN) network bridge adapter card.

Wireless network adapter cards are installed inside a PC in a PCI slot on the motherboard. There are also 802.11 cards for notebook PCs that allow the PC to move about inside the WLAN's coverage area.

A wireless bridge can be used to connect two or more wired or wireless networks as much as a mile apart. Each network has a wireless bridge that's connected to an external antenna that has a clear and direct line of sight to the antenna connected to a wireless bridge on the other network. A wireless bridge can be used to create a CAN by interconnecting the buildings on a business or school campus.

Bluetooth

Deriving its name from an ancient Swedish king, Bluetooth is another emerging wireless technology. *Bluetooth* is used to connect PCs with external peripheral devices, such as modems and printers, to create a wireless personal area network or WPAN (pronounced *double-you-pan*).

Bluetooth wireless devices must be within 10 meters of a PC or other host device to work effectively. Bluetooth technology transmits encrypted data at 721 Kbps by using frequency-hopping, which helps to secure the data from other Bluetooth devices that might be nearby. Bluetooth has become very popular for use with personal digital assistants (PDAs), such as the Palm Pilot and Visor, and is being built into or can be added to several models. Like other RF devices, a Bluetooth transceiver can be connected to a PC through a USB or serial port, but many newer PCs, keyboards, mice, and other peripherals are available with built-in Bluetooth capability.

IrDA

The Infrared Data Association (IrDA) is a trade and standards organization dedicated to establishing and preserving the standards and usage of devices that use an infrared signal (light spectrum) to communicate. There isn't much in the way of IrDA networking except in a PAN setup in very close proximity.

Working with a NIC

The device used to connect a PC to a network is typically a network interface card (NIC), which is also referred to as a *network adapter*. Typically, a NIC is installed inside the PC (and in some networkable peripheral devices) in an expansion bus slot. The NIC provides the active connecting point between the network (meaning the network cabling) and the PC. The active ingredient in the NIC is its transceiver (transmitter/receiver), which serves as the intermediary between the PC and the network media and the network operating system (NOS).

Getting to know NIC

Network interface cards and network adapters are manufactured by a wide variety of computing equipment manufacturers. Each brand or model of NIC is somewhat unique in its design and even a bit of its functionality. However, nearly all NICs share the same major characteristics, which include

- *Data bus compatibility:* Most newer NICs are designed for the PCI bus. However, many ISA NICs are still in use.

- *MAC address:* Every NIC is assigned a universally unique ID number that's also used as its unique identifying address on a network. The MAC address is used to identify the PC housing the NIC to the network.

- *System resources assignments:* A NIC requires an interrupt request (IRQ), an input/output (I/O) address, and a direct memory access (DMA) channel. The commonly used resource assignments for a NIC are IRQ3, IRQ5, or IRQ10; I/O address 300h; and an available DMA channel.

- *Transceiver type:* Special NICs are available that have different ports for two or more cable types. For example, a NIC can have separate ports and transceivers for UTP and thin coax. This provides flexibility to environments transitioning from one media to another.

Addressing the network

Two levels of addressing are used on networks: physical and logical. The *physical address* of a NIC is its MAC address, which is supplied by the manufacturer. The *logical addressing* of a workstation or node includes its network name and, if Transmission Control Protocol/Internet Protocol (TCP/IP) is in use, its IP address.

MAC ADDRESSING

The MAC address assigned to every NIC or network adapter is universally unique. A *MAC address* is a 48-bit address, expressed as 12 hexadecimal digits. The MAC address is burned into the NIC's firmware during manufacturing and cannot be altered. A NIC's MAC address is used for physical-level LAN addressing of the workstation, and all the other LAN addressing schemes are cross referenced to it.

The WINIPCFG command can be used on Windows 9.x and Me systems to display the PC's MAC access, which is actually the physical address of its NIC. Figure 22-10 shows a sample of the WINIPCFG display. The MAC address shown, 00-A0-CC-34-0A-CE, identifies the manufacturer (the first three segments), and the remainder is the unique number assigned to the NIC.

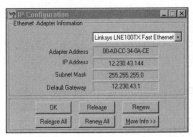

Figure 22-10: The WINIPCFG command displays
the MAC (adapter) address of a PC's NIC.

On a Windows 2000/XP system, the IPCONFIG /ALL command is used to
display the system's MAC address.

IP ADDRESS

If a network is using the TCP/IP suite (and most do), each workstation is also
assigned an IP address. This address is a logical address in that software is used to
interpret and direct messages to and from IP addresses.

An *IP address* is a 32-bit address expressed in four 8-bit octets (or sets of eight).
The IP address (as well as other IP addressing information) for a PC can be displayed by using the IPCONFIG /ALL command. The information displayed by
IPCONFIG /ALL (see Figure 22-11) includes the IP address (00-A0-CC-34-0A-CE), a
subnet mask (used to determine how much of the address is used to designate the
network), and the IP address of the default gateway of the network.

Figure 22-11: Use the IPCONFIG /ALL command to display
the IP address configuration of a PC.

Naming a network

On a Windows network, a PC is assigned a Network Basic Input/Output System (NetBIOS) name – also called a *network name* – by the network administrator. Users can also create network names by assigning share names to workstations and other networked devices. The Windows name conversion protocol Windows Internet Name Service (WINS) correlates the IP and NetBIOS names of each network node so that messages can be directed to the correct workstation.

The *NetBIOS name* is a unique 15-character name that is periodically broadcasted over the network to be cataloged by the Network Neighborhood function. The NetBIOS name is the one that shows up on the Windows Network Neighborhood. Figure 22-12 illustrates the use of NetBIOS and share names on a Windows PC.

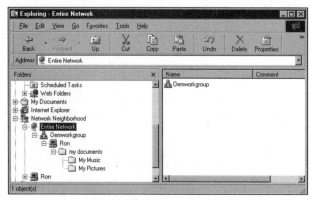

Figure 22-12: NetBIOS (Ron) and share names (My Music and My Pictures) as displayed in Windows Explorer.

Displaying the MAC Address of a Windows PC

To display the MAC address on a Windows 9x PC:

1. From the Windows desktop, choose Start → Run.

2. In the Run dialog box that appears, enter **WINIPCFG** in the Open text box to display the WINIPCFG information, shown in Figure 22-10.

As shown in Figure 22-10, WINIPCFG shows more information than just the MAC address. This command can also be used to troubleshoot Dynamic Host Configuration Protocol (DHCP) conflicts.

Display the IP Address of a PC

Many LANS and virtually all WANs use IP addresses to identify their nodes. An IP address for a networked workstation combines the addresses of the network and the node into a 32-bit address that is expressed in four 8-bit octets (sets of eight).

To check the IP address assignment on your networked PC:

1. Open an MS-DOS command prompt.

2. Enter **IPCONFIG** on the command line and press Enter.

3. Information like that shown in Figure 22-11 is displayed.

4. Enter **EXIT** to close the MS-DOS window.

Figure 22-11 shows the display of an IPCONFIG /ALL command. The display includes the IP addressing information for a networked PC — in this case, a PC with two NICs, one of which is disabled.

IPCONFIG /ALL displays the IP address assigned to the workstation (in this case, 12.230.43.144), its subnet mask (used to determine how much of the address is used to designate the network or the node), and the default gateway of the node.

Dealing with Networked PC Issues

For the most part, the problems that can occur on a networked PC (at least those that have anything to do with it being networked) concern its network adapter (NIC), its cable connection, or its immediate upstream network device (such as a hub, switch, or the like).

In this section, I include the more common issues that you might encounter when supporting user nodes on a network. What I haven't included are those issues that concern the operation, configuration, and troubleshooting of a network server or any of the network devices.

Installing and configuring a NIC

A NIC is installed in a PC to connect the PC to the network or to replace a failed NIC. To install a NIC in a PC, follow these steps:

1. If you're replacing an existing NIC, before physically removing it — even if it's the very same manufacturer and model — it should be uninstalled from the operating system.

   To do this, open the Network dialog box from the Control Panel, highlight the adapter to be removed, and then click the Remove button.

2. Before you insert the NIC in an expansion slot, check the documentation to determine whether any physical configuration steps are necessary.

   Most PCI cards are Plug and Play (PnP) but might still require a Dual Inline Packaging (DIP) switch or a jumper to be set. You absolutely want to do this before inserting the card in a slot. And be sure to handle the card only by its non-connecting edges.

3. Install the NIC in the appropriate expansion slot.

   NICs are usually PCI cards, but you might still find some ISA or Enhanced ISA (EISA) cards around.

4. From the Windows Control Panel, click the Network icon.

5. From the Network dialog box that opens, click the Add button to display the Network Component Type list.

   Four network components can be configured from the Network window. They are

   - *Adapters:* This choice identifies and loads the device drivers for a NIC. To configure a PC to a network, a NIC must already be installed. A NIC installed in a PCI slot should already be listed.

   - *Protocol:* A *protocol* is a set of rules that communicating devices must follow when transmitting data, controls, and commands to one another. To communicate with other network nodes, the PC must use the same protocols as the other nodes.

   - *Client:* Network *clients* allow a PC to communicate with specific network operating systems, such as Windows NT, Windows 2000, or Novell NetWare. To communicate with the network, a PC must have at least one client configured.

   - *Service:* Network *services* include specialized drivers that facilitate specialized capabilities (such as File and Print Sharing) and support for file systems on non-Windows systems.

6. On the Configuration tab of the Network window, click the NIC in the list and then click the Properties button to open the Properties window for the NIC.

   - The *Driver Type tab* should indicate an Enhanced mode (32-bit and 16-bit) Network Device Interface Specification (NDIS) driver for the NIC. The other choices are for cards without 32-bit NDIS support or NICs requiring Open Data-Link Interface (ODI).

   - The *Bindings tab* shows the protocols that have a binding to the NIC. In most cases, these are pre-configured, but they can be modified. A *binding* is a network term for two protocols that perform different networking functions that have an active connection. If you're on an

Ethernet network that has access to the Internet, your bindings will reflect your NIC with a binding to TCP/IP protocols.

- The contents of the *Advanced tab* vary by NIC and the characteristics of the network. The properties list can reflect the media and connector in use, or it can be used to turn on a log file.

7. From this point, click any Apply or OK buttons that appear.

You will be asked for other network information, IP address, gateway, and DNS. The user or the network administrator should provide this information. The system will update its information database, and you might be asked to restart the system.

Troubleshooting a NIC connection

If a newly installed NIC is having problems connecting to or communicating with a network, check the following items:

1. If the NIC has a NIC diagnostics disk or utility, run the diagnostic program to determine whether the problem is on the NIC, PC, or network. If a diagnostics disk or utility wasn't supplied with the NIC, move on to the next step.

TIP   Nearly all NICs come with a NIC diagnostics disk or utility, which is usually included on the disk with the device drivers.

2. Assuming that the NIC is connected to the network (that is, the cable is connected to the NIC, and the device drivers are installed), check the NIC's exterior light-emitting diodes (LEDs).

The LEDs actually do have meaning beyond indicating a connection.

Table 22-3 lists the descriptions for a 3Com dual-speed (meaning 10Mbps/100Mbps) NIC. Because the meanings of the LEDs vary by manufacturer, check the NIC's documentation for the meanings for your particular NIC.

TABLE 22-3 NIC LED DISPLAY MEANINGS

LED	Meaning	Color	Purpose	Flashing	On	Off
LNK	Link signal	Green	Link integrity	Reversed polarity	Good connection	No connection
ACT	Activity	Yellow	Port traffic	Traffic present	Heavy traffic	No traffic

If the LNK LED doesn't light, check the following:

- Make sure that the correct device drivers are loaded.

- Check the cable and connections to the NIC and hub to ensure that they're properly and securely connected.

- Change the hub port.

- Check the duplex mode settings on the NIC and hub for compatibility.

If the ACT LED doesn't light, check the following:

- Make sure that the correct device drivers are loaded.

- Check for network activity because the network might just be down or idle.

- Replace the NIC.

- Check the connection of the RJ-45 to the cable.

3. Check the physical installation of the NIC, making sure that it's properly seated in the expansion slot.

   If the NIC is an ISA or EISA card, verify that jumper or DIP switch settings, if required, are correct. If all looks good, you might want to try a second identical card to eliminate the possibility of a bad card. Check the expansion slot for broken contacts or move the card to another slot.

4. Check the Windows Device Manager to look for an indication of a problem.

   If either a yellow or black exclamation point or a red X is showing on the NIC, look at the NIC's properties for an indication of the problem.

5. Check the cables and connectors.

   In addition to problems with the connector or the cable, the cable could be too long. Verify that the workstation is not beyond the maximum segment length or that there aren't more nodes than the cable medium can effectively support. If the problem is on a peer-to-peer network where two PCs are directly connected without a hub or switch, make sure that a crossover cable (see Table 22-2 earlier in the chapter for cable length parameters) is being used.

6. Check the PC's BIOS.

   Verify that you're running the latest version of the BIOS. If not, check with the motherboard or BIOS manufacturer to see whether upgrades affecting PCI ports or NICs have been made.

7. Verify that the correct device driver is installed.

Use the driver that came with the NIC or one downloaded from the manufacturer's Web site to reinstall the driver from the Windows Device Manager. You might want to check the compatibilities of the driver as well because not all drivers work with every operating system.

The computer hangs when the NIC's device drivers are loaded

This problem is probably caused by the NIC's PCI interrupt settings in the BIOS. Check the NIC and BIOS documentation for the correct settings.

Another cause could be the high memory device driver. If the PC is running EMM386.EXE, many PCI NIC device drivers require version 4.49 or later.

The Wake on LAN (WOL) feature is not working

Wake on LAN (WOL) is a feature supported by many NICs that allows a PC to be powered up by the network server or from a remote location on the network. If WOL is not working, check these items:

1. Check the BIOS to ensure that it supports WOL.

   If it does, enable it by changing its setting to Enabled. If it doesn't, check with the BIOS or motherboard manufacturer for a BIOS upgrade that includes this support.

2. Check the WOL cable connection between the NIC and the motherboard by verifying the documentation of the NIC and the motherboard to determine where this connection is made.

   In order for WOL to be functional, a WOL cable must be connected between the NIC and the motherboard. Without this cable, the WOL signal cannot be passed to the motherboard.

3. Check the network cable connection on the NIC.

Verifying a local network connection

If you wish to test a newly installed network PC to see whether it can connect to another computer on the local network using the TCP/IP suite, follow this procedure:

1. On a Windows PC, open a DOS command window:

   Windows 9x or Me computers: Open an MS-DOS prompt window by selecting the appropriate icon after choosing Start → Programs.

   Windows NT, 2000, or XP systems: Enter **cmd** in the text field of the Run dialog box (choose Start → Run) and then click OK.

2. Enter the `ping` command along with the IP address (or the NetBIOS name) of the computer that you wish to reach.

This command should look something like the following. (Of course, the IP address shown might be different in your specific case.)

```
C:>ping 192.168.2.100
```

3. The response should look something like the following:

```
Pinging 192.168.1.7 with 32 bytes of data:

Reply from 192.168.2.100: bytes=32 time<1ms TTL=12
Reply from 192.168.2.100: bytes=32 time<1ms TTL=12
Reply from 192.168.2.100: bytes=32 time<1ms TTL=12
Reply from 192.168.2.100: bytes=32 time<1ms TTL=12

Ping statistics for 192.168.2.100:
Packets: Sent = 4, Received = 4, Lost = 0
Approximate round trip times in milli-seconds:
Minimum = 0ms, Maximum = 0ms, Average = 0ms
```

However, if the computer IP or NetBIOS name entered is incorrect or if the PC cannot connect to the network, you might see something along the line of this:

```
C:>ping GILSTER
Ping request could not find host GILSTER. Please check the
name and try again.
```

TIP On Windows 9x, Me, and NT systems, you should always be able to ping another network PC by using its name because TCP/IP uses NetBIOS broadcast messages to find the destination node. However, if you're on a Windows 2000 or XP system, verify that NetBIOS is enabled in the Advanced TCP/IP Properties.

Verifying a connection to a remote site

If you're having trouble connecting to a remote site over the Internet, two TCP/IP tools can be used to check out the connection: `ping` and `tracert`.

PING

You can read more about using ping to verify a local network connection in the previous section. To verify a connection to a remote site, the remote site's IP address or DNS name is used. For example, to ping the `rongilster.com` Web site, you enter

```
C:>ping rongilster.com
```

Or

```
C:>ping 64.35.138.3
```

TIP

To learn the IP address of a site on the Internet, use the IP Whois service at www.samspade.org.

If a host unknown message is returned, chances are that the site no longer exists, it's down, or you have a DNS problem. Or maybe the DNS server on the network isn't configured properly or is offline. Check with the network administrator or the ISP to resolve this problem.

If you wish to verify that your PC's NIC is connected and operating, try pinging your own machine. To do so, enter the following command:

```
C:>ping localhost
```

Or

```
C:>ping 127.0.0.1
```

NOTE

IP addresses that begin with 127 are reserved for loopback testing, which allows you to send out a test message and have it loop back to the NIC.

A good response means that you're able to reach the loopback functions on your PC's NIC. If you don't get a reply, the problem is likely with the NIC, network configuration, or cabling. Run the NIC's diagnostics; if all is well, verify that the cabling is connected properly to the NIC. Beyond that, you need to coordinate with the network administrators.

If the NIC and cabling check out, verify the network setting on the PC. This can be done by using the IP configuration utility of the operating system. On a Windows 9x or Me system, use the WINIPCFG command. On a Windows NT, 2000, or XP system, use the IPCONFIG command. Figures 22-10 and 22-11, earlier in the chapter, show the output of the WINIPCFG and IPCONFIG utilities, respectively.

TIP Always check the NIC's link and activity lights to see whether they show a connection and network activity.

TRACERT

The `tracert` utility is used to identify any problems that might exist along the IP path between your network and the remote site. To display the route and response times along the routing path between you and a remote site, enter the following (substituting the IP or host name of the site that you wish to trace):

```
C:>tracert rongilster.com
```

The results displayed should look something like those shown in Figure 22-13. If any hop displays asterisks and the message `Request timed out`, that location could be a bottleneck or a barrier to reaching the destination site.

```
TRACERT                                                    _ @ x

C:\>tracert rongilster.com

Tracing route to rongilster.com [64.35.138.3]
over a maximum of 30 hops:

  1    10 ms    10 ms    18 ms  10.128.32.1
  2    28 ms    11 ms     9 ms  12.244.81.97
  3    74 ms    31 ms    16 ms  12.244.64.53
  4    24 ms    70 ms    81 ms  12.244.72.14
  5    72 ms    21 ms    24 ms  gbr2-p70.st6wa.ip.att.net [12.123.44.61]
  6    21 ms    79 ms    32 ms  gbr3-p80.st6wa.ip.att.net [12.122.5.165]
  7    50 ms    31 ms    32 ms  gbr4-p10.sffca.ip.att.net [12.122.2.61]
  8    61 ms    59 ms    79 ms  gbr3-p50.dvmco.ip.att.net [12.122.2.66]
  9    55 ms    67 ms    55 ms  gbr2-p20.dvmco.ip.att.net [12.122.5.26]
 10    70 ms    96 ms    55 ms  gar2-p370.dvmco.ip.att.net [12.123.36.141]
 11    55 ms    82 ms    66 ms  12.124.158.46
 12    56 ms    94 ms    81 ms  den-core-02.tamerica.net [205.171.16.17]
 13    52 ms    54 ms    77 ms  sea-core-01.tamerica.net [205.171.8.82]
 14    53 ms   106 ms    51 ms  sea-core-03.tamerica.net [205.171.26.54]
```

Figure 22-13: Use `tracert` to track the routing path between a source network and a destination site.

Resolving host name resolution issues

If you can't ping NetBIOS names on a network, the problem is possibly with WINS or LMHOSTS in most cases. If you can't ping DNS host names over the Internet, the problem is either a local HOSTS file issue or a network DNS problem.

Windows 2000 and XP systems include a number of TCP/IP tools that you can use to troubleshoot address and name resolution issues: the `ping` command (see

"Verifying a connection to a remote site" earlier in the chapter), the `ipconfig` command (see the sidebar entitled "Display the IP Address of a PC" earlier in the chapter), and the `nslookup` command.

HOSTS FILE

The *HOSTS file* is used to support name resolution on a local network and is located on one or more network servers. If the HOSTS file is local, it's typically located in the \System32\Drivers\Etc folder. Unfortunately, this file is not dynamically maintained, and any entries must be manually entered. An entry in the HOSTS file looks like this:

IP Address	Friendly Name
192.168.2.10	rgilster # Remarks are preceded with a #

Problems with resolving host names can include the following:

◆ A particular host name is not included in the HOSTS file or DNS server

◆ A HOSTS file entry or DNS command has a misspelling of the host name

◆ The IP address associated with the host name is invalid

◆ The HOSTS file contains more than one entry for the same host (in which case the first entry is always used)

NSLOOKUP

Although only on Windows NT, 2000, and XP systems, the `nslookup` command is used to search DNS name servers to display information about either an Internet host name or an IP address (reverse lookup). Its format is

```
C:>nslookup rongilster.com
```

NBTSTAT

The `nbtstat` (NetBIOS over TCP/IP Status) command is used to resolve a NetBIOS (local host name) to its IP address on TCP/IP networks. Typically, the `nbtstat -n` (the – parameter lists the NetBIOS names for the local host) command is used as follows:

```
C:>nbtstat -n
```

The information displayed by this command (as illustrated in Figure 22-14) lists the names that the NetBIOS server has registered on the network.

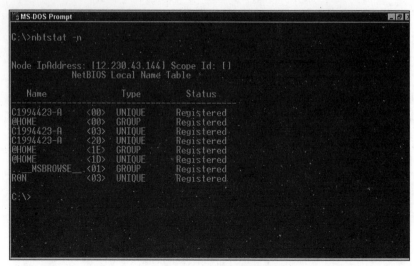

```
MS-DOS Prompt                                              ▬ ▢ ▯

C:\>nbtstat -n

Node IpAddress: [12.230.43.144] Scope Id: []
            NetBIOS Local Name Table

     Name               Type        Status

C1994423-A    <00>  UNIQUE     Registered
@HOME         <00>  GROUP      Registered
C1994423-A    <03>  UNIQUE     Registered
C1994423-A    <20>  UNIQUE     Registered
@HOME         <1E>  GROUP      Registered
@HOME         <1D>  UNIQUE     Registered
.__MSBROWSE__.<01>  GROUP      Registered
RON           <03>  UNIQUE     Registered

C:\>
```

Figure 22-14: Using the nbtstat -n command displays the registered names of a network.

Part VIII

Configuring the PC

Chapter 23

Expansion Cards

IN THIS CHAPTER

The challenge of an expansion card, beyond getting the right one, is getting it installed, configured, and operating. I discuss the following in this chapter:

◆ Installing an expansion card

◆ Troubleshooting expansion cards

◆ Dealing with choke points

◆ Installing a SCSI host adapter

◆ Installing serial and parallel add-on ports

◆ Resolving resource conflicts on Windows PCs

◆ Resolving resource conflicts with Plug and Play devices

ADDING ANY ADDITIONAL FUNCTIONS to the mix can create conflicts and introduce problems in areas that were perfectly fine before the card was inserted.

Expansion Basics

Since the early days of the PC, you've been able to add to or alter its capabilities by adding expansion cards inside the PC's case. *Expansion cards*, also called expansion boards, adapters, add-in cards, and daughterboards, allow you upgrade the quality of the PC's graphics and sound, control internal devices, or connect to the outside world. Figure 23-1 shows a typical expansion card, which is in this case a network interface card (NIC).

In the context of the PC, *expansion* means broadening the capabilities of the system by inserting special purpose circuit cards into the expansion bus on the motherboard.

At the risk of sounding obvious, expansion cards are inserted into expansion slots on the motherboard. *Expansion slots* are connector receptacles located on the PC's motherboard that connect the inserted card to the motherboard's input/output (I/O) bus structures. Inside an expansion slot are metallic (typically copper) spring fingers that clamp onto the expansion card when it is inserted in the slot. Each of the fingers matches up with one segment of the card's edge connector to complete one of many different connections of the slot-and-card combination. Figure 23-2 shows a card being inserted into a slot.

Figure 23-1: An expansion card is added to a PC to increase its capabilities.

Figure 23-2: An expansion card and an expansion slot on a motherboard.

On early PCs, expansion cards were used to add some of the basic functions of the system, including memory, hard disk and floppy disk controllers, video controllers, serial and parallel ports, modems, and even the clock and calendar function of the PC. Today's PCs still add some of these functions through expansion cards, but many of these capabilities are now built into the motherboard's chipset. On modern PCs, expansion cards are used to improve or add to the capabilities of the system, to add controllers and adapters for special purpose hardware, and to connect to a network. Expansion cards can allow a PC to have video capture, sound, fax, scanners, and network capabilities.

As I mention earlier, the challenge of expansion cards, beyond getting the right one, is getting it installed, configured, and operating. Because a PC is configured to the set of features included when it was manufactured, adding any additional functions to the mix can create conflicts and introduce problems in areas that were perfectly fine before the card was inserted. The world of expansion cards is one of interrupt requests (IRQs), direct memory access (DMA), I/O ports, Dual Inline Packaging (DIP) switches, and jumper blocks. But before I get to that, review the expansion buses and the unique expansion slot used by each.

Reviewing the Expansion Buses

Bus structures, also called *bus architectures*, define the length, width, number of contacts, and interface used to add expansion cards to the motherboard. Why one bus would be used over another can be a matter of preference, but each of the popular bus structures, illustrated in Figures 23-3 through 23-6, has a unique set of operational features that differentiates it from the others.

Here are the PC bus structures that have been the most popular over the years:

♦ *Industry Standard Architecture (ISA):* This bus structure has been around the longest of all the buses still in use. In fact, it is now largely obsolete, but most motherboards still have at least one ISA slot to provide some backward compatibility to support older hardware. The 8 MHz ISA bus is a 16-bit bus that also supports 8-bit cards. Some ISA cards (newer cards) are Plug and Play (PnP), and others (typically older cards) are not, which means an ISA device might need some or a completely manual configuration and setup. The ISA bus is also called the *AT bus*, for the IBM PC AT on which it was featured. Figure 23-3 shows a drawing of an ISA card. Compare its edge connectors with those of the expansion cards for the other expansion bus structures shown. ISA expansion slots are typically black.

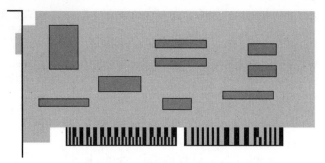

Figure 23-3: An illustration of an ISA bus expansion card.

◆ *Extended ISA (EISA):* This PC bus extends the 16-bit ISA bus to 32 bits and adds bus mastering (see "Mastering the bus" later in the chapter). EISA expansion slots are backward compatible to ISA and can run at the same slow 8 MHz speeds of the ISA bus to maintain the compatibility. The PCI bus has largely replaced EISA, which is still available on some motherboard designs. Like the ISA slots, EISA slots are black and are placed next to the ISA slots on those motherboards that include them.

◆ *VESA local bus (VL-bus):* The VL-bus architecture was developed by the Video Electronics Standards Association (VESA) for use with the 486 processor. A *VL-bus* is a 32-bit bus that supports bus mastering and runs at speeds up to 40 MHz. If you have a PC with a VL-bus expansion slot, you can't mistake it for anything else. VL-bus slots are similar in appearance to ISA slots but have an extra slot added to the end and are four inches long in total. The PCI bus has essentially replaced the VL-bus on modern PCs. Figure 23-4 shows an illustrated view of the relative size of the most common expansion slots.

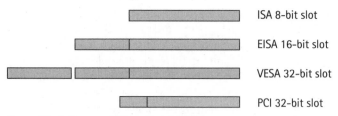

ISA 8-bit slot

EISA 16-bit slot

VESA 32-bit slot

PCI 32-bit slot

Figure 23-4: Common PC expansion slots.

◆ *Peripheral Component Interconnect (PCI):* The PCI showed up with the first Intel Pentium computers and is the de facto standard for add-in cards on virtually all motherboards since then. PCI, which is commonly used on PCs, Macintoshes, and workstations, provides a high-speed data path between the CPU and the peripheral devices connected into it. The PCI bus, which is a local bus (see "Taking the local bus" later in the chapter), usually includes some devices mounted or connected directly to the motherboard as well as in the PCI expansion slots. Most motherboards include three or four of the white PCI expansion slots. PCI provides 32- and 64-bit interfaces that support either 33 MHz or 66 MHz data bus speeds. PCI also supports full PnP capability, which provides nearly foolproof installations and configurations. The shorter slot length helps make motherboards smaller. Figure 23-5 shows a PCI expansion card.

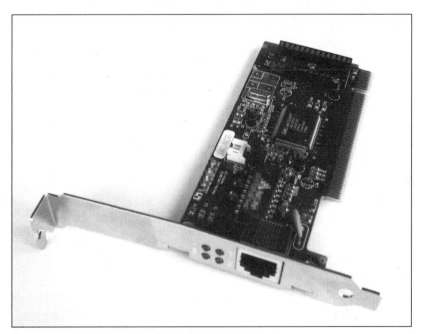

Figure 23-5: A PCI bus network interface card.

- *Accelerated Graphics Port (AGP):* This expansion bus is a little different than the ISA and PCI buses in that it was invented for one purpose only: the support of video cards. Its primary purposes are to improve the performance of 3-D graphics on the system and to make video cards less expensive by removing the need for memory on the video card. However, video systems have become less expensive, and although the AGP interface does help, it no longer really provides the benefits it was intended to deliver. AGP, with data speeds up to 133 MHz, does run at faster speeds than the legacy PCI bus.

However, different speed ratings exist for AGP video cards: 264 Mbps or 1xAGP, 528 Mbps or 2xAGP, 1 Gbps or 4xAGP, and 2 Gbps or 8xAGP. The AGP slot is a brown slot that's just a little shorter than the white PCI slot. Figure 23-6 shows the placement of the AGP slot on an AT form factor motherboard in relationship to the ISA and PCI slots.

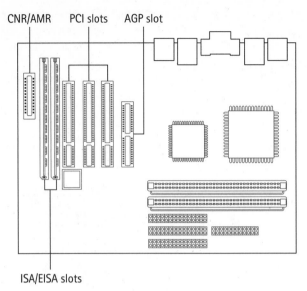

CNR/AMR   PCI slots   AGP slot

ISA/EISA slots

Figure 23-6: The placement of the expansion slots on a motherboard.

◆ *Communications and Network Riser (CNR)*: Some newer motherboards now include a CNR slot that can be used to extend the motherboard with a riser card that supports audio, modem, and local area network (LAN) using specialized riser board chipsets.

◆ *Audio/Modem Riser (AMR)*: Although less common on motherboards than a CNR slot, an AMR slot is used to extend the motherboard using a riser card that packages audio and modem support along with a compressor/decompressor (codec) used to convert analog and digital signals back and forth. The equivalent of AMR for portable PCs is the Mobile Daughter Card (MDC).

Mastering the bus

The PCI bus architecture features a technology called *bus mastering,* which allows expansion cards to directly access the PC's main memory (random access memory, or RAM) and other peripheral device controllers without the need to pass through the CPU. Bus mastering allows the PCI bus controller to transfer data from a PCI device directly to memory while the CPU is executing other instructions.

Taking the local bus

Bus architectures that are connected directly into the same internal bus structure that supports the CPU and run at its data speeds are said to be *local* to the CPU. Local bus, also called *system bus,* structures are largely in the past because the system bus of most motherboards now has data speeds well above that of the peripheral devices and expansion buses.

Expanding the portable PC

Portable PCs, most notably notebook computers, have a special expansion bus that allows expansion cards to be inserted while the system is running and without the need to open the computer's case. The PC Card interface, formally called the Personal Computer Memory Card International Association (PCMCIA) interface (after the standards body that developed it), uses a 68-pin socket that connects directly to the computer's expansion bus. PC Cards are inserted into this socket to add resources or devices to the computer. Figure 23-7 shows a notebook computer with a PC Card network adapter being inserted.

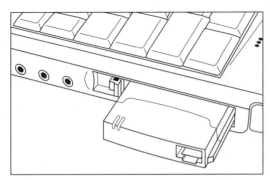

Figure 23-7: A PC Card is the expansion card for notebook computers.

PC Cards use a special socket in which credit-card-sized expansion cards that can encompass entire peripheral devices are inserted. These expansion cards can contain additional memory, a hard disk drive, a modem, a network adapter, a sound card, or more.

The PCMCIA has established standards for three PC Card slots (and the devices that fit into them):

♦ *Type 1:* This slot and card is 3.3 millimeters (mm) thick and is used to add additional RAM and Flash memory. Type 1 slots are most common on very small computers, such as palmtops.

♦ *Type 2:* This slot is 5 mm thick, and its cards are typically able to perform I/O functions, such as modems and network adapter cards. Figure 23-8 shows a Type 2 PC Card network adapter with its dongle connector.

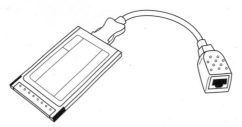

Figure 23-8: A Type 2 PC Card network adapter.

◆ *Type 3:* This slot is a whopping 10.5 mm thick and is used mainly for add-on hard drives and 802.11 wireless network devices.

PC Cards are *hot swappable,* which means that they can be inserted and removed while the system is running and that they don't require the system to be restarted to recognize the card. Not all PC Card devices totally adhere to the PCMCIA specifications: Some require a software driver before they are fully functional.

Working with SCSI

The Small Computer System Interface (SCSI) is not actually an expansion bus structure, but it can be used to add both internal and external devices to a PC. SCSI (pronounced *skuz*-zee) devices are more commonly found on network servers rather than personal computers because they tend to be more expensive than ISA or PCI devices. However, SCSI adapters provide a very easy way to connect multiple devices together on a single interface, both inside and outside of the system unit. SCSI has been around for some time and has a variation to fit just about every system, including both ISA- and PCI-compatible host adapter (expansion) cards.

For more information on SCSI, see Chapter 11.

A SCSI host adapter card can handle up to seven devices in addition to itself, counting both internal and external devices. Newer versions, like the SCSI-3 standard, now handle up to 15 devices, but these cards are almost prohibitively expensive for a home computer. A SCSI interface with multiple devices must be terminated at each end of the chain. Each device on the chain is assigned a unique identity number that's used by the host adapter to communicate with it.

Adding serial and parallel ports

Since their inception, PCs have had at least two ports: a serial port and a parallel port. On older PCs, such as PC XTs through and including most 486s, these ports were added through expansion cards, which were inserted primarily into ISA slots.

 See Chapter 24 for more information on these and other I/O ports and connectors.

Interfacing with USB and IEEE 1394

Two of the newer connector and interface types used to connect external peripherals to a PC are the Universal Serial Bus (USB) and the Institute of Electrical and Electronics Engineers (IEEE) 1394 standards.

USB

USB devices can be connected to external USB hubs, which can be daisy-chained together to the point of 127 devices on a single USB bus. This means that 127 devices can share one bus but also one set of system resources as well. Figure 23-9 shows a USB port and connector.

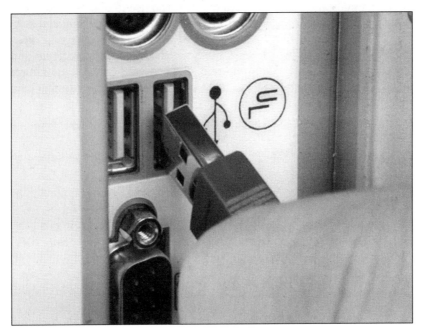

Figure 23-9: A USB port and connector.

IEEE 1394

The IEEE 1394 standard is more commonly known as FireWire (Apple), i.Link (Sony), or Lynx (Texas Instruments) proprietary interfaces, or by its generic name High Performance Serial Bus (HPSB). FireWire (its most common name) and USB are flexible device interfaces that can support both low-speed devices (such as keyboards and mice) as well as high-speed, high-end devices (such as video cameras, scanners, and printers).

Like USB, FireWire is hot swappable and PnP compatible, which means that FireWire devices can be added to or removed from a PC without the need to reboot the system or extensive installation procedures. IEEE 1394 (FireWire) is a slightly faster interface than USB 1.0 (however, USB 2.0 will regain its title) and is designed to handle the bandwidth and data transfer speeds and requirements of devices requiring an *isochronous* (real-time) interface. The IEEE 1394 interface supports up to 63 devices that can have different device transfer speeds on a single bus.

 All versions of Windows since Windows 98 directly support the IEEE 1394 standard.

Sorting Out Expansion Cards

For all the different bus and interface types that you can use to plug an expansion card or device into a PC, there really aren't that many types of expansion cards. At one time, any additional function that you wished the PC to have beyond those included on the motherboard (which wasn't very much beyond the processor and BIOS) had to be added via an expansion card. Today's motherboards now have quite a few of the functions that once required a separate adapter or controller card built into the chipset or its Super I/O chip.

 For more information on chipsets, see Chapter 3.

Each of the following sections gives a quick overview of one of the many common expansion card types that can be added to a PC.

Adding a controller card

A *controller card*, also know as an *adapter card*, is an expansion card that contains the circuitry and components needed to control the operations of a peripheral device, such as a disk drive. Controller cards are now less common on newer PCs because device controllers are typically included in either the system chipset or the Super I/O chip.

Controller cards are fairly easy to find in the PC. They are the ones with flat ribbon cables attached to them that run to the hard disk, CD-ROM, DVD, and floppy disk drives. In most older PCs, the disk controller card supports both the hard disk drive and the floppy disk drives – and usually more. If a CD-ROM device were installed in an older PC, it typically had its own controller card but could also share the common (multi-purpose) controller card.

The SCSI host adapter is not a controller card, although it might appear to be one. SCSI devices, like IDE (ATA) devices, have their controllers integrated into the device itself. (See Chapter 11 for more information on IDE and SCSI storage devices.)

Communicating through I/O cards

I/O cards are used to add I/O ports, such as serial and parallel ports, to a PC. Although these cards were once a mainstay of PC configurations, they are nearly obsolete today because the ports that they support are typically included as a part of the motherboard.

INTERFACE CARDS

This is the most nondescript of the expansion cards. In fact, just about any expansion card can be and usually is classified as an interface card. But in general use, an *interface card* connects a PC to any external device, network, or gadget. An interface card connects a mouse, an external CD-ROM, scanner, camera, or other device to a PC, including the PC Cards used to connect external devices to portable PCs.

MEMORY CARDS

Most PC technicians don't think of memory modules as expansion cards, but in the strictest interpretation of an expansion card, the memory modules used to add memory to a PC are just that. See a Single Inline Memory Module (SIMM) being installed in its slot in Figure 23-10.

Figure 23-10: A SIMM being installed on a motherboard.

MEMORY EXPANSION CARD (MEC)

Higher-end PCs, like those in use as network servers or graphics workstations, often fill up their memory module slots and still require additional memory. Many of these systems are able to install a special expansion card, called a Memory Expansion Card (MEC), that can add up to 16GB of additional RAM (usually synchronous dynamic random access memory [SDRAM]) to the system. This is where the amount of RAM that the CPU can address becomes important. Figure 23-11 shows an illustration of a MEC for a workstation line of computers.

As Figure 23-11 illustrates, a MEC is able to mount a number of memory modules (usually Dual Inline Memory Modules, or DIMMs). The card illustrated has 8 memory slots, and some are available to handle as many as 16 DIMMs. One drawback, although slight when weighed against the advantage of the additional memory, is that the MEC sits on the system bus and is therefore slower than the memory mounted in the SIMM or DIMM slots on the motherboard.

PC CARD MEMORY CARD

Memory can be added to a portable PC, virtually on the fly, with a PC Card Type 1 memory card. Remember that the standards organization for PC Cards is named the Personal Computer Memory Card International Association (PCMCIA), with the emphasis on *memory card*.

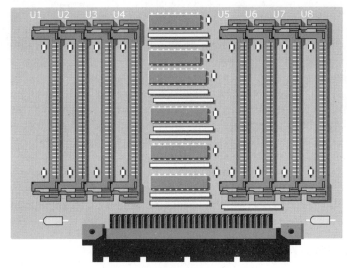

Figure 23-11: A memory expansion card.

PC Card memory cards are credit-card-sized memory modules that incorporate Flash memory (static RAM, or SRAM). When a Flash memory card is added to a portable PC, the memory added should not be used as a substitute for a disk drive but used to extend the working storage of the PC. PC Card memories are available with 8MB to 1GB of Flash memory.

PC Card memories are available in Type 1 packaging or in compact flash (CF) cards that can be added to the PC through a Type 1 adapter card. Figure 23-12 shows a CF card and its PC Card adapter.

Figure 23-12: A PCMCIA Flash memory card.

MODEM CARDS

A *modem* (short for *modulator/demodulator*) allows you to connect to and communicate with other computers over the public telephone network. An *internal modem* is one that plugs into an expansion slot on the motherboard. *External modems,* which connect to the PC via a serial or USB port, have indicator lights that are lit to signal the activity of the mode. However, when using an internal modem, because it's mounted inside the system case, the user must rely on a software interface to control the modem and view the status of a communications session.

Internal modem cards, like most other expansion cards, are available for either the ISA or PCI expansion buses. Installation of the modem card might require some COM (serial) port assignment, but typically the modem will have an installation disk that also includes its device driver. Any problems that are created with the installation of the modem usually involve system resource conflicts.

Just about all notebook computers and other portables have a modem built into the system. If you wish to use an external modem, you typically add it to the system in the form of a PC Card Type 2 card. The telephone cable is attached with an *X-Jack,* which is a connector that pops out of the end of the card to allow the phone cable's RJ-11 connector to plug in.

Chapter 21 deals specifically with the functions and configuration of modems, both internal and external.

SOUND CARDS

Although sound (audio) processing is included on the motherboard of some newer PCs, it's usually a feature added through an expansion card. Sound cards are fairly standard in their basic function: producing sound. However, the number of voices — meaning the different distinct instruments or sounds that the sound card can reproduce — continues to grow.

The number in the sound card name, such as Sound Blaster *16,* Soundwave *32,* or Sound Blaster AWE *64,* refers to the number of voices that the sound card can reproduce, not the number of bits that the sound card uses to decode the sound samples. Many sound card manufacturers now produce PCI sound cards with 128 voices, but read the specifications because many "128" sound cards still have only 64 voices.

Like with most expansion cards, probably the only snag that you'll run into when installing a sound card in a PC is system resource conflicts, especially interrupt requests (IRQs). See the "Troubleshooting expansion cards" section of this chapter for more information on resolving resource conflicts for expansion cards.

Nearly all sound cards use a 16-bit digital sound resolution, which is the same that's used on all CD players and CD-ROM drives.

More information is available about sound cards in Chapter 16.

VIDEO CARDS

The video card in your PC could arguably be the most important expansion card in your system, depending on how you look at it. The video card provides your PC with the ability to display a picture on the monitor. True, some newer motherboards now integrate the video processing into the chipset or on the motherboard itself, but for the vast number of PCs in use, a video expansion card is used to drive the video signal.

The video card must be matched to the monitor. Don't buy a screaming video card to drive a wimpy monitor. These two components must be matched in their capabilities. The video card must be able to drive the monitor, and the monitor must be able to display the output of the video card.

When choosing a video card for a PC, you should look at three important features or components: its processor or chipset, its bus, and its memory.

See Chapters 14 and 15 for more information on video cards and monitors, respectively.

Installing and Configuring Expansion Cards

This section of the chapter covers what could be the most common maintenance and repair activity on a PC: installing the card. With most cards now PnP-compatible, most of the work is accomplished when you install the card. However, on some (it just never fails), you might need to perform additional or corrective configuration. The following sections provide the processes and steps used to install and configure expansion cards.

Installing an expansion card

Assuming that you are following the electrostatic discharge (ESD) protection guidelines (outlined in Chapter 27), follow this general procedure to install an expansion card in a PC:

1. Create a backup of the hard disk's contents.

   Typically, installing an expansion card shouldn't have any effect on the hard disk, but you just never know.

2. Turn off the computer's power and remove the AC power cord from the outlet.

3. Open or remove the system case, depending on the case design of the PC.

4. Identify an available slot of the appropriate expansion bus.

   Remember that expansion cards are manufactured to fit the slot style of a certain bus structure. If the PC is fairly recent, as well as the card, more than likely either an ISA or a PCI slot is what is needed. An older 8-bit card will fit into an ISA 16-bit slot. To make room for the card, you might need to rearrange the existing cards.

5. Remove the screw holding in the metal slot cover for the slot in which you will be inserting the new expansion card.

   Hang onto the screw; you'll need it to secure the expansion card.

6. Before inserting the card, read its documentation to verify its configuration and settings.

   Setting DIP switches and jumpers after the card is inserted into a slot and fastened down is very difficult: Be sure to do this before inserting the card.

7. Handle expansion cards only by their edges and avoid touching their circuit side (the one with the electronic stuff on it), their pin side (the backside), or the edge connector.

   That doesn't leave much, I know, but the top and side edges do give you enough of the card to hold.

8. Insert the card by aligning it to the slot (as shown in Figure 23-13), and then with steady pressure, press the card into the slot.

   You might need to rock it very slightly front to rear to get it to settle into the slot. *Don't force it.* It should be snug, but you can also damage the slot or the card (or both) by forcing the card into the slot too fast and too hard. As you work, keep the card from rubbing or touching other cards already installed. Figure 23-13 shows a very realistic situation for installing an expansion card.

Figure 23-13: Installing an expansion card in a PC.

9. When the card is evenly and securely in the slot, fasten it with the slot screw.

10. You might want to plug the PC in and test it for a very short time with the system case covers off.

   If you test with the cover off, if there is a problem, it's a much shorter path back to where you were.

11. When you're sure that all is well, replace the system case cover.

Troubleshooting expansion cards

Several situations in which you might encounter a problem relating to an expansion card are

♦ After you install an expansion card.

♦ Some time after you install an expansion card.

♦ Getting a boot error with a Power-On Self-Test (POST) beep code or error message indicating a possible expansion card problem. (See Chapter 3 for more information on beep codes.)

♦ An expansion card doesn't perform as it should.

When these problems arise, three possible scenarios could be to blame:

♦ A bad connection, meaning that the card was improperly installed

♦ A system resource conflict

♦ A malfunctioning (or just plain bad) expansion card

Here is a troubleshooting regime to track down which of these scenarios is causing the problem:

1. Always begin by organizing a workspace around the PC as much as possible and preparing the workspace, the PC, and yourself against ESD (as outlined in Chapter 27).

   I can't emphasis this too much. Even the smallest static discharge can inflict enough damage to the expansion card to have caused the problem that you're now trying to track down.

2. Turn off the PC, unplug it from its electrical outlet, and turn off any peripheral devices attached to the PC, unplugging their power cords from their AC outlets as well.

   Just turning off the plug strip is not enough. If any phone cables, network cables, or any other telecommunications lines are connected to the PC, disconnect them, too.

3. Remove enough of the PC's case to allow as much of an unobstructed access to the expansion slots on the motherboard as possible.

4. Check that each expansion card – not just the one last installed – is firmly seated in its slot.

   Cards can creep out of their slots over time *(chip creep),* or you might have accidentally pushed a card out of its slot slightly when installing another. If any of the cards are loose or not seated completely, you might have found the problem. Without putting the case back on, power on the PC and test whether the error condition is gone.

5. Check the connecting cables on each of the expansion cards to verify that each end of the cable is snuggly connected.

6. Disconnect the cable connector one end at a time and then reconnect it tightly.

   Never force connectors and always pay attention to the keys on the connectors that are meant to prevent you from connecting it incorrectly.

   You have a choice now: You can power the PC up after reconnecting each card or wait until you have done so for all the cards. If the error is gone when you reboot the system, the problem was obviously a loose connector.

7. If you've gotten this far in this procedure, the problem is not a generic one, like loose cards or connectors.

   At this point, you need to gather some tools: a Phillips screwdriver, the documentation for your expansion cards, and possibly a probe, a stylus, or needle-nose pliers.

8. If you've just installed an expansion card, start with it and verify any DIP switch or jumper settings that you made to the card against the documentation.

   A common error here is that when you set the jumpers or switches, the card wasn't oriented as the documentation assumed. For example, you might have had the card upside down. ISA cards have configuration settings for all three of the system resource settings (IRQ, DMA, and I/O address). Verify that you've set all three, if applicable, against the recommended settings in the card's documentation. Retest the system after verifying each expansion card.

9. If the problem persists, use the operating system's Device Manager to verify that no system resource conflicts exist.

   If any conflicts are identified, which are likely to be IRQs, reconfigure the newer device or the one used less frequently to an available resource setting and retest the system.

   On a Windows system, you would use the Device Manager (accessed through either the Properties window of My Computer or via the System icon of the Control Panel). Figure 23-14 shows the Computer Properties screen. To view the system resource assignments for an individual device, display the properties for the device and then click the Resources tab, as shown in Figure 23-15. A red X or a yellow exclamation point in front of the device or resource name indicates conflicts in the Device Manager.

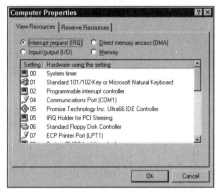

Figure 23-14: System resource values on the Computer Properties window of the Windows Device Manager.

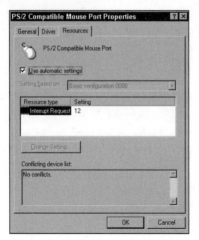

Figure 23-15: The system resources for an
individual device are displayed in the
Properties window for the device.

10. If the problem persists, it's all or nothing time. Write down the order and
slot placement of each card in the PC, label each cable, and then proceed
as follows.

I recommend sketching the expansion slot area to show where the cards
and cables are connected. You should also enter the system BIOS configuration data and record all the BIOS settings for the PC.

a. Get a supply of anti-static bags or make lots of room on a clean static-
free surface. Leaving only the hard disk controller card (if one is in
use), remove all the expansion cards from the PC. Place each card in an
anti-static bag or where it will be safe. (*Never* stack expansion cards on
top of each other, whether they are in anti-static bags or not.)

b. Install one expansion card at a time and test the system after each
card. This procedure tries to isolate the card that's causing the problem.
It's your call, but to test for the fault with this process, you really
should put the case cover back after installing each card. The problem
could actually be something like the card grounding to the case. If you
find the suspect card, retest it without the case on, just to be sure.

c. You might need to change the system BIOS setup data to indicate that
one or more of the cards have been removed and then reconfigure the
BIOS data after it's installed using the data that you recorded prior to
starting this procedure.

11. If you find the card that caused the original problem – and not some new
problem – you might want to verify that the slot isn't the problem by
retesting the slot with a different and compatible card.

12. If the problem persists, the problem is probably related to the motherboard.

    See Chapter 1 for procedures to use to test the motherboard. It might also be time to contact the technical support folks at the manufacturer of the PC or the motherboard.

Dealing with expansion card choke points

A *choke point* on a PC occurs when too much data is trying to get through too small of a passageway. A common choke point is using an inappropriate expansion card for a system. For example, on a Pentium PC, using an ISA video card will likely cause a choke point when the monitor display graphics tries to run over the low-speed ISA bus.

If an expansion card is performing poorly or very slowly, it might be bound by a choke point of its own causing or one caused by too much traffic on a bus.

Some things that you can do to prevent or eliminate a choke point for peripheral devices and expansion cards are

1. Upgrade to a motherboard with built-in controllers for the floppy disk and hard disk and as many other ports as possible to eliminate controller and adapter cards on the expansion bus.

2. If one isn't available on the motherboard, install a USB or IEEE 1394 port expansion card and use it for future peripheral devices that you add to the PC where possible.

    Some USB devices provide additional serial and parallel ports, which can also save expansion bus slots.

Installing a SCSI host adapter

Follow the procedures outlined earlier in "Installing an expansion card" to install the SCSI host adapter. Be sure that you have the appropriate card for the type of expansion bus slot available on your PC.

1. Before inserting the SCSI card, verify its termination settings.

    Use the card's documentation to find these settings. Some cards use a switch or jumper to enable or disable termination, and others use a firmware utility that's included on the card that runs at boot up to configure termination. Also verify any system resource settings that must be made physically on the card. In the documentation, find any resource settings that must be entered into the BIOS setup data or an installation program and make a note of them for later.

2. Before you insert the card into its slot, attach any internal SCSI device to the adapter card.

It's much easier and safer for the connectors and neighboring cards to do this now than after the card is seated. External devices should be attached after the card is seated and secured.

3. Make any configuration changes to the BIOS configuration data and reboot the system.

   If all is well, you should see a SCSI BIOS boot message immediately after the POST completes.

See Chapter 11 for more information on the SCSI interface bus.

Installing serial and parallel add-on ports

Follow the procedures outlined earlier in "Installing an expansion card" to install the SCSI host adapter. Be sure that you have the appropriate card for the type of expansion bus slot available on your PC.

1. Because most serial and parallel port expansion cards are 8-bit cards, you can get by with using an ISA slot, if one is available.

   Because little else will fit this slot anyway, this is a good use for it, and it leaves the long (16-bit) slots available.

2. From the card's documentation, check the configuration settings, which for serial and parallel cards are typically set on the card through jumpers and DIP switches.

   If other serial or parallel ports are installed on the system, verify which system resources are assigned to them. The IRQ and I/O addresses assigned to these ports determine which logical port (COM1, COM2, LPT1, and so on) that they will be assigned during the boot sequence.

3. After the card is installed and secured, reboot the system and install any device drivers required.

See Chapter 24 for more information on serial and parallel ports and their uses.

Installing a USB or IEEE 1394 expansion card

Although I refer to USB ports in this procedure, the same process can be used to install IEEE 1394 (FireWire) expansion cards:

1. Follow the procedures outlined earlier in "Installing an expansion card" to install the SCSI host adapter.

   Be sure that you have the appropriate card for the type of expansion bus slot available on your PC.

2. Because USB expansion cards are installed in PCI slots, make sure that one is available before getting too far along and then install the card as you would any other.

   These cards are Plug and Play, so you shouldn't have any configuration to perform. If you're on a Windows NT system, you might need to enter the System Devices area to add the card. When the system reboots, you'll be prompted to load the device drivers, which you probably need to get from the manufacturer of the USB device. Windows 98 and 2000/XP will most likely have the driver that you need onboard, but the card should also have a disk or CD with it that contains the driver needed.

 See Chapter 24 for more information on USB and IEEE 1394 interfaces.

Resolving resource conflicts on Windows PCs

If a PC has system resource conflicts, one of the following is probably happening:

♦ The system fails to boot, sounding an error beep code or displaying an error message that indicates an error on the motherboard or expansion bus.

♦ During the boot sequence, the system freezes and will not complete the boot.

♦ The system halts or freezes during an I/O operation or for no apparent reason while an application program is running.

♦ An I/O device performs erratically or intermittently.

The only cause for a resource conflict is a recent hardware upgrade, and if the answer to any one of the following is "Yes," the problem is probably a system resource conflict:

◆ Have you recently added a new internal device, expansion card, or device driver?

◆ Did the problem show up after a new component was added to the PC?

◆ Was the PC operating fine before the new component was added?

If you have at least one Yes to the above questions, you need to troubleshoot the system resources to resolve the problem. And you can just about count on the problem being a system resource conflict if the device added was a sound card. To check:

1. Write down the current resource settings and assignments, including those in the BIOS' configuration data.

2. Run a virus checker on the system before making any changes.

   Make sure that the PC isn't suffering from a virus, which can appear to be system resource problems.

3. Open the Device Manager and select the device (expansion card) that was recently added to the PC.

   If the device has a yellow exclamation mark or red X symbol in front of its name, it is conflicting with another device or its configuration cannot be resolved by the BIOS.

4. Open the Properties window and display the Resources tab information.

   At the bottom of the display (refer to Figure 23-15), you should see information regarding the device with which there is a conflict. You need to change the conflicting resource (probably an IRQ, and definitely an IRQ if the device is a PCI card) to another available setting.

   If there are no available resources of the kind you need, you might need to share with another device that's not in use at the same time as the new device. You might also need to change the settings on the expansion card using jumpers or DIP switches, using the card's documentation as your guide to the new values or positions. The system BIOS of the PC might support the reassignment of IRQs (for PCI slots) in the setup program. Most resource conflicts exist between expansion slots, and many can be resolved in the BIOS settings.

Resolving resource conflicts on PnP devices

Plug and Play (PnP) devices can cause IRQ conflicts because the PnP processes in the operating system and BIOS might not detect all other devices or they might not correctly detect a new device. There are standards, but standards are open to interpretation. PnP devices are configured after all the other devices are squared away during the boot cycle.

To resolve a resource conflict on a Plug and Play device, perform the following:

1. Remove the new device's configuration using the Windows Device Manager and then restart the PC to see whether the problem was a one-time thing.

   You cannot just disable the device in the BIOS configuration data; it must also be removed from the Device Manager's settings as well.

2. If the device is still having problems, verify that the most current device drivers are installed.

   Visit the manufacturer's Web site to find the latest drivers and then install them on your PC.

3. If the new device is not being detected, use the Add New Hardware Wizard from the Control Panel to install it.

   If the Add New Hardware Wizard isn't able to install the device, you need to configure the system resources manually.

   a. Open the Device Manager, highlight the selection for the device in question, and then click the Properties button.

   b. On the Properties window that appears, choose the Resources tab.

   c. Clear the Use Automatic Settings check box.

   d. Choose the system resources that are in conflict and use the Edit Resource function to reassign them to available or unassigned resources.

      The Device Manager will keep you inbounds by not letting you assign values outside the assignable range. If you assign a resource already in use, you get a warning.

   e. When all is well, click OK and close it out.

4. Restart the system, and the problem should be solved.

   If not, repeat this process until you arrive at a workable set of system resources.

   If the manufacturer has technical support available, don't be too stubborn to call or e-mail the company.

Installing a video card

Follow the procedures for installing an expansion card detailed earlier in the chapter. The steps listed in this project are specific to video cards.

1. Before you remove the old video card, remove everything listed under Display Adapters in the Device Manager and then shut down the PC.

You can access the Device Manager through the System icon of the Control Panel.

2. Remove the monitor connection from its plug on the old video card.

3. Open the system case and remove the old video card.

If the card doesn't pull out easily, rock it gently front to back — *never side to side* — until it frees up and pulls out. Some systems have video systems integrated into the motherboard. Check the motherboard's documentation on the procedure to use to disable this system before installing a new video card. Typically, a jumper plug or switch is used to disable this circuitry.

4. Insert the new video card and connect any external parts that are a part of the video card system, like those with some Matrox cards.

The system should detect the new card and ask for device drivers. Always use the drivers that came with the video card in lieu of the stock drivers included with the operating system.

You might want to check the manufacturer's Web site for updated drivers after the installation is complete.

Chapter 24

Ports and Connectors

IN THIS CHAPTER

Because very few users have exactly the same peripheral devices on their PCs, the PC must provide for as many options as possible. Users have a wide range of peripheral device choices available that they can use to turn their standard PC into a customized workstation, entertainment unit, or publishing center. To accommodate these choices, the PC must provide for a variety of input/output (I/O) ports that accept the various connector types employed by the different peripheral devices that could be attached to it.

In this chapter, I cover the following:

◆ Troubleshooting a serial port

◆ Troubleshooting a parallel port

◆ Dealing with serial port system resource conflicts

◆ Dealing with printing problems

◆ Troubleshooting a USB connection

◆ Assigning an IRQ to the USB host controller

◆ Enabling IRQ steering

THE PC ESSENTIALLY COMPRISES its core components: the processor, the motherboard, and the chipset. All other components (peripheral devices) connect to the core components through some form of a port or connector. This chapter focuses on the ports and connectors used to attach peripheral devices, whether internal or external devices.

Connecting a PC

To connect to the PC, two components, a port and a connector with complementary matching but opposite features, must be connected. The *port* is the part attached to or incorporated into the PC. The *connector* is typically on the end of a peripheral device's cable or, on many recent devices, a part of the device itself.

A connector is plugged into a port to make a connection between the PC and the peripheral device, making the peripheral device available for use.

The ports, also called *connectors* in some uses, are mounted either directly on the motherboard or on an expansion card installed in a motherboard slot. I/O ports extend through the back panel template on the back of a PC's case. However, a PC is not limited to only these external ports. The motherboard and many expansion cards also have internal ports, also called *connectors*, which are used strictly for connections between internal devices.

Motherboard connectors

In the past, nearly all device connections were made through expansion cards. However, virtually all Pentium-class PCs have many, if not all, of their standard internal and external ports and connectors integrated into the motherboard. Not all motherboards, including some newer ones, include all the connectors discussed in this section, but most do.

Motherboard connectors are classified into three groups: back panel, onboard (mid-board), and front panel connectors. These connector groups (see Figure 24-1) are used to connect the motherboard to core internal devices, such as the power supply, system speaker, and the front panel switches and light-emitting diodes (LEDs), as well as external peripheral devices, such as a printer, modem, keyboard, and a mouse.

BACK PANEL CONNECTORS

As illustrated in Figure 24-2, the motherboard's back panel typically includes several I/O ports that support a standard set of peripheral devices. Other ports can be added with an expansion card. The standard set usually found on most current PCs is shown in Figure 24-2. Each of these connectors is discussed in more detail later in the chapter.

ONBOARD CONNECTORS

Several connectors are located on the central part of the motherboard to provide support for onboard device and bus services. The onboard, or mid-board, connectors are divided into five functional groups:

◆ *Audio/video:* Motherboards that have built-in support for sound, video, and CD-ROM include an auxiliary sound line in, a telephony connection, a legacy CD-ROM connector, and an AT Attachment Packet Interface (ATAPI) CD-ROM connection. These connectors and their uses are explained in more detail in Chapter 13.

◆ *Peripheral device interfaces:* Virtually all new motherboards have a standard set of connectors located on the board to provide support for several internal devices. Typically, these connectors are Integrated Drive Electronics/AT Attachment (IDE/ATA) interface connectors, illustrated in Figure 24-3, that support the hard disk, CD-ROM, and floppy disk. These connectors are discussed in more detail in Chapter 8.

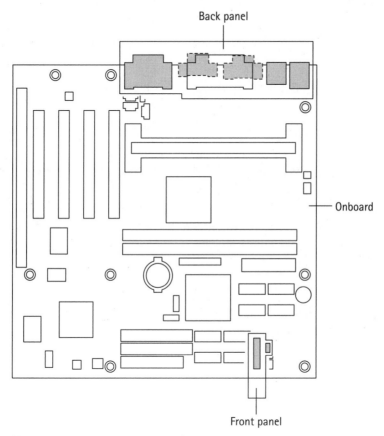

Figure 24-1: The general location of the motherboard's connector groups.

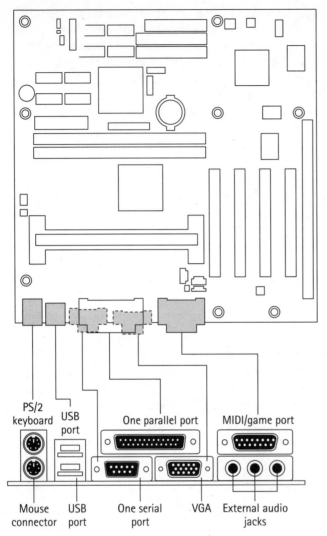

Figure 24-2: The common ports on the back panel of the motherboard.

◆ *Hardware power and management:* These connectors attach the power supply to the motherboard, connect system and processor fans, and provide an interface for Wake on LAN or Wake on Ring technologies.

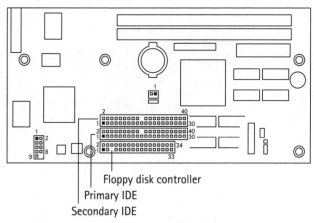

Figure 24-3: Peripheral device connectors located on a motherboard.

◆ *Memory slots:* Every motherboard includes some form of connector, mounting, or slot for memory chips or modules. Newer boards include mounting slots (shown in Figure 24-4) for RDRAM Inline Memory Modules (RIMMs) and Dual Inline Memory Modules (DIMMs). Older motherboards can have slots for Single Inline Memory Modules (SIMMs) or even Dual Inline Packaging (DIP) sockets. See Chapter 6 for more information on memory modules.

◆ *Expansion slots:* The expansion slots (see Figure 24-4) on the motherboard are used to add peripheral device adapters and interface cards to the PC. Motherboards support a variety of expansion slot types, but Industry Standard Architecture/Enhanced ISA (ISA/EISA), Peripheral Component Interconnect (PCI), and Accelerated Graphics Port (AGP) are the most common. See Chapter 23 for more information on expansion cards.

CONNECTORS ON THE FRONT PANEL

As I describe in Chapter 8, the front panel of the system case can have a variety of LEDs and switches that attach to the motherboard for power and activity signals. The front panel connector group typically includes a connection for hard disk LEDs (power and activity), the main power On/Off button, a reset button, and a few power and grounding connections. Separately, the motherboard also has a connection for the system speaker that is also mounted either on or near the front panel. The motherboard might also have an infrared (IR) or Infrared Data Association (IrDA) serial port connector as well (more on IR connections later in the section "Infrared ports").

Expansion slots   Memory slots

Figure 24-4: The location on memory and expansion slots on a Slot A motherboard.

External ports and connectors

The external ports mounted on a motherboard's rear panel are set by its form factor. Because most of the PCs in use today are built to the ATX form factor, most of them have a basic set of external ports. As shown in Figure 24-5, the ATX standard set includes a serial port or two, a parallel port or two, Universal Serial Bus (USB) ports or FireWire ports, a video port, a game device port, and speaker and microphone jacks. This set of ports is the real focus of this chapter.

For more on form factors, read Chapter 8.

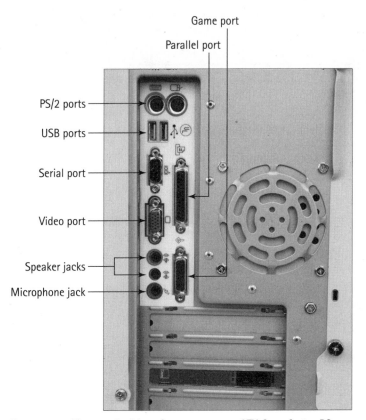

Figure 24-5: The standard interface ports on an ATX form factor PC.

Reviewing Interface Technologies

Before I go deeper into each of the interfaces listed in the preceding section, I want to review some of the "how and why" of the operations of interfaces and the different types of data that they support. Each of the specific interfaces is explained later in the chapter.

Characterizing data

Data is stored on a PC in the American Standard Code for Information Interchange (ASCII; pronounced *as*-kee) format. ASCII defines the standard character set of PCs, including a number of special command, inquiry, and graphics characters with the upper- and lowercase alphabetic characters, special characters, and numbers of the American English language.

Table 24-1 includes a sample of the ASCII character set, including the binary and decimal values for each character.

TABLE 24-1 SAMPLE ASCII CHARACTERS

Character	Decimal	Binary
Null	0	00000000
Backspace	8	00001000
Line feed	10	00001010
Form feed	12	00001100
Space	32	00100000
!	33	00100001
Dollar sign ($)	36	00100100
0 (zero)	48	00110000
1	49	00110001
2	50	00110010
: (colon)	58	00111010
; (semicolon)	59	00111011
?	63	00111111
A	65	01000001
B	66	01000010
C	67	01000011
X	88	01011000
Y	89	01011001
Z	90	01011010
a	97	01100001
b	98	01100010
c	99	01100011

Character	Decimal	Binary
x	120	01111000
y	121	01111001
z	122	01111010

Figuring out serial and parallel data

Data is transmitted and moved in and out of the PC by using one of two formats: parallel or serial. A *parallel transmission* sends its data one character at a time with the bits of a character transmitted at the same time over parallel wires. On the other hand, *serial* data is transmitted one bit at a time over a single wire. Figure 24-6 illustrates the difference between these two transmission formats.

Parallel data

Serial data

Figure 24-6: Character bits are sent at the same time in a parallel transmission and one bit at a time in a serial transmission.

Configuring for full, half, and simplex modes

A communications connection can be set up for one-way only or two-way simultaneous transmissions depending on the transmission mode configuration established between two communicating devices.

A communications line can be configured with one of three transmission modes:

◆ *Simplex:* A *simplex line* can communicate in only one direction. A speaker wire is an example of a simplex communications line.

◆ *Half-duplex:* Whereas a *duplex line* carries data in two directions, a *half-duplex line* carries data in two directions but can only transmit in one direction at a time. A citizen's band (CB) radio is an example of a half-duplex line – one party must wait until the other party is finished before speaking.

◆ *Full-duplex:* A *full-duplex line* carries data in two directions simultaneously. An example of a full-duplex line is your telephone.

Transmitting serial data

Serial ports and connectors were used on the very first PCs to connect modems and early dot matrix printers. Serial ports transmit data one bit after the other in a series. All serial devices, cables, ports, and communications transmit their data this way. To transmit a single byte of data through a serial port, eight separate 1-bit transmissions are sent. Serial transmissions are somewhat like sending data down a pipeline just big enough for a single bit.

Although an ASCII character can be defined with either 7 or 8 bits, more than this number is sent for each character, regardless of the transmission format. The extra bits are used for data integrity, data block identification, and data synchronization.

BITS THROUGH THE PORT

External serial devices connect to a PC through a serial or COM port. The terms *serial* and *COM* are used interchangeably, and most operating systems refer to the serial ports as COM ports, with the first serial port labeled COM1 and subsequent serial ports designated as COM2, COM3, and so on. Serial ports are also called *EIA232* (Electronics Industries Association standard 232) *ports* or by the legacy name *RS-232* (Reference Standard 232) *ports*. EIA is an industry association that develops standards for the communications lines, ports, and connectors used to transmit standard serial data communications.

TIP

COM is a legacy term for communications.

A typical PC has one serial port mounted on the motherboard. Serial ports are easily recognized because they use either 9-pin or 25-pin male D-type connectors that are designated as DA-9 and DB-25 connectors, respectively. Figure 24-5 includes a single DA-9 serial port.

Because a serial transmission uses only 9-pin connectors and wires, most PCs use the DA-9 port in place of the larger DB-25. The DA-9 connector is smaller and has fewer pins, reducing both the potential for damaged or bent pins and the space required for the port area on the PC. Older PC models typically included a single DB-25 serial port on a multipurpose card that could also include a second serial port, typically a DA-9 port, a parallel port, or a game port. The DB-25 connector is also popular on external modems and serial printers.

SERIAL CONNECTOR PINOUTS AND CABLE CONNECTIONS

Table 24-2 shows the pinouts for the DB-25 and DA-9 serial connections. Note the difference in the pin assignments between the two connectors. For a cable that has a DB-25 connector on one end and a DA-9 connector on the other end, the pins must be cross-matched to carry the signals to the appropriate pins on each end.

TABLE 24-2 DB-25 AND DA-9 CONNECTOR PINOUTS

Function	DB-25 Pin	DA-9 Pin
Ground	1	Not used
Transmit	2	3
Receive	3	2
RTS (Request to Send)	4	7
CTS (Clear to Send)	5	8
DSR (Data Set Ready)	6	6
Signal Ground	7	5
Carrier Detect	8	1
DTR (Data Terminal Ready)	20	4
Ring Indicator	22	9

A serial cable has as few as 2 wires and usually not more than 20 wires, but having 8 wires is very common. The wires in the cable are color coded to make connecting connectors to the cable consistent by making it easier to find the same wire on each end of the cable. The connector is attached by soldering the wires to the back of a connector's pins. Plugging the connector into a matching port completes the connection when the pins in the port make contact with the holes in the connector. With the serial connection established, the PC and peripheral device can send signals back and forth to communicate and control the transmission.

Communicating asynchronously

Asynchronous communications are used to connect to a printer, modem, fax, and other peripheral devices. Asynchronous transmitters and receivers operate independently and are not synchronized to a common clock signal or each other. Data blocks are separated by arbitrary idle periods on the line, as illustrated in Figure 24-7.

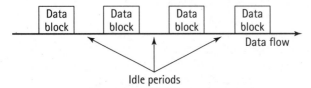

Figure 24-7: Asynchronous communications send data in 5-byte to 8-byte blocks that are separated by variously sized idle periods.

Asynchronous data blocks are fixed in size and format. To the 8-bit ASCII character is added a start bit before the character and one or two stop bits after the character. These bits indicate the beginning and ending of each character to the receiving device. Typically, the start bit is a 0, and the stop bit is a 1. If parity is in use, the parity bit is tacked on to the data block as well.

Checking parity

The parity used with asynchronous communications is very much like that used with memory (see Chapter 6). The parity bit is used to force the count of 1s bits in the transmitted character to either an even or an odd number. For example, when an uppercase A is transmitted, its binary value (01000001) is transmitted. If even parity is in use, the parity bit added to the end is set to 0 (zero) because there are an even number of 1s bits in the character. If odd parity is in use, the parity bit is set to 1 to force an odd number of 1s bits in the character. If the receiving device detects an error in the number of 1s bits, it sends a request for the character to be resent.

With everything added to the ASCII binary character (start bit, stop bit, and parity bit), the asynchronous data block is 11 bits long. Here is what this might look like:

```
Transmitted character:       A

Start bit:                   0
ASCII binary data pattern:   01000001
Even-parity bit:             0
Stop bit:                    1

Transmitted data block:      00100000101
```

Using the UART

A specialized integrated circuit called a *universal asynchronous receiver/transmitter* (UART; pronounced *you*-art) is used to control all serial ports and most serial device connections. A UART is located on a device adapter card, directly on the motherboard, or integrated onto a serial device's internal controller.

A UART controls all of a serial port's or device's actions and functions, including

◆ Controlling all the connectors' pins and their associated signals

◆ Establishing the communication protocol

◆ Converting the parallel format bits of the PC's data bus into a serial bit stream for transmission

◆ Converting the received serial bit stream into parallel data for transmission over the PC's internal data bus

On the PC, a UART interprets and translates the data coming into and being sent out of a serial port by examining the incoming data, looking for the start and stop bits, and verifying the parity bit counts. The UART inserts the start and stop bits and parity bit (if needed) into outgoing data. The UART also controls the data speed of the serial port or device. Table 24-3 lists the UART chips that have been used in PCs, modems, and other serial devices over the years by their identity numbers. Most modern PCs use the 16550 UART chip, which supports speeds up to 115.2 Kbps.

TABLE 24-3 UART CHIP CHARACTERISTICS

Chip	Maximum Speed (bps)
8250	19,200
16450	38,400
16550	115,200
16650	430,800
16750	921,600
16850	1.5 Mbps
16950	1.5 Mbps

Communicating with synchronicity

Synchronous communications have a bit more overhead than asynchronous transmissions. Synchronous transmissions have a fixed interval length between data blocks. The data blocks and the intervals of a synchronous transmission are synchronized to a clock signal that's sent right along with the data. The communicating devices also carry on a running dialog that confirms and acknowledges that each data block has been received. If the acknowledgement doesn't come back in the proper time interval, the sending device automatically sends it again. Because synchronous devices must complete one operation before beginning the next, this communications mode is very accurate. However, most serial communications on PCs use asynchronous technology.

Configuring a serial port

Virtually all PCs have at least one serial port, which is designated as COM1. If a PC has additional serial ports, they're designated as COM2, COM3, and COM4. If you need to add more serial ports to a PC for some reason, you can add them one at a time or in sets of two or four. Individual serial ports require individual system resource assignments, and two such cards require two sets of system resources. However, a multiport serial card shares a single interrupt request (IRQ) among its ports with an onboard processor handling the traffic management. If a PC requires multiple serial ports, it's probably more efficient to install a multiport card (or consider using USB; more on this later in the section "Utilizing a USB Interface").

Most PCs have default assignments for up to four serial ports. Table 24-4 lists the default system resource assignments for PC serial ports. COM1 shares an IRQ with COM3, and COM2 shares an IRQ with COM4, which means that you must be careful when assigning devices to COM ports to avoid competing devices. See Chapter 7 for more information on system resources. Typically, COM1 is a DA-9 male port, and COM2 (if present) is a DB-25 male port.

TABLE 24-4 SERIAL PORT SYSTEM RESOURCE ASSIGNMENTS

Logical Device Name	IRQ	I/O Address
COM1	IRQ4	3F8h
COM2	IRQ3	2F8h
COM3	IRQ4	3E8h
COM4	IRQ3	2E8h

Understanding Parallel Ports

A parallel transmission sends the bits of a character at one time using parallel wires, which means that a character is transmitted much faster than it would be over a serial connection. The internal bus structures inside the PC use parallel transmissions, which is why a serial port needs a UART to convert the internal parallel format into a serial format for transmission over a serial line.

Parallel ports are female DB-25 connectors into which a male DB-25 connector is plugged. Although originally used almost exclusively by printers, other devices have been adapted to the parallel port, including external CD-ROMs, external tape drives, scanners, and Zip drives. These devices take advantage of the bidirectional capabilities of the newer parallel port standards.

The IEEE has combined parallel port standards into a single standard: IEEE 1284. This standard incorporates the two pre-existing parallel port standards with a new protocol to create an all-encompassing parallel port model and protocol standard.

The separate parallel port standards included in the IEEE 1284 standard are

♦ *Standard Parallel Port (SPP):* Defines a simplex parallel port that allows data to travel only from the computer to the printer.

♦ *Enhanced Parallel Port (EPP):* Defines a half-duplex parallel port that allows the printer to signal that it's out of paper, its cover is open, and other error conditions.

♦ *Enhanced Capabilities Port (ECP):* Most PCs that list an IEEE 1284 port as a feature indicate support for an ECP port. The ECP standard allows bidirectional, simultaneous communications between a parallel device (usually a printer) and a PC. The IEEE 1284 standard also defines an ECP standard cable. When shopping for a printer ECP cable, be sure that you get an ECP cable because some EPP cables won't work properly.

Utilizing a USB Interface

The *Universal Serial Bus* (USB) is a newer hardware interface standard that supports low-speed devices (such as keyboards, mice, and scanners) and higher-speed devices (such as digital cameras). USB, which is a serial interface, provides data transfer speeds of up to 12 Mbps for faster devices and a 1.5 Mbps subchannel speed for lower-speed devices. A newer version of the USB standard, USB 2.0, supports up to 480 Mbps for data transfer speeds.

A USB port offers the following features:

♦ The flexibility of Plug and Play (PnP) devices

♦ Standard connectors and cables with a wide variety of devices available, including keyboards, mice, floppy drives, hard disk drives, Zip and Jaz drives, inkjet printers, laser printers, scanners, digital cameras, modems, and hubs

◆ Automatic configuration of USB devices when they are connected

◆ Hot swapping (USB devices that can be connected and disconnected while the PC is powered on)

◆ The capability to support up to 127 devices on one channel

Connecting with USB

USB uses a unique pair of connectors and ports, as shown in Figure 24-8. USB *Type A* connectors are used to connect devices directly to a PC or USB hub. You'll find USB Type A connectors on devices with permanently attached cables. USB *Type B* connectors are found on those devices that have a detachable cable. The cable uses a squarish Type B port on the device and connects to either a Type A or Type B socket (the cable usually has both on the other end) on the PC or hub. Figure 24-9 shows a USB Type A connector being connected to a PC USB port.

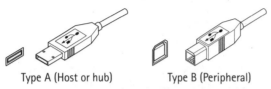

Type A (Host or hub)   Type B (Peripheral)

Figure 24-8: The two types of USB connectors and ports.

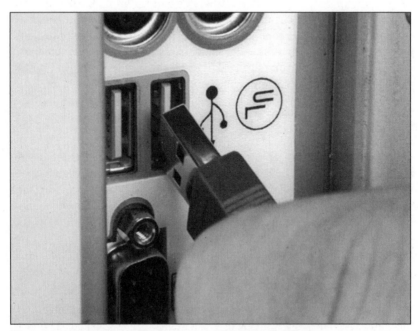

Figure 24-9: Connecting a USB device to a USB port on a PC.

A single USB channel can support up to 127 devices. To add more devices to a USB channel, a USB hub is used. The hubs are daisy chained to add more devices to the channel. Some newer devices, including monitors as illustrated in Figure 24-10, also have USB channels. A USB port carries .5 amps of electrical power, which is usually enough to power most low-power devices, such as a mouse or keyboard. No additional power source is required. This adds to the flexibility of the USB channel because additional devices can be added without regard to location. Those USB devices that require more power than is carried on the channel have AC/DC adapters.

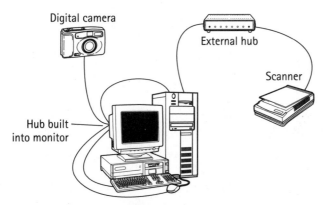

Figure 24-10: Multiple USB devices can be connected to a single PC.

Interfacing to USB

A USB interface has three essential components:

- ◆ *USB host:* The *USB host* device carries operating system, chipset, and Basic Input/Output System (BIOS) support for the USB interface. Typically, the PC is the USB host.

- ◆ *USB hub:* A *USB hub* serves as a collector device to cluster USB devices onto a USB channel. USB devices can be added to the channel in a tiered fashion with one hub plugged into another and a connection to the USB host from the first hub.

- ◆ *USB devices:* Typically, a PC has only one or two USB devices plugged into its USB channels, but a USB channel is limited to 127 devices, counting USB hubs.

IEEE 1394 (FireWire)

The IEEE 1394 standard defines another high-speed serial bus, officially known as the High Performance Serial Bus (HPSB) but more commonly called *FireWire*. This serial interface supports data speeds between 100–400 Mbps (which is the equivalent of 12 to 50 megabytes per second). Newer versions of the 1394 standard, which are being developed by the 1394 Trade Association (www.1394ta.org), are promising data speeds of 800 Mbps to 1.6 Gbps.

An IEEE 1394 connector looks something like a USB connector (see Figure 24-11), except that it's just a bit larger.

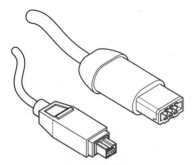

Figure 24-11: A IEEE 1394 (FireWire) cable showing its connectors.

The IEEE 1394 bus is similar to the USB interface in many ways. Both are high-speed, PnP, hot-swappable interface buses. One major difference is that 1394 supports isochronous (real-time) data transfers. An *isochronous* transfer moves data so that all of its parts arrive together, which can be very important for audio/video data, like with multimedia data or images directly from a video camera. Other differences are that the 1394 standard is a peer-to-peer interface that doesn't require a host system, and an IEEE 1394 bus can support up to 63 external devices.

Working with Wireless Ports

Wireless or cordless interfaces are becoming more popular for PCs and can be used to connect peripheral devices to the PC or, as I explain in Chapter 22, even to connect the PC to a local area network.

Two types of wireless connection technologies are in use on PCs: infrared (IR) and radio frequency (RF).

Infrared ports

An IR port uses an invisible band of light to carry data between a peripheral device and a transceiver on the PC. *IR* light is just outside the light spectrum that humans can see. Infrared contrasts with *ultraviolet (UV),* which is another invisible band of light at the other end of the light spectrum. IR devices are also called IrDA devices. IrDA is the trade organization for the infrared device industry that has established the standards that define the use of an IR connection. An IrDA port is the small oval-shaped dark red plastic window built into a PC's case.

An IR device is a line-of-sight device that must have a clear, unobstructed path between its transmitter and receiver. With an IR connection, a portable PC or a personal digital assistant (PDA) can connect to another PC, a keyboard, a mouse, or a printer without using a physical cable connection. Built-in IR ports (receivers) are common on portable PCs, notebooks, and PDAs, but an external IR receiver can be attached to a PC through a serial or USB port.

Here are some tips for working with IR devices:

◆ Two IR devices must have a clear, unobstructed line of sight between them.

◆ The devices that you're trying to connect via IR must be at least six inches apart but not more than three feet.

◆ The transmission pattern of the IR signal is a cone about 30° wide. Make sure that the devices are oriented to one another inside the transmission cone.

◆ Avoid competing IR devices in the vicinity – such as a TV remote control – that could interfere with the connection.

Radio frequency interfaces

Many cordless peripheral devices, especially those that are typically used in close proximity of the PC's system case, use RF transmitters, receivers, and *transceivers* (the combination of a receiver and transmitter) to send data to the PC. RF devices include mice, keyboards, modems, and even network adapters for desktop and portable PCs.

Cordless RF mice and keyboards transmit data to a receiver attached to a PC through either a serial or PS/2 connection. The operating range of these devices is around 6–10', despite claims of 50' ranges. In most cases, the performance of the cordless RF keyboard and mouse is as good as a wired device inside its effective operating distance.

RF networking devices, which are defined in the IEEE 802.11 wireless, are also known as *Wi-Fi* (wireless fidelity). Networking standards and other wireless networking standards, such as Bluetooth and HomeRF technologies, are discussed in more detail in Chapter 22.

Understanding PS/2 and DIN Connectors

The 5-pin DIN connector and the PS/2 (mini-DIN connector) are the two most popular connectors for connecting keyboards, mice, and external IR and RF receivers. These connectors have become the standard for virtually all keyboards and mice on PCs.

Here is a brief description of these two connectors:

♦ *5-pin DIN connector:* This connector, often called the *AT-style connector,* has been in use since the very first PCs. Deutsche Industrie Norm (DIN), a German standards organization, developed the round connector style used on this and the 6-pin version of this connector. Only four of the five pins are used and carry the clocking (pin 1), data (pin 2), and provide a ground (pin 4) and +5 volt (v) of power (pin 5).

♦ *6-pin mini-DIN (PS/2) connector:* This DIN-style connector (shown in Figure 24-12) is a smaller version of the 5-pin DIN connector. Keyboard and mice connections use only four of the six available pins to connect the data signal (pin 1), ground (pin 3), +5v of power (pin 4), and a clocking signal (pin 5). This connector, which is now the de facto standard for all cabled keyboards and mice, was first introduced on the IBM PS/2, which is why it is commonly referred to as the *PS/2 connector.*

Nearly all mice sold today use the PS/2 connector, but some serial mice still around use the DA-9 serial connector. However, because newer PC systems rarely offer more than a single serial port and have specially designated PS/2 connectors for the keyboard and mouse, the serial mouse has all but disappeared except on some older systems.

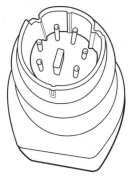

Figure 24-12: A 6-pin mini-DIN (PS/2) connector
is standard on most PC keyboards and mice.

Checking Out Video Connectors

Regardless of the type of internal interface a video card uses (see Chapter 14 for more information on video adapters and the video interfaces), virtually all video ports use a female 15-pin DB port and connector, like the one shown in Figure 24-13.

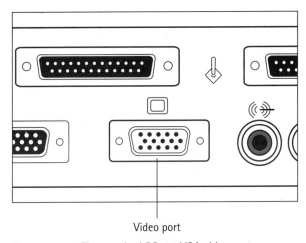

Video port

Figure 24-13: The standard DB-15 VGA video port.

The standard port and connector used for Video Graphics Array (VGA), Super VGA (SVGA), and Extended Graphics Array (XGA) monitor connections is the DB-15, which is also called a *mini-sub D15 connector*. Figure 24-14 shows the pin configuration of this connection, and Table 24-5 lists its pin assignments.

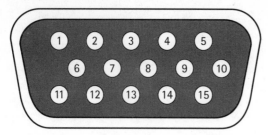

Figure 24-14: The standard VGA video connector has
15 pins arranged in three rows.

TABLE 24-5 PIN ASSIGNMENTS IN A VIDEO CONNECTOR

Pin	VGA/SVGA/XGA
1	Red video
2	Green video
3	Blue video
4	Monitor ID 2
5	Ground/Not used
6	Red video return
7	Green video return
8	Blue video return
9	Not used
10	Ground
11	Monitor ID 0
12	Monitor ID 1
13	Horizontal sync
14	Vertical sync
15	Not used

Dealing with Port Problems

Problems with I/O ports are typically problems with the device attached to the port, a problem with the cable, a bad connector or connection, or a system resource conflict. The following sections deal with how to troubleshoot and resolve problems with the various I/O ports.

Troubleshooting a serial port

When troubleshooting a serial port problem, first try connecting a different serial device to the port in question. Next, check for system resource conflicts using either the System Information applet or Device Manager on a Windows system.

The System Information utility can be found by choosing Programs → Accessories → System Tools, and the Device Manager is best accessed by right-clicking the My Computer icon on the desktop, choosing Properties from the pop-up menu that appears, and then choosing either the Device Manager tab in Windows 9.x or Me or the Hardware tab in Windows 2000 or XP.

If you believe that you have a problem with the serial port, use the pinouts listed earlier in the chapter and a multimeter to check the voltages of the serial port on the PC and the continuity of the cable.

RESOLVING SYSTEM RESOURCE CONFLICTS

System resource conflicts cause a serial device to fail intermittently or perhaps not work at all. Other symptoms are that an existing serial device stops working when a new additional serial device is installed or the PC locks up during the boot sequence.

CHECKING THE SERIAL PORT

To troubleshoot a serial port problem, check the following:

- *Inspect the port for bent pins.* Certain pins absolutely must be straight in order for the device to work properly. If you have a bent or broken pin, you should replace the connector (or cable) because the damage might compromise the connection of other pins as well.

- *Check the connection and connectors.* Make sure that the cable wires are properly soldered to the pins in the connector and that the connector fits snuggly and correctly to the port. If any of the wires are touching each other (it takes only one strand to cause a problem), either replace the cable or repair the connector.

- *Test the port with another device.* A serial mouse is a very good tool to have for testing serial ports. If the port is the problem and it's mounted on the motherboard, disable it and install an additional serial port with an expansion card — that is, if you truly must use a serial port.

- *Test the serial device on a different known-good serial port.* Test the serial device by connecting it to another PC on which you know the serial port is working. If the device works, you know that the problem is not the device. However, you still have some troubleshooting to do on the original PC to isolate the problem.

- *Ensure that the cable is appropriate for the device.* Some serial devices can't use a straight-through or null modem cable. Check the pin and configuration requirements of the device and use the appropriate cable.

- *Check the length of the serial cable.* You might hear stories of successfully using longer cable lengths, but the nominal maximum length for a serial cable is 50' between two devices. Beyond 50', you might suffer *attenuation* (the distance at which the signal begins losing its strength) and begin seeing data errors.

- *Check the BIOS settings.* COM ports can be enabled and disabled in the BIOS setup configuration data. Make sure that the port is enabled. A disabled port will not work.

- *Check the Windows Device Manager or System Information applet for system resource conflicts.* An IRQ conflict is the most common error with serial devices. **Remember:** Only one active device should be using an IRQ at a time.

- *Check the software setup.* In most cases, application software is used to manage or control the serial device, such as dialup software for a modem. Check the configuration of the software and the settings that it uses to configure the serial device.

Dealing with serial port system resource conflicts

The symptoms for a system resource conflict on one or more serial ports are fairly straightforward. Here are the most common:

- The modem on COM3 fails when the serial mouse on COM1 is used or vice versa.

- The system locks up when the serial devices on COM2 and COM4 are used at the same time.

TIP

There are many variations of these two problems, but they boil down to a system resource conflict and probably a specific IRQ conflict. If the device on COM2 is having or causing the problem, it should be reconfigured either to a different COM port or IRQ. If the COM ports were installed on a multiport I/O controller card, change the configuration of the card through its jumpers, as specified in the card's documentation.

Troubleshooting a parallel port

Because parallel ports are virtually featureless and either work or don't work, most parallel port problems are caused by the physical part of the connector or port (bent pins or blocked holes), the cable (wrong type: SPP, EPP, or ECP), or the attached device.

Here are some steps that you should use to troubleshoot and isolate a parallel port problem:

◆ *Check for resource conflicts.* There is an outside chance that the problem is a system resource conflict, but this problem is usually caused by another device that was just added to the PC. See Table 24-6 for the default system resource assignments made to parallel (LPT) ports.

TABLE 24-6 PARALLEL PORT SYSTEM RESOURCE ASSIGNMENTS

Port	IRQ	I/O Address	DMA Channel
LPT1	IRQ7	378h	DMA 3 (ECP capabilities)
LPT2	IRQ5	278h	NA

◆ *Check the cable and connectors for physical problems.* If a commercial printer cable is in use, make sure that it's tightly fitted on both ends to the port and printer. If a homegrown cable is in use, make sure that the cable wires are properly soldered to the pins in the connector and that the connector fits snuggly and correctly to the port. If any of the wires are touching each other (it takes only one strand to cause a problem), either replace the cable or repair the connector. If the parallel port is attached to a pass-through port where two parallel devices are connected in tandem (like on a scanner or Zip drive), I suggest disconnecting one of the devices and testing again. The problem could be the pass-through connector.

◆ *Verify that the device is working properly.* To test the printer, try printing a plain text file to avoid issues on the printer itself. If the printer appears to be receiving data but doesn't print, try the printer on another PC. If it still doesn't work, you know that the problem is with the printer. Otherwise, check to make sure that you have the proper device drivers and configuration for the printer or other device.

◆ *Verify system resource settings.* If the PC is equipped with more than one parallel (LPT) port, use the Windows Device Manager or System Information applet to rule out system resource conflicts.

◆ *Check the BIOS setup configuration.* You can set the IRQ assigned to the LPT ports in the BIOS setup configuration data. Make sure that it's set to IRQ7 (default) for LPT1 and IRQ5 for LPT2. If the problem is with the port assigned to IRQ5, check for a conflict with the sound card.

◆ *Verify the communications mode of the parallel port.* Check the device's documentation to verify that the port is configured to the correct communications mode (SPP, EPP, ECP). Many printers require at least an EPP mode to be configured to the port in the BIOS setup configuration data.

◆ *Check ECP settings.* If ECP mode is enabled on a parallel port, it can cause system resource conflicts that are avoided by other parallel modes. Although the LPT ports are assigned an IRQ, most parallel devices (such as printers) don't use it. However, if ECP mode is enabled and the IRQ has been assigned to another device, it can cause a resource conflict. ECP mode also requires a DMA channel and could be in conflict with the sound card.

◆ *Verify the device drivers.* Check the device manufacturer's Web site for newer versions of the device driver. Make sure that the device drivers in use are compatible with the operating system in use on the PC. Many Windows 9*x* drivers won't work on a Windows 2000 system.

Dealing with printing (parallel port) problems

In most cases, if a printer is producing garbled or distorted print or if part of a page or image is missing, look for a problem with either the hardware or the software associated with the printer itself. However, if all appears to be right with the printer, the LPT port can cause one or two things as well.

To diagnose this problem, check the following:

◆ *Check the print mechanism on the printer.* Although the focus is on the cable and the connector, perhaps the printer itself isn't functioning. This is a good place to start when printing problems occur. The problem is rarely on the parallel port or the cable.

◆ *Verify that the most current printer driver is in use.* The printer driver must be compatible with the printer as well as the operating system on the PC or the network. An installation disk or CD-ROM comes with most printers, but you should visit the manufacturer's Web site to download the most current driver for the printer and operating system.

◆ *Try changing the parallel port mode.* Not all printers are compatible with the latest standards. Some printers can have problems with the ECP communication mode and work much better with EPP mode. Check the printer's documentation to verify its communications mode requirement and configure the port accordingly in the BIOS setup configuration.

◆ *Verify that the cable is appropriate.* Check the cable for problems, sharp bends, cuts, indications that it might have been crushed, or loose connector heads. Also check to see whether the cable is the right one for the printer. If the printer requires an IEEE 1284-certified ECP printer cable and the cable in use is only an EPP, you could have a problem.

Troubleshooting a USB connection

If you're having problems with a USB port, here are some things that you can check to make sure that the USB ports are active on the system. The first place to look is in the Windows Device Manager to ensure that the USB ports are actually installed on the system. Figure 24-15 shows where the USB ports are listed in the Windows Device Manager.

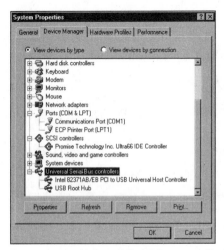

Figure 24-15: Universal Serial Bus controller information in the Windows Device Manager.

If all appears to be normal in the Device Manager (no conflicts or missing drivers), check the following:

◆ *Check the device connections.* Although it might seems obvious, this should always be the first troubleshooting step when dealing with device problems. Make sure that the device is connected to the PC – and if it requires power, that it's plugged into a power source. Some USB devices (such as keyboards and mice) get their power from the USB channel, but others require additional power.

◆ *Enable the USB connection.* Make sure that the USB ports are enabled in the BIOS setup configuration data. Although the PC should be shipped from the factory with its USB ports enabled, you never know until you try to use one. It could be that the PC has USB ports, but the BIOS system doesn't support them. In this case, you might need to upgrade the BIOS (see Chapter 4) to support USB ports, if such an upgrade is available.

◆ *Verify the devices installed.* If both the host controller and the root hub are installed (and listed on the Device Manager), all is well. However, if one or the other is missing, the problem is in the .INF file used to install the device drivers. Try removing the device from the Device Manager and then clicking the Refresh button to have the system automatically detect the devices. If this fails, open the device's Properties window and update the device driver, which you'll find in the USB.INF file in the INF folder (a subfolder to the Windows folder), and then re-install it.

◆ *Check for system resource conflicts.* The USB host controller shares its IRQ with other devices. Rarely does this cause a problem; however, on occasion, this can cause the USB device from being recognized when attached to the USB port. If this happens, you should reassign the USB host controller to a different IRQ (providing that one is available).

Assigning an IRQ to the USB host controller

Use these steps to force the USB host controller to a different IRQ setting:

1. With the Device Manager displayed, double-click Computer at the top of the device tree.

   This displays the Computer Properties window, shown in Figure 24-16.

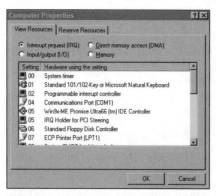

Figure 24-16: The Windows Computer Properties window.

2. On the Reserve Resources tab, click the Add button, enter the number of the IRQ currently in use by the USB host controller, and then click OK to close the window.

3. On the Device Manager window, select the USB host device and click the Remove button.

4. Restart the system.

   The USB host controller will be detected and assigned to a different IRQ.

5. Return to the Device Manager's Computer Properties windows and remove the reservation of the IRQ reserved in Step 2.

6. Click OK on each succeeding window and restart the PC when requested.

Enabling IRQ steering

The USB host controller requires IRQ Steering to be enabled on the PCI bus in order to support multiple devices. To enable IRQ steering, perform the following steps:

1. From the Device Manager, choose the PCI Bus entry and then click the Properties button.

2. Choose the IRQ Steering tab and then select the check box for Use IRQ Steering as illustrated in Figure 24-17.

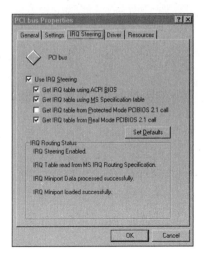

Figure 24-17: The IRQ Steering tab in the Windows PCI Bus Properties dialog box.

3. Under the Use IRQ Steering check box are four IRQ steering options: The first two and the fourth settings should be marked.

4. Click OK on each succeeding window and restart the PC when requested.

Part IX

PC Operating Systems

CHAPTER 25
The Windows Operating System

CHAPTER 26
Unix and Linux Operating Systems

Chapter 25

The Windows Operating System

IN THIS CHAPTER

I know that this is essentially a hardware book, but a PC technician absolutely must be able to install and configure an operating system on a user's PC because it's just a part of the overall installation and configuration process. As much as you and I would like to concentrate on hardware and the really challenging physical elements of a PC, in effect, there is no PC without its operating system (OS). Okay, I should include application software along with the OS to make a PC truly usable, but there is so much application software and so little time.

In this chapter, I cover the following:

◆ Installing and configuring Windows 98 (and Me)

◆ Installing and configuring Windows 2000

◆ Installing and configuring Windows XP

◆ Starting Windows in Safe mode

MY VIEW OF OPERATING SYSTEMS is the product of my experience, which tells me that when talking about operating system software, the first name out of the box is Microsoft, which automatically leads to Windows. Microsoft Windows has the largest installed base of any of the OS providers, so it's essential that a PC technician have a working knowledge of the processes used to install and configure this system.

 No, I haven't forgotten about other operating systems, but because this book is for PC technicians, I'm not covering network operating systems (NOS) — and, in a fairly bold stand, I'm not including Apple Computer's operating systems (Mac OS) as well. However, Chapter 26 does cover some essential Unix/Linux topics that every PC technician should know.

Looking at the Different Versions of Windows

Microsoft Windows has been around for nearly a decade and in that time (and despite a somewhat shaky start) has grown to be the most popular PC OS in the world. Regardless of what you, I, or the Justice Department think of it, the Microsoft Windows (hereafter, just plain Windows, please) OS is as much a part of the PC world as the hard disk on which it resides.

Over the years, Windows has released several versions. Some versions were just patches and fixes to the previous version, whereas others, such as Windows NT, 98, and XP, have effectively re-invented the system's look – and to a lesser extent, its function.

I think little is to be gained by covering the versions prior to Windows 98 in this book. It always surprises me how much information is still available on the Web about Windows 3.*x* and Windows 95. If you need further information on these systems, I suggest that you use Google or a similar search engine to hunt for what you need.

In the following sections, I cover the installation and configuration processes (along with a few troubleshooting tips) of Windows 98 (occasionally referred to as Windows 9*x*, when the information also covers Windows 95 OEM SR2), NT, Millennium Edition (Me), 2000, and XP. In the case of Windows NT, 2000, and XP, the discussion is limited to desktop (Professional or Home) versions rather than the Server versions.

Installing and Configuring Windows 98/Me

For an obsolete operating system, Windows 98 is sure hanging on. Many users and IT departments are approaching Windows OS updates with the attitude that if it ain't broke, don't fix it. If you ever need to install Windows 98 for the first time on a PC (or reinstall it after some catastrophe), follow the steps in the next few sections.

 For the sake of simplicity, I use *Windows 98* in this section to indicate Windows 98, 98 SE, and Me.

Installing Windows 98/Me

Using a clean installation is the best way to install Windows 98. A *clean installation* means that the hard disk drive on which you wish to install the system has been partitioned, formatted (see Chapter 10 for more information on formatting and partitioning a hard disk drive), and cleaned of all pre-existing data. If another OS has been on the PC, you should definitely create a full backup of the system prior to deleting or formatting the old partitions. Nothing goes wrong in 99 percent of the cases, but that 1 percent can ruin you.

To install Windows 98, use the following procedure:

1. Before beginning the installation, assemble the following items:

   ■ The Windows 98 CD-ROM release media.

   ■ A valid Windows 98 product key ID number.

   ■ A Windows 98 boot disk (just in case things do go wrong during the installation) — see "Creating a Windows 98/Me boot disk" later in this chapter.

   ■ Current and up-to-date device drivers for the peripheral devices and controller cards in the PC.

   With these items assembled, you're ready to start the installation.

2. Insert the Windows 98 boot disk in the floppy disk drive and power the PC off and on to boot the system from the floppy disk drive.

 If the system bypasses the floppy disk drive and boots from the hard disk, enter the Basic Input/Output System (BIOS) setup program and change the boot disk search sequence to add or move the floppy disk drive into the first position.

3. After the Windows 98 Setup menu appears, insert the Windows 98 CD in the CD-ROM drive.

   The Windows Setup menu gives you three installation options:

   ■ Start Windows 98 Setup from CD-ROM

   ■ Start computer with CD-ROM support

   ■ Start computer without CD-ROM support

4. Choose the second option, which will load the CD-ROM device drivers and make it accessible.

   When the drivers are installed, a list of the detected hard disk drives on the PC is displayed, followed by a DOS command prompt.

5. Repartition the system hard disk, if needed, and format the partitions that you wish to clean for the installation.

You aren't required to repartition the hard disk(s). If you've had trouble with them in the past, you might wish to do so.

6. At the command prompt, enter **A:\>FORMAT C: /Q** to format the C: disk partition.

Remember, DOS commands aren't case sensitive; you can enter them as upper- or lowercase characters.

If you're using a different partition, replace the C: with the appropriate drive designation.

Understand that formatting the hard drive will erase all data and programs on the hard disk partition.

When the formatting is completed, you have the option of naming the hard disk partition or pressing the Enter key to skip this step.

Unless you're planning to install an application system in a particular partition, such as DB2, Sybase, or the like — or will be dual-booting the PC with a Linux system — there really are no hard and fast rules for naming partitions. However, make sure that the application software or second operating system doesn't specify a particular partition naming convention.

7. At the command prompt, enter the drive designator for the CD-ROM drive.

   It should typically be something in the range of D:, E:, or F:. I'm assuming that it is D:; if not, use the drive designator assigned by the system. Press Enter to move to the next step.

8. At the command prompt, enter **D:\win98\setup**.

   The Windows 98 Setup program starts and displays a message that it will now run the ScanDisk utility. Accept this action (by pressing the Enter key) and then start a scan of the hard disk partition for any media errors.

9. When the ScanDisk completes, the Setup program displays installation options. Choose the Typical Installation option to start the file installation process.

10. When the basic installation is completed, restart the system as requested, making sure that you remove the boot disk from the floppy drive before doing so.

11. After the system restarts, install the device drivers for any motherboard-related components, including Peripheral Component Interconnect (PCI) bus mastering, interrupt request (IRQ) routing, and Accelerated Graphics Port (AGP) miniport drivers, if needed.

    These drivers are typically found on the CD that shipped with the motherboard, but if not there, they can be downloaded from the Web beforehand. The best place to find drivers for the motherboard-related components is on the manufacturers' Web sites.

12. Before installing the peripheral device drivers, run the Disk Defragmenter utility to further clean up the system.

    Disk Defragmenter can be found by choosing Start → Programs → Accessories → System Tools.

    After the device drivers are installed, you've completed the installation of the Windows 98 operating system and just about its entire configuration. Any remaining configuration steps are usually proprietary or locally defined, so follow the instructions for each device to the letter.

Controlling a Windows 98 setup

The Windows 98 Setup program has a variety of parameter switches that you can use to control the function and actions of the setup process. Table 25-1 lists the major options available to you.

TABLE 25-1 WINDOWS 98 SETUP SWITCHES

Value	Action
/?	Lists the available switches for the setup program.
/na	Bypasses the program check based on the value substituted for n. 0 = Default. 1 = No Windows-based program checking; MS-DOS programs are blocked. 2 = No MS-DOS program checking; Windows programs are blocked. 3 = No Windows or MS-DOS program checking.
/nd	Ignores the presence of a Migration.dll file and forces the setup program to overwrite newer files. The exception is that Windows Setup will keep newer "x32" files. (See /na for values of n.)
/nf	Omits prompting to remove the floppy disk drive (when installing from a bootable CD). (See /na for values of n.)
/nm	Bypasses the minimum hardware requirement test (486DX66 and 16MB RAM). (See /na for values of n.)
/d	Bypasses using any existing Windows configuration files (Win.ini and System.ini).
/ie	Bypasses the Windows 98 Startup Disk wizard screens, and the Windows\Command\EDB folder is not created.
/ig	Allows Windows 98 to be installed on legacy Gateway and Micron PCs with older BIOS.
/in	Bypasses the installation of the network wizard pages, and the network setup routines won't run.
/ir	Bypasses the updating of the Master Boot Records (MBRs).
/m	Bypasses the setup sound (.wav) files.
/n	Bypasses the mouse drivers to run setup without a mouse. (This switch is the letter *n* and not a value.)
/t<dir>	Assigns a location for the setup temporary files.

Configuring Windows 98

Actually, after Windows 98 is installed, there really isn't that much more to configure. However, the following sections include a few things that you might want to tweak to ensure that it operates like it should.

DEALING WITH DEVICE MANAGER ERRORS

Immediately after installing a Windows system of any version, check the Windows Device Manager (see Figure 25-1) to ensure that no hardware errors have been created in the process. On a Windows 9x system, the Device Manager is accessed by right-clicking the My Computer icon on the desktop, choosing Properties from the pop-up menu that appears, and then choosing the Device Manager tab of the Properties window.

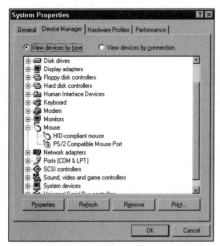

Figure 25-1: After a Windows installation, check Device Manager for hardware errors.

If a device problem exists, Device Manager flags either the device class (such as hard disk controllers, mouse, or display adapters) or a specific device (such as the PS/2-compatible mouse port) with one of three symbols (not counting the symbol used to mark an operating device):

- *Exclamation point inside a yellow circle:* Indicates a device that's in a problem state. A device in a problem state could be working, yet something isn't quite right with it – for example, an incompatible device driver.

- *Red X:* Indicates a device that's been disabled by either the system or the user. A disabled device is physically installed in the system and has system resources assigned to it but doesn't have a protected mode driver installed.

- *Blue i:* Indicates that automatic resource settings aren't in use on the device. This isn't necessarily a problem but more of a reminder.

If a device is flagged with one of these symbols, look at the device's properties (click the Properties button) to see whether a conflict exists or a system error code has been assigned to the device. Here are a few of the Device Manager's error codes and their appropriate resolutions:

♦ *Code 1: The system hasn't configured this device.* Follow the instructions in the Device Status box for removing the device from the Device Manager, restarting the PC, and running the Add New Hardware Wizard from the Control Panel.

♦ *Code 2: The device wasn't loaded by the device loader (DevLoader).* This error is typically displayed when the device is a Root Bus DevLoader (for example, PCI or BIOS). It typically includes the message `Windows could not load the driver for this device because the computer is reporting two <type> bus types (Code 2). Contact your computer manufacturer to get an updated BIOS for your computer.` The `<type>` will be `ISAPNP`, `PCI`, `BIOS`, `EISA`, or `ACPI`.

If the device is not a Root Bus DevLoader, the message is `The <type> device loader(s) for this device could not load the device driver (Code 2). To fix this, click Update Driver to update the device driver.` In this case, `<type>` is `FLOP`, `ESDI`, `SCSI`, and the like.

♦ *Code 3: The device driver is bad or the system is running low on memory.* Update the device driver or delete the device from Device Manager and use the Add New Hardware Wizard from the Control Panel to add the device again.

♦ *Code 4: The* `.inf` *file for the device is incorrect or the registry entry is corrupted.* Remove the device from the Device Manager and use the Add New Hardware Wizard from the Control Panel to add the device again.

You'll find around 35 of these error codes, some indicating very critical problems and some only minor system nuisances — but all should be investigated and resolved. Visit the Micosoft Knowledge Base at `http://support.microsoft.com/default.aspx?scid=KB;en-us;q125174` for a complete listing of the error codes.

If a device's problem appears to be that a real-mode driver is being used in place of a protected-mode driver (the driver you really want to have loaded), check the entries in the `Ios.log` file in the Windows folder, which can only be found if you're experiencing this problem. Real-mode device drivers are 16-bit drivers compared with the 32-bit `.vxd` (protected-mode) drivers. Because Windows log files are in text format, you can use the Notepad utility to open and read them.

The first line in the `Ios.log` file, if present, should indicate why the protected-mode driver didn't load. If the `Mbrint13.sys` file is mentioned, you can be almost sure that a virus is causing the problem (that is, unless you're using a device driver that replaces the Master Boot Record).

ACCESSING THE CD-ROM AFTER INSTALLING WINDOWS 98 OR ME

If you cannot access the CD-ROM driver after installing Windows 98/Me, the problem is linked to a dual-channel Integrated Drive Electronics (IDE) controller on the system. Use the following steps to resolve this problem:

1. Choose Start → Settings → Control Panel, click the System icon, and then choose the Device Manager tab.

2. Expand the Hard Disk Controllers group.

3. Click the IDE controller to highlight it, click the Properties button, and then choose the Settings tab on the window that opens.

4. In the Dual IDE Channel Settings drop-down list box (see Figure 25-2), choose the Both IDE Channels Enabled option from the list and then click OK.

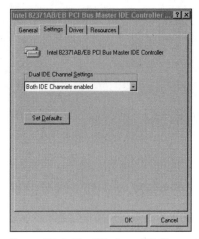

Figure 25-2: The Windows IDE Channel Setting dialog box is used to control the availability of IDE channels.

5. Restart the PC.

PHANTOM USB

Even if the PC's USB ports aren't in use, you might want to enable two BIOS settings (in the BIOS setup configuration data) anyway:

◆ *OnChipUSB:* For some reason, this setting on the Chipset Settings menu allows the system to shut down properly and display the It is now safe to turn off your computer message on some PCs.

◆ *Assign IRQ for USB:* This setting on the Plug and Play (PnP)/PCI Configuration menu allows a system shut down to complete properly on some motherboards, but especially on motherboards manufactured by Abit Computer Corporation.

OPTIMIZE THE SWAP SPACE

On PCs with 128MB or more of memory, the size of the hard disk swap file is less critical than on PCs with low memory. So to optimize (conserve) the hard disk space used by the virtual memory swap file, make the following change to the registry:

1. From the Windows Notepad utility, open the SYSTEM.INI file from the Windows directory.

2. In the section following the subtitle [386Enh], insert the following entry:

```
ConservativeSwapfileUsage=1
```

3. Save the file and restart the PC.

MINIMIZE THE DISK CACHE

The *disk cache* – the buffer allocated in system memory to the caching function of the hard disk drive – can slow down the system and cause some low memory problems. This problem is especially noticeable on PC's with 16MB or less of RAM that run Windows 98/Me.

To control the minimum and maximum amount of memory allocated to the hard disk cache on a PC, use the following steps:

1. Open the SYSTEM.INI file in the Windows folder from the Notepad utility.

2. In the [vcache] section, locate and modify, or add if needed, these two lines:

```
MinFileCache=0
MaxFileCache=4096
```

On PCs with more than 16MB of RAM, you can increase the MaxFileCache to about 25 percent of the total RAM size. For example, if you have 256MB of RAM, you could set MaxFileCache=64000000.

Installing and Configuring Windows 2000 Professional

If you've recently passed the Microsoft Certified Systems Engineer (MCSE) 70-210 (Installing, Configuring, and Administering Microsoft Windows 2000 Professional) exam, you can probably skip this section. However, if you've never installed or configured the Windows 2000 Professional (Pro) operating system on a PC, the following information could be helpful. Understand that the most common form of installing Windows 2000 is as an upgrade, typically over Windows 98/Me.

Installing Windows 2000 Pro

Installing Windows 2000, at least in terms of installing the basic operating system, is actually quite easy. Just follow two basic steps: Insert the release CD in the CD-ROM drive and then restart the PC. A small run-time version of Windows 2000 is copied into RAM and started, which then loads and starts the setup program. You need to answer a few questions and enter the software ID key (found on the release booklet), but that's about it, especially for Windows 2000 Pro.

VERIFYING WINDOWS 2000 MINIMUM REQUIREMENTS
The minimum system requirements for installing Windows 2000 are the following:

- *Processor:* A 133 MHz or higher Pentium-class CPU; Windows 2000 supports either single or multiple processors.

- *Memory:* At least 64MB of RAM, but more is better.

- *Hard disk space:* At least 2GB with 650MB of available free space.

CHECKING WINDOWS 2000 HARDWARE COMPATIBILITY
Before installing Windows 2000 (NT or XP, as well), you should verify that the hardware, software, and BIOS of the PC are compatible, which means that they have been tested and found to perform like they should on a Windows 2000 system.

Microsoft includes a list of compatible devices and systems in its hardware compatibility list (HCL). For the latest list, visit

www.microsoft.com/windows2000/professional/howtobuy/upgrading/compat

This Microsoft Web site provides search tools for computers, hardware devices, and software that you can use to see whether a PC and its components will work properly with Windows 2000 Pro.

Here are two reasons why you should check the BIOS first:

♦ The existing BIOS version might not support the advanced power management and device configuration features of Windows 2000. In order to take advantage of the power management features in Windows 2000, the PC must be compliant with Advanced Configuration and Power Interface (ACPI) BIOS.

♦ The wrong BIOS version on a PC could cause the PC to stop working like it should, with Windows 2000 installed or not.

See Chapter 4 for information on PC BIOS and the procedures used to update a BIOS system.

PREPARING TO INSTALL WINDOWS 2000

Windows 2000 can be installed three different ways:

♦ *Clean install*: Install Windows 2000 as the only operating system on a PC on an empty or formatted hard drive. This section focuses on the clean installation procedure.

♦ *Dual boot install*: Install Windows 2000 on a PC with another operating system, such as Windows 98, Windows NT 4.0, or Linux, so that the PC can be booted to either system from a menu of operating system choices displayed when the PC boots. Windows 2000 must be installed either on a separate hard disk drive or into a separate partition from the other operating system.

♦ *Upgrade install*: A PC running Windows 9x or Windows NT 4.0 can be upgraded to Windows 2000. This type of installation replaces the existing operating system files with new ones.

To install Windows 2000 using a clean install, you first need to prepare the hard disk drive for it. The three different ways to accomplish this task are the following:

♦ *Using Windows 2000 boot disks:* To create a set of four Windows 2000 boot disks, you must first boot the system (this can be done on any computer, not just the one on which you'll be installing Windows 2000) to a DOS prompt using either a Windows 9x or MS-DOS boot disk. See "Creating Windows 2000 boot disks" later in the chapter for information on creating the boot disks. Insert the first of the four boot disks and reboot the PC. The installation will then proceed.

◆ *Using a Windows 9x boot disk:* This is the faster of the two methods that you can use, but it will only work if the boot disk has `SMARTDRV.EXE` on it: Without it, the installation can take hours instead of minutes. After booting the PC to the boot disk, use the DOS `FDISK` command to create one or more partitions on the hard disk drive. Reboot the system, enabling CD-ROM support, and then use the DOS `FORMAT` command to format the system (active) partition, which is usually the C: partition. Next, enter the DOS command `SYS C:` to make the C: drive bootable (this step might or might not be necessary, but it provides a bit of insurance that the system will reboot to the active partition). See "Creating a Windows 98/Me boot disk" later in the chapter for information on creating a boot disk.

RUNNING WINDOWS 2000 SETUP

The following steps detail the process used to install Windows 2000:

1. Before inserting the Windows 2000 release CD in the CD-ROM drive, enter the BIOS setup program and set the CD-ROM driver as the first boot device. See the earlier section "Installing Windows 98/Me" for instructions on how this is done.

2. Place the Windows 2000 CD in the CD-ROM drive and restart the PC.

   If the hard disk drive is partitioned and formatted, the message `Hit Any Key to Boot from CD-ROM` is displayed.

3. The AutoRun feature on the CD starts up and runs the setup program and begins to load the device drivers needed to proceed.

4. Continue through the Welcome to Setup menu and read the license agreement. If you agree to abide by the license agreement, which you should, press F8 to continue.

   The next display is the partition screen where you can indicate the area of the disk on which you'd like to install Windows 2000.

   You can assign Windows to an unpartitioned part of the disk or set up partitions on an unpartitioned disk drive. See "Preparing to install Windows 2000" earlier.

   The format screen displays where you can specify how you wish to format the disk drive space, meaning which file system you wish to use.

5. Normally, you should choose FAT from the list if you're installing Windows 2000 on a standalone PC, or you can choose one of the other options available, provided that you know what they are and when you should use them. See "Configuring Windows 2000" later in this chapter for more information on files systems.

After you make your choice, the setup program confirms it and begins formatting the partition. On a very large disk drive (more than 4GB), this can take awhile.

After the partition space is formatted, the PC restarts and displays the Setup Wizard.

6. Continue through the first wizard screen to start the hardware detection phase of the installation.

   After the system has detected and configured the attached and compatible hardware, it runs through a series of screens to set the regional settings; the user's name and organization; product key ID; administrator's password; and the date, time zone, and local time.

   If the PC is networked, Windows 2000 then detects and installs the networking settings. The typical settings work just fine for nearly all workstation PCs.

7. When asked which type of installation you wish for Windows 2000, unless you have specific reasons not to, you should click the Express Setup button. The Custom Setup option requires knowledge of Windows 2000 and its elements.

8. When the Setup Wizard completes, click the Finish button to restart the PC.

   After the system restarts, the Network Identification Wizard starts. You can configure the PC's network ID and workgroup at this time or wait and do it later.

9. The basic installation and configuration are done.

   If needed, you should enter the Control Panel and configure the PC for the user or the network, depending on the peripherals, dialup, networking, and features desired by the user.

Configuring Windows 2000

For most users, after the Windows 2000 installation process is completed, their PC is essentially good to go. However, you can do a few things to optimize the system for performance and to avoid future problems.

SETTING MAXIMUM VOLUME AND FILE SIZES FOR WINDOWS 2000

Windows 2000 supports three different file systems: File Allocation Table (FAT), FAT32, and New Technology File System (NTFS). When defining the partition size for Windows 2000, use the information in Table 25-2 as a guide.

TABLE 25-2 WINDOWS MAXIMUM VOLUME AND FILE SIZES

File System	Windows Versions	Max Volume Size	Max File Size	Max Files (Folders) per Volume
FAT	All Windows versions	2GB on Windows 95; 4GB on all later versions	4GB	512
FAT32	.NET 2003, XP, 2000, 98, 95 OSR2	2TB	4GB	65,534
NTFS	.NET 2003, XP, 2000, NT (NTFS 4 only)	256TB	Volume capacity	4,294,967,295

The use of long filenames reduces the volume and file size numbers. Check the documentation of the Windows version in use.

CONVERTING A FAT FILE SYSTEM TO NTFS ON WINDOWS 2000

Which file system a system should use depends primarily on the application programs running on it. Many legacy programs will only run with an FAT file system. However, if the decision is made to convert an FAT or FAT32 file system to NTFS, you don't need to reformat the disk partitions affected, but you should back up the data on the file system to be converted.

You would convert an FAT or FAT32 file system to NTFS because it's more powerful than FAT or FAT32, it's required for hosting Active Directory, and it supports many very important security features of Windows 2000, such as domain-based security.

To convert the FAT or FAT32 file system on a Windows 2000 system to NTFS, use the following steps:

1. Open a command prompt window by entering **cmd** in the Run dialog box (from the Start menu) and then clicking OK.

2. At the command prompt that appears, enter **convert drive_designator: /fs:ntfs.**

Installing Windows XP

Nearly all newer PCs come with Windows XP pre-installed, but that doesn't mean that you can just replace perfectly working PCs with new ones just to get an upgraded system. As simple as that might sound, the money issue typically prevents it from being that easy.

Upgrading to Windows XP

Not every system can be upgraded to Windows XP. Table 25-3 lists the versions that can be updated to Windows XP Home or Windows XP Pro, which are the versions that I'm assuming you would install on a user's PC.

TABLE 25-3 WINDOWS VERSIONS UPGRADEABLE TO WINDOWS XP

Windows Version	XP Home	XP Pro
Windows 3.x	No	No
Windows 95	No	No
Windows 98	Yes	Yes
Windows NT Workstation 4.0	No	Yes
Windows 2000 Pro	No	Yes
Windows Me	Yes	Yes
Windows XP Home	-	Yes
Windows XP Pro	No	-

 With the Windows XP version, Microsoft has made Upgrade Advisor available. This online utility checks a PC for its compatibility for an upgrade to Windows XP. In addition, Upgrade Advisor checks your system for required updates and then downloads and installs them. You can find more information on Upgrade Advisor at www.microsoft.com/windowsxp/pro/howtobuy/upgrading/advisor.asp.

Upgrading to Windows XP from an eligible Windows version (see Table 25-3) is actually fairly easy. Insert the Windows XP CD-ROM; when you're asked which type of installation you'd like to perform, choose Upgrade. If all is well, the Windows XP setup program will perform the upgrade installation automatically.

Installing Windows XP Pro or Home editions

To install Windows XP on a clean PC (one that's had its hard disk drives formatted clean), use the following steps:

1. Boot the PC from the Windows XP release media CD.

2. If the PC has any devices not supported by Windows XP (XP doesn't have drivers for them), obtain the drivers before starting the installation and press F6 when the XP installation first starts up.

   The setup program begins loading the Windows XP files and displays a series of screens, most of which you should continue through (accepting the End-User License Agreement [EULA] along the way).

   Eventually, a screen displays that asks you to select the hard disk partition on which you wish to install Windows XP.

3. Choose the partition and then click Next to proceed.

 If you wish to have two operating systems on the PC, you should create two hard disk drive partitions, one for the existing operating system and one for Windows XP, either beforehand or at this time.

4. If you're installing Windows XP into a partition that has existing data, be sure to choose the Keep Current File System Intact option on the next screen displayed.

5. If the installation is on a clean PC (recommended), select the partition and then click Next.

6. On the next screen displayed, select either a quick format for FAT or NTFS as the file system for the PC.

   - If no data on the PC requires security, choose FAT because FAT is the faster file system choice.

   - Choose NTFS if security is required for the existing data or for future data to be stored on the hard disk drive.

   After choosing the file system appropriate for the PC, the Windows XP Setup continues to load its files. After it copies the files that it needs for the configuration that you've indicated, the system restarts itself.

After rebooting, you'll be asked for the Regional and Language options along with a few bits of other information for its files and its product ID key.

Because Windows XP assumes that it will be networked, the remainder of the setup requests a workgroup or domain and an automatic check for the type of network on the PC.

7. The final installation step asks you to create the user name account for the user or users of the PC. XP creates user name accounts without passwords, so that's something you must do later via the Users icon of the Control Panel.

Starting Windows in Safe Mode

If a PC has a serious boot problem, such as freezing during startup or a device that fails to load its device driver, you should boot Windows into Safe mode as the first step in your troubleshooting process. In *Safe mode*, Windows loads only the device drivers that it needs in order to function, which excludes most of the peripherals attached to the PC. The process used to start Windows in Safe mode varies by its version. The following sections detail the steps used to start Safe mode for the different Windows versions.

 All Windows versions, with the exception of Windows 3.*x* and Windows NT, can be started in Safe mode.

Opening Windows 9x/Me/2000 in Safe mode

To start Windows in Safe mode, the first couple of steps depend on whether Windows is running. Here's what to do

◆ If Windows is running:

1. Close all open programs.

2. Choose Shut Down from the Start menu.

3. Click Restart and then click OK.

◆ If Windows is not running:

1. If the PC is powered on, turn off the power switch.

2. After a few seconds, power the PC on.

The next set of actions is common to all versions of Windows (including Windows XP):

1. Watch the screen and its display carefully. As soon as the Starting Windows bar appears at the bottom of the display, begin tapping F8.

   This should cause the Options menu (called the Advanced Options menu on Windows 2000) to display.

2. Select the Safe Mode option (typically the first option on the menu) and press Enter.

   The system will start up in Safe mode, which might take a few minutes to complete.

3. After you complete your troubleshooting, restart the PC, and it will return to normal mode.

Opening Windows XP in Safe mode

If you can start the PC in Windows, here are the recommended steps to use to set up Windows XP to restart into Safe mode (SAFEBOOT):

1. Close all running application programs.

2. Run the System Configuration Utility by entering **msconfig** into the Run dialog box (from the Start menu) and then clicking OK.

   The System Configuration Utility window (see Figure 25-3) displays.

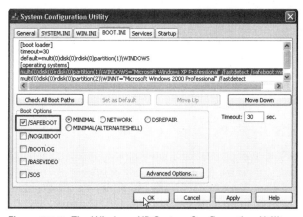

Figure 25-3: The Windows XP System Configuration Utility.

3. As shown in Figure 25-3, mark the /SAFEBOOT check box and then click OK.

4. When prompted to restart the PC, click the Restart option.

    The PC restarts and loads Windows XP into Safe mode.

5. After you complete your troubleshooting and wish to return Windows XP to its normal mode, run the `msconfig` utility again, clear the /SAFEBOOT check box, and then restart the PC.

Another way that you can reach Safe mode on a Windows XP system is to press the F8 key during startup, but you have to do it at just the right time or you'll have to try again. That's why I prefer the /SAFEBOOT method — I never seem to hit the key at just the right time.

Creating a Windows Boot Disk

Creating a diskette to use to reboot a Windows system when it can't otherwise be started is always a good idea. Users will think that you can walk on water if you can boot a PC that has been unbootable. Plus, it's tough to fix a PC that you can't get up and running.

Creating a Windows 98/Me boot disk

To create a Windows 98 boot disk, access the Add/Remove Programs icon on the Control Panel and choose the Startup Disk option to create the disk. The boot disk that's generated (on your blank diskette) provides all the required files, including CD-ROM support, needed to boot a Windows 98/Me system.

TIP   I recommend that you copy the DOS commands `FDISK`, `FORMAT`, and `SMARTDRV` to the boot disk, if you will be using it to install either Windows 2000 or Windows NT 4.0.

Creating a Windows NT boot disk

To create a Windows NT boot disk, use the following steps:

1. Use the Windows Explorer to open the i386 folder on the Windows NT release media CD or in the WINNT folder on the hard disk drive.

2. Format a blank floppy disk and copy the following files to the diskette:

    ■ `boot.ini`

    ■ `ntdetect.com`

- `ntldr`
- Also copy to the diskette any Small Computer System Interface (SCSI) or other devices that you wish to access after you boot the PC with the boot disk that you're creating.

Creating Windows 2000 boot disks

To create a Windows 2000 Pro boot disk, you need to have four 1.44MB diskettes and the Windows 2000 Pro release media CD available. Follow these steps to create the boot disk:

1. Insert the CD in the CD-ROM drive.

2. Open the Run dialog box (from the Start menu) and then click the Browse button to browse the CD.

3. Open the Boot Disk folder on the CD and double-click the `makebt32.exe` program.

4. Click OK to start the program, which will guide you through the steps needed to create the boot disks.

Obtaining Windows XP setup boot disks

Windows XP setup boot disks are created through a file that you must download from the Microsoft Web site. Visit the following URL for information on which file to download for your XP version and instructions on creating boot disks:

`http://support.microsoft.com/default.aspx?scid=KB;en-us;q310994`

Chapter 26

Unix and Linux Operating Systems

IN THIS CHAPTER
Surprisingly enough, for some people, there *is* life outside the world of Windows.
Users who (for myriad reasons) don't want to use Windows can opt to install and
use Unix (which is not an acronym for anything) or Linux (likewise) as an alternative to Windows.

I don't propose in this chapter to give you an in-depth Linux tutorial, but I do
want to provide you with the following information on Linux hardware support so
that if you encounter a PC running Linux, you have some idea how to identify the
source of a problem:

- An overview of Linux hardware systems

- Dealing with Linux hardware issues

- Managing hardware configurations in Linux

UNIX AND LINUX (hereafter I use *Linux,* which is the most common of the two on
PCs, to represent both) are among the most popular operating systems in the world
on several levels of computing. Unix can be found on supercomputers, mainframes,
minicomputers, network servers, and specialized networked workstations. Linux is
more often found on network servers and frequently on standalone user PCs. Linux
has grown in popularity because of its source accessibility, which is especially
popular with operating system purists and operating system hackers. Unix is still
very expensive to run at the PC level (as much as $1,500 per machine), but the
freely distributed Linux is available in an open source form at no cost. Commercial
versions of Linux are also available from Caldera, Red Hat, Slackware, and others.

Understanding a Linux Installation

If you're a Windows-trained technician who has never had the fun of working with
MS-DOS or the like, Linux might seem a bit overly complicated to you when you
first encounter it. Unless the PC is running X-windows (a Windows-like user interface for UNIX and Linux systems) or its equivalent, you'll probably be greeted by
its standard command prompt, which is typically a dollar sign ($).

This command prompt tells you that you are logged in as a user and are currently in the root directory. (No folders on this system!) In essence, the Linux command prompt shown is very much like the MS-DOS command prompt: `C:>\`.

Logging on as the supervisor

If you're working on a PC that has a Linux operating system, you need to have the user log you onto the system as the supervisor. To modify the system, you must work at the supervisory level, much like you need to be the administrator to make significant changes to a Windows NT/2000/XP system.

You'll know that you're in supervisory mode when the prompt changes to a pound or number sign (#).

Operating in dual mode

A Linux system can operate as either a single, standalone operating system or in a multiboot (dual boot) mode. You'll commonly find a system that can boot into either Windows or Linux. On these systems, if a problem shows up on Linux, it must be resolved in Linux. The problem could also exist on the Windows side as well, but regardless, any problem identified in Linux must be resolved there. However, I recommend testing for the same problem on the Windows side, also.

On a dual boot PC that has Linux installed along with Windows NT/2000/XP, the Windows NTLDR routine resides on the master boot record and loads the Linux loader (lilo [Linux loader] or grub [grand unified boot loader], depending on the Linux version) that boots the Linux system.

Viewing the hardware configuration

The hardware configuration files on a Linux system are stored in a system directory on the root (/) file system under the pathname `/dev`. This directory holds the files that define and link to the peripherals, both active and inactive.

The commands used in Linux to navigate between directories are `cd` or `chdir` (change directory), just like the commands in MS-DOS.

READING THE /DEV FILE LIST

The information on the configured hardware devices on a Linux system are in the `/dev` directory. To display the file properties for the device files (or the files in any directory, for that matter), the command `ls -l` (long list) is used as follows:

```
$ ls -l /dev/*
crw-rw-rw-  1  root   root 1,   3 Dec 5 2002   /dev/null
brw-rw-rw-  1  root   root 3,   0 Dec 5 2002   /dev/hda
brw-rw-rw-  1  root   root 3,   1 Dec 5 2002   /dev/hdb
crw-rw----  1  root   root 6,   0 Dec 5 2002   /dev/lp0
brw-rw----  1  root   disk 8,   0 Dec 5 2002   /dev/sda
$
```

To decipher the preceding sample display of the files in the /dev directory, reading left to right, the entry values are the following:

◆ *File mode character:* The first character in the file listing represents the mode of the file. A c designates a character mode file, and a b indicates a block mode file. The primary difference between a character mode file and a block mode file is that a *character mode file* can be displayed as text, and a *block mode file* is a buffered file that contains information on the configuration and link to a particular peripheral device.

◆ *File permissions:* The *file permissions* on a Linux file indicate the rights and actions assigned to the file's owner, the group to which the owner belongs, and all users. The permissions consist of three sets of three characters (such as the rw- for the /dev/hda file in the preceding sample). Each of the three characters represents an action and can contain either a dash (hyphen) to mean that no permission is granted for a particular action, or an r, w, or x, which indicate, respectively, that read, write, and execute permissions are granted to the associated user level.

 A group in Linux is very much like a group in Windows and is used as a mechanism to assign permissions to a collection of users simultaneously.

◆ *File ownership:* The first text word in the file properties – root in each case in the above example – indicates the user login or administrative level that owns the permission set on the file. Only a user logged in at that user level is allowed to effect changes to the permission set or location of the file. The first set (three characters) of file permissions indicates the permission set for the file owner.

◆ *Group ownership:* The second text word, following the file owner ID, is the name of the group to which the file owner belongs. All users that are members of the group named in this entry assume the permission set of the group. The second set of file permissions indicates the permissions of the group.

As is often the case on a Windows system, if a user complains that he either can't find or can't open a particular file or directory, that user probably doesn't have the proper permissions assigned to do so.

◆ *Major number:* The first number to the left of the group name (the one with a comma following it) indicates the device category of the peripheral device. The *major number* is used to categorize devices that require similar handling or addressing. For example, notice that the first hard disk drive (/dev/hda) has a major number of 3, and the first parallel port (/dev/1p0) has a major number of 6. A hard disk drive requires different access methods than a parallel port.

On a Linux or UNIX system, /dev/hda is the first disk drive; /dev/hdb is the second disk drive; /dev/hdc is the third disk drive; and so on.

◆ *Minor number:* If more than one device of the same type is on a system, such as the /dev/hda and /dev/hdb, the system must have a means of distinguishing them. The minor number is like a sub-identification for devices in the same major number category.

◆ *Maintenance date:* The date indicated in the file properties is the date of the creation of the file or its last modification that required the file to be rewritten.

◆ *File pathname:* The last entry is the pathname of each device file.

CREATING A DEVICE ENTRY

Although not a common occurrence, sometimes you need to create a new or additional device file in Linux. The Linux command used for this purpose is makedev (make device), which is located in the /dev directory.

The makedev command can be used to create a set of standard (std) devices for the system architecture or one or more devices specific to a single PC. The command structure for makedev is

```
# makedev device_parameter
```

Table 26-1 lists the more commonly used device parameters for the makedev command.

TABLE 26-1 DEVICE PARAMETERS FOR THE LINUX MAKEDEV COMMAND

Parameter	Action/Usage
all	Creates a standard number of device files for all known devices, including local devices
console	Creates virtual terminal files associated with the system console
std	Creates standard device files (console, floppy disk, memory, standard input, standard output, and null)
acd#	Creates AT Attachment Packet Interface (ATAPI) CD-ROM drive files
ad#	Creates ATAPI Integrated Drive Electronics (IDE) disk drive files
ast#	Creates ATAPI tape drive files
busmice	Creates a set of standard bus mouse device files, including logimouse (Logitech), psmouse (PS/2), and msmouse (Microsoft)
da#	Creates Small Computer System Interface (SCSI) hard disk drive files (# represents drive number – 1, 2, 3, and so on)
fd#	Creates floppy disk drive files
hdx	Creates hard disk drive files (x represents the drive hierarchy a through d)
isdns#	Creates Integrated Service Digital Network (ISDN) device files
js#	Creates joystick device files
loop#	Creates loopback device files
lp#	Creates parallel port device files
sa#	Creates SCSI tape drive files
tty#	Creates standard COM port (serial) device files
ttyS#	Creates serial COM port device files
usbs#	Creates Universal Serial Bus (USB) device files
vty#	Creates virtual console device files
wd#	Creates Winchester hard disk drive files

Correcting Hardware Woes

The different versions of Linux that can be installed on a PC can create some hardware situations that you might need to correct to get a user's workstation up and running properly. The following sections include only the more common of these problems. For more information on hardware issues that can arise from a Linux installation, visit the Web site of the Linux version or supplier.

Configuring IDE/ATA drives

If IDE/ATA hard disk drives are in use, the Linux /boot partition must be located on the hard disk drive attached to the primary controller, or the PC might not boot properly. If the PC has two IDE/ATA hard disk drives, they should be attached to the primary IDE controller as master and slave, and any CD-ROM drives should be installed on the secondary controller.

If the hard disk drive on a PC is a SCSI device, the /boot partition must reside on SCSI ID 0 or 1.

Preventing drive letters from changing

When you add a new disk drive to a PC and then boot to Windows, Windows reassigns the drive letters of the disk drives, including assigning new drive letters to existing drives. If the new disk drive is a hard disk installed to hold Linux, you should boot to Linux first, where you can assign the hard disk drive a Linux-only drive letter. Later startups into Windows ignore the Linux disk drive and do not reassign the drive letters of the Windows-recognized devices.

Resolving device access issues

If a user can't access a particular hardware device on a Linux system, the problem is typically device file permissions. To determine whether this is the problem, log onto the system with the root username and attempt to access the problem device. If you can access the device, the problem is the permissions on the device file in the /dev directory.

 The root username is *omnipotent* (a fancy word for all powerful) and should be used only for system administrative purposes. For normal user access, each user should have a user-level account created by using the mkuser command.

CHANGING DEVICE FILE PERMISSIONS

You need to change the access permissions on the device file with the chmod (change mode) command. The chmod command, which can be entered in octal format or alpha format, allows you to set the permissions of the owner, group, or user (or all). The syntax for the `chmod` command is

```
chmod mode file(s)
```

The `mode` parameter is a string that represents *who* is to be changed and *what* access is being granted or removed. The *who* part of the mode parameter is represented with one of the following choices: a for all, o for owner, g for group, or u for users. (See "Reading the /dev file list" earlier in the chapter for information on the device file permissions structure.)

The first character in the *what* part of the mode parameter indicates whether you're adding or removing permissions by using a plus (+) or minus (-) sign, respectively. Next are the permissions that you're adding or removing, which are indicated with an r for read, w for write, or an x for execute. For example, the following command adds read (open) and write permissions to the user permission level of the first hard disk drive:

```
chmod +rw /dev/hda
```

To remove access to a device file, a minus sign is used with the permission being removed; the command should look something like this:

```
chmod u-r /dev/hda
```

GRANTING DEVICE FILE ACCESS

If a user can't open or access a particular device, access might have been denied to the user's group or to all users in general. Listing the /dev directory contents (use the command `ls -l`) allows you to verify whether this is the case; if the permissions should be changed, the `chmod` command can be used to alter the permissions.

Some device classes are commonly owned by a user group created especially for controlling access to the device. For example, the groups `floppy` and `cdrom` are commonly used as the owners of the floppy disk and CD-ROM disk drives, respectively. This arrangement provides a means to assign global access to these devices.

UNDERSTANDING FILE SYSTEM NAMES

A file system is not necessarily a file system . . . when you compare a Linux file system with a Windows file system, anyway. Linux organizes data files in a hierarchical tree-like structure that starts at the top with the root (/) directory. All other directories, subdirectories, and files are subordinate to the root directory.

The /etc/httpd directory is an example of the Linux file structure and its hierarchy. The /etc (root/etc) directory (pronounced *et-*see, not et-*cet-*er-a) is subordinate to the root directory, and the httpd directory is subordinate to the /etc directory.

Each storage drive, whether a hard disk, CD-ROM, floppy, tape, or other type of drive, is associated with a file system. A file system is *mounted* (attached and made available) to the file system tree; after it's mounted, it appears to seamlessly be a part of the same directory system. In place of the A:, C:, and E: drives of a DOS/Windows system, you have /disk1, /floppy, or /cdrom. In fact, a mounted disk drive might not even be physically inside the PC but on another computer across the network.

Table 26-2 lists the standard file systems and directories of a Linux system.

TABLE 26-2 LINUX FILE SYSTEM DIRECTORIES

File system	Detail
/ (slash)	The root directory, which is equivalent to the C:\ directory on an MS-DOS/Windows PC, must be present to start or run a Linux system.
/bin	This directory contains the majority of the binary executables of the Linux system.
/boot	This directory includes the base kernel (core) and the information needed to start the system.
/dev	This directory contains the device files. (See "Viewing the hardware configuration" earlier in this chapter.)
/etc	This directory holds the majority of the system configuration files. Typically this directory requires administrator (root) permissions to access its contents.
/usr	This directory contains the globally available general-use commands and programs of the Linux system. It is also where new application software is installed by default.
swap	In a Linux system, you need to create a swap space on a separate hard disk drive partition, which contrasts to the use of the Win386.swp file in Windows.

Resolving sound card problems

A common problem on Linux systems is a sound card that won't make sound. When this happens, enter the Basic Input/Output System (BIOS) configuration (during the system boot sequence) and disable plug-and-play (PnP) support by changing the PnP setting to Disable.

Adding a hard disk drive to a Linux system

After you physically install a new hard disk drive in a Linux PC (see Chapter 10 for information on installing hard disk drives), you still have a few steps to perform to complete the installation for Linux.

1. After booting the system and logging in as `root`, run the display message command `dmesg | more`.

   This command displays information about the disk drives that have been detected on the PC, including the new drive (provided that it's properly installed).

2. Find the drive in the information listing.

   The second hard disk drive should be listed as `/dev/hdb`; the third drive should be listed as `/dev/hdc`; and so on. Remember this name for later.

3. The new disk needs to be partitioned. Assuming that it's the second hard disk drive, enter the command `fdisk /dev/hdb1`. The parameter `/dev/hdb1` indicates the hdb (second hard disk drive) with a sub-device number of 1.

   A new command prompt displays that reads `Command (m for help):` or something very similar.

 The `fdisk` command in Linux, although performing the same actions as the Windows/MS-DOS `fdisk` command, has a completely different syntax in Linux. The Linux `fdisk` command uses single letter commands to indicate the action to be taken.

---

4. At the `fdisk` command prompt, enter **p** to display the existing partitions, if any. If partitions need to be deleted, enter **d**; and at the next prompt, enter the number of the partition to be deleted.

5. Enter **n** to create a new partition, and at the next prompt, enter the number 1 (if it's the first partition on the drive).

   You'll be prompted for the cylinder number on which you wish to start the partition. If the new partition is the first partition on the disk, enter the number 2. Trust me on this: You don't want to start the partition on cylinder 1. (It is reserved for the system.)

   You're asked for the number of the ending cylinder of the partition.

6. If you wish to use the entire drive in a single partition, press Enter to accept that as the default. If you wish to use only a part of the disk, you need to calculate the number of cylinders that you wish to allocate to this partition.

7. Linux requires that you place a file system on the disk, which is a process very similar to formatting the disk in the MS-DOS/Windows world. To create a new file system on a newly partitioned hard disk drive, enter the `make filesystem` command indicating the device on which the file system should be created: `mkfs /dev/hdb1`.

8. Create a mount point for the partition (and its file system).

   As long as the directory name isn't duplicated on this partition, you can use virtually any name you'd like, with the exception of those in the `root` partition. For example, to create a mount point of `/prtn1`, use the make directory command, like this: `mkdir /prtn1`.

9. Edit the `/etc/fstab` file to add your partition and file system to the system. In a text editor (Linux has `vi` or `ed`, which are globally available commands), create an entry at the end of the file, similar to this one:

   ```
   /dev/hdb1   /prtn1   ext2   defaults   1   1
   ```

   Save the file.

10. Enter the command `mount -a` to mount (activate) the partitions listed in the `/etc/fstab` file.

    That's it.

Optimizing a hard disk for 32-bit and DMA operation

Many Linux versions need some tweaking in order to speed up hard disk performance by enabling 32-bit input/output (I/O) and direct memory access (DMA) operations. To perform this operation, use the following procedure:

1. Log on with the root user ID.

2. With the following command, list the current parameters of the hard disk drives on the system:

   ```
   hdparm -c /dev/hda
   ```

   which returns the information:

   ```
   /dev/hda:
   I/O support = 0 (default 16-bit)
   ```

3. Repeat the `hdparm -c` (query) command for each hard disk drive that you might wish to optimize, replacing `/dev/hda` with the filename of the other disk drives (`/dev/hdb`, `/dev/hdc`, and so on).

4. Query each hard disk drive with the `hdparm -t` (timing buffer) parameter:

```
hdparm -t /dev/hda
```

which returns the following:

```
/dev/hda:
Timing buffered disk reads: 64 MB in 17.58 seconds = 3.64
MB/sec
```

From the information displayed in Steps 2 and 4, the `/dev/hda` hard disk is set to 16-bit I/O with no DMA enabled.

5. To turn on 32-bit I/O and DMA for this device, use the following command:

```
hdparm -c1 -d1 /dev/hda
```

which returns the following information:

```
/dev/hda:
setting 32-bit I/O support flag to 1
setting using_dma to 1 (on)
I/O support = 1 (32-bit)
Using_dma = 1 (on)
```

6. Display the timing information for the drive by using the `hdparm -t` command (see Step 4), which should now display

```
/dev/hda:
Timing buffered disk reads: 64 MB in 11.77 seconds = 5.44
MB/sec
```

Modifying a disk drive for 32-bit and DMA operations results in an increase in throughput of 50 percent, which makes it worth doing in most cases.

However, the setting changes that you've just made are temporary and will be reset to their default values the next time you reboot the system. To make these changes permanent, use the `hdparm -k` (keep) command:

```
hdparm -k1 /dev/hda
```

which will respond with the following:

```
/dev/hda:
setting keep_settings to 1 (on)
keepsettings = 1 (on)
```

Part X

Maintaining a PC

Chapter 27

Preventive Care

IN THIS CHAPTER

A PC is essentially just a machine or an appliance with moving parts, electronics, and glass and plastic surfaces that all require care. Dirt, dust, and other debris can get in and on the components of the PC – in the best case, just making it dirty and dusty. In the worst case, dust and dirt can damage or destroy a PC's components, especially those inside the system case. Just like you perform scheduled maintenance on your car, you should also perform preventive maintenance (PM) on a PC to avoid failures and repairs and to extend the PC's life.

In a perfect situation, a PC should be operated in an environment that is relatively dust, moisture, and smoke free. In this perfect world, nothing would ever be spilled into or onto its components; the PC would never be bumped or dropped; and the electrical power source would always run at a perfect 110 volts (v).

Unfortunately, PCs don't operate in perfect worlds because they're used in homes, offices, and factories. These environments have dust, smoke, and other airborne debris that can get inside the unit and clog up the works. Because multiple users pull from the same supply system, electrical power fluctuates and on occasion, blackouts and brownouts occur. Because the world of the PC is not perfect, you must develop a PM program that provides preventive, proactive, and corrective actions against the hazards of the PC's environment.

Scheduling Maintenance

TO BE EFFECTIVE, A PM PROGRAM must be applied on a regular basis. Just like the required maintenance schedule in your car's owner's manual, many PCs now include a similar maintenance schedule in their owner's manuals that detail the maintenance, adjustments, and cleaning that should be done, along with a suggested schedule for when these tasks should be done. Table 27-1 includes a sample version of this type of schedule:

TABLE 27-1 A SAMPLE PC MAINTENANCE SCHEDULE

Frequency	Component	Activity
Daily	PC	Perform a virus scan of memory and hard disk
	PC	Restart or shut down Windows
	Hard disk	Create a differential/incremental backup
Weekly	Hard disk	Run a disk cleanup utility
	Hard disk	Create a full/archive backup
	Web browser	Clear browser cache, history, and temporary Internet files
	Windows desktop	Empty the Recycle Bin
	Antivirus software	Update antivirus data files
	Inkjet printer	Run printhead nozzle cleaning utility
Monthly	Hard disk	Defragment the drive and recover lost clusters
	Hard disk	Uninstall all unnecessary applications
	Keyboard	Clean the keyboard with compressed air; check for and repair stuck keys
	Mouse	Clean ball and rollers and check for wear
	Monitor	Turn off and clean screen with soft cloth or antistatic wipe
	Dot matrix printer	Clean with compressed air to remove dust and bits of paper
	Laser printer	Use cleaning kit to clean interior rollers
On failure	Floppy disk drive	Clean floppy drive head
	System	Troubleshoot and replace (if necessary) failed component
Yearly	Case	Clean with compressed air to remove dust and other debris
	Motherboard	Check chips for chip creep and reseat if needed
	Adapter cards	Clean contacts with contact cleaner and reseat

Frequency	Component	Activity
As required	CMOS	Record and back up CMOS setup configuration
	PC	Keep written record of hardware and software configuration of system
	Printer	Check ink and toner cartridges or ribbons and replace (if needed)
	Hardware	Clean the keyboard, mouse, monitor, and case

Developing a common sense approach

A very good start to protecting your PC is to apply some common-sense guidelines that can protect the PC and extend its service life. Here are a few general tips for keeping your PC in working order:

♦ A PC should be located in a room that is as cool and dry as possible.

 TIP Two major hazards to the PC's electronics are heat and humidity.

♦ The PC should have an airflow buffer space all around it. It doesn't need to be more than a few inches wide, but make sure that you allow ample air space around the PC, avoiding drafty and dusty areas.

♦ Because the PC's cords and cables can be a hazard to you and other people, keep them together and tucked away to protect the cords, the PC, you, and others.

♦ When a PC is powered up and down frequently, the heating and cooling can stress the motherboard and other electronics, leading to intermittent problems from degradation and eventual catastrophic failures. Avoid powering the system on and off frequently.

♦ Most newer PCs have many energy-saving features built into the Basic Input/Output System (BIOS), chipset, and operating system, such as suspending the hard disk and monitor. These features not only save electricity, but they also extend the life of the PC and its components.

◆ Always connect the PC to the alternating current (AC) power source through a surge suppressor or an uninterruptible power supply (UPS) to protect the PC from possible damage caused by electrical spikes, blackouts, and brownouts.

◆ Always wear an antistatic wrist or ankle strap when working inside the PC's case to avoid possible damage from electrostatic discharge (ESD).

 Never wear an antistatic device when working on the monitor or inside a power supply. In fact, you should never work on a monitor or inside a power supply.

◆ Always close any open applications, shut down the operating system, and power off and unplug the PC from its power source before beginning work on your PC or its peripherals.

◆ Never place a PC, and especially its monitor or stereo speakers, near any strongly magnetized objects, which can distort the image and sound produced by the monitor or speakers and possibly eventually damage disk storage devices as well.

◆ Always power down the PC before connecting or disconnecting a serial, parallel, or video device. Universal Serial Bus (USB) and FireWire devices can be hot plugged and are a better choice for devices that need to be removed and replaced often.

◆ Always shut down the operating system before powering down the PC. On a Windows system, use the Shut Down option on the Start menu.

Gathering tools and cleaning supplies

To properly care for your PC, you need a few simple tools, cleaning supplies, a boot disk, an Emergency Repair Disk (ERD), and a PC maintenance schedule. The tools and supplies that you need can be obtained from computer, hardware, and even grocery stores (for some items). The maintenance schedule for your PC is likely included in the documentation for your PC. See Table 27-1 earlier in this chapter for a sample schedule.

The tools and supplies that you should have on hand to care for and maintain your PC are

◆ *A quart bottle of 70 percent isopropyl alcohol:* Use this to clean plastic, the case, and many of the smaller parts of the PC, keyboard, printer, connectors, and mouse. Unless you use more than you should, a quart should last you a few months or longer.

◆ *A can or two of compressed air:* This is a very versatile tool to have in your cleaning kit. Compressed air is very useful for blowing dust and small bits of paper and other debris out of hard to reach places. Also use compressed air for cleaning those areas of the PC and its components that cannot have water or liquid on them.

◆ *A clean, lint-free cloth:* Every PC cleaning instruction calls for you to use a clean, lint-free cloth. A piece of an old T-shirt works very nicely, but you can also use non-shredding cleaning tissues. A recently introduced product that's excellent for use on a PC is the Scotch-Brite High Performance Cleaning Cloth (HPCC) made by 3M (www.3m.com).

◆ *A package of high-quality cotton swabs:* Get the ones whose cotton tips stay on the swab. These are used for cleaning just about any small object inside or outside of the PC with alcohol and other liquid cleaners.

◆ *A #8 Chinese bristle artist's brush or any other soft bristle brush that has bristles about two inches long:* This brush, which you can typically find at craft stores that sell tole painting supplies, is used to brush dust and other particles from hard to reach areas inside the PC.

◆ *An inexpensive pair of pointed-tip tweezers:* These are useful for removing bits of debris from between the keys on the keyboard, inside the mouse ball chamber, or inside the computer case.

◆ *A small brush-head vacuum cleaner:* This is an excellent investment if you care for two or more computers on a regular basis. Several models are available with a gooseneck brush head that allows you to clean the keyboards and inside the system case easily. The danger of using a standard type of vacuum inside the PC is that some generate a lot of static electricity, and their cleaning nozzles are large and can easily damage the electronics on the motherboard and expansion cards.

◆ *A medium-size Phillips screwdriver:* Use this for case, keyboard, and adapter board screws.

◆ *A small-head Torx screwdriver:* Many newer cases use Torx screws to hold the case parts together as well as to anchor expansion cards.

◆ *A bottle of non-ammonia window cleaner:* Use this to clean the glass on the monitor. Although they are a bit more expensive than window cleaner, you can also purchase special cleaning solutions made just for monitors. The Scotch-Brite HPCC cloth is also excellent for cleaning a monitor without liquid.

◆ *An ESD grounding strap:* You can use either a wrist strap or a heel strap. If you have a permanent workstation on which you work on PCs, you want to equip it with an ESD mat.

Performing Data Backups

Backing up data is definitely a preventive maintenance step. You should create a copy of the data on the hard disk on a removable storage media that can be stored outside the PC but in a remote location as well. Data backups protect you from the loss of the data in the event of a hard disk failure, other PC problems, or disaster. Should some catastrophic mishap, such as a fire, earthquake, or tornado, destroy the building, the hardware can usually be replaced, but too often the data cannot be. Creating a backup copy of your data files and storing it off-site is a safety precaution that ensures the data can outlive its internal storage device.

Choosing the backup media

Any removable storage medium, such as a floppy disk, tape cartridge, CD-R or CD-RW, optical disk, another PC's hard disk, or even a storage service located on the Internet, can be used to hold a backup copy of a hard disk's data. The best medium depends on the amount of data to be backed up and your preferences. If you're backing up a 40GB hard disk, you probably should consider using a tape drive, but if you're only creating a backup of a 100MB hard disk, a Zip disk is probably adequate. If you trust your Internet connection and the transmission of your critical data across the network, you might even consider an online data warehousing service.

Picking the backup software

The popular operating systems in use today all include a utility for creating a backup. Windows has its Backup utility, Unix and Linux have the `tar` (tape archive) command, and Novell has its NetWare Backup Service utility.

In addition, most tape, recordable CD, and other writable media drives include backup software with their product. A variety of software packages specifically designed to perform backups are also available for purchase, such as Computer Associates' ARCServe (www.ca.com), Dantz' Retrospect Backup (www.dantz.com), and VERITAS' Backup Exec (www.veritas.com).

Backup software offers some advantages over just copying a file to a removable medium, including data compression techniques that reduce the number of tapes or disks needed to hold the backed up data. Most also provide cataloging routines and single directory or file restore capabilities.

Determining the best type of backup

The type of backup that you should use depends on the volatility of your data. If a high percentage of all your data is added or modified each day, you might want to consider taking a full backup every day. However, if only a small percentage of your total data store is created or modified each day, a backup scheme that involves an incremental or differential backup daily and a full weekly backup might serve your needs.

TIP When a directory or file on the hard disk is added or modified, it's flagged as such by turning on (setting high) its archive bit. The *archive bit,* which is one of four attributes (the others are read-only, hidden, and system) assigned to each directory and file, is used by backup utilities to determine which files should be included in the backup.

The four types of data backups that you can use in your backup scheme are

◆ *Full (or archive) backup:* This type of backup copies every directory, folder, file, and program from the hard disk to the backup medium regardless of the archive bit's status. However, all archive bits are reset off (set low).

◆ *Incremental backup:* This type of backup includes only those files that have been modified or added since the last full or incremental backup and resets the archive bit on the files copied to the backup medium.

◆ *Differential backup:* This type of backup includes only those files created or modified since the last full or incremental backup without changing the value of each file's archive bit. If used daily, a differential backup accumulates the new or changed files since the last full or incremental backup, which clears the archive bit.

◆ *Copy backup:* This backup type selects the files and directories specified in the command line parameters and copies them to a particular location or drive. For example, copying a hard disk file to a floppy disk creates a copy backup.

TIP The DOS command XCOPY is commonly used to create copy backups because it will copy a directory along with its files and subdirectories.

A common backup scheme includes a full backup weekly and a differential or incremental backup daily. The choice between a differential and an incremental backup depends on the amount of data affected each day. If the daily backups are large, an incremental backup might be the better choice to avoid a huge differential backup at week's end.

However, if the amount of data that must be backed up daily is small, the differential backup has its advantages. The idea behind using a combination of full and partial backups is that to recover in the event of a hardware failure, you need to load only the last full backup and the last differential or each of the incremental backups made since the full backup.

Protecting Against Viruses

A *computer virus* is software that attacks a PC with the intent of disrupting its operations, destroying its data, or erasing part or all of its disk drives. A computer virus attaches itself to another file or piece of code on a floppy disk, downloaded file, or e-mail attachment. It can also take the form of an executable file that runs when opened on the target system. A computer virus typically has a built-in propagation scheme that allows it to replicate itself and infect other systems, duplicating itself from one computer to another on removable media or e-mail.

Here are some (but not all) of the signs that your PC may be infected with a virus:

♦ All your e-mail address book contacts receiving copies of the virus via e-mail

♦ Application crashes

♦ Boot disks that won't boot

♦ Corrupted or missing data from disk files

♦ Disappearing disk partitions

♦ Distorted, misshapen, or missing video on the monitor

♦ Sound card or speaker problems

♦ Spontaneous system reboots

♦ System crashes

The best defense against a virus on your PC is antivirus software. Several antivirus offerings are on the market, such as Norton AntiVirus (www.norton.com), McAfee VShield (www.mcafee.com), and Trend Micro's PC-cillan (www.trendmicro.com). These companies provide you with the ability to update the virus database about as often as new viruses show up, which is almost daily.

Protecting Against Power Problems

Several levels of protection are available to protect a single PC, a group of PC equipment, or an entire network. How much protection you need is based on the amount of equipment that you're trying to protect against electrical over-voltage and under-voltage conditions.

The first line of defense is a surge suppressor. The entry-level surge suppressor is a plug-strip that includes a varistor that is designed to absorb spikes and surges on the electrical supply line and not pass them on to any devices plugged into it. Higher-end models protect your phone lines, modems, and network connections. The best protection from electrical problems is an uninterruptible power supply

(UPS), which also provides backup power should the power fail or run below normal voltage levels.

See Chapter 9 for a more detailed discussion of surge suppressors and UPS units.

Disposing of Hazardous Materials

A PC has several components that by law or environmental common sense require special handling or disposal procedures, including batteries, the power supply, and the cathode ray tube (CRT) in the monitor.

Disposing of batteries

Special handling is required to handle or dispose of PC batteries, which are usually very small lithium batteries used to power Complementary Metal-Oxide Semiconductor (CMOS) memory. (No battery of any kind should be disposed of in fire or water.)

In fact, no battery should be casually discarded. They should be disposed of according to whatever local restrictions and regulations are in effect regarding the disposal or recycling of all batteries. Leaking batteries should be handled very carefully. If you must handle a leaking battery, be very sure not to get any of the *electrolyte*, the stuff oozing out from the inside of the battery, into your eyes or mouth.

Discarding a monitor

A CRT in a monitor (just like the picture tube in your television set) contains the following contaminants: solvents and solvent vapors, metals (including a very high level of lead), mercury switches, photoresist materials, deionized water, acids, oxidizers, phosphor, ammonia, aluminum, carbon slurry, and a long list of other chemicals and caustic materials. This is why a monitor should not be just thrown in the dumpster, trash can, or landfill but should be disposed of carefully and properly. The best and most environmentally conscious way to dispose of a monitor is through a disposal service that handles computer equipment.

Nearly 70 percent of a CRT contains lead, which is why it comes under the Land Disposal Ban Program of the Resource Conservation and Recovery Act (RCRA) administered by the U.S. Environmental Protection Agency (EPA), the same act that created all the Superfund toxic waste dump sites. This law requires that old CRTs (and old television sets as well) be dismantled, crushed, and encapsulated in cement. This isn't something that everyone with an old monitor is able to do, so many salvage and recycling companies now exist that are equipped to properly dispose of your old CRTs for a fee.

Dumping chemicals

The liquid cleaning compounds that you use to clean your PC (or your home or car) can pose a safety or environmental problem or might require special handling. Many of these solutions are poisonous or hazardous in other ways. If you're unsure of the safety, handling, storage, or use of a cleaning product, the best reference available for information on any particular chemical solution or cleaner, including household cleaners, is its Material Safety Data Sheet (MSDS). Every chemical product that has any possible hazard has an MSDS prepared and readily available. Typically, information on how to obtain an MSDS for a product is included on the product's label.

 The best place to look for product safety information is the product label or any documentation included inside its packaging. Hazardous products from reputable manufacturers always list the hazards and handling requirements for their products on the product's label. If the label for a cleaning solution or solvent doesn't list a hazard or other product safety information, don't just assume that it's safe.

The cleaning supplies that you should be concerned about include the solutions used to clean the contacts and connections of adapter cards, glass cleaners, and plastic- or metal-case cleaning products.

Other PC and peripheral components that should be disposed of using special procedures are laser printer toner cartridges and refill kits and the used or empty containers of chemical solvents and cleaners. The best place to find information on the proper way to dispose of an item is in its documentation, like the information that comes with a printer cartridge, or the MSDS or the Workplace Hazardous Materials Information System (WHMIS, which is Canada's equivalent to MSDS) information on a chemical product. You can take a look at the WHMIS Web site at www.hc-sc.gc.ca/hecs-sesc/whmis/.

Preventive Maintenance Procedures

The sections that follow list the recommended steps to use in developing and performing a preventive maintenance program for a PC. The key words that you should remember when planning, designing, and implementing a PM system are *consistent* and *regular.*

Cleaning a keyboard

The standard keyboard is an open-faced device that collects whatever falls or spills on it. A keyboard can develop a number of problems when dirt, food, or liquid gets

What's Inside an MSDS?

A standard MSDS includes the following information:

- Section 1. Chemical Product Section
- Section 2. Composition/Information on Ingredients
- Section 3. Hazard Identification
- Section 4. First Aid Measures
- Section 5. Firefighting Measures
- Section 6. Accidental Release Measures
- Section 7. Handling and Storage
- Section 8. Exposure Control/Personal Protection
- Section 9. Physical and Chemical Properties
- Section 10. Stability and Reactivity
- Section 11. Toxicological Information
- Section 12. Ecological Information
- Section 13. Disposal Considerations
- Section 14. Transportation Information
- Section 15. Regulatory Information
- Section 16. Other Information

You can also obtain a copy of a product MSDS from the Internet. Two Web sites, among others, that list many of the products that you might use and need information about are

- The Northwest Fisheries Science Center of the National Oceanic & Atmospheric Administration (NOAA): `http://research.nwfsc.noaa.gov/msds.html`
- The Vermont Safety Information on the Internet (SIRI): `http://siri.org/msds/index.php`

between and under its keys, including keys that stutter, stuck keys, or keys that just stop working. A *stuttering key* isn't stuck down permanently but sticks for a few keystrokes and repeats its character a few times. A *stuck key* is stuck down and does not issue its character.

The best way to care for a keyboard is to keep food and beverages completely away from it. But because that's probably unlikely, a keyboard needs cleaning regularly. Along with the PC's monitor, the keyboard should be cleaned more frequently than the PC's other components.

Use the following steps to clean a keyboard and to perform its preventive maintenance:

1. The easiest way to clean a keyboard is to simply turn it upside down and shake it.

    Make sure you're not over your PC when you do this. Just about anything that has fallen under the keycaps should fall out, unless it's a larger item that's stuck behind the keys, such as a paperclip or the like.

2. To open a "cleaning hole" to let larger debris fall out, remove the keycaps of the last three keys on the right-hand end of the keyboard: the – (minus/dash), + (plus), and Enter keys on the Numeric keypad.

    To remove the keycaps, use a flat-blade screwdriver and gently pry the keycap up and off the key switch.

Before removing the keycaps, disconnect the keyboard from the PC. Keyboards get their power from the PC over the connection cable.

3. Use compressed air to blow out the keyboard, using the air stream to sweep the debris toward the removed keys or toward one end of the keyboard.

Always wear safety glasses or other eye protection when working with compressed air.

4. Use a non-static blower brush, brush vacuum, or a probe to lightly loosen any large or stubborn debris and then shake the keyboard or use compressed air to blow it out.

5. If one or two keys are sticking or have stopped working, disconnect the keyboard from the PC, pry off the keycap, and clean under and around the keyswitch by using a cotton swab and a small amount of isopropyl alcohol to remove whatever is jamming the key. Then use compressed air to blow the area dry and replace the keycap.

If the key doesn't begin working after cleaning, you can replace the keyswitch, but replacing the keyboard is far easier — and in most cases, less expensive.

6. If liquid spills on a keyboard, immediately disconnect it from the PC and turn it upside down to allow the liquid to drain.

If the keyboard had soda pop, fruit juice, or any other sugary drink spilled on it, the keys might stick or stutter. Your choices to fix the problem are to replace the keyboard or wash it.

Putting water on any electronic device is always risky, but if you are careful, you can wash a keyboard. Newer keyboards are sealed under the key switches to protect the keyboard grid. Anything that spills in the keyboard will either settle on the keyboard membrane as sticky gunk or simply run off.

To clean any sticky residue resulting from a spill, use warm, clean water to rinse it out of the keyboard. By continually testing the keys, you can tell when you've rinsed the keyboard long enough. In an extreme case, you can wash the keyboard in the upper tray of a dishwasher — but don't use any soap. Even after the dishwasher's dry cycle, let the keyboard sit face down for a few hours and then blow it out with compressed air. Before connecting it to the PC, be absolutely sure that the keyboard is completely dry.

7. After you clean the keyboard, replace any key caps that you removed or replace the keyboard's cover.

8. If you really want to get the keyboard clean or want to also do a close visual inspection of it, remove the keyboard cover.

Between 4 and 16 screws hold the keyboard's cover in place. Unless you have a very serious cleaning problem on the keyboard, avoid removing the cover, especially on older PCs with mechanical switch keys (see Chapter 19). If the problem on the keyboard is serious enough for major surgery, you might want to consider just replacing it.

9. Use a soft, lint-free cloth and a little isopropyl alcohol or a non-sudsing, general-purpose cleaner to wipe away any body oils, ink, or dirt on the keys or keyboard case.

Alcohol works best because it evaporates without leaving moisture behind to seep inside the keyboard, but never pour the alcohol directly on the keys or case. Pour a small amount on the cloth and then wipe the keys and case. The same goes for the cleaner, if you choose to use one. A cotton swab dipped in cleaner or alcohol will get tight spots. Again, be absolutely sure that the keyboard is dry before connecting it to the PC and powering it up.

10. After cleaning the keyboard and ascertaining that it's completely dry, reconnect the keyboard to the PC and reboot the system.

    Watch the Power-On Self-Test (POST) process carefully for keyboard errors. After the PC is running, test the keyboard by pressing each key and verifying its action.

Cleaning a mouse

When the ball or insides of a conventional mouse get dirty, the mouse can begin working erratically or not at all. Dirt from the mousepad or work surface gets on the ball and is transferred to the sensors and rollers inside the mouse. The sensors are used to detect the movement of the mouse and translate it to movement of the pointer on the screen. If the sensors are dirty, they can't translate your movement precisely.

To care and clean the mouse, use this procedure:

1. First check the mousepad.

    If the mouse ball is dirty, the mousepad is probably also dirty and needs to be either cleaned or replaced. The mousepad sits in the open where it gets dusty, dirty, wet, and suffers any accidents that happen on the desk-top. If the mousepad isn't cleaned or replaced regularly, the mouse picks up the dirt and transfers it inside to the rollers and sensors. To clean the mousepad, just wipe it with a damp cloth, but make sure that it's dry before using it with your mouse.

2. Check the mousepad for wear, both to its fabric or plastic surface and for places where a track, dent, or dip might have been worn into it.

    A worn-out mousepad can cause lint, bits of rubber, or threads to get pulled up inside the mouse.

3. I recommend shutting down the PC when cleaning the mouse because in most cases, the mouse has either a serial or PS/2 connector, neither of which should be removed nor inserted while the PC is running.

    If you have a USB mouse, you can disconnect the mouse to clean it and reconnect it when you're finished while the PC is running. However, remember that open applications, including Windows, can do some strange things if you clean the mouse while it's connected and the PC is running.

4. Inspect and clean the mouse ball and its chamber.

    a. Place the mouse on its back and remove the ball access slide cover. As illustrated in Figure 27-1, the mouse ball is held in place by a locking cap that rotates to its locking or release positions. Turn the cap in the direction of the arrows printed or molded on it.

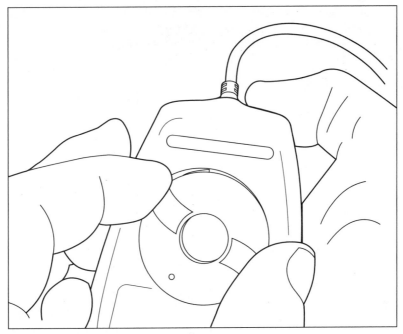

Figure 27-1: A mouse ball is held inside the mouse by a rotating locking cap.

b. Tip the mouse up to drop the ball into your palm, cupping your hand so that the ball doesn't fall on the floor or table. Examine it for pits, cracks, or flat spots, making sure that the ball isn't lopsided or oval-shaped. If the ball has any of these problems, the ball needs to be replaced, but because spare mouse balls are not always easy to get, you should probably just replace the mouse.

c. Use a slightly damp, lint-free cloth or a Scotch-Brite HPCC to clean the mouse ball. If you do use a damp cloth, use only water. Do not use cleaners or alcohol on the mouse ball because they can shrink or distort the ball. Don't soak it or scrub it — just wipe it clean, let it dry, and then reinsert it in the chamber and replace the locking cap.

 Wash your hands thoroughly before touching the mouse ball.

d. Inspect the mouse ball chamber (see Figure 27-2) for lint, dirt, and even threads. Carefully remove debris that you find with tweezers or a cotton swab with just a drop of alcohol on it.

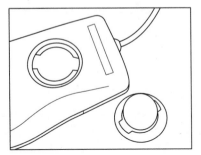

Figure 27-2: The mouse ball chamber with its cover removed.

e. Inspect the rollers inside the ball chamber for dirt or lint, and if needed, use tweezers or a swab with a small drop of alcohol to remove it.

f. Use compressed air to blow out the mouse ball chamber, directing the air stream to one side. Try not to blast the rollers to avoid causing damage to the small electronic parts inside the mouse.

 You shouldn't blow out the mouse ball chamber with your mouth for two reasons: You can get saliva in the ball chamber, and you can get dust in your eyes.

5. If needed, use isopropyl alcohol or a general-purpose, no-rinse cleaner to clean the exterior of the mouse.

6. Reconnect the mouse and restart the PC.

Watch for any POST problems with the mouse or connector. Give the mouse a complete test, including its buttons.

 An alternative to a conventional mouse is an optical mouse. An optical mouse eliminates most of the cleaning and care required of the conventional mouse with a ball. See Chapter 20 for more information on optical mice.

Caring for other input devices

Other types of PC input and data capture devices should be cleaned regularly as well. How frequently depends on the device and how often it's used. Here are some cleaning hints for several of the more common input devices:

- ◆ *Scanner:* The biggest issue with a flat-bed scanner is its inside glass surface. Use either a non-ammonia glass cleaner and a lint-free cloth or the Scotch-Brite HPCC for Electronics.

- ◆ *Digitizing tablet:* Follow the cleaning instructions included in the device's documentation. Some of the rubber-like materials used for the touchpad can be cleaned with a general-purpose cleaner and a damp, lint-free cloth. Take care not to get the unit too wet and to dry it completely.

- ◆ *Digital camera:* Clean the camera lens with a lens cleaner solution, like you would use for eyeglasses, and a soft lint-free cloth or the Scotch-Brite HPCC for Electronics. Use either isopropyl alcohol or a general-purpose cleaner to clean the exterior of the camera. Avoid getting the unit very wet.

- ◆ *Microphone:* Use the same steps used for the digitizing tablet above. Be very careful not to get water or alcohol in the openings and down inside the microphone.

Cleaning and caring for a monitor

The monitor's glass screen requires cleaning more often than any other component on a PC. Because the monitor's screen produces a lot of static electricity, it attracts and holds dust and flying lint. A dirty screen can put a strain on your eyes if you view the screen for extended periods.

Most PC users take a safety risk when cleaning a monitor's screen. Because the screen holds a large amount of static electricity, if you place your hand flat on the screen with a wet cloth, you invite the monitor to ground itself through you. The following steps detail the process that you can use to safely keep the monitor screen clean and clear.

1. Turn the monitor's power off and unplug it from its power source before beginning to clean it.

   You don't need to disconnect it from the PC. After turning the monitor off, wait a few minutes before beginning to clean it to allow the built up static charges to dissipate a bit.

 TIP Do not wear an ESD ground strap when working with a monitor, even to clean it. You could become the grounding circuit for all of the electricity stored in the monitor's capacitor, which is a very shocking experience.

2. Use compressed air to clean any dust on the top of the monitor's case, blowing the air stream across the top of the monitor and not directly down to prevent any dust from blowing into the monitor's vents.

Never open and remove the cover of a monitor! Every monitor, regardless of its size, poses an extreme high-voltage hazard.

3. Use a soft cloth and either isopropyl alcohol or a general-purpose, no-rinse cleaner to clean the outside of the monitor case.

    The alcohol is probably the better choice because it won't create a safety hazard if it drips inside the case.

4. Use an antistatic cleaner or a Scotch-Brite HPCC for Electronics to clean the glass of the monitor.

    Never use an ammonia-based glass cleaner on the monitor glass because the monitor screen is coated with filtering chemicals to help improve the image and reduce eyestrain. Using a harsh cleaner can remove these coatings, thus harming the monitor and potentially harming your eyes.

Never use water or a liquid cleaner to wash the monitor's glass with the power on. Water is an excellent conductor of electricity; if your hand makes sufficient enough contact with the screen, you could be the ground for the electricity in the monitor.

5. Reconnect the monitor and test the video.

    If nothing displays, check the power switch, the power cord, the video connection, and the brightness and contrast settings, any of which could have been accidentally dislodged, moved, or turned while you were cleaning the case.

Cleaning and maintaining a printer

The cleaning procedures and the supplies used vary by the type of printer in use. Laser printers have completely different cleaning and maintenance requirements than inkjets and dot matrix printers. This section gives a general overview of the cleaning and preventive maintenance steps that you can use for each type of printer. However, you should follow the specific instructions provided by the manufacturer of your printer in the owner's manual or on the manufacturer's Web site.

LASER PRINTERS

Because of the many different designs for how the laser toner and drum cartridge fit into laser printers, the process varies for different printers. Check your printer's documentation for specific cleaning instructions. See Chapter 18 for more on cleaning laser printers.

1. To clean a laser printer thoroughly, you need

    -   A laser cleaning kit for your printer's make and model

    -   A small vacuum cleaner that is specifically designed to handle laser printer toner

    If the cleaning kit doesn't include cleaning paper, you should purchase a package from your local computer supply store or online. Cleaning kits typically contain cartridge cleaning sheets, cleaning solution, lint-free swabs, an antistatic cloth, plastic gloves, and a few ink- and toner-remover hand wipes.

 Laser printer toner is made of minute particles of ferrous oxide (iron) coated with a plastic resin material. During the printer's fusing process, the plastic resin is melted to bond the toner to the paper. A standard vacuum will pass these particles near or through a very hot motor where they can melt and clog the system. Special models of vacuum cleaners are available just for toner. You can also contract with an office supplies company to have somebody come in to clean the laser printer for you.

2. If the printer has been in use very recently, let the printer sit idle for at least 15 minutes to allow the fusing assembly to cool before removing or opening the covers.

3. Switch off the power on the laser printer, unplug the printer to prevent the power from being accidentally switched back on, and then remove any paper or paper cartridges from the printer.

4. After you open or remove the part of the printer's case that exposes the fusing assembly, follow the printer manufacturer's instructions for cleaning the fusing rollers.

    Typically, this is done with a lint-free cloth and either the cleaning solution that came in the cleaning kit or some denatured alcohol (which is not the same as isopropyl alcohol).

5. Wipe the rollers lightly and do not rub, taking care not to touch any of the gears inside the printer.

6. Using an appropriate vacuum with a soft brush attachment, clean the fusing area of any debris — or at least use compressed air to blow out any debris in this area.

   In either case, you should wear eye protection. Be very careful not to snag or pull any wires in the fusing area.

7. Clean the transfer roller area. (See the printer's documentation for the specific instructions on how to clean the transfer rollers.)

   The transfer rollers are typically located under the toner cartridge, so you must remove the toner cartridge and set it on some newspaper or other large sheets of paper. You can then easily dispose the paper if any of the toner spills.

8. Use the soft brush in the laser printer cleaning kit to clean the transfer rollers. After brushing the rollers, use a vacuum or compressed air to clean away any debris in this area of the printer.

9. Check the paper path and use a soft brush to clean the feed rollers if needed. Replace the toner cartridge, if needed, and replace the cartridge and any of the printer's cover parts that were removed in earlier steps.

10. Before reconnecting the printer to its AC power source, clean the exterior.

    The best cleaner is a mild liquid detergent, such as one used for dishes. Mix a solution of the detergent with water and, using a cloth dampened with the solution, wipe the printer clean. Never pour or spray water or cleaners directly on the printer. If you're using a prepared cleaner, spray or pour a small amount on the cloth and wipe the printer with the cloth.

11. If you cleaned the printer's exterior, wait a few minutes to make sure that the printer is dry before replacing the paper supply and reconnecting the printer to its power source.

12. If you have laser printer cleaning sheets, run one or two through the printer, following the instructions on the sheet pack to clean the components inside the cartridge.

    You should run a cleaning sheet through the printer each time you change the toner cartridge. In normal operations, if the printer is smearing or smudging the print, use a cleaning sheet to clean the toner cartridge, transfer rollers, and fusing rollers. You might also want to be sure that you're using laser printer paper.

 Be sure not to use hot water to wash toner off your hands: It can melt the toner onto your skin. Use slightly warm water instead.

INKJET PRINTERS

Chapter 17 explains the inkjet printing process in detail, especially how the inkjet cartridge works to print a page. The most common problem of an inkjet printer is a clogged printhead on the inkjet cartridge. Other than that, inkjet printers are fairly simple printers that are largely considered disposable technology. Several inkjet models are now on the market costing between $40 and $100, which is not all that much more than the ink cartridge itself. Should anything major happen to an inkjet printer, such as the feed rollers getting misaligned or the cartridge gearing that moves the print cartridge side-to-side failing to operate, it's usually less expensive just to get a new printer.

The following are some cleaning and maintenance tips that can help you to extend the life of your inkjet printer:

- *Clean the print nozzles on the cartridge regularly:* Most inkjet printers have a built-in utility to clean or unclog the printhead nozzles, and you should use it regularly as a part of your preventive maintenance program and when the printer has sat idle for a couple of weeks or longer. If the cleaning utility is unable to unclog the nozzles, remove the ink cartridge and use a swab or lint-free cloth (one you don't mind staining permanently with the ink) dampened with a small amount of isopropyl alcohol and wipe the print head lightly. Don't rub back and forth across the nozzles; instead, wipe lightly across the nozzles in one direction. Reinstall the print cartridge and redo the printhead cleaning utility. If the cartridge is still clogged, replace it.

- *Never turn the printer off at a plug strip, surge suppressor, or other power source:* Always use the printer's power switch to turn it off. The printer has some built-in functions, such as parking the printhead, that are tied to the power-off function of the printer's on/off switch.

- *Use inkjet quality paper:* Standard bond paper, which is not treated for inkjet inks, absorbs too much ink. On black and white printing, the result might be a fuzzy or blurry print image. On color prints, the result might be light or blurred images. Inkjet paper is treated to provide the best possible image. The printer's owner's manual most likely has a recommendation for the paper that should be used.

- *Dust and paper scraps and bits can collect in the bottom of the paper path in an inkjet printer:* On a fairly regular basis, you should check the inside of the paper path and bin to remove the paper scraps and blow out any dust or paper bits that have accumulated. Always wear eye protection when using compressed air, especially when blowing about bits of paper.

DOT MATRIX PRINTERS

After the noise and the slow speed, the main problem with a dot matrix printer is its ribbon. The ribbon is messy to install and replace and also messy to operate. Because dot matrix ribbons aren't evenly coated with ink, they drop bits of dried ink down inside the printer's case.

Dot matrix printers typically use a forms tractor to pull tractor-feed paper through the printer using the pinholes along the sides of the paper. Unfortunately, as the paper is pulled through the printer, bits of paper from the holes and the perforations along the edges of the paper fall down inside the printer.

The paper and dried ink bits should be cleaned from the printer regularly with either a vacuum or compressed air (definitely wear eye-protection). Follow the manufacturer's documentation on how to remove the cover and the ribbon in order to get down into the printer. Typically, a ribbon release lever unlocks the ribbon cartridge so it can be lifted up and out of the printer. However, because dot matrix printers and their setup vary greatly by manufacturer, check the documentation before cleaning the printer, especially the printhead.

 There is some controversy over whether a dot matrix printhead should be cleaned. The printhead can get very hot and should not be touched while in operation. And because it prints by pushing pins that are mounted on very thin wires into the ribbon, you could possibly bend a wire when cleaning the printhead and render the pin useless. You should never lubricate the printhead because the oil or lubricant could stain your paper during printing. However, using a cotton swab to remove bits of ink and paper fuzz from the printhead, if done very gently, probably won't damage the head and will likely improve the function of the printer.

Cleaning the system case

Because the system case is rarely (and in many cases, never) opened, the inside of the system case isn't usually cleaned regularly, if at all. However, I recommend that you do clean the system case regularly, especially if the PC is located in a dusty environment or in one with airborne particles that could be sucked inside the PC's case, such as oil mist or metal particles.

The power supply's cooling fan either pulls air into or pushes air out of the system case, depending on the age of the system. Regardless, air passes in or out the air vents on the case, which is reason enough for the system case to be on your list of regularly cleaned items. For example, a mid-tower PC case that sits on the floor in an office, bedroom, or family room accumulates dust either around its air vents or on the grill or blades of the fan, or both. If not cleaned, the dust could eventually clog the cooling system, accumulate on the processor's heatsink and fan or on the motherboard, and cause the processor and memory to overheat and malfunction.

At minimum, you should clean inside the PC's case at least once every six months. Use a soft brush vacuum cleaner made for cleaning PCs or compressed air to blow the dust out of the case (wear eye protection).

Use the following steps to perform preventive maintenance inside the system case:

1. After properly shutting down the operating system, power off the PC and remove the power cord from the AC power source.

2. After you carefully remove the case cover, watching for cables and cords inside the PC that might get snagged on the case cover, examine the inside of the case cover for dirt streaks that indicate an air leak caused by a badly fitting case, which can be the cause of an overheating processor.

3. Perform a visual inspection of the inside of the case to determine how much cleaning is needed.

   - On virtually every PC, the inside and outside vents should have some dust accumulations. If dust is collecting where it shouldn't, the cooling system might not be working as well as it could. The case might be cracked or a part (perhaps an expansion slot filler) might be missing.

   - Examine the interior of the case thoroughly for dust, corrosion, leaking battery acid, and other problems. If the case has only a light accumulation of dust, use compressed air to clean it. Use a vacuum with a brush head to clean away any larger accumulations of dust.

4. Check the data and power cables on the motherboard, power supply, disk drives, and so on for loose connections. Check the adapter cards to make sure that they're properly seated. Also check for any signs of corrosion on the edge connectors of the memory modules and expansion cards. If you find any, use contact cleaner to clean them.

5. Use compressed air to blow off the outside vents of the power supply and then the inside vents. Also use the compressed air to clean the drive bays, adapter cards, and finally the outside vents of the case.

6. Replace the case cover, taking care not to snag any cables when placing or sliding the cover into place.

7. Use a general-purpose cleaner to clean the outside of the case, using caution not to get any moisture inside the case.

8. Power on the PC and monitor the POST process for errors.

   If any errors occur, they will probably be adapter data cable, power connector, or expansion card errors. Open the case and check these connections for a snug fit.

 Always wear ESD wrist or ankle straps when working inside the PC case and ground yourself with one of the metal chassis parts even when wearing ESD gear.

Housekeeping for a hard disk drive

Other than checking its connectors and removing any dust that might have accumulated on the Head Disk Assembly (HDA), you can't physically do much for a hard disk drive in terms of preventive maintenance. HDAs are sealed units, so no physical cleaning needs to be done; the preventive maintenance actually centers around the optimization of the drive's storage space.

To perform housekeeping and optimization on a hard disk drive, you need to include the following activities in your preventive maintenance program:

- ◆ Create full and partial backups of the data on the hard disk. Always create a full backup of the hard disk drive before doing any work on it and create backups according to your needs or those of the organization.

- ◆ Run ScanDisk regularly to check the hard disk for media and file errors.

- ◆ Run the Disk Defragmenter disk optimization program.

- ◆ Empty the Recycle Bin on the Windows desktop at least monthly.

- ◆ Run the Disk Cleanup applet weekly to remove unneeded files from the hard disk.

On a Windows 9x or Windows NT system, the utilities named in the preceding list are found on the System Tools menu, which is accessed from Start → Programs → Accessories → System Tools. To access the ScanDisk utility on Windows 2000 or XP systems, open the My Computer folder. From the Desktop, select Properties from the File menu and then click the Tools tab.

Optimizing a hard disk

The Windows System Tools applets used to improve the performance of the hard disk drive are ScanDisk (Chkdsk on Windows 2000/XP), the Disk Defragmenter, and Disk Cleanup.

RUNNING SCANDISK

The *ScanDisk utility* is used to scan the disk surface for media errors, to scan files and folders for data problems, or both. The ScanDisk utility runs automatically each time that Windows isn't shut down properly to ensure that no disk and data problems were created when the system was powered off. Windows assumes that the only reason that the system wouldn't have been shut down properly is a power failure, and so it runs ScanDisk to check for disk problems that might have been caused by the sudden loss of power.

You should run ScanDisk at least once a week to search for and repair small errors on the disk before they become big problems. See Chapter 28 for more information on ScanDisk.

DEFRAGGING THE HARD DISK

The *Disk Defragmenter utility* is used to rearrange your disk files and combine and organize unused disk space to help applications run faster. During the course of working with the operating system and your applications, files are opened, modified, and removed from the hard disk, which causes the files on the disk to become fragmented.

 See Chapter 10 for more information about how data is stored on the hard disk drive.

Disk Defragmenter reorganizes the data files and eliminates the fragmentation so that a file is readily available to programs asking for it.

Removing unused files on a disk drive

Another Windows System Tools applet that can be used to remove unnecessary files from your hard disk and free up valuable hard disk space is the Disk Cleanup utility. This tool scans the disk that you designate (it works on every type of disk drive, including diskettes and Zip disks) to find files that can be removed without seriously affecting the operation of the PC and Windows operating system.

Caring for a floppy disk drive

About the only preventive maintenance that you can perform on a floppy disk drive is to clean its read/write head, and you really shouldn't do that until the drive begins having read/write errors. A floppy disk drive's read/write head can be over cleaned and worn out in the process. Other than blowing out the drive with compressed air to remove dust or bits of media, there isn't much to be done on a floppy disk drive.

When the drive begins exhibiting signs of reading or writing problems, use a cleaning kit to clean the read/write heads, following the directions in the kit. You can buy a drive cleaning kit at virtually all computer supply stores for less than $10. A typical cleaning kit has a special diskette and a small vial of cleaning solution.

Caring for CD-ROM and DVD drives

Two things should be regularly cleaned on a CD-ROM or DVD drive: the disk tray and the CD-ROM's read/write lens. The tray is cleaned with some general purpose cleaner or isopropyl alcohol by applying the solution to a soft, lint-free cloth or cotton swab and gently wiping down the tray. Avoid pressing down on the tray. A swab is good for getting down into the creases of the disk tray without pressing down on it. Allow the tray to completely dry before closing it.

To clean the lens, you need to purchase a CD drive cleaning kit that's designed for tray-based CD players. Many versions of CD cleaning kits are available, including those for caddy drives, automobile drives, and others. The cleaning kit typically contains a CD that has a set of very small brushes built into it and perhaps some CD cleaning wipes. The brushes on the cleaning CD sweep across the lens and clean it as the disc spins in the drive. Follow the directions on the package exactly to avoid damaging your CD drive.

To clean a CD-ROM, remember to wipe the silver side (gold side on a DVD) with a soft, lint-free cloth or a Scotch-Brite HPCC. Don't use paper towels or other textured paper that can leave streaks or scratch the disc. To wipe the disc, start from the center and move outward from the inside edge to the outside edge; don't use a circular motion.

Cleaning expansion slot connectors

The connectors in an expansion slot should be cleaned at least twice a year by using the following steps:

1. Typically, all you need to do is wipe the contacts with a soft cloth, like the Scotch-Brite HPCC.

2. Remove the expansion card from its slot without touching its contacts and wipe each contact gently from top to bottom.

   To avoid dislodging the contacts from the card, do not wipe from the top of the contact down or across all the contacts. Blow out the expansion slot with compressed air.

3. If signs of corrosion or oxidation appear on the contacts, use a *contact cleaner,* a solution made especially for cleaning metallic electronic connectors.

4. Also check the contacts in the expansion slots — *gold fingers* — for discoloration and oxidation.

   Figure 27-3 shows the gold fingers (contacts) in the expansion slots of a motherboard. Use a cotton swab and the contact cleaner to clean the gold fingers, but avoid rubbing them with a cloth because they're easily bent or broken.

Cleaning external ports

About all you can do for the external ports that extend through the case's rear panel is to keep them from getting too dusty when not in use. A very dusty port can make a poor connection when you need it.

Use compressed air to blow the dust from any unused external ports, especially the USB ports. Don't use water or alcohol on female ports because it can get down inside the pinholes and possibly corrode the connection.

Figure 27-3: The contacts in the expansion slots on a motherboard should be cleaned regularly.

Phot courtesy of Silicon Integrated Systems Corporation.

Caring for a portable PC

Portable PCs, including laptops, notebooks, and palmtops, have many of the same preventive maintenance requirements as a full-sized desktop PC. For the peripheral devices on a notebook PC, such as the hard disk, floppy disk, CD-ROM, keyboard, mouse, and ports, use the same cleaning and maintenance procedures used on non-portable PCs. On a notebook or portable PC, the batteries, video display, and case have special care requirements.

PORTABLE PC BATTERIES
The battery in a portable PC probably won't last the life of the PC. These batteries are expendable, and they all lose their ability to be recharged. Although the life of the battery ranges from 600 to over 1,000 recharges, eventually the battery won't be able to be recharged and must be replaced.

The most popular battery type used on portable PCs is the nickel metal-hydride (NiMH) battery. This very heavy battery can be recharged around 600 times, or about one year of use, before it begins having recharge problems.

TIP

The best way to get the most out of a battery is to discharge it completely before you recharge it.

The newest form of portable PC batteries is the Lithium-Ion (Li-Ion) battery, which has a rechargeable life of about 1,200 charges. This battery type is used primarily on more expensive systems because of its cost, which is higher than the NiMH battery.

When a battery begins having recharge problems, the best thing to do is to replace it. However, here are some tips for getting the most out of your portable PC battery:

- Use a port replicator or the AC power adapter whenever possible.

- Because disk drives are the biggest drains on a battery, avoid disk access when you can, if possible.

- Enable and use the built-in power-saving features or software on the portable PC.

  These power-saving features typically include slowing the processor speed, suspending the hard disk, display, and on many systems, the entire PC, when idle for a specified period. If you don't need the speed, save the power by turning on these features.

- If the portable PC is designed for the Energy Star energy standard, it reduces its power consumption as much as 99 percent when it goes into Sleep or Suspend modes, which simulate a shutdown of the PC. The downside to suspending the PC is the time that it takes the PC to reawaken when you're ready to work again.

CARING FOR AN LCD DISPLAY

To clean an LCD display on a portable PC, don't use harsh cleaners: an LCD display is easily scratched. You shouldn't use anything more harsh than a general window cleaner (without ammonia) on a soft, lint-free cloth (such as an old T-shirt) or a Scotch-Brite HPCC.

CLEANING A PORTABLE PC'S CASE

Portable PC cases, except those on ruggedized portables, are fragile and are designed for lightness rather than strength. Dropping a portable PC can very well damage just about all its components.

To clean the portable PC's case, avoid using any liquid in or around the keyboard. Use a soft, damp, lint-free cloth to wipe over the keyboard and the exterior of the case. Use compressed air to clean the keyboard. The floppy disk and CD-ROM drives are cleaned by using cleaning kits just like on a desktop PC.

Chapter 28

Optimizing the PC

IN THIS CHAPTER
If a PC doesn't run as sprightly as it once did or if it's unable to keep pace with the demands of newer software, you might want to consider updating or optimizing the PC to enhance its performance. You can optimize any number of parts of your PC. Those I cover in this chapter include

- The BIOS and boot process

- The hard disk drive

- Expansion cards

SOME OPTIMIZATION steps cost money, but many only involve using software that you might already have, or software that's readily available for downloading from the Web.

Optimizing the BIOS and Boot Process

Dozens of settings in the Basic Input/Output System (BIOS) setup configuration data are stored in the BIOS Complementary Metal-Oxide Semiconductor (CMOS). Whether these settings reflect the actual hardware environment of the PC can make a difference in how quickly the system boots and performs. Chances are that you can or should change few settings, but a valuable feature that you do have, such as system caching or using the QuickPOST (Power-On Self-Test) process, might be disabled and should be re-enabled for optimum performance of the PC.

Tweaking the BIOS settings

The following are some simple BIOS setting tweaks that can optimize the performance of a PC (see Chapter 4 for information on how to access BIOS settings):

- *Auto-Detect IDE:* Use Auto-Detect Integrated Drive Electronics (IDE) to detect the IDE hard drives on the PC. After you know the IDE drives that are in use, enter the BIOS setup and disable those IDE channels not in use.

If you're reluctant to disable an IDE channel that has a CD-ROM or another device attached, remember that the system uses a different way of detecting those devices that is separate from these BIOS settings.

- ◆ *Floppy Seek at Boot-Up:* This setting tells the PC to search for new floppy disk drives each time that it boots. Disabling this feature significantly speeds up the boot process.

- ◆ *QuickPOST:* Enabling this feature speeds up the startup processes of the PC.

- ◆ *Shadow System BIOS:* If this setting is enabled, the PC copies the BIOS program from the BIOS ROM into system memory (RAM), which speeds up the process. The increase in speed isn't large, but every little bit helps.

- ◆ *Turbo Frequency:* This setting is a form of *overclocking,* or running the system clock at a speed higher than its nominal speed. If the PC is already overclocked, leave this setting as is. However, this setting can be used to increase the clock speed of the PC.

Flashing the BIOS

Flashing the BIOS (see Chapter 4) can add or enable features that provide faster performance for the PC's primary components (processor, chipset, memory, and the like).

Be sure that you follow the BIOS or motherboard manufacturer's instructions to the letter when performing this operation. Flashing the BIOS ROM is one operation you can't afford to mess up or have interrupted; that is, if you want to reboot the PC anytime in the future.

Optimizing the Hard Disk Drive

The best tools available for optimizing a hard disk drive (in terms of usage and access speeds) are included as utilities of the Windows operating systems. The big two of these tools are ScanDisk and Disk Defragmenter.

Scanning the disk

ScanDisk for Windows 9*x* and Me, shown in Figure 28-1, or Chkdsk for Windows 2000 or XP systems, is used to check a disk for errors in the media and file structure and then repair them or remove unrecoverable areas of the disk from the usage tables to prevent future errors.

Here are the two levels of scans you can use:

◆ *Standard test:* This option checks for file and folder integrity and runs about 10 minutes to completely check a disk drive. A standard check should be run at least once a week. Also, this test runs automatically anytime Windows is not shut down properly.

◆ *Thorough test:* This option also checks for file and folder integrity, and scans the disk surface for defects. Completely checking a hard disk drive takes about 25 minutes to an hour. A thorough test should be run every two to four weeks.

Both the standard and thorough ScanDisk versions have an Advanced features button, which can be used to add options to deal with lost file fragments, invalid file types, and files that have become cross-linked. You can also choose to keep a ScanDisk log file.

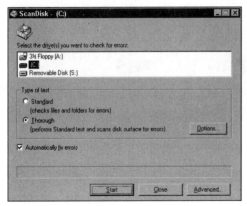

Figure 28-1: The Windows ScanDisk utility's opening window.

Defragmenting the disk

The *Disk Defragmenter* utility (see Figure 28-2) organizes data file fragments into a more optimized and logical format that provides for faster access times and less read/write head movement. While files are written and rewritten to the hard disk, data file fragments can become scattered about the disk in non-contiguous areas. The Disk Defragmenter should be run about once a month, depending on how frequently disk files are modified or deleted. The Disk Defragmenter can be found at Start → Programs → Accessories → System Tools → Disk Defragmenter.

You should run ScanDisk before running the Disk Defragmenter because if Disk Defragmenter finds any errors that ScanDisk could fix, it will stop and recommend that you run ScanDisk anyway.

Figure 28-2: The Windows Disk Defragmenter utility.

Optimizing Expansion Cards

The best way to optimize input/putput (I/O) controllers and other types of expansion cards is to install them in the correct physical order. No harm is done to the PC if expansion cards are installed in any order, but some benefit can be gained from putting them in the proper sequence to take advantage of the priority order in which they are detected during the boot process.

Putting the cards in order

When installing expansion cards in a PC, put the video card in the first slot, followed by the NIC, modem, and sound card, in that order. If you're unsure of which PCI slot is the first PCI slot, you should consult the motherboard's documentation or download a PCI-numbering utility from the motherboard manufacturer's Web site. PCI *slot 0,* the first slot, is not necessarily the first one on the left or right on the motherboard, but instead is the first one detected by the BIOS during the boot process.

Using PCI

On a Pentium-class system, try to use Peripheral Component Interconnect (PCI) cards and avoid Industry Standard Architecture (ISA) cards, if possible. Just about all I/O adapters, including video cards, sound cards, network interface cards (NICs), modems, and Small Computer System Interface (SCSI) host adapters are available in a PCI expansion bus format. The Pentium processor is designed to work with the PCI bus natively, but the 8-bit ISA cards require additional overhead, which will slightly slow down the system.

Optimizing the Processor

You can optimize the processor for speed in three ways:

♦ Replace it with a faster speed or higher-level processor.

♦ Use a utility from the processor manufacturer to apply patches or fixes to the processor logic.

♦ Overclock the processor.

Replacing the processor

The requirement for replacing your processor with a higher-level or faster processor is that the motherboard and chipset must support the new processor both logically and physically.

Logically, the chipset and motherboard must support the bus speed of the new processor and have the supporting circuitry that it requires. You should check with the processor manufacturer or the motherboard manufacturer to verify these compatibilities. Replacing the motherboard is often a much better option to ensure compatibility.

Updating the processor

The manufacturer of the processor might have some utilities available for download that can be used to improve some aspect of the processor's capabilities, such as video processing, buffer handling, and other processor-based functions. You can also find many of these utilities on several Web sites, such as www.motherboard.com and www.tomshardware.com.

Overclocking the processor

Overclocking a processor means running the processor at a clock speed faster than it is released to support. Most processors are capable of running at speeds higher than their nominal (or rated) speeds. The *nominal speed* of a processor is the speed at which it has been tuned to run with a certain chipset, motherboard, cooling system, and other components of the PC.

Raising the clock speed of the processor can create heat issues and lead to frequent system lockups, memory problems, and other heat-sensitive issues. Overclocking the processor can also harm the processor itself.

The speed of the processor is controlled by the internal clock, which is controlled by the internal clock multiplier. To change the internal clock multiplier, you need to locate the CPU to Bus Frequency Ration Selection jumper on the motherboard. Consult the motherboard's documentation or refer to an overclocking guide on the Web, such as Tom's Hardware Overclocking Guide at `www.tomshardware.com/guides/overclocking` for more detailed instructions on overclocking a processor.

When overclocking a processor, you also usually need to change the bus speed on the motherboard and perhaps the processor voltage level as well.

Part XI

Appendix

APPENDIX A
About the CD

Appendix A

About the CD

System Requirements

Make sure that your computer meets the minimum system requirements shown in the following list. If your computer doesn't meet most of these requirements, you could have problems using the contents of the CD.

◆ A PC with a 486 or faster processor.

◆ Microsoft Windows 95 or later.

◆ At least 16MB of total RAM installed on your computer.

◆ At least 32MB of available hard drive space to install all the software on this CD. (You need less space if you don't install every program.)

◆ A CD-ROM drive — double-speed (2x) or faster.

◆ A sound card for PCs.

◆ A monitor capable of displaying at least 256 colors or grayscale.

◆ A modem or broadband link with a speed of at least 14,400 bps.

If you need more information, some of the best sources are in my favorite books (all published by Wiley Publishing, Inc.):

◆ *Fix Your Own PC*, 7th Edition, by Corey Sandler

◆ *PC Upgrade and Repair Bible*, 3rd Edition, by Barry Press, Marcia Press

◆ *PCs For Dummies*, 8th Edition, by Dan Gookin

◆ *PCs All-in-One Desk Reference For Dummies*, by Dan Gookin

♦ *PC Upgrade & Repair Simplified*, 2nd Edition, by Paul Whitehead

♦ *Troubleshooting Your PC For Dummies*, by Dan Gookin

♦ *Troubleshooting Your PC Bible*, 5th Edition, by Jim Aspinwall and Mike Todd

♦ *Upgrading and Fixing PCs For Dummies*, 6th Edition, by Andy Rathbone

Using the CD with Microsoft Windows

To access the content of the CD, follow these steps:

1. Insert the CD into your computer's CD-ROM drive.

2. A window appears with the following options:

   ■ *Explore:* Enables you to view the contents of the CD-ROM in its directory structure.

   ■ *Software:* Gives you the option to install the supplied software on the CD-ROM.

   ■ *Files:* Allows you to view the bonus files provided with the CD.

   ■ *Links:* Opens a hyperlinked page of Web sites.

   ■ *Exit:* Closes the AutoRun window.

If you do not have AutoRun enabled or if the AutoRun window does not appear, follow the steps below to access the CD.

1. Choose Start → Run.

2. In the dialog box that appears, type **D:\SETUP.EXE**, where D is the letter of your CD-ROM drive.

   This brings up the autorun window described earlier.

3. Choose the Explore, Software, Files, Links, Exit option from the menu.

   See Step 2 of the preceding list for a description of these options.

What You'll Find on the CD

This CD-ROM contains bonus content from *PC Repair Bench Book*, plus third-party software to help you diagnose, solve, and protect yourself from common PC problems.

Bonus content

The following is a summary of the bonus content included on this CD:

- A searchable version of this book in PDF format
- Bonus Appendixes in PDF format:
    - Bonus Appendix A, "Troubleshooting PC Problems"
    - Bonus Appendix B, "The PC Technician's Toolkit"
    - Bonus Appendix C, "Glossary"
- Find-a-Fix, a guide to the most common PC problems and some suggested troubleshooting steps and resolutions
- A links page that includes links to all of the Web pages mentioned in this book, organized by chapter

Third-party software

These third-party programs are included to help you get the most out of this book:

- Adobe's *Acrobat Reader:* Free software that lets you view and print PDF files on all major computer platforms
- PC Certify Inc.'s *PC Certify Pro* (trial): Software that allows you to conduct diagnostic testing of PCs
- PC Doctor OnCall Inc.'s *PC Doctor* (trial): Software that performs a series of diagnostic checks to locate file errors and problems, including all types of software errors, registry problems, leftovers from incomplete uninstalls, and much more
- Iolo Technologies, LLC's *System Shield* (trial): Software that defends your computer against unauthorized attempts at recovering information
- Iolo Technologies, LLC's *Macro Magic* (trial): Software that helps you create macros to simplify repetitive tasks into a single step

- ◆ Iolo Technologies, LLC's *System Mechanic* (trial): Software to clear junk files from your PC, clean your registry, speed up your Internet connection, ensure your privacy, fix broken shortcuts, and find and remove duplicate files

- ◆ Pro Tech Diagnostic's *ToolStar Test* (demo): Universal PC diagnostic software (written in assembly language) that uses its own operating system to independently test PC hardware

- ◆ Pro Tech Diagnostic's *ToolStar Windows* (demo): An addition to ToolStar Test that enables you to analyze resources and configurations and test the various components in Windows

- ◆ CST Inc.'s *DocMemory Pro* (trial): Software to evaluate your computer's RAM for errors

- ◆ Rarsoft's *WinRAR* (trial): Software for using and manipulating compressed and archived files

- ◆ e-merge GmbH *WinACE* (shareware): Software for using and manipulating compressed and archived files

Troubleshooting

I tried my best to compile programs that work on most computers with the minimum system requirements. Alas, your computer could be somewhat different, and some programs might not work properly for some reason.

The two most likely culprits are that you don't have enough memory (RAM) for the programs you want to use or that you have other programs running that affect the installation or running of a program. If you get error messages such as Not Enough Memory or Setup Cannot Continue, try one or more of the following procedures and then try using the software again:

- ◆ **Turn off any antivirus software monitor that you might have running on your computer.** Installers sometimes mimic virus activity and can make your computer incorrectly believe that it's being infected by a virus.

- ◆ **Close all running programs.** The more programs that you run, the less memory is available to other programs. Installers also typically update files and programs; if you keep other programs running, installation might not work properly.

- ◆ **Close the CD interface and run demos or installations directly from Windows Explorer.** The interface itself can tie up system memory or even conflict with certain kinds of interactive demos. Use Windows Explorer to browse the files on the CD and launch installers or demos.

◆ **Add more RAM to your computer.** This is, admittedly, a drastic and somewhat expensive step. However, if you have a Windows 95 PC, adding more memory can really help the speed of your computer and enable more programs to run at the same time.

If you still have trouble with the CD, please call the Customer Care phone number: (800) 762-2974. Outside the United States, call 1 (317) 572-3994. You can also contact Customer Service by e-mail at techsupdum@wiley.com. Wiley Publishing, Inc. will provide technical support only for installation and other general quality control items; for technical support on the applications themselves, consult the program's vendor or author.

Index

Symbols & Numerals

continued

continued

continued

continued

Wiley Publishing, Inc.
End-User License Agreement